BASIL
MOREAU

"In this era of the New Evangelization, we can learn much from the inspiring example and writings of Blessed Basil Moreau, a holy priest who embraced with passionate zeal the mission of the new evangelization in nineteenth-century France, facing challenges not unlike our own. This wonderful collection of his writings provides rich material for spiritual reflection. Moreau's spirituality, focused on the imitation of Christ, trust in divine providence, and hope in the victory of the cross, reveals to us the necessary foundation for all our evangelizing endeavors: prayer and friendship with Christ."

Most Reverend Kevin C. Rhoades
Bishop of Fort Wayne-South Bend

"This much-anticipated and brilliantly compiled volume responds to the need for an English-language anthology of the writings of Blessed Basil Moreau, the founder of the Congregation of Holy Cross. For students of history and religion, as well as for anyone seeking to understand and benefit personally from the profound spirituality of Father Moreau, this book is an absolute treasure."

Most Reverend Charles J. Brown
Apostolic Nuncio to Ireland

"Blessed Basil Moreau had a singular ability to address problems with a combination of intellectual acuity, spiritual wisdom, and practicality. His thoughts on Catholic education and the virtues of teachers are especially noteworthy. We would do well to reread them at the beginning of each academic year. Grove and Gawrych have assembled a wonderful introduction to the mind and character of the founder of the Congregation of Holy Cross."

John Garvey
President
Catholic University of America

"In their steady, nonintrusive editing and organization of Basil Moreau's key writings, Grove and Gawrych make tangibly near the wide-ranging and energetic thoughts of a man notable for his ability to live deeply into his own time yet beyond it. . . . In accessible and smooth translation, these essential writings reveal that Moreau's spiritual vision is powerful, ongoing, edifying, and gritty, the contribution of a man whose consequences have remained anything but hidden over the ages, under the standard of the cross, to the greater glory of God."

Robert Geisinger, S.J.
Procurator General, Society of Jesus
Professor of Canon Law, Pontifical Gregorian University

"By retrieving the words of their sainted founder—Basil Moreau—two young Holy Cross religious help us to understand the mind and heart of a man who provided (and still provides) the deep impetus that urges the Holy Cross family to proclaim the Cross as our only hope. This inestimable collection will help sustain the Congregation in its charism and give ample encouragement to those who share in its mission."

Lawrence S. Cunningham
John A. O'Brien Professor of Theology (Emeritus)
University of Notre Dame

"These writings are a rich bequest to the Holy Cross family by Blessed Basil Moreau, who shared his vision and design of a Holy Cross education; urged the imitation of Christ as the way to know, love, and serve God; and lived the motto of Holy Cross as he accepted his own cross in his darkest hour and deepest anguish. Amidst chaos and during a time of religious persecution, Moreau showed how the passion and faith of one man brought God back into a world that had rejected him and into the new world that did not know him."

Carolyn Y. Woo
President and CEO
Catholic Relief Services

"Holy Cross Fathers Kevin Grove and Andrew Gawrych are to be congratulated for this excellent, rich resource into the life, vision, and ecclesial contribution of Blessed Basil Moreau. This book beautifully integrates the academic, spiritual, liturgical, and apostolic dimensions of a great pastor and thinker who lived during a time of seismic shifts in the Church and in the world. To anyone who seeks to understand Moreau, a 'simple instrument in the hands of divine providence, and the history of Holy Cross, this collection of essential writings is a must!"

Rev. Thomas Rosica, C.S.B.
CEO, Salt and Light Catholic Media Foundation
Consultor, Pontifical Council for Social Communications

"*Basil Moreau: Essential Writings* is a much-needed addition to the corpus of contemporary Moreau scholarship. . . . This work can be highly recommended for study and spiritual reading to the religious of Holy Cross and their colleagues, and to all those seeking support and guidance along the pathways of their journey toward union with God."

Br. Joel Giallanza, C.S.C.
Author of *Praying from the Heart of Holy Cross Spirituality*

"This collection of the essential writings of Blessed Basil Moreau offers extremely valuable insights into the life of the remarkable founder of the Congregation of Holy Cross, whose writings on education and evangelization are as valuable now as they were in the wake of the French Revolution and whose spiritual vision provides a meaningful path to a rich life in Christ."

Rev. Thomas J. O'Hara, C.S.C.
Provincial Superior
Congregation of Holy Cross, United States Province of Priests and Brothers

"This superb and much-needed work makes accessible to us, in their historical and theological context, the writings of Blessed Basil Moreau, someone who has profoundly shaped the University of Notre Dame and many other educational institutions throughout the world, along with countless other good works—all of which exist because of his vision for the Congregation of Holy Cross."

Rev. John I. Jenkins, C.S.C.
President
University of Notre Dame

BASIL MOREAU

ESSENTIAL WRITINGS

An Introduction to the Life and
Thought of the Founder of the
Congregation of Holy Cross

Edited by Kevin Grove, C.S.C.,
and Andrew Gawrych, C.S.C.

Foreword by John C. Cavadini

Christian Classics   *Notre Dame, Indiana*

Contents

Foreword by John C. Cavadini ix

Preface and Acknowledgments xv

Introduction 1

    Moreau's Context: Two French Revolution Sketches 2
    Moreau's Intellectual Formation 7
    Moreau as Scholar and Teacher 11
    Intellectual and Spiritual Influences on Moreau 16
    The Early Developments of Holy Cross 23
    Moreau's Leadership and Development of Holy Cross 29
    Moreau from 1860 to 1866 40
    Moreau's Resignation and Last Years 42
    Moreau's Spiritual Emphases 45
    Conclusion 53

Chapter 1: Sermons 55

    Meditation 57
    Community Spirit 78
    Confession 106
    Holy Communion 120
    Renewal of the Vows 131
    The Sacred Heart of Jesus 151
    The Immaculate Heart of Mary 167
    St. Joseph 175
    Reception of the Habit for Carmelite Sisters 191

Chapter 2: Spiritual Exercises 201

    Second Week: The Illuminative Way 203
    Meditations for the Feast of the Sacred Heart 239
    Fourth Week: The Unitive Way 248

Chapter 3: Christian Meditations 259

    Epiphany: Meditation on the Mystery 261
    Third Sunday after Epiphany: Meditation on the Leprosy of Sin 267
    Sixth Sunday after Epiphany: Meditation on the Minor Virtues 271
    Sexagesima Sunday: Meditation on the Word of God 277
    Friday after the Third Sunday of Lent: Meditation on the Mystery of the
        Five Wounds of Our Lord 282
    Fourth Sunday of Lent: Meditation on the Behavior of Jesus Christ and of the

People in the Multiplication of the Loaves and the Fishes 285
Friday after Passion Sunday: Meditation on the Mystery of the Transfixion or
    Compassion of the Blessed Virgin 288
Quasimodo Sunday: Meditation on Interior Peace and Exterior Peace............ 292
Fourth Sunday after Easter: Meditation on Silence 298
Fifth Sunday after Easter: Meditation on Mental Prayer 304
Sixth Sunday after Easter: Meditation on Preparing for the Holy Spirit 310
Pentecost: Meditation on the Mystery 313
First Sunday after Pentecost: Meditation on the Mystery of
    the Most Holy Trinity 317
Thursday after the Most Holy Trinity: Meditation on the Procession of
    the Feast of the Blessed Sacrament or of the Most Holy Body of Christ........... 322

Chapter 4: Christian Education   329

Preface.. 331
Introduction 333
Part One: On Teachers and Students.. 334
Part Three: On the Formation of School Children in the Christian Life and
    the Means to Ensure Their Perseverance.. 361

Chapter 5: Circular Letters   377

Circular Letter 14 (September 1, 1841) 379
Circular Letter 23 (January 4, 1845) 387
Circular Letter 25 (January 5, 1846) 403
Circular Letter 34 (June 19, 1848) 413
Circular Letter 36 (April 15, 1849)... 415
Circular Letter 79 (January 1, 1857) 424
Circular Letter 96 (June 16, 1858) 439
Circular Letter 137 (January 3, 1861) 444
Circular Letter 179 (January 10, 1865) 449
Circular Letter 8 to the Sisters (January 22, 1858).. 456
Circular Letter 16 to the Sisters (January 2, 1859).. 466

Moreau Chronology   476

Map of Moreau's France   483

Notes   484

Selected Bibliography   507

Index   510

Biblical Index   519

FOREWORD

by John C. Cavadini
University of Notre Dame

Ave Crux, Spes Unica!

In their excellent introduction to this volume, the editors feature this motto as the heart of the spiritual theology of Blessed Basil Moreau. They observe, "Learning to love the cross as a sign of real hope was the spiritual core of Moreau's theology" (p. 45).[1]

This makes me wonder how best to translate the phrase *Ave Crux, Spes Unica*. The most common translation is "Hail the Cross, Our Only Hope!" but the word *only* in English is deceiving. Especially in the phrase, "only hope," it often signifies, ironically, a nearly hopeless situation—a hope that is slim, desperate and unlikely. And when the *cross* is said to be such a hope, the phrase also seems to carry a strong world-rejecting resonance, as though there are no glimmers or indications of hope anywhere in the world. The cross being the lone slender hope left against all contraindications. Further, someone only casually acquainted with Blessed Basil might expect just such a spirituality from him. Hadn't his hopes been wrenched out of the world by the French Revolution and its wholesale persecution of the Church? Could there be a tinge of Jansenism here?

What this collection of the Blessed Basil's writings shows is that nothing could be further from the truth. Perhaps, then, we should translate *unicus* in its classical sense as not simply "only" but "matchless." *"Hail the Cross, Hope Unsurpassable!"* or even, *"Hail the Cross, Our One, Most Awesome Hope!"* could be paraphrases, and maybe, *"Hail the Cross, Our One Supreme Hope!"* could be a translation. In any event, the phrase is intended as an act of praise, not an act of desperation. One may certainly utter it in desperate situations, but as an act of praise, gratitude, and love—an act of one who "gives thanks always for all things to God the Father in the name of our Lord Jesus Christ" (Eph 5:20).

For Blessed Basil, the cross was a mystery of hope because, first of all, it *was* a mystery, something essentially "hidden," something without obvious grounding in any human work, be it one of reason or one of power. Its cause is an unimaginable love, the origin of which is not traceable by human reason, and of which human reason cannot be "proud" as though it were one of its most magnificent achievements. Hope placed in the cross is hope placed not in human reason or human power but, in the first instance, in God. Blessed Basil comments that, "without neglecting the natural means of learning," we should imitate the saints who "learned more at the foot of the crucifix than in discussions with others or in books" (p. 314).

Second, the cross was a mystery of hope because it, especially, sums up all of the mystery of the Christian life under the aspect of its essential "hiddenness." To have hope in the mystery of the cross is to believe scripture when it says (in Col 3:3), "You have died and your life is hidden with Jesus Christ in God" (p. 234). The religious life is the "hidden life" *par excellence*, but only because, for Blessed Basil, it is an intensified form of the hidden life "which is that of every Christian" (p. 233).

The life of Jesus Christ is the paradigmatic hidden life, not only in its more obviously hidden stages, meaning those hidden from view by the Gospel narrative, but in an essential and irreducible sense. To consider the life of Christ as "hidden" is to consider the Incarnation itself, "how this God of glory first hid himself under the veil of human nature" (p. 234). Even in the midst of wonders that revealed his divinity, "Jesus Christ remained a hidden God for almost everyone" (p. 236). It is easy not to notice, or else to have contempt for, even the miracles of someone who identifies himself "with all the privations associated with the poor and the outcast of society" (p. 244), people who are never noticed anyway. In the Passion, he is hidden, too, for he is "covered by sins" for which, though not his own, he is abandoned by his father, "as if the

Lord were no longer his father" (p. 237). The extent of the "hiddenness" of God in Christ is the extent of his self-emptying gift of himself as Love.

The Third Meditation for the Feast of the Sacred Heart contains a meditation on the hiddenness of Christ's life, because the Incarnation itself, and all the hiddenness of God's status and privilege as God that flows from it, *is* the revelation of God's love. The Sacred Heart is the "symbol, source, and center of his love" (p. 239). It is a "furnace of love," the "height, width, and depth" (p. 155, citing Eph 3:18) of which cannot be measured. Ephesians 3:18 was frequently taken by St. Augustine to indicate the dimensions of the cross, and as such a summary of the whole Christian life as a life of love in its configuration to the cross. This, not Jansenism, is the Augustinianism of Blessed Basil.

"Love causes love" Blessed Basil reminds would-be teachers (p. 339). As love presently works, still hidden, *par excellence* through the sacraments, but also through devotion to the Sacred Heart of Jesus, through studying the "language of the Gospel" (p. 414), through the work of teachers and the inspiration of the Spirit, it "causes love." The life of the Christian is configured to the love that is revealed by the "life hidden in God or rather God hidden in Jesus Christ" (p. 235).

To say *Ave Crux, Spes Unica* means to not be afraid to live the life of love, even though it is inescapably hidden, for though hidden, it is not erased and is not erasable. Instead, *hid with Christ in God,* it is the risen life of the risen Lord. One does not have to be afraid to leave behind "esteem and honor" (p. 99) and the obsessive quest to be noticed and noteworthy. "Therefore," Blessed Basil invites us, speaking in the voice of Christ, "Hide yourself in God with me, and do not dream of appearing again before I show myself to the world. Hide yourself. Bury yourself willingly in the dust of a classroom or in the obscurity of a rural parish church" (p. 238). This is life in the midst of a "beauty ever ancient and ever new," that is, the "loving kindness" of God's own Trinitarian life (p. 319), the beauty "hidden" in the life of Christ, and all lives configured to His life.

Thus, those who say *Ave Crux, Spes Unica*, who have placed their hope in the mystery of the cross, can live life with confidence in the future. It is the same confidence that Blessed Basil expressed when he said he had not "even for so much as one moment lost confidence in the future" despite terrible scandals, betrayal, and incompetence (p. 452). To say *Ave Crux, Spes Unica* is to place one's confidence in the love of God and the life of love, no matter how hidden or counter-intuitive it may seem. *Ave Crux, Spes Unica* is an empowering message, enabling us to embrace life fully with a heart like an anvil (p. 390) in the workshop of God, who can forge on it works both great and small, even turning the small into the great, just as he turned the work of an unknown local French seminary professor into the work of the founder of a fully global religious order, the Congregation of Holy Cross.

The editors of this volume have done an excellent job of choosing representative texts from Blessed Basil Moreau in a variety of genres. Their selection reminds us that the charism and vision of the founder of Holy Cross also set the tone for renewal, for the founding was itself a renewal of sorts, a reorientation to the originating newness of Jesus Christ, whose newness is intrinsic and perpetual. Blessed Basil's founding vision is local, in that it is the foundation of a specific religious congregation at a specific time to meet a specific need. It was successful, however, precisely because the newness of the foundation was an authentic fruit of Blessed Basil's openness to the timeless newness of the One who "makes all things new." Returning to the vision of the founder will mean not a return to the oldness of a time past, but an encounter with the fountainhead of newness and renewal, and not only for Holy Cross, but for anyone seeking a vision of renewed life in the Church. "Hail the Cross, Our Matchless Hope!" means that we have died to all that is old, to death itself and all its power to frighten and shame and paralyze, and that our life, hidden with Christ in God, is bursting with an irresistible newness that transfigures everything it touches. May we return to the sources our editors have so carefully laid open for us, and allow Blessed Basil to teach us to be open to that beauty which, though indeed ever ancient, is nevertheless ever new and ever renewing!

PREFACE AND
ACKNOWLEDGMENTS

Since his beatification on September 15, 2007, Basil Moreau has become a historical person of increased interest. The variety and number of his works broadly available, however, have remained minimal by any account. The result is that contemporary thinkers have little access to the writings of a man who is credited with saintly accomplishment. This book represents but the beginning of a response to that need. In addition, this book aims intellectually to aid further research concerning the mission and charism of the Congregation of Holy Cross and its apostolates. We have chosen the texts printed here in order to show not only the breadth of Moreau's works but also the depth of consistency with which he worked out various theological and practical matters.

To be certain, nineteenth-century France is not our own day. In editing the translations of Moreau's writings, we have resisted the temptation to update him or to make the translations themselves relevant by criteria that would inevitably be arguable. Where possible, we have tried to explain the references Moreau was making to other theological sources as well as to current and congregational events.

Moreau often quoted scripture from memory, cited the Latin Vulgate, or translated from a scriptural language himself. For this reason, scriptural citations in the translations are not standardized in accord with any current English version of the Bible. We have supplied the scriptural allusions indicated by parentheses, as well as the parenthetical English translations of Latin Vulgate citations.

***

We are first and foremost grateful to the Congregation of Holy Cross, and in particular to Superior General Fr. Richard Warner, C.S.C., for permission to use the congregational archives and to publish Blessed Basil Moreau's writings.

Many other confreres have supported this effort. Though it is not possible to name them all, we are especially grateful to Fr. Jim Connelly, C.S.C.; Br. Joel Giallanza, C.S.C.; Fr. Jim King, C.S.C.; Fr. Steve Lacroix, C.S.C.; Fr. Thomas Looney, C.S.C.; Mr. Patrick Reidy, C.S.C.; and Benjamin Rusch for their content and editorial help. Mr. Adam Booth, C.S.C., provided archival support, a bibliography, and a timeline.

We acknowledge in gratitude the enduring quality of the translation work of M. Eleanore, C.S.C. (Sermons), and Edward Heston, C.S.C. (Circular Letters). Further, the brothers of the Holy Cross Institute have provided a modern translation of part one of *Christian Education*. The introduction and part three of *Christian Education* were translated afresh by Fr. Gregory Haake, C.S.C. The remaining texts by Moreau were translated anonymously by members of the Congregation of Holy Cross. Perhaps the broader readership of Moreau will serve as partial reward for their humble and careful service.

We are further indebted to Kevin Cawley at the University of Notre Dame Archives. The introduction benefitted greatly from the comments of two University of Notre Dame faculty members: Professor Larry Cunningham of the Department of Theology and Professor Kathleen Sprows Cummings, director of the Cushwa Center for the Study of American Catholicism.

Finally, we are grateful to Tom Grady, publisher of Ave Maria Press, and his staff, including Editorial Director Robert Hamma, Managing Editor Susana Kelly, and Creative Director Kristen Hornyak Bonelli, who have continued to dedicate vision and effort not only to Christian classics but also to the subset of those writings that has emerged from the Congregation of Holy Cross.

K. G. and A. G.

January 20, 2014

The Feast of Blessed Basil Moreau

INTRODUCTION

For Basil Moreau, life was an imitation of Christ. The cross was his only hope. Moreau strove not only to live but also to teach these truths. From the sermons he preached to the spiritual exercises and circular letters he wrote for the Congregation of Holy Cross, his writings bear witness to this primary concern—becoming a living copy of the crucified Savior.

A respected professor of philosophy, dogmatics, and scripture, Moreau founded what quickly became an international religious congregation. As a devoted superior of a fledgling community, he nevertheless continued his study and scholarship. The bulk of Moreau's theological work can be categorized as practical, and he certainly produced much of it to fulfill the apostolic needs of the Holy Cross community. Even so, many of these same texts exhibit a sophisticated and overarching grounding in scripture and tradition, so that Moreau's writings reveal not only careful theological treatment but also markedly consistent application.

This integrated theology flows from Moreau's belief that to imitate Jesus Christ is "to seek to know Jesus Christ. By studying him, you will come to know him. By knowing him, you will come to love him. By loving him, you will be imbued with his Spirit and thenceforth you will imitate him."[1] Thus, for Moreau, a faith that seeks understanding is also a faith that practices imitation. It is this combination of study and imitation that then yields a "knowledge of Jesus Christ that is life-giving, profound, luminous, and practical" (p. 224).[2]

What makes Moreau's writings so profitable to study, however, is also what can make them difficult to read. Accessing the depths of his works and unraveling their interwoven influences, concerns, and themes requires understanding of the French Revolution and how it affected the Catholic Church of Moreau's time. It also demands familiarity with the French School of Spirituality, which gave Moreau a theological and spiritual framework that guided his life and ministry. Finally, studying Moreau requires a grasp of the complex history surrounding the work that defined his life for almost four decades—founding and leading the Congregation of Holy Cross. This introduction provides an overview of each of these complex areas.

Moreau's Context: Two French Revolution Sketches

The French Revolution was nearing its conclusion when Basil Anthony Mary Moreau was born on February 11, 1799. By the end of that year, Napoleon Bonaparte (1769–1821) had come to power and declared an end to the Revolution.[3] Revolutionary fervor and fears nevertheless continued to grip and shape France for decades, including unrest and uprisings in 1830 and 1848. The latter, which led to the overthrow of the monarchy, became a source of significant concern and trial for Fr. Moreau as superior of his still-nascent religious community.[4] Even beyond continued political instability, the cultural and religious upheaval of the Revolution cast a long shadow over post-Revolution France and the Catholic Church. What follows are two brief sketches of the political and cultural scene of the time, one national and one local. The first is a glimpse of the overall relationship between the Revolution and the Church; the second shows how this relationship played out for one priest, Jacques-François Dujarié (1767–1838), who came from the same region—and the same diocese—as Moreau and who played an important role in the early life of Moreau and the Congregation of Holy Cross.

1. The French Revolution and the Catholic Church

When King Louis XVI (1754–1793) assembled the Estates-General in May 1789, there was a widespread sense, even among clergy and nobility, that reform of French society was necessary.[5] The state was facing bankruptcy, much of the population lived in poverty, and a heavy tax burden on the poor, along with a concentration of power among noble and clerical elites, was leading to growing agitation.[6] Fueled, in part, by the Enlightenment ideas of Voltaire, Diderot, d'Alembert, Rousseau, and others, the reform many envisioned quickly ignited into full-blown revolution in the summer of 1789, reaching into all corners of French society.[7] After the storming of the Bastille on July 14 and Louis XVI's subsequent withdrawal of troops, power now rested with the National Assembly.

The Revolution quickly came into conflict with the Catholic Church.[8] In many ways, the Church dominated pre-Revolution French society: clerics ranked above nobles as the first order of the realm, the Church owned 10 percent of all land and was exempted from most taxes, and all the king's subjects were legally Catholics. The Catholic Church had founded and administered virtually the entire educational system, as well as most hospitals and services for orphans, the poor, and the sick. As a result, any reorganization of French society required a transformation of the Church in France, and many within the Church saw both the need and the opportunity for such transformation.[9] The thinking among members of the clergy was not uniform, however, since parish priests, many of whom lived in poverty, favored some sort of revitalization, while the powerful and often-wealthy members of the episcopacy, many of whom came from nobility, were largely opposed to such a change.[10] Despite these differences, most of the clergy agreed that the Church should retain its control over education, its power of censorship, and its standing as the state religion.[11] It was these societal influences that had most upset the leading thinkers of the Enlightenment, however, and had, in turn, upset many members of the Revolution.

Consequently, the Revolution ushered in swift and extensive changes throughout the Church in France. Less than a month after the storming of the Bastille (1789), the laws providing monetary assistance for the Church had been overturned, from the tithes and vestry fees for parish priests to the feudal dues for bishops and ecclesiastical corporations, including charitable and educational organizations. Then the Declaration of the Rights of Man and the Citizen did not declare Catholicism the state religion, thereby stripping the Church of much of its political power and privilege.[12] The National Assembly did not stop there, believing it had the authority to reshape and restructure the French Church for the better. Next it dissolved all contemplative monasteries and convents and banned new religious vows. Then, in the Civil Constitution of the Clergy, the National Assembly enacted its most sweeping reform; it reorganized Church structures and even provided for the election of bishops without papal approval.[13] When the constitution, made law on July 12, 1790, met with strong resistance from the Church and began to engender public polarization, the National Assembly on November 27 imposed an oath by which all clergy had to declare their allegiance to the new constitution and government.[14]

Responses to the oath varied widely. In Paris, the center of the Revolution and therefore the most anticlerical sector of the country, most priests took the oath. In some regions outside the city such as Western France, the "nonjurors" (clerics who refused the oath) outnumbered the "constitutionals" (clerics who took the oath) more than three to one.[15] At the same time, many monks and canons, who had been evicted from the cloister when their monasteries were dissolved, found in the oath a means to secure a salary and even a chance for advancement in the constitutional church.[16]

The ensuing chaos within the Church continued without official response from Rome until May 4, 1791, when two private letters from Pope Pius VI (1717–1799) to the French bishops became public. The first, dated March 10, criticized the Civil Constitution, and the second, dated April 13, formally asked the bishops not to take the oath. Though the letters did not explicitly condemn taking the oath, everyone interpreted them as doing so.[17] Spurred on by the letters, nearly 10 percent of the clergy who had previously taken the oath rescinded it. Thousands of priests went into exile, and many others were forced underground to avoid imprisonment or execution.[18] By forcing people to side with either the Revolution or the Catholic Church, the clerical oath divided the two irreconcilably, thereby marking a decisive turning point in the relationship between them.[19]

2. Fr. Jacques-François Dujarié and the Diocese of Le Mans

Jacques-François Dujarié, a key figure in Moreau's life, came from a region of France in which most of the clergy remained nonjurors. Born on December 9, 1767, in Rennes-en-Grenouilles, Dujarié was a seminarian in Angers when the Revolution began. When news of the oath of the Civil Constitution of the Clergy reached Angers in January 1791, all of the Sulpician seminary directors refused to take it. Within days of the constitutional bishop's arrival on March 19, most of the seminary's 240 residents, including Dujarié, left.[20] Upon returning home to Rennes, Dujarié found the people confused, confronted with both priests who had taken the oath and those who had refused. Although in Rennes and the surrounding region the constitutional priests were regarded as intruders and the people supported the nonjurors, it still was not safe for Dujarié to remain at home; other nonjuring clerics and their supporters at times were tracked down and persecuted.[21] Dujarié first sought refuge with his sister in Lassay, taking up the weaving trade. That stint was brief, however, and he soon began traveling from village to village, at times needing to disguise himself as a shepherd or lemonade salesman for safety.[22]

Although the most violent period of the Revolution, the Reign of Terror, ended on July 28, 1794, any reprieve was short-lived. The National Convention in 1795 reaffirmed the penalty of death for nonjuring clergy and imposed a new oath. Religious ceremonies in private houses involving more than ten people were banned, as were religious garments and emblems.[23] In the midst of these still-dangerous conditions, Dujarié went to Ruillé-sur-Loir in July 1795 to resume in secret his studies for priesthood under the tutelage of the pastor, Fr. Jacquet de la Haye.[24] In December, disguised and admitted by password to his rendezvous point—necessary precautions because other seminarians had been arrested while making the trip—Dujarié went to Paris to be ordained. He was ordained on December 26, becoming one of twenty-nine priests ordained in secret for the diocese of Le Mans between 1792 and 1801.[25] After his ordination, Dujarié returned to Ruillé where, side by side with de la Haye, he ministered underground until Bonaparte came to power in 1799.

The four-year span from 1796 to 1799 was marked by continued attempts by the Revolution to bring the Church under its authority, including the institution of new oaths. As a result, Dujarié, de la Haye, and other nonjuring clerics still had to minister largely in secret, careful of the persecutions that flared up.[26] At the same time, Catholic culture was far from gone; indeed, some places experienced revitalization. The people became bolder during less violent periods and began to engage in public acts of worship, such as ringing church bells and making processions.[27] An increasing number of priests who had taken the oath retracted it and were reconciled with the Catholic Church.[28] Nevertheless, the situation for the Church remained tenuous. In the department of La Sarthe alone, which encompasses the diocese of Le Mans, forty-five priests were arrested in the last year of the period known as the Directory (1798–1799), including one who was murdered by the citizen group that arrested him.[29] The danger persisted, not fully dissipating until after Napoleon came to power in November 1799.

On July 15, 1801, Napoleon signed a concordat with the Church that was later celebrated in a solemn Mass on Easter Sunday in 1802 in Notre Dame Cathedral in Paris. The concordat restored public worship and reconstituted the Catholic Church in formal relationship with the state, but it did not restore the pre-Revolution Church by any means.[30] The Catholic Church had been stripped of much of its land, its wealth, and its political power. Monastic orders had been disbanded and cloisters of nuns closed. Almost half of the parish clergy had been killed, deported, or had fled into exile. The clergy and hierarchy who remained were left to wrestle with reconciling the schism brought by the Civil Constitution of the Clergy, and much of the Church's institutional infrastructure—particularly in education and health care—had been decimated. As the French Revolution historian William Doyle writes, "No wound of the revolutionary years went deeper."[31]

Education statistics provide a useful metric for assessing one aspect of the Revolution's effect on the Church and society; the Revolution's suppression of the Church produced an entire generation that was essentially unschooled. Although the Revolution declared education a basic human right and envisioned a new educational system, it was never able to achieve its goals. An 1801 *Report on Public Education* observed, "Public education is practically nonexistent everywhere. The generation now reaching the age of twenty is irrevocably sacrificed to ignorance."[32] Prior to the Revolution, in the diocese of Le Mans alone, there were 321 parochial schools—180 for boys and 141 for girls.[33] The crumbling of the Church's extensive network of primary schools during the Revolution, schools that had taught not just the Catholic faith but also reading, writing, and mathematics, led to more than a 70 percent drop in the number of students in universities and a decrease in the national literacy rate from 37 to 30 percent.[34]

Moreau's Intellectual Formation

The aftermath of the French Revolution affected the education of the children of the Moreau family. Much as the time before the Revolution, the parish pastor played a key role in education, especially in small villages. In Laigné-en-Belin at the time of Basil Moreau's birth (1799), the pastor was a constitutional priest, and the Moreau family, along with many others in the town, rejected the constitutional clergy and sought the sacramental care of nonjuring priests in hiding.[35] By the time that Basil received his own religious instruction, the parish was back under the care of a nonjuring pastor, Fr. Julien Le Provost. Le Provost opened a school for boys and taught the catechism, reading, writing, and mathematics.[36] Having identified Basil as intelligent and a candidate for the priesthood, Le Provost took it upon himself to educate him in the study of classics and Latin. He assured Louis Moreau, the boy's father, that either a benefactor or Le Provost himself could provide Basil further education at the College of Château-Gontier, a twelfth-century college known for its educational quality.[37] Basil studied there from October 1814 until 1816, when he entered major seminary at St. Vincent's Seminary in Le Mans.[38]

The intellectual culture in the seminary at the time was marked by a strictly determined doctrinal content.[39] Faculty had to submit their notes for inspection by superiors, and students likewise could have their class notes examined. Etienne and Tony Catta, biographers of Moreau, describe the quality of education at the seminary as likely quite low. For instance, they describe one philosophy text used in the seminary as "a manual in three small volumes, written in shabby Latin and marked with a very Cartesian touch."[40] The seminary education was further marked by Gallicanism, which, since its codification in the Declaration of 1682, affirmed the spiritual authority of the papacy but proscribed the pope's temporal authority in favor of French control.[41]

Four years after entering the major seminary, Moreau was ordained a deacon by Bishop de la Myre and then ordained a priest on August 12, 1821.[42] Moreau's first solemn Mass was in his hometown with his own pastor, Le Provost, assisting. As a newly ordained priest, Moreau asked his bishop to send him to the Foreign Mission Seminary, but Jean-Baptiste Bouvier (1783–1854), his seminary director, and Bishop de la Myre had already decided that Moreau would continue his studies in order to become a faculty member at the seminary. De la Myre sent Moreau to Paris to continue his studies under the guidance of the Sulpicians, from whom Moreau received exposure to the ideas of the French School of Spirituality, especially those of Pierre de Bérulle and Jean-Jacques Olier.[43] During the first phase of his studies in Paris (1821–1822), the young Moreau wrote to a friend that he had "never taken so many notes" as he had at Saint-Sulpice.[44] The faculty also was able to offer training in Hebrew for more sophisticated study of scripture, as well as in-depth exposure to dogmatic and moral theology.

While studying with the Sulpicians, Moreau kept a correspondence with Fr. Louis-Jean Fillion (1788–1861), the rector of the seminary in Tessé, where Moreau himself later became a member of the teaching faculty. Moreau wrote to the rector:

> If I fall into your hands, I shall sing a *Te Deum* even while trembling, for I am frightened by the prospect of hearing seminarians' confessions and passing judgment on their vocation. But if they send me to preach in some country parish, I shall thank God and my bishop. I am burning with this desire, and should love to be already engaged in this work. Need I tell you? At times, this desire is so strong that I feel my whole heart on fire. When I get into my bed, which I regard as my grave, I should like to wake up and find myself in the midst of some poor peasants. How I would teach them! How I would bring them back to God! Do these sentiments indicate a desire to be prominent, betray self-love or pride, or are they pious sentiments and holy inspirations? God alone knows. But I know that this desire is consuming me. While I am studying *Beth* and *Resch*, while I am toying with an *atqui* and an *ergo*, the soul of my brother is being lost. As for the rest, God will take care of everything, and at the first signal.[45]

This letter gives early evidence of the importance of teaching for Moreau, beginning with the continual development of his capacity to teach scripture by working on languages. Even though he grew frustrated with the amount of time that it required, he devotedly worked on his Hebrew (*Beth* and *Resch*) and wrote his own scholarly texts in Latin (*atqui* and *ergo*). One interpreter of Moreau described this letter as exhibiting a stifled desire to evangelize, but a more plausible interpretation is that the letter reveals an early connection for Moreau between teaching and evangelizing.[46] When he writes of "preach[ing] in some country parish," he exclaims, "How I would teach them!" As became more evident in his leadership of Holy Cross, Moreau saw education as the key to evangelization.[47] Whether this happened in a country parish—as the young Moreau's pastor had done for him—or in the seminary, Moreau's apostolic desire was to spread faith through teaching.[48] The letter indicates that Moreau knew he was going to be a seminary professor and looked forward to working with Fillion. Moreau's reservations were simply that he would have to make judgments about the vocations of young men, and thus make judgments concerning their call from God to the priesthood.

From what he later communicated to his own seminary students, we can get a sense of Moreau's own approach to learning. Moreau suggested to them that the study of theology be undertaken with a spirit of zeal, humility, and love of God. Zeal was ardor for the task of learning. Humility meant both resisting the temptation to study for the sake of reputation and admitting that some divine truths would remain shrouded in mystery. Love of God required plunging the heart ever more deeply into the fire of charity; Moreau believed meditation on divine truth was impossible without it. He had concerns in particular about the danger of the study of theology—namely, that a topic inherently concerned with divine truth did not always provoke a correlative response of increased prayer or charity, both fruits of a deepening encounter with and knowledge of God.[49] This caused Moreau consistently to suggest to students that their study of theology must be coupled with markedly consistent work at its daily application, both in their lives and in their ministry.[50]

Moreau did not immediately begin as a seminary professor after finishing in Paris; he spent a further year at the Sulpician Solitude of Issy (1822–1823). This year provided Moreau with a time of prayer, solitude, study, and labor analogous to a religious novitiate, which is a dedicated time of apprenticeship in the religious life in preparation for the profession of religious vows. At this point, however, Moreau was still a diocesan priest. Years later, as part of his work founding Holy Cross as a religious community, Moreau would publicly profess the vows of poverty, chastity, and obedience, thereby entering religious life and becoming a religious priest.[51] During this period Moreau committed himself to silence, rose during the four o'clock hour of the morning, studied scripture and Hebrew daily, and engaged in a rigorous rule of life that included prayer, fasting, and mortification.[52] He also made a very detailed and deliberate effort to stem his vices of pride and anger in day-to-day activity.[53] He continued to attend theology classes in the mornings, using the afternoons to study French history, Church history, and geography, and to write his own compositions.[54] Not a requirement, this was Moreau's personal rule of life encouraged by the Sulpician spirituality of the Solitude. Moreau also began weekly spiritual direction with the Solitude rector, Fr. Gabriel Mollevaut (1774–1854), a relationship that would remain important for Moreau until Mollevaut's death more than three decades later. Mollevaut was a confidant to the young scholar in his personal life and a guide during his early years as superior of Holy Cross, often offering advice on how to set up the governance of his young society.[55]

Moreau as Scholar and Teacher

1. Formation in a Time of Debate

Moreau's scholarly development took place alongside a contemporary debate in Parisian theology concerning the inadequacy of human reason in ascertaining truth.[56] Hugues-Félicité Robert de Lamennais (1782–1854) wrote the four-volume work *Essai sur l'indifférence en matière de religion* from 1817 to 1823. Consistently critiquing the work of Rousseau and other philosophers—such as Descartes, Kant, and Locke—Lamennais argued that the philosophical social contract, emerging especially from Rousseau, was insufficient to ground a free society. In Lamennais's understanding, after dethroning God and then the king, the concept of a general will in such a contract would ultimately "dethron[e] man and reduce him to the level of an animal."[57] In such a society, he thought, "force alone" would be "the final arbiter."[58] The ruin of religion and the ruin of society were coterminous for Lamennais.[59] Moreau's engagement with the Lamennais controversy, seen in letters from Moreau to the director of his first seminary, provides a glimpse of how the young scholar wrestled with a complex issue involving theology, philosophy, politics, and a reconsideration of the French Revolution. In these letters, Moreau details all of the current scholarly objections to Lamennais's work and the responses to those objections.[60] Moreau himself took up the intellectual questions of the certainty of belief, continuing to follow the debate through his time in the Solitude and later as a new professor, beginning with teaching philosophy at the minor seminary in Tessé.

The debates surrounding the work of Lamennais and Moreau's involvement in them likely began to solidify his Ultramontane, or pro-Roman, position.[61] The division between Ultramontanism and Gallicanism was a French manifestation of the inherent tension within the Catholic Church between its local and universal aspects. Ultramontanism valued the universality of the Church, in part, by upholding papal authority, whereas Gallicanism favored the autonomy of the local Church, temporally and sometimes theologically.[62] This theological division undergirded a number of significant personal frustrations and struggles in Moreau's life. Moreau experienced Gallicanism firsthand through Jean-Baptiste Bouvier (1783–1854), the seminary rector during Moreau's time at St. Vincent's Seminary and then bishop of the diocese of Le Mans when Moreau was leading his newly formed religious community. Bouvier's Gallican perspective manifested itself in concrete actions, particularly when dealing with Holy Cross and the monastic foundations (e.g., Solesmes) of the Le Mans diocese. The bishop forestalled Holy Cross's recognition at the papal level, preferring a more localized, diocesan oversight. There were smaller disagreements as well. Bouvier shuffled Moreau between seminary professorial posts in an apparent attempt to suppress the teaching of Ultramontane theology.[63] Moreau, in obedience to Pope Pius IX himself, stopped wearing a Gallican clerical collar in favor of a Roman one.[64] Moreau also ceased using Bouvier's own theology manual for the instruction of Holy Cross seminarians.[65] The disagreements between Moreau and Bouvier had a personal component, but also exemplify the ill will that was caused by fundamentally divergent theological dispositions.

2. A Personal Rule and a Professor

Moreau was keenly aware and strikingly forthright about how his conversations concerning Lamennais and other thinkers affected his own spiritual life and that of his students. Moreau writes about his personal reactions to these debates and how they stirred his anger. Consequently, he tried to keep such debates within the bounds of his seminary classroom, since conversations outside, at his own initiation, had caused "tempers [to] flare, and charity [to be] wounded in more ways than one."[66] Moreau did not avoid complex positions and continued to treat them in his philosophy courses at Tessé, but he reflected often on his reactions to them, writing to Mollevaut with concern for his own spiritual disposition and that of his students. In this sense, his scholarship was never isolated from the rest of his life; he rigorously committed himself to a spiritual life in continuous dialectic with the difficulties and joys of intellectual engagement.

As a young professor, Moreau continued much of the rule of life he had established at the Solitude of Issy. He evaluated his own actions in correspondence with Mollevaut and continued habitual scholarly practices, including beginning each day with a regimen of Hebrew-language studies. He also maintained a regular routine of prayer and fasting. After just a short time teaching philosophy at the minor seminary at Tessé (1823–1826), Moreau was sent to the major seminary of St. Vincent's as a professor of dogma under the direction of Bouvier. Then, after nearly four years in that post, Bouvier informed Moreau that he would be moved to teach sacred scripture. Moreau's writings indicate that he knew Bouvier was the driving force behind the change.[67] The dogmatic theology post was the one in which Moreau's understanding and articulation of the position of Lamennais in favor of the papacy ran most afoul of the strong Gallican commitments of Bouvier.[68] This move both surprised and disappointed Moreau, but—with Mollevaut's help—he came to appreciate the skill he brought to the study and teaching of scripture. Moreau wrote that he was pained by the "lack of straightforwardness" and "distrust" with which he was treated. Nonetheless, he accepted the new position in "a spirit of obedience," though his Ultramontane intellectual commitments did not change.[69]

3. Moreau's Exegesis

The best treatment to date of Moreau's exegetical work is Cécile Perreault's *To Become Another Christ: Identification with Christ according to Basil Moreau*.[70] She develops her thesis concerning Moreau's vision of the imitation of Christ around his exegesis of Galatians 2:20. When teaching Galatians, Moreau relied on Bernardin de Picquigny's *Explication des épîtres de saint Paul* (1706).[71] By lining up a particular Galatians verse from the Vulgate, the Picquigny commentary, and Moreau's notes, Perreault identifies where Moreau's exegesis either departs from or builds on the work of Picquigny. In one instance, Moreau connects the "I live" statements in the Vulgate text with a baptismal reading, suggesting that Christ living in the disciple precipitates transformation in virtue. Picquigny had suggested this living in Christ meant a "spiritual and divine life." Moreau made this connection more concrete and connected it to the sacramental life as *imitatio*. Christ comes to live in a disciple through baptismal death and rebirth as well as the Christlike practice of virtue. In later writings, Moreau would point to explicit examples of this change, such as in the life of St. Vincent de Paul (1581–1660). In spiritual writings, Moreau would encourage retreatants to consider Christ from Galatians 2:20 as speaking through their mouths, praying on their lips, and acting in their limbs.[72]

As Moreau developed a synthesis of former teachers' courses, material recommended to him by Mollevaut, and his own reading of scripture and commentaries, he began to emerge as a more mature scholar.[73] His sophisticated library went beyond the manuals of his time and included many patristic sources and spiritual writings.[74] His own treatise entitled *De religione et ecclesia* is perhaps the clearest evidence of this scholarly maturation. Written specifically for seminarians in Holy Cross, the work is, in many respects, a paradigmatic example of Moreau's thinking. First, it acknowledges a specific, local theology (i.e., the Gallican theology of Le Mans)—even if only to state its limitations. Secondly, it addresses the broader Catholic tradition as well as the philosophical underpinnings of natural religion. Finally, it includes a historical treatment of salvation, the nature of the Bible, *creatio ex nihilo*, the flood, and Abraham, before it segues into the life of Christ, including his plan of redemption, birth, infancy, and public actions.[75] Thus, a treatise that represents the grand synthesis of Moreau's work as both a scholar and teacher, *De religione et ecclesia* demonstrates Moreau's sensitivity to local theology, his concern for the universality of the theological enterprise, and the presentation of these concerns so as to be accessible to student members of Holy Cross.

4. Developing a Pedagogy of Christian Education

Moreau's experience as a seminary professor, both in teaching and in curriculum development, laid the foundation for his philosophy of education. After Bouvier was made bishop of Le Mans in 1834, Moreau served as the vice-rector of St. Vincent's. In this capacity, Moreau made a genuine innovation in seminary education at St. Vincent's by establishing a course in physics and by hiring a physics professor.[76] This action satisfied a dual need. It assumed that those educated to be clergy would need to teach, but also—unlike Moreau's parish priest who taught him Latin lines—assumed that the new generation of teachers needed to be conversant with the demands of science as well. It also satisfied Moreau's perceived need for broad intellectual inquiry and engagement in Christian education. Moreau, in a later conference on how to study, cited scripture, Aquinas, Cicero, and Francis Bacon in the same lecture. He saw no reason that a seminary education—and later a Holy Cross education—should not have the same breadth and depth as other types of education.[77]

This concern is also evident in Moreau's writings as superior of Holy Cross. In some of his most famous lines on education, the mutually demanding synthesis of faith and reason is quite plainly stated in a way remarkable for Moreau's time:

> No, we wish to accept science without prejudice and in a manner adapted to the needs of our times. We do not want our students to be ignorant of anything they should know. To this end, we shall shrink from no sacrifice. But we shall never forget that virtue, as Bacon puts it, is the spice which preserves science. We shall always place education side by side with instruction; the mind will not be cultivated at the expense of the heart. While we prepare useful citizens for society, we shall likewise do our utmost to prepare citizens for heaven. (p. 417)[78]

While the *telos* of education for Moreau was heavenly beatitude, he understood that both the rigorous education of the intellect and the formation of virtue were constitutive in the development of students. Preparing them to be citizens of heaven meant training them to be contributing citizens in this world.

Intellectual and Spiritual Influences on Moreau

As a young professor, Moreau revealed himself as a thinker with diverse abilities and interests. His intellectual influences came primarily from three sources: Sulpician and French School spiritualities, Ignatius of Loyola, and liturgical spirituality through Dom Guéranger at Solesmes (Benedictine) and silent retreats at La Trappe (Cistercian).

1. Sulpician Spirituality and the French School

Through his education at Saint-Sulpice and his year at the Solitude of Issy, Moreau incorporated a great deal of Sulpician and French School spiritualities into his own prayer and writing. He later instilled this spirituality into his religious community. Sulpician and French School spiritualities are not synonymous, but rather the former is one example of the latter. Moreau's encounter with both came through the Sulpicians, first in Paris and Issy and then through his ongoing relationship with Mollevaut, his spiritual director.

The French School first originated in the thought of Pierre de Bérulle (1575–1629). A French cleric and later cardinal who participated in an early seventeenth-century mystical circle, Bérulle formulated an abstract mysticism that then underwent a Christological turn around 1605–1610.[79] As a "school," however loosely termed, the French School responded to a number of influences. The Council of Trent had instituted seminaries for priestly education, but they had not become law in France.[80] Those considered primary members of the French School—including Bérulle, Jean-Jacques Olier (1608–1657), and St. John Eudes (1601–1680)—were all somehow involved with the education or spiritual formation of priests.[81] Bérulle said that authority, holiness, and doctrine concerning priests—that is, the priestly office, spirituality, and learning—had been divided. The priestly office was relegated to bishops, spirituality to the religious, and learning to professors. None of these included the regular or secular clergy for whom all three were intended.[82]

Bérulle's solution was in part a theological one. He returned to central theological mysteries for insight into daily life that would reintegrate priesthood, spirituality, and learning for the regular cleric. He stressed the Incarnation as an extension or expression of the Trinity. Echoing the prologue of the Gospel of John, Bérulle wrote, "He who is, becomes: the Uncreated is created . . . the One who enriches the world becomes poor."[83] Pope Urban VIII (1568–1644) later called Bérulle the "apostle of the incarnate Word," since Bérulle argued that Jesus Christ was God's unique and highest revelation.[84] Echoing the Irenaean and Athanasian formulae on divinization, Bérulle believed that God became man in order to make humans divine. This Christology formed something of a metaphysics of the Incarnation, because the love in which humanity was assumed by the divinity of Christ could not, for Bérulle, pass away. Consequently, the effects of the Incarnation resonate in all human beings and prompt the need for direct meditation on, and participation in, the life of Christ.[85] Though this meditation would take different forms in the work of Olier and Eudes, both exhibit a strong incarnational focus with a clear Trinitarian background. These themes are also present in Moreau. The unity of the family of Holy Cross, for example, was inspired in part by the relations of the three persons of the Trinity.[86] Further, the *telos* of life in Holy Cross was imitating, loving, and thereby becoming another Christ.[87] Teaching this end would be the purpose of its educational mission.

The theology of Bérulle was made practical by the work of Olier. Olier knew St. Vincent de Paul (1581–1660) and St. Francis de Sales (1567–1622), both models for Moreau in his own life and in his teaching. Olier was a pastor and a founder of seminaries. His primary foundation was Saint-Sulpice in Paris, but he also organized a missionary society that went to modern-day French Canada. His *Introduction à la vie et aux vertus Chrétiennes* provided a programmatic manner of following Christ in fifteen chapters, focusing on the removal of vice and the cultivation of virtue.[88] This and other works of Olier put into perspective the rigorous rule of life that Moreau established for himself during his year at the Sulpician Solitude of Issy.

Eudes, a third figure from the French School, would shape Moreau's devotional practices. Although passages about the heart of Jesus can be found in both Bérulle's and Olier's writings, Eudes presented meditations on the Sacred Heart of Jesus and connected the heart of Mary with the heart of Jesus—a union laid out most completely in the culminating work of his life, *The Most Admirable Heart of the Most Sacred Mother of God.*[89] In order to categorize that which Mary held in her heart (Lk 2:19, 51), Eudes spoke of interconnected divisions within the hearts of Mary and Jesus. These divisions allowed him to maintain distinctions between earthly and divine, and between bodily and spiritual, within the context of human flesh's incarnational sharing in the heart of Christ.

Accordingly, the French School described the mysteries of Christian salvation in strong, affective language for the purpose of shaping an individual's relationship to Christ and his body, the Church. For instance, the heart became a central trope for the description of God's love for humans and humans' love for God, as well as for the meeting of both.[90] Francis de Sales would describe the Mount of Calvary as a "mount of lovers," a martyrdom of love that takes place primarily in the heart.[91] Conformity with Christ brought about a union of hearts, not only between the person and God, but also between the person and the Church. The corresponding ecclesiology of the period was strongly tied to the Pauline imagery of the head, body, and members; it was precisely together that believers were growing to full stature as the whole Christ.[92] This affective language was derived from and gained its strength of expression from careful exegesis of scripture and patristic commentaries. Though Moreau did not utilize all of the divisions within the Eudist system, he nevertheless placed the various constituencies of Holy Cross under the heart of Jesus (priests), the heart of Mary (sisters), and the heart of Joseph (brothers). Union within Holy Cross stemmed from a union of hearts with one another and with the Holy Family.[93]

In addition, from the time of Bérulle onward, the French School thinkers—and subsequently Moreau—were committed to an understanding that the mystery of the Church was lived in liturgical prayer and mission.[94] Liturgical prayer, particularly grounded in an emphasis on preaching the scriptures and praying before the Blessed Sacrament, provided the most important way to contemplate and conform one's life to Christ's Incarnation and the paschal mystery. The work of missions or retreats was the extension of the Incarnation into their own day. Examples of these two principles abound in the writings and activity of Moreau as he organized parish missions—and shortly thereafter, international missions—to enrich the life of the Church. In addition to preaching, Moreau's missions and the later missions of Holy Cross also involved a rich liturgical experience: reciting the Stations of the Cross, praying benediction, and celebrating the sacraments—all for the purpose of education in the way of imitating Christ.[95]

2. St. Ignatius of Loyola

Along with the French School, St. Ignatius of Loyola (1491–1556) became another major influence on Moreau. Moreau had read Ignatius in the past for personal spiritual nourishment, but he now turned to him with a new and quite practical purpose: the ongoing development of the spiritual lives of the members of his religious community.[96] Moreau's *Spiritual Exercises* are structured around the model provided by Ignatius with Moreau's own added insights. The *Spiritual Exercises* of Ignatius are set out in a series of four weeks, each with different spiritual emphases in relation to the life of Christ.[97] Moreau follows an essentially Ignatian meditation structure with a series of two or three preludes drawn largely from scripture but occasionally from other sources. The exercise invites the retreatant to engage the imagination in drawing closer to Christ, through a meditation either on an action of Christ or on one's own sin and need for repentance. The retreatant then works through the exercises as they are helpful; the object is less efficiency or completion than a deep engagement with Christ. Finally, at the end of the exercises, Moreau, like Ignatius, often writes either a colloquy—a conversation of gratitude with Christ or Mary—or a preparation for sacramental action, such as confession or Holy Communion. Although Moreau borrowed from the structure and writing of Ignatius, he did not consider himself strictly bound to its content or form. His first and most significant departure from Ignatius was to write directly for the retreatant, rather than for the spiritual director or retreat master. Moreau's model eliminated the intermediary.

Moreau was not the first in the French School to borrow from Ignatius. Bérulle himself had integrated Ignatius into his own spirituality after making his early seventeenth-century incarnational and mystical turn.[98] Vincent de Paul used Ignatian ideas in setting up the rules of the Congregation of the Mission and the Daughters of Charity.[99] The French School and Ignatius also shared a common affinity for Thomas à Kempis's *Imitation of Christ* because of its emphasis on the interior life and the active modeling of one's life on Christ's.[100] Ignatius provided the French School a mode of contemplating the human Christ that complemented their incarnational spirituality. Perreault rightly summarizes that "Moreau's thought focuses on Christ, the Word made flesh, through whom God's life is restored to us."[101] Ignatian structures provided a natural fit as Moreau worked out ways for his religious to become more "conscious" of and "committed" to this central, spiritual insight.[102]

3. Solesmes and La Trappe

Given Moreau's liturgical interests, he also found inspiration in two nearby monasteries—the famous abbey of Solesmes and La Grande Trappe of Mortagne. An eleventh-century Benedictine foundation in the area, Solesmes had been abandoned during the French Revolution but was revitalized under the vision and leadership of Prosper Guéranger (1805–1875). Contemporaries, Moreau and Guéranger became personally acquainted. At one level, they had a great deal in common: both were leaders of religious communities near Le Mans, and both struggled with Gallican Bishop Bouvier. Some of their correspondence survives in sixteen brief letters in the Solesmes archives (addressed from Moreau to Guéranger).[103] For example, Moreau's letter of February 12, 1852, to Guéranger indicates shared advocacy on the part of both Moreau and Guéranger for the Roman liturgy in the diocesan synod of 1852 in Le Mans. Catta and Catta suggest, however, that a deeper connection and friendship between the two would have been impossible, since a relationship between the two would have been threatening to Bishop Bouvier.[104] Ultimately, it was Guéranger's liturgical thought itself that would have the most profound intellectual effect on Moreau. The abbot's *Liturgical Year* prompted the overhaul of Moreau's own meditation writing, bringing it more in line with the rhythm of the liturgical year.[105]

Another religious foundation in the Le Mans area, the Trappist monastery La Grande Trappe of Mortagne, provided Moreau with spiritual retreat and solace.[106] As a young priest, he had made a retreat at a different Trappist foundation, and he often sought out the silence of La Grande Trappe for his own prayer. His last spiritual testament of 1867 was written from his retreat at La Trappe. Moreau even took the Auxiliary Priests there in October of 1836 to discern how they would live and work together, and thus La Trappe played an important role in the founding of Holy Cross. Moreau later wrote to the abbot: "Holy Cross began in your monastery."[107]

4. Synthesis

Moreau was able to draw on any number of these theological influences, integrating them into his own synthesis. A good example is his sermon to his religious on how to meditate.[108] In an attempt to cultivate a life of prayer, he taught that those who pray will be just, have love for those around them, look hopefully to heaven, and yield rich fruit in the harvest of the Lord. Those who neglect meditation are "tepid" and "languishing." They "are like plants on an arid plain, withered by the heat of a torrid sun." In an effort to cultivate a habit of meditation, or drinking in of the "dew of God's grace," Moreau presents his religious with a number of options. Moreau walks carefully through a modified form of Ignatian prayer, giving exercises for memory, understanding, and will. He is able to shift quickly, however, and explain that while directed at the same end, the Sulpician mode of prayer is somewhat different, addressing prayer directly to the Savior. Moreau mentions the differences that the Visitandines and the Carmelites, especially St. Teresa of Avila (1515–1582), offer on these two methods and explains them accordingly. Moreau's concern in setting forth a spiritual program for his religious was first and foremost that they were praying. He knew well the various prayer resources at his disposal and presented them all.

The fluidity with which Moreau drew from different parts of the tradition ought not be seen as scattered or diffuse. Moreau was actually marshaling all the resources at his disposal in order to promote a singular goal: the complete conformity of his disciples to Christ. This singularity of purpose reveals the enduring influence of the French School on Moreau. Even years removed from Saint-Sulpice and the Solitude, the French School—particularly its incarnational Christology—remained the most defining characteristic of Moreau's intellectual formation and subsequently his theological thinking. To understand Moreau's writings means to look at them through the lens of imitating Christ, a practice he first and most deeply learned from the Sulpicians and the French School thinkers, even as he enriched it with the wider tradition.

The Early Developments of Holy Cross

With this understanding of Moreau's intellectual formation and his spiritual influences, one can now consider the work into which Moreau would apply much of his theological study and thought: the Congregation of Holy Cross. He dedicated twenty-nine years—over half of his priesthood, from 1837 to 1866—to founding, shaping, teaching, and leading this international congregation of educators. The roots of the Congregation of Holy Cross, however, actually predate Moreau and go back to Jacques Dujarié and the Brothers of St. Joseph. When Moreau was given charge of the Brothers of St. Joseph, he joined them with his own Auxiliary Priests, and Holy Cross was born. Within a few years, Moreau added a branch of sisters, and his new association was complete. This complex history will set the stage and provide the context for his greatest theological works.

1. The Brothers of St. Joseph

After the ending of the French Revolution and the signing of the concordat, Dujarié was appointed pastor in Ruillé-sur-Loir in 1803. Within
three years, he had assembled a group of ten young women to assist
him with the instruction of children and care for the sick—two immense
needs in the wake of the French Revolution.[109] At a diocesan retreat in
1818, with his community of women growing quickly, Dujarié was
approached about founding a community of teaching brothers.[110] By
September 1820, he had received his first three recruits (although one
was quickly dismissed, and neither of the other two persevered beyond
the first few years).[111] The lack of training and formation, coupled with
poor living conditions, led to a lack of retention and a high turnover
rate. Given the pressing need for brothers in parishes and schools, many
of his recruits, including some as young as sixteen years old, received
only a few months of rudimentary training before they were sent out
to teach.[112] Moreover, although they took the title "brother," the Brothers of St. Joseph did not take formal religious vows, and their spiritual
formation was often as lacking as their educational training.[113] These
departures, setbacks, and challenges, however, were offset by a steady
stream of new candidates and new schools. Within five years of their
founding, the Brothers of St. Joseph had seventy-three members, and
they worked in thirty-two schools.[114]

Moreau's connection with the Brothers of St. Joseph goes back to
their earliest days when Dujarié asked him to preach the community's annual retreat in 1823.[115] He returned multiple times to lead the
retreat, and Dujarié also relied on Moreau for guidance in stabilizing his
community when the political instability in 1830 lowered retention.[116]
At Moreau's encouragement, the brothers drew up a "Pact of Fidelity"
at their annual retreat in 1831, seeking to deepen the moral bonds
of the members to the community and its work.[117] The following year,
again largely at Moreau's inspiration, the community developed a plan
for improvement, aimed at both structural reorganization and spiritual

renewal, including a proposal to examine the addition of religious vows. The plan also called for a spiritual director, and Moreau was chosen for the position.[118] Many of these other proposals, however, would go unfulfilled.[119]

Given his strong connections with the organization, the brother-directors who helped lead the community unsurprisingly turned to Moreau in 1835 when it came time to find a successor to their ailing, virtually bedridden leader.[120] Moreau expressed his willingness to serve in a letter to Br. Leonard on June 17, provided that he was given full authority and that the brothers' headquarters was moved to Le Mans.[121] Two days later, on June 19, Moreau met with Bishop Bouvier, who asked him to assume leadership of the Brothers of St. Joseph. Over the ensuing weeks, Moreau worked carefully and respectfully with Dujarié to ensure a smooth transition, which would take place at the community's annual retreat.[122] On August 31, the last day of the retreat, Dujarié formally asked the bishop, in the presence of the assembled community, to name Moreau his successor. With the approval of Bishop Bouvier, Moreau responded with characteristic trust in divine providence: "Abandoning myself entirely to God, I accept the burden of this task out of obedience, and I hope, my very dear Brothers, that, as I make this sacrifice of myself, I shall find in you men who will be docile and ready to cooperate with my efforts to insure the welfare of this congregation."[123] Dujarié died less than three years later on February 17, 1838, after spending his last years with the community at Moreau's invitation.

Moreau quickly implemented many of the proposed spiritual and temporal reforms that had not been fully realized, and he moved their novitiate to the Sainte-Croix quarter of Le Mans.[124] Moreau's post as professor of scripture and vice-rector at St. Vincent's Seminary in Le Mans certainly was a factor in the move. The proximity with Sainte-Croix allowed him to direct the brothers personally while he continued to work at St. Vincent's, at least for another year. The move also allowed Moreau to "procure for the novices the kind of training demanded by the needs of the day."[125] Moreau utilized St. Vincent's professors to provide the Brothers of St. Joseph a more thorough academic training, and he secured other instructors who provided the brothers "lessons in reading, writing, arithmetic, geography, linear drawing, surveying, architecture, singing, sacred and profane history, not to mention book-keeping and the courses on Christian Doctrine and the religious life."[126] The breadth of their education reflected not just the needs of a rural teacher, but also Moreau's vision of the completeness of a Christian education. In addition, Moreau ensured a more thorough spiritual training for them before sending them out to teach and work.[127]

2. The Auxiliary Priests and the Fundamental Act of Union

Also significant in the decision to move the brother's novitiate to Sainte-Croix was a new initiative that Moreau was undertaking in Le Mans. The land for the new novitiate had been originally slated for this other undertaking—a group of Auxiliary Priests. The first associates of this new group had been gathered by Moreau on retreat at La Grande Trappe just before he received charge of the Brothers of St. Joseph in 1835.[128] Moreau had been interested in forming a group of priests to preach parish missions and retreats since his time as a newly ordained priest at Saint-Sulpice, where he witnessed firsthand the missions in Paris.[129] Dujarié had also harbored a similar idea, but the association never came to fruition.[130] Moreau initially envisioned the Auxiliary Priests as an autonomous association focused both on revitalizing parish life through missions and on instructing the youth, especially in preparatory seminaries and colleges.[131] Once given leadership of the Brothers of St. Joseph, Moreau's vision began to broaden. On March 1, 1837, less than two years after becoming the superior of the brothers and founding the Auxiliary Priests, Moreau brought the two groups together in the Fundamental Act of Union, which was signed by fifty-four brothers and seven priests.[132] This document gave birth to the new association that became known as Holy Cross, named after the village of Sainte-Croix where it was founded.

3. The Religious Family of Holy Cross

Moreau, however, was not done assembling his religious family. The auxiliary needs at the new boarding school in Sainte-Croix, including the infirmary and clothes room, were continuing to grow. After contacting two communities of religious sisters that declined his request for assistance, Moreau began to assemble a group of young women to work at Sainte-Croix in 1838 and 1839.[133] Although originally gathered to assist with the auxiliary services, they soon came to teach and administer their own schools.[134] Moreau's intent from the earliest days of gathering together these women was to include them as an integral and essential part of Holy Cross. He even attempted, unsuccessfully, to include the sisters in his association's preliminary constitutions.[135] Whether or not this was a part of his original plan at the time of the Fundamental Act of Union, Moreau grew to see the inclusion of a branch of sisters as God's plan for Holy Cross. Once again, Moreau relied on divine providence:

> If I could have foreseen the development of the Congregation of Holy Cross from the outset, I could then have regulated and coordinated everything in advance. If such were the case, however, this Congregation would have been a merely human combination and not the work of divine providence. The fact of the matter is that it began and developed in a manner so mysterious that I can claim for myself neither credit for its foundation nor merit for its progress. Therein lies the indubitable proof that God alone is the Founder of this Congregation.[136]

Moreau always maintained that joining the Brothers of St. Joseph with his Auxiliary Priests was in conformity with Dujarié's intentions for the brothers.[137] Dujarié had envisioned a society of priests to lead the Brothers of St. Joseph and the Sisters of Providence. That said, Moreau did more than simply bring to fruition what Dujarié never could. The association Moreau formed at Holy Cross bore his unique stamp, particularly as an expressly religious community living the vows of poverty, chastity, and obedience.[138] Although the Brothers of St. Joseph had an annual promise of obedience (which not all took), Dujarié never permitted them to profess religious vows.[139] Moreau, though, had encouraged the brothers to profess vows since 1832, because he saw religious life as a means of not only stabilizing but also energizing their community.[140] Once he assumed leadership in 1835, Moreau instituted religious vows as part of the community, and the first brothers professed their perpetual vows at the 1836 retreat.[141] Despite other obstacles in gaining permission for the priests and sisters to profess vows, Bishop Bouvier received Moreau's own perpetual profession on August 15, 1840. Later that evening, four Auxiliary Priests, including Fr. Edward Sorin, made their profession.[142] The first profession of vows by the sisters came in 1843.[143]

The religious life, with its communal living of the vows of poverty, chastity, and obedience, was central to Moreau's vision for Holy Cross, and it was connected to two other significant departures from Dujarié's vision. First, whereas Dujarié's vision of the mission field remained local, responding to the immediate and immense needs that pressed upon him in the wake of the French Revolution, Moreau's vision, like his understanding of the Church, was international. Although at the time Holy Cross was an association of diocesan right and thus subject to the authority of the local bishop, Moreau began sending his priests and brothers to missions outside of France in 1840, just three years after the Fundamental Act of Union.[144] The first sisters sent on international mission left for the United States in 1843.[145]

Second, as previously mentioned, Dujarié had envisioned a society of priests to govern the Brothers of St. Joseph and the Sisters of Providence. At this time in the Church in France, such a vision was not uncommon. There were other associations that were comprised, at least loosely, of societies of priests, brothers, and sisters.[146] Moreau's contribution was to envision, notwithstanding the role of the priests as ecclesiastical superiors, a common dignity among the members of the institute—an equality rooted, not only in their shared religious life, but also in the models of the Holy Trinity and the Holy Family that Moreau held up for his association and its union. Accordingly, the priests, brothers, and sisters were all to share in the work entrusted to the association in different yet complementary ways.[147]

Moreau's Leadership and Development of Holy Cross

During nearly three decades as the head of Holy Cross, Moreau transformed his religious family from its humble beginnings in Sainte-Croix into an international religious congregation, approved by the Vatican and serving on four continents. Even while overseeing this time of rapid growth, he was an extraordinarily productive writer. These years were also marked by intense spiritual strife for Moreau, both in his personal life and in the life of his community. The keys to understanding his life and thought can be roughly divided around five central themes: the evolving structure of the association; the growth of the community and its work; the impact of Moreau's "dark night" on his spiritual writings and leadership; his work in Christian education; and the long struggle for and reception of papal approbation of Holy Cross.

1. Circular Letter 14 and the Association of Holy Cross

In September 1841, Moreau substantially laid out his overall vision for Holy Cross in a circular letter, which is a letter addressed to all members of the community to provide them with news, exhortations, and spiritual guidance. By then, Moreau had led the various branches of his fledgling association for six years. He had watched as the events of those years, especially in response to the need for education, slowly gave shape to the Brothers of St. Joseph, the Auxiliary Priests of Holy Cross, and the Marianite Sisters of Holy Cross. Bolstered by a growing wave of vocations, the community was starting new foundations within France in tandem with undertaking its first foreign missionary endeavors to Algeria in 1840 and to the United States in 1841.[148] By September of that year, Moreau was finally ready to spell out the aims and organization of Holy Cross in Circular Letter 14.[149] Former superior general of Holy Cross Fr. Thomas Barrosse referred to Circular Letter 14 as the "Magna Carta of Holy Cross."[150] This letter reveals Moreau's intellectual and spiritual formation synthesized in the service of his missionary interests.

Holy Cross had grown more quickly and fruitfully than Moreau had imagined. He explains his own role in what he would refer to throughout his life as the "work" of Holy Cross. The work, according to Moreau, was God's, and God alone would see it to completion.[151] In keeping with this conviction, Moreau consistently and unfailingly writes about divine providence guiding Holy Cross, even at his darkest hour.[152] Moreau understood himself at the service of Holy Cross, as an instrument in the hands of God that might be used according to the Lord's purposes. He believed that the work given to Holy Cross was far from complete, calling "for many sacrifices and much labor . . . to afford [the association's members] an intellectual formation in keeping with the needs of the times, and to establish uniformity in their conduct and their teaching methods" (pp. 379–380).[153]

The work of education, the topic of Moreau's statement above, was the daily labor of Holy Cross. That work could only be undertaken if members were striving at the same time to live "a perfect life," which for Moreau was imitating Christ with the ultimate goal to reach heaven. Perfection literally meant being "finished" or "completed," which included moral perfection but also included the broader concept of the *telos* of Christian life and, in particular, the religious life.[154] Perfection came from a purity of intention that sought not oneself but God alone and that required a continual imitation of the acts and dispositions of Christ. Spiritually, this imitation meant patterning one's own life on both the inner and outer lives of Christ, described by Moreau:

> It will be a life of devotion to the work of teaching or of any other
> employment, to punctuality to the common exercises, and to the
> shunning of idleness. Lastly, it will be an interior life, elevated to
> God by the habitual practice of acts of faith, hope, and charity,
> after the example of Jesus Christ, who is to be the particular
> model of our conduct. Unless we wish to ruin the work of Holy
> Cross, it is absolutely essential for us to lead with our Lord a life
> hidden in God. (pp. 380–381)[155]

Though Moreau outlined an apostolic life rather than a monastic
one for his religious, he structured the values of such a life with the
disciplines he learned during his own quasi-monastic year with the
Sulpicians at the Solitude of Issy. He focused on the manners and actions
of Jesus' life later in the letter, but the general principle of close imitation of Christ's acts and dispositions remained important and consistent
throughout all Moreau's writings.

For Moreau, the individual modeling of one's life on Christ forms the
foundation for union in Holy Cross. Personal union with Christ happens
through imitation. Union *with* Christ brings about more perfect union
with one's neighbors *in* Christ. Moreau describes this unity with different
images. When speaking about the highest form of unity, he always gives
recourse to the Trinity.[156] In practical discussions, he holds up "the Holy
Family wherein Jesus, Mary, and Joseph, notwithstanding their difference
in dignity, were one at heart by their unity of thought and uniformity of
conduct" as a vision of union for Holy Cross (p. 384).[157] The members
of the Holy Family are the principal patrons of the three societies, with
the priests consecrated to the Sacred Heart of Jesus, the brothers to the
heart of Joseph (which Moreau changed later simply to St. Joseph), and
the sisters to the Sorrowful Heart of Mary.

At other times, Moreau uses the Johannine image of the vine and
the branches or the Pauline image of the body with Christ as head.[158] He
was giving his community images of union that emphasized its power to
accomplish good, since union had such an essential part in the mission

and work of Holy Cross. Spurred by political movements that achieve
their own designs by harnessing the power latent in the masses and
joining them together in a single cause, Moreau wanted his religious to
harness the greater power latent in union with each other in Christ to
achieve God's designs:

> In fact, why are the political parties that are disturbing society
> today powerful enough to bring about revolutions and upheavals?
> Is it not because they know the secret of uniting and working for
> one same end? Would it not, then, be disgraceful for you and
> for me not to do for the cause of good, for God, and for eternity
> what the children of the world do every day for the cause of
> evil, for the world, and for the short day of this life? Ah, we who
> are disciples of a God who died for the salvation of souls who
> are perishing, we do not realize all the good we could do for
> others through union with Jesus Christ in the spirit of our rules
> and constitutions. It is this touching mystery of religious union
> that our Savior unveiled for us in the Gospel when he explained
> the incorporation of all the faithful with his divine person in the
> mystical body of which he is the head and we the members. Since
> we form with him but one body and draw life from the same
> Spirit, he urges us to remain united in him, like the vine and the
> branches, borne by the same root and nourished by the same sap,
> and forming together but one plant. (p. 383)[159]

For Moreau, although union—stemming from incorporation in Christ
and modeled in the persons of the Trinity—was first a spiritual and salvific matter, it also held the key to the success or failure of the work God
had entrusted to Holy Cross. Moreover, in a time when the Revolution
had driven many religious practices into the recesses of homes and
schism had fractured the unity of the Church in France, Moreau was
making strong claims on the communal and universal dimension of
Christianity.

2. Growth of the Congregation

The years from the community's founding until its official recognition by the Vatican were a time of great growth in Holy Cross. After its initial missionary endeavors to Algeria and Indiana, USA, subsequent missions began from Sainte-Croix in rapid succession to Quebec, Canada (1847), Louisiana, USA (1848), Rome (1850), East Bengal (present-day Bangladesh and Northeast India, 1852), and Poland (1856).[160] In France, new schools were being added, and a conventual church, Notre-Dame de Sainte-Croix, was completed and consecrated in 1857.[161] Not all of these missions (i.e., Algeria and Poland) endured, but rapid expansion from France brought with it both ministerial successes and practical hardships. The most pressing of these difficulties concerned leadership and personnel. While the quick spread of Holy Cross demanded the ingenuity and zeal of religious in particular areas, the governmental structure of the community remained centered on Moreau and his council in France. This arrangement became increasingly difficult in matters of international communication and finance.[162] Moreau had to decline requests from bishops in Argentina and Australia for Holy Cross religious, since the community was already struggling to cover its greatly expanded commitments.

Despite these issues, the 1850s were a time of great productivity for Moreau. In addition to overseeing this missionary expansion and continuing to work for the association's recognition by the Vatican, Moreau also did a substantial amount of writing and preaching, aided in part by a knee infection he suffered in 1853, which limited his mobility and kept him from travel.[163] During this time, Moreau revised the constitutions for the priests, brothers, and sisters. He wrote *Christian Education* and revised his *Spiritual Exercises* and *Christian Meditations*. Moreau also remained active as a preacher. Both within and outside of Holy Cross, he would continue to preach retreats even in the final year of his life.

This period was not without difficulties for Moreau, particularly his ongoing conflict with Bishop Bouvier. Even in light of Pope Pius IX's otherwise favorable view of Holy Cross, Bouvier refused to recommend the association for Vatican approval, which would have given Holy Cross greater freedom and standing in the wider Church to pursue its international mission and growth. In its ongoing process of seeking formal approbation from Rome, Holy Cross was established by the Vatican as a missionary institute, under the supervision of the Propaganda Fide, the office in Rome responsible for the Catholic Church's missionary work and related activities.[164] Bouvier's own theological work, *Institutiones theologicae ad usum seminariorum*, started to draw suspicion in Rome for its Gallican agenda. Bouvier went to Rome in 1853 and promised to make amends to his theology as necessary. Vatican authorities were reluctant to acknowledge a new association in the diocese of a bishop who had just demonstrated a willingness to revise his theology on account of its Gallican content.[165] Bouvier's disposition toward Rome was less malleable in local practice.[166] Papal approbation of the Constitutions of Holy Cross and the community itself would not happen until after Bouvier died in 1854 and the incoming bishop offered his support to Moreau and Holy Cross.

Intracommunity tensions also plagued Moreau during this period. Moreau's and Sorin's relationship soured when Sorin refused to leave Notre-Dame du Lac and take over the new foundation in Bengal.[167] This period was also marked by many community deaths from disease, with significant outbreaks in Holy Cross communities abroad in Montreal (1853), New Orleans (1853), and Notre Dame (1854).[168] Moreau saw these conflicts and tragedies (along with other financial problems experienced by the community during this time) as crosses, and this trying period in the life of Holy Cross set the stage for Moreau's own experience of Christ's cross in his spiritual life.

3. Basil Moreau's Dark Night: October 1855

In 1855, Moreau underwent a "dark night" that marked a decisive event in his life.[169] He would refer to this event often, even at the end of his life.[170] Moreau never wrote an account of his dark night, but he described it aloud to his community:

> I never see the return of the month of October without being deeply moved because it recalls that frightful trial which God allowed to befall me either in the interests of the congregation or in order to give me a greater insight into the spiritual sufferings of others. For several years I had been without my spiritual director, M. Mollevaut, and my regular confessor was absent. It all began when I allowed myself to become terribly worried over the political revolution which I feared was imminent and over the high cost of living, which gave rise to serious concern. I saw, or thought I saw, very clearly the impending doom of the entire congregation, even abroad.[171]

Moreau, the superior who reminded his religious that no work inspired by faith can last without crosses, was experiencing perhaps the heaviest cross of his own life.[172] Those close to him asked Moreau how he allowed himself to become so discouraged, one "who used to have such great confidence in providence." Moreau's reply was humble: "I could find no satisfactory answer. I could only say that there are moments when those who undertake the works of God must be broken and humiliated—times when everything must be crushed." Moreau continued in this state, even questioning the work of the Holy Cross as he heard the stones being put into place in the conventual church: "Fool that you are, what a scandal you have caused in the Church of God." He did not think that in good conscience Holy Cross could take in students or take money from their parents on account of financial injustice. Moreau wrote to Sorin during this time: "I am in a continual state of affliction and extreme distress. May God have pity on us and watch over you in a very special way."[173]

Spiritually the matter reached its darkest moment in Moreau's prayer. He recounted:

> But [the community] never abandoned prayer, and you recall
> how we went sadly every evening to beg Jesus, father of the
> poor, for bread for the next day. Then, when the community had
> retired, I remained in the chapel for long hours. What did I do
> there? I went from station to station, searching for a light, for an
> inspiration, and I found nothing, absolutely nothing. I came back
> to the sanctuary, went up to the altar, and knocked on the door
> of the tabernacle. I waited and received no answer, not the least
> encouragement. At that moment I understood something of our
> Lord's abandonment in his agony as he went from his father to
> his disciples without finding any consolation. I then understood
> perfectly the suicide of Judas, and it would have been a real favor
> if someone had taken away from me two objects which I had
> procured and which were on my desk—a passport, which I had
> requested for the Ministry of Foreign Affairs, and five hundred
> francs to pay my passage. I would have yielded to the temptation,
> had I not kept my eyes fixed on the crucifix. I kept looking at it
> for days.

Moreau himself recounted that a rumor started to spread at the time
concerning his sanity, which he vehemently denied: "Nothing could be
more false. I was just as calm as I am today, and I enjoyed the use of all
my faculties. But I saw no escape; I thought it was all over."

A letter from Countess de Jurien, a friend and benefactress of Holy
Cross who had been informed of Moreau's spiritual state, brought his
despair to a close. Moreau wrote of this moment:

> The trial had been going on for about two months, and the com-
> munity had never ceased to pray for me, when I received a letter,
> which came from a distance of more than fifty leagues from a
> person who, at least as I supposed, could not have known of my
> condition. In this letter I found the phrase: "I see you in the same
> state as Peter, when he was sinking in the water." In the twinkling

of an eye light flooded my soul and all my confidence returned.
The trial was over.

The actual text of the letter exists, dated from Paris on October 30,
1855. De Jurien's letter continues after describing Peter sinking in the
water:

Our Lord held out his hand to him and scolded him. "Man of little
faith," he said, "why do you doubt?" And I, father, repeat these
same words to you with the authority of the master who spoke
them first, and I tell you also: "Why do you doubt?" Renew your
courage and peace. Peace, but in abandonment to God. This
work is from God and *not from you*.[174]

Remarkably, Moreau's circular letter written to the community during
that time shows his trust that the experience was part of God's providence. On October 25 of that year, Moreau wrote to his religious:
"Impenetrable are the designs of providence, and we must bow our
heads in resignation even under its most painful blows."[175] His trust did
not wane, but the cost had been great. Nevertheless, this experience of
conformity to Christ through the suffering of his cross was the event that
Moreau chose to reflect upon on for the occasion of the fiftieth anniversary of his priesthood, celebrated in 1872, the year before his death.[176]
The experience also represents, in many ways, the core of his spiritual
thinking concerning the cross of Christ, which will be taken up more
explicitly in the section "Moreau's Spiritual Emphases."

4. Christian Education

His dark night behind him, Moreau prepared "in haste" a work he saw
as vital for unity within Holy Cross's increasingly far-flung international
missions.[177] Although education had been at the heart of the community's
work since its founding, until 1856 Moreau had written sparingly and in
broad strokes about the contours and characteristics of a Holy Cross education. The rapid expansion of the community, however, began to raise

concerns for Moreau about the quality and consistency of the education provided by Holy Cross. He asked local houses to give him "specific information on their methods of teaching, their textbooks, etc." When those responses arrived, Moreau's suspicions were confirmed: "One fact is evident from these various reports, namely, the almost general lack of unity and cooperation, which are of such prime importance in this field." Moreau's solution was to "[prepare] a treatise on *Christian Pedagogy* for use in all our primary schools."[178]

In that treatise, entitled *Christian Education*, Moreau opens by describing education as "the art of forming youth—that is to say, for a Christian, to make of youth people who are conformed to Jesus Christ, their model" (p. 333).[179] He then outlines the specific virtues required of a Holy Cross teacher, as well as the personal style and character of the relationships to be fostered with students, especially those with particular needs. "If you show them greater care and concern, it must be because their needs are greater and because it is only just to give more to those who have received less" (p. 338).[180] Moreau then describes in detail the practicalities of classroom layout and management. He concludes *Christian Education* by calling on the community to "make haste, therefore; take up this work of the resurrection, never forgetting that the particular goal of your institution is, above all, to sanctify youth. By this, you will contribute to preparing the world for better times than our own, for these children who today attend your school are the parents of the future and the parents of future generations" (p. 376).[181]

5. Papal Approbation and Moreau from 1857–1860

In 1856, Moreau took a census of Holy Cross and reported to the community in Circular Letter 77 that the association had grown to 648 religious (72 priests, 322 brothers, 254 sisters). Together, they were educating ten thousand students on four continents.[182] In just under two decades, Holy Cross had grown significantly from the fifty-four brothers and seven priests who had signed the Fundamental Act of Union. The following year, with the positive interventions of Bishop Nanquette, the Holy Cross rules and constitutions received papal approbation from Propaganda Fide on May 13, 1857.[183] Just more than one month later, on June 17, Holy Cross's conventual church, Notre-Dame de Sainte-Croix, was consecrated.

This was a time of real joy for Moreau. He had stood in desolation at the tabernacle of a church not two years earlier. But now he approached the tabernacle of his own conventual church in tears of joy, a joy he expressed to his fellow Holy Cross religious:

> As for myself, I could not read the telegram announcing this solemn act without exclaiming with David: *Oh! How good is the God of Israel, to those who are upright of heart!* In this same church which has just been consecrated, it was only on my knees, at the foot of the tabernacle, and while shedding tears of happiness, that I could read the decree which makes the Congregation of Holy Cross an officially recognized body in the Church.[184]

It is easy to appreciate Moreau's joy after almost two decades of working tirelessly to receive approval of Holy Cross from the Vatican.

The approbation of the constitutions of Holy Cross signaled the beginning of the final nine years (1857–1866) that Moreau would lead Holy Cross. Moreau continued to write, including revising and updating the rules for Holy Cross (1858), publishing the second edition of his *Christian Meditations* (1859), and composing a new *Catechism* for religious life (1859) based on the writings of St. Robert Bellarmine (1542–1621).[185]

In the summer of 1857, Moreau made his only trip to North America, visiting the Holy Cross foundations in Canada and the United States. Overall, the apostolic visit was a great success, and from aboard the ship returning to France, Moreau wrote his next circular letter, addressing the Holy Cross religious in North America:

> Although we are far away from one another, you will be ever present to me, even to my last sigh, and I shall never forget even

the details of my sojourn in your midst. I could have described
for you one after another the various places I visited, and could
have set down the memories I brought away with me. . . . Since
I cannot record here the many houses and names which are all
dear to me, I beg them all to receive this expression of my satisfaction and of my thanks for their touching welcome.[186]

The circular letter also announced the 1860 General Chapter, which
would mark the escalation of Moreau's difficulties and foreshadow his
resignation as superior general of Holy Cross in 1866.

Moreau from 1860 to 1866

The 1860 General Chapter, a regular legislative meeting that constitutes
the highest governing body of Holy Cross, did not go well for Moreau
or his standing as superior general of Holy Cross.[187] Two key constit-
uents were missing: Sorin and the bishop-elect of Eastern Bengal, Fr.
Pierre Dufal, who both arrived in France only after the chapter was
finished.[188] The chapter did not accept Moreau's 1858 *Rules* without
modification and set up a committee chaired by Moreau's nephew, Fr.
Charles Moreau, to gather input on the rules and have a finished version
prepared for the next chapter in 1863.[189] Moreau also proposed that the
chapter address very contentious issues, including budgets, the creation
and suppression of foundations, and civil lawsuits. Ultimately, Moreau
offered his willingness to resign to the chapter, should he become an
obstacle to "peace and union of hearts."[190] The chapter did not accept
his offer.

1. Financial Woes

Although the causes for Moreau's rockiest years abound, two dynamics
remain essential for understanding the period that led to his resignation
as superior general of Holy Cross. Financially, as the work of Holy Cross
quickly spread to different lands, the use and administration of funds

became a matter of tension between the missions and the headquarters in Sainte-Croix. These tensions were sometimes procedural (e.g., waiting for approval from Moreau to build or undertake new loans), and other times they related to frustrations beyond congregational control (e.g., legal battles over donations).[191]

The most crushing of these financial troubles came from the actions of Br. Marie-Julien, the steward of the Holy Cross school in Paris, at the beginning of 1861. Br. Marie-Julien, a member of Moreau's administration and with power of attorney, made a number of loans that yielded no returns. The largest loan supported a foundation called "The Good Samaritan," which claimed to be supported by the Vatican and to offer aid to prominent persons who might "eventually be visited by misfortune."[192] This organization and its subsidiaries, however, were a scam. Even though Sorin had dealings with one of the leaders of these organizations, his reaction to the situation was well stated: "O God, dear Father, what a catastrophe! What will happen to the congregation unless God has pity on us?"[193] Matters would get worse, however, since Marie-Julien controlled not only funds for the house in Paris but also part of the funds for the missions to the United States and Bengal.

A net result of this complex affair, involving Holy Cross religious in both Indiana and Rome, burdened the congregation with a massive 210,000 franc debt.[194] The cardinal in Paris, wishing to avoid a public scandal, resisted Moreau's request to undertake fundraising to alleviate the debt and was grateful when Moreau assumed complete responsibility for it. Moreau was forced to mortgage the property of the congregation in France and to withhold funds meant for the missions. Holy Cross in France would never recover from the debt, and a later general chapter opted to sell Notre-Dame de Sainte-Croix.

2. Disagreements concerning Governance of the Sisters

The second major area of difficulties for Moreau in his later years of leadership surrounded governance of the sisters. Moreau's vision for

Holy Cross, as noted from Circular Letter 14, was that of priests, brothers, and sisters working together under the model of the Holy Family.
In its approval of the Constitutions of Holy Cross, however, the Vatican
required a separate governance structure and constitution for the sisters.
The Vatican suggested the sisters operate under the authority of the local
bishop, but Moreau pressed for them to have their own superior general
and be responsible, as the men were, to the Propaganda Fide in Rome.
Constitutions were not approved for the sisters until February 1867, and
this delay precipitated governance disputes, specifically whether the
sisters were an international congregation or a group of local associations controlled by the bishop in the area in which they served.[195] For
example, Bishop John Henry Luers (1819–1871) of Fort Wayne, Indiana,
wanted authority over the sisters in Indiana. Moreau wrote to the sisters
and to Luers that if the bishop instructed the sisters not to follow the
rules or constitutions of Holy Cross in any way, they were free to leave
the diocese.[196]

The difficulties over the relationship between the sisters in Indiana
and in France continued without resolve on a number of levels. American bishops interceded on behalf of American interests to postpone
Vatican approval of the sisters' constitutions. The relationship became
a significant source of conflict between Moreau and Sorin, as well as
between Moreau and Drouelle, who lived in Rome and was in communication with the Vatican.[197] This decade-long debate over governance of
the sisters contributed to a growing concern among the members of Holy
Cross regarding Moreau's ability to lead an international congregation.

Moreau's Resignation and Last Years

News of the congregation's misgivings about Moreau's leadership
reached the Vatican in late 1860 via an anonymous letter, which historians have since attributed to Holy Cross priest Louis-Dominique
Champeau.[198] The Vatican eventually responded in August 1861 by
calling for an official visitation of Holy Cross by the French Bishops.

Completed in September 1862, the visitation revealed the frustration of several important Holy Cross religious who were involved in Holy Cross from its earliest days.[199] Bishop Charles-Jean Fillion, who led the visitation, realized that Moreau had too many functions—he served as superior general, provincial of France, local superior, master of novices, and professor of theology.[200] Over the next four years, Moreau attempted on more than one occasion to resign as superior general of the Congregation of Holy Cross. His resignation, however, was accepted neither by the general chapters of Holy Cross nor by the Vatican until June 14, 1866, when Cardinal Barnabo from Propaganda Fide sent a letter accepting Moreau's resignation on behalf of Pope Pius IX.[201]

Moreau announced his resignation to the community in his last circular letter to Holy Cross in June of 1866.[202] This began Moreau's transition into the final era of his life, one marked by a rigorous preaching schedule, the revision of his *Christian Meditations* (1872), and his continued defense of local creditors who had financed Holy Cross's debt. These last years of Moreau's life were certainly difficult, and his writing reflects a driving concern about the treatment of the creditors, emotional pain from what he perceived to be slanders against his own name, and care for the future of Holy Cross. Moreau nevertheless visited Rome for one final audience with Pius IX, and the pope granted him freedom to spend his last years as he chose.[203] Moreau chose to live near Sainte-Croix with his biological sisters, though this decision, too, was a painful one.[204] Sorin, the newly elected superior general of Holy Cross, considered the future of the congregation to be in North America and subsequently moved the general administration to Notre Dame, Indiana. Though Sorin invited Moreau to live at Notre Dame, Moreau could not forgive Sorin for moving the community's headquarters despite the decree from the last general chapter that stipulated it should remain in France.[205] Moreau remained in France, and the Marianite sisters provided him with meals and remained with him through his hour of death on January 20, 1873.

Moreau wrote a last spiritual testament at La Grande Trappe in June of 1867, the year after he resigned, and supplemented it with a final statement in August of 1871. He asks forgiveness from God for his faults but expresses his pardon to all those who hurt him in the exercise of his ministry. Moreau also asks for pardon from those he unintentionally hurt and then gives thanks to both his natural family and religious family in Holy Cross. He closes his 1867 testament as follows:

> I sincerely thank all those who were kind enough to assist me in the foundations of which I was the instrument. I recommend myself to their faithful prayers, promising not to forget them before God if, as I hope from his infinite mercy, he deigns to make me live and die in his love.
>
> But it is to you that I address myself in conclusion, my dearest friends, priests, brothers, and sisters of Holy Cross, beloved sons and daughters in Jesus Christ, who, in the midst of my trials, have never ceased to show for me the deepest interest, the most tender attachment, and the most generous devotion. Receive here the last expression of my gratitude, esteem, and affection. Although separated in body, let us remain united in spirit and in heart and by constant fidelity to your Rules, by your devotion to the Sacred Heart of Jesus and the Immaculate Heart of Mary, obtain the grace of entering into eternal union with God and his elect. It is there that we shall meet after the farewells of this earth, if you are faithful to your vocation and acquire its spirit and its virtues daily in an ever increasing degree. To this end, observe inviolably the three vows of your religious profession, meditate on your Rules and my circulars and, lastly, pray for the poor priest who has been to you a father and who has turned his dying looks and last thoughts to each one of you, to bless you all. Fiat, Fiat![206]

Moreau's Spiritual Emphases

As mentioned previously, Moreau was a product of French School formation and concerned with education in the context of post-Revolution
France. Central themes emerge in Moreau's writings, and yet they all
spring from one central source: the imitation of Christ, and in particular
the crucified Christ. After addressing the centrality of the imitation of
Christ and his cross, we will treat three other related themes that deserve
separate comment: divine providence, union, and zeal.

1. Imitatio Christi: *the Centrality of the Cross*

The imitation of Christ is at the core of Moreau's theology and spirituality.
He writes that if the imitation of Christ is our duty, it is also our glory.[207]
For Moreau, this meant becoming another Christ, a work that begins in
Baptism and ends only in resurrection. Between Baptism and resurrection, however, for both Christ in the gospels and those who share in his
life, stands the cross. Learning to love the cross as a sign of real hope
was the spiritual core of Moreau's theology. Learning entailed practice,
and walking the way of the cross meant recognizing three things for
Moreau: that Christ represents the only possible reconciliation between
interior dispositions and exterior actions, that union with Christ means
union not only with his life but also with his death, and that those who
learn the mystery of the cross of Christ are also learning his resurrection.

Moreau introduced the concept of imitation of Christ to new religious by focusing on conforming their interior and exterior lives to Christ.
Moreau displays this clearly in his sermon to new Carmelites about to
receive their religious habits:

> Therefore, it is to each of you that, after first addressing these
> words to myself, I say: "Learn from Christ to put aside the old self
> and to put on the new self." But I am addressing you in a particu-
> lar way, since that is the purpose of your receiving the habit and
> the grace to ask for as you begin your novitiate. This is not merely

> a question of changing worldly fashions for clothes of a different
> quality, style, and color; that would not need to be blessed by the
> Word of God. It is, rather, a question of effecting in your life, in
> the eyes of faith, the transformation symbolized by the changing
> of attire, which will take place before this assembly. (p. 191)[208]

The habit was to be the outward expression of an inner transformation,
one to transfigure the entire life of the religious—thoughts, dispositions,
and ultimately actions.[209]

Such complete conformity, Moreau reminded the novices, was only
possible because of the Incarnation. In the Incarnation, the second person of the Trinity assumed human nature, being born in human flesh,
and thereby reconciled the divide between exterior and interior that sin
causes in humans. Moreau continues:

> This is not enough; you must identify yourselves with your model,
> not only in order to become a faithful copy, but to become some-
> what another Christ, according to his request to the father for his
> followers, that they become one with me as I am one with you,
> Father, and that they be in me as I am in them (Jn 17:21). Is this
> possible? Yes, and this is how. Just as intelligence and will in the
> body and soul of Jesus Christ are united by divine nature through
> the Incarnation, so is our spirit united to the spirit of Jesus Christ
> through faith, our heart to his heart through charity, and our body
> to his body through Communion. He also invites you to develop
> this union within you by saying: I am the life, the way, and the
> truth—life through my sacraments, truth by my doctrine, and the
> way by my example (Jn 14:6). (p. 199)

Moreau wanted those who heard him to seek union with Christ, not only
with their minds, but with their hearts and bodies as well. Therein was
the reintegration of their exterior and interior lives.[210]

Wearing religious garb and dedicating oneself to union with Christ
were only the first steps toward imitation of Christ. As a scholar, Moreau
had commented on Galatians 2:19b–20, and he continued to cite it with

frequency throughout his life: "I have been crucified with Christ; and it is no longer I who live, but it is Christ who lives in me. And the life I now live in the flesh I live by faith in the Son of God, who loved me and gave himself for me" (NRSV).[211] Union with Christ requires union not only with his life but also with his death. For Moreau, this too was eminently practical and emerges frequently in writings to his congregation.

The cross provided Moreau with a spiritual framework for speaking about the difficulties of the work of Holy Cross and the difficulties in his own life.[212] In Circular Letter 34 he writes to his religious:

> Thus is Jesus Christ pleased to try his work; only a religious spirit that understands the power of his cross can sustain our courage in the midst of all these trials. Happy, indeed, are we if we know how to profit by them and to understand the unspeakable advantage of becoming more and more conformed to the image of the divine Christ crucified. For those who live by faith, the cross is a treasure more valuable than gold and precious stones. If we were truly worthy of our vocation, far from dreading these crosses, we would be more eager to accept them than to receive a relic of the very wood that our Savior sanctified by his blood. Let us not allow ourselves, then, to be discouraged by trials, no matter how numerous or bitter they may be. Afflictions, reverses, loss of friends, privations of every kind, sickness, even death itself, "the evil of each day," and the sufferings of each hour—all these are but so many relics of the sacred wood of the true cross that we must love and venerate. We must enclose these precious souvenirs in a reliquary made of charity that is patient, resigned, and generous, and which, in union with the divine master, suffers all things and supports all things. Thus will we appease his justice. (pp. 413–14)[213]

Moreau is exhorting his religious to map their own trials and sufferings onto those of Christ. Rather than desiring a relic of the true cross, Moreau believes the sufferings his religious were enduring were relics themselves. Those sufferings and ills are to be cherished and guarded with love, patience, resignation, generosity, and union with God. Beneath the lofty language lies a very challenging teaching on the cross of Christ. Ultimately, imitation of Christ is not merely a way of coping with difficulties in the world; it becomes the way of faith seeking to approach them with love.

Moreau's theology, however, does not end at the cross; the presence of the cross indicates that resurrection follows. In more than one important instance, Moreau points to moments of resurrection and new life on account of conformity to the cross. In Circular Letter 11, following the departure of some of the members of Holy Cross, Moreau writes: "As you see, my dear sons in Jesus Christ, the tree of the cross has been planted in the land where our worthy religious dwell. . . . But these religious have learned to savor its life-giving fruits; and if God in his goodness preserves them in the admirable dispositions which they have shown thus far, they will never taste death, for the fruits of the cross are the same as those of the Tree of Life which was planted in the Garden of Paradise."[214] The scripture scholar is playing on the description of the Tree of Knowledge of Good and Evil, which had fruit pleasing to the eye, good for food, and that would cause wisdom (Gn 3:6). By alluding to Genesis, Moreau is claiming that the cross would not simply be something upon which people suffer, but it would itself become a new tree of life. Holy Cross's work is cultivating the growth that should emerge from where the cross is planted.

Moreau also connects the cross and the resurrection to his congregation's mission in education. He describes the work of Holy Cross educators as a "work of resurrection."[215] A true education, or preparation for heaven, is one that allows experiences of the cross to teach students, not only about a better life in this world, but also about life in its fullness in the world to come. Moreau's *Christian Education* concludes with an exhortation to contemplate their goal:

This is what you can and must do for your students, if you truly have zeal for their salvation. Make haste, therefore; take up this work of the resurrection, never forgetting that the particular goal of your institution is, above all, to sanctify youth. By this, you will contribute to preparing the world for better times than our own, for these children who today attend your school are the parents of the future and the parents of future generations. Each one of them carries within him or her a family. Influence them, therefore, by all the means of instruction and sanctification that I have just explained. Then, and only then, will you be able to hope to achieve the end of your vocation by the renewal of the Christian faith and of piety. Fiat! Fiat! (p. 376)[216]

For Moreau, those who dedicated themselves to imitating the life of Christ could not shirk crosses. Conformity to the cross was not intended as morose duty, but as a way to live in real anticipation of resurrection, as a way to practice authentic hope. Accordingly, Moreau placed his congregation under the motto *Ave Crux, Spes Unica*, which means, "Hail the Cross, Our Only Hope!"[217]

2. Divine Providence

The cross undergirds and sustains Moreau's trust in divine providence. His writings about providence—a topic of interest for the French School—show that, in his mind, God's designs need not only be found in those experiences of life that are of consolation and sweetness.[218] Moreau recognized experiences of sweetness as gifts from God, and he frequently exhorted his community to give thanks in the midst of blessings.[219] At the same time, Moreau writes more often of seeing the hand of providence in the midst of crosses, believing that "just as divine providence has willed its greatest works to begin in humility and abjection, it has also decreed that they should expand only at the price of difficulties and contradictions, trials, crosses, contempt, calumny, and detraction" (p. 450).[220] Moreau presents the cross and divine providence as so intertwined that divine providence, like the Christian life itself, is cruciform at its core. For Moreau, as Fr. Robert Kruse points out, "the presence of the cross is, therefore, characteristic of the work of God."[221]

This trust in divine providence naturally leads Moreau to a robust understanding of God's sovereignty over the world and world events, to the point that "it is [God] who, up to the present, has directed all those events which appeared most contrary to the execution of his holy will."[222] At the same time, Moreau never minimized the human will, which often gives in to sin and needs healing. He constantly urged his religious "to second the designs of this merciful providence which destines us for such great things."[223] Moreau did not believe in an automatic unfolding of God's will in an individual's life or in the life of his religious community, yet God's will could be found in all things. Trials and crosses were not immediately or instantly blessings, but they could "be changed later into the many precious stones that will make up the crown of glory reserved for those who have been faithful to the duties of their vocation and have worn lovingly, even to the end, their Savior's crown of thorns" (p. 390).[224] In this paradox of God's sovereignty and human freedom, God did not "[forbid] foresight and human initiative. He recommends elsewhere work, order, and economy in the use of temporal things, but he forbids all anxiety, because this is a reflection on his paternal providence."[225]

For Moreau, cooperating with the designs of providence draws Christians both into union with Christ and into union with each other. As he exhorted his fellow religious, "Let us, then, dear sons and daughters in Jesus Christ, continue to remain thus united in our Lord, and let us often come together in spirit in spite of the distance which separates us. By these relationships of mutual friendship and dependence we shall help one another correspond with the designs of providence in our regard and make a holy use of the rapidly succeeding years."[226] The key was to become a "simple instrument" in the hands of divine providence. In this way, one's life and one's work, much as the life and the work of the larger community, were transformed into "God's work."[227]

3. Union: Holy Trinity and Holy Family

From the pulpit of the cross, as Moreau styled it, Christ exhorted his followers to a particular sort of union:

> This is why Jesus Christ so earnestly recommended union to his disciples and why in his last moments from the heights of that pulpit of which, so to speak, one side rested on the Cenacle and the other on Calvary, he made of union a formal command, his command of predilection. For this reason also, addressing himself to his father in a most sublime and moving prayer, he earnestly asked that his disciples might be united with one another, as are the three divine persons of the Trinity, making them all as one. Oh, who will grant us this grace?[228]

Moreau was speaking in the context of the religious vows—poverty, chastity, and obedience—which represent the clearest way for the members of Holy Cross to remain in a union that might reveal God's providence in the world.[229] Two significant aspects of Moreau's thinking take shape in the text. First, the cross stands as a central connection for a number of spiritual realities. The cross reveals Christ's relationship to his father and his desire that his disciples might be united. For Moreau, following Christ requires a particular sort of union, a union perfectly exhibited in the Trinity.[230] Just as important, Moreau explains that the pulpit of the cross, from which Christ spoke to his apostles a command of unity, had a side that rested on the Cenacle, where Jesus hosted the Last Supper.[231] In a subtle allusion, Moreau reveals an enduring teaching throughout his writings: spiritual union is fostered in devotion to the Eucharist.[232]

Moreau was a fervent advocate of frequent Communion for his religious.[233] He urged his religious to throw themselves back into the arms of the God who "wants to be our father, not our judge. He is our friend, our brother who has for us only words of mercy and bounty, provided always we bring him a contrite and humble heart" (p. 122).[234] Theologically, Moreau believed that the Eucharist nourished and perfected the union he saw as necessary for Holy Cross to undertake the work of God. The Eucharist brings about immediate union with the person of Jesus: "Instead of acting like a royal personage before whom we must abase ourselves and from whom we must keep a respectful distance, Jesus even wishes to let our hands touch him, our hearts melt into his own, our whole being be filled with his" (pp. 121–122).[235] Moreau explains that the Father and the Spirit, the other members of the Trinity, are put completely at our disposal in the Eucharist as well. We dwell in the Trinity, and the Trinity dwells in us.[236] Though perhaps more difficult for individual contemplation, the end of Holy Communion, the end of religious life in Holy Cross, and the end of the Christian life in general was a sharing in the beatific vision of the Holy Trinity.[237]

Without diminishing emphasis on the perfect union of the members of the Trinity, Moreau supplied his religious with a second, more practical, image for the union of Holy Cross. In consecrating the priests, sisters, and brothers to Jesus, Mary, and Joseph, the interactions of the Holy Family could provide a pattern for the relations of Holy Cross in its communal life and ministry. This practical guide was important for Moreau, who believed that union also served a practical purpose in discipleship. He wrote of union becoming "a powerful lever with which we could move, direct, and sanctify the whole world, if the spirit of evil, who has been allowed to exercise his power over this earth, does not set himself up against the wondrous effects of this moral force" (p. 382).[238] Union with Christ brought those who, by the force of sin, had become divided against themselves, their Church, and the communion of the triune God into right relationship again.

4. A Virtue: Zeal

Moreau believed that interior and exterior conformity to Christ and his cross should be lived with zeal. Zeal became the virtue that characterized the work of Holy Cross. Moreau defines zeal most clearly in his treatise on *Christian Education*, describing it as "the great desire to make

God known, loved, and served, and thus to bring knowledge of salvation to others" (p. 337).[239] Zeal, as a virtue of religious life, encompasses both prayer and study. Times of retreat and prayer rekindle interior zeal, yet zeal is primarily about carrying out Christ's mission exteriorly in the world today. Zeal could be wrongly directed, falsely funneled into self-serving pursuits. True zeal must be fostered and constantly refined in humble, faithful imitation of Christ crucified, seeking to second the designs of divine providence, and striving for greater union in the Body of Christ.

Conclusion

To read Moreau is to engage a serious and committed priest, scholar, and educator who integrated the academic, spiritual, liturgical, and apostolic parts of life into his thinking and writing. Theological nuance permeates his letters and educational instruction, as well as his meditations and sermons. Moreau was a remarkably consistent thinker in a time and place when both society and the Church were shifting. Consistency, however, did not mean Moreau neglected these cultural shifts; it allowed him to guide others through them. Thus, a reader of Moreau must prepare to see his incarnational Christology at play and applied in response to political instability, community setbacks, and international missionary achievements.

An introduction to Moreau ought to end by setting forth what benefit Moreau might offer the modern reader, and to this question, the simple answer is hope. Moreau was convinced that in Christ are the mysteries of salvation that directly inspire the daily cultivation of virtue in imitation of him. He believed this was possible because sin and darkness had already spoken their strongest word. The reader of Moreau does not need to go looking for hope. By looking at Christ alongside Moreau, the reader realizes what Moreau had learned so thoroughly: in Christ, hope has once and always come to us. *Ave Crux, Spes Unica.*

Chapter 1

SERMONS

Almost immediately after his ordination to the priesthood, Moreau began preaching retreats and missions. He quickly developed a reputation as a gifted preacher and was frequently sought out by parishes and religious communities alike. Moreau continued this ministry personally throughout his priesthood, even during his busiest days leading the Congregation of Holy Cross, and up until the last days before his death.

Much of Moreau's preaching, including the sermons in this collection, came in the context of retreats or missions, which accounts for both their length and their topical or thematic nature. His sermons reveal not only the breadth and depth of his study and grasp of the faith, but also his training as an educator and his belief that education lies at the heart of evangelization. Whether preaching for religious or for lay men and women, Moreau weaves quotations and references from scripture, as well as from a wide variety of saints and theologians, throughout his sermons. He also shows a keen desire for incorporating dogmas, doctrines, and other teachings of the Church. For Moreau, this theological depth and breadth provides the firm foundation on which to draw practical import as well as courses of action, so as to build a life of virtue and become another Christ.

Since Moreau used these sermons on more than one occasion, he often left places and dates out of the texts. Scriptural quotations and allusions have been marked with parenthetical references in the text, and to the extent possible, references to the writings of saints and theologians have been marked with footnotes. The subheads have also been added.

K.G. and A.G.

Meditation

· · · · · · · · · · · · · · ·

With desolation is all the land made desolate; because there is none that considers in the heart. (Jer 12:11)

The truths of religion have notably depreciated in the eyes of men. It would seem that if this depreciation continues but a little further, it will verify the prediction of the Savior: "The Son of Man, when he comes, do you think he shall find faith on earth" (Lk 18:8)? Then will follow that frightful allurement of the antichrist from which not even the elect can escape, if God, in his mercy, does not shorten its duration. Therefore, it is more necessary than ever before that the few souls still faithful meditate on the truths of religion. It is ignorance or forgetfulness of these truths that causes the ruin of so many and all the upheavals in human society.

Our principal duty, my dearly beloved, after the sanctification of our own souls, is to bring the truths of religion again before the eyes of men and women by teaching and by example. We can, however, teach only what we know well ourselves, and our living example must be ever the outward expression of our inner life. In a very real sense, we become what we think upon, and so it is particularly necessary that we learn how to meditate well. Meditation should serve a twofold purpose: to enrich our mental life by its subject matter and to inspire us to the practice of the virtues of our state of life. Only when we are constantly renewing and conserving our faith in the great truths of religion by well-made meditations can we do anything to preserve the souls of our brothers and sisters from the seductive doctrines of our times and to advance godliness in general.

To get ourselves into the frame of mind essential to making the best possible use of our meditations, we should often ponder on the requirements for spiritual progress: to reform what has been deformed by sin, to conform our lives thus reformed to that of Jesus Christ, to confirm ourselves in that conformity, to transform ourselves into the divine model. St. Paul explains it thus: "Those whom he foreknew, he also predestined to be made conformable to the image of his son; that he might be the first-born among many brothers and sisters. And those whom he predestined, he also called. And those whom he called, them he also justified. And those whom he justified, them he also glorified" (Rom 8:29–30). Herein is the whole mystery not only of the predestination of the elect but of their justification and their glorification as well.

In order, however, to achieve the transformation of our life into that of Jesus Christ, we must, according to the teaching of St. Ignatius of Loyola, proceed in varied and successive ways.[1] The first of these is called the purgative way, because it is the one that purifies the soul from its sins. The second is known as the illuminative way, because it enlightens the soul by the doctrines and the examples of the Savior, who is the light of the world. The third is called the spiritual way, a name which is given it to distinguish it as that period of the Christian life when the soul, risen with Jesus Christ, is so lifted above the senses as not to be subject to the allurements of the flesh. The fourth is named the unitive way, because it enables the soul to affect with God an intimate union — preparatory to the beatific union of eternity.

Each of these ways requires its special meditations and spiritual exercises. We must learn our particular needs and make our meditations accordingly. If the road we are taking be the purgative way, in which we are trying to detach ourselves from sin and to reform our conduct, we should think on sin, the last end of humanity, death, judgment, hell, divine mercy, heaven, and Holy Communion. If it be the illuminative way, we should think on the private life, the public life, and the passion of Jesus Christ, in order to find out our duties and to set ourselves to the performance of them, despite any difficulties they may involve. If it be the spiritual way, we should think on the resurrection, the manifestations, and the ascension of the Savior, modeling our new life so as to get rid of the "old man."[2] If it be the unitive way, we should think on the Holy Spirit, who is by charity the bond between God and the soul; his seven gifts; the sweetness of the service of Jesus Christ; his transfiguration; and everything that helps to lift our thoughts and desires to the Lord, to inflame us by his love, and to make us taste in advance the delights reserved for the saints in paradise.

Though the whole scheme of using these four ways of spiritual progress is usually thought of as confined to the exercises of a spiritual retreat, we may pursue almost the same order in adapting our cycle of meditations to the Office of the ecclesiastical year. There is an analogy between these ways and the various seasons of the liturgical year in that the purgative way seems to correspond to Advent, the illuminative way to Lent, the spiritual way to Easter time, and the unitive way to the season of Pentecost. Furthermore, these grand divisions of the ecclesiastical year correspond to the four natural seasons — winter, spring, summer, and fall. In like manner the life of the Christian here below has, as does the life of the Church, its period of infancy, youth, maturity, and old age. But the old age of the Christian and of the Church retains the energy of the years of virile strength and leads in the end to eternal life rather than to death. Can one not say, indeed, that the life of Jesus Christ reproduces itself unceasingly in his mystical body, the Church? Like him, it had its hidden life in the catacombs during its first three centuries; it had its public life through its exterior development from the conversion of Constantine to the sixteenth century, when Luther began the era of rebellion against it by its own children; it had and is still having its suffering life; and at length will come its glorious life, when there will be but one shepherd and one flock in its triumphant existence in heaven.

Such are the admirable harmonies that God has established between our two lives, the physical and the spiritual, between the moral order and the physical, between the procession of the religious festivals and that of the seasons.

The spiritual ways that we have explained are not, however, so definitely marked off from one another that each may not include some exercises proper to the others. Nor do they differ in that respect from the various stages of Christian life, which are also subject to reversals as a rule. Even the greatest saints, after traveling successively along the four ways, have more than once lapsed from the unitive, the spiritual, or the illuminative way to the purgative. St. Paul, for example, after he had been ravished even into the third heaven, was humbled by the sting of the flesh in order that the sublimity of his revelations might not make him proud (2 Cor 12:7).

St. Ignatius on Mental Prayer

According to the teaching of St. Ignatius, there are three kinds of mental prayer: meditation, which consists in the exercise of the three faculties of the soul—the memory, the intelligence, and the will; contemplation, which consists in considering the persons involved in the subject before the mind, their words, and their actions; and application of the five senses to the details of the subject. We shall try to explain and illustrate these three methods.

No one should go into a meditation unprepared. There are three parts to the preparation for the morning meditation practiced almost universally among religious. There is first the remote preparation, which consists in avoiding sin and its occasions, in mortifying the passions, and in guarding the senses. The proximate preparation consists in reading the subject matter of the meditation on the evening before and recalling the matter to mind before going to sleep and again immediately on awaking. The immediate preparation consists in an act of faith in the presence of God—an act of contrition, of humility, and of confidence. Then the preludes come. In the first, one recalls to mind the subject matter of the meditation. In the second, one makes a mental picture of the subject matter; and in the third, one asks for the fruit he wishes to draw from the meditation. Then the meditation proper comes. We shall now illustrate this method of meditation.

In all those communities that have morning prayers in common, there is undoubtedly the common design of prayers preparatory for meditation. I have chosen the following prayers for the communities that God gave me the honor of bringing into existence, and I beg your indulgence for inserting them here:

V. Come, O my soul, let us adore God. Let us prostrate ourselves in his presence and bend our knees before the Lord who created us.[3]

R. Because he is the Lord our God, and we are his people and the sheep of his flock (Ps 100:3).

V. May the Blessed Virgin, her worthy spouse, St. Joseph, our guardian angels, and all the saints intercede for us before God.

R. That we may adore the Lord in spirit and in truth through Jesus Christ, that we may deserve to be assisted and heard by him in this meditation, and that we may gain all the indulgences attached to our actions this day (Jn 4:24).

Prayer:

O supreme majesty, my Lord and my God, I am not worthy to raise my eyes to your eternal throne, on account of my numberless iniquities. I am but dust and ashes, and yet I will dare to speak to you my homage, O Lord my God, because you are infinitely good and merciful. I will call upon your holy name and meditate on your commandments, that I may learn and keep your justifying ordinances.

O God, Father, Son, and Holy Spirit, enlighten my mind that I may know what I must do or omit in order to procure your glory, my own perfection, and the salvation of others. Move my will that I may detest all the faults and negligences of my past life, that I may desire and accomplish what I know is my duty during this day, and that I may love you above all things, O you, my God, who are infinitely amiable. Assist the powers of my soul that I may courageously and constantly do and suffer, after the example of Jesus Christ, my guide, whatever and in whatever manner you choose, because it is pleasing to you.

R. Amen.

Here say the Our Father, the Hail Mary, and the Apostles' Creed.

For an example of the Ignatian method of meditation, let us choose the time of Advent for our subject matter. We shall take the first prelude from the invitatory of the Office: "Come, let us adore the Sovereign King who is about to come."[4] In our second prelude, let us regard the Church as addressing this invitation to the Jews, to the pagans, and especially to her own children. For our third prelude, let us ask, as the fruit of this meditation, for the invisible coming of the Savior into our hearts through his Holy Spirit.

The first part of our meditation is an exercise of the memory. We should recall in detail the subject matter of our meditation, considering in due order the persons, actions, places, means, motives, manner, and time involved in it. We shall proceed thus. The Church, at the beginning of Advent, invites us to prepare to celebrate the anniversary of the first coming of its divine spouse, and for this purpose the Church recalls to us the longing of the patriarchs and the prophets for that coming. To attract our attention to this preparation, it unites in its liturgy today the threefold coming of the Savior on the earth: his coming into the manger of Bethlehem, his invisible coming into the hearts of men and women, and his final coming at the end of the world. Its desire is that we draw from the frightful spectacle of the last judgment that salutary fear which is the beginning of wisdom (Prv 9:10; Ps 111:10).

In the proper of the Mass, the Church prays with the same expressions as those used in the Old Law to beg for the manifestation of the eternal Word in the flesh.[5] For Christ would surely have been born in vain at Bethlehem more than nineteen centuries ago did he not return yearly, or better, hourly, to renew unceasingly or to develop his divine life in us by the communication of his Holy Spirit.

That we may respond as we should with sentiments of fear and of hope to the sight of God become both judge and Savior, the Church requires of us during this season the spirit of recollection, prayer, and penance. It invites us to this spirit by the example of the just of the Old Testament and also by repeating the words of St. John the Baptist to the Jews: "Prepare the way of the Lord, make straight his paths" (Mt 3:3). It invites us also by the rites and practices proper to this holy season. The four weeks of Advent recall to us the four thousand years of waiting for the promised Messiah. The fast of the Ember Days, the purple vestments, and the suspension of the *Te Deum* and the *Gloria in excelsis*, except on the festivals of saints, are means by which the Church keeps before us the idea of penance.[6]

The next step in the meditation is the exercise of the understanding. We should reason on our subject and draw consequences from it applicable to ourselves, which must not be vague and abstract, but must be motivated by their fitness, agreeableness, facility, utility, or necessity for our own needs. We must see how we have acted in those circumstances of our lives that the subject under meditation recalls. In this case, we should look into the way we have kept Advent heretofore and how our observance of its practices can be improved. We must find out the obstacles that have prevented us from getting all we might from the spirit of this holy time and then see how we can overcome them during the present Advent.

We know how the Church would have us pass the time of Advent — in a deeper recollection, a more fervent spirit of prayer, and a greater mortification of our senses. Now we should think of the many reasons why we should enter into these dispositions: the fitness of this preparation for the coming of God to us, the pleasure that is ours in receiving him well that we may in turn be welcomed by him, the need we have to correspond with the intentions of the Church, and the ease with which we may do so.

Let us first find out what has been our attitude toward this period of the ecclesiastical year and then see how we should like to pass this time and whether there is anything that can keep us from doing everything in a holy way.

We are now ready for the exercise of the will. By this time, certain pious affections ought to have been induced in us by the thoughts we have been entertaining. These affections should lead us to form resolutions. Let us not be vague and impractical in this matter. Let us form resolutions that are practical, personal, humble, and founded on solid motives. We should first ask pardon of God for having so poorly responded thus far to the intentions of the Church for Advent, for most of us have likely failed in some measure. Then let us determine to enter into its spirit and, for this purpose, to form the resolution to pray with all the attention we can command, to observe the fast and abstinence as rigorously as we are permitted, to be present at every religious exercise, to bring a docile mind to our spiritual reading and other instruction, and to communicate with all the fervor we can rouse in ourselves. These rather general resolutions we all need to renew frequently. Each of us will find, on earnest self-examination, that there is some particular resolution we need to add to these, one which we can practice every day during Advent to aid us toward perfection. Having made our resolutions, we should beg of Jesus Christ, through Mary and Joseph, the grace to be faithful to them.

We come now to the conclusion of the meditation. This consists of a colloquy, with our Lord or with some saint to whom we have devotion, of our needs and desires, of a brief examination of the way in which we have meditated, of a recapitulation that will fix the high points of the meditation in our memory, of a glance at the possible difficulties the day may put in the way of our resolutions, of a spiritual bouquet or ejaculatory prayer, and of a notation of the graces we have received during the meditation.[7] In this particular meditation, the words of the first prelude, "Come, let us adore the sovereign king who is about to come," will furnish a suitable spiritual bouquet. In fact, the first prelude of any meditation will usually serve this purpose. A suggestion for the colloquy in this meditation is the prayer, "O Jesus, living in Mary, come and live in your servants, by the spirit of your holiness, by the fullness of your power, by the perfection of your ways, by the truth of your virtues, and by the communication of your mysteries. Triumph over all enemies by your spirit for the glory of the father. Amen."[8] Pope Pius IX attached an indulgence of three hundred days to the recitation of this prayer (October 14, 1859).

There are doubtless many religious who will find this method of meditation too complicated and who will need some simpler way. St. Ignatius teaches another method, called contemplation, which applies chiefly to the use of the mysteries of our Lord and his mother as subject matter. It consists in picturing both the good and the bad persons connected with the subject, in listening to their words, in trying to understand their thoughts and sentiments, and in observing their conduct. While we are reflecting on each of these points, we should make frequent applications to ourselves and try to draw fruit from the considerations suggested by the various individuals under contemplation.

The following example will serve for an illustration of this method. Let us take our first prelude from the gospel of the first Sunday: "They shall see the Son of Man coming in a cloud, with great power and majesty" (Lk 21:27). The scene we should picture is laid in the Valley of Josaphat at the foot of the Mount of Olives. As the fruit of this contemplation, we should try to secure from the Holy Spirit the fear of the Lord. For this purpose we should say the prayer of David the penitent: Lord, "pierce my flesh with your fear" (Ps 119:120).

Let us think first on the persons involved in our subject matter. Thousands of men and women on earth at the end of the world, as at the time of the flood, will be living careless or even sinful lives with no thought but of this present life. These may be surprised during sleep, since there are many Doctors of the Church who say the end of the world will come in the night. Let us contemplate their agonized confusion in that tremendous hour. Then let us think of the despairing wicked in hell, whose misery will be increased by the public ratification of the decree of their damnation. Let us look now at the happy souls awaiting in purgatory their solemn glorification on this day when all the elect will be canonized by Jesus Christ himself as he appears in clouds of glory. Let us look at our Lord in his robes of justice as he holds aloft the banner of his cross. Truly will he show himself both God and Savior in this overthrow of the whole world by his sacred standard. Judgment will be visibly exercised by him with his Father and the Holy Spirit, though the divinity will remain invisible to the eyes of the reprobate. What will be the fate of each of us in that hour?

Let us think now of the words we shall hear on that great day. God will "send his angels with a trumpet, and a great voice, and they shall gather together his elect from the four winds, from the farthest parts of the heavens to the utmost bounds of them" (Mt 24:31). Let us imagine we hear this great voice resounding to the ends of the universe: "Arise, you dead, and come to judgment." Immediately, the "dead will rise again incorruptible," all changed in their flesh to a common immortality and yet keeping their widely varying and distinguishing characteristics, and will be brought "in the twinkling of an eye" to the Valley of Josaphat at the foot of that tribunal on which Jesus Christ will be seated "in his power and majesty" (1 Cor 15:52). His face will be filled with sweetness for the just but will be terrible for the reprobate.

At the right hand of the Savior will be his Blessed Mother and at his left St. Joseph. Around him will be the apostles, who are to judge with him, and his angels, who will be made visible to the eyes of men and women at this time when they are to separate the just from the wicked as the shepherd separates the sheep from the goats (Mt 25:32). On which side will they place us?

Let us think further on this great spectacle we have set before us. On that great day the inmost consciences of all will be made manifest, and all their external works, whether good or evil, will be made known. Christ will address himself first to the just with ineffable sweetness: "Come, you blessed of my father, possess the kingdom prepared for you from the foundation of the world. For I was hungry, and you gave me to eat; I was thirsty, and you gave me to drink" (Mt 25:34–35).

O lovely words! Shall we deserve to hear them? The elect, in their astonishment at receiving the eternal kingdom in return for the little they have done for God in the person of his poor, will utter cries of admiration at his bounty. But, oh, the terror of the lost! The sovereign judge, turning eyes of eternal wrath on them, will pronounce their doom in a terrible voice: "Depart from me, you cursed, into everlasting fire which was prepared for the devil and his angels. For I was hungry, and you gave me nothing to eat; I was thirsty, and you gave me nothing to drink." The lost, hearing this reproach, will wish to justify themselves. They will urge that they did not hear him ask for anything whatsoever (Mt 25:41–44). Some of them will cite their good works of other kinds, but their pleas will be vain because they will have done these works either in the state of sin or with an evil intention. What will Jesus Christ, who has thus declared failings in charity to be sufficient cause for damnation, do about the positive crimes with which people have soiled their lives? Let us think on our own sins which will one day be made known in this assembly of all the world.

Let us look now at the actions of the various persons involved in this contemplation of the last judgment. The master has told us that sinners will wither away from fear at the mere sight of the signs that will precede the final judgment. What, then, will happen when they hear the decree of their eternal damnation, which will be immediately executed? Let us imagine we see the sovereign judge ascending again into heaven with all the elect. Then let us watch the devils, pitiless executors of God's justice, while they seize the souls of the damned and drag them, cursing one another, into hell, which yawns before their feet. Then let us watch the seal of eternity being set upon that horrible sepulcher.

Surely we must now resolve to expiate our sins and to shun henceforth whatever would expose us to that reprobation should we at this moment die. Then let us recite in conclusion some strophes of the *Dies irae*, and often say the following:[9]

> Judge of justice, hear my prayer,
> Spare me, Lord, in mercy spare,
> Ere the reckoning day appear.

For those who find both meditation proper and contemplation too difficult, St. Ignatius teaches a third method of arriving at the desired result of mental prayer. The application of the five senses to the subject matter under consideration is an exercise as simple as it is useful. It is based on the fact that the soul is able by the aid of the imagination to represent any object as present and to act as if the object considered were really seen, heard, tasted, smelled, or touched. This application of the senses to a truth of faith, or to a mystery of our Lord, is a vivifying method of occupying the mind usefully during prayer, provided we join to it reflection, making some of those short and appropriate uses of reason that are conducive to awakening the will. Application ordinarily involves five points, unless the senses of taste and smell are used together.

The signs foretelling the last judgment, though not strictly the matter of a mystery, can serve us for an example of the application of the five senses. St. Luke tells us that "there shall be signs in the sun, and in the moon, and in the stars" (Lk 21:25). We cannot limit ourselves to a particular scene, for the entire universe will be involved in this frightful spectacle. To get some idea of how terrifying this occasion will be for those living at the time, let us imagine that the end of the world is beginning.

Let us ask that the fruit of this work of the imagination be the fear of the Lord.

Let us consider first what we shall see on this great day. At the last judgment, Jesus Christ will confirm universally and publicly the sentence he has already pronounced on every soul at its particular judgment. Thus, he will honor his friends and will confound their enemies and his own in the sight of the entire world, and he will justify the mysterious workings of providence, now so little understood. This occasion will be preceded by terrifying signs. Some of these signs are remote, and some are immediate in that they will immediately precede the coming of Christ.

The remote signs, according to holy scripture and tradition, are the ruin of the Roman Empire, now long disintegrated; the preaching of the Gospel throughout the world, which has been fairly well done; the weakening of faith and charity, and almost general apostasy through the abandonment of the Holy See and of Christian practices; and, finally, the coming of the antichrist.

The immediate signs are the appearance of Enoch and Elijah to preach penance and make a last effort to convert the Jews, the eclipse of the sun, the absence of all light through the changing of the moon into blood, the visible falling of the stars, the shaking of the props of the firmament, the convulsion of the earth, the collapse of buildings, the bellowing of the waters as they rise to flood everything, the unchaining of the furious winds to raise tempests, the appearance of horrible specters in the air, the burning of all the earth, and then the resurrection of the dead and the coming of Jesus Christ in clouds of glory. Let us look at the whole of this spectacle and see whether Jesus Christ had not reason to declare that men and women will wither away from fear.

Now let us listen to the din of this general upheaval, to the noise of the sea and of the winds, to the shrieks and howls of perishing animals, to the piercing cries of people roasting alive in the flames, to the fury of the devils, to the blasphemies of the damned brought back again to life.

Now let us breathe in the stench of the fire that consumes everything, the sulfurous and bituminous odors exhaled from burning things, and the infected smell of decomposing bodies.

Now let us imagine that our palates and our tongues taste the disgusting mold of death, the bitter tears of the dying.

Now let us put our hands into that fire from which there is no release, into that mass of death for which there is no name in any language.

Then let us ask ourselves: Who is the God that will bring about this terror, the God that will call us to such a judgment? What will the rigor of everlasting punishment be if this preparation for it is so frightful? This exercise can be concluded, as are the meditation proper and the contemplation, with the colloquy, the recapitulation, and the spiritual bouquet.

If we wish to follow a sequence in our meditations, it will often be well to use a subject first for a meditation proper and then use it again the following day for a contemplation or for the application of the five senses. On the second day, however, instead of going over all the points, we should dwell on those that attracted us most on the first day and gave us greatest ease in conversing with God and arousing our affections.

St. Ignatius offers another manner of mental prayer to those who find meditation too difficult or who need to refresh their minds by an occasional change. After the morning prayers have been said, we should seat ourselves or remain kneeling according as health and devotion dictate. We should then begin a prayer, for example, the Our Father, pausing on the first two words. We should think on them, search into their meaning, bring in comparisons, and hold them in our minds so long as they furnish thoughts and affections. Then we should go on to the next phrase, "who art in heaven." It may happen that some phrase or even single word will furnish reflections and feelings sufficient to occupy the whole time destined for the mental prayer. If so, we should say the rest of the prayer rapidly and save it for the next day's meditation, repeating the first part without pausing on this occasion and taking up the meditation where we left off the day before. The exercise is concluded by a conversation with God or the saint to whom the prayer is addressed, in which we ask for the virtue or the grace we feel most in need of.

A variation of this method, which is still easier, is to pronounce a vocal prayer with a brief pause after each word, to think on the meaning of the words, or on the one to whom the prayer is addressed, or on our own unworthiness. We might, for example, say the Hail Mary, thinking of each word, or of the Blessed Virgin, or of our imperfections that make us so different from Mary. Oftentimes we shall find our devotion aroused by one of the words and shall be able to go into the preceding method of praying. In case we are given to distractions in our ordinary prayers, we shall find this last method very helpful to accustom ourselves to say attentively and piously our required prayers. Thus we shall practice the counsel of St. Paul: "I will pray with the spirit, I will pray also with the understanding. . . . I had rather speak five words with my understanding, that I may instruct others also, than ten thousand words if in a tongue" (1 Cor 14:15, 19).

Perhaps it will not be out of place here to consider the remaining method of prayer offered by St. Ignatius, since we religious so often make retreats, for which this method is especially designed. It is more of a spiritual exercise than a prayer. Its purpose is to assist the soul to become more agreeable to God. It consists in meditation on the commandments of God and of the Church, on the seven deadly sins, on the three faculties of the soul, and on the five senses of the body. We should first ask ourselves questions and answer them: What am I going to do? I am going to pray. Before whom? Before God. Why? For his glory and my salvation. The preparatory prayers are the same as for the meditation.

Let us first go through the commandments, pausing on those we transgress most frequently, and then the deadly sins, to see what share our three powers of soul and our senses have had in our sins. Let us find out the reasons for our sins and see what steps we must take to prevent their recurrence. Then let us humble ourselves and beg God's pardon and his grace to avoid falling again into our sins, and let us conclude with a colloquy, which our dispositions will suggest, ending the whole with an Our Father.

The time to be spent on each commandment, deadly sin, faculty of the soul, and sense of the body is about what it takes to say three Our Fathers. We have to be careful not to let this exercise degenerate into an examination of conscience such as we make for confession. Our purpose, too, should not be merely contrition; it should be not so much to learn our faults in detail and be sorry for them as it is to learn our duties and get to know ourselves. Hence, we should think on the excellence, justice, and holiness of each commandment, the advantages its observance has procured for individuals and for society, and how we have kept or violated it. So too, we should consider the excellence of the faculties of our soul and of the senses of our body; the advantage we should reap from them; the purpose for which they were given us; the way in which Jesus Christ, the Blessed Virgin, or St. Joseph used them; and then what service we ourselves have put them to.

The Sulpician Approach to Meditation

The method of the Sulpicians is somewhat different from the Ignatian method of meditation, though its purpose is the same—that of enriching the mind with the truths of faith and moving the will to seize on the good by means of directive resolutions. For an example of this method, let us take a sentence from the gospel of the second Sunday of the first week of Advent: "Relate to John what you have heard and seen" (Mt 11:4). Jesus Christ here refers to the fulfillment of the prophecies in and by himself, particularly those of Isaiah concerning his miracles. "Then shall the eyes of the blind be opened, and the ears of the deaf shall be unstopped" (Is 35:5). "The spirit of the Lord is upon me, because the Lord has anointed me; he has sent me to preach to the meek, to heal the contrite of heart" (Is 61:1). In the presence of two disciples of his precursor and a crowd of people, our Lord declares that he has fulfilled to the letter these prophecies concerning his work in the world, and this is sufficient to convince John the Baptist that Jesus Christ is really the long-awaited Messiah. As the fruit of this meditation, let us ask for a living faith in the coming of Jesus Christ in the flesh, which will better prepare us for Christmas.

After the foregoing preludes, this method takes us immediately into the body of the prayer, which is addressed directly to the Savior:

"I adore you, O my Jesus, who, with your Father and the Holy Spirit, did prepare for your coming into the world by figures, prophecies, and events of such character that not to recognize you as the Messiah would be impossible. The figures of the Old Testament unmistakably

delineated your portrait, the prophecies completed it, and the great political events concurred to point to your coming."

Point 1: "In most striking figures do I first see, you, O Jesus. You
are in Adam as the Father of all people, according to the Spirit; in Abel
as the Lamb immolated for the salvation of the world (Gn 4:1–16); in
Noah as the builder of your Church, outside which no person is saved
(Gn 6:5–9:17); in Melchizedek as the high priest offering yourself on our
altars under the species of bread and wine (Gn 14:18–20); in Abraham's
son Isaac as the bearer of your own cross to Calvary (Gn 22:1–19); in
Jacob as one stronger than the divine justice roused against us (Gn 32:4–
33:20); in Joseph as one sold by your brothers and sisters (Gn 37:1–28);
in Moses as one rescued from the massacre of the innocents (Ex 1:8–
2:10); in Joshua as one appointed to lead us into heaven (Nm 27:12–23);
in Jonah as one buried in the tomb and come back to life on the third day
(2:1–11)."

Point 2: "Even had these lineaments not been sufficient to render
incredulity inexcusable, you did so complete your portrait by the prophets that no one can mistake it. David proclaimed your eternal generation (Ps 2:7) and foretold the Magi's adoration (Ps 72:10–11) and your
passion, resurrection, and ascension (Ps 16, 22). Ezekiel and Solomon
predicted the virginity of your mother and her divine maternity in the
Incarnation (Ez 44:1–3). Jacob prophesied your descent from the tribe of
Judah (Gn 49:8–10); Micah, the place of your birth (Mi 5:1); Daniel, the
precise time of your coming (Dn 2:44); Malachi, your presentation in the
Temple (Mal 3:1–4); Hosea, your flight into Egypt (Hos 11:1); Jeremiah,
the massacre of the innocents (Jer 31:15), your return from the land of
exile (Jer 46:27–28), and your sojourn in Nazareth (Jer 23:5); Isaiah,
the coming of your holy precursor (Is 40:3), your preaching (Is 61:1–3),
your miracles (Is 35:4–6), and your passion (Is 52:13–53:12). How, after
all this, O my Jesus, can I fail to adore you as my God and my Savior?"

Point 3: "You have done even more than this to accomplish the prophecies. Your providence has raised up four great monarchies. The first of
these, the Babylonian, chastised the people destined to conserve your religion till they left off idolatry. The second, the Persian, brought this people
back from Babylon to Judea. The third, the Greek, through translating

the scriptures into their language and incorporating the Jews into their army, made your sacred oracles known to the Gentiles and facilitated the preaching of the Gospel in the language the apostles and evangelists were to use. The fourth, the Roman, prepared the way for the Gospel by laying great routes through all the then-known world, and by an edict of Caesar—who had something entirely different in mind—obliged Joseph and Mary to go to Bethlehem at the very time you were to be born."

Here follows what is called the "communion." "Truly, O my Savior, who from the height of heaven did make all things conspire to the execution of your designs, you are worthy of my adoration. Adore, O my soul, admire, praise, love, and thank this good master for calling you to his service." Plunge yourself often into the heart of Jesus that there you may find all these sentiments and may clothe yourself in his virtues, as one dips cloth into dye to color it, and then offer the whole to him through Mary and Joseph.

The next step is called "cooperation." "That I may cooperate in the preparation for your coming to me, O my Jesus, by the workings of your Spirit, I dare to ask you, through the intercession of your holy mother and your foster father, to make me share their sentiments at the approach of your birth at Bethlehem and to bless my resolution to be entirely united in disposition with them during this holy time."

Now the conclusion comes. "Be ever blessed, O my God, for the graces you have given me during this exercise, and forgive me for the distractions I have put in your way. O Mary, my Mother, do supply whatever has been lacking in this prayer and obtain for me the blessing of your divine Son to accomplish my resolutions. For my spiritual bouquet I shall often repeat: May the clouds rain down the just one."

Other Approaches to Meditation

The method of meditation of the Redemptorists and the Visitandines differs from that of the Jesuits only in that, after the ordinary preparation and preludes, St. Alphonsus de Liguori and St. Francis de Sales both give more liberty to the will, devoting less time to reason than to the affections, though St. Ignatius, too, would have us pass on to the activity of the will as soon as reason has prepared us to do so, even though this consume but a moment. The method of the Carmelites, as explained by St. Teresa, consists in acts of adoration, offering, thanksgiving, and petition made according to the attraction of the Holy Spirit, whether in dwelling on the point of meditation indicated the evening before or in devoting the time to some other subject prepared in advance.

For an example of these methods, let us use another sentence from the gospel of the second Sunday of Advent: "Blessed is he who shall not be scandalized in me" (Mt 11:6). For our second prelude, let us think on St. John the Baptist, prevented by his imprisonment from person-ally making the Messiah known to his disciples, sending two of them to Jesus. For the fruit of this meditation, let us ask our Lord to make us comprehend better the mystery of his humiliations and to give us grace to bear our own with resignation. For those preceding acts of faith in the presence of God, of humility, and of petition for grace that St. Francis de Sales always uses, the prayer "O Supreme Majesty" will do very well.[10]

This method now has a consideration. "Consider, O my soul, how Jesus Christ became a subject of scandal." The Jews, and after them the Gentiles, deceived by the letter of the prophecies and by their own too-natural sentiments, awaited the messiah as a powerful king who at the head of great armies would deliver them from the yoke of the Romans and would conquer the world. And yet, they knew that this would keep away from him the poor and unhappy, for whom so many of the prophe-cies said he was to come. On his coming, the Jews and the Gentiles, far from seeing him wrapped in royal purple, saw in him only contempt for human grandeur and love for poverty. From this they concluded that he did not fulfill the promises made by the prophets, and this conclusion became for them an occasion of scandal.

St. John the Baptist, to get this false notion of the messiah from the heads of his disciples, sent two of them to his divine master that they might learn from his own lips the meaning of the sacred oracles, the pur-pose of which Jesus achieved by recalling for them the prophecy of Isa-iah concerning his miracles and especially his preaching of the Gospel to the poor. He said to them: "Go and relate to John what you have heard and seen. The blind see, the lame walk, the lepers are cleansed, the deaf hear, the dead rise again, the poor have the gospel preached to them. And blessed is he that shall not be scandalized in me" (Mt 11:4–6). The Savior knew that from these signs St. John would understand who he was. He blessed all those who would understand with the precursor and would not take as occasions of scandal his poverty, his humiliations, and the contradictions that assailed him.

From this consideration should arise affections. "Now I understand, O my Savior, how you did become at first a subject of scandal to the Jews. They contradicted maliciously all your words and acts. The doctors of the law never approached you without seeking to surprise, injure, or embarrass you. When you did heal a paralytic on the Sabbath, instead of seeing a manifestation of your divine power, they accused you of violating the Sabbath. When you did drive out devils, instead of seeing your divine power over even the powers of darkness, they proclaimed that you did use the devil's power to drive out devils and were, therefore, an enemy of the Temple. Truly indeed, O my Jesus, you are the one of whom Simeon said when he held the Redeemer in his arms: "This Child is set for the fall . . . of many in Israel, and for a sign which shall be contradicted" (Lk 2:34).

Now we may take up a second consideration of the subject. Scandal was taken from the doctrine and from the humiliations of the Savior, not alone by the Jews but by the pagans as well. Regarding his Gospel and his cross as folly, they persecuted him by all sorts of cruelty in the person of his apostles and martyrs (1 Cor 1:18–24). Far from being scandalized by him, they should have recognized in him the true Messiah from his treatment by the Jews. Isaiah had announced the promised one to be a stumbling block against which those who would stumble would bruise themselves (Is 28:16). David had said that he was the cornerstone which would be rejected (Ps 118:22). Moreover, even among those who became his disciples, many heretics and schismatics have stumbled and been "broken in pieces" against his adorable person. Many Catholics, even ecclesiastics and religious, live in such a way in the bosom of the Church that the Gospel scandalizes and shocks them, since they do not want to conform their conduct to what it prescribes.

Affections peculiar to each of us must arise from this consideration. "Why, O my God, do you permit that even today your adorable Son has so many enemies and contradictors and so few servants? You do wish me to appreciate more fully the grace of being kept faithful to you in the midst of the defections and scandals of the times. You do wish that in the confusion of all those who contradict the Savior, my faith may be more living, my hope more firm, my charity more ardent, my gratitude more generous, and my zeal to imitate him more adequate to make up to him for so many ungrateful people."

My resolution inspired by all this is that I may henceforth make a heroic effort to be a better disciple of my master. "Since you will publicly punish at the last judgment all those who have been scandalized by your cross and will reward your faithful servants, I shall try so to live that on that great day you will recognize me as your disciple and admit me to the company of the elect. In conclusion, I thank you, O my God, for the sentiments and good purposes with which you have inspired me. Deign to accept and bless them."

The importance of the holy practice of meditation cannot be over-estimated in the religious life. St. Vincent de Paul used to say: "Give me a man of prayer, and I can do anything with him. Such a one can say with the apostle: 'I can do all things in him who strengthens me'" (Phil 4:13).[11] Very different is the lot of those who are faithful to meditation from that of those who too easily neglect it. The first are daily refreshed with the dew of grace. They drink in the rays of the Sun of Justice, and they grow up and become strong in denial of self and in detachment from creatures. Their hearts are warm with love for those around them and full of respect for their superiors. They burn with the love of God, look hopefully to heaven, and sigh for the end of their exile on earth. They are like vigorous and sap-filled shoots, rooted in the soil into which they have been transplanted by providence. The nourishing sap penetrates to every part, the buds swell, the leaves unfold, the flowers expand, and in the time of harvest they are laden with rich, ripe fruits. Those who hate meditation are tepid, weak, languishing, annoying to others, troublesome to themselves. They have no relish for spiritual things and are dissatisfied with everything. They are of no use to religion or to their neighbor. They soon become slaves to the world, the devil, and the flesh. They are like plants on an arid plain, withered by the heat of a torrid sun, scorched by the burning reflection of the desert sand.

Oh, my dearly beloved, I would conjure you never to omit your daily meditation. Study the methods well and persevere, no matter how weary you may become. If meditation proper proves too difficult for you, and you cannot use the other methods offered, confine yourself to a few simple acts, for example, to adoration of Jesus Christ; to studying and trying to practice some special virtue in imitation of him; to offering him your admiration and joy and love because of his goodness, your compassion for his sufferings, your gratitude for past favors, and your humble plea for necessary graces.

No matter how difficult it is to learn and use the Ignatian method, the advantages to be gained from it will abundantly repay any amount of trouble in becoming familiar with it. We cannot insist too strongly on the remote preparation for this holy exercise, which is avoidance of sin, mortification of the senses, and interior and exterior recollection. This continued disposition to mental prayer should extend through our whole lives and, thus, serve also as a constant preparation for frequent Communion, without which we cannot be genuine and sterling religious. If we meditate well, we shall say or hear holy Mass well, and we shall communicate well. Thus, we shall prepare our minds and hearts for everlasting contemplation of the infinite beauty of God and of our union with him when we shall have exchanged faith for vision.

Community Spirit

· ·

*I pray . . . they all may be one, as you father are in me, and I
in you; that they also may be one in us: I in them, and you in
me. (Jn 17:20–23)*

If the outward expression of the bond of brotherly love among the
early Christians was so new and strange to the pagans as to cause
them to comment, "Behold how these Christians love one another,"
we can surmise to what degree they had lost the concept of charity.[12]
Even to the Chosen People, Christ's Gospel of charity was an unaccus-
tomed message: "You have heard that it has been said, 'An eye for an eye,
and a tooth for a tooth.' But I say to you not to resist evil, but if one strikes
you on your right cheek, turn to him also the other. . . . You have heard
that it has been said, 'You shall love your neighbor and hate your enemy.'
But I say to you, love your enemies, do good to them that hate you that
you may be the children of your father who is in heaven" (Mt 5:38–44).
All people, however, were to know Christ's disciples by their love for one
another, as unusual and perhaps even as unwelcome as was this sign in
the world.

It would scarcely seem necessary to note that this sign of the Christian should be most evident in a religious community, whose members are
vowed to become other Christs even more perfectly than are other members of his mystical body. Sad experience, however, has taught most of
us that the flame of brotherly love is sometimes almost smothered among
religious by the cold ashes of pride, envy, vainglory, ambition, and intol-
erance. Of some of these enemies to community spirit we shall have something to say later. I should like first to explain to you what I consider the
indispensable foundation of this beautiful spirit.

It is, of course, God who builds every religious house, God who
founds every religious community, no matter how great in himself be its

founder and how fervent be its early apostolic members. It is God who carries on the work to its completion. If the work fails, it is always because the members fail in the constant effort to live the perfect life. What is the perfect life? It is a life submissive, social, regular, interior, edifying, laborious. It is made perfect by pure intentions that aim only at heaven and at nothing earthly. It makes us aspire to the happiness of possessing Jesus, of belonging only to him and his Blessed Mother. It makes us use all interests, goods, and rights only for the honor of our divine master and for the salvation of souls. It makes us exactly obedient by constant and universal fidelity to the rules and constitutions of our community, a fidelity inspired by love and not by fear, by faith and not by human expediency. It makes us social by humility, meekness, and charity, so that the advice of the author of the *Imitation*, "mutually supporting, consoling, aiding, instructing, and admonishing one another," is accomplished to the letter.[13] It is a life edifying in its modesty, in its avoidance of all criticism, raillery, and levity. It is a life of labor. It is an inner life elevated to God by the habitual practice of the acts of faith, hope, and charity after the example of Jesus Christ, whom we are especially bound to imitate in our conduct. It is a life in every sense hidden with Jesus in God.

This perfect life, upon which I cannot too strongly insist, will remind us of the entire divine life of our Savior: his life of obedience; his life subject to the miseries of our humanity, even to infamy, sufferings, and death; his life of rule, conformable in all things to the will of his father; his social life; his life in the company of our Blessed Lady, St. Joseph, and his apostles; his edifying and laborious life; his life of inspiration in the midst of the world, his labors, and his passion; his inner life; his hidden life at Nazareth, so full of instruction and so calculated to excite a just dread of all exterior ministry. Oh, what marvels of grace would our community produce if we but succeeded in renewing in ourselves the life of Jesus Christ.

In every active community, there are necessarily disintegrating elements, due to the diverse works and interests of its members. Yet, the same spirit that guided the wheels of the mysterious chariot seen by Ezekiel (2 Kgs 2:11–12), the same spirit that moved the symbolic animals of such varied forms, one before the other, so that without ever pausing in their onward course, without ever retracing their steps, they tended to

the same end, though by ways apparently most opposed to one another—
that same spirit can so relate and bind all the activities of the members
of religious communities that no friction need arise. Regardless of the
difference of employments, zeal for the glory of God will, by means of a
pooling of efforts, bring about a union of hearts of which it is the bond
and the strength.

For in a great work of charity, as in the erection of a great building,
one worker alone does not build it, nor is it constructed out of a single stone or single beam of wood. On the contrary, the various workers
make their separate contributions, each stone is cut to fit into the place
for which it was destined, and each piece of wood is arranged and placed
so as to add to the beauty and the strength of the entire building. Union,
then, is the powerful lever with which we can move, direct, and sanctify
the world, if the spirit of evil, who is permitted to exercise his power over
this earth, does not oppose successfully the wondrous effects of this moral
force.

The political parties that disturb society have power to cause revolutions and disorder simply because they know how to unite and work
for the same end. Would it not, then, be a shame for us not to do as much
good for God and for eternity as the children of the world do for the
world and for the short day of this life? Ah, we do not know, we disciples
of a God who died for the salvation of souls in danger of perishing, how
much we could do to save them if we but united ourselves to Jesus Christ
through the scrupulous observance of our rules and constitutions.[14]

It is this touching mystery of religious union that our Lord reveals
to us in the Gospel when he explains the incorporation of all the faithful
with his divine person. In this incorporation, he is the head and we are
the members with one and the same life. He tells us that we should remain
united to him, that we may be but one with him, just as the branches
attached to the trunk, depending on the same root and nourished by the
same sap, form with the trunk but one and the same tree.

The beautiful parable in the fifteenth chapter of St. John gathers
together all the motives capable of inducing us to tighten the cords that
unite the works of our community. There is, first of all, the motive of
honor, for we should strive to escape the shame of sterility by procuring

for ourselves the glory of numerous followers. As the branch of itself, however, cannot bear fruit unless it be united to the vine, neither shall we attract others to our mode of life unless we be united in Jesus Christ, who is the vine of which we are the branches. Then there is the motive of fear. If we separate ourselves from this mystic vine and become divided among ourselves, we expose the work of God to ruin, and we therefore deserve the chastisements of his eternal justice. There is, moreover, our own personal and common interest, for from this union will flow down on us, as from an abundant source, all kinds of graces and blessings. Finally, there is the motive of gratitude toward the author of our vocation. God will be glorified by the fruits of justice and sanctity we produce as he who plants a tree is glorified by its fruits. Hence, beholding the fruits of our union, the world will glorify God.

The devil, jealous of so many spiritual and temporal blessings, will consequently try to annihilate them in their first cause, seeking to destroy these works by sowing division in the minds and hearts of the members. For he knows well that he can do us no harm if we preserve a holy union among ourselves. Woe and anathema, then, to any religious who helps the devil to sow discord in a community.

It follows from all this that there should be but one mind and one heart among all the members of a community. Between the highest authority and the members, there should be a replica of Christ and his mystical body, of the head of the Church and the faithful. Between the local superiors and the superior general, there should be the same dependence as exists between the branches of a tree and its trunk, between the sun and its rays, between the river and its source—under penalty of seeing all disintegrate and come to naught. But this trunk, this sun, this source—being but the instrument used to create and preserve the rest, being of itself without strength, light, and water—it ought to be intimately united to God through Jesus Christ, and to Jesus Christ through Mary and Joseph, in order to receive light, the sap of the spiritual life, the salutary waters of divine grace. My dearly beloved, I beg of you, pray for your superiors, pray especially for the one on whom rests the burden of the general administration, and give them and him your unquestioning loyalty and your unfaltering support. Love one another; help one another;

pray for one another. Remember that you are to be known as followers of
Christ by this sign: "Behold these religious, how they love one another."

Pride

As humility is the foundation of charity, pride is its ruin. The proud man
does not even know the meaning of the words "community spirit." He
cannot enter into its daily give and take; he is forever wearing a chip on his
shoulder and, as it were, daring someone to knock it off. In every change
of employment, he finds a reason for personal offense. He is never happy,
and he often keeps others from being so. Let us meditate on the malice of
pride, the first and worst enemy of community spirit. Pride is a vain and
deceitful thing. It spoke its first lying words in the Garden of Eden, "You
shall be as gods" (Gn 3:5). By this deceitful message, Lucifer, under the
form of a serpent, led our first parents into his revolt, by way of compen-
sating himself for not being able to win all the angels and also because of
his jealousy of humanity, who, he saw, was destined to be seated on the
thrones of which he and his unhappy accomplices had been dispossessed.
Surely he was worthy to be called the "father of lies," that wretched and
fallen angel, who dared to promise deification as the reward of pride and
independence, when he had just made such disastrous trial of the shame
and abasement that was their fruit.

Behold that impostor. Jealous of the happiness of humanity in
whom the image of God shone as in the angelic nature, although to a
lesser degree, he came to us in the midst of the terrestrial paradise, and,
as the cause of his own downfall was vainglory, he dragged us into the
abyss into which he was himself plunged, communicating to us his passion for false greatness. He told us to disregard the prohibition given, cast
off the yoke of obedience, and thus become a god. We believed him and
in our vain thought were raised above our natural condition. Hence, that
sentiment which makes us want too much elevation is called *superbia* by
the scriptures, from the Latin word *super-ire*, "to go above." Thus, the rule
of pride, begun in heaven and extended to our first parents by a single

temptation, spread over all the earth and became the cause of idolatry. From that moment men and women always wished to raise themselves to the level of divinity and thus rob God of a portion of his glory. Hence, I think we should consider here this species of parent malady that is more or less born with us, this passion for esteem and honor that is the source of all our mistakes and evils, so that we may see it as it is: the most criminal and yet most common of all the tendencies we have to combat — also the most dangerous, though the most vain and frivolous of them all.

To understand the crime of pride and the nature of a vice so inherent in our fallen nature, we must consider it as a true act of independence on humanity's part toward its Creator. Hence, we must go back to the sin of Adam. In his state of innocence, the first human was united to God by complete dependence, and he drew from this union the clear light of his intelligence, the firm rule of his will, the spiritual life of his soul, his absolute empire over his body, his sovereign authority over creatures, and the immortality that allowed him to aspire to eternal glory. All this was because our first parent saw himself in God, who was always with him as the source of all his happiness through his perfect submission to the divine will. But that permanent regard of humanity toward its Creator — humanity in whom God mirrored himself, so to speak — which referred all humanity to God suddenly was lost through the deviation of the human mind turned away from God and upon itself. Man and woman, seeing their souls so beautiful, instead of continuing to behold in them only the image and reflection of the divine beauty, turned their eyes from their Creator to fix them on themselves. They grew complacent and delighted in contemplation of their excellence. Then, forgetting from whom they were separating themselves, and repudiating their dependence, they attributed to themselves all they found of worth within their nature. Knowing that they had power to act, they made a deadly trial of their liberty, freeing themselves from the rule of the eternal, whose laws they violated, to act only of their own volition.

Truly was it blind and madly abstracted to withdraw from God, who alone is the light and strength of his creatures, in order to seek outside him the chimerical perfection offered by other creatures, and to desire to dethrone him by wanting to equal him, instead of recognizing his absolute dominion. And yet, strange to say, both angel and human dared to commit such a stupidly foolish crime. The angel, self-deceived into loving himself more than God, cried out in his pride, "I will rise even to the high heavens and will be as the Most High." Humans, refusing to obey God because they wanted to be their own master even as God, dared to try out for themselves the promise made by that proud one who brought revolt into heaven: "You shall be as gods."

Such is the origin and the criminal character of vainglory. Divine glory was elevated above both angel and human, even though, being the glory of God, it was independent and incommunicable in its essence. Lucifer aspired to it in his audacious pride, and then, failing to acquire it, he made it shine before the eyes of the first human being, who, in his foolish vanity yielding to its illusion, reached out after it. Thus egoism rules the straying heart, worshipping the ego as its divinity and seeking on every side victims and altars for itself and for the devil whose slave it has become.

Satan, elated by this success in the terrestrial paradise, carried on his plan of making himself equal to God. Openly declaring himself the rival of God and trying to turn everything from the divine majesty to himself, he adulterated, as Tertullian says, all the works of the Creator. Teaching men and women a corrupt use of creatures, he turned stars and elements, plants and animals, into objects of idolatry. He practically abolished the pure worship of God outside Judea and made himself adored elsewhere throughout the earth. Hence, David sang: "The Lord . . . is to be feared above all gods. For all the gods of the gentiles are devils" (Ps 96:4–5). Hence, Jesus Christ called Lucifer the "prince of the world," and St. Paul called him "the god of this world" (2 Cor 4:4). In the words of Bossuet, everything was a god except God himself.[15] Thus, through the pride of a fallen angel, God was banished to a large extent from his creation and the rule of Satan was established in the world. What a strange and criminal upheaval.

Not less criminal and even more unbelievable is the sight of human beings wishing in their turn to pass for gods, and yet such was the result of the first of the three forms of concupiscence, which is called vainglory. Numberless martyrs went to their death for refusing adoration to vile and corrupt mortals. History commemorates the three Hebrew children cast into the furnace by the unconquerable king of Babylon (Dn 1–3), so proud in the midst of his conquests, so luxurious amid his immense treasures, so vain because of the powerful suzerainty imposed by his sword on the nations, because of the chains weighing down these peoples, and because of the groaning of his captives. Raised by ferocious and barbaric grandeur to the position of a divinity of this world, he looked over his vast empire and found complacency in himself and his pomp. Maddened with pride over the foaming seashores, the broken cities, the thousands of corpses beneath his throne, the vases of gold and brass plundered from the Temple of the true God, the innumerable armies spread over great fields of combat, the plentiful booty for his soldiers, he thought himself indeed a god: "You shall be as gods." Yet, we know of his terrible downfall from that supposedly imperishable grandeur into an animal state, which rightly punished his pride: "People when they were in honor did not understand; they are compared to senseless beasts, and become like them" (Ps 49:13).

We need not go so far back into history for instruction, however. In these present days of anarchy, we have made a god of our own reason; we have usurped the sanctuaries of divinity for the caprices of our mind and heart. No Christian Frenchman will ever forget the goddess of reason, exalted to the opprobrium of our ancestors and the shame of a beautiful country. To overthrow the established order, this goddess had to be surrounded with bloody hatchets, savage bodyguards, and mad leaders. Under the rule of this sovereign, France had made its god. There was no law except arrests, no rule except death, no ministers except executioners. For it is true that whenever human beings try to steal divine authority under pretext of securing greater liberty, their vainglory makes them the slave of disorder and sin, and yet we go madly on trying to realize the promise, "You shall be as gods."

We would go so far as to rule God entirely from our creation. God can no longer command the nations to adore him alone in the way he prescribes. Governments claim the right to choose a divinity of their own making and to trace the rules of their religious worship, if they do not altogether deny divinity. God must be content with whatever homage they deign to give him. He must not presume to teach them what is good and what is evil, what is permitted and what is forbidden. Philosophers have the right to fix limits and write moral laws. And what a morality theirs is! God could surely apply to them the cutting irony spoken against the same disorder of the human mind and heart at the beginning of the world: "Behold, Adam is become as one of us" (Gn 3:22). Pride thus leads us so far that we wish to withdraw from our Creator and the light of revealed religion, to find truth for ourselves and invent our own worship and rules of conduct.

Experience shows us people once brilliant for their very Christianity, ornamented even more by their knowledge of religion than by their great secular learning, who obtained renown under the standard of faith by the victorious eloquence with which they overthrew heretics—and who yet suddenly fell into deplorable disorder. We wonder how this evil can happen. A bit of vain complacence, a light which they thought they perceived by their own genius and without God's assistance, was sufficient to lead them astray. Yielding to their imprudence, they trusted first to the artificial brilliance of their intellect and then fell in love with its deceiving luster. Sure self-opinion followed, and with it perseverance in error, despite the warning of that legitimate authority which is the sentinel of the faith and could still have reclaimed them. Stubborn with the pride that characterizes all heretics, they fell into schism and heresy and sought glory in their wrong opinions.

And yet, it is evident that heresy has always produced only a dark night of error and of contradictory doctrines, with attendant relaxation or positive disorder in morality. There is no peace where pride rules, for it creates an interminable tempest of raging waters that rise and fall in mad confusion with no result except frothing waves that bring destruction till they die away to nothingness. Pride spends itself in tempestuous contradictions whose outcome, contrary to the promised deification of humanity, merely shows the nothingness of the creature, powerless in its efforts to withdraw from the rule of the Creator. Who of us, after these thoughts, will again surrender to the disastrous and criminal passion of pride? Yet, so much is it part of our fallen nature that we must cry out with St. Paul: "Who shall deliver me from the body of this death?" (Rom 7:24). Pride is of all passions the most common, being the first form of concupiscence, which is called vainglory.

In running after vainglory we shall never be satisfied. We shall rather resemble that fabled sinner who the poets represent as striving always to satisfy his thirsty throat in waters his lips can never reach. We shall be wretched with cares and regrets because, following pride only to discover its illusions, we shall lose the hope of being raised one day to the true glory that God reserves for the humble of heart. Truly this devouring thirst for vainglory has been our punishment ever since our first parents tried to make themselves equal to divinity through the lying promise of the devil: "You shall be as gods."

Oh, my dearly beloved, let us tear from our hearts that concupiscence that St. John calls the "pride of life" and which, in leading us to try to elevate ourselves unduly, hurls us, along with Lucifer and our first parents, into an abyss of humiliations. For God gave his word, and he has seen to its fulfillment from age to age: "Those who exalt themselves shall be humbled, and those who humble themselves shall be exalted" (Mt 23:12). If we but avail ourselves of all the holy practices of humility offered by our community life in opposition to the suggestions of our self-love, we will enable God to exalt us to share in his eternal glory and make us really like himself: "I have said, 'You are gods and all of you the sons of the Most High,'" (Ps 82:6). Let us raise our thoughts even to this glory, which alone is worthy of our ambition, because it alone is assured, permanent, and unlimited, whereas that offered by the world is uncertain, fleeting, and limited. After the example of Jesus Christ and all the saints, let us trust the care of our reputation to him who alone can give it solidity and patiently await the day of triumph when, in the face of heaven and earth, justice will be solemnly rendered to all according to their works. Our merits will be recompensed with the happiness even of God, who will then, St. John tells us, make us "like to him" and, consequently, "other gods" (1 Jn 3:2).

Happy are those who understand and practice this doctrine. Freed from human judgments, calm and immovable as a rock in the midst of the waves of opinion that come and go, they let the world move about them and spend its malignity against them, and yet they keep their interior peace, because they have learned to count as true glory only that which awaits the humble of heart in heaven.

Pride is not only the greatest enemy to true union with God; it is also the greatest enemy to the true community spirit. Seldom do we witness among religious the public downfalls on which we have just meditated, for religious are more often the victims of a lesser species of pride, which is, nevertheless, in many ways just as destructive to the harmony of community life. I refer to what is forbidden by St. Paul: "Let us not be made desirous of vainglory, provoking one another, envying one another" (Gal 5:26). This passion of the heart is so much the more dangerous in that the vain prejudices of the world seem to ennoble it. It is so common that, far from being ashamed of it, worldly people regard it as scarcely a defect. It is so much the more deadly because it was not only the first cause of all humanity's sorrows and difficulties, but it is still the source of most of the disorders that dishonor the sanctuary and afflict the Church of God. This species of pride I would call the love of the glory that comes from the honors and dignities of earth.

The germ of this evil passion is in all of us; it needs but the least circumstance to develop it, and there is not one of us in whom its pernicious roots do not more or less extend and its bitter fruits do not grow easily. Who of us can say that we have never felt in our hearts the desire to be overesteemed by our companions? No greater service could be done our community than the cure of this malady and the raising of the members forever beyond the suggestions of self-love. So I say to you, as I have said to myself, with all the zeal I have for our happiness in eternity: "Let us not be made desirous of vainglory." Let us not run after the esteem of the world, but let us root out from our nature, so corrupted by sin, that absurd attachment to praise and that eagerness to curry favor with human judgment. "Let us not be made desirous of vainglory." Let us courageously combat a passion that, by making us lose the merits of our works, paralyzes our ministry among others.

To better get rid of this passion, it will be well to consider first what it is in itself, as the most common, most dangerous, and most vain of all the passions we must conquer, and then what it is with reference to God, as reproved by his express word in the scriptures, by the example of Jesus Christ his Son, and by that of all the saints animated by his Spirit.

"O Jesus, meek and humble of heart, bless my words, give unction to my voice, and make us all sharers of your humility. Jesus, meek and humble of heart, have mercy on us."

Of all the passions that tyrannize over us, the passion for esteem is the most common because it constantly pursues every one of us, the most dangerous because it leads to every sort of evil, and the vainest because it seeks a frivolous object it can never attain. It follows us always, leaving us no permanent peace or even temporary truce. It waits forever at the door of the heart, watching its chance for entrance. The imprudent person who is not on guard receives a thousand wounds from it without even suspecting them. Let us go over the details of our life day after day, and likely we shall find not even one moment when it does not more or less exercise control over our actions.

We naturally desire esteem of our origin, for example. Suppose our birth was advantageous through station or wealth. We speak of it complacently and adroitly turn conversation to our family, our relatives, our friends. Suppose, on the other hand, our birth was obscure or mean in the eyes of the world. We dissimulate, hiding what is true and telling or inferring what is not true. And yet, the Son of God, with a lineage far nobler than ours, did not blush at being born in a stable of parents who were very poor.

We desire esteem for our talents. We take great care to see to it that they are not ignored. We air them on every occasion, today by a fine bit of banter, a biting satire, tomorrow by a bit of history recounted with ease and to the point because we prepared it before the conversation. Sometimes we talk of the sciences and the languages we know. We are eager to learn more merely for the purpose of airing it afterward. Sometimes we pretend to know that of which we are really ignorant. When with those who might find us out by their knowledge, we dissemble our ignorance by the use of vague terms that will not betray us or by a silent air of approval which signifies that we know all about what is being discussed. At other times, for fear of betraying our ignorance, we refuse to ask necessary questions from those who could instruct us and fall into grave error that harms our ministry. Or, with a view to appearing learned, we affirm doubtful matters as if we knew them certainly and even support them when we have no fear of contradiction.

Desire of esteem makes us dominate others in conversation. We form the habit of contesting and contradicting others because we want to seem important and estimable. We want to spread news obtained from those in authority, and we speak familiarly of them in jest and with wit. We are adroit at using the least circumstance that can be turned to our advantage and at insinuating our own praise, never, of course, speaking it openly lest we be thought vain. Yet, we are bound to end by carelessly dropping words that show what we think of ourselves and our secret joy in every advantage to ourselves.

Desire of esteem creeps even into our solitude. Even when we are alone at the foot of our crucifix, our imagination with its avidity for praise ferments vainglory within us, inspires us with desires, suggests projects to us, and makes us conceive hopes. Sometimes it so disquiets us about the opinions of others that we try to enter into the minds of our superiors and fellow religious to see what is there concerning us, and we even assist afar at conversations in which they speak of our virtues and talents. Sometimes it surrounds us with a brilliant public atmosphere of homage and applause and shows us the steps by which we might rise to such a reputation and how, on returning to our community, we might bring it along as our just due.

Desire of esteem enters into our works and sufferings. Whenever we have anything to do, we publicize its difficulty in order to publicize our merit. If we are suffering, we recount our woes that others may pity us and admire our patience. Desire of esteem has its part in our very faults. When we do something wrong that we cannot hide, we hasten to avow it for fear others might reproach us more severely otherwise; sometimes we even exaggerate it, so that at least they may think us humble. This passion is, indeed, everywhere and breeds preferential attachment on the one side and aversion for those of superior talents on the other. From these come agitation of mind after a humiliation; malignant joy over those small successes of others that make our own achievement, as we suppose, seem so much greater; and painful feelings when the praise and honor we so much covet go to others. The most inconceivable effect of vainglory is the way in which it warps our judgment so that we are puffed up over the esteem even of some poor obscure person whose opinion on other matters is beneath our notice. Surely there is not another enemy whose insidious attacks should command greater vigilance.

We must conclude, then, that no refuge is safe from vainglory. It lurks in the shop of the artisan as in the atelier of the artist, in the obscure hut of the poor as in the brilliant academy. All men and women, great, wise, or ignorant, weary themselves to be admired and exalted in the opinions of others as they are in their own imaginations. Almost all people's vain occupations have this end. To increase self-esteem one ravages the land, another devotes his life to study, another writes a book, another travels a thousand leagues from home to get a bit of decoration. Thus, by raising self-esteem, men and women try to distract themselves from the importunate remembrance of their misery and nothingness. Truly, we have reason to say that the passion for vainglory is the commonest of all passions.

This passion is as dangerous as it is general, because we so easily pardon our secret complaisance in the esteem of others. We smile at such sweet sentiments or we ignore them, not realizing that in acting thus we nourish a mortal enemy which can lead us to every evil and finally to hell. St. Teresa saw one day the place reserved for her in hell if she did not reject the first inclination to vanity. St. Francis Xavier had so great an aversion against this passion that he was often heard to cry out: "O esteem of human beings, what evil you have done, are doing, will yet do!"

In the history of the world we likely could not find a single country in which the ravages of self-love have not written their terrible tale. Vanity has presided over all the bloody wars that have desolated society. Vanity has inspired all the wicked ways to fortune, for people want wealth as a means to gain esteem. Vanity has sacrificed duty to the intrigues of ambition, for people want prominent places to attract attention and provoke admiration. Vanity breeds envy, hate, jealousy, human respect, cowardly yielding of principle, and all attendant vices.

Most of us need not go outside ourselves for examples of the effects of vanity. Was it not the passion for esteem that caused most of the blunders we remember with distress? Was it not this passion that inspired in our conversations every reticence, evasion, perhaps a lie, whether to justify ourselves when we were blameworthy or to remove ideas disadvantageous to ourselves? Was it not vanity that made us feel aversion against those who esteemed us slightly and too much attachment to those who seemed valuable to us? Was it not the passion for esteem that made us envious of others, that made us complain when we did not receive what we thought our due of honor, that so often altered the purity of our intentions, that distracted the prayers of our minds and hearts? We who have the care of others should be especially careful of this passion lest we realize the fear of St. Paul: "Lest when I have preached to others, I myself should become a castaway" (1 Cor 9:27).

Religious animated by the passion for esteem are apt to complain of the post they are assigned to, to murmur against authority, and to demand their supposed rights. If they can get a higher post, they will—for the sake of their vain ambition—leave the one providence gave them. If labor be their portion, not content with the obscure functions that are their duty, they seek the brilliant ones that are not asked of them. If they teach, they do not deign to abase themselves to the level of the little ones but prefer to make themselves admired rather than understood, to establish a reputation for cleverness rather than produce fruits of knowledge. Their exterior is ruled by luxury, studied elegance, affectation, and vanity of habit and belongings. Their interior is agitated by self-love and pride if they succeed, by discouragement and sadness if they fail. They brought to the community certain resolutions on the preparation and decency due to the Holy Sacrifice, to prayer, to religious customs, and to zeal for the salvation of souls; but later they ask themselves: "What will they think of me if I am too pious, if I withdraw too much from worldly amusement?" Hence, not to seem singular, to avoid the criticisms of lukewarm religious, they ignore their resolutions till they themselves become lukewarm or even give scandal. Such are the dangers of this passion for esteem and praise. How we should work to tear it from our souls!

Another consideration that should help determine us to destroy it is that it runs after a frivolous object it can never attain. With all its efforts and agitation, all that it pretends to is to win here and there the good opinion of human minds, some expression of esteem, be it only a word, gesture, or glance. Surely nothing could be more futile in both its causes and its effects. As to its causes, self-love tells us when we are praised that this homage is given our merits—in payment of a debt, as it were—though very often the merits are only imaginary ones. Very often the praise is mere flattery, or pure civility rising from fear of wounding our suscepti- bility, or desire to give us pleasure because we are known to love praise. Very often it is just an encouragement to our weakness, an aid to our cowardice, since, without it, we would have no courage at all. Sometimes it is the charity that thinks no evil and sees only the good that honors Jesus Christ in our person and hence treats us courteously, speaks to us honorably, loves us cordially. Often it comes from prejudice in our favor, born of blind friendship, or family, or social bonds, and those who judge us let their hearts so rule their heads that they find all we do and say wor- thy of approval; they see only virtue and spiritual wealth where God sees miserable poverty, and they discover rare talents where truth perceives only a very ordinary mind. More often still, praise is given us because of ignorance; we are esteemed because we are not really known but are judged by deceitful appearances. Oh, how rare would be the language of praise in our ears did the eyes of others uncover what we are!

This ignorance in those who praise us is excusable, of course. But we who know what we are have no excuse for being complacent over it. Let us imagine a beggar reduced to the last degradation, with only rags to cover his wounded flesh, to whom people bend the knee and speak thus flatteringly: "We all admire you, sir, for your prodigious wealth, your grace and beauty of person, your magnificent clothes." We should think such a person had lost his reason if he took pleasure in these words and consider them his due when knowing the contrary to be true. Yet, that is our history, yours and mine. We are so poor that we have nothing and can do nothing, and we are covered with the wounds of our sins and the marks of our passions; and yet, we take pleasure in seeing ourselves thought rich in merits, virtues, and talents. However false be the praise given us, we are delighted to hear it, since we care more about what we seem to be to others like ourselves than about what we truly are before God. Were we not so stupidly foolish, these compliments and marks of esteem would rather emphasize our misery and be considered by us, as they were by the saints, as injuries done to extreme poverty. "Receive praises as banter and affronts," said St. Francis Xavier. Could we, if we knew ourselves, judge otherwise than as he did? Surely we must conclude that we do not merit esteem and that the opinions of those who flatter us are, therefore, of little consequence.

Vainglory is not less undesirable in its effects than it is in its causes. Are we greater or lesser in character when we are praised or blamed, esteemed or despised, forgotten or well-known? Are we less miserable because today the world happens to call us famous? Those of us who are honest feel that this thinking but adds to our miseries and reasons for ridicule since we take complacency in esteem we do not deserve, that the swelling of our pride, which puffs us up without really adding to our moral physique, is a dangerous malady of soul. Have we lost anything when tomorrow the world pricks the bubble it made and sees us as little, miserable creatures unworthy of any esteem? If we see straight, we shall regard what we lost as nothing but useless amusement, a bit of reputation enormously dangerous for our self-love and vanity. Do most of us need anyone to talk of the good there is in us? Have we not grown eloquent about it far too often ourselves?

Human judgments are only wind and smoke, which give us nothing and take nothing from us, which make us neither better nor worse. Besides, most of us are ashamed when we find ourselves so greedy for praise. Much as we like to be brought into public recognition and hear things advantageous to ourselves, we always want others to think we do not care for it. We boast of our humility and appear to suffer on hearing certain compliments, and yet our very way of rejecting them shows that we think we merit still more of them. Truly, this is a strange thing—the esteem of others is so vain that it makes us ashamed when we like it, and yet it flatters our poor hearts so sweetly.

The purpose of our creation, on the other hand, is for the glory of God and for the praise and esteem he alone can rightly bestow because he alone can appreciate matters truly. If we can only win this precious esteem, if our great master will proclaim us one day in the assembly of the saints, it will not matter if the world ignores us or despises us. If, on the contrary, the blessing of God fails us, the honorable testimonials of approval of all the world will avail us nothing. Though our glory be durable enough to survive us, the praises given us on earth will assuage our eternal torments not at all. Truly, the esteem of others, both in its causes and in its effects, is an illusion, a shadow, a nothingness. Why, then, do we make it the object of our ambition as if it were a serious and true thing? Why does its possession delight and transport us, its loss trouble and disquiet us?

It might be something if all our lives we could attain and enjoy this esteem, all futile as it is, but we cannot. No person escapes censure and criticism. Somehow, all people, as if they were at war with one another, observe and remark the failings of their neighbors to make them the object of their satire. They seem to take pleasure in seeing the faults of others or, if they can find none, in misinterpreting their intentions in their good deeds. It is a truly remarkable thing that there is perhaps not a person on earth against whom lying and calumny, suspicion and criticism, have not sent their poisonous breath. It is an incontestable truth, so well received as to be a proverb, that one cannot please everybody. Why, then, should we hesitate to renounce so frivolous a thing as the esteem of others and fail to practice henceforth the advice of the apostle: "Let us not be made desirous of vainglory" (Gal 5:26)? Let us determine to rid our hearts of this passion that we have just seen to be so dangerous in itself, and let us confirm our hatred of it by considering how God looks upon it.

The Example of Jesus

To know how God condemns the passion for esteem, we have only to glance at the holy scriptures, at the example of Jesus Christ, and at the conduct of those whom the Church honors with public veneration. The Bible tells us: "The Lord is the King of Glory" (Ps 24:10); "To the only God be honor and glory" (1 Tm 1:17); "I will not give my glory to another" (Is 48:11); "For all flesh is as grass" (1 Pt 1:24). Here is evidence that honor and praise belong to God alone and that no poor creature has the right to them. With Peter of Blois we must conclude that to wish for esteem is to attempt to make our own the right of the Creator and to practice theft on God's domain. It is written: "The Lord hath made all things for Himself" (Prv 16:4). He created the nations only to confess his name. He gave them intelligence for "his own praise, and name, and glory" (Dt 26:19). He formed the heavens to tell his glory and the earth to preach his providence. Hence, to try to attract esteem to ourselves is to profane vessels destined to enclose the praises of God; it is to pervert the order of God, to frustrate the end he proposed in giving existence to intelligent creatures. The teachings of the gospels are especially formative. In the first pages, we find an anathema launched against the passion for esteem: "Woe to you when others shall bless you" (Lk 6:26). On the contrary, you are happily blessed "when they shall revile you, and speak all that is evil against you" (Mt 5:11). We surely believe the words of wisdom incarnate. Yet, shall we, if in the immediate future we hear someone speak evil of us, bless God for it? Do we sincerely fear to have good spoken of us? Alas, O my God, we have a speculative belief in your Gospel, but we are far from having a practical faith in it.

Let us listen further to our divine master speaking against the passion for vainglory. From the principles just enunciated flow numerous consequences, but we perhaps should not have had the courage to deduce them, and so God deigned to do it for us. "Take heed that you do not your justice before others to be seen by them" (Mt 6:1). Take care of what, Lord? Not to sin, not to give scandal? No, take care of an evil more dangerous in a way than even sin; take care not to do your justice to win the esteem of others. "When you give alms, let not your left hand know what your right hand does, that your alms may be in secret, and your father who sees in secret will repay you. When you fast, anoint your head, and wash your face, that you appear not to others to fast, but to your father who is in secret; and your father who sees in secret will repay you" (Mt 6:3–4, 16–18). If the ordinary Christian must avoid esteem this scrupulously, what of the religious? St. Paul, scarcely knowing how to qualify the crime of those who even in the functions of the ministry seek their own glory to the falsifying of the Gospel, declares that they "adulterate the word of God" (2 Cor 2:17). Instead of "begetting children of the gospel" (1 Cor 4:15), such priests misrepresent it to engender admiration for their persons and praise of their minds. This is more than adultery; it is an attempt at felony against the Lord, a crime of divine *lèse-majesté*.[16]

God, the great king of the universe, seeing from his throne on high that infidel peoples refuse to give him due honor, sends his priests to recall their wandering hearts to duty, somewhat as a powerful prince delegates his ministers to rebellious provinces to rally round themselves their unsubmissive subjects and thus strengthen the bonds that unite them to their monarch. And yet, these priests, making themselves leaders of the revolt, seek to rule minds instead of making God reign therein, to win esteem for themselves rather than procure honor for God. Though they claim to look only to the Lord, they yearn from the bottoms of their souls to turn eyes from him to themselves. Though they seem in religious ceremonies and chants to be occupied solely with the glory of the Most High, they are dreaming only of making themselves noticed and admired. This is truly a sacrilegious revolt, and of those guilty of it we could truthfully write this epitaph: "They loved the glory of others more than the glory of God" (Jn 12:43).

The Lord has also reproved the passion for vainglory by the example of Jesus Christ, his adorable Son. If the esteem of others were a true good worthy to occupy human hearts, God would not have refused it to his incarnate Word, in whom he had all complacence. Yet, what do we see? The second person of the ineffable Trinity, eternal wisdom, who housed all the splendors of the divinity, was concealed for nine months in the womb of the virgin. He who could call himself equal to God hid himself under the form of a slave and "in the likeness of sinful flesh and of sin" (Rom 8:3). When he had been born, a stable was his palace, a manger was his throne, shepherds were his courtiers. In his childhood, he had all the treasures of wisdom and knowledge, but he kept them hidden rather than let them make him famous (Col 2:3). Even in beginning his mission, he let himself be thought unlearned: "And the Jews wondered, saying: How doth this man know letters, having never learned?" (Jn 7:15). He was thought but the son of a carpenter, a carpenter himself (Mt 13:55; Mk 6:3; Jn 6:42). While he was carrying on his mission, the world held him in wavering esteem. When some proclaimed him prophet and Redeemer, others said he was a liar and impostor. He was accused of loving pleasure and wine; of being a Samaritan, a heretic, an impious enemy of the Temple and all holy people; of casting out devils by the power of Beelzebub and having a devil; of being seditious, more criminal than Barnabas. At length they cried: "Away with him. Away with him. Crucify him!" (Jn 19:15).

Such things were thought and said of the Son of God with all his titles to a good reputation and to esteem and praise. What were his thoughts, sentiments, and dispositions when he was attacked by so many cruel shafts at a time? Did he abandon himself to shame and desolation as we should do in like circumstances, we whom the least suspicion casts down and disconcerts, we who cannot accustom our ears to the language of reproach? Did he at least desire praise to make up for the unfavorable gossip? Ah, far from this. When a certain Jew approached him and called him "good master," Jesus, from whom calumny had never won a word of self-defense, could not restrain himself on hearing such praise: "Why do you call me good? None is good but one; that is God" (Mk 10:18). Furthermore, the thirst of Jesus Christ for contempt was not yet satisfied: "I have a baptism wherewith I am to be baptized, and how I am anguished until it be accomplished" (Lk 12:50). What was this baptism, O my Savior? They will cover me with blows, spittle, stripes; they will punish me as a blasphemer; they will mock me as a masquerading king; they will crush me as a worm on the earth. My heart has expected reproach and misery (Ps 69:21). I shall give my cheek to him who strikes me; I shall be filled with reproaches (Lam 3:30). He wanted disgrace and reproach without any mixture of praise.

Being God, Jesus could have dissipated the clouds of calumny by the brilliance of his miracles, but let us note that he did not use them so. When he worked them, preferring contempt to esteem, he commanded that they be made known to no one (Mt 8:4). After his resurrection, he had power to remedy the obscurity of his earlier life, but—how remarkable a thing, as if he feared being seen by others in his glorious and immortal state and receiving the praises due his triumph—he showed himself only to certain ones, and then but for a short time. He could, after his ascension, have sheltered himself entirely from forgetfulness and insults, but he shut himself into the silence of the tabernacle and has dwelt there for nineteen hundred years, exposed to the contempt, the outrages, of blasphemers.

Shall we not be ashamed, after all this, to wish for esteem and honor? Shall we not come even to understand that maxim of the Gospel, "Blessed are you when they shall revile you, and persecute you, and speak all that is evil against you, untruly, for my sake" (Mt 5:11)? St. Bernard says that either it was folly for the Son of God to wish to be an object of disgrace, reproach, and contempt, or it is folly for us to have a passion for the esteem of others. The Jews were scandalized by Christ's conduct, and the Gentiles took it for madness, but in the eyes of those who are called, it is nothing less than the wisdom and the virtue of God (1 Cor 1:20–25). It is, then, a true folly for us to care so much for the opinion of the world, for glory and reputation. Has our heart never felt the force of this reasoning? Ah, if we had really understood it even once, we should not have so often sighed after human judgment and the honors of earth; we should not have desired so much to be seen, to have a place among the eloquent, distinguished for their learning and power; we should not have sought to win minds to us, to merit praise and flattery by certain arts of speech and action, by studied sweetness and affected manners.

God not only reproves vainglory by the example of his adorable Son; he further condemns it by the conduct and maxims of saints whom his Spirit animates, as the apostle says (Rom 8:14). Indeed, even before Jesus Christ had revealed his sublime doctrine to the world, the royal prophet penned these beautiful words: "I have chosen to be at the threshold of the house of my God" (Ps 84:11). I will demean myself more (2 Sm 6:22). Already the queen of all saints, Mary had consented to be forgotten in her tribe, and that royal daughter of Judah was content to remain always in the obscurity of a cottage. Jesus Christ appeared. Whom did he choose to overthrow the monstrous giant of idolatry, to abase the hauteur of Rome and Athens, to convert the world? People poor and despicable in the eyes of the world, and he inspired them with love of greater poverty and further humiliation. "They went from the presence of the council, rejoicing that they were accounted worthy to suffer reproach for the name of Jesus" (Acts 5:41). This great lesson teaches us that with the passion for praise we can never be true Christians, still less priests and apostles. Though St. Paul was a Roman and a savant, rather than seeking esteem for his birth and talents, he immediately caught the true Christian spirit: "If I pleased men, I should not be the servant of Christ" (Gal 1:10); "To me it is a very small thing to be judged by you, or by humanity's day" (1 Cor 4:3); "I please myself in my infirmities, in reproaches, in necessities, in persecutions, in distresses, for Christ" (2 Cor 12:10).

After the apostles appeared the martyrs, thousands in number, who joyfully lost their reputations on this earth in the belief that they began to be disciples of Christ only at the moment when they were humiliated and despised. Then came the solitaries, who hid forever from the eyes of others and concealed their virtues from human esteem. Then came saints of both sexes, of every age and condition, who, when forced by providence to remain in public places, sought solitude in their hearts and were dismayed when surprised in a good act which could give some idea of their holiness — so much did they fear esteem as a danger to humility and praise as a death-dealing scourge. When calumny and persecution came upon them, they were calm, content, even joyful. St. Vincent de Paul, for example, published widely that he was the son of a peasant and had kept flocks in his boyhood, and he let the public think him a thief and a hypocrite, and this for many years. St. Francis de Sales also was content with a reputation shattered for two whole years.

When we see what the saints thought of worldly esteem, we do not dare to call ourselves their children and imitators — we who experience so sweet a feeling when someone gives us honorable mention; we who know so well how to hold the approving silence that makes pass for true the false praise given us; we who are so prompt to excuse ourselves when we are wrongly blamed and cannot be reproached for the least fault without making reply; we who have such a horror of humiliations, though these are in the judgment of saints the greatest grace God can give us and the sole means to cure our pride; we who carry our vanity so far as to speak to our own disadvantage in order to insinuate that we are really humble, but not at all to win credence for what we are saying; we who, after a ceremony or public function in which we think we have been successful, go out of our way, when no one mentions it to us, to ask someone in what we have failed, or even find fault with the part that seemed best to us, to provoke a complimentary rejoinder. Ah, let us be ashamed and afraid lest we have one day as our accusers those saints whose blood flows in our veins and whose ravishing examples we have thus far so poorly imitated.

We have just seen that no passion is more common, dangerous, and frivolous than that of vainglory, a passion God has reproved by his express word and by the example of Jesus Christ his son and of all the saints animated by his Spirit. Let us combat it, then, with unfailing courage. In the way of the Savior and his true disciples, let us lift our gaze on high. Let us no longer try to feed our souls on the phantom food pursued by a mad self-love but have a nobler desire. Let us aspire, not to an uncertain glory, fleeting and limited, such as the world gives its partisans, but to an assured glory, endless and unlimited, such as the Savior gives his elect in eternity. Trusting, as did our divine master, all care for our reputation to him who alone can give it solidity, let us wait with confidence and humility the day of triumph when, before heaven and earth, justice will be solemnly rendered to each according to his works, and our merits will be recompensed by God with his own happiness.

Thus, freed from human judgments, calmly immovable as a rock while waves of opinion come and go, our interior peace will not be troubled though the world dashes its malignity against us, because we shall have learned to count as true only what the sovereign judge sees and approves in us. Then only shall we be fit to labor toward the consummation of the elect, because St. Augustine says, the more one is emptied of self, the more one is filled with grace and capable of doing great things in the order of salvation.

The Virtues

As humility is the base of all fraternal generosity, pride and vainglory are the most destructive forces against community spirit. From these vices rise envy, criticism, gossip, uncharitable talk. They not only occasion sin in their possessors but provoke it in others. The proud are either feared or ridiculed, and the result in either case is the occasioning of rash judgments and of judgments that are true but foster cruelty of mind. Where all the members of a house are humble, there can be but few sins against charity. Where charity is not violated, a religious house is a foretaste of heaven on earth.

To follow the precept of Jesus Christ on fraternal charity, we must pay particular attention to the practice of this virtue as it is described by St. Paul. Our charity must be "patient," so that everything may be suffered from others, and others may not be made to suffer by us, that thus there may be no murmurings or complaints (1 Cor 13:4ff.). It must be "full of kindness," so that we are always reasonable, obliging, civil. It must "not envy," so that we shall not be jealous of the advantages others enjoy but shall rather wish them greater good. As charity "never works evil," we must be vigilant, circumspect, and attentive to avoid indiscreet language, misplaced pleasantry, and unpleasing voice and gesture. Should we unwittingly give offense by word or deed, we must not let the day pass without asking forgiveness.

As charity is "not puffed up," whatever be our rank, we must avoid haughty airs, ostentation, and pride, and we must never speak contemptuously to others or take a superior tone with them. Knowing that charity is "not ambitious," we should not expect extra consideration or make known that we receive it if we do, and we should not desire preference or positions of authority. As charity does not "seek her own," we should treat our neighbor with truly Christian affection, sincere attachment, unselfish zeal, and no wish for return of service.

As charity is "not carried away," we should be willing to admonish others or explain ourselves when necessary, but always without passion, because otherwise we should be carried away by eagerness. As charity "thinks no evil," we should never be distrustful or suspicious; we should never form aversions or rash judgments. Instead of always looking at the worst side of things and coloring them to the disadvantage of others, we should take all in good faith—not, of course, approving anything wrong, but slow to believe there is anything wrong. Charity "rejoices not in injustice but much in truth," and so, far from being pleased when others are blamed and mortified or when people turn against them, we should lament such a thing. When others do good and are justly treated, we should thank God for it. Charity "endures all, believes all, hopes all, bears all," and so good intentions must be readily believed and whatever tends to the justification of our neighbors received with eagerness and simplicity; or, when they cannot be justified, we must pray for them and hope they will soon amend.

Recreation is a great aid or a great hindrance to community spirit. Religious should always practice the gentle culture of refined family life. Politeness, the true politeness that comes from loving hearts, should always set the tone of community recreation. Christ, who is our model, had royal blood in his veins, and his training in courtesy was at the hands of Mary and Joseph. Need I say more? And we should be other Christs. Remembering that Christ is the listener to every conversation, we should try to be as the two disciples on the way to Emmaus, who had no need to shift the subject of their conversation to let the Savior join in with it and who were prepared by their thoughts to let him make their hearts burn with zeal while he conversed with them.

If a religious community be, as faith teaches it is, a family knit by the closest bonds, the loyalty of its members to one another should be manifest to the entire world. In conversations and in correspondence with outsiders, the true religious is most careful not to betray any of the weaknesses of his brothers and sisters; in fact, loyalty to the community is one of the first marks by which a true religious is known, just as love for others is the first mark of a Christian, the sign by which one is known to be a disciple of Christ.

Every member should try to secure the reign of a pious emulation in the community in regard to discipline, regularity, silence, obedience, and charity. To assist one another to climb the difficult ladder of religious perfection, those more advanced in age and rank should reach down their hands to the younger by good example first and by good counsel second. The greater glory of God, their own sanctification, and the edification of their brothers and sisters should be motives that grow stronger with advancing years. For the sake of both charity and humility, all should look on others as superior to themselves, should give others the respect and honor due to their station, should see in the neighbor the image of

God and honor the guardian angel attending him. Everyone should be zealous for the preservation of that unity of mind, heart, and conduct which is the principle, not only of peace, but of the very existence of the community. This should not be difficult where all have the same God, the same faith, the same sacraments, the same rules to observe, the same establishments to maintain—where the good of one must be the good of all, and the evil of one must be the evil of all.

There are three great virtues on which the unity of a religious house must rest: humility, charity, and mortification. The third of these is well taken care of by the vows. Those who observe every detail of his rules on poverty, chastity, and obedience cannot but lead a mortified life. Such as these are like well-disciplined soldiers, who are in no way distinguishable from others in the ranks by eccentricity of dress or behavior. One of the greatest mortifications is to lead the common life perfectly. Such mortification protects the vows. Religious who keep their clothing and other possessions strictly within their vow of poverty will never let themselves hurt that uniformity which is the outward expression of community spirit. Those who are content with what the common life provides in food and other necessities in accordance with the spirit of poverty will be safeguarded against manifestations of sensuality that single out unmortified religious from the more temperate ones. Those who keep strictly to the prohibition of their vow of chastity against particular friendship will not form any of those defensive and offensive alliances that so often breed discord in communities. Those who have really the spirit of obedience will fit into the daily routine of community life as a well-oiled part of a machine.

Oh, my dearly beloved, could we all but observe forever and everywhere the maxim of St. Jane Frances de Chantal, "Everything for grace, and nothing for nature"; could we but always distinguish the inspirations of grace from those of nature and then follow only the first; could we but do everything in obedience and nothing simply for personal inclination— our community would soon be welded into a perfect army, fighting the good fight of salvation, keeping all the treasures of faith intact, until at length we should finish our course and hear those blessed words: "Well done, good and faithful servant, . . . enter into the peace of your Lord" (Mt 25:21).

In regard to mortification, communities are like individuals, prone to great exactness and even to austerity in their youth but apt to grow lax as years go on. This is why so many communities have needed reform after a lapse of time. Mortification has never been relaxed among the Carthusians, and so they still have their primitive fervor. It is all too easy to adopt the worldly attitude, to become overfearful about health, to let agreeable work take the place of prayer and penance. It is all too easy to dry up the heart to the advantage of the intellect, to fall into easy routine in the use of the sacraments and the saying of the Office. It is all too easy to come to believe that the active life does not permit any supererogatory acts of devotion or mortification. It is true that religious who keep the letter of their rule deserve canonization, but religious who do not also keep its spirit never keep its letter.

There are so many aids to this mortification that is the third great pillar of the community spirit. Let us think often of our interior graces and good inspirations that deter from evil and urge to good, of our preservation from grave faults and from many venial ones deliberately committed, of our ever-increasing ease in triumphing over obstacles to our sanctification, of our ever-increasing love of vocation. Oh, it is most true that the Lord is good, that his mercy endures forever. "O my soul, bless the Lord, and never forget his benefits" (Ps 103:2). What return shall I make to him for all he has done for me? Let me follow him, let me be known as his disciple by the love I have for those who walk with me the difficult road to religious perfection.

Confession

. . . .

Whose sins you shall forgive, they are forgiven them; and whose sins you shall retain, they are retained. (Jn 20:23)

The sacraments are the most tangible proof of the love of Jesus Christ for us. They are as the last effort of his tenderness toward those he came to save, for they serve as the channels through which he communicates his grace and gives us his own life and spirit. They are the sacred fountains of which the prophet spoke, from which we joyfully drink the waters that purify our souls from all stains of sin and that give them sweet peace, divine strength, and new ardor to go forward in the ways of salvation (Jl 3:18).

Especially in the sacrament of Reconciliation do we prove in a most remarkable way the mercy of the Lord. In it are united many precious advantages: assurance of pardon for sin through the priestly absolution; repose and tranquility of conscience in the happy impressions of grace that God makes us feel deep in our hearts; nourishment and support for our weakness in the advice given us by the priest.

There are two kinds of confession: that made to God alone and that made to a priest. Confession is almost as old as humanity. In the terrestrial paradise, God exacted of our first parents an avowal of their disobedience. Later, we see the Jews offering the emissary goat in public confession of sin. The use of confession existed also among the Egyptians, the Greeks, the Romans, and the Japanese. The right of God to exact confession can surely not be questioned. It is not for the sinner but for the one outraged to determine the conditions of pardon. There is no need to prove the divine establishment of the tribunal of penance to you, my dearly beloved, but a review of its origin and history is always able to increase our understanding of this saving gift and our gratitude to God for it.

Scripture, reason, and tradition all prove the divine origin of auricular confession as now practiced among Christians. In the Bible we read: "Whatsoever you bind upon earth, it shall be bound also in heaven; and whatsoever you loose on earth, it shall be loosed also in heaven" (Mt 16:19). "Whose sins you shall forgive, they are forgiven them; and whose sins you shall retain, they are retained" (Jn 30:23). The apostles and their successors were thus established as judges and physicians of souls. To judge, one must know the matter. To cure, one must know the state of soul and its needed remedy. Hence, sinners must confess their sins to these judges and physicians, who otherwise could not know them.

An analogy may make this matter clearer. A king, to render individual justice to each of his subjects, calls about him the most virtuous available and bids them: "Go into all my provinces to settle matters of justice. I shall delegate my authority to you, and I shall forgive all those you forgive and condemn all those you condemn." What would be thought of those judges if, without being thoroughly informed concerning the crimes of the subjects, they should send some to the guillotine and should release others and restore them to their families? This very situation would be true if the apostles had been sent out with power to absolve and retain sins without at the same time having the opportunity to hear declarations of sin.

Here is another analogy. Skillful physicians are employed in the hospital to cure diseases. Without opportunity for exact information concerning the nature of the various maladies, they prescribe certain remedies. What is to be thought of them? Let us suppose the apostles and their successors had to employ the same method in treating sicknesses of the soul. Surely the power to absolve or to retain supposes the obligation on the part of the penitent to confess his sins. And yet, eager as all are to be assured of the forgiveness of their sins—all too many of them—even those most willing to reveal their most loathsome physical maladies to a physician find auricular confession a heavy if not insupportable burden.

Even were the scriptures less formal, tradition should suffice to prove the divine origin of the sacrament of Penance. If we go back through the centuries, we shall constantly hear repeated the equivalent of the command that all sinners must confess their sins humbly, at least at the paschal time. In the first century of the Christian era, Pope Clement I in his epistle to the Corinthians begs the seditious to "submit themselves to the presbyters and receive correction so as to repent," and St. Ignatius of Antioch promises the mercy of God to sinners if they will return "with one consent to the unity of Christ and the communion of the bishop," who, he adds elsewhere, "presides over penance."[17] So too, the *Didache*, written at the end of this century or the beginning of the next, prescribes: "In the congregation you shall confess your transgressions."[18] In the second century, we have the testimony of Irenaeus, Tertullian, and Origen, and the prayer used at the consecration of a bishop, as recorded in the Canons of Hippolytus, shows that this power of forgiving sins came by a process of transmission from earliest times: "Grant him, O Lord, the episcopate and the spirit, of clemency and the power to forgive sins." There are countless other testimonials to the traditional belief in auricular confession. One must either say that confession dates back to Jesus Christ or abjure all belief in tradition.

Historically, one would indeed display ignorance if he did not accept the continuous existence of this institution. No one can find a time since Christ when this universal custom has not prevailed. No one can tell when, where, and how it began if not with Christ, though we know the origin of all human institutions and of all heresies. Let the unbelievers tell us in what country, at what period of history, and in what way the practice of auricular confession began. Let them tell us what sort of priests they were who dared to impose this obligation on kings, emperors, soldiers, and priests themselves, for all these have been obliged to go to confession. Let us suppose that in our particular city confession is unknown and that some priests come into the city and try to impose it on the citizens. Have human passions been different from ours in any past age or human beings been more ready than we to confess the excesses of these passions?

The necessity of confession is evident. In all history no one except the Savior ever dared to utter such words as these, "Which of you shall convict me of sin?" (Jn 8:46), because he alone is truth and holiness and hence exempt from all falsehood and sin. Happy are the people who have ceased even to love sin. Happier still are those who have ceased to commit it habitually and who, purifying themselves by a good confession, can henceforth defy their enemies by their conduct. And yet, such is the mysterious effect of confession and penance, that, rightly used, it can enable us thus to live. Hence, the necessity of confession should seem to us a sweet and loving law.

Nothing could be more unjust and insulting to Jesus Christ than the unworthy prejudice that makes us regard confession as an insupportable yoke. If we paid only a little attention to the views of our Savior in instituting it, we should find that his only designs were those of peace and mercy. His one wish was to furnish an easy and infallible remedy for our weakness, to enable us to expiate by the pain we feel in confessing our sins a part of the penance they deserve, and to let us find in the shame, which accompanies their avowal, a capable bridle to control the furious impetuosity of our passions.

We know that heaven, the place of peace and innocence, will not admit anything sinful. To enter the banquet hall of our celestial spouse, we must have on the wedding garment of grace or be banished in dishonor (Mt 22:11–14). We know also how few of us would escape the many perils of the world and the deluge of sin sweeping over it and be able to gain our celestial inheritance if the Lord, who knows all the weakness of our nature, had not taken care of our feebleness, provided for all our needs, and supplied in the tribunal of penance, to which we have easy recourse, the remedy for our sins.

What do we mean by going to confession? Do we mean wasting all our strength of mind in an endless search into our least actions? Do we mean preparing by long and learned discourse to give our faults an appearance of equity and justice and plead our cause face-to-face with the minister of the Lord? There are those, it seems, who think so. But to go to confession means to let a conscience speak, a conscience that bears witness against itself and does not forgive itself the least sin. It means to follow up on that interior feeling of our miseries which leads us to put a happy confidence in the judge of our conscience. It means to discover the wounds of our soul to a charitable physician who knows the art of genuine healing. It means to avow our sins and ask pardon of a good father who desires nothing so much as to see himself disarmed by the humiliation and repentance of a rebellious child.

Despite the uncertainty and weakness of our human resources, we do not hesitate to have recourse to them when in trouble. In sickness of the body, we submit to operations and other severe remedies that often mean great danger to our lives. We find comfort in confiding the bitterness of our troubles to a friend, sometimes an unfaithful one who is secretly glad of our sorrows and may use them for his or her own benefit. And yet, some of us think it unbearable to cast ourselves on the mercy of a minister of Jesus Christ, who has infallible remedy and consolation for our sinful souls. We forget that one of the primary objects of the Savior in establishing confession was to allow us to use the very violence we do ourselves in declaring our sins as a part remission of the punishment due them. Through confession, eternal punishment is turned into temporal pain, and the very difficulty of confession takes care of part of that temporal pain. It seems strange that, with the great horror most of us have of penance, we should reject this infallible means of acquitting some of the great debt we have contracted toward divine justice. If we add this reason to all the other advantages of confession, we shall see why many of the saints went frequently, even daily, to confession.

The Fruits of Frequent Confession

We who are obliged by our rule to frequent confession and who practice it faithfully need no further explanation to urge us to determine never to abandon this saving practice. We do need, however, reflections on its advantages to stir us to make better use of our opportunity. Before we enter into these reflections, let us glance at the subject of general confession. During retreats and missions, a general confession or a review of the time since the last general confession is sometimes advisable. So too, even though there be no absolute need of it, a general confession is of much practical value before some very important step in life is taken, such as entering the religious state. Certain prescriptions for making such a confession can well be stated here.

A general confession is necessary when at some time in the past there has been deliberate omission of a mortal sin from a confession and this has not been repaired in a succeeding confession, or when there was such serious negligence in the examination of conscience that the sin was not mentioned, or when the nature of the sin was concealed through unwillingness to describe necessary circumstances. It is also necessary when mortal sin was confessed without sorrow and without resolve to refrain from it in the future. It is necessary when a confession was divided, that is, part of its grievous matter revealed to one priest and part to another. It is necessary when there was refusal to perform the penance enjoined at a past confession. A confession must be suspected as likely invalid when almost immediately after it there was relapse into some habitual sin, without any effort to withdraw from the immediate occasion or to resist the temptation, because so early and so easy a fall is indication that there was neither contrition nor firm purpose of amendment.

I know, my dearly beloved, that such necessity can scarcely exist in the case of any of you. Some of you will need rather to be warned against making general confessions because of the delicacy or even scrupulosity of your consciences. The scrupulous are always to be advised against general confessions, except in such rare cases as the confessor sees reasons for recommending otherwise.

It is well for us to meditate occasionally on the advantages of frequent confession in our religious life, since one of the most efficacious means to keep from sin and to make solid and rapid improvement in virtue is to use frequently this sweet and loving means of salvation. Indeed, independent of the grace of reconciliation it contains and of the all-powerful efficacy of the merits of Jesus Christ, which in confession are applied to our souls to purify and heal them, we find in this sacrament a salutary force to resist the tempter, wise counsels to guide us, and the encouragement of a paternal voice to animate and console us. He who speaks to us knows all the infirmities of our souls and, hence, can talk of our personal wants and enlighten us as to our past and our future.

Père Bourdaloue writes thus in his *La Rétraite*, which is acknowledged by enlightened thinkers to be a masterpiece of reason, wisdom, and faith: "Frequent confession is a very efficacious means, not only to obtain the remission of our actual sins and, thus, maintain us in innocence and purity of heart, but also to enable us to know ourselves, to make us foresee the dangerous and personal occasions of sin we should avoid and teach us how to put a stop to them, and to prevent our imperfections from becoming through unfortunate repetitions rooted habits."[19]

Frequent confession is advantageous both to sinners and to the just. It is advantageous to sinners because it is one of the most powerful means to uproot within us the beginnings of sins and to arrest the unfortunate consequences of our downfalls. After we have obtained in this sacrament forgiveness of our avowed offenses, we still have the same enemies to contend with, both within and without ourselves. Though they are weakened by a good confession, they are not destroyed. The wounds they have given us are closed but are ever easy to open. Hence, the most efficacious means to conquer these enemies and keep our wounds closed is to go frequently to the tribunal of penance. By means of medicines the deepest wounds may be healed and all their infection removed; and so too use of the remedies for sin furnished by our confessor—after we have humbly accused ourselves of our sins and weaknesses and have promised to make satisfaction for them—will, with the divine assistance, deaden by degrees the most violent passion, unbind the tightest knots sin can tie, and overcome any habit or temptation.

Nothing is more suitable to the just than frequent confession, which purifies them ever more and more before God and constantly renews their fervor. According to the testimony of God, even the just fall as often as seven times a day. The reason for their falls is that they are subject to human frailties, since all are weak and imperfect. No one can doubt that by frequent confession he or she can be purified of the last stain of sin. The more often the soul reflects on itself in a serious examination of conscience, the more clear-sighted it becomes to see its sins and the more eager it becomes to blot them out by penance, so that they may not develop into more grievous ones.

Frequent confession not only purifies the just more and more in the eyes of God; it also renews their fervor constantly. If there be no fire so bright that it does not dim when care is not taken to keep it alive, there is no piety so fervent that it does not cool if it is not fed and developed.

To maintain our souls in the best condition by constantly rekindling and stirring them up, nothing is better than frequent confession. The more often we approach the sacrament of Penance, the more we shall draw from its graces, and it is the holy movements of grace that animate fervor. The more often we go to confession, the more will our minds be filled with pious reflections and our wills with lively affections. And such reflections and affections are the food proper to keep the fire of piety burning. We do not leave the sacred tribunal without carrying away a certain unction that seeps into our hearts and fills every crevice of our souls.

After a good confession, we feel interiorly recollected, filled with heavenly internal joy. Sometimes we are even so moved with devotion that our hearts are filled with happy sighs and our eyes with tears. Our spiritual pace is quickened by new ardor. We run along the path of perfection. We become more regular and devoted in all our exercises of piety. Because of the effects of frequent confession, it is required in every religious community as the necessary safeguard not only of piety and morals but also of the rule itself.

Despite all the advantages offered by frequent confession, however, there is a danger in it: that of routine. When confessions are frequent, the members of a religious community, being surrounded with many protective precautions by the paternal vigilance of their superiors and by their rules, should hardly ever have great faults to confess. In fact, their faults are usually slight ones. They may, therefore, easily be liable to confess without contrition, without a firm resolve, and, consequently, without utility for their souls; for the frequentation of the sacraments in general can be useful only when it is holy, and confession can be holy only when the penitent brings suitable dispositions. When confession is frequent, we are apt not to be so attentive as we should be. Hence, we must take great care, for there is nothing less than a sacrilege to avoid. It would be a strange subversion if, far from being purified in the holy tribunal, we should go forth more guilty in the sight of God than we were on entering. The faults we confess may be only venial, but sound theology tells us that in this supposition there is a strict obligation under pain of mortal sin to have true repentance for at least one sin confessed and a firm resolution to avoid it; otherwise, the confession is null and there is abuse of the sacrament. To make sure of proper contrition, it is well to add some past sin for which one is certainly sorry.

Another efficacious means to keep from a fatal routine is not only to make known our slight sins—the avowal of which is ever being repeated in most cases and so does but little to enlighten the confessor and let him see the real interior of his penitent—but also to acquaint him honestly with the spiritual state of our souls. Of course, we must confess our daily faults, but another matter well worthy of attention is to make known to our spiritual father the actual state of our dispositions, the efforts we have made, the good or bad will we feel within us. Then, when we have rendered this account of the week, he will know what he must think of us and prescribe for us.

Considered thus, confession cannot be too frequent. If penitents ask themselves seriously before confession, "What is my real state in the eyes of God?" and if they really give an account to themselves and to God, this investigation is very useful to them. General confession in the case of religious should be made only with the express permission of the confessor. As I said before, in the case of timorous and scrupulous souls, it may be prejudicial; for thinking themselves obliged, for instance, to tell everything even in an unnecessary general confession, they are exposed to the danger of concealing some mortal sin that they have already confessed with great difficulty and are not really obliged to repeat, and they only find their difficulties and anxieties increased instead of lessened. When a general confession is unnecessary, the penitent is free to confess such sins only as he or she desires to confess. To make a necessary general confession requires more care than to make only an advisable one, and the sins committed since the last confession should be separated from those preceding it to give the confessor a better knowledge of the state of the penitent's soul.

Making a Good Confession

To make a good confession, we should first ask for the grace of doing so. The following prayer is suggested: "O Lord, who has promised us the forgiveness of our sins if we sincerely do penance for them, grant me, if it pleases you, light to know those I have committed, humility to accuse myself strictly of them, love to feel contrition for them, and grace to avoid them in future."

As a prelude to the examination of conscience, the following prayer is offered:

"O my God, by the words of your prophet, you assure us that you will not the death of sinners but rather their conversion and life in you (Ez 18:23). Behold me, then, a poor sinner prostrate before your sovereign majesty. Weeping and ashamed of my sins, I want to come back to you. From the depth of my misery, I dare to raise my imploring voice to the throne of your infinite mercy. Open your heart, O God, to my prayer. I ask of you only the entire knowledge of myself as you see me. O Lord, show me my heart. Let me know myself as you know me; let me see all my sins, their number, their malice, their gravity.

"O Holy Spirit, source of light, dispel the darkness that blinds me. Enlighten my mind that I may know all my faults as I shall know them on the day when I shall appear before my judge to give an account of my life. Soften my heart that I may abhor my sins as I shall abhor them on the day that will be so terrible even for the innocent soul. Perhaps that day is not far distant; perhaps this confession will be my last one. O my God, may it reconcile me perfectly with you.

"O Mary, sweet refuge of sinners, you also I invoke in this circumstance which will perhaps decide what my eternity will be. Obtain for me the grace that it may efface from my soul the name of sinner, the infamous mark that I would willingly destroy by the greatest sacrifice, even by that of shedding my blood. O Mary, Mother of my God, pray for a poor sinner who places all his confidence in you."

To excite our souls to fervent contrition for all the sins of our lives, it is well to make four brief meditations: the first at our own open grave;

the second at the tribunal of God; the third at the gate of hell; the fourth at
the foot of the cross, which holds all our hope of pardon and of the joy of
heaven. Then, we should examine our consciences on the sins committed
since our last confession and recall the sins of our past lives for which we
have greatest sorrow.

The following prayer may help to excite contrition: "Look upon me,
dear Lord, covered with confusion and filled with grief at the sight of my
sins. I detest them with all my heart, and I am sincerely sorry that I have
offended you, who are so good, so loving, and so worthy of my love. You
did not expect from me such ingratitude after you did love me so dearly
as to shed your blood for me. How could I have let myself be led by such
malice and be guilty of such thanklessness? I humbly implore your forgiveness, and I beg you, through that same goodness which has helped
me so often before, to grant me the grace to do penance from now until
the day of my death."

Next we should make an act of resolution to amend our lives: "How
I wish, O my God, that I had never offended you! But since I have had
the misfortune to do so, I will try to show you how sorry I am by conduct entirely opposed to that which displeased you. I renounce from this
moment all sin and every occasion of sin, especially the sins into which
I have fallen so often and the occasions that caused me to commit them.
I know that in your mercy you will give me the grace to carry out this
resolution, which I offer you with a will determined to fulfill faithfully all
my duties and to let nothing stop me from serving you to the best of my
powers. Amen."

Before entering the confessional, let us say this prayer: "Abide, O
my God, in my heart and on my lips, that I may make a sincere and entire
confession of all my sins. Abide also in the heart and mouth of your minister, that, filled with your spirit of light, wisdom, and charity, he may
discover the depth of my wounds and apply to them the healing merits of
the charitable physician of my soul, Jesus Christ my Savior, who alone
can heal me and can teach me the way I should follow to attain salvation.
Amen."

After these prayers, we should kneel humbly at the feet of the priest
and tell him all our sins. Let no false shame make us conceal any mortal

sin, for it would but be a new sin, a horrible sacrilege that we should add to our burden, instead of the forgiveness we hoped to obtain. Let us take courage from the thought of the advantages we shall reap from a humble, sincere, and entire confession. We are assured that the momentary confusion we undergo in disclosing our sins to a priest, bound to inviolable secrecy, will merit their remission, quiet our consciences, and spare us on the day of judgment from the unbearable confusion of having our sins made known to all the world. The more courageous we are in accusing ourselves and emptying all the infection from our hearts, the greater will be our comfort and peace afterward. Therefore, let us confess all, making known necessary circumstances, that our confessor may understand the depth of our wounds and apply proper remedies to them. If we are afraid of forgetting some of our sins through timidity, let us tell all we can remember and then ask the confessor to interrogate us, should he think it expedient.

The priest should absolve only well-disposed penitents. The grace of healing cannot be applied to those who preserve enmity against their neighbor without desire of being reconciled, who do not make restitution of property when possible, who have a habit of sin they will not break off, who will not avoid proximate occasions of sin, who remain in voluntary ignorance of their greatest duties, who have no contrition and no purpose of amendment. These may indeed confess, but they must make known these bad dispositions so as not to receive absolution and, thus, add sacrilege to their other crimes. They should beg the priest to put off absolution until their hearts be changed and they have broken the ties that bind them to sin. The priest will pity them, give them good counsel, and try through his own prayers, fasting, and alms to draw on them the grace of a true conversion.

The accusation of our sins being finished, let us humbly accept the penance given us and fulfill it faithfully as soon as possible afterward. We know that, however great it may be, it cannot be in proportion to the enormity of our sins, except by union with the sufferings and satisfactions Jesus Christ has offered for us to his father. Let us return thanks to God for the grace he grants us to satisfy in this world by so light a punishment his justice—which chastises so severely in the world to come—for the very sins he has just remitted. Let us be attentive to the advice the priest gives us for future safeguards against the passions that have made us sin, especially the predominant passion that rules us often so entirely.

If this passion be attachment to the things of the world, the confessor will likely tell us to show contempt for them by dividing them liberally with the poor members of Jesus Christ. If it be luxury, he will advise us to shun the places, renounce the companions, burn the books that have given rise to it and keep it alive. He will remind us with St. Paul that those who belong to Jesus Christ have chastised and crucified their flesh with its concupiscence (Gal 5:24). Is it not shameful that under an innocent head, crowned with thorns, the members should live in impurity? If it be pride that has intoxicated us, he will bid us to contemplate the Son of God, equal to the father, who humbled himself even to the death of the cross, to draw us from vain horrors (Phil 2:6–8), and he will remind us that only in the annihilation of all pride, only in complete humility, can we be exalted and only when we love to be forgotten by others and be esteemed as nothing can God find ways to exalt us. He will bid us especially to have no trust in our own strength, for we should soon fall again. He will induce us to have recourse to prayer, so just and easy a means to keep from sin.

During the absolution, we should try to feel as Magdalene must have felt at the feet of Jesus, try to imagine the blood of Jesus flowing down on our guilty souls, try to hear the voice of Jesus in the voice of the priest. Then, after the absolution, let us say with the priest: "May the passion of our Lord Jesus Christ, the merits of the Blessed Virgin and of all the saints, the good that I may do, and the evil that I may suffer serve for the remission of my sins, the increase of grace, and life everlasting. Amen."

When we have left the confessional, let us say to God: "Dare I hope, O my God, that from the sinner I was but a moment ago, I have now become pure and agreeable to you? Yes, O God of goodness, your merciful words of pardon have justified me in your sight and washed away all my sins. Ah, Lord, you must be mild and merciful to be so gentle to me, a poor, miserable sinner. Your forgiveness increases my love for you and my regret for offending you. I shall spend all my life in atoning for my sins and in glorifying and loving so good a God, so tender a father."

What could the dear Lord Jesus do to save us that he has not done? Truly have the words of the prophet been realized in this tender sacrament: "If you be driven as far as the poles of heaven, the Lord your God will fetch you back from there and will take you to himself. The Lord your God will circumcise your heart. His word is not above you, nor far off from you: it is very near to you, in your mouth and in your heart. I have set before you life and good . . . death and evil. Choose, therefore, life, that you may live" (Dt 30:4–19). Truly is "this promised propitiation" in the mouth and in the heart of sinners who repent and accuse themselves of their departures from the commandments of God. By this propitiation, sinners who are "touched with repentance" will once more "abound in all the works of his hands, and in the plenty of all good things" (Dt 30:4–19). Oh, it is most true that "the Lord is sweet to all, and his tender mercies are over all his works" (Ps 145:9).

Every one of us can but praise forever the God who has provided this saving sacrament for our weak and sinful souls. "Blessed be the God and Father of our Lord Jesus Christ, the Father of mercies, and the God of all comfort" (2 Cor 1:3). Blessed be the goodness and kindness of God our Savior, who "saved us by the laver of regeneration and renovation of the Holy Spirit" (Ti 3:5). Blessed be the Holy Spirit, in whom, my beloved, we build ourselves upon "our most holy faith, in whom we pray and keep ourselves in the love of God, waiting for the mercy of our Lord Jesus Christ unto life everlasting" (Jude 20–21).

Holy Communion

· ·

He sent his servant . . . to say to them that were invited, that
they should come, for now all things are ready. (Lk 14:17)

A
t every dawning, our heavenly father prepares for us a divine
banquet at which the Lamb without blemish is offered for the
nourishment of our souls. When the priest at the altar pronounces the words of consecration and all heads are bowed in adoration at the astounding mystery, Jesus Christ, obedient to his voice, comes
down from heaven upon the altar with accompanying angels to form on
earth a celestial court. There, in his role of sacrificial victim, Jesus is as
truly present as he is in heaven, and through the Eucharistic veil he looks
longingly at us in his burning desire to give himself to us. He is entirely
at our disposal. He himself has prepared the delicious food he offers us,
and yet he must await our pleasure to partake of it. His flesh will be our
food, his blood our drink, his divinity our gift, all at the same moment (Jn
6:55). His preparations are finished; his holy table is set. It is for us to
come to our Communion.

We can but marvel at God's goodness. See how he loves us! We
might have wandered about like sheep without a shepherd, with no one
mindful of our needs (Mt 9:36; Mk 6:34), but the sovereign master of the
universe deigned from his throne on high to look down tenderly and mer-
cifully on our youth (Is 63:15). He was not content with giving us life and
with conserving our existence in preference to so many others who had
not the happiness of receiving Baptism. He made us be born of Christian
parents, and he taught us little by little the consoling truths of religion.

Despite all the blessings that marked the days of our childhood,
we perhaps offended him, using our minds wrongfully to learn forbidden
evil, our hearts to love the sin he detests, our tongues to blaspheme his
adorable name, and our senses to outrage him. Yet, he, touched by our

misery and pitying our woes, absolved us from our sins by the hand of the priest. Now he invites us to a mystic repast in which he gives himself to us with all the fullness of his gifts. He says to us: "Come, ungrateful but always beloved child, take your place among my elect, eat this supernatural bread, and drink the mysterious wine I have prepared for you. This bread is my body, which was crucified for you; this wine is my blood, which I poured out for you even to its last drop. 'Eat, O friends, and drink, and be inebriated, my dearly beloved'" (Sg 5:1).

The Generous King

Let us suppose that a king invites us to dine at his table. Should we not be almost beside ourselves with joy, especially if he should load us down with magnificent presents and set us among the most distinguished members of his court, as did Nebuchadnezzar to Daniel and his worthy companions (Dn 2:48)? Yet, the king of heaven and earth, the prince of time and eternity, Jesus the Lord God himself, summons us daily to his table and honors us in a far more ideal and generous way than any earthly king could do. Though our eyes see nothing but the white color and round shape of the bread, the consecrated host is nevertheless the divine master in the full splendor of his glory, surrounded by blessed spirits, and eager to enrich us with all he has.

Would that for one moment I could take away the veil that hides him from our sight! We then could see him as he is, as he appeared to his disciples after his resurrection, radiant with glorious majesty, and as he will appear amid clouds of glory when he will come to judge the living and the dead. The sight of such splendors would terrify us, however, and so he acts as if they were not, keeping profound silence and giving no external sign of life. He would rather be forgotten and even despised by the unbelieving than separate himself from his faithful children by an imposing display of his divinity. Provided we love him and he can shower blessings on us, he is satisfied.

Instead of acting like a royal personage before whom we must abase ourselves and from whom we must keep a respectful distance, Jesus even wishes to let our hands touch him, our hearts melt into his own, our whole being be filled with his. When we think that he actually gives us his body to eat, his blood to drink, that he communicates his own virtues to us and applies to us his own merits, we shall begin to see how he loves us. But vision falters when we think that it is truly God who thus gives himself personally to us and that, thus, the Father and the Holy Spirit, who are inseparable from the Son, are also put entirely at our disposal, along with all heaven, so that the adorable Trinity dwells in us and we in the Trinity.

This admirable union was begun for us in Baptism, and it was reestablished in us by confession if we had the misfortune to destroy it by sin. It was not truly perfect, however, until Jesus came to us in Holy Communion, because Holy Communion unites us to the loving Savior more directly than two balls of wax are united when melted together or the ordinary food we eat is united to our body by becoming its substance. O prodigy of charity! O miraculous invention of the love of God for his creatures! Could Jesus love us more tenderly and generously? How gratefully we should come to his table in response to his loving invitation.

Gratitude is not enough, however. We should appear in his presence with most profound humility and sincere sorrow. Who are we to dare to receive him into our souls? Who is this Jesus who comes to us? He is and always will be the most excellent being, and we are but nothingness. He is holiness itself, and we have only sin, darkness, and corruption. No matter how young we are, we cannot count the number of our imperfections and acts of disobedience to his law, so sinful are we all in his eyes. Hell would have been both our lot, had he consulted only the rights of his justice and our desert from his vengeance. But he wants to be our father, not our judge. He is our friend, our brother who has for us only words of mercy and bounty, provided always we bring him a contrite and humble heart.

Let us, then, throw ourselves into his arms as other prodigals. Let him see our shamed faces, our tear-wet eyes, while we strike our breasts with the penitent publican and cry out to him the words of the centurion: "Lord, I am not worthy that you should enter under my roof" (Mt 8:8). Let us tell him that if we heard only the voice of our consciences, we should say as did the prince of the apostles: "Depart from me, for I am a sinful man, O Lord" (Lk 5:8). Then, let us remind him that we cannot bid him to go, that we can never leave him. It is written that "they that go far from you shall perish" (Ps 73:27), for "you have the words of eternal life" (Jn 6:69). Let us remind him that he has commanded us under pain of death to eat his adorable flesh and drink his precious blood, and so we must come to him, repentant of heart and filled with confidence in his infinite mercies. Let us beg him to purify us more and more and prepare in our souls a place of dwelling less unworthy of his majesty. With these dispositions, we can be sure that he will take no account of our past infidelities and will treat us with all the sweetness he shows to those who have never abandoned him.

Jesus asks still more than gratitude and contrition from us. He wants us to respond to the eagerness with which he gives himself to us with a burning desire to receive him and be forever united to him by the bonds of love. Jesus is our king, our Savior, and he alone can make us happy in time and eternity. Jesus is full of grace and truth, and all the treasures of wisdom and knowledge are found in him, and yet he wants to share these favors with us, to enrich us with these gifts, to make his own raptures grow within us (Col 2:3). Can we not, after all this, feel an ardent desire to partake of this celestial banquet?

Let us say to him with all the fervor of our souls: "Come, O my God, come into my soul that sighs after you as the thirsty stag pants for the water. Do not delay, O my Jesus, for I languish far from you, my salvation and my life. Since my waking, I have turned my thoughts and affections toward you, O well-beloved of my heart, and my flesh trembles with eagerness at the hope of possessing you. Tell my innermost soul that you wish to visit it, fix in it your abode, and honor it with your sacramental presence. Then, filled with your grace, illumined by your light, and set on fire by your charity, my soul will rejoice in you and sing your praises."

If these be our sentiments, let us come without fear to partake of the happiness that awaits us; but if, unhappily, our consciences reproach us with failing to make known to our confessor all our grievous sins, woe—a thousand times woe—if we dare to receive Holy Communion in such a state. We should only eat and drink to our own condemnation, and the blood of Jesus Christ, which we should profane, would one day serve to make the fires of hell feed on our flesh and blood. But why should I speak thus, O my Savior, to trouble the peace of those now reconciled with you, those whom you cherish as children brought back to you by repentance? Far from me is the thought that any Judas hears my word. I know that you, my dearly beloved, are friends of Jesus and privileged members of his flock. Before he gives himself to you for food, our good master requires only of you that you profess your love for him, and so he asks you now, as long ago he asked St. Peter, "Do you love me?" (Jn 21:16). Let your heart reply. If it can say, "Yes, Lord, you know that I love you," thank him and come fearlessly to the altar. Thus, you may reply publicly to the God who asks you whether you have resolved to love him in the future, whether you want to love him forever and ever.

One of the Savior's parables relates the sad fate of one who came to a wedding feast without having on a wedding garment (Mt 22:1–14). Since it undoubtedly refers to the robe of sanctifying grace that we should wear when we approach the holy table, let us meditate on this parable. Let us imagine the festal table, the king who has invited many guests. The first chosen are the Jews; the second are the Gentiles. Among them is one who has dared to come without the garment made especially for this occasion. Oh, when sin tempts us to make our reception of Jesus impossible, let us think on the terrible fate of this man as Jesus describes it: "Bind his hands and feet, and cast him into the exterior darkness; there shall be weeping and gnashing of teeth" (Mt 22:13). If we could but realize what it would mean to be cast away from Jesus into the outer darkness, sin would no longer charm us, temptations would avail nothing against us, and virtue would seem far less difficult to obtain.

Let us think now of the happy lot of those who were pleasing to the king when he saw them at his banquet table. Let us see God in this king, the Church in the banquet hall, the true body and blood of Christ in the feast. Immediately, we can but thank God for selecting us, from among thousands who have no faith in his presence, to come to this feast. Jesus Christ concludes this parable by saying that many are called but few are chosen (Mt 22:14). History has verified his words. There were but few of the Jews in comparison to the Gentiles who embraced Christianity, and most of the leaders and chiefs of the once-Chosen People rejected the Messiah. "He came unto his own, and his own received him not. But, as many as received him, he gave them power to be made the sons of God, to those who believe in his name" (Jn 1:11–12).

Let us now enter the banquet hall to which we have been invited. Who gave us this invitation? Jesus Christ, God and man, our judge and our Savior. He comes to greet us and make us feel welcome, and we can but cry out with St. Elizabeth: "Whence is this to me, that my Lord should come to me?" (Lk 1:43). And with the centurion we must protest: "Lord, I am not worthy" (Mt 8:8). Why does Jesus come? He wants to be our companion in our exile, our victim, our food, our strength, the pledge of our final happiness. Will he give us this blessed food and drink but once and then bid us to depart from him to go our way alone? Ah, no, he bids us to stay always in his banquet hall that he may be our daily bread. The Church wants her children to receive Holy Communion every time they hear holy Mass, as it explains in the Council of Trent, to imitate, thus, the example of the early Christians who received every day and to reanimate in themselves the fervor of the apostolic ages.[20]

We should bring certain dispositions of mind and heart to the reception of Jesus in the sacrament of his love. With lively faith, we should say to him: "I do believe, Lord; help my unbelief" (Mk 9:23). We should give him profound adoration: "Come, let us adore and fall down and weep before the Lord who made us. For, he is the Lord our God, and we are the people of his pasture and the sheep of his hand" (Ps 95:6–7). With sincere humility we should acknowledge: "Lord, I am not worthy." We should have true contrition: "Father, I have sinned against heaven and before you. I am not worthy to be called your son" (Lk 15:18–19). We should bring great gratitude: "What shall I render to the Lord for all the things that he has rendered to me?" (Ps 116:12). We should come in entire confidence: "If I shall touch but his garment, I shall be whole" (Mk 5:28). We should feel ardent desire: "Come, Lord Jesus, come" (Rv 22:20). We should feel the transport of love: "Who then shall separate us from the love of Christ? Neither height, nor depth, nor any other creature, shall be able to separate us from the love of God, which is in Christ Jesus our Lord" (Rom 8:35, 39). All these dispositions we should try to keep alive in our hearts day after day, so that we may never miss a Holy Communion through our fault. If, happily, we can receive Holy Communion every day, the first half of each day should be spent in thanksgiving and the second in preparation for the next reception.

Sacramental Presence

Jesus wants us to come into his sacramental presence as often as we can. On each happy occasion when we can visit him in the Blessed Sacrament, we should make a spiritual Communion. This invitation to Jesus to come spiritually into our hearts, however, may be given him at any time—even when we are not in his sacramental presence. Since Jesus remains on our altars night and day that we may visit him, such visits become our pious duty. It is a case of rendering to God the things that are God's (Mk 12:17).

Let us imagine ourselves among the courtiers in the throne room of a king, or better, among the poor and oppressed who wait outside his door for an audience to tell him their needs and receive his generous help. How willing we should be to wait long hours for our turn. Now, let us think of the court of Jesus. In many of our churches, he is left alone all day long, waiting and longing to have his needy children come to him. We need no letter of recommendation to him. We need not wait our turn to have audience with him. Usually, we can enter his presence immediately and have him all to ourselves. Jesus wants our visits, and we have need of them. Why, then, do we stay away from him?

Even if Jesus were present in the Holy Eucharist only in his humanity, he still would attract us to his feet, for he is beautiful above all the children of the human race, with a mind that holds always the beatific vision and a will set always on the good. Though it is true that, wherever we are, we may talk with God in his divinity, we can come actually into his human presence only in the Blessed Sacrament. There we visit Jesus just as truly as did those who walked and talked with him in Galilee. Oh, if for but one moment he would lift the veil and let us see him there in the beauty of his humanity, even though he should still veil his divinity, we should run to him with childlike eagerness and love. Let us console ourselves for the blindness of our physical eyes: "Blessed are they that have not seen, and have believed" (Jn 20:29). Let us go, then, to adore him, not only because he permits us, but because he invites us: "Come to me, all you who labor and are burdened, and I will refresh you" (Mt 11:28). He has told us so definitely: "My delights are to be with human beings" (Prv 8:31). And this desire to be with us will never cease: "I am with you all days, even to the consummation of the world" (Mt 28:20).

Though it is true that Jesus ascended into heaven, he did not leave us orphans. He is still with us, though invisibly, for he can no more separate himself from us than we can live without his bread of life. Why can we not respond to this loving desire for union with us, especially when he only entreats though he has the right to command? Nothing we could do would please him more than a visit to him. Oh, why do we not go as often as we can to see him and stay with him as long as possible each time we go?

We all need Jesus for our difficult spiritual advancement. From these holy, saving, and consoling visits, we can gain strength for progress in virtue. Even the comfort and inspiration of a human being like ourselves can often sustain us in the unending combat against the demands of fallen nature, and yet the wisest of our friends can do no more than sympathize with us, guide us, and pray for us. Jesus need not stop with words or even prayers. He lifts our fainting courage with his grace, arms us with his power. He wraps us in the armor of his love which no arrow can pierce. Our visits to him put at our disposal the very source of all graces, which are enclosed in the sacrament of his adorable body and his precious blood. Our Savior works on our maladies of soul the very same miracles of healing he worked on the sick and broken bodies of Judea long ago. He is our consolation, and by his bruises we are healed (Is 53:5; 1 Pt 2:24). Experience of this truth made many of the saints give testimony of how their pains were solaced in his presence. St. Alphonsus put his record into the helpful prayers of his *Visits to the Blessed Sacrament and to the Blessed Virgin.*

Institution of the Eucharist

To awaken new devotion to Jesus in the sacrament of his love, let us often go back in thought to the institution of this sweetest of the sacraments. Let me take you for a little while into that upper room wherein Jesus ate the Pasch with his apostles. Let us kneel humbly in a shadowed corner to watch and pray. "Jesus rose from supper and laid aside his garments, and, having taken a towel, girded himself. After that, he put water into a basin and began to wash the feet of the disciples and to wipe them with the towel with which he was girded. He came, therefore, to Simon Peter, and Peter said to him, 'Lord, are you going to wash my feet?' Jesus answered, and said to him: 'What I do you know not now; but you will know hereafter.' Peter said to him, 'You will never wash my feet.' Jesus answered him, 'If I wash you not, you will have no part with me.' Simon Peter said to him, 'Lord, not only my feet, but also my hands and my head.' Jesus said to him, 'He who is washed need not but to wash his feet, for he is clean wholly. And, you are clean, but not all'" (Jn 13:4–10).

St. Peter doubtless understood at that moment that obedience and purity are the indispensable virtues for participating in this holiest of ceremonies, the celebration of the Mass, and he knew that his humble acceptance of the "hard saying" that commanded the disciples of Jesus to eat his flesh and drink his blood was now in some mysterious way to be exercised (Jn 6:56). Jesus had carefully prepared the apostles for this hour. "After he had washed their feet and taken his garments, he, being sat down again, said to them: 'Do you know what I have done to you? You call me master and Lord, and you speak well, for so I am. If then I, being your Lord and master, have washed your feet, you also ought to wash one another's feet. For, I have given you an example, that as I have done to you, so you do also'" (Jn 13:12–15). Thus, Jesus added two more indispensable virtues we must bring to Holy Communion, humility and brotherly love.

When the master had made the apostles understand that he knew who would betray him, he instituted the Holy Eucharist, the sacrifice and the sacrament of the altar, as a memorial of his passion and death.

"Taking bread, he gave thanks, and broke it, and gave to them, saying: 'This is my body, which is given for you. Do this for a commemoration of me.' In like manner, the chalice also, after he had supped, saying, 'This is the chalice, the new testament in my blood, which shall be shed for you'" (Lk 22:19–20).

At last had come the moment to which may be applied the words of David: "In your sweetness, O God, you have provided for the poor" (Ps 68:11). "Let the just feast and rejoice before God and be delighted with gladness" (Ps 68:4). O my Savior, this is no figure, no representation, no part of yourself. It is your whole person, with all your satisfaction for sin and your merit, which you offered for me as well as for your apostles, because you gave them and their successors in the priesthood through all the centuries to come the power to change bread and wine into your body and blood. You bid them and us to eat this bread and drink this chalice to "show the death of the Lord, until he comes" (1 Cor 11:26). O incomprehensible invention of your wisdom, power, and love!

Fear and adore, O my soul! We need not listen to reason, which might well ask how Jesus Christ could hold his own body in his sacred hands and distribute it to his happy apostles. Yet, for even reason, it suffices to remember that Christ's sacramental body is not his natural physical body but is his body spiritualized as it was after his resurrection. Consequently, his body could be on this occasion both visible and invisible, almost as the thoughts that are invisible in the soul may at the same time be visibly written on paper.

Oh, let us love this Lord who has found a way to penetrate the wall of flesh that is usually an obstacle between human hearts. Only God could have devised so sweet a way of enabling the loving soul to contract an actual union with the beloved, and yet, this union that he meant for all is realized by such a comparatively small number. Let us make up to him for all those into whose hearts he can never come in his humanity. Let us adore him now and forever, not only for Catholics who do not adore him, but also to supply the place of all—heretics, schismatics, infidels, atheists, blasphemers, Muslims, Jews, and idolaters who do not adore him.

"O my Jesus, may I help to make you known to all; may I cause you to be adored, loved, and thanked at every moment in your most holy and divine sacrament of love. Only a God could love as you love—with a love beyond death; with a love that depends for return upon the very creature you made; with a love that survives a thousand outrages; with a love that comes as tenderly into a hovel as into a palace, that welcomes with equal goodness the monarch and the shepherd; with a love that unites two things so remote by their natures, humanity, vile and weak, and the infinite majesty of God, before which the heavens and the earth are as if they were not. To love thus, one must be God.

"My Jesus, teach me how to love. Teach me to use each sacramental union with you as a preparation for the next, so that when my last Holy Communion comes I may but exchange one heaven for another, the heaven of you in my heart for the heaven in which I shall see you in all your beauty face-to-face. Amen."

Renewal of the Vows

· ·

This day shall be for a memorial to you, and you shall keep it a feast to the Lord in your generations with an everlasting observance. (Ex 12:14)

B y this ordinance, God enjoined the children of Israel to perpetuate the remembrance of their departure from Egypt and their freedom from servitude. During the night, a destroying angel had slain all the firstborn of the Egyptians, both of humans and animals. The Israelites had eaten the paschal lamb, with their loins girt, with shoes on their feet and staves in their hands, to be ready to set forth for the promised land; and they had, as also commanded, put the blood of the lamb on the side posts and the upper doorposts of their houses (Ex 12:3–11). The moment had come for them to depart for the desert in which would be worked such prodigies of power and mercy as the passage of the Red Sea (Ex 14:15–20), the promulgation of the Law from Mount Sinai amid thunder and lightning (Ex 19:16–20:17), the miraculous water from the rock (Nm 20:1–11), the column of fire (Ex 13:21–22), and the celestial manna (Ex 16:3–15). The Lord, wishing the Hebrews to keep forever the memory of so extraordinary an event, bade them do so by yearly observing the anniversary with appropriate pomp.

In a sense less striking but just as real, God has inspired founders of religious communities to have their members celebrate yearly, after a preparatory retreat, the anniversary of their profession, since this event marks their departure from the world, that other Egypt, and their entrance into the land of blessing. Let us imagine, then, my dearly beloved, that Jesus Christ himself, our God and Savior, on this occasion says to us all in general and to each in particular: "Remember your vows, and renew them on this day, which is as a sensible and everlasting memorial of them."

The words of my text undoubtedly look more to the Christian Pasch than to that of the Jews because, besides solemnizing it by worship and

ceremonies that will end only with time, we renew the memory of the
spotless Lamb immolated for our sins, we celebrate the feast of our freedom from the tyranny of the devil by virtue of the blood shed for us,
and we eat the holy victim in the unleavened bread of justification. They
apply, furthermore, to our profession. Did we not shake off anew the
yoke of the prince of darkness when we sacrificed ourselves by irrevocable contract to the glory of the Most High? Did not the blood of the
Savior seal this new covenant and his flesh become our food? Oh, to the
eyes of faith, it was indeed a true pasch, which we took from one state of
life to another.[21] Thus, it is but just that we should prepare in solitude to
celebrate its memory by solemnly renewing our vows with deepest gratitude, humility, and generosity.

Gratitude

We should renew our vows with gratitude. What do the promises we
renew recall to us? They recall our vocation to religious life and, consequently, all the graces that preceded it, accompany it, and will follow it.
Who could tell all we have received of blessings and singular favors from
him who chose us for his spouse? Having given us Christian parents, a
preference over so many others who are born into the bosom of paganism
and other errors, he regenerated us by Baptism and protected us since
early youth by the sweetness of his blessings. With paternal solicitude, he
guarded our infancy, sheltering it from all the accidents that could have
ended our life. Then, as our intelligence developed, he illumined our mind
with the light of faith and kindled in our heart the fire of his love. Thus,
he disposed our soul to the secret communications of his grace, inspiring
us with taste for virtue, with horror of vice, and with the beginning of our
attraction to religious life.

To fortify us in these happy dispositions, he guided us into the
school of religion to receive catechetical instructions and to partake in
the imposing ceremonies of the Church, but this was only the beginning
of his loving predilection. As we grew older and the enemies of our salvation consequently redoubled their efforts and the world grew ever more

dangerous to us, he invited us to his table where he gave himself to feed our souls as the bread of the strong—and not merely once, but yearly, monthly, weekly, daily. Then came the moment to decide our vocation. What did his providence then do to execute the designs he had conceived on us from all eternity?

Perhaps at that period of our life, levity, want of reflection, and liberty of the senses altered the purity of our conscience and opened our heart to sin. His grace sought us, and when it had enlightened, purified, and inflamed us, it pointed out to us our community. Soon, it suggested new thoughts, desires, and hopes. Then, docile to the voice that said to us, as of old to Abraham, "Go forth out of your country, and from your kindred, and out of your father's house, and come into the land that I shall show you" (Gn 12:1), we consulted the man of God who answered all our uncertainties, and we had no thought but to carry out our project. If we had not the means to defray the expenses of our new state of life, we found protectors provided by heaven. Then, all obstacles being removed, we found our community waiting with the open arms of disinterested charity to receive us among its children.

Forever associated therein with the spouses of Jesus Christ, we have had every means and aid to sanctification in good example, in the rules of our community, in the advice of our superiors, in frequentation of the sacraments, and in all the exercises of piety proper to our vocation. Our desires were foreseen, our pains divined, our difficulties removed. What, then, has our whole life been but a marvelous chain of graces and favors? What are we in the eyes of faith except children of mercy and predilection? Oh, my dearly beloved, we should be so grateful on this anniversary of the day of our consecration to God, and we should renew our vows most lovingly.

What might we have become without the singular blessing of vocation? Thrown into the midst of a world, which, under attractive guise, conceals so many horrors, and left to ourselves and surrounded by scandals, we might have lost our innocence and have surrendered, as many do, heaven for earth. But no, the Lord prevented us and brought us into the safe harbor of our community. Here, we are in the ark, with the family of the elect. We can sail with full canvas to a happy eternity, while so many in the world are swallowed up in the waters of a deluge of iniquities. Oh, let us give everlasting thanks to the Good Shepherd, to the gentle Savior, to the tender and generous father who has given us such great proofs of his love. Let us cry out with David in transports of gratitude: "What shall I render to the Lord for all the things that he has rendered to me?" (Ps 116:12). He has not given such grace to many others or treated them with such bounty. He chose me, the least of my kindred, to raise me to the rank of his favorite spouses and to let me sing his praises in the assembly of his elect. O my soul, bless the Lord your God and exalt forever his holy name, for he has done great things to you (Lk 2:46–49).

It is less by words, however, than by works and by exemplary conduct that we can testify to our gratitude and devotion to our divine spouse. Can we truly say on reviewing the past that we have been constantly faithful to all our duties, fulfilling to the letter each of our vows, and making continuous progress in religious perfection? This is a certain mark by which we may know whether we have been truly thankful for the grace of our vocation, and reflection on it will likely cause us to renew our vows with humility. If, during the days of preparatory retreat, we examine our conduct since our entrance into religious life, we shall doubtless find motives to humble and confound ourselves.

By the promises of our Baptism, we contracted to destroy the "old man of sin" within ourselves, to die to ourselves, and to live only the life of Jesus Christ, as he lived on earth only the life of his father. If a tree be known by its fruits and a Christian by works and fulfilled obligations, we may perhaps find reason for weeping and saying with David, "O Lord, the sins of my youth and my ignorances do not remember" (Ps 25:7). We shall not treat here of the obligations we took at the baptismal fount. However extensive these were, they were only the prelude to and trial of those we contracted on the day of our profession. Oh, how joyful and eager we were on that day. We can but love to recall our ardor in ranking ourselves under the standard of Jesus Christ and in becoming members of our community. O blessed day! O moment of salvation! The rule had, then, nothing too difficult for nature, and all our sacrifices seemed as nothing. All the monsters barring our entrance into the promised land were unable to frighten us. More courageous, more faithful than the Israelites, who soon wearied in the desert of pursuing the conquest of that happy land, we had a holy impatience to enter the most difficult places of our community.

Filled with gratitude for the divine mercies, we had such thoughts as these: "What shall I do for God in return for all he has done for me? How shall I repay him for that gratuitous preference of mercy by which he has chosen me among many more worthy than I of such ineffable bounty? He has snatched me from the soul-slaying Egypt to lead me into the loving solitude of religious life, and from it into the land of promise. To him alone belong the homage of my mind and the affection of my heart. I wish to live only for him and sigh only for his glory. Yes, I wish so to unite myself to him that I may be a complete sacrifice, immolated for his sovereign majesty. I wish to make him solemn promises and pay him my vows before all the world. Nothing can turn me aside from this purpose. Reason, hold your tongue. False lights of worldly glory, be snuffed out. All personal interests, be gone. Even you, sweet love of relatives, friends, and acquaintances I have cultivated so eagerly—you will vainly oppose yourself to the attractions of grace and the wooing of the Holy Spirit.

"High heaven, you have heard and bear witness to the great words I have uttered. I have vowed forever to God my poverty, chastity, and obedience, according to the constitutions of my community. I have vowed poverty; that is, I will own nothing and will not be attached to the conveniences of this life or to the objects destined for my use, and I will receive and keep nothing without the permission of my superiors. I have vowed chastity; that is, I will never permit my eyes the least immodest look, my tongue the least unguarded word, and my heart the least movement capable of wounding purity. I have vowed obedience; that is, I will do in everything the will of those who have the right to command me, and I will do it simply, promptly, without exception, and without relaxation. I will obey their voice as the voice of God; I will love their orders and submit to them blindly. I will observe my rules and constitutions from point to point, meditating on them day and night, forming my conscience on them, and keeping them for my guide even until death. Thus will I be able to labor for the instruction and salvation of souls."

Such were the obligations we contracted by pronouncing our vows. The words our lips spoke are irrevocable; the great promises we made to God are everlasting. Have we ever lost sight of these sacred obligations? Have we always kept them faithfully with the same fervor we had in pronouncing them? Have we not lost the first brilliant beauty of our early zeal and pure charity? In the quality of our religious life, we are supposed to be noble children of Zion, bright and precious vessels of election of the celestial Jerusalem. Can we be reproached for changing ourselves into clay vessels of poor value? Perhaps we deserve to have God say to us what St. John once said on his behalf to the angel of Ephesus: "I have something against you, because you have left your first charity. Be mindful, therefore, from where you have fallen, do penance, and do the first works" (Rv 2:4–5). These "first works" are those of humility without disguise, penance without chagrin, repose without slothfulness, modesty without affectation, submission without murmuring, labor without inquietude—the works of an ever equable and uniform conduct.

It is not rare to see fervor relaxed in proportion as one grows older in the service of God. The ways of the just, like the rays of the sun, increase from brilliance to brilliance, but many in religious life seem to proceed by contrary ways, decreasing in piety as they advance in age. Have we perhaps experienced this humiliating truth since the day of our profession? Have not care of our health, search for ease, and fear of lacking something we want weakened the spirit of poverty that should constantly animate us? Have attachment to creatures, attraction to a particular friendship, wanderings of a too-little-guarded imagination, and liberty of the senses never tarnished the luster of a complete purity? Have not too much self-opinionatedness, weariness of dependence, and distaste for continual subjection made our yoke less supportable and aroused sentiments against obedience and its blind simplicity?

Obedience

Jesus Christ is our model of obedience. "He humbled himself, becoming obedient unto death, even to the death of the cross" (Phil 2:8). The bloody standards of this unacknowledged king are unfurled before our eyes, and the mystery of his cross shines everywhere. Such a spectacle can but revive our faith, reanimate our confidence, inflame our charity, and bruise our hearts with compunction. These are, at least, the happy effects that should be produced in us by contemplation of Jesus crucified. The scriptures pronounce woe to the one who does not feel sorrow on the anniversary of his passion: "Every soul that is not afflicted on this day shall perish from among his people" (Lv 23:29). Nevertheless, sentiments of Christian piety and holy affections at remembrance of Calvary are often without merit before God and fruit for ourselves because they remain sterile and do not influence our conduct. To certain Christians, to religious especially, the crucifix says more than it says to the general population. From the height of that instrument of torture, the Savior says to each of us, as in olden times he said to his apostles and disciples: "If any will come after me, let them deny themselves, and take up their cross daily, and follow me" (Lk 9:23).

Let us obey today the voice of our divine master and follow him. The cross he bids us carry under pain of not being numbered among his disciples can be for us only fidelity to the rules prescribed for us on our entrance into religious life. Do we actually carry it as real disciples of Jesus Christ? Let us examine this in our meditation, and let us consider the qualities that our obedience to rule should have for the purpose of being a faithful imitation of the obedience of the Son of God. To be perfect, our obedience must be pure, prompt, universal, and constant.

Our obedience must be pure, that is, undertaken and carried out for a good motive—for love of God and his greater glory, as St. Benedict says. Charity makes our submission of will come from the heart and gives us no other end in obeying but the accomplishment of the divine will. It makes us honor and love those who command us and despise their faults, so that to their voice we answer as did the beloved disciple to the voice of Jesus: "It is the Lord" (Jn 21:7). The holy religious says to himself: "Whatever be the conduct of the ones who have authority over me, though they seem to me not to have the light and the experience necessary for the place they occupy, it is the Lord who addresses me through their mouths. Whether they be young or old, commendable or not for their spirit and talents, it is the Lord. Whether they have lovable or repellant qualities, even if they be imprudent, unfair, insincere, indiscreet, and capricious, it is the Lord, and I must obey." Animated by the fire of divine love, such religious trample underfoot all the unworthy motives that could rob them of the merit of obedience: all vain respect, all human considerations, and all self-interest. They purify their souls more and more by the "obedience of charity," according to the counsel of the prince of the apostles (1 Pt 1:22).

Have we learned thus to obey? Do not some of us, on the contrary, obey through vanity, habit, pure politics, human respect? Have not some of us had as motives to avoid reprimands, to acquire the reputation of being fervent religious, to win the good grace of those charged to watch over our conduct, to merit the esteem and confidence of our brothers and sisters, to look after our own interests, and to procure ourselves some notable employment? Some among us, perhaps, obey as humanly as did the Jews; some in a mercenary way, as servants and slaves; some in a mechanical way, as inanimate beings; some as those of whom the apostle spoke, "serving to the eye" (Col 3:22) and forgetting that when we are alone the eye of God contemplates us. Oh, may divine charity be the sole motive and principle of our submission! Then, obeying only to please the Lord, we shall make our superiors carry easily the weight of their charge and shall edify our brothers and sisters. But that our obedience may thus be a matter of habitual and mutual edification, it is not sufficient that it be pure in its motive; it must also be prompt.

Our obedience must be immediate, because to defer obedience is obviously to refuse it during the time of delay; to do God's work negligently; to give the first fruits of our acts to the devil; to resist grace, which, as St. Ambrose says, cannot suffice for sloth and delay; to lose all the fruit of our sacrifice; and to scorn all the examples given us by scripture and the lives of the saints as models of prompt obedience. How could we act thus toward the great master we serve? Would it be reasonable to deprive ourselves thus of the many merits we could gain daily? Rulers of this world will not keep in their service lazy, indolent, slothful servants who are always late and carry out orders with great slowness. Neither will God, and so we should do immediately what is given us to do.

The promptness with which we should obey is comparable to an arrow that, when released from the bow, flies swift and straight to the mark without deviation to either side. It is comparable to those mysterious wheels of which Ezekiel speaks, which rapidly follow the movements of the spirit guiding them (Ez 1:15–21). It is comparable to the eagerness with which a starving child runs to its mother when she calls it to eat. Hence, in all communities, the members are exhorted to leave everything at the sound of the bell, not pausing to finish the task in hand but hastening to the place designated. Let those who are writing leave their letters unfinished; let those who are reading or meditating quit their task. The sound of the bell is the voice of God. Will the religious refuse to hear it? "'The master . . . calls for you.' She, as soon as she heard this, rose quickly, and came to him" (Jn 11:28–29).

Why all this haste? Because a faithful servant knows not the meaning of delay. Those truly obedient people of whom Cassian speaks, those angels of the desert in whom true perfection shines, give us marvelous lessons and confound our daily sloth with their fervor. At the first signal, they could be seen hastening in holy rivalry from their cells as a swarm of bees from their hives. Always ready of mind, prepared of heart, with eyes open, ears alert, feet light, and hands eager, they awaited only the command, or even anticipated it. "Oh, what is our life, if compared to theirs?"[22] "Now, he is thought great who is not a transgressor."[23] Surely such ardent vivacity will excite our indolence and make us prompt in rising and leaving our rooms in the morning. Surely it will make us resolve no longer to be the last to arrive at the various exercises of the day and thus begin them without a moment's preparatory recollection.

There are religious among us, it is true, who could be our models. Since, however, our obligations are common with theirs, since our reasons for promptness in obeying the rule are theirs, since the punishments we have to fear and the rewards we hope for are theirs as well, our perfection should already equal theirs. Then, too, the holy religious who have preceded us in our community should urge and drive us by their zeal. Let us imagine them all radiant in glory bidding us from the height of heaven to run as they did in the way of obedience. From their place of happiness they tell us: "Courage, good and faithful servants, if you persevere in exactitude, God will say to you as he did to us: 'Because you have been faithful over a few things, I will place you over many things. Enter into the joy of your Lord'" (Mt 25:23). Let us run, then, in the way that lies open before us. Let us so run that we may obtain the incorruptible crown (1 Cor 9:24–25).

To arrive at this happy end, however, we must practice a universal obedience, that is, extended to all matters without exception, embracing all times and places. Otherwise, it would be slow, servile, and imperfect. Let us obey without reserve, in secret as in public, in little things as in great, in silence as in recreation, in rest as in labor, in prayers as in mortifications, in health as in sickness. Thus, we shall practice that abnegation indispensable to any disciple of Jesus Christ; thus, we shall live only by our rule; thus, we shall carry our cross daily after the Savior and walk in his footsteps.

This hourly obedience calls for constant denial of self. To rise at the first sound of the bell when we are tired and sleepy, to leave recreation for work or study, to be refused a desired permission to go to town—these mean denial of self. Obedience which is without reserve costs sacrifice at every moment. Surely it is painful always to renounce self and act contrary to our will, but for our consolation it is written: "The kingdom of heaven suffers violence, and the violent bear it away" (Mt 11:12). "How straight is the way that leads to life" (Mt 7:14). "Through many tribulations, we must enter into the kingdom of God" (Acts 14:22).

How can we, without this heroic obedience, one day appear beside those intrepid martyrs whose history we read so easily and yet in whom nature was so mercilessly crucified? Let us never forget that "there is no other way to life and to true internal peace but the holy way of the cross and of daily mortification."[24] To follow any other way is to take the wide way that leads to death. Ah, let us listen to those brave models who say to us with the apostle: "You have not yet resisted unto blood" (Heb 12:4).

Our obedience should be constant, with that perseverance which is its perfection and its crown. What will it avail us to have been for some time models of obedience if we end in relaxation? Would not our many efforts to break and subdue our will be vain? Would this not be to abandon the harvest after we have sowed it, to renounce the reward after fighting for it? Let us be consistent and faithful, then, even unto death, after the example of Jesus, the author and consummator of our obedience as he is of our faith: "He was obedient unto death" (Phil 2:8).

God grant that our last days as religious resemble or even surpass in this regard our first ones. For this purpose, let us often renew our retreat resolutions. Of what account have they been thus far? Do not our consciences reproach us about them? Where would our virtues be, where the fruit of our many graces, should we now hear the words, "Render an account"? Because of our instability in the ways of perfection and our daily transgressions of rule, to some of us the days that have slipped away since our entry into religion must seem as so many degrees by which we have descended into a state of lukewarmness.

The habit of violating the rule when we are not under the eyes of others causes us to observe it only through decorum or fear of arousing unfavorable comment. In neglecting obedience, we lead a relaxed life; we are inattentive to our faults; we lack zeal and piety and the interior spirit; we are softly indulgent to our evil tendencies; we even go backward, because not to advance in the way of perfection is to retreat. This relaxation of fervor is as a slow fever, which diminishes our spiritual strength, withers our hearts, destroys all sentiments of devotion, alters all our good dispositions, and daily consumes the life of our souls. O my God, let not this strange state be ours; let us not end in that lukewarmness which will cause you to vomit us out of your mouth (Rv 3:16).

St. Bernard cried out amid his tears: "What do I see here? I see a sluggard who needs the goad, a timorous creature who has lost courage, a lazy person who makes bitter and heavy the loving yoke of the Savior, a voluntary weakling who is immediately tired, a continual opening of the heart to worldly and sensual thoughts, an imprudent and untimely conversation, an imperfect and wholly human obedience, prayers without attention and respect—in a word, people going to the sacred tribunal with a will indifferent and insensible to their faults. They make a cold recital of their ordinary sins and profit neither by the accusation nor by the absolution. They are a thousand times reconciled and never penitent. They approach the holy table almost as the common one, and the bread of heaven is for them almost as the bread of earth."

This is the misery to which habitual infidelities to our general and particular rules reduce us, we who should be always animated by a new fervor, and these are the consequences of our daily disobedience. Happy are we if we have not come even to the pass of censuring the conduct of those who force themselves to remain faithful, of turning them from their exactitude by our talk after we have scandalized them by our example. Is this the way—I will not say a religious—a Christian should act? What can we answer when, at the last judgment, our brothers and sisters whom we have made lax will reproach us for being the first cause of their woe and for making them lose all the fruit of their exercises of piety? What can we answer when the souls who were entrusted to them and were lost through their negligence will blame us as the first authors of their reprobation? What can we answer when the founders, the benefactors, and the superiors of our community will accuse us of retarding, harming, and perhaps destroying the work they began, and thus making useless their gifts and their labors? What can we answer when our Lord himself will make us see all the good of which we shall have deprived his Church and all the evils to which we shall have exposed it? "Ah, the lukewarmness and negligence of our state, that we so quickly fall away from our former fervor, and are now even weary of living through sloth and tepidity."[25]

If the examples of Jesus Christ and of the saints touch us, if the glory of the Church interests us, if our spiritual advancement is dear to us, let us recover ourselves and say to the God who will gladly hear us, "Now have I begun" (Ps 77:10).[26] "I have sworn and am determined to keep the judgments of your justice" (Ps 119:106). Why this determination? Should we who have trampled the world and its vanities underfoot—we who have cut off commerce with worldly people to shut ourselves into a monastery wherein we submit our will to that of superiors—should we render these great sacrifices useless and expose our final perseverance for the sake of slight infidelities? Give us grace, O my God, give us grace to keep from such evil, or withdraw us from it if we have already fallen into it. "Confirm, O God, what you have wrought in us" (Ps 68:29), finish the work you have begun in us (Phil 1:6), that you may crown us at the end of life (2 Tm 4:8). As for us, we resolve, henceforth, to practice an obedience that is pure, prompt, universal, and constant.

This pure, prompt, universal, constant fidelity to what is prescribed for us daily, weekly, monthly, yearly, will make of us so many victims of divine love, so many living hosts. Oh, how I should bless divine mercy for this. Permit me to borrow the language of St. Paul to address you, my dearly beloved: "I am jealous of you with the jealousy of God, for I have espoused you to one husband that I may present you as a chaste virgin to Christ" (2 Cor 11:2). Let us be obedient, then, with the obedience we vowed at the foot of the altar, obedient to all the commandments of God and of the Church; obedient to our baptismal promises; obedient to the evangelical counsels of our state of life as determined by our rules and constitutions; obedient to the least desire of the supreme head of the Church and to the faithful interpreters of his will; obedient to the bishops who deign to employ our labors in conformity with our rules, being respectful, submissive, and united to them and through them with the Holy See; obedient to the civil authorities in all that is within their jurisdiction; obedient to our superiors with what St. Paul calls obedience unto justice (Rom 6:16). Without obedience to superiors, we shall be unhappy ourselves and make our superiors unhappy; we shall hinder God's work and incur a frightful responsibility.

Let no one say that obedience is the hardest and heaviest yoke in the community, that it suffices to obey God without subjecting oneself, not only to the wisdom and charity of good superiors, but even to the passions, whims, and ill treatment of imperfect ones who are jealous of domination. We may reply that either the superiors acquit themselves of their office in accordance with the rules, or they do not. If they faithfully govern and direct us, we obey God in obeying them, and so, far from being rulers, they are but our servants, since they must occupy themselves with all our needs of body and soul; must be all things to all people; must forget themselves and their liberty to become, by devotedness and charity, the servants and debtors of their brothers and sisters (1 Cor 9:19). If, on the contrary, superiors are capricious in exercising their power, if they even abuse it and become guilty in the eyes of him who will judge those in authority most severely, they yet give us opportunity of humbling ourselves; of renouncing and mortifying our will and our self-love; and, so long as they command nothing wrong, of reaping abundant merit and eternal reward.

Though they do wrong in acting thus, their unjust and capricious will yet becomes in a mysterious and important sense the will of God for us, since we are in greater need of dying to our own will and judgment than of being enlightened, edified, and consoled by faultless superiors.

After all, the worst that bad superiors can do to us is to humiliate us and make us do penance. But should we not strive for humility and always do penance? Is not the life of the ordinary Christian, even more of the religious, a sacrifice of love, humiliation, and continual penance, without which he would be unable to satisfy the justice of God for his countless sins? If, then, our superiors command kindly or cruelly, let us obey like little children, without stopping to reason on their commands, without questioning, without worry, and we shall be safe.

Chastity

The psalmist tells us that they are happy, indeed, whom the Lord has chosen and taken under the cover of his wings, for "they shall be inebriated with the plenty of his house and shall drink of the torrent of his pleasure" (Ps 36:8–9). This abundance of pleasure is all the more precious in that it is spiritual and celestial. Far from the world and its dangers, sheltered from its errors and misfortunes, living in the company of wise virgins who keep their lamps always lit for the coming of their divine spouse, such as these can delight in the Lord and receive the requests of their heart. Like the bees that make their honey from various flowers, they can grow in perfection by imbibing the good example of their brothers and sisters, imitating the humility of one, the patience of another, the mildness of this one, the charity of that one. Hidden in the secrecy of the heart of the Lord, they know a peace, a repose, which is troubled only by the thought of those who have it not because of sin. Truly do they know how lovely are the tabernacles of the Lord, tabernacles not of ivory and gold but of the warm breathing bodies consecrated by the vow of chastity.

Let us be chaste, then, with a chastity that makes pure all our thoughts and affections, all our words and acts, our bodies and our souls.

This sacred obligation is not a hard and heavy yoke; it is not a punishment. It is, as St. Paul assures us, an extra liberty, a sweet exemption from the distressful cares and bitter tribulations that so often afflict the married (1 Cor 7). Marriage is, as he teaches, a holy state, but the state of virginity is a higher and holier state. This freedom of virginity we have all experienced. All of us who compare our lot to that of our families, no matter how happy and holy its members may be, know that we do not have their share of sufferings, cares, anxieties, contradictions, and self-denials. Every one of us can but cry out with the royal prophet: "The lines are fallen unto me in goodly places. I will bless the Lord, who has given me understanding" (Ps 16:6–7).

Let us deem ourselves happy, then, in being rid of the tribulations of the flesh of which the apostle speaks, and far from soiling ourselves with earthly and animal affections, let us lift ourselves up on the wings of divine love into the ways of the angels. If impurity makes people something less than human, purity makes them something more. If vice lowers humans to the level of the beast, virtue raises them to the height of the angel. Let us seek all our joy of love in the bosom of him who promised heaven and the sight of himself to the pure of heart and who chose for his best beloved on earth a Virgin Mother, a virgin foster father, and a virgin disciple. Let us live in him who "purchases us from the earth" as virgins who will "follow the lamb wherever he goes" in paradise, singing "a new canticle before the throne" (Rv 14:3–4). To keep ourselves in this sublime state, we must submit more and more to the law of supernatural love that refers all things to God, that undertakes and suffers all for his glory.

To remain on this exalted plane it is literally necessary that we follow the injunction of St. Paul: "Put on the Lord Jesus Christ and make not provision for the flesh in its concupiscence" (Rom 13:14). You recall the way in which Jacob at the persuasion of his mother took by trickery the blessings of Isaac, his father. She clothed him in Esau's good garments that she had with her and put the skin of a kid on his neck and hands. If we translate this from the physical to the moral order, we shall put on the new man or Jesus Christ to win new graces from our heavenly father, not by trickery but with his consent and with our elder brother Jesus to clothe us in himself. This means that we must not limit ourselves to the wearing of the religious habit, which recalls the garb formerly worn by penitents, but we must let the change of dress produce in our souls and our whole exterior conduct the sentiments and the manner of action of Jesus Christ (Phil 2:5). We have for guarantee that this is to put on the new man St. Paul, who bade us put on the Lord Jesus. Our whole life should have for its end to assimilate so perfectly the thoughts, judgments, desires, words, and actions of Jesus Christ that we can say with the great apostle: "I live, now not I, but Christ lives in me" (Gal 2:20). Let us be as the limb that lives on the sap of the tree to which it has been grafted, as real members of Christ's mystical body.

We must so identify ourselves with our divine model as not only to be a faithful copy of him, but to become, as it were, another him. This he asked for his own from his father: "That they all may be one, as you, Father, are in me, and I in you; that they also may be one in us: I in them, and you in me" (Jn 17:21–23). Is this possible? Yes, and it is accomplished thus: As the intelligence and will, the soul and body, of Jesus Christ are united to the divine nature by the Incarnation, so our mind is united to that of Jesus Christ by faith, our heart to his heart by charity, and our body to his body by Holy Communion. He invites us to contract this union with himself: "I am the way, and the truth, and the life" (Jn 14:6). He is the way by his example, the truth by his doctrine, and the life by his sacraments.

What is the wonderful transformation worked in us by this union with Jesus Christ, and what are its wonderful characteristics? It is an entire union of mind, will, and body. It is an intimate union which makes us live the very life of Jesus Christ. It is an efficacious union, since it restores all we lost in Adam and makes us one moral person with the Savior. It is a glorious union which gives to our actions supernatural merit and the right to eternal glory. How the soul dilates with joy at the thought. How could we ever surrender such a body, a body fed on the Body of Christ, to impurity? How could we ever divide a heart, a heart that is one with his, between him and a creature?

Of all our vows, chastity is the most glorious for our community, but it is also the most delicate and difficult to keep perfectly until death. Our youth was trained to obedience, and we were accustomed from infancy to ask for the means to satisfy our corporal needs. Thus, we were in a way ready for the obligations of our vows of obedience and poverty. If, however, we had a happy family life, we were not so well prepared for that complete detachment required by genuine chastity of the heart. Virginal integrity is only the first requirement of this consecrated virtue, though; alas, by all too many, it is supposed to satisfy even the spirit of the vow. Being other Christs, we must love all our brothers and sisters with a boundless love. Possessive love of one of them narrows this wide love in proportion to its exclusiveness.

Since there is no state of life so holy as to escape the onslaughts of the evil one, and since even the greatest saints were not exempt from temptations of the flesh, we shall look for a moment here at the essential malice of impurity. Christian philosophy describes a human being as an intelligence served by bodily organs, or, if you like this better, a soul created to the image and likeness of God, which gives form to a body that it should govern. If there be one of the passions of the body that, upsetting this natural order, subjects the soul to the senses and directs all its desires to the flesh so as, in a way, to materialize it, that passion may be said to turn a person into a kind of brute. Such is precisely the degrading effect of the vice we are discussing. It even degrades a person below the brute, since animals have no useless desires outside the purpose of reproduction, being chaste by instinct.

Because of the character of a Christian, the profanation of his body takes on the nature of a sacrilege. His body is as the ciborium and the chalice for the flesh and blood of Christ; he is the living temple of the Holy Spirit. Hence, the apostle writes: "For this is the will of God, your sanctification—that you should abstain from fornication; that every one of you should know how to possess his vessel in sanctification and honor, not in the passion of lust like the Gentiles that know not God" (1 Thes 4:3–5). These words were addressed, not to consecrated religious especially, but to the Christian living in the midst of the world as well. Impurity is a blasphemy against the three persons of the most adorable Trinity—against the Father whose image it defaces, against the Son whose members it defiles, against the Holy Spirit whose living temple it profanes. We can look to both faith and reason to measure the horror of this sacrilege.

We need not enter here into the kinds of impurity, those of thought, word, and deed. Nor need we dwell on the distinction between temptation and sin. Our purpose is rather to acquire a greater love for the virtue, a greater detestation for the vice, and to learn the means of safeguarding ourselves from yielding to temptation. There are but three means, but we shall find them efficacious. They are fear, avoidance of occasions, and prayer.

St. Augustine tells us that if we do not wish to be rejected from the presence of God, we must fear the fire of concupiscence. "Blessed is the one that is always fearful" (Prv 28:14). This fear should be founded primarily on the rigor of the chastisement God has always used and will everlastingly use against the impure. Are we tempted to commit one of those secret sins by which the body is despoiled of its sanctity? Be it only a word, a single voluntary thought, a deliberate glance, let us remember that everlasting hell is its punishment. St. Augustine teaches that to be forever damned, it suffices to take pleasure in one evil thought, to retain willfully in the mind one sinful desire, without actual intention of putting the thought into act. Our Lord Jesus Christ said: "Whosoever shall look on a woman to lust after her has already committed adultery with her in his heart" (Mt 5:28). Let us judge, then, the deceit of that pretended strength of mind that treats all these secret matters as mere trifles and see whether we have not reason to urge on ourselves, as the first means to avoid this sin, a great fear of it.

We should fear this vice also because of the great facility with which we fall into it, for it flatters so much our corrupt nature. Age is no protection. Wealth or poverty makes no difference. Holiness of life is no infallible guarantee. David, before his sin, was perhaps more holy than any of us, and yet he fell and, without a miracle of grace, would now be in hell. What caused his ruin? An indiscreet glance. St. Paul tells us to flee from this danger (2 Tm 2:22; 1 Cor 6:18). We must not go into this kind of combat; we must flee from it. The only way in which to keep our treasure is to run away with it. St. Ambrose tells us that the characteristic of a chaste soul is to be afraid of the unguarded look of a person of the other sex.

Our paramount duty, then, in regard to this treasure we carry in a fragile vase is to avoid all occasions of harming it. We surely need no warning against intimacies of a dangerous kind, for our holy rule forbids not only such physical manifestations of love but even those outpourings of the heart in particular friendships which sully its complete virginal consecration to our divine spouse. Our rule takes care also to save us from dangerous reading with its almost limitless power to harm chastity.

Let us add to this salutary fear and to the continual avoidance of occasions fervent, frequent, and humble prayer. Let us ask God with all our hearts to save us from every sin. Let not a day go by without our asking for grace to keep our chastity, and, along with our prayer, let us practice that continual temperance in all things which is prescribed by our vow of poverty. The vows supplement one another, and so both obedience to the rule and the poverty of the common life are safeguards to chastity.

Poverty

It is a happy self-denial that begets the peace and the liberty of the children of God. It is a desirable poverty of spirit by which we divest ourselves of our own wisdom and of our own will and of our own body. Happy are those who understand it; happier still are those who open their hearts to this poverty of spirit. For such, command becomes easy and subjection seems right and good. It is very easy, nevertheless, to have illusions regarding the vow of poverty. Though we all promised God, by a public promise made before the altar, to renounce the use of anything without the consent of legitimate superiors, many of us have since fallen into the snares of our desires. How few of us are really poor in spirit and in heart, poor in detachment from created things, especially as regards our ease and convenience? Do not many of us give with one hand and take back with the other?

Self-love is prolific in pretexts to excuse its laxity in this matter. It winds in and out of all we do like a serpent, hiding when we grow suspicious of it. It takes all kinds of forms and repays itself in little details for the great sacrifices it had to make. It had to surrender home and wealth, perhaps, and now it clings to a piece of furniture, an article of clothing, a book, or some trifle not worth naming but capable of showing how much alive nature still is.

Far from being poor in food, in clothing, in the simplicity of our room, in every detail of life, some of us wish to have everything to our taste. We feel the least privation; we will not want for anything. If our food is not so good as we have been led to expect, we grumble. Ah, the rules we promised at the altar to observe do not regard poverty thus; nor did the founders of our community so regard it.

Let us look back on the history of the monastic orders. The early members proposed to themselves as models the toilers in the fields who earn their living by the sweat of their brow and manage only the bare necessities of life. In this true poverty many delicate virgins lived and, thank God, still live, virgins often of noble birth who were brought up in ease. They sleep on hard beds; they wear coarse clothing; they walk barefoot; they eat poor and scanty food; they fast frequently; they rise to sing the Office at midnight; they bear the cold and suffer the heat; they keep silence; they remain long on their knees in prayer; they wear hair shirts and perform other bodily austerities; they work like common servants; and they do all this with submission and joy. Ah, this is, indeed, to practice the poverty of Jesus Christ, who was born on straw, had no place to lay his head during his journeys, and died naked on a cross.

"O my God, shall not we, without going beyond our rules, imitate your poverty generously? At least, suffer not among us those who complain about food and clothing. Instead, give us new hearts, hearts worthy of you, hearts that are enemies to sensuality and that freely enjoy only what the rule permits us, hearts for which you suffice, hearts that delight in detachment and increasing privation. Keep in our minds the memory of your cross and your sufferings. Teach us what a lovely thing it is to be truly free, to be detached from everything, to cling to nothing that will pass with time. Grant that when the anniversary of our profession comes yearly, each new one may find us more and more filled with the spirit of our vows, so that our renewal of them may indeed be a feast to you and an everlasting remembrance of your great mercies in choosing us to come into your land of blessing."

The Sacred Heart of Jesus

· ·

One of the soldiers with a spear opened his side, and immediately
there came out blood and water. (Jn 19:34)

To prove how dearly the Son of God loves us, no part of his innocent flesh was left unhurt by the passion. His august head was
crowned with thorns and his whole body cruelly scourged. His
hands and feet were pierced with nails, his joints torn, his veins emptied.
His mouth was seared with vinegar and gall. Finally, a soldier opened
his side with a long spear and brought forth the blood and water that yet
remained therein. It is generally believed that the point of the death-dealing iron was thrust so violently into the breast of Jesus as to enter even
his heart. Even had the Savior not been already dead, the tearing open of
his heart would have caused his death.

Thus was accomplished the prophecy of Zechariah that the Jews
should look upon him "whom they had pierced" (Zec 12:10). This bar-
barous act has served for all time to demonstrate to the incredulous the
death and, consequently, the true resurrection of the Messiah. It was not
without mystery, however, or by chance, that Jesus Christ accepted this
new wound. By it, he wished to show us the ardor of his love and his
burning desire to gather us all into his heart as into an assured refuge.
Let us, therefore, enter with loving respect into this sanctuary of divine
charity. It is our Lord himself who invites us therein and who, says St.
Bernard, for this reason, let his side be opened with a lance, that the
bloody wound may be as a door through which we may enter the more
easily into his heart.

Oh, my good master, would that I might draw today into your adorable heart all those to whom your grace permits me here to speak and
thus assure you an eternal conquest over them. How I should then bless
heaven for deigning to choose me as the instrument of its mercies. But, to

fulfill worthily such a mission, I should need the eloquence of the prophets, the ardor of a seraph, and the burning language of divine love. The
voice of God, however, can speak through my feeble tongue and thus
make its triumph but the more glorious.

So I would implore you, dearly beloved, to listen for this voice
within my own and "harden not your hearts" (Ps 95:8). Let the heart
of Jesus triumph and our hearts be trophies to his glory. We owe him
the tribute of our homage and solemn devotion to worship him under so
many titles. We owe our adoration of his Sacred Heart also to his Church,
which urges us to it, and we owe it to ourselves for our personal interests.
Let us try to understand these three powerful motives more completely,
that they may influence us more irresistibly. "Heart of my Jesus, speak
to our hearts and convert them to you forever. We ask this by the wound
given you on Calvary, and by that counterthrust which at the same time
transpierced the living heart of Mary, your mother, who stood beside
you."

Justice, Gratitude, and Obedience

We owe it to Jesus Christ to honor his heart in a special manner. Let
us try to comprehend it well under the titles of justice, of gratitude, and
of obedience. The virtue of justice is a great love of order that makes us
render to all what is their due and, consequently, the kind of honor that
belongs to them. Surely in the eyes of faith, nothing more deserves our
respect and adoration than does the Sacred Heart.

If we contemplate the heart of Jesus in itself, we see it as a part of
the flesh of our Lord, the principle of a life consecrated entirely to the
salvation of the world, and the source of the precious blood that redeemed
us. If we look at it from the view of the love animating it, with which by
the nature of its functions it is made but one, we see it as the principal
organ of the affections and the center of the most perfect virtues that
have existed, as a true treasury of candor, innocence, purity, meekness,

patience, and humility—in a word, as the living mirror of the most admirable human perfections and the rarest gifts of grace.

If we consider the Sacred Heart relative to ourselves, we see it as the heart of our friend, our brother, our father, and our Savior; as the mysterious heart in which justice and peace have kissed (Ps 85:10) and in which prodigies of power and of mercy unite to renew the face of the earth (Ps 104:30); as the immense heart that embraces all the children of Adam to love them without end—the most beautiful masterpiece of the hands of our Creator. Yet, it is also, I must say it, the most afflicted heart, basely outraged by people in the very sacrament of the altar wherein it consumes itself with love for them.

If we consider the Sacred Heart with respect to the Word, to whom it is hypostatically united, we see it as the heart of Jesus Christ, the only Son of God and true God himself, as a heart divinized, the very heart of God, since it encloses really the plenitude of his divinity.

Is it not just to adore such a heart? If everything that was an instrument of our redemption—the cross, the nails, the crown of thorns—merits from the children of the Church a special veneration; if we reasonably venerate the relics of the saints; if we believe we should render to the hearts of great men and women who are dead honors proportionate to the virtues that distinguished them during life, we should be most inconsistent to refuse our adoration to the Sacred Heart of Jesus, in comparison to which all that is most perfect in the heroes of the ages is but weakness and imperfection.

Ah, if the prodigious riches of the Sacred Heart were known to us now as they will one day be to each of us in eternity, or even as they have been known to certain saints in this life—if, drawing aside the veil that hides it from our gaze, Jesus should deign to show us here his heart as it is or only as he once showed it to a privileged soul, that is, opened by the lance, surmounted by a cross, crowned with thorns, surrounded by flames, and blessed spirits adoring silently—at that sight we should not be able to restrain our sentiments but would annihilate ourselves in profound adoration. And yet, faith teaches us what that miracle and what those supernatural revelations would reveal of the heart of our great master. Come, then, let us adore his heart, truly worthy of adoration forever from angels and humans, and let us embrace with rapture the practices of devotion to it. This is our indispensable duty not only in justice but also in gratitude.

The virtue of gratitude obliges us to render love for love, or at least to recognize, as much as is in our power, the benefits we have received. Who has ever loved so generously as has Jesus? How can we measure the boundless effects of his charity on us? Let us reflect on how this tender father sacrificed himself for his children, how he was exhausted, consumed, to show his affection for us. The love with which his heart burns for us robbed him of his glory by making him put on the form of a servant and be born in a stable; it made him live amid labor and suffering; it made him sorrowful unto death in the Garden of Olives; and it crucified him on Calvary. Love keeps him still in the midst of us, hiding him under Eucharistic symbols, and unites him so directly with our souls that we become actually one with him. *Ecce quomodo dilexit.* ("Behold how he loved [him]" [Jn 11:36].)[27]

What are we, O my God, that you treat us with such goodness, and what is it that can draw you to so close a union with us? Ah, it is that Jesus loves us, that his heart has for us all the sentiments of the most affectionate and compassionate charity. For this reason, he wished to unite himself with us and even become as one of us by his Incarnation, that he could take us up, in a way, and hold us in his arms and lavish caresses on us. Let us, then, contemplate gratefully this divine heart all burning with the love that suggested to our Savior so many sacrifices to make us happy, and all filled with that mercy to which we owe our redemption. *Ecce quomodo dilexit.*

Let us be mindful that this is the very heart that felt so keenly all our miseries, which was so cruelly afflicted for our sins, and in which were formed so many ardent desires for his father's glory and for the sanctification of our souls. Let us recall that immense ocean of sorrow into which the heart of Jesus was plunged during his passion and abandonment on the cross. Who could fathom the unending sufferings that tore and wounded it then? Hear how Jesus cries out his woe through the mouths of the prophets: "My heart is become like wax melting in the midst of my bowels. My strength is dried up like a potsherd, and my tongue has cleaved to my jaws. . . . I have called for my friends, but they deceived me. . . . They have heard that I sigh, and there is none to comfort me" (Ps 22; Lam 1). Can we fail to have compassion for the sufferings of a heart that languishes and dies for love of us? Should not the remembrance of all that the Savior endured for us from the crib of Bethlehem to the cross of Golgotha move us even to tears and transports of gratitude?

It is this incomparable heart that Jesus Christ presents today to our homage, my dearly beloved. He offers it to us, not only as the supreme symbol of his charity for us on Calvary, but also as an offering constantly consumed with love for us in the august sacrament of the Eucharist, wherein he is continually exposed to our outrages. O admirable invention of the bounty of our Savior. There, yes, there on the altar, to console the weariness of our exile, he gives us a bread more delicious than that of the desert; there he gives us his flesh to eat and his blood to drink; there the incarnate Word becomes present in our souls, communicates to us his heart with all its affections, and thus forces ours to open themselves within his own. Think of such inconceivable tenderness and such blessings. God though he is, could he love us more? *Ecce quomodo dilexit.*

To explain the mysteries of a heart so lovable and so loving, one would have to measure all the height, width, and depth of that furnace of love, but that, O my Jesus, is not the privilege of a soul so cold and feeble as mine. No, it belongs to the saints, your intimate friends, to plunge with delight into that ocean of graces and favors. Even were it given me to comprehend such great matters, I could not—as your apostle recalled from his ecstasy could not—find expressions to bring them to earth, because they surpass infinitely all our conceptions and words. But shall I, O my Savior, because I am incapable of comprehending how you love me and of showing my gratitude as I should, be so ungrateful as to ignore your love and refuse you my heart? No, this shall not be. From this very moment, condemning all my past ingratitude, I wish to put all my pleasure in loving you and making your Sacred Heart honored on the earth. Your love will be, henceforth, the center of my canticle of thanksgiving. Yes, I will live and die in the faith of him who has loved me even unto death to redeem me.

Can I suppose that you, my dearly beloved, have sentiments other than mine at this moment? Come, then, once again, let us prostrate ourselves in spirit before the heart of Jesus and vow ourselves irrevocably to the practices of devotion to it.

Christian obedience also makes it a duty to practice a devotion that has Jesus Christ himself for its author, which heaven has confirmed by the authority of miracles, and which the Church proposes to its children. Such is the devotion that I have the honor to treat with you. To convince us first that it comes from our Lord himself, we may reason thus: Without wishing to base the solidity of the worship we give the Sacred Heart on the revelation made to that privileged soul of the seventeenth century, that event appears, nevertheless, to be sustained by witnesses sufficiently respectable to merit our belief, and to be cited in an assembly of the faithful as a manifest sign of the divine will concerning this devotion.[28] Jesus Christ one day showed his divine heart to that holy religious, as it is ordinarily represented in pictures, and told her that his desire was to have it honored in a special way and that he had chosen her to propagate this devotion. His pious daughter wrote to her director, the Jesuit Father de la Colombière, that if it were known how agreeable to Jesus is the worship given his heart, there is not a Christian who would not hasten to give it to him at once.[29] Can it not be said, after this, without rashness, that it is the Son of God himself who has revealed the devotion I am preaching to you?

This devotion was familiar to a great number of saints who have recorded it in their writings. Among them particularly are Sts. Bernard, Bonaventure, Lawrence, Justinian, Thomas of Villanova, Francis de Sales, Peter of Alcantara, Philip Neri, and others not less illustrious in learning and virtue. Moreover, since the time has come in which the Lord resolved to have rendered to the heart of his divine Son its deserved honors, we have seen this devotion spread throughout Europe and even into the New World with such swift success that we can but recognize in it the finger of God. In so short a space of time, one can count in its favor more than seven hundred public mandates by various bishops in their respective dioceses and more than eighty briefs of indulgences accorded by diverse popes who have permitted the celebration of the feast. The immortal Pius VI solemnly approved this worship by a bull, which was eagerly received by all Catholic prelates.[30]

France, the land of Margaret Mary, was not backward in this matter. As soon as the devotion was made known to her toward the end of the seventeenth century, it was widely practiced in this country. A thousand monuments of thanksgiving and love were raised in its honor, altars were erected, solemnities were celebrated, and associations were formed in great number. All the bishops of the kingdom united to encourage, teach, and confirm it, and did so on the invitation of the virtuous queen, Marie Leczinska, wife of Louis XV. Immediately after, the Revolution, though it wrought such evils, only served to augment this salutary practice in the Church in France. Persecuted Christians had need to seek in the heart of their divine master consolation for the evils they suffered for the faith, evils whose bitterness could not be sweetened by human remedies. Since that disastrous period, the bishops of France, becoming freer for a moment, propagated this growing devotion with more zeal than before, and many dioceses were consecrated to the Sacred Heart of Jesus for special protection, such as those of Paris and Poitiers. In 1823, Bishop de la Myre of Le Mans fixed the day of the feast in his diocese, which is to be solemnized with suitable pomp.[31]

Every one of us who truly loves Jesus has experienced in some measure the boundless fruits of grace and salvation true Christians have received since the pious institution of this devotion. Besides these personal motives, we know we could have the devotion presented to our faith by no authority more venerable and imposing. When the will of the Church and her divine spouse has been so authentically expressed in this regard, we need desire nothing further. To refuse to surrender to this will would show a lack of obedience and a contempt for the commands of heaven. Far from yielding to such blindness, my dearly beloved, and thus saddening our tender mother by criminal resistance to her invitation to adore the heart of Jesus, let us rather anticipate her desires and second her efforts in order to assuage her sorrow over her many ungrateful and rebellious children. If we really wish to respond to her intention, moreover, we shall not limit ourselves to mere affections and exterior practices, for these are of no value if we do not labor courageously and perseveringly to imitate the heart of our divine master.

The Heart of Jesus

Let us now consider how much it is in our interest to practice such exercises of devotion. By becoming for us an abundant source of blessings, they will lead us to virtue. On the other hand, when they are neglected or disdained, they will expose us to deadly consequences.

This devotion leads us to virtue, for one of its principal ends is to offer us a model to imitate, a model of such a sort that, when we look at this adorable heart, the Lord may be supposed to say to us, as in olden times he said to Moses when presenting him the form of the Ark of the Covenant and of the tabernacle: "Look and make it according to the pattern" (Ex 25:40). We are shown the heart of him who has been given us for a master, and we are assured that our duty is to conform our own hearts to his. Let us, then, study his adorable dispositions toward his father, the world, and himself—from his Incarnation even to his triumphant ascension into heaven. "Look and make it according to the pattern."

Are we tempted to pride? Let us contemplate the heart of Jesus. When we see how our Lord bore humiliations, calumnies, and outrages, his example of humility will help us to repress our sentiments of self-love and vainglory. "Look and make it according to the pattern." Does the memory of an injury or some other trial inspire us with thoughts of revenge? Let us look at the heart of Jesus. When we remember how he pardoned his enemies and prayed for his executioners, his example of patience will help to stifle in us every sentiment of hate, anger, and passion. "Look and make it according to the pattern."

Do vice and luxury charm us even to the point of seducing our innocence? Let us think on the heart of Jesus. When we consider how it was pure and stainless to the extent of choosing to be formed of the blood of an immaculate Virgin and how Christ never let his enemies raise the least doubt of his innocence, his example of a purity more than angelic will help to extinguish within us the fire of a passion as criminal as it is degrading. "Look and make it according to the pattern."

Does love of gold and silver make us insensible to the misery of the poor and needy? Do we find it difficult to endure the sacrifices demanded by our vow of poverty? Let us look at the heart of Jesus. When striving to enrich ourselves for eternity, if we consider how our Lord was reduced to poverty so far as to be born in a stable and not to have even a stone on which to rest his head, his example of generous charity and voluntary indigence will soften us to the fate of the unfortunate and will help us bear cheerfully all the privations of our state of life. "Look and make it according to the pattern."

Do we suffer as the object of contradiction, the victim of deceit and calumny, and are we, consequently, tempted to murmur against divine providence? Let us glance at the heart of Jesus. When we see how he suffered during his whole life, especially in the passion, in his honor, in his soul, and in his body—and all this without ever complaining—his example of submission to most difficult orders from heaven will make us in future more patient and resigned in our sufferings. "Look and make it according to the pattern."

Briefly, in whatever dispositions we be, in whatever situation in life we be, we must look at our model and set ourselves to imitate him. We can be assured that in imitating him we shall attain perfection and shall find in that imitation a certain pledge of salvation, for the apostle tells us that our predestination to glory depends on our resemblance to Jesus Christ, the head of the predestined. "For those whom he foreknew, he also predestinated to be made conformable to the image of his son, that he might be the first-born amongst many. And those whom he predestined, he also called. And those whom he called, them he also justified. And, those whom he justified, them he also glorified" (Rom 8:29–30).

Let us, therefore, walk in Christ's footsteps and make our sentiments conform to those of our divine master, "letting this mind be in us, which was also in Christ Jesus" (Phil 2:5). Let us be as he was, zealous for the interests of God and religion, detached from the world and its vanities, dead to the flesh and its concupiscence, dead to pride and its suggestions. Otherwise, all the homage we give the Sacred Heart will not be pleasing to him. He will reprove our devotion as hypocritical and lying because we honor him only with our lips, as did that unbelieving nation of which he said, quoting the prophet: "This people honors me with their lips, but their heart is far from me" (Mt 15:8).

Are there, perhaps, some among us to whom our Lord could utter this humiliating reproach? It is not unusual to encounter even in the religious life hearts whose dispositions are wholly opposed to those of the heart of Jesus. There are fierce and haughty hearts whose sensitive pride is irritated or even shocked by the least affront. There are hard and unsympathetic hearts whom religion and humanity cannot make interested in the needs of the unfortunate. There are hearts spoiled and wallowing in the mire of shameful pleasures, whose chains nothing can break. There are hearts filled with anger and bitterness, which abuse the patience of others with the extravagances of their disposition, the transports of their wrath, the stubbornness of their hate, and the scandalous uproar of their quarreling. There are lazy, lukewarm, and sluggish hearts with energy for nothing, in which faith casts only a feeble and dying glimmer.

How could anyone pretend to honor the heart of Jesus Christ, holiness itself, and enter into the designs of the Church with a heart fruitful in crimes and dominated more or less by the passions I have just described? No, the Lord does not accept the worship and prayers of one who comes before him with a heart hardened by sin. I seem to hear him cry today to these false and hypocritical adorers as he did in olden times to the carnal Jews: "Of what avail are these sterile praises whose vain show reassures but does not convert you? Your solemnities oppress me because they bring me, under their cover, iniquities that wound by their very nearness the purity of my eyes. 'This people honors me with their lips, but their heart is far from me' (Is 29:13; Mt 15:8)."

Can it be that the devotion of some of us is only superficial and that we merit these bitter reproaches? I believe I should do you an injustice, my dearly beloved, if I should harbor this thought concerning any of you in particular. But would it insult an audience so numerous to suppose in it one religious unfaithful to his duties and enslaved by the devil? We all know how easy it is to be led into sin in a world wherein everything is a snare and a seduction. If, then, any of you now weep over the weight of your sins, in the name of the heart of Jesus that you have so saddened, break your chains and thus give glory to the Sacred Heart. Hear him who cries to you from the depths of the sanctuary wherein he awaits you day and night: "My son, my dear son, give me your heart. I have given you mine with all its affections, and I offer it to you again today. Is it not just for you to give me yours in return? Do you not know that far from me you will have no peace, no happiness? Return, then, to your father, ungrateful but always eagerly sought son."

Can you still resist the touching invitation of your God and refuse him the heart he asks for so insistently? Have you not too long and too boldly rejected the solicitation of his grace and the inspirations of his Holy Spirit? Yield now to the remorse of your conscience and the paternal pleadings of your Savior by consecrating to him your heart with all its inclinations. Thus, through your example you will confirm the truth I have just advanced, that devotion to the Sacred Heart leads to virtue. This is the only means to experience for yourself the second advantage it procures us, which is an abundant source of blessings.

The Church effectively proclaims this advantage in the sublime preface of the Mass of the feast: "We give thanks to you, O holy Lord, Father Almighty, everlasting God, who willed that your only-begotten Son should be pierced by the soldier's lance as he hung on the cross, so that from his open heart, as from a treasury of divine bounty, he might pour out on us torrents of mercy and grace, and in that heart, always burning with love for us, the devout might find rest and the penitent a saving refuge." From this divine heart the saints have drawn those extraordinary gifts of grace which we admire in them. The afflicted have found comfort in it, the sick have found healing, and the true faithful still daily draw from it their virtues and their merits. In this adorable heart the just find their happiness, their wealth, and their consolation.

From the Sacred Heart of Jesus, St. Bernard drew the generous love and tender piety that breathe through his works. In it, St. Bonaventure tasted those interior joys, those ineffable delights, that united him so directly with God. In it, the penitent St. Augustine found strength and courage to conquer himself. By it, St. Francis of Assisi was inflamed with all the seraphic ardors of divine charity. In it, the holy Bishop of Geneva formed himself so perfectly to evangelical meekness. From it, the apostles drew their zeal, the martyrs their triumph, the virgins their purity, and all the elect of the New Covenant their enlightenment and their holiness.

Entering the Heart of Jesus

Happy, then, are the Christians who direct their eyes and their longings to the heart of Jesus Christ. They will find therein a fertile source of love for God and for their neighbor, because in devotion to the Sacred Heart everything breathes and inspires love. It has love for its object, the heart of Jesus, in which are consummated all the mysteries of divine charity. It has love for its end, which is especially to testify to our thanksgiving and to make him honorable amends for all the outrages he has received and is still receiving from us. It has love for its practices, which include only exercises of love, as, for example, that invocation, which the associates should recite at least once daily: "O heart of my Jesus, make me ever love you more and more." Let us enter, then, into this ever-loving heart so filled with blessings.

Above all, let those of us who are honored by the priesthood seek refuge in this loving heart, for we are particularly charged to bring others therein. Let us celebrate the holy mysteries in the heart of Jesus; let us recite in it the Divine Office; let us hear in it the avowals of our penitents; let us announce from this safe point of vantage the Word of God—let us do all our priestly functions in the Sacred Heart, and it will spread over the exercise of our ministry the most abundant blessings. But let us not enter alone, bringing only ourselves to partake of this precious treasure; let us draw along all those whose salvation is confided to us and compel them with holy violence to enter with us.

Yes, whoever we are, rich or poor, great or small, young or old, just or sinner, let us all lose ourselves lovingly in this heart which knows only the excess of tenderness, in this heart in which all the seraphim humble and annihilate themselves, in this heart whose activity has not been diminished by nineteen hundred years of ingratitude. Where could children

better be than in the heart of their father? Come, then, let us all hasten
into this waiting heart, no matter what the state of our soul. If we are in
sin, here is the heart that received the prodigal son, pardoned the penitent
Magdalene, made the apostate disciple weep repentantly, and converted
a thief on the cross. If we are lukewarm, here is the source of charity, in
which we can renew our arms, warm our hearts, and draw new strength.
If, after being converted to the Lord for many years, we are tempted to
abandon him, if the spirit of darkness and our own evil impulses torment
us by continual assaults, the heart of Jesus is our retreat and refuge, for
it will lift us above the senses and enable our feebleness to win glorious
victories. If we fear being lost in the deluge of crimes flooding the earth or
being shipwrecked on the stormy sea of the world, here is the ark of salvation and the vessel that will carry us to the harbor. Let us enter once more,
then, and the heart of Jesus will be everything to us in life and in death.

Let us ponder well this last word: the heart of Jesus will be everything to us in death. When our last hour strikes, when as we wait on the
edge of eternity our past, our present, and our future rise up to trouble
and confound us—where will then be our resource? To whom, then, shall
we go if not to the heart that holds all our hope of eternal life? Where
shall we, then, turn our eyes and our sighs for help if not to that heart
which wants only our contrition to forgive us? Yes, heart of my God, into
you will I throw myself at that terrible moment, and in your protection I
hope to find grace and mercy before the awful tribunal at which I must
appear.

But what will happen in that dreadful hour to those blind sinners
who, despising the favors of this heart, unceasingly outrage it by their
anti-Christian conduct and irritate it by their infidelities? Here I wish to
explain how, by despising the devotion with which I would inspire us,
they are exposed to the deadliest consequences. The day will come that
must end the earthly career of the impious and that, despite them, will fix
all their attention on the heart of Jesus Christ. What a frightening spectacle for those wretches will be the sight of the heart that has loved them
so much and so long and yet has met only vile rebuff from them. What
will be their consternation when at the moment of death they will face a
heart filled with vengeance against them and when at the judgment they

will see burning in the air that eternal monument of divine charity! What will become of them when they have to look at the scar of the deep wound made by the spear in that heart so prodigal of itself, a scar which will be as an open mouth to reproach their ingratitude and insensibility. What will become of them when the savior God, who will be their judge, shows himself to them in all the apparel of his majesty and uncovers for them his wounds, and thus reproaches them?

"Answer me, O ungrateful and ever-rebellious hearts: What could I have done to move you and win you to me that I have not done? See this open side from which the blood and water flowed for you on Calvary. By it, I wanted to give you entrance into my heart, but you only sought to plunge new darts into it and lifted against me the hands I had filled with my gifts. You were urged to submit to the sweet yoke of my Gospel. My ministers begged you to practice a devotion, which, by carrying you to virtue, would have made you participate in my most precious graces. I myself urged you to this devotion with the touching secrets of my Holy Spirit and waited for you to come to me even until you drew your last breath on earth. But my patience served only to increase your audacity and multiply your sins. Now open your eyes and look at this heart whose love you have disdained and whose wrath you have braved. Now it cries vengeance against you and calls upon your head the thunders of celestial anger. 'The day of vengeance is in my heart' (Is 63:4)."

What will judgment mean to those lax and apostate Christians who do not comprehend and do not wish to comprehend the love of Jesus Christ and his holy religion? Ah, in that dreadful moment, they will invoke death, will beg the divine justice to annihilate them and thus take from them the look of angered love. Awful and useless despair will be theirs who must expiate in everlasting hell the injuries done to the Sacred Heart. "They shall look upon him whom they have pierced" (Zec 12:10). And they shall say to him, "What are these wounds in the midst of your hands?" And he shall say, "With these I was wounded in the house of them that loved me" (see Zec 13:6).

But you are already convinced, my dearly beloved, that no one can neglect or ignore, without risking the deadliest consequences, the worship we should render to the heart of our great master. Slighting this pious devotion would be the more dangerous for us today, moreover, since the Sacred Heart is our only resource in the evils that have so long afflicted the Church. Who of us is ignorant of the countless outrages done the Catholic religion and of the unheard-of blasphemies of which its adorable author is the constant object in many parts of the world? Christ and his religion are outraged by forgetfulness of evangelical truths and abandonment of the sacraments. The Church is outraged by the vast plan of persecution hatched for many years and in many countries against bishops and priests. Religion is outraged by the battering down of crosses and the profanation of churches. Worse than these outrages, from those who have never been of the true fold and who have grown up in the abuse of grace and that almost universal hardness of heart so characteristic of this generation, are the outrages of hypocritical sinners who go to Communion unworthily and sacrilegiously, who are irreverent before holy altars and during the Office — or, in a way, the outrages of negligent, lukewarm souls who receive Holy Communion often with no increase of fervor. Is there any place, at any moment of the day or night, when someone is not outraging the Sacred Heart?

It is not only in our interest but also should be our keenest joy to try to repair so many outrages, to disarm the divine wrath they rouse against the world. To whom can sinful humanity have recourse if we force the heart of Jesus to close against us, if we despise its all-powerful mediation, if we set against us the very one who alone can satisfy for our offenses and merit us pardon for them? Should we not expose ourselves to the terrible measures of that justice which finally punishes ingratitude by the withdrawal of blessings, continued resistance to the light of the Gospel by the extinction of the torch of faith, and the impiety of a whole nation by its overthrow and final ruin? "Jerusalem, Jerusalem, . . . how often would I have gathered together your children, as the hen gathers her chicks under her wings, and you would not. Behold, your house shall be left to you, desolate" (Mt 23:37–38).

Ah, let us address ourselves now and henceforth to him who wishes to avenge himself only in pardoning, and his heart will soften to our personal woes and to those Christian nations once so fruitful in martyrs and saints and now so desolated by atheism and libertinism. Let us prostrate ourselves before this merciful heart, and as those mountains whose lofty summits cleave the sky, dissipate the storm, and make fall the beneficial rain, so its prayer will penetrate even to the breast of God, will abate the thunderbolts of his vengeance, and will bring down on us the abundance of his blessings. As we have seen, we owe it to Jesus Christ, to his Church, and to ourselves to give due homage to the Sacred Heart, and we cannot honor it better just now than by lovingly "pouring out our hearts before him" (Ps 62:9).

Come, then, once again let us adore this Sacred Heart that is so good to us. Let us adore, and let us weep over the outrages we have done it and those it has received and is still receiving from our straying brothers and sisters. Let us prostrate ourselves before the Lord Jesus and make him an authentic and solemn reparation, and then let us beg of his father: "Forgive us, Lord, in the name of the love of the heart of your divine Son who cries for mercy to us, and forgive all your people." *Parce, Domine, parce populo tuo.* ("Spare your people, O Lord" [Jl 2:17].)

"O heart of Jesus, heart outraged by incredulity, by forgetfulness, and by the contradictions of humanity, have pity still on your heritage, and do not abandon it to the fury of your enemies. We know well that not all these enemies are those who do not know you or who deny your presence among us; some of them even partake of your sacred banquet with cold and indifferent souls or even with souls infected by the hideous leprosy of sin, thus wounding your heart most dolorously even in the house of those who love you. But, O generous Savior, you are so good that you will pardon all and so powerful that you will take from among us hearts unworthy of your tenderness. Change these hearts, make them conformable to yours, O divine master, and forget so many offenses. *Parce, Domine, parce populo tuo.* We would now make you honorable and solemn amends. May the sentiments of sorrow, thanksgiving, and fidelity, which you send now into our hearts, make recompense to you for the injuries of a world that incessantly crucifies you anew. For this purpose we consecrate to you and vow to your adorable heart our thoughts, desires, and affections, our souls and bodies, that you may possess them forever and that we may merit to possess you in heaven. Amen."

The Immaculate Heart of Mary

. . . .

Mary kept all these words, pondering them in her heart.
(Lk 2:19)

T he references of the Gospel to the heart of the Virgin Mother can but make us wonder lovingly about it. In its chaste depths, Mary treasured faithfully every least thing she saw and heard of the Savior to make of it the habitual subject of sublime meditation and to nourish the flames of her charity on it. After the heart of her adorable Son, there is, it appears to me, no more worthy object of all time—both for the complaisance of the Most High and for our veneration and love—than the Immaculate Heart of Mary.[32]

We know that the Lord, after he had created our first parents in justice and sanctity, fixed his gaze pleasurably on their pure and innocent hearts. We know that he does not disdain to avow that he is smitten with even our feeble hearts and loves them to the limit of jealousy, going so far as to use entreaty and even threat to submit them to his empire. We know that he has promised to show himself unveiled to the chaste heart, to be prodigal of blessings to the right of heart, to pour out his mercy to hearts that are tender and compassionate, and to pardon the contrite and humble heart. We know that his eyes are always turned on the human heart, no matter how degraded by original sin, to observe all its emotions and desires, and that he sees and esteems in people only their hearts, because from the heart come generous sentiments and saintly dispositions. With what satisfaction, then, does he contemplate the heart of Mary, which was never, for an instant, disfigured by sin, and which he has enriched with all the treasures of his grace.

At the thought of the stupendous things worked in that incomparable heart by the power and the mercy of the Creator, one experiences complete amazement and a new sense of the divine. At the spectacle one falls into an ecstasy of admiration, which feebly mirrors that of Mary as she lived in perpetual contemplation of the marvelous riches of the heart of her divine Son and of the mysteries of his life, both hidden and public. "Mary kept all these words, pondering them in her heart" (Lk 2:19). Let us then, my dearly beloved, enter with religious respect into this august sanctuary, wherein divinity dwelled corporally. The Church itself invites us, and we are but obeying the voice of the Holy Spirit, who tells us that all the merit of the mother of Jesus Christ comes from within, having its source in her heart. All the glory of the king's daughter is within (Ps 45:14). Would that I might lead you at this moment into that heart from which come so many virtues and perfections and fill you with the holy ecstasy that transported it when Mary cried out her canticle of thanksgiving: "My soul magnifies the Lord" (Lk 1:46). Thus would I assure the conquest of your hearts by that of the divine mother.

After the humanity of the eternal Word, the heart of Mary is the most beautiful masterpiece of the hands of the Creator. Let us not be astonished at such a statement. Once the adorable Trinity had resolved that the mystery of the Incarnation should be accomplished in the womb of Mary, it was for the divine glory that nothing be lacking to the perfection of a person called to so high a destiny. The Holy Spirit, therefore, sanctified not only her birth but even her conception by preserving her from the stain of original sin and by an infusion of grace without example and almost without measure.

Immaculate Conception

It is true that we question the gospels in vain to find whether the heart of the Blessed Virgin was conceived without the stain that dishonored our own souls in the first moment of their existence. It is true also that we do not hear the Fathers of the Church in the first ages proclaim this truth or the Doctors pronounce it to the faithful by common accord. The heart of Mary resembled a sanctuary filled with mysterious obscurity. The Holy Spirit through the angelic salutation and the evangelists revealed to us her holiness and also some of her thoughts, words, and actions, which have been proposed to the meditation of the faithful so as to teach them to venerate and love her and to imitate her virtues. But the divine plan seems to have been that Mary was to be glorified through the centuries by having each generation add to her homage and to the number and brilliance of her feasts. Thus was magnificently and literally accomplished her own prophecy that all generations would call her blessed (Lk 1:48). Devotion to Mary did, indeed, grow from age to age, and the praises of earth rose to her heart in a concert ever more perfect, ever more worthy to be united to the songs of the angels that celebrate her in eternity. The prime devotion of our age is the Immaculate Heart of the mother of the Savior, and it is the principal object of the praise I would render her here. It will be for me a great consolation at death to be able to say to the Blessed Virgin that I have spoken for her during my life and prayed for the increase of her glory.

Let us not think at all, however, that the homage we give today to the sinless heart of Mary was entirely unknown to our fathers in the faith or that the Catholics of the first ages ignored the doctrine of the Immaculate Conception. Truth will not be hidden. It was recounted from parents to children, and each age transmitted it to the following one. The doctrine of the Immaculate Conception was not formally and generally taught, because the minds of men and women were directed to other objects to find food for their piety. In a world given over to paganism and idolatry, the dogma of the Incarnation and of the God-Man needed to be established first in the minds of humans. Only after making known minutely the adorable person of Jesus Christ did the Church begin officially to add to the crown of Mary ever-virgin, of whom was born the Savior, the last and richest jewel: the definition of her Immaculate Conception. Hence, though every age furnished glorious testimonies to this doctrine and helped to raise up her edifice of glory, it was not completed until our own day.

One cannot doubt that the apostles left by word of mouth to their disciples precious teachings on the privileges and the virtues of Mary and that these were to be preserved along with numerous other traditions, without the help of the scriptures, by the loving piety of the faithful.

From where, otherwise, would have come this admirable tradition? All the churches proclaimed the mother of Jesus immaculate, all brilliant with innocence and purity.

When the Fathers of the Council of Ephesus defended Mary against the blasphemies of the impious Nestorius, they at the same time pronounced the beautiful truth that Mary, mother of God, was always preserved from all sin.[33] St. Augustine said that she should be excepted whenever there is question of sin. If the heart of the august Virgin be not immaculate, I no longer understand the councils or the Doctors of the Church, for they show her to me as a flower that shines with a living luster, as a beautiful lily in the midst of thorns, and as a ray of light coming out from the divinity. Then, too, the theologian teaches it to his disciples, the preacher announces it to the faithful, the universities bind themselves by solemn oath to sustain this truth, and the Seraphic Order seems destined to propagate it everywhere and to carry it to the ends of the earth.[34] Feast days establish it, confraternities are formed to promote it, and miracles set on it the seal of divine authority. Finally, the Church herself declares it, after eighteen centuries during which, in the designs of God, faith in it was left free to be prompted spontaneously in each of the faithful as the fruit of love for the Sacred Heart of Jesus.

What has been lacking to make this tradition an article of faith? Bishops put their hopes and found their consolation in this belief, and they roused their flocks to accept it. From the apostolic throne itself, the Vicar of Jesus Christ encouraged it by his words and rewarded pastors and the faithful with indulgences for accepting it. Charged to feed the sheep as well as the lambs, the Holy Father proposed to us, in order to nourish our piety, devotion to Mary conceived without sin. After all this, we cannot, we dare not, fail to accept as an article of faith belief in the most holy and most Immaculate Heart of the mother of the Savior.

We can never, in view of all this, comprehend the merit of the heart of Mary. We can but begin to imagine the holiness of that heart in which the eternal Father prepared a dwelling for his only Son and in which the Holy Spirit celebrated his ineffable espousals. God must have united therein all the purity of the heart of Susanna, all the fortitude of the heart of Judith, all the piety of the heart of Esther, all the faith of the heart of

Abraham, all the hope of the hearts of the prophets, all the zeal of the hearts of the apostles, all the heroism of the hearts of the martyrs, and all the innocence of the hearts of the virgins.

Think of the impressions of grace Mary's heart must have received during the nine months the incarnate Word passed in her chaste womb. With what fire must it have been kindled by that sun, held during so long a time, within so small a space, without one ray escaping to the outside! Think of the emotions of that heart when the Blessed Virgin held the divine infant in her arms and received his caresses. Think of the way holiness developed in Mary's heart during the thirty years of daily and mutual confidences between her and her dear Jesus and during the three years of the Savior's apostolate, the least details of which she recalled with delight in the silence of her profound meditation (Lk 2:19).

Truly, it is impossible to reveal her many virtues and perfections. There is nothing better to say than what the archangel Gabriel uttered: Mary was full of grace. Consequently, her heart always responded in its sentiments and desires and merits to her sublime titles of Daughter of the Eternal Father, Spouse of the Holy Spirit, and Mother of the Son of God.

The Lord was pleased to embellish her heart with the most pure gold of charity, as in olden times he had the ark of the desert covered with the finest gold, because this Ark of the New Covenant is the far-more favored possessor of the reality of which the ark of the desert possessed only the figure. Mary's mind was nourished on divine thoughts, her heart fed always on the divine love, her body obeyed the inspirations of her soul and thus preserved always perfect integrity. She was, then, truly the tabernacle of God, the Ark of the New Covenant, the house of gold, and the source from which flowed the river of life. Is it not a matter of justice to honor such a heart?

The Love of Mary's Heart

Who could tell all the effects of her charity on us her children? When Jesus Christ wished to express the great prodigality of the father's love for us, he said that he loved the world even to delivering his only Son to death for it (Jn 3:16). This St. Paul calls the excess of the divine "charity for humanity" (see Eph 2:4). The heart of Mary is capable of the same sort of excess, since she likewise delivered her only son, the adorable fruit of her womb, for the redemption of humanity: *Sic enim dilexit mundum* ("For [God] so loved the world" [Jn 3:16]). Yet, there is this difference: So great a sacrifice could cause no pain to the eternal father, who is essentially impassible, whereas it caused the august Virgin a woe so bitter, so profound, that we can never find an expression which will give a just idea of the martyrdom she endured, a martyrdom which began not merely on Calvary but at the very moment she received the visit of the archangel.

To understand this fact better, let us remember that the heart of Mary was the most tender and most charitable that can be imagined after that of the Savior, for it was the heart of a mother whom God himself was pleased to form as a pattern of the Sacred Heart of Jesus, a mother he destined for his son. Let us think how this heart had to love, how the joys and the sorrows of the son were vitally felt by the mother. It was for her dear son that Mary lived and her heart beat. To contemplate his adorable traits and keep as a most precious treasure all the words that came from his mouth was her happiness, her life.

It is doubtless that the intrepid disciple who encouraged the others to follow Jesus to Jerusalem to die with him loved the Savior, but the heart of Mary loved still more. It is doubtless that the apostle who quit all to follow him and who, after protesting his love three times, was commissioned to feed the flock loved Jesus, but the heart of Mary loved still more. It is doubtless that the disciple who was the witness of the glories of Jesus and the confidant of his sorrows and who rested his head on the Savior's heart and drew from it new fires of love loved him, but the heart of Mary loved still more. If, to give a better idea of the love of the heart of Mary for her divine son, it is necessary to add something further, let us unite the hearts of the celestial intelligences that chant the praises of the Lamb, assemble all their flames of love, add to the love of the angels that of the archangels, to the ardors of the cherubim those of the seraphim, and without doubt we shall have a gigantic sum of love. But the heart of

Mary is more loving and compassionate than all theirs, not only for Jesus, but also for each one of us in particular.

We are all acquainted with that sentiment called maternal tenderness — that love of a mother for those to whom she gave life, a love that makes her think and labor unceasingly for their happiness. What is more tender, more ardent, more generous, more heroic? This love is but a feeble image of that which the heart of Mary feels for each individual soul and of the charity with which it has burned ever since she became our mother and took us for her children.

Here we shall take a glimpse into the excess of her tenderness in seeing all she has suffered to make us eternally happy. Knowing from the first instant of the Incarnation of the Word in her womb that she was called to give to the world the victim for the human race, Mary never ceased to suffer all the desolation inseparable from such a destiny, being powerless to put from her mind prevision of the sorrows of the Garden of Olives, of the Praetorium, and of Calvary.

Mary cooperated in the sufferings of her adored son and, in our favor, became the minister of the rigorous designs of his father upon him. She presented him for the ceremony of the circumcision, that his blood might begin to be shed for us. She brought him to the Temple to offer him as our future victim, and she heard the holy old man speak of the sword of sorrow that must one day pierce her soul (Lk 2:35). She met him on the dolorous way to Calvary and mounted with him the hill of sacrifice. Oh, there we shall see to what a point she loved us. She stood at the very foot of the cross, among the executioners and soldiers, so near her dying son that no detail of his death could escape her. "There by the cross of Jesus stood his mother" (Lk 19:25). What did she do in this circumstance, so devastating for her mother's heart, in that attitude of priest and minister before the altar on which was consummated the sacrifice of our redemption? Truly did she fulfill to the final measure her part in the work of Christ, to "fill up those things that are wanting of the sufferings of Christ, in her flesh, for his body, which is the Church" (see Col 1:24).

While Jesus Christ offered himself to his father for our salvation, Mary offered him also for the same end, and we were then so much the sole object of the thoughts of the son and the mother that the Savior, turning upon her his dying eyes still filled with love, addressed her a last word, which was not of himself or of her, but of us. Christ saw at his feet, below the cross, one of his disciples, whom he made represent all the others and the whole world. Thus, enfolding us all in the person of St. John, he presented us to Mary, saying, "Woman, behold your son" (Jn 19:26). It was as if he said to her: "New Eve, here is your family. You are, henceforth, alone the true mother of all the living. You have borne all these children in your sorrow, and I wish you to love them even as you have loved me: 'Woman, behold your son' (Jn 19:27)." Then, with a loving look at St. John, he said to him: "Behold your mother." It was as if he said to us all in that sublime moment: "Most happy children of Adam, know your new mother. I yield thee all my rights over her, so have recourse to her in all your needs. If her womb did not bear you, her heart has given birth to you in this great hour, and if anything could equal my tenderness for you, it would be her own: 'Behold, your mother.'"

One can but bow in humble adoration before such admirable charity and such blessings bestowed on humanity. Who could, O Mary, reveal to the world all there is of tenderness in your heart for us? Who could ever love enough a heart so lovable and so loving?

In olden times, when infidels menaced the Christian peoples, the sovereign pontiffs, to encourage pious knights, dictated to them some invocation to Mary, which would serve as a motto and countersign. Then the soldiers went to combat full of confidence, and victory was granted their arms. We need such a Christian word today. It is true that they are no longer barbarians who declare war on us today, but Christians, our brothers and sisters, who are divided and who destroy one another. Nations are shaken, rulers unite against the Lord and his Christ, and peoples plan vain conspiracies. To whom shall we have recourse? To the heart of Mary. Let others trust in their horses, arms, and chariots (Ps 20:8–9). As for us, strong in our faith and strength from on high, we cry to the heart of Mary. She will have pity on us, for she is compassionate and will not permit that we perish.

St. Joseph

. . . .

Go to Joseph, and do all that he shall say to you. (Gn 41:55)

While the seven years of famine were desolating the land of Egypt, its starving people came to the court of Pharaoh to beg for food. The monarch bade them go to the faithful governor of his palace and do whatever he commanded them. Because Joseph had prophesied to Pharaoh this terrible famine, which was to follow the years of plenty, and had in many ways shown his virtue, the prince loaded this illustrious son of Jacob with royal favors, making him the general steward of his household, the governor of all Egypt, and the keeper of the seal of authority (Gn 41:15–37). "And, he made him go up into his second chariot, the crier proclaiming that all should bow their knee before him" (Gn 41:43). Then he laid on him the care of his people in their need.

In this history, with its many symbolic figures, we find a prophecy of what God's gifts of grace wrought in our holy patriarch St. Joseph. Or we might say the virtues and the achievements of the older Joseph are but the shadow of those we honor in our glorious patron. Such is my confidence in his power with God and the veneration that fills me at the sight of his picture or statue, that the words, "Go to Joseph, and do all that he shall say to you," seem no longer those of the olden king but those of our mother Church. Seeing her children about to perish from material want, or from diseases of body and soul, or even from loss of faith, she bids them in her grief: "Go to St. Joseph."

However this thought appeals to you, I am resolved to try to communicate my own devotion to any of you, my dearly beloved, who will have the goodness to hear me. With this end in view, I wish to talk with you about the virtues and prerogatives of St. Joseph.

"O Mary, I have so often invoked you in the course of my labors and preaching, but never, perhaps, with more confidence than at this moment when I am moved to reveal to my brothers and sisters my thoughts on the holiness and the privileges of the worthy companion of your sublime destiny. Daring to count on your assistance, I humbly implore it in the name of the most pure and faithful heart of your spouse. Hear me for your joy in the angelic salutation. Heart of Joseph, most pure and most faithful, pray for us."

The Virtues of St. Joseph

In this meditation on the virtues of St. Joseph, we shall not present them in detail and historical sequence. For this we have not the means, since both the gospels and tradition keep an extraordinary and almost absolute silence on the subject. This very silence, however, says the utmost to us and makes our incomparable patron greater in our eyes than many words could do. Surely the one who conceals what he could advantageously make known to the world, who hides marvels most fitted to awaken its admiration, is truly virtuous and worthy of highest esteem. Such a one deserves the eulogy offered to the first Christians by the apostle, "You are dead; and your life is hidden with Christ in God" (Col 3:3). Think, then, of the prodigious matters our saint could have revealed to the world—he who was the intimate confidant of the Virgin Mother of God, the recipient of visits from angels, the foster father of the infant Lord, he who was initiated into the plan of the redemption of the human race. The hidden life of the new Joseph and the silence of the gospels in his regard are, then, proof of his very great holiness, and they make him the more worthy of veneration in that they show him more like to Jesus and Mary. What was said of Jesus during the thirty years while the Holy Family lived obscure and inseparable? Only that he grew in age and wisdom before God and men and that he was submissive to his parents. And what was said of the Virgin of Nazareth? Only that she kept and pondered in her heart all that she saw and heard said of her divine son.

The very same gospels tell us that our immortal patriarch was a just man. This eulogy, though we knew nothing further, suffices to give us the most exalted idea of him and to console us for the silence of scripture and tradition on this subject. When we reflect on the etymological value of the word "just," it seems like one of those brilliant stars that throw a living light on all about them, and it also recalls that rich coat of varied colors with which Jacob clothed his dear son Joseph. The word "just" comes from the old Latin verb *iustare*, meaning to "adjust" or "put in order." Being "just" before God must mean, therefore, to adjust or order one's thoughts, judgments, desires, words, and actions to the divine will that is the eternal rule of all perfection. In proclaiming the spouse of Mary "just," the Holy Spirit spoke, then, the greatest eulogy, declaring Joseph perfect in every respect. Though we could apply this word to each of his virtues in particular, let us limit ourselves to a study of his perfection in his purity, his obedience, and his poverty. So perfect is he in these virtues that, if his incomparable spouse is the greatest of all saints, their very queen, St. Joseph is undoubtedly the greatest of all these saints.

St. Joseph excels all by his purity. I believe, with the pious Gerson, preaching of our saint to the Council of Constance, and with several worthy Doctors of the Church, that St. Joseph was sanctified in his mother's womb, as were Jeremiah and John the Baptist, and was then confirmed in grace, though this is not saying that he contracted exemption from all sin.[35] I believe, with Suárez, that concupiscence of the flesh was dead in him from his birth, so that he was exempt from this law of the members of which the apostle complained and from those disorderly impulses which humbled the greatest saints (Rom 7:14–25).[36] With St. Peter Damien, St. Peter Chrysologus, Hugh of St. Victor, Alcuin, St. Albert the Great, St. Bernardine of Siena, and St. Thomas, I believe that he made in early youth a vow of perpetual chastity. I believe with these same authorities, and with St. Francis de Sales, St. Teresa, and at least 350 other historians and eulogists, that spirit and flesh preserved in him virginal integrity.

Surely it is fitting that this should be so. If Jeremiah had to be purified from original sin shortly after his conception because he was to announce the Messiah; if John the Baptist was accorded this favor because he was actually to point out the Savior; if Jesus Christ wanted the best beloved of his disciples to be a virgin, and his mother as well — surely anyone can see that there was the strongest reason for great purity in the man who, passing as the father of Jesus, was to carry the Messiah in his arms.

It is true that Mary espoused Joseph, but she did so under the formal condition that she would remain a virgin and that, in giving each other mutual empire over their hearts, they would not give each other their bodies. The Gospel tells us that they "knew not" each other (Lk 1:34). According to the chancellor Gerson, by this exemplary marriage Joseph was given to Mary as the witness, the protector, the guide, and the spouse of her virginity. What a holy alliance. One virginity is united to another. Here are two creatures in whom the Holy Spirit, the mysterious bond between the Father and the Son in eternity, becomes the conjugal bond in time. Far from Mary and Joseph is every desire, every thought, of flesh and blood; all is pure, all is spiritual. On the one side is, according to St. Denis, the most beautiful creature on whom the sun has shone; she has such majesty on her countenance, such brilliance in her eyes, and so divine an air, that one has almost to force himself from adoring her. On the other is a man disengaged from all the senses, superior to all inclinations of degraded nature, one who lives amid flames but is not burned, who is surrounded by an ocean of lights but is not dazzled, who feels the arrows of the most perfect love but is not wounded. I seem to see the cherubim charged to watch the gate of the terrestrial paradise, or better, the two cherubs of gold who, on the two sides of the oracle, spread their wings and covered the mercy seat to form the throne of the divine majesty above the Ark of the Covenant (Ex 25:18–22).

It is not surprising, after such consideration, to hear a pious commentator, Cornelius a Lapide, cry out that St. Joseph seems rather an angel than a man.[37] Nor can we doubt that if, to become the mother of Jesus, Mary had to be the purest of virgins, Joseph had to be the purest of men to become the spouse of Mary and the reputed father of the Savior. If another more just than he in this regard could have been found, that one would have been preferred for so noble a union. Hence, we conclude that the holy patriarch was the most pure, most modest, most chaste among the sons of Adam, and consequently the most perfect in his virginity, which exalted him as much above other saints as the lily excels other flowers by its whiteness.

St. Joseph practiced obedience also in the most perfect manner. While he was enjoying at Nazareth the delights of the most sacred union ever contracted and was practicing all the virtues of the hidden life, heaven heaped on him the worst trials to which the human will can submit. Let us note the dolorous events that came upon his heart as father and spouse. To carry out the command of the emperor Augustus concerning the numbering of his subjects, St. Joseph was obliged to go to Bethlehem, traveling the thirty leagues and crossing steep mountains probably on foot in December, the most inclement season of the year. And he did all this when his virgin spouse was ready to give birth to her child. When they finally arrived in the city, they found all the inns closed against them. The only refuge they could find in the city their ancestors had governed was a cave, which had been hollowed in the rock to serve as a shelter for the flocks. Here began new sufferings for the Holy Family, and especially for St. Joseph, who had the care of Jesus and Mary. Did he let himself complain or even be distressed? Assuredly not. Rather, he makes us admire his resignation to the ruling of providence and his obedience to every trial God asked of him.

The infant God, who came to earth to redeem the world and teach it obedience, wished to fulfill the Jewish law and thus furnish example of this difficult virtue. He was presented in the Temple on the fortieth day after his birth. His blood flowed in the Jewish circumcision. The old man Simeon spoke of the sword of sorrow that would pierce the soul of Mary because of the obedience of Jesus even unto death (Lk 2:34–35). This sword went also into the heart of St. Joseph, even though he was not actually at the passion of Jesus, for the terrible future which was then announced was from that moment present to his mind to afflict his compassionate soul.

Scarcely had the Holy Family settled again in their home when an angel appeared to St. Joseph in a dream to bid him: "Arise, and take the child and his mother, and fly into Egypt; and be there until I shall tell you. For it will come to pass that Herod will seek the child to destroy him" (Mt 2:13). That jealous and angry prince, having seen the Magi come from the Orient to adore at the crib of the newborn king and being fearful for his throne, ordered the massacre of the innocents. It might well have

seemed strange and even bewildering to St. Joseph to be ordered to take
such a flight. He might well have asked why the Son of the Most High
was obliged to flee before a man, let alone such a man. He might well
have questioned why he must go into a distant and unknown country and
expose a frail infant to the weariness and perils of such a difficult journey;
why he must set forth during the very night when he received the order,
without preparation and provisions; why he must take refuge among a
people who were idolatrous and avowedly unfriendly to the Jews and live
there until it pleased providence to have him return, with no word at all
from the angel as to the duration of the exile. These were questions that
would naturally arise in such circumstances, at least in the minds of most
of us. Could religious obedience offer a more difficult trial? Yet, without
a word from Joseph, Mary, or Jesus, the Holy Family obeyed.

So we see that the obedience of our glorious patriarch was not less
perfect than his purity. Let us remark on its qualities. It is blind obedience
which does not stop to reason about the expediency of the command.
Joseph did not allege that he was ignorant of the way to Egypt; that
Jesus, still so young, could not endure such a journey; that he could not
set out in the night and run such risks on the way; that he could not find
means of livelihood when he would reach Egypt; and that, after all, God
could save his son from Herod without subjecting his parents to such
difficulties. Joseph's obedience is prompt and unhesitating. The Gospel
tells us that he arose and took the child and his mother by night and went
into Egypt (Mt 2:14). It is generous and constant obedience. Nothing
stopped St. Joseph; nothing discouraged him, though it seemed that he
lacked everything necessary. But he was sufficiently rich because Jesus
and Mary were with him. Even had he lacked this consolation, he would
have obeyed unto death, the death of the cross.

It is evident that our incomparable patron surpasses all other saints
in his purity and his obedience. He is also the greatest of them all in
his love of poverty. Joseph, as well as Mary, was of the tribe of Judah,
descended in direct line from David, and hence he was an heir to the
throne of Israel. Since he was destined to be the foster father and guardian of Jesus Christ, however, it was fitting that he be poor like the Savior,
first, out of respect for the divine sentence commanding humans to labor

and penance, and second, in order to be conformed to his divine son, who had not anywhere to rest his head and who was to proclaim voluntary poverty one of the evangelical beatitudes (Mt 5:6).

Far from trying to reclaim his ancestral crown, therefore, St. Joseph did not even seek to leave his obscure and poor state of life. He, rather, cherished his condition, which was so mean and humiliating in the eyes of the world. Submitting gladly to the decree of eternal justice that condemns us to earn our bread by the sweat of our brow, he lived as a simple artisan, a day workman in wood and iron. Even more, when his angelic spouse gave birth to the Savior, though he suffered to see Jesus born into such woeful misery, he contemplated in silent and perfect resignation the stable that served the little king for a palace, the manger that did for a cradle, the straw that formed his couch, the swaddling clothes that formed the royal mantle, and the animals that warmed Jesus with their breath while they did duty for courtiers.

Could poverty go further? What is the poverty of prophets, apostles, solitaries, and religious in general compared to the destitution we have just seen? Had we not reason to say that, in the praise of St. Joseph by the Holy Spirit, the word "just" is equivalent to the word "perfect"? And is it not right to conclude that, if he surpassed all other saints in purity and obedience, he was also the greatest in poverty, not in mind and in heart alone but in reality? Yes, with no fear of being considered rash, we may conclude that if Mary is queen of all saints through her virtues, through her glory in heaven, and through her privileges on earth, St. Joseph, though assuredly inferior to his celestial spouse, is after her the greatest saint we can honor on earth.

How could it be otherwise? When the adorable Trinity resolved to elevate the Virgin of Nazareth to the highest imaginable dignity, by accomplishing in her womb the mystery of the Incarnation and making her the finest masterpiece of grace after Christ's own humanity, God could only honor her further by making the man destined to share her supreme destiny the most worthy of all men in incomparable holiness. And Mary herself, by consenting to enter into her most holy marriage with Joseph, could but make him a sharer in all the gifts of the Holy Spirit, which she possessed in their plenitude, since in virtue of this unparalleled marriage whatever belonged to the one had to belong to the other. Hence, it follows that there was no sentiment, however noble; no affection, however pure; no faith, however living; no charity, however glowing, in the heart of the Virgin Mother that was not also in the heart of her virgin spouse. This was the reasoning of St. Bernardine of Siena, and it seems that everyone must see the justice of his reasoning.

We give praise, therefore, to your merits, O holy patriarch of the New Covenant, and we congratulate you on such great treasures. We bless God, who has shown himself so admirable in your sanctity. Be moved by our misery, and give us something from your abundance. As priests, some of us are privileged to bring onto the altar him whom you saw born in the stable and to receive into our hands and hearts him whom you carried in your arms. Make us, therefore, to share in your angelic purity that we may be less unworthy. Religious brothers and sisters, walking in your footsteps, vow themselves to a life of obedience, chastity, and poverty, that they may serve better and cause to be loved him whom you called on earth your adopted son. Obtain for them fidelity to their vows and perseverance in their vocation. Grant, also, that the young confided to our care may imitate your spotless purity and obedience so as to be distinguished always by pure morals, perfect docility to those directing them, and love for their duties. We ask this of you through the power of all those virtues we have just admired in you, and especially in the name of the glories that are their recompense. "Heart of Joseph, most pure and most faithful, pray for us."

The Glories of St. Joseph

The glories of St. Joseph are our next consideration. In the long genealogy written by St. Matthew and St. Luke to show that St. Joseph was of the most illustrious blood in the world and counted among his ancestors, patriarchs, prophets, heroes, and kings, we might find sufficient reason to attest his glory. We do not wish to seek therein, however, the titles to his glory. We would seek them, rather, in the prerogatives that faith reveals in him by reason of his alliance with Mary, and this despite the obscurity of his life in Nazareth. Though in that poor retreat of Nazareth his was not the power with which David defied so many enemies of his country, though he was not clothed with the purple or surrounded with the pomp of Solomon, though the crown of Josaphat was not on his head nor the scepter of Judah in his hand, we can only believe that he was superior to all his illustrious ancestors by the fact that he merited to be the spouse of the queen of heaven and earth, the foster father of Jesus Christ, and the trustee of the authority of the eternal father over his incarnate Word.

Think on the unimaginable glory of St. Joseph in sharing the honors, the spiritual wealth, and all the sentiments of the mother of God. This ineffable privilege was given him by the Lord through his uniting Joseph in marriage to the mother of his own son. The result is that when the Church proclaims Mary queen of patriarchs, prophets, apostles, martyrs, confessors, and virgins, Joseph is as a king, sharing all these glorious titles. The Congregation of Rites, in deciding that the name of this great saint could always be added to the prayer *A cunctis*, permitted it to be placed before those of St. Peter and St. Paul, so certain is the Church of the greatness conferred on him by his function of spouse of the adopted daughter of the Most High, the mother of the Word made flesh, and the spouse of the Holy Spirit.[38] Though the apostles were, indeed, called to preach the Gospel, the martyrs to combat for the faith, the doctors to instruct the people, the pastors to govern, the confessors and the just to fill the world with the good odor of Jesus Christ, St. Joseph alone was destined to be the guardian of the whole economy of the mystery of the redemption. The adorable Trinity initiated him into the plan of the Incarnation, not only in confiding to him all the destinies of the holy Virgin, which constituted his first glory, but even in making him the foster father of the Savior.

Surely we cannot refuse him the title which the Gospel gives him, which Mary recognized in him, and with which the divine infant glorified him, the title of "father of Jesus." St. Luke tells us, "His father and mother were wondering at those things which were spoken concerning him" (Lk 2:33). Mary, on finding Jesus in the Temple, cried out, "Your father and I have sought you, sorrowing" (Lk 2:48). St. Bernardine of

Siena says in his beautiful panegyric: "Oh, what sweet melody to the ears of St. Joseph, when he heard the infant God lisp his name, call him father, hold out to him his little arms, and put them about his neck to embrace and caress him." Of this same matter, St. Basil says that all the angels and highest seraphim in heaven bear the name only of servants of God. Joseph alone of the whole Church militant and triumphant has the honor of bearing the name of father of the savior of humanity.

Not only did St. Joseph bear this glorious name; he fulfilled all its functions by clothing and feeding Jesus Christ through his labor, his weariness, and the sweat of his brow. Scarcely had the eternal father seen his only son under the form of a sinner when he abandoned him to the tender charity of St. Joseph. In the Savior's poverty and woe, St. Joseph accepted his guardianship, took care of his needs, showed him the affection of his heart, and fulfilled all the duties of a father toward him. It was Joseph who procured for Jesus the food that made his sacred body grow to its full strength and stature and that filled his veins with the precious blood which was shed for the salvation of the world. Thus, God the Father gave divinity to Jesus Christ, Mary furnished him his body, and our patron saint preserved his existence. We can but marvel at such a plan of cooperation and the everlasting glory it gave St. Joseph. He was only a man, and yet, by his daily toil, he earned the means to clothe, support, and even feed his God. One can conceive that the older Joseph was praised for saving Egypt in the time of famine, that Jacob was blessed by his father for once giving him food, that Abraham was rewarded for giving hospitality to three angels who entered his tent, that celestial spirits could congratulate themselves on being allowed to bring food to Jesus in the desert after his temptations. But what are these praises, blessings, and favors compared to the privilege of nourishing for almost thirty years the sovereign Lord of angels and of humans?

We read in the Gospel that at the end of the world our Lord will say to the elect on his right hand: "I was hungry, and you gave me to eat; I was thirsty, and you gave me to drink; I was a stranger, and you took me in; naked, and you covered me" (Mt 25:35–36). We can but imagine that all the predestined, turning their gaze on our holy patron, will avow that these words are verified absolutely only by Joseph and Mary, because the needs of the child Jesus were the personal needs of his humanity and he actually received all these helps from his parents.

How happily did St. Joseph lavish his care on such a son! Think of his joy in having such a child for his own, to carry in his arms, to press against his heart, to cover with kisses, to protect as another guardian angel. I wish I could picture for you his loving transports, his sweet raptures, his delicious exaltations, his divine ecstasies in the midst of such privileges. Besides these dear intimacies so precious to his heart, he knew that he was really the delegate of the Holy Trinity, the virgin spouse of Mary, the foster father of the second person of the Trinity. To see the God, before whose throne they trembled as they adored, seated and eating at a poor table on earth between Mary and Joseph must have been a spectacle creating envy in the celestial court. One cannot even feebly conceive of those meals. One cannot begin to imagine the conversations that were the outward manifestation of the admirable accord, the ravishing union of hearts, in this visible and created trinity.

How your breast must have burned, O blessed father of my Savior, how fast your heart must have beat, and how living and intoxicating your emotions must have been when Jesus smiled at your paternal solicitude and rewarded it with new caresses. O Jesus, O Mary, O Joseph, little trinity of mutual lovers, what charms and pleasures were yours. No human words can ever express what passed in that house of Nazareth, which angels later carried into Italy, so as better to show the entire world the services that Mary and St. Joseph rendered in it to Jesus Christ.[39]

The crowning glory to which our illustrious patron was elevated now breaks on our eyes with more radiance than the noonday sun. St. Joseph held on earth the delegated authority of the eternal father of his divine son, who respectfully obeyed Joseph and Mary. One dares to say that Jesus was even more obedient to Joseph than to Mary, since Mary, while commanding Jesus, obeyed Joseph as the head of the Holy Family. To help us understand more exactly the authority of this great patriarch over Jesus Christ, the Gospel tells us that Joseph was charged with naming the divine infant (Mt 1:21). Mark the thought that flows from this fact. God the Father produces the Word by his understanding, but he gives him only the divine nature. Mary produced him in her virginal womb, but she gave him only the human nature. Joseph reproduced him entirely by his lips in naming him Jesus, since this sacred name includes both the divine and the human nature. See how Joseph appears again in this glorious privilege, as always, clothed with paternal power. To Joseph the angel pointed out the danger threatening the infant God from the jealousy of Herod; to him was given the command to take the child into Egypt; to him was indicated the time of the return to Nazareth; and for thirty years, his will served as the rule for the will of the Savior: "He was subject to them" (Lk 2:51).

Yes, it was principally our glorious patron who directed all the movements of Jesus Christ during his hidden life. In this regard, Joseph appears as the cherub who guided the triumphant chariot of Ezekiel (Ez 10:14–19), or better, as that angel who is charged with the sun, to direct his rising rays and withdraw his light seasonably. With infinite respect but also with all the authority of a father, Joseph, after seeking the divine will in sublime contemplation, would say to his adorable son, "Do this," and Jesus would do it. He would say, "Go there," and Jesus would go. "Work," and Jesus would work. "Rest," and Jesus would rest. Meanwhile, all the angels were in admiration of a God acting in blind obedience to a human being, to "the Lord obeying the voice of a human being" (Job 10:14). Though it was amazing in the time of King Hezekiah to have the sun put back ten degrees and stand still at the command of Joshua, it was not so much that a man commanded the sun as it was God who acceded to the prayer of Joshua.[40] Here, however, by a strange reversal, it was really the creature who was giving commands to the Creator. As God had to expiate by his obedience the disobedience of the human race, the Lord obeyed the voice of a human being. Could St. Joseph have been elevated to a more glorious dignity?

St. Augustine tells us that this mystery is represented by the astonishing dream of the older Joseph, who saw the sun, the moon, and the stars adoring him (Gn 37:9). He explains the matter as follows. Eleven stars adore, since the saints who are the bright stars of the firmament venerate the patriarch of the New Covenant as the father of their Savior. The moon adores him when Mary, figured by that queen of night, respects him as her spouse. The sun adores him when Jesus, the divine Sun of

Justice, obeys him as his father. Surely no one could refuse veneration to this great saint when he sees the master of heaven and earth, before whom all tremble and are as nothing, receive with docility the commands of this poor artisan and render him and Mary services that are humbling in themselves.

As for me, I fall at his feet. I am enraptured by such glory, and I willingly believe St. Joseph equal to the guardian angels. Did he not watch over the divine child committed to his care? I believe him equal to the archangels. Did he not communicate to Jesus and Mary the commands from heaven? I believe him equal to the virtues. Did he not govern the Holy Family? I believe him equal to the powers. Did he not manifest to the Egyptians the power of the Word made flesh, who would overthrow their idols? I believe him equal to the principalities and the dominions. Did he not command the king and queen of heaven? I believe him equal to the thrones. Did he not carry Jesus in his arms? I believe him equal to the cherubim. Did he not penetrate the deepest mysteries of wisdom incarnate? I believe him equal to the seraphim. Was he not raised on wings of fire to the heights of contemplation and did he not love Jesus Christ with a love so burning that, like the love of these blessed spirits, it transformed him, as St. Bernard says?

This supernatural transformation made St. Joseph worthy to be one of the visible trinity that the house of Nazareth sheltered. In this trinity, Mary held the place of God the Father, since she became the mother of the Savior just as he is the Savior's father. Jesus kept his rank in this trinity of earth, between Mary and Joseph, as between the Father and the Holy Spirit in the Trinity of heaven. St. Joseph held the place of the Holy Spirit, being the love of the mother and the infant God, as the Holy Spirit is the love of the Father and the Son. These three persons, who represent so visibly the invisible Trinity, represent also the unity of God, for the three of them have morally but one heart and one soul.

Do you think, my dearly beloved, that God could have elevated St. Joseph to a higher degree of glory and crowned him with greater honor? What may have been said in the conversations of this adorable family, what were the thoughts that enlightened their minds, the sentiments that animated their hearts—this is not given us to understand or even to know.

I can say only that I think the whole celestial court was attentive to this ravishing spectacle of heavenly love and listened devoutly to the conversations of Jesus, Mary, and Joseph.

What more can we add to make clear the glorious privileges of St. Joseph? Let us conclude with that happy and unique privilege of our illustrious patron, the one that makes him the universally recognized patron of a happy death. St. Joseph had the unimaginable privilege of dying with Jesus and Mary close by his deathbed to assist him in his last moments. These two, in gratitude for the tireless services he had given them with such loving zeal, now gave him theirs, vying in tender care to lavish on him the aids of a divine tenderness. Surely in this supreme moment, troops of angels came to make St. Joseph's blessed dying joyful with their songs.

St. Bernardine of Siena says he does not know how to express the consolations, the sweetness, the lights, the tender emotions, and the flames of love that moved this soul, blessed above all souls, in its passage to eternity. Undoubtedly, Jesus held one of his arms beneath the weary head and the other he placed on that heart on which he had so often rested in his infancy, piercing it with the darts of his charity as he treasured its every beat. Therefore, the Church compares the death of St. Joseph sometimes to a peaceful sleep, such as that of a child on its mother's breast, and sometimes to an aromatic torch that in dying breathes out an ever-sweeter odor.

After considering all these privileges, one readily admits the opinion of those who think that this great saint rose with Jesus Christ, for he was dead at least three years before the passion of the Savior. St. Bernardine of Siena, preaching at Padua, authorized this pious belief by crying out before a great audience: "I assure you that St. Joseph is body and soul in heaven, shining with glory." Fact added confirmation to this belief, for there appeared immediately above the head of the celebrated speaker a miraculous cross of gold, which was seen by all the listeners.[41]

However this came to be, we can now very easily imagine this glorious patriarch in the height of heaven above all the saints and angels. For so many virtues and privileges on earth, for so many services rendered to the mother of God and the son of the Most High, he must, as

St. Augustine says, be placed immediately after Mary and very close to Jesus. It is indeed fitting that the Holy Family be in paradise as it was on earth. Who could dare to separate in eternity what grace so tightly bound in time? We must definitely conclude, from all we have just meditated, that he whom we honor, having been during his life the greatest of saints, is also in heaven the most elevated in glory after Jesus and Mary.

The New Joseph

Let us go, then, to the new Joseph. Oh, let us give him the homage of a sincere devotion. We cannot refuse this honor when we see him honored by angels, by the queen of virgins, by Jesus Christ himself, and by the whole Church, which proclaims him the protector of Christians in general, and in particular of religious orders. We can but run to his protection when we hear St. Teresa of Avila assure us that she never invoked him without being heard immediately. She put under his protection the first monastery of her reform, saying that since Jesus Christ had refused him nothing during the time he submitted to him on earth, he will refuse him even less now that he reigns with him in glory. Should one not, therefore, see all Christians at his feet, glorifying him by their devotion?

Let us cast ourselves into his arms, then, as in olden times the children of Jacob cast themselves into the arms of their brother. Just as the older Joseph comforted them in their needs and loaded them with gifts, the new Joseph will care for us (Gn 42:1–45:25). "Go to Joseph, and do all that he shall say to you" (Gn 41:55). Alas, like the Egyptians of that time, we have had also our years of abundance and growth, happy years which scarcely passed the number seven. During this time we amassed treasures of virtue; but without foresight and wisdom, we have perhaps dissipated our spiritual wealth, lost all our merits. Now our soul, sterile and dry, is a prey to scarcity or even famine. Let us cry for mercy to St. Joseph, and he will open the granaries of grace to enrich us.

"O chaste spouse of the Virgin and foster father of my Savior, you open your ears to all who implore your assistance, and so from this moment, I invoke you with new confidence for the priests, brothers, and sisters who have the honor of belonging to a community of which you are the powerful protector. I implore you also for the young whose minds we are charged to develop and whose hearts we are to form. Can you be deaf to my prayer when its end is to make us more worthy of you, your divine son, and our own sublime destiny? Ah, I beg you in the name of your celestial spouse, who is our mother, and through the love of your adorable son for our souls, hear our prayers on this day consecrated to your memory. Hear especially the prayer I address you and shall often repeat: to show yourself always my defender and my father, and when the moment of my death comes, when my soul, about to quit my body, will pour out its last sigh, O Joseph, show yourself to it as its advocate before its judge, and refresh my dying eyes with your dear presence. Amen."

Reception of the Habit for Carmelite Sisters

· ·

I am the Way, the Truth, and the Life. (Jn 14:6)

In the school of Christ you learned to put aside your old self, and put on the new self. (Eph 4:21–24)

As I was prostrate before the Lord who was preparing me for this ministry among you, I felt that the Holy Spirit was placing on my lips the lovely passage of the great apostle's letter to the faithful of Ephesus: In the school of Christ you learned to put aside your old self, and put on the new self. What could be more appropriate to the spirit of this ceremony in your honor and to the needs of this assembly than the explanation and practice of this mysterious divesting and transformation demanded, by the doctor of nations, of all Christians in general and of those called to the religious life in particular?[42]

Therefore, it is to each of you that, after first addressing these words to myself, I say: "Learn from Christ to put aside the old self and to put on the new self." But I am addressing you in a particular way, since that is the purpose of your receiving the habit and the grace to ask for as you begin your novitiate. This is not merely a question of changing worldly fashions for clothes of a different quality, style, and color; that would not need to be blessed by the Word of God. It is, rather, a question of effecting in your life, in the eyes of faith, the transformation symbolized by the changing of attire, which will take place before this assembly. This is what I will try to explain, with the help of grace, by meditating on this passage with you. What is this old self that you must put aside and this new self that you must put on?

The Old Self

What is this old self, which is so important for you to put aside? To ponder deeply this truth, we must first of all recall what Adam, the first man, was like when he came from the hands of his Creator. Fashioned in the image of the adorable Trinity, he resembled the Father by his memory, which retained the notions of God he had received and which is still within us as the principle of our knowledge of God, the world, and ourselves. He resembled the Son by his intelligence, for he was given the necessary light to understand these very notions. And he resembled the Holy Spirit by his will or his heart, for he loved this knowledge and became attached to it in such a way that his soul was enlightened by the deepest faith and tasted a sweet friendship which was totally divine. His body, which was impassive, immortal, and totally submissive, brought him the homage of all creation. Through his vision, he enjoyed all physical beauty; through hearing, all melodies; through smell, all odors; through taste, all flavors; through touch, all pleasant sensations.

In this happy state, the first man was truly his own master, king, and pontiff of the universe. Since he was destined to see God in heaven, his soul, enriched by all the gifts of the Spirit, was in touch with the angels, linking him to the invisible world. Meanwhile his body, nourished by the fruit of life, put him in communication with the visible world, which he governed wisely and justly, without being dominated by any material object. He was, therefore, a person of interiority, held to this earth by nothing other than the tips of his toes. He was caught up in God, whose perfections he could see in all creatures as in a mirror, spiritualized, as it were, totally celestial. In this glorious condition, his innocence was like a mantle of honor, concealing his nudity from his own eyes, and like a ray of his future glory, serving as clothing. This is Adam created by the Lord in justice and holiness, that is, indeed, perfect. The word "justice" derives from an old Latin verb *iustare*, which means "to be adjusted"—that is, conformed to the eternal rule or infinite perfection.

But many important advantages were dependent on the union of humanity with God, who communicated life in this way. Once this covenant was destroyed, Adam lost all his treasures, without being able to reclaim linkage to his brilliant destinies. As you know, this supernatural union did not last long. The spirit of our first father was soon separated from that of his Creator through disbelief, when he chose to believe more in Satan, who promised him deification if he ate the forbidden fruit, than in the very truth threatening him with death if he touched it. His will was diverted from that of the eternal one when he followed the desires of lust, and his body, influenced by sensuality, revolted against his soul after he ate fruit from the tree of knowledge of good and evil.

From then on, his intelligence, deprived of the light of the Word, was dulled and fell into the darkness of error. His memory lost the notions it had received from God as from its principle. His will, having been tainted, was no longer guided by the Spirit. His heart became corrupt. His emotions deteriorated, and a sense of degradation made him ashamed of his nudity. At the same time, the creatures which had been submissive until then rose up against him and hastened his death. By losing his innocence, he lost his glorious immortality, and through his gross desires, he became like a brute.

Then, after this degenerate man had girded himself with large fig leaves to hide his shame, much more than to protect himself from the dangers of the climate, God, in his mercy and without doubt to remind him constantly of his degradation, gave him clothing made of animal skin. This shows that our clothing is a visible sign and like a sacrament of our humiliation. How foolish to let it become a subject of vanity!

That is why, when I see you dressed as the people of the world, it is like seeing beggars covered with tattered clothes, admiring themselves and believing themselves very rich because they are hidden under a piece of used material that has been dyed a scarlet color.

Leave these worldly fashions, as a detachment from foolish pride, but in doing so, put aside your old self, which hides this shame and deprivation. This old self is comprised of a triple concupiscence, which we have inherited with original sin—that is, the inclination to pride, ambition, and sensuality—which was the downfall of our first parents. These inclinations made them want to be equal to God, using a fruit, which God had reserved as a sign of their dependence, to satisfy their carnal desire, like an animal satisfying instinct (Ps 49:13). This is the source of self-indulgence. In writing to the Galatians, St. Paul describes the sad results: "The works of the flesh are antagonisms, factions, dissensions, divisions, idolatry, drunkenness, jealousies, cruelties, apathy, quarrels, and other crimes about which I have spoken to you already. I declare to you that those who do such dissolute things will never enter the kingdom of heaven" (Gal 5:20–21).

No doubt, you have not known such disordered ways, and the Christian education you received in your early years has protected you from such humiliating and criminal passions. It does not follow, however, that you have not had to groan under the weight of the old self, because it is like a poisoned root that spreads its branches in all directions and spoils our actions. Does not sight expose us to carnal love, by seeing natural and created beauties, rather than beauty which is uncreated and eternal? Does not hearing expose us to licentious words and erotic songs? Does not smell weaken our will by breathing the sweetness of perfumes? Does not taste dull the spirit by eating well, and does not touch make our body a heavy burden that bends us toward the earth when we should be breathing nothing but heaven?

Have you never experienced these involuntary tendencies toward physical things? St. John says that in the world all is pride, because most of our behaviors or actions are spoiled through self-love; through concupiscence of the eyes, because they want to see and to possess all that flatters; and through lust of the flesh, because everything on earth tends to sensuality (1 Jn 2:16–17). It is true that you have been protected from these worldly tendencies from your youth. You did not have to be concerned only about dignity and honors, rich clothes, beautiful homes, valuable furniture, delightful gardens, gold and silver, entertainment, theater, and carnal or sensual pleasures. Have you never given in to the desire of being esteemed by others, of having the merit of thinking only of God and of acting only for his glory?

If the greatest Carmelite saint, St. Teresa, saw in the image of a cluster of spoiled grapes her virtues and her best actions impaired by self-interest or by lack of truth and purity of intention, what reasons do you have in this regard not to fear pride or the desire for esteem and praise?

Consider briefly the details of your life, one day even, and perhaps you will discover that there is not a moment when this passion, this child of pride, does not exercise its power on our words and actions.

I ask you, could there be an enemy whose constant attacks require more vigilance? If pride alone already causes so much conflict in life, even in the silence of retreat, then what will be the consequences of the concupiscence of the eyes and flesh? All this is part of the old self, which you have inherited through original sin just as Adam's other children, and which, according to St. Paul, "makes all creatures groan, like those suffering the pains of giving birth, until all creation is delivered from this bondage" (Rom 8:22–23).

But let all creation be consoled. The day of freedom is near since, by reducing all his enemies to serve as his footstool, Jesus Christ, the new man, must renew, with the earth and the heavens, human nature in his chosen ones and restore it to its original state. Therefore, struggle with courage against yourself, for you have a share in this religious renewal. You must triumph over the world and its vanity, the flesh and its concupiscence, pride and its prompting, so you can truthfully say, as this virgin martyr of the early centuries: Among us, the soul commands and the body obeys.

Christ, the New Self

In fact, it is precisely this to which you have committed yourselves through your Baptism, since you are, therefore, dead to sin and have been buried with Jesus Christ in the waters, which, by flowing on your head three times, purified your soul: In Christ . . . put off your old self. Therefore, in triumphantly placing at the foot of the altar these remains taken from the enemy of your salvation, these worldly pomps, this sumptuous luxury of the old self which you are wearing for the last time, divest yourselves of the triple concupiscence and clothe yourselves with the new self who is Christ: In Christ . . . put on the new self.

Who will deliver me from this body of sin (Rom 8:24)? Such was the cry of St. Paul as he endured the burden of the old self, and no doubt such is the cry that would escape from your hearts, if you were to speak in my place. The answer, which the great apostle was then given, is also the one I would give at this moment: "My grace is enough for you," said the divine master (2 Cor 12:9).

It is, in fact, while expecting the dissolution of the old self through death that grace is sufficient to triumph over its corruption. You will surely triumph if you know how to put on the new self, as you were taught in the school of Christ (Eph 4:21).

But, who is this new self, and how can we be united to it to the point of wearing it like clothing? Listen again and admire the means of your salvation. This new self is Jesus Christ, the second Adam, created more perfectly than the first in justice and holiness. By taking the form of a serpent, Lucifer succeeded in separating us from our Creator and preventing us from going to heaven by tempting us through pride, ambition, and sensuality. Then, it was decided in the eternal counsels that the Word, by hiding himself, in turn, under the veil of our humanity, would reestablish the degenerate self in his own person by returning it to its original state. He would do so by teaching us to overcome pride through humble obedience, ambition through poverty, and lust through mortification, which entails the destruction of the old self or the triple concupiscence.

In fact, since the old self had become carnal, preferring nothing but the flesh, the Son of God became flesh in order to draw us to him by his glory, grace, and truth (Jn 1:14). But through the Incarnation he took only the resemblance of the old self, because he was born of a virgin and had no more a father with regard to his body than he had a mother with regard to his divinity. In this he resembled more fully the first Adam who did not owe his body to human generation either. From then on, he was neither soiled by original sin, nor subjected to the triple concupiscence, which is the consequence in each of us. He would have neither suffered nor died if he had not resolved to do so for us before entering into the glory promised to the innocent and if he had not conquered Satan for us beforehand by repairing the pride of human nature through his humiliation, ambition by his total divesting of self, and sensuality by his mortification.

This is the old self renewed or the new self, the second Adam, even more perfect than the first, since he has in himself all the treasures of knowledge and wisdom; he is truth, justice, and the very author of grace. Therefore, his intelligence is more enlightened, his will has more uprightness, and his body has more submission to his soul than had the first man. This is truly the new self that you must put on (Eph 4:24). Gladly acknowledge these aspects in Jesus Christ, your model. Admire how he overcomes the old self of which he has but the resemblance.

The old self is proud, disobedient, and wants to be equal to God; Jesus Christ is humble and submitted to the father unto death, after having hidden under the veil of flesh and coming for us to the very depths of degradation where we had fallen (Phil 2:6–8). For this he was born in a stable between two animals. The old self is ambitious, greedy, miserly, always wanting more; Jesus Christ is poor, dispossessed of all, and having nothing but a crib to lie in, the earth as a resting place, and a cross for a deathbed. Finally, the old self is sensual, an amateur of carnal pleasures, good food, and its own comfort; Jesus Christ mortified his chaste body through work, fasting, and suffering. He also told his disciples: Blessed are the poor, blessed those who mourn, blessed those who have a pure heart, blessed those who suffer (Lk 6:20–22). Consequently, and this concerns all Christians in general, we cannot belong to the Savior and then enter heaven without renouncing here below—at least in heart and spirit—honors, riches, and pleasures. In fact, that is what we promised through Baptism, when we renounced Satan, his pomps, and his works.

But other than this affective renunciation, there is another which Jesus Christ demands of those he calls to religious life. One day, he said to someone who asked him what he must do to obtain eternal life: Observe the commandments. Since the person told Jesus that he had observed them since his early childhood, the divine master added, "If you would be perfect, go, sell everything you possess, and give it to the poor, then come and follow me" (Mt 19:21).

There are, therefore, two different ways and two different forms of life to follow in order to go to heaven: that of the commandments, which constitute the Christian life, and that of the counsels, which are included in the religious life or a perfect life. You wish to embrace the latter. In this way, you will put aside the old self much more efficiently than the simple faithful, because this does not mean merely renouncing the three objects of concupiscence through love. In reality, it means being obedient by renouncing your will, chaste by having no other spouse than Jesus Christ, and poor by having nothing of your own and using nothing without permission.

This is also the example given by your divine master, since he lived in absolute renunciation of his will, in virginity, and in poverty. He came to us in this state, saying to each one: "If any want to be my disciple, let them renounce themselves and take up their cross and follow me" (Mt 16:24). And again: Those who do not renounce everything they possess cannot be my disciples—everything, without exception, including their father, mother, brothers, sisters, their fields and their house (Mt 10:37–38).

So much does this constitute the religious state in which you will suffer trials that we cannot see it otherwise, since this state is impossible without the three vows of poverty, chastity, and obedience. Furthermore, our Lord himself vowed to live poverty, chastity, and obedience before inviting his closest associates to do so. It is, therefore, in his footsteps, and in the company of Mary, his Blessed Mother, the apostles, and a multitude of religious saints, men and women, that you commit yourselves by entering this monastery. In this way, therefore, you will put on the new self.

Recall that when Jacob plotted to have the blessing of Isaac his father, following his mother's persistence, he put on his brother Esau's robe and covered his neck and hands with goatskins (Gn 27:15–16). Transfer this physical action to a moral one, and you will put on the new self or Jesus Christ. That is, do not limit yourselves to one tunic, one belt, and sandals, which recall so well the clothing of the old penitent self as well as that of the Savior; instead, let your soul and your exterior behavior be filled with the mind and manner of Jesus Christ (Phil 2:5). This is what it means to put on the new self, and St. Paul is my witness: "Put on the Lord Jesus Christ" (Rom 13:14).

It follows that your whole novitiate, rather, your whole life, must have as its purpose to assimilate so well the thoughts, judgments, desires, words, and actions of Jesus Christ, so that you can say with the great apostle: "I live; rather no, I live no more; it is Christ who lives in me" (Gal 2:20). This is how the tree, which has been grafted, lives from the sap of the trunk on which it has been grafted.

This is not enough; you must identify yourselves with your model, not only in order to become a faithful copy, but to become somewhat another Christ, according to his request to the father for his followers, that they become one with me as I am one with you, Father, and that they be in me as I am in them (Jn 17:21). Is this possible? Yes, and this is how. Just as intelligence and will in the body and soul of Jesus Christ are united by divine nature through the Incarnation, so is our spirit united to the spirit of Jesus Christ through faith, our heart to his heart through charity, and our body to his body through Communion. He also invites you to develop this union within you by saying: I am the life, the way, and the truth—life through my sacraments, truth by my doctrine, and the way by my example (see Jn 14:6).

How admirable the transformation that will take place in you through your union with Jesus Christ, and how wonderful the characteristics of this union. Total union in being, intelligence, will, body—an intimate union, since it goes as far as living the life of Jesus Christ; an effective union, since it restores to us all we had lost in Adam and through it we become the same moral person with Jesus Christ; a glorious union, giving supernatural merit to our actions and the right to eternal glory. With this in mind, how could you not expand your soul?

This very union is proposed to you today in the name of Jesus Christ, by the chapter of this community; this is what I myself am offering to you on their behalf, by opening the doors to this charitable dwelling.

The deep emotions of your heart, the happiness that fills your soul, and your tears of tenderness speak eloquently of your eagerness to respond. Rejoice, therefore, and sing the canticle of your deliverance, saying with David: "My father and my mother have abandoned me, but the Lord has taken care of me" (Ps 27:10). You have wanted so long to enter this community, which is so regular and edifying. You longed for the day when you could divest yourselves of the ignominy of this world to take the habit of Our Lady of Mount Carmel. Your hopes are accomplished. The minister of Jesus Christ is now ready to bless the veil that will hide you from our eyes and the habit with a form and color that will remind you that you have left the old self to put on the new self. Amen.

Chapter 2

SPIRITUAL EXERCISES

The selected exercises that follow are examples of the spiritual program that Moreau adapted for Holy Cross religious from the *Spiritual Exercises* of St. Ignatius of Loyola. Here, Moreau summarized in practical methods of prayer how he envisioned his religious could conform their lives to Christ. He would write more than one set, adapting them, with slight variations, for priests, brothers, and sisters. These come from the exercises for the Salvatorists or priests (1859 edition). More specifically, these exercises are tailored for novices in Holy Cross, although they were also used by seminarians and priests after their novitiate. The novitiate is a year of intensive prayer, reflection, and spiritual formation in preparation for religious vows.

As Moreau explains, St. Ignatius divided his exercises into four weeks. Moreau maintains that structure, though on occasion he adds multiple meditations for the same day. While Ignatius designed the *Spiritual Exercises* primarily for spiritual directors or retreat directors, Moreau is writing directly for the individual Holy Cross novice. He eliminates the intermediary, mainly by providing more direction and guidance through the meditations. For this reason, Moreau's exercises are longer than those of Ignatius.

Moreau also spreads out the weeks of meditation according to the liturgical calendar of Holy Cross feast days. The first week makes up the purgative way and corresponds to the beginning of the novitiate. The second week, or illuminative way, is the week leading up to the Feast of St. Joseph. The third week, which continues the illuminative way, corresponds to the week leading up to the Feast of the Sacred Heart of Jesus. The fourth week, or unitive way, happens either at the end of the academic year or before the Feast of the Assumption of Mary.

This meditation style specifically works the imagination. The prelude structure prepares one for prayer; the colloquy (literally "conversation") and the spiritual bouquet serve to draw it to a close.

Biblical references have been added in parentheses. Where Moreau provides a scriptural text from the Latin Vulgate, the editors have supplied the English in parentheses. The biblical quotations in the text attempt to preserve Moreau's translation of scripture. References to nonbiblical sources are indicated in footnotes where possible.

K.G. and A.G.

Second Week: The Illuminative Way

. . . .

During the novitiate, preceding the Feast of St. Joseph

S aint Ignatius divides his *Spiritual Exercises* into four parts, each of which is assigned a separate week (and that makes for four weeks). It is important not to begin the succeeding ones without having completed the preceding parts, but for beginning the novitiate, it is not necessary to have undertaken each in its entirety or to have spent the full eight days with it as indicated. The purpose of that first "week" is to attain contrition for sins, to be reconciled with God or at least to be strengthened in the spirit of repentance. Some people reach these goals in less time than others, and so the exercises need to be shortened or lengthened depending on the needs of each person. The usual length of time needed for each of the four parts, however, is one week.

If it meets your needs better, for example, you could spend the first three days of the retreat meditating on the first three topics of the previous week's exercises for the purgative way; the next three days could be spent on the first three topics of the exercises for the illuminative way; and the final two days could be given over to the first two exercises of the last section, which we will present later on, for the unitive way. This sort of method would be useful for the annual community retreat at the motherhouse each year.

Some of those called to make these exercises will only be ready to begin the purgative way. They will be cleansed of their bad habits and sins through the tears of repentance and the practice of mortification. They will need to meditate on what can lead them to heartfelt compunction, to detesting their faults, and to the necessary improvements in their lives. All of that is the fruit of meditating on the offense done to the divine majesty, on the shame and the punishment of sins, and on a human being's ultimate purpose in life.

Others will have already made some progress. They are already on their journey along the illuminative way, as it is called. Freed from the slavery of concupiscence that clouds the mind, liberated from bad habits that prevented them from seeing the good, assisted by the Holy Spirit who dwells in them with his special gifts, these people have deep insights into the works of justice and piety. They find they are strongly drawn to practice all the virtues until they arrive at the vision of God in heaven. The topics of meditation fitting for them are those drawn from the mysteries of both the public and private life of Jesus Christ, exemplar of all virtues and source of all justice. This is the subject of the second part of these exercises.

Still others will have already reached the summit of perfection and now walk in the unitive way. It is given this name because the will of these people is, so to speak, united with that of God, and they are united to him by bonds of the most ardent love. Such as these need to meditate preferably on the glorious mysteries of Jesus Christ, for example, his resurrection and his ascension.

Preliminary Exercise

The evening before the retreat, around 5:30 p.m., do some meditative reading or at least pay close attention to the following reflection.

I presuppose that you are reconciled with God by means of the exercises for the purgative way. They comprise the "Retreat to Begin the Novitiate," which you ought to have already completed. If you were already in the state of grace, I presume that you are now strengthened in the spirit of repentance and eager to walk more zealously on the way of salvation. Here we want to shed some light on what you are to do and to help you do it in the fullness of God's designs for your soul. This is also the goal that St. Ignatius proposes in the exercises, which you will soon begin, known as the illuminative way.[1] What could be more apt than to teach you the obligations of being a Christian and the path you need to follow to reach God, your ultimate goal, or to show you Jesus Christ walking on ahead of you? He himself has done first what he now asks of you, inviting you to follow him as the most perfect exemplar you could imitate.

That is the goal of this second part of the retreat during which you will place yourself under the gaze of the divine Savior. He is the heavenly original of which you need to become a living copy. Each day you will hear the equivalent of these words of the eternal God to Moses: "See that you make them according to the pattern shown you on the mountain" (Ex 25:40). For, as the apostle says: "Those whom he foreknew he predestined to become true images of his son, that the son might be the firstborn of many brothers and sisters; these are the ones he justified, and those he justified he also glorified" (Rom 8:29–30).

If you want to attain the glory of paradise, imitate Jesus Christ insofar as it depends on you. Let yourself be deeply permeated not only with the good intentions of reaching that end but also of putting that imitation of Christ into practice. Moreover, the first meditations of this week are for teaching this to you.

St. Ignatius calls this meditation foundational because all the other meditations of this week of retreat and even the exercises of the following week are based on it and follow directly from it, for they all have as their subject matter Jesus Christ as seen in the different events of his life and death. St. Ignatius entitled it "On the Reign of Jesus Christ" because the divine Savior is presented there as a powerful king.[2] Wanting to increase the number of his subjects, this king proposes that all who already live under his sway would also reign with him in heaven, provided that they follow him on the expedition that he is preparing and that they share with him the work and the dangers of the conquest he is considering. Would you hesitate to place yourself under the standard of such a leader? Hesitation at this point would make me fear either that you are refusing to respond to the end for which you were created or at least that you are taking a route not leading directly to that end. Jesus Christ is the way that leads to God, your goal. Refusing to follow Jesus would be like a wayfarer lost in a vast wilderness who continues to walk on the shifting sand that can give no indications of where the road is.

And so, try to think over the topic of your first prayer period for tomorrow so well that you could truly say, without ever going back on your word, what the scribe in the Gospel said to Jesus Christ: "Master, I will follow you wherever you go" (Mt 8:19).

After having put off your old self with all its bad habits, if you truly want to follow Jesus wherever he goes, this second retreat, which is about to begin, will form in you the new self, that is, Jesus Christ. You are about to be clothed with the mind and heart of the master, reproducing in yourself his thoughts, his feelings, his wishes, his words, and his actions—in short, everything about his life that relates to your vocation. From now on, your conscience will give you the evidence that the apostle of the nations gave about himself when he wrote: "It is no longer I who live but Jesus Christ who lives in me" (Gal 2:20). Jesus Christ speaks using my mouth, prays using my lips, acts using my body. St. Vincent de Paul used to put this into practice very well. He had the habit of asking himself even about the details of his actions: What would Jesus Christ do now in my situation?

Note well that it is not yet my intention to speak to you about that mystical life which focuses on thinking, loving, speaking, and acting the way Jesus did and which is the fruit of this entire retreat. No, for the moment it is a question only of what constitutes the life of a Christian. You have to be a Christian before you can become a perfect Christian.

And so we are led to ask in what this life, which makes a person a Christian, consists, what its purpose is, and what its obligations are. These are three things you need to know if you are to know the very basis of our religion. I will now try to help you understand what these three things are.

First of all, Jesus Christ himself taught us in what his life in us consists when he said that he is the vine and that we are the branches (Jn 15:5). St. Paul puts it in another way when he writes that "the Church is but one body of which Jesus Christ is the leader or the head and we its members" (1 Cor 12:27). Likewise with a vine. The branches receive life from the sap that the main stem brings to them. They are united with it and together are but one vine. And just as the limbs of a human being have no other life except the one they receive from the head with which they are but one body, so does the life of a Christian come only from being one with Jesus Christ. Together they form, so to speak, but one composite, one moral entity, one person.

This union of the individual with Jesus Christ came about in you through Baptism, which grafted you, so to speak, onto this divine head of the body. Confirmation then strengthened and sealed, as it were, this union. Eucharistic communion renders this union more and more intimate and indissoluble, for Jesus Christ says that he dwells in whoever eats his flesh and drinks his blood (Jn 6:56). The conclusion of this is that mortal sin is like a paralysis that prevents the flow of life from head to limbs or like a string tied so tightly around a stem that sap cannot rise from the roots through the trunk to the branches.

Furthermore, even though venial sin is not as great an obstacle to life, it attacks the source of life nonetheless. It is like a body fluid thick and noxious that hinders the free flow of nutrients to the body. But thanks to sacraments instituted by Jesus Christ, Penance and Extreme Unction, which is the perfect completion of Penance, destroy the obstacles and give the life of Jesus Christ complete freedom to flow into our soul.[3]

And so, do you now have a better inkling of the purpose of Jesus Christ's life in you? It is the fount of all your greatness, the source of all your merits, and the foundation of all your hope.

1. The fount of your greatness. For what are you, really, in and of yourself? Nothingness, wretchedness, and sin. But united with Jesus Christ, how noble and preeminent! You may consider this situation as if it were the marriage of a poor peasant girl with a king who is ruler of the whole world. Would we not forget everything she used to be and see now only the splendor of her high rank? Similarly, by your union with Jesus Christ, you have become his brother, coheir along with him, friend of God, and God's adopted son. Separated from Jesus Christ, however, by mortal sin, you were the object of God's contempt and wrath, the plaything of the demons, and a victim destined for hell. Reflect on all this attentively and learn the priceless benefits of your union with our Savior.

2. Next, consider this union as the source of all your merits. Even though it is true that your actions, separated from Jesus Christ, are not always sinful, it is also certain that they cannot merit heaven for you any more than all the virtues we admire in the most illustrious pagans of old.

They were, says St. Augustine, among the great people of the earth but not among the heroes, for they were not following the true path.[4] You, on the contrary, are united to your divine master by habitual grace. The least of your acts, even as small a thing as a sigh, enjoys the influence of that union and will take on an infinite value. It will merit for you paradise or a higher degree of eternal glory. The reason for this is quite simple. It will not be you who are acting all alone but Jesus Christ acting along with you (Gal 2:20). You will share, therefore, in his merits, almost as a graft from wild stock shares in the nature of the tree onto which it has been grafted (Rom 11:17).

3. Now you can understand how the life of Jesus Christ in you becomes the foundation of all your hope, that is, of your glorious resurrection and your eternal happiness. Paul says in his letter to the Romans: "Now that we have been justified by faith, we are at peace with God . . . and we boast of our hope for the glory of God. But not only that—we even boast of our afflictions. We know that affliction makes for endurance, and endurance for tested virtue, and tested virtue for hope. And this hope will not leave us disappointed, because the love of God has been poured out in our hearts through the Holy Spirit who has been given to us" (Rom 5:1–5). "There is no condemnation now for those who are in Christ Jesus" (Rom 8:1), who no longer live according to the tendencies of the flesh but to those of the Spirit (Rom 8:4–6). "Consequently, if Jesus Christ is in you, the body is dead because of sin while your soul lives because of justice. If the spirit of him who raised Jesus Christ from the dead dwells in you, then he who raised Christ from the dead will bring your mortal bodies to life also, through his Spirit dwelling in you" (Rom 8:10–11). "The Spirit of adoption himself gives witness with our spirit that we are children of God. But, if we are children, we are heirs as well, heirs of God, heirs with Christ, if only we suffer with him so as to be glorified with him" (Rom 8:16–17).

Such is henceforth your consolation in the midst of all your work throughout life and the trials that accompany your vocation. Filled then with the liveliest yet tender confidence, you will go straight to God when you die—to God as judge, to be sure, but also to God as your father. If he is united with you now, if he lives in you because of the faithful accomplishment of the many obligations required of you by this divine life, have you anything to fear? No, of course not. Is not your life holy even now? This new life in you compels you not just to preserve yourself in a perfect purity of heart and body lest you banish Jesus Christ from your soul or break your union with him. It also makes you love always and tenderly everyone who has become Christian because of the same faith and use of the same sacraments as you.

This union with Jesus Christ gives an impulse to look more closely at him in the gospels and in the letters of St. Paul, to love him, and to make others love him as much as you can, in order to atone for insults against him, to rejoice in the success of whatever makes him better known and adored, and to give yourself wholeheartedly to work for that purpose according to your vocation and to obedience. These, then, will be the dispositions you want to foster in yourself during this retreat, if you are to take full advantage of it.

And so, put your whole self into acquiring and keeping this divine life in you. Remember that you need only to will it for this great undertaking to be successful for you. What is unavailable to a will that is genuine, strong, and full of life? Do not forget to include trust in God and to carry out very carefully the directives at the end of this first exercise, the end of day one. Doing so will ensure your success for this retreat, for you are now aware of the three main dispositions upon which it is built.

Week Two: Day One

Foundational meditation: the call of Jesus Christ and his kingdom

Jesus Christ came to establish his kingdom on earth, but we realize that it is not a sovereign, inalienable domination that God exerts on every creature. *Quis enim potest resistere voluntati eius?* ("Who can resist his will?" [Rom 9:19].) It is rather the realm of love that his free-willed creatures build for him in their heart by their voluntary submission to him and which gives so very much glory to God. This is the meaning of the prayer, *Adveniat regnum tuum* ("Your kingdom come" [Mt 6:10]).

All Christians are obliged to work toward that end in accord with the graces given them, by first of all resisting in themselves the world, the flesh, and the devil—enemies of Jesus Christ and their own as well. All who are called to a life of great perfection will have to begin the battle there and never lay down their weapons.

First Prelude

Put yourself consciously in the presence of God.

Second Prelude

Reflect on your topic of meditation in these words of our Lord to St. Matthew, "Follow me," and in the response of the apostle who "got up and followed the master" (Mt 9:9).

Third Prelude

Place before your eyes the image of Jesus Christ who, during the thirty three years of his life on earth, sought to form his own disciples by the force of his teachings in order to win souls for him through their own example and teaching. "He even went through all the stages of human life," says St. Irenaeus, "that he might be an example for everyone."[5] Then, represent him to yourself as a completely humble and loving man. According to St. Jerome, there was something celestial in the way he looked and the way he looked at you. St. Bernard adds that he enthralled the people around him.

Take these characteristics of Jesus and add to them the notion of a great king to whom was given all power in heaven and on earth. In your imagination, hear him invite everyone, and you in particular, to imitate his way of life and his zeal. Listen to him closely. He promises to help you with his grace and to ask of you nothing that he himself has not done first.

Finally, hear him assuring anyone who responds to his gentle invitations a hundredfold in this world, especially peace of heart, and a crown of victory in eternity whose shining brilliance will correspond to how closely we have each followed his example on earth (Mt 19:29).

The prince of this world, one formerly chosen by God who now calls on the services of his own subjects, is a sham. The stipulations he exacts and the promises he makes are all impossible.

But in Jesus Christ, those promises are real and true. He introduces himself to the world, addressing these words to every human being:

"My plan is to drive out all my enemies from my realm, to establish my reign on earth, and thus to win my kingdom.

"Assured beforehand of victory, I have no need of foreign assistance. *Torcular calcavi solus et de gentibus non est vir mecum.* ("I have trodden the wine press alone, and from the peoples, no one was with me" [Is 63:3].) But because, in the course of this expedition, there will be glory and rich spoils to be had, I am here inviting you to take part in it.

"No one will be lost in battle. Victory is certain. But the person who would follow me will have to be satisfied with what satisfies me. Moreover, I never require something of anyone without first giving an example by doing it myself, choosing for myself whatever is more difficult: in work, the hardest part; in combat, the most dangerous assignment.

"After victory comes the sharing of the spoils in proportion to how much each person will have shared in the weariness of the war."

Given these conditions and these proposals made by such a distinguished person, a refusal would be nothing other than a cruel insult, the height of ingratitude and despicable cowardice. To enlist with a firm commitment in the troops of so bounteous a general will be the response of everyone with courage and common sense.

In the crowd of people invited by this victorious king will be some who feel they want to show him an even greater dedication by making him a still more costly proposal.

I suggest that you now envisage our Lord walking along, here on earth, at that time. Crowds of people throng around him. Just to see him is their most ardent desire. To have actually touched him is cause for envy. A glance or a word from him is complete happiness.

Meanwhile, he reaches the city as the din of the crowd was already announcing his imminent arrival. He stops in front of a certain house. Who are these mortals living in that house who are blessed with such a favor? It is precisely the house where I am at that time.

He enters. I see him move forward surrounded by his disciples. It is he, with his kind smile and a look on his face full of love. What unspeakable gentleness is evident in his features, moderating the divine brilliance. He pronounces a certain name. His eyes look around for someone. He is looking for me! I see him coming directly toward me. He stretches out his hands toward me and opens his arms to embrace me. What transport of joy rushes over me! I fall at his feet, clutching them tightly. *Dominus meus et deus meus!* ("My Lord and my God!" [Jn 20:28].) But he raises me up and holds me close to his heart. Oh, my own heart breaks at the remembrance of my sins. My tears flow, but they are sweet because I shed them on his breast. My God, will you forgive me? He answers only: "My child, there is still one place available among the apostles (Acts 1:15–26). Do you want it? I am here to offer it to you." Ah, Lord, it is more than I could ask for. "Oh, so you know where I intend to lead you?" Lord, following you I will go anywhere. *Sequar te quocumque ieris.* ("I will follow you wherever you go" [Mt 8:19].) *Amorem tui solum cum gratia mihi dones et dives sum satis.* ("Give only your love and your grace; that is enough for me.")[6]

But suppose I fail? "I will die with you. Nevertheless, there are going to be difficult battles to be won." Your presence, Lord, will enliven my strength, as long as I do battle in your presence. "The birds in the sky have nests, foxes have lairs, but the Son of Man has nowhere to lay his head" (Mt 8:20). *Non est servus major Domino suo.* ("No servant is greater than his master" [Jn 13:16].) *Sufficit illi si sit sicut Dominus ejus.* ("It is enough for him to be like his master" [Lk 6:40].)

"But what reward do you expect?" *Nullam aliam nisi te, Domine.* ("None other than you yourself, Lord" [Est 14:14]).[7]

"My child, I am satisfied with your dedication. You know, of course, that, far from fearing for myself, for my life, or for the outcome of the battle, I am certain of victory. And I promise that no one who follows me will perish in my service. As for the reward you desire, I see that you recognize the better part (Lk 10:42). You will, indeed, share in my glory to the extent that you will have shared in my sufferings (Phil 3:10). I promise you one of the thrones reserved for my apostles (Lk 22:30), at the head of the entire army of the elect."

What can I say? What dare I think about the honor given to me by my Lord and king—to me, a rebellious subject and convicted of disloyalty and notorious cowardice? It would have been enough to count myself blessed if he were to let me live humbly among the least of his subjects.

Chosen as his guard of honor and brought together as the best of his warriors, these blessed companions will be allowed to share his riches and to sleep in his tent and to eat his bread. They will assist him *per magna et fortia* ("with mighty signs and wonders" [Rom 15:19]) in winning his kingdom on earth and in bringing hearts under his sway. For this distinguished post of command, he let his eyes fall on me as if he no longer remembered anything of my past. And it is true that he washed everything away in the shedding of his blood (Rv 7:14). Ah, there is enough here to soften a rock and to give heart to the cowardly.

Well then, it has been decided, and nothing will hold me back from my resolve. From this moment on, I commit myself without reservation to the lot of this leader. Henceforth, my king is everything for me. His glory is my glory, his armament is my armament, his sufferings my sufferings, his setbacks my setbacks. He is poor, and I will be poor, too. He is brought low and persecuted, and that is what I will look for, too. He seeks out souls, sacrificing himself for them, and I will do the same.

"All for him and nothing for me." What a great honor to fight at his side, to be worn out in his service, to die in order to ensure that he is enthroned in people's hearts.

God forbid that I should ever ask for rest or retirement or pension. I vow to live and die under his standard along with my fellow comrades in arms. God forbid that I should ever seek out high rank or distinctions for my service. His victory is all I want.

And so, if these warlike images stir up the imagination, let us recall that it is the Lamb of God himself who sends us out like lambs among wolves (Lk 10:3). His meekness brought him victory; his cross and his long suffering were his only weapons. By this, the heroic Christian will understand the sort of bravery required. He will need a lion's courage to overcome himself, to suffer and triumph by self-sacrifice. *Non est colluctatio nobis adversus carnem et sanguinem.* ("For our struggle is not against enemies of blood and flesh" [Eph 6:12].)

Leaving aside the petty and ephemeral part of a soldier's glory, what we have for ourselves is the part of that glory which is lovely, noble, and heroic. We are, indeed, on a veritable expedition to give hell some severe blows. One day we will see glisten every noble feat of this war, which God alone witnesses now.

Colloquy

Kneel at the feet of your Savior, and make your offering to him *corde magno et anima volenti* ("with a strong heart and a willing spirit" [2 Mc 1:3]).

"Oh sovereign king and ruler of the universe, I recognize my lowliness. But buoyed up by your grace, I offer myself entirely to you, along with all that I have. I proclaim before your infinite bounty, in the presence of the Blessed Virgin Mary, my Mother, and before all the heavenly choir, that it is my desire, my intention, and my deliberate will to follow you as closely as possible, willingly accepting affronts, insults, and poverty, whether of spirit or of goods, if only your majesty is thereby glorified and that you yourself are pleased to call me to this excessively great honor."

Week Two: Day One

The *first consequence* of the foundational meditation: the imitation of Christ

First Prelude
Adore your Lord who very much wants to be your exemplar.

Second Prelude

Listen to your divine Savior who says to you: "I have given you an example so that you may imitate what I have done" (Jn 13:15).

Third Prelude

Ask the Lord to make you open to his invitations and to make you say, with even greater purity of intention than that doctor of the Law who hoped that the miracles of the God-Man would give him the means for being enriched by following him: "Master, I will follow you wherever you go" (Mt 8:19). To obtain this grace from Jesus Christ, turn to the Blessed Virgin who imitated him more faithfully than anyone else. Turn to the apostles and the other disciples who, after the descent of the Holy Spirit, followed the example of his life as closely as possible.

Consider now the reason why you ought to imitate your divine exemplar and to have him reign as absolute king in your heart. This meditation is to convince you that the imitation of Jesus Christ is (1) your duty, (2) your glory, and (3) your happiness.

1. Your duty. Is it not, in fact, your obligation to benefit from the Incarnation of the Word by living and acting as a true Christian and to see to it that you are counted among the elect? If you do not imitate Jesus Christ, (a) his Incarnation is of no use to you, (b) you will be unworthy of being called "Christian," and (c) you can never be numbered among the predestined.

   a. The Incarnation is useless for you. If the eternal Word was enfleshed to reconcile the world with the father and to free it from slavery to the devil, that is only one part of his mission. One of the main reasons for this divine Incarnation was to give mortal human beings a teacher, a master, and a model of all virtues, as Jesus Christ himself proclaimed when he said that he is not only the truth because of his teachings and the life because of his death and the sacraments, but he is also the way because of his example (Jn 14:6). Was that not his reason for wanting to go through all stages of human life: to be born, to live, to suffer, and to die just like all the children of Adam? In God's plan, therefore, every action on the part of the incarnate Word is a trait to be imitated. His life is such a genuine mirror of what ours ought to be (2 Cor 3:18) that there is nothing at all in the life of Jesus Christ about which he could not say to us as he did once to his disciples: "I have given you an example that you should do what I have done" (Jn 13:15).

And study well the divine model. Imitate him in your chosen vocation by your poverty, obedience, and chastity. Imagine him saying to you now, as he once said to the disciple who asked leave to go first and bury his father, of whose death he had just been informed: "Follow me" (Mt 8:22). Unless you follow him, you render useless for yourself that great mystery of the Incarnation.

b.   Unless you imitate Jesus Christ, you cannot truly be a Christian. The first Christians of the Gospel received this name from the pagans only because they confessed themselves as followers of the Christ and his teachings (Acts 11:26). To be called a Christian is to be called a faithful follower of Jesus Christ. Is it not true, then, that our Savior came to be the guiding rule of our morals, our behavior, and our faith? Without following his way of acting, in other words, without imitating his virtues, we cannot be his disciples. Thus does he invite us all: "Let whoever wants to belong to me follow me" (Mt 16:24).

St. Paul also teaches us that when we become Christians, we become adopted children of God by grace, just as Jesus Christ is son by nature (Rom 8:14–15; Gal 3:26–27, 4:5; Eph 1:5). Therefore, we need to be the image of our heavenly father, just as children are the image of their father in the order of nature. But because the image of God is not something we can see, we can express it in ourselves only by becoming visibly like his son, God's image by his very nature (2 Cor 4:4) and, therefore, made visible for us (Rom 8:39). Just as we received from Adam the beginnings of bodily life, which, as it develops, makes us pass through the different stages of human life until we are fully grown and resembling that first father of ours, so it is that in Baptism we received a kind of spiritual life, which needs to grow and be strengthened until Jesus Christ is formed in us (Gal 4:19). And this needs to take place in us in such a way that, alive with his own life and reinforced with his own strength (2 Cor 12:9), we are truly another Jesus Christ whose life is lived out in ours (2 Cor 4:10–11; Gal 2:20).

c. Unless we imitate Jesus Christ, we cannot be counted as predestined. St. Paul teaches that, through Baptism, the faithful are transformed into Jesus Christ and become one with him (Rom 6:3–5; 1 Cor 12:12–13). Consequently, they are living members of the one body of which he himself is the head (Eph 4:15). In this admirable work of art wrought by divine wisdom, everything needs to be in proper proportion. The holiness of the head needs to radiate also from all the members of the body. Likewise, in the human body, it is the same divine Spirit that binds together all the different parts. Paul then adds: "All of you who have been baptized into Christ have clothed yourselves with him" (Gal 3:27).

It is as if St. Paul were saying this: the virtues of our divine Savior—his charity, his patience, his chastity, his obedience, and his humility—in some way ought to be our clothes as well. It follows that the whole Christ is morally made up of the God-Man and his faithful people who are one body with him. It is in this way that branches are attached to the trunk, kept in place by the same roots, and nourished by the same sap and so together form but one and the same tree. Given that no one can be saved if he does not belong to Jesus Christ and is not alive with the very life of Jesus by imitating him, your conclusion must be that, if you forgo the imitation of Christ, you also forgo your predestination and your eternal glory. For the same apostle says that "God predestined his elect to be conformed to the image of his son" (Rom 8:29). It is this reality that made St. Gregory of Nyssa say that "a Christian ought to be another Jesus Christ."[8]

Look very carefully now to see if you are a living copy of this divine exemplar. Are your eyes as pure as his, your ears as chaste as his, your mouth as discreet as his, your gait as modest and unpretentious as his? Alas, what a contrast, perhaps, between the life of Jesus Christ and your own. What a great difference between his humility and your ambition, his warm love and your cold indifference, his courage and your weakness, his calmness and your outbursts of emotion, his virginal innocence and your unruly passions, his recollection and your distractions, the wisdom of his words and your excessive babbling!

2. Imitating Jesus Christ may be your duty, but it is also your glory. And just what makes for the glory of a disciple? Attaining the perfection of the master. See with what burning zeal people endowed with brilliant minds work at updating the thinking of the great geniuses of old, with what courage they travel far and wide to study under the most renowned masters, with what attention an artisan learns the techniques of even the most everyday kind of mechanical arts apprenticed to a more skilled worker than himself, and what degree of glory awaits that artisan who develops his skills to the point of imitating the masters and producing works as perfectly executed as those of the masters themselves.

For human beings, imitation is a necessity. It is also their life. Children retrace in their own persons the good as well as the bad characteristics of their parents; servants, those of their master; soldiers, those of their captain; friends, those of their closest friend. The remarkable thing is that all of these people consider it an honor to have developed a resemblance between themselves and those they admire or esteem.

Understand, then, to what great glory your God wants to raise you up when he calls you to imitate his only son, who became human like you so that you might all the easier imitate him. For if he remained only God, you could then say either that it is impossible to imitate his perfection or else that it would be sinful pride to become really and truly like God, which was Lucifer's dream. If he had shown himself to you only as a human being, you could be afraid of straying from the path of following in his footsteps. And so, to remove all pretext of fear and cowardice, he willed to unite our human nature with his divine nature.

Oh, who could ever imagine how glorious it is for us lowly mortals to have no other feelings, no other desires, conversations, or actions, than those of an incarnate God? Do you not see now why St. Paul boasted of his sufferings (2 Cor 11:16–30)? Why the apostles parted from the members of the Sanhedrin full of joy at having been ill-treated and flagellated (Acts 5:41)? Thus it was that they came to be like their divine master in still one more way.

Give some thought to this example. If Mary is the one enjoying the highest degree of glory in heaven, is it not because, while she lived on earth, she was the one most perfectly conformed to her divine son? Imitating Jesus Christ will bring you also this heavenly glory.

3. Your happiness also depends on your imitating Jesus, both now and for eternity. Here on earth you can be the object of God's blessings, love, and kindness only to the extent that he sees in you the image of his beloved son. When you die, you can claim the joys of paradise only to the extent that the divine justice finds you conformed to Jesus Christ.

To end this meditation, take yourself in thought to that great day when consciences will be publicly revealed. Imagine the Lord coming on the clouds of heaven (Rv 1:7) to crown the members of his body who are alive because of grace and to condemn those members who are dead because of sin. He will then say to those in whom he finds his own likeness: "Come, you whom my father has blessed" (Mt 25:34). To those who did not imitate him, he will give the contrary sentence: "Depart from me, you wicked people, to the eternal fire" (Mt 25:41). To make this point more vivid for you, recall the consolation felt by St. Martin, Archbishop of Tours, when he was about to die and could say to the devil: "You will find nothing in me that belongs to you."[9] Why did he say this? St. Martin did all in his power to make himself like our Savior. Overwhelmed by the weight of his advanced age, his works, and his austerities, the saintly bishop thus announced to his followers that his last moments had at last arrived.

This news filled them with very deep sorrow. They could not be consoled because of the tremendous loss they were about to experience along with the entire Church. St. Martin mingled his tears with those of his followers and spoke this noble prayer: "Oh Lord, if I am still of any use to your Church, I do not refuse to continue working." Burning with fever, lying on a hair shirt, covered with ashes, his eyes and his hands raised up toward heaven, he never stopped day and night addressing his prayers and supplications to God. His attendants wanted to turn him onto his other side to give him, if possible, greater comfort. But he said: "Let me look toward heaven rather than toward the earth, so that my soul may take its flight up to the Lord with whom it will soon be united." What calmness. What profound peace. What heavenly joy at the moment before going to appear before the sovereign judge. The devilish lion, roaring about the saint in his last hour, was seeking to devour him (1 Pt 5:8), trying with all his might to instill fear and terror in his soul. Powerless efforts, however. "What are you looking for here, cruel beast that you are?" said this undaunted soldier of Jesus Christ. "You will find nothing in me that belongs to you!"

As you complete this meditation, ask yourself: Could I boast of myself in the presence of Jesus Christ for being conformed to him in anything? If, at this very moment, I had to appear before his majesty and hear him pronounce the sentence that would decide my eternal lot, could I hope to be among the saints who will be glorified because they resemble the Son of God? Truly, these questions are worthy of consideration throughout life, no matter how long I should live, a pursuit a thousand times more important than what is pursued each day by many people of renown in the world.

Have I taken time for solitude and afterward come out with the dispositions which motivated Jesus Christ? Have I lived and worked in the spirit of penance, of surrender to the will of God, of zeal, and of the willingness with which Jesus Christ gave himself to the difficult tasks he undertook for love of me? Are my prayers and other exercises of devotion enlivened by the same holy fervor, profound humility, tender piety, and limitless trust that Jesus Christ brought to all his religious acts before his father? Does my behavior toward superiors and directors correspond to that of Jesus Christ toward Mary and Joseph, his parents, to whom he was subject for thirty years without doing anything except obeying in silence?

Jesus Christ sat in the Temple amid the doctors of the Law, listening to them and asking them questions with unassuming simplicity (Lk 2:46). And yet, it was he who could have revealed to them the mysteries they were most interested in. Is this the kind of model I take for myself when I begin any lessons to increase my knowledge? Can Jesus find in me, in my relationship with my confreres, the same strengths and virtues he has in conversing with others: compassionate understanding, gentleness, thoughtfulness? In the course of his ministry, Jesus had nowhere to lay his head (Mt 8:20), lacking at times even what seems necessary. Can he see in me some similarity to his own needs and hardships?

On the contrary, does he not find rather a certain love of luxury, ease, the comforts of life, and a secret strong dislike for work and anything painful? Are you now coming to see how important it is for you to narrow the gap between your attitudes and those of Jesus Christ? If God were often to grant all novices the grace of conforming their dispositions to those of Jesus Christ, would not this Solitude, already quite fervent, take on a new form?[10] Everyone who lives here at the Solitude would be among the saints and the elect in whom the Lord would never cease to be well pleased. In time, he will shower his grace on them, giving them the power to imitate Jesus Christ. In eternity, these saintly imitators of the incarnate God will share his peace and his happiness.

And now resolve to do all you can to imitate Jesus Christ. Review once more the reflections and motives which underlie this resolution you just made. Converse openly and freely with God about your needs.

Spiritual Bouquet

Make up a short saying or a spiritual bouquet that sums up in a few words the entire topic of your meditation, using, for example, these words which you read when you began this meditation: "You have learned to put off the old self and to be clothed with the new" (Col 3:9–10). And then recall these words from time to time throughout the day.

Week Two: Day One

The *second consequence* of the foundational meditation: the means for imitating Jesus Christ or for establishing his kingdom in oneself

After having roused or at least strengthened in your heart the desire to imitate Jesus Christ and to see him reign in you, you will no doubt want to become familiar with the means of being successful in this imitation. You can sum them up in a single means that encompasses all the others, provided that you are blessed with being habitually in the state of grace, or with returning to it through the sacrament of Penance as soon as you have fallen: seek to know Jesus Christ. By studying him carefully, you will come to know him. By knowing him, you will come to love him. By loving him, you will be imbued with his Spirit, and, thenceforth, you will imitate him. Therefore, fill yourself full of this truth by the following meditation, which is but the sequel to the previous one as well as its development.

First Prelude

Coming to know Jesus Christ. You are reminded of it in these words of St. Paul to the Corinthians: "I decided to know nothing other than Jesus Christ" (1 Cor 2:2).

Second Prelude

Imagine to yourself the sight of the Savior wandering through the synagogues, towns, and villages of Judea to preach the Gospel there, and, in your imagination, listen to him call you to follow him as he once called his disciples and apostles.

Third Prelude

Entreat your divine master not to let you be deaf to his voice but, on the contrary, to grant you the grace of imitating him on your journey as you follow him.

No doubt you have already come to know Jesus Christ in the sense of your not being ignorant of his life or his mysteries. You have studied your catechism. You have been to different churches and can recall the homiletic instruction you heard preached in them. Then there are the crosses set up after parish missions at road intersections throughout the countryside. You have prayed your morning and evening prayers, recited the Creed every day, and celebrated the feast days of the Church. Has not all of that come together to give you this knowledge of Jesus Christ?

You are very well aware, then, that the Son of God became man by uniting himself with human nature, that he was born in a crib at Bethlehem, that he lived in poverty. You are also aware that he left his hidden life to spread the Good News among the inhabitants of Judea, that he instructed them by his teachings, edified them by his examples, got their attention by the brilliance of his miracles—everywhere leaving behind traces of his blessings, healing the sick, consoling the sorrowful, helping people in their need, welcoming sinners with kindness. You know that he made twelve poor men his associates and endured their ignorance and their rough manners.

You know that his virtues stirred up the hatred of the hypocritical Pharisees who were persecuting him and that, betrayed by one of his apostles, he was handed over to his enemies and condemned to death like a wicked criminal, he who was justice itself. You know that he let himself be led to torture like a lamb to the slaughterhouse. You know that he died

on the cross to expiate the sins of the world, that he rose again on the
third day and ascended into heaven forty days later, that finally there in
heaven he intercedes continually with his father for us, showing him his
meritorious wounds. You have known all these facts a long time already,
and it is precisely because you have read them and heard them so often
that perhaps your heart is now less than sensitive to them.

But what we are talking about is not at all this general and superficial knowledge, which is the same for you as for all other Christians. That
same knowledge is found even among the enemies of religion. No, it is not
enough for you to be merely acquainted with Jesus Christ, his sayings,
and his life as one takes pride in knowing the history of a famous celeb-
rity, which after all is of little real interest to us. Instead, you will need
to study in detail the events of the Savior's life and the sentiments that
buoyed him up in order to fill your mind with these examples.

You will need to fill and nourish your heart with his teachings, to
meditate on these mysteries in silent recollection as well as on the abundance of his mercies. You will also need to ask God to enlighten your
mind and heart so that you may understand and savor them in such a
way that you may come to that kind of knowledge of Jesus Christ that
is life-giving, profound, luminous, and practical, and which make his virtues almost palpable, so to speak, his lessons familiar, and remembrance
of him as habitual as it is enjoyable.

That is the kind of knowledge with which you need to become thoroughly familiar, and it is of such a knowledge that St. Paul spoke to the
Ephesians when he wrote: "I remember you in all my prayers, that the
God of our Lord Jesus Christ, author and giver of glory, may grant the
spirit of wisdom and of light to bring you to full knowledge of him" (Eph
1:16–17). Have you seriously applied yourself to all this? See with what
eagerness the children of this world study the deceitful teaching of philosophers, and then really ask yourself if you are studying with as much
diligence the Gospel of Jesus Christ whose every word is written for your
salvation.

Consider what those artists do who want to be very good at their
profession, how they try to copy the works of the great masters. Then,
recall to yourself that, following St. Gregory of Nyssa, you ought to be

the painter of the Savior's life.[11] For as this Father of the Church says, your will must be like the hand that holds the paintbrush. The virtues that you reproduce in yourself will be the colors of the painting, and Jesus Christ will be the model whom you copy.

Indeed, just what does a painter do? He studies his subject. He fills himself with it totally in order to reproduce it and, in a manner of speaking, to create it anew on canvas in a very close imitation of the subject's features. Is it in this way that you try to make Jesus Christ live again in you, to the point of his being totally remade or formed again in you?

Ah, if you loved him, this divine master, you would stake your happiness on trying to become like him, and you would soon become a faithful image of him. Indeed, look at what happens in day-to-day life. Sometimes you meet people whose thoughts, feelings, sense of taste, tone of voice, and mannerisms all resemble one another. How is that? It is just because the custom they have of living familiarly with one another, the close friendship that unites them, intermingles them and unites them in such a way that they have but one heart and one soul. Therefore, love Jesus Christ, and before long his thoughts, his feelings, and his way of living will be your own. Indeed, is not the best way to arouse in you love for him simply to understand well, by studying him more and more, that he is your own greatness, your hope, your salvation, your refuge, and your life?

For if you are Christian, is it not through Jesus Christ? If you have any claim to the kingdom of Jesus Christ, is it not through Jesus Christ? If your sins have been forgiven, is it not through Jesus Christ? These are truths that thankfulness ought to carve forever into your heart. If you were to meditate well on them and feel them deeply, they would set on fire in you love for your Savior, for it is from such thoughts that St. Paul derived that ardor that made him say: "Cursed be anyone who does not love Jesus Christ" (1 Cor 16:22). It, likewise, made him write to the Romans that "anyone who does not have the Spirit of Christ does not belong to him" (Rom 8:9).

To know better whether you love Jesus Christ and, consequently, whether you imitate him or not, now put those questions to your conscience without deluding yourself and see what kind of spirit it is that gives you life. Then, let the conclusion of that series of questions be the need you have for studying your adorable model and for preferring so much more that kind of study to all others to which you give yourself all the more easily.

In this holy Solitude, indeed, every day you are reading the Gospel or are hearing it read. Therefore, it is in this heavenly book that you can contemplate him and admire how, in the womb of an immaculate virgin, Jesus was developing into a child and was making John the Baptist holy, too. You can contemplate and admire how even in the crib he was giving you lessons of humility, simplicity, and poverty; how in his presentation in the Temple he offers the most perfect model to those who, at still a tender age, want to consecrate themselves wholly to the Lord; how at Nazareth he preaches to you obedience and manual labor—all these even though he was still far from the world which does not yet know him and whose esteem and praises he was not seeking.

After having thus gone through these different mysteries of his hidden life and his public life, take his cross in your hands and say to yourself: "Who is this who died thus in the midst of most dreadful sorrows? It is Jesus Christ, my God and my Savior. And why these sufferings? Ah, it is his love for me that crucified him. See, then, to what great depths he loved me! It is both in this moving written account, available for all eyes to see, and at the foot of the crucifix that are taught and formed all those great saints who will be the admiration of all ages: St. Bernard, St. Francis of Assisi, St. Thomas Aquinas, St. Bonaventure, St. Teresa—in a word, all the disciples of the Gospel with the holy ambition of becoming other Jesus Christs."

Like them, study your model in this admirable book and meditate especially on the dispositions of his heart, whether toward his father or toward the world or toward himself, in an effort to make them your own.

It is in the letters of the apostles, particularly in those of St. Paul, that you can do this study, the most essential one of all the exercises to which you apply yourself during this holy retreat. Read, therefore, the translation and commentary given by Fr. R. Bernardin de Picquigny.[12] Also read and reread *The History of the Life of Our Lord and Savior Jesus Christ* by Fr. de Ligny, as well as the *Book of the Chosen Ones*, if you can, or the book *On the Knowledge and the Love of Jesus Christ* by Fr. Saint-Jure.[13] Take pride in a holy desire to know, understand, meditate on, and study thoroughly the Gospel as well as the letters of the great apostle. These inspired writings will make you enter into the deepest mysteries of Jesus Christ. Reading them will make well up in you a very lively eagerness to become another Jesus Christ, and then, by the examples set before you rather than by catechetical explanation, you will be filled with a truly apostolic zeal to make known and loved the childhood of the divine master.

Colloquy

Cry out with St. Augustine: "Let me know you, oh my God. I burn with the desire to meditate on your sacred books, and I do not want to use the time I have at my disposition for any other purpose. Yes, my Lord, your scriptures will always be my chaste delight. Bend down, therefore, and uncover for me their meaning, revealing yourself in them to my heart and making me drink unceasingly at your salvific waters."[14]

Finally, bring an end to this conversation by adding the words of St. Ignatius in the desire of answering the invitation of Jesus Christ, who calls you to follow him by a faithful imitation of his virtues: "Here I am, sovereign monarch, absolute master of all that exists. Counting on the help of your grace, even though no one, alas, is more unworthy of it than I am, I offer myself wholly to you and without reserve. All that I have, all that I possess, I submit absolutely to your most holy will. At the feet of your supreme majesty and in the presence of your noble mother and of all the celestial court, I declare that my intention, my desire, my firm and unchangeable determination, is to follow you as closely as I can, as much as your glory and my own salvation require it. I want to be like you in your patience when undergoing insults and injuries, to be like you in your courage of suffering all kinds of tribulations. Furthermore, I submit myself to spend my entire life in poverty, obedience, and charity, if your adorable majesty is pleased to call me to live in this way."[15]

Week Two: Day One

The *third consequence* of the foundational meditation: what the imitation of Jesus Christ means for you in practice

If you are truly convinced of the obligation to establish in yourself the reign of Jesus Christ by imitating his virtues, you must now give yourself over to the study of his teaching and of the examples he gives, because you cannot imitate what you do not know. But because your divine model was brought to completion in all aspects and because his teachings are as numerous as they are sublime, a purview as weak and limited as your own could not, especially in so short a retreat, cover in all its details such a perfect painting. Therefore, you will need to stop at a few of the principal features of the divine original and work at reproducing them in yourself. Such is the goal of this meditation whose preludes now follow.

First Prelude

Remember that the subject here is to know in what you ought to make your imitation of Jesus Christ consist.

Second Prelude

Represent to yourself the Savior surrounded by his apostles. After washing their feet, he says to them: "I have given you an example, that you also should do what you have seen me do" (Jn 13:15).

Third Prelude

Pray that your divine master will make you open to his invitation and make you know in what special way he wants you to imitate him.

To guide you in the choice you have to make from among the virtues that such an appealing model offers you, look first at those of which you have a more pressing need and then at those which he himself very admirably put into practice quite often. That is of supreme importance. Also, reflect on this truth: that God who is all wisdom and all goodness, our Lord, necessarily had to give us by his own example more frequent lessons on those virtues that would be more indispensable for us and which could better heal the particular inclination we feel toward evil. Once you have acknowledged that truth, ask yourself what it is that impels you most strongly toward evil. It is this threefold concupiscence of which St. John speaks (1 Jn 2:16), consisting in love of pleasure, love of honor, and love of our own will. Yes, how true it is that sensuousness, ambition, and pride are for you the great battlefield, just as they are for all the poor children of Adam.

And so, these three deadly tendencies are fought against by means of the three virtues that shine so brilliantly in the life and the teachings of Jesus Christ, namely, poverty, humility, and obedience. Poverty, in fact, regulates the love of well-being by stripping us of those riches whose absence exposes us to need, inconveniences, privations, and sufferings, just as it happens to the indigent poor of the world. Humility regulates excessive love of honor by making us love it, long for it, and accept it only as much as God insists on it. Finally, obedience regulates and directs our own will by subjecting it in everything and in every case to the will of God manifested by the will of duly-appointed superiors. Once these three virtues are in your heart, there is nothing else that can hinder you from going to God, because, thanks to these virtues, you are no longer bound to the flesh and its concupiscence, nor to pride and its suggestions, nor to your own will and its whims.

Furthermore, in how many encounters our Savior practiced and specially recommended these three virtues of poverty, humility, and obedience! It will be easy to convince you of this by meditating on his mysteries, his teachings, and his entire life. Without doubt, there is not even one encounter in which our master did not excel to the point of always being an excellent model, even though he did not put that fact into an explicit statement. He put into practice the other virtues at proper times but in a way that was less evident, with the exception of charity, which was the first and universal rule of all his conduct on earth. As for charity, it is perhaps better learned in the school of the Holy Spirit than by contemplating the external conduct of Jesus Christ.

From all the above, your conclusion ought to be that, in order to establish in yourself the kingdom of the Savior by imitating him, you need (1) to learn in this school to become humble, poor, and obedient, and (2) to devote your retreat to understanding the moving lessons and examples of his virtues that he left for the world. "Thus it is that you will put off the old self and will be clothed with the new self" (Col 3:9–10). This old self is nothing else than the threefold concupiscence by which Adam, in sinning, contaminated our nature.

Look with wonder at how the Savior of the world, who is the new Adam, remedied the evil of our sinful beginnings by expiating the transgressions of our first father through actions contrary to that evil. Pride had blinded our ill-fated father to the point of his thinking that he wanted to be like God (Gn 3:5). Jesus Christ, however, was obedient and humbled himself from the time of his Incarnation to his death on the cross (Phil 2:7–8). Sensuality had roused the former to eat some of the forbidden fruit, which brought about in him the rebellion of the flesh against the spirit. The latter mortified his senses at every turn and subjected them to the spirit by the most perfect chastity there ever was.

Finally, avarice and ambition brought the hand of the former to take hold of something that did not belong to him, the fruit of the tree of knowledge of good and evil. Jesus Christ, on the other hand, emptied himself to the point of considering himself a worm and letting himself be treated as such. He died to himself, was poor, and was stripped of everything so thoroughly that he could truly say: "Foxes have dens but the Son of Man has nowhere to lay his head" (Mt 8:20). Because of that, do you not have a sense of what you need to do now to "put on the new self" (Col 3:10)?

Colloquy

Here then is what you have been thinking up to now about humility, obedience, and poverty. Be humbled at seeing yourself so far removed from your model, and for your colloquy, cry out with a fervent desire of being heard: "Come, Lord, come and take possession of a soul that belongs to you in so many ways and has been acquired for you more than ever by the gift it makes to you of itself. Enter a heart where you alone ought to reign, and banish from it everything that would separate me from you or you from me, for you are a jealous God. You want me entirely for yourself, and you have told me in your Gospel that I cannot serve two masters (Lk 16:13). Whom else but you can I choose? What else must I renounce for you?

"That is what I have wanted, oh Lord, ever since I withdrew into your holy house, which is your kingdom on earth, and ever since I began to serve you by putting on the religious habit. How is it that this awareness of duty has not been stronger and more enduring? Yet, there is still time to renew it and to learn it over again. 'You are my Lord and my God!' (Jn 20:28). Such is the homage given to you by one of your apostles as he moved beyond his unbelief, and such is the homage now given to you by me, filled with lowly confusion and yet alive with true repentance.

"Command what you will, and see that I am ready to do anything in order to obey you. No matter how you reveal yourself to me, in the splendor of your glory or in the humiliation of your cross, you remain my Lord and my God. No matter what road it pleases you that I take alongside you or following behind you, you will find me both always ready to obey and always ready to march on farther. If you call, I will answer you. If you inspire me, I will act accordingly. If you make me hear your heavenly desires for me, I will conform myself to them. I will do all of that out of love, for you are a God of love, and it is through love that you reign over faithful souls and that you exercise in them your most powerful dominion. Be master, then, especially of my whole being by means of your virtues, especially by your obedience, your chastity, and your poverty, so that I may live only with your life and not with the life of the senses."

Remain with the colloquy for a while with such strong fervor that, having been called to religious life, you will find in this colloquy its true foundation. Religious life, in practice, essentially means stripping yourself of the life of the flesh by means of mortification and chastity, stripping yourself of the life of pride by obedience and humility, and stripping yourself of the life of comfort and ambition by poverty.

Thus, you will establish in yourself the kingdom of Jesus Christ, which consists in banishing from your inner depths every spirit except that of Jesus Christ, so that all the virtues of Jesus Christ may come alive in you by putting them into practice constantly and habitually, especially those virtues on which you have just meditated.

May Jesus Christ govern you in everything. May he rule over you in everything and be the source of all you undertake and accomplish, along the lines of this prayer, which you ought now to recite with greater enthusiasm than ever: "Oh Jesus, living in Mary, come and live in your servants by your Holy Spirit, by the fullness of your justice, by your perfect ways, and by communion in your mysteries. Conquer all enemy powers by your Spirit and the glory of your Father. Amen."

· The better to succeed in establishing this kingdom of Jesus Christ in you, apply yourself to three things that will be, as it were, the practical consequences of your reflections: (1) Make a thorough study of the life of Jesus Christ in the Gospel, so that none of the features of his life that pertain to yours is unavailable to you; (2) work at becoming a new self in love and thankfulness for this divine Savior, so that you may work with greater generosity at imitating him; and (3) from time to time during the day, deliberately bring your way of acting into line with his, saying to yourself along with St. Vincent de Paul, "At this moment, what would Jesus Christ do if he were in my situation?"

Spiritual Bouquet

Your spiritual bouquet could be this saying of Jesus Christ: "I have given you this example, that you should act as you have seen me act" (Jn 13:15).

Week Two: Day Two

Meditation on the hidden life of Jesus Christ in general

Because details make a greater impression than an overview, St. Ignatius first lays the foundation of everything you are to look at in the second and third weeks of these exercises, and then he sets before the eyes of the retreatant each of the most important mysteries of the life of Jesus Christ. First of all come those of his hidden life, because that is where he spent a greater number of years, and you ought, therefore, to have a greater affection for this hidden life. Afterward come the mysteries of his public life. And so, you will begin with the mysteries of his hidden life.

You ought to have a greater attraction to his hidden life, because it is more like your own situation right now. You are not yet exposed to the dangers of public life but rather are enjoying all the advantages of the Solitude. Because all the merit of a life that is simple and communal consists in the observance of the commandments of God, you must be absolutely determined to embrace this way of living, which is that of every Christian.

You must, then, further discern whether God is calling you to the other kind of life that leads to evangelical perfection and determine how strongly he is calling you to it. This retreat, therefore, will be divided into two parts. In the first part, you will make a resolution to practice faithfully what is essential to being a Christian, to which you are held responsible because of your baptismal promises. Your resolution will be to imitate the thirty years of the hidden life of Jesus Christ, which he lived totally in obedience and obscurity.

Only the first four days will be taken up with his hidden life in these exercises. The rest of the retreat, which forms the second part, will be used to discern what God is asking of you. At the end of this second part, you will have to choose a state of life, if you have not already irrevocably made that decision. In that case, you need to be renewed in that state which you have embraced, if it is irrevocable.[16] Your resolution will be to fulfill exactly the duties which that life requires. And to do that, you will meditate on the example which Jesus Christ has given to you in his public life up until his passion.

First Prelude

Find your topic of prayer in these words of the apostle St. Paul to the Colossians: "You have died and your life is hidden with Jesus Christ in God" (Col 3:3).

Second Prelude

Picture for yourself the Savior during his life hidden from the world, whether in his mother's womb by his Incarnation, or in the stable of Bethlehem at the moment of his birth, or at Nazareth where he spent almost his entire life.

Third Prelude

Entreat the Savior to grant you the grace of understanding well and of tasting the advantages of the life hidden with Jesus Christ in God. To obtain that grace, invoke Mary and Joseph, who had the blessed joy of being witnesses to all the mysteries of Jesus' own hidden life.

Now, you must pour out your heart in silence and in peace as you meditate on the hidden life of Jesus Christ. Therefore, be in wonder at how this God of glory first hid himself under the veil of human nature, "although all the treasures of wisdom and knowledge were in him" (Col 2:3).

See him, next, hidden in the womb of the Virgin, even though the marvel of his virginal conception escapes detection under the veil of the holiest marriage that ever existed. As Mary visits her cousin, notice that, if Jesus Christ made John the Baptist feel his presence, his power penetrating the womb wherein lay the holy precursor, it is only at the sound of his noble mother's voice that the wonder took place. "At the sound of your voice," Elizabeth cried out, "the infant leaped in my womb" (Lk 1:41).

It is true that in coming into the world he made himself known, but it was to poor shepherds, and, therefore, you could say that "he came into the world and the world which was created by him did not know him" (Jn 1:10). In fact, the stable of Bethlehem held him, but the rest of the world did not know him. But, then, it is true that his childhood had nothing spectacular. Whereas notice is taken of other children, especially if they are born princes of the earth, not a single thing is said about Jesus Christ. "Where did he get all this knowledge, seeing that he has never studied" (Jn 7:15), for no one had seen him in a school?

He does, indeed, make an appearance, but only once, at the age of twelve, in the midst of the doctors of the Law, and even there the Gospel says nothing about his doing any teaching. Rather, he listened to them, asking them questions about truth in an astonishing manner, but it did not seem that he had settled any matters for them at that time, even though part of the reason he came into the world was to teach. Nevertheless, we must admit that all who listened to him were "amazed at the wisdom of his answers" (Lk 2:47). He began by listening and asking questions, and yet none of that came from any of his childhood training.

Again, after he had burst onto the scene for a moment like a sun that breaks through a thick cloud cover, he quickly returned to his voluntary obscurity and remained there many a year—so that during thirty years no one knew anything of him except that he was the son of a carpenter (Mt 13:55) and a carpenter himself (Mk 6:3), working in the shop of the man people considered his father (Lk 3:23) and obeying his parents (Lk 2:51), being of help to them around the house and using his mechanical skills as is the custom of the children of all other artisans.

What was this, then, if not life hidden in God or rather God hidden in Jesus Christ? Is it possible that you would not want to share in the perfection and the happiness of this hidden God? Learn then in the same way "to hide your life in God with your divine master" (Col 3:3), cherishing your place in the Solitude and leaving it only under obedience.

Then came the moment when the Savior had to reveal himself to the Jews. Although he went forth from that holy and heavenly obscurity, he continued to remain hidden even in the midst of his public life. Though he appeared as the light of the world, the world—enemy of the light that could uncover the wickedness of its works (Jn 3:19) — began to hurl out from all sides calumnies, which darkened the "sun of justice" (Mal 4:2) in the eyes of whoever received its divine rays. There is no kind of deceit that does not try to cover up the truth which Jesus brought to human beings or to cover up the glory which was his because of his sublime teachings and his miracles.

Given that deceit, there now comes a moment when you no longer know whether you ought to believe in his divinity, if you listen to the people and the false teachers: He is a prophet (Lk 6:15; Jn 9:17); he is a fake (Lk 7:39; Jn 7:52). He is the Christ (Jn 7:41); he is not the Christ (Jn 10:24). He is a man who loves pleasure, the good life, and good wine (Lk 15:2; 7:34; Mt 11:19). He is a Samaritan (Jn 8:48), a heretic, a blasphemer (Jn 10:33), an enemy of the Temple and of the nation (Lk 23:2; Jn 11:48). He frees the possessed by the name of Beelzebub (Mt 12:24); he is himself possessed (Jn 8:48), and an evil spirit is at work in him (Jn 10:19). Can anything good come out of Nazareth (Jn 1:46)? No one knows where that one comes from (Jn 9:29), but he is certainly not from God because he does not observe the Sabbath (Jn 9:16). He even heals people and performs miracles on that holy day (Lk 13:14). What sort of man is this who comes into Jerusalem and the Temple today with so much loud acclaim? No one knows him. And the crowd was greatly divided concerning him (Jn 9:16).

It is quite true, then, that even in the midst of the wonders which revealed his divinity, Jesus Christ remained a hidden God for almost everyone. He did that out of love for that very hidden and lowly life which you perhaps have so much trouble putting up with. Look at your model with admiration; humble yourself at his feet. Beg him to give you the grace of appreciating and cherishing the obscurity of your solitude or of your work.

At last, the hour to save the world had come, and as if to make us better understand that salvation is found in humiliation and self-forgetfulness on the part of creatures, Jesus Christ never seemed so hidden. He is the least among humans (Jgs 6:15), or rather not a human at all but a worm (Ps 22:6); he no longer has any beauty or human features (Is 53:2). No one recognizes him, and he seems to have been forgotten. For do you not hear him cry out, "My God, my God,"—as if the Lord were no longer his father— "why have you abandoned me?" (Ps 22:1; Mk 15:34)? Covered with sins, he seems to have become sin in place of us (2 Cor 5:21). It seems that he sees only the debt he paid as Savior of the human race. And he has to pay the entire debt, which makes him say through the mouth of the psalmist: "My sins," the sins of the world which I have taken upon myself, "my sins do not let me hope that you would deliver me from the evils I endure" (Ps 38; 40). They heaped upon me injury and insult (Lk 23:11).

Yes, Jesus Christ died. He went down to the tomb and even to the shades of the dead. Can he ever hide himself more or vanish from sight more than this? Soon afterward, he came out of the sepulcher, and Magdalene did not find him there (Jn 20:13). She had lost even the dead body of her divine master. It is true that he did appear after his resurrection in glory and triumph, but he showed himself only in secret and in passing, not to his enemies to gloat over their confusion or in the main square of Jerusalem, but only to his disciples and apostles.

Finally, a cloud took him up from their sight (Acts 1:9). They would see him no more here below, and until the end of the ages, he will remain hidden in the solitude of our tabernacles. There, he will be insulted and will be trod under foot, but he will make neither his thunder boom out nor his great power felt.

"Human beings will forget about you, oh my Savior. With impunity, they will blaspheme against you. The entire earth is full of your enemies and blasphemers. Every day scandals increase, and charity grows cold. Do they not believe that we are now in the times you had foretold when you said: 'Do you think that the Son of Man will find faith on the earth?' (Lk 18:8).

"Yes, you are misunderstood even by those who profess to be your disciples, and your glory among us continues to subsist only in God, where you are hidden. As for me, I, too, want to hide myself in God along with you, for the world is not worthy of my searchings nor my aspirations. What sort of case can I make in favor of this world after it has judged you and treated you so unworthily, you and all who belong to you, oh my divine master? Let it despise me, too, and let it speak against me as much as it wants. Let the world treat me as demented, ambitious, dominating, or hypocritical, and I will be grateful to it for doing so, because in that way it will make me share in your own life. No matter the cost, I will seek in everything, everywhere and always, to be 'hidden with you in God' (Col 3:3), your father, until truth triumphs over all."

Go now to the foot of the altar. Contemplate Jesus Christ in the reserved sacrament where he is hidden. Remain there in silence, saying nothing to him. Just look at him, waiting eagerly for him to speak to you. Listen to what he says to you in the depths of your heart:

"You see, here have I died, and my life is hidden in God until the time comes for me to appear in glory to judge the world. Therefore, hide yourself in God with me, and do not dream of appearing again before I show myself to the world. Hide yourself. Bury yourself willingly in the dust of a classroom or in the obscurity of a rural parish church. If you are alone, I will be your companion; if you are weak, I will be your strength. If you are poor, I will be your treasure; if you are hungry, I will be your food. If you are afflicted, I will be your comfort and joy. If you are sluggish, I will lift you up; if you are exhausted, I will be your support.

"I am at the door, and I knock. Whoever hears my voice opens the door. I will enter the house and dwell there along with my father, and I will take my meal with those who open the door, and they with me (Rv 3:20). I will give them the fruit of the tree of life (Rv 2:7), which is in the paradise of my God, and I will also give them the hidden manna whose taste no one knows except those who receive it" (Rv 2:17).

Spiritual Bouquet

End your meditation with these words which will also serve as your spiritual bouquet: "Come, Jesus, come and do not delay" (Rv 22:20; Heb 10:37). Hide me, oh my God, in the hidden mystery of your face.

Meditations for the Feast of the Sacred Heart

. . . .

First Meditation for the Feast of the Sacred Heart

The object of this meditation: devotion to the Sacred Heart

First Prelude

"My child, give me your heart" (Prv 23:26).

Second Prelude

Imagine that you see Jesus Christ showing you his heart today as once he did to a holy religious of the Visitation.[17] He showed it to her on a throne of flames, crowned with thorns, and nailed to a cross. Now hear the divine Savior ask you, as Jehu asked Jehonadab (2 Kgs 10:15), whether your heart reciprocates his feelings for you.

Third Prelude

Consider now the object of devotion to the Sacred Heart.

This meditation's object is the very heart of the Savior, not in a material sense separate from the rest of his humanity, but considered as one with his body, soul, and divinity and understood as the symbol, source, and center of his love for us humans. What could be more worthy of your reverence, your thanksgiving, your adoration?

Is it not true that, in virtue of the hypostatic union, the human nature in Jesus Christ shares in the honor due to his divinity? Is that not also why we adore his body and blood in the Blessed Eucharist? Is it not likewise because of that same principle that a special feast was instituted to honor his precious blood and his sacred wounds? Do we not also revere the thorns which crowned his sacred brow, the nails which pierced his hands and feet, the cross on which he died, the shroud in which he was buried, the very name of Jesus before which every knee must bend in heaven, on earth, and in hell (Phil 2:10)? How then could you refuse your homage to this Sacred Heart, the most noble and most touching part of his humanity, to this heart of the Word incarnate, the greatest, the most generous, holy, tender, and compassionate heart to have come from the hands of God? In him are contained all the treasures of knowledge and wisdom (Col 2:3) and all the riches of love. In him dwells bodily the fullness of the Godhead (Col 2:9). In him is the origin of all the mysteries of our salvation. This adorable heart is the source of all graces, from which there never cease to flow out over us with inexhaustible abundance the graces of expiation, of reconciliation, and of sanctification, and especially of your spiritual rebirth in the sacrament of Baptism and your reconciliation with God in the sacrament of Penance. The heart of Jesus is the true gate of heaven, which is closed by our sins and which his adorable heart never ceases to open for us. It is the spiritual bath that washes away our stains — makes us white as snow, pure and pleasing in the eyes of God — and restores to us all the privileges of the state of innocence.

The heart of Jesus is the burnt sacrifice yet always alive, never ceasing to burn for us, always making the incense of his sacrifice rise up to the throne of the divine majesty. His heart disarms the justice of God, so often inflamed by our sins, and obtains for us, through pardon of our sins, a new superabundance of graces and merits. A holy religious once said: It is in this adorable heart that we will find weapons to defend ourselves, remedies to cure us, powerful aids against temptation, very sweet consolation in our hurt, and the purest of delights in this valley of tears. It is a secure asylum, a refuge for the afflicted, and protection for all Christians.[18]

Ah, if it is delightful to be one in heart with those we love, if we taste so much happiness in the intimate exchange of deep affection, if we eagerly honor the name of heroes or the ashes of saints, how can we not consider it both a duty and a blessing to give homage to the heart of our Savior? With love as gentle and kind as any father's, he joins together in himself the sovereign majesty and the incomprehensible grandeur of God. Go to him, therefore, with a confidence complemented with holy reverence. Prostrate yourself before him. Adore him by offering him your own heart, which he never scorns, unworthy though it is. In this way, you will begin to enter into the spirit of this wonderful feast.

End your meditation with a truly affectionate colloquy with the heart of Jesus. Offer him your homage in union with his Blessed Mother and St. John, the beloved disciple, both of whom had the happiness of leaning back on his heart, just as you will in a little while when you receive Holy Communion.

Spiritual Bouquet

"My child, give me your heart."

Second Meditation for the Feast of the Sacred Heart

The object of this meditation: devotion to the Sacred Heart

First Prelude

"I will speak to his heart" (Hos 2:14).

Second Prelude

Let us give ear to the voice of the eternal father, who is saying to us: "Jesus is my beloved son; listen to him" (Mt 17:5).

Third Prelude

Enter in spirit into the Sacred Heart of the Savior, and hear the voice of Jesus saying to you: "I have given you an example, my child, that you should do as I have done" (Jn 13:15).

Consider now your Lord and master in the course of his hidden life or his public life. Is he not the divine model of all perfection? What humility and what gentleness! What obedience, not only to his heavenly father whose will is like his daily bread, but also to Mary and Joseph in the humble abode of Nazareth! What poverty! Not even a place in which to lay down his head. What a spirit of penitence and mortification. He was always busy doing the heaviest and most tiring of chores; he spent whole nights in prayer. He fasted forty days without taking any nourishment at all. He thirsts for insults and sufferings. There is a baptism of blood for which he longs because he knows that that alone is the price of our salvation.

And yet, what burning love, what inexhaustible mercy, what unflagging zeal for souls. And now, going through the different events in the life of our Savior in as great detail as possible, can you find even one word, one action, or one desire on which charity did not leave its mark? Charity followed him wherever he went, from Bethlehem to Nazareth, from Nazareth to the desert, from the desert to Calvary, from Calvary into the arms of death. And in the midst of contradictions, what patience. In trials, what resignation. In insults, what calm. What silence even in the midst of torture.

If you now take a look at yourself, if you plumb the depths of your heart and contrast it with the heart of your model, how red would your face be in your humiliation? What, in fact, do you find in your heart most of the time if not indifference, worldly attachments, distaste for heaven, resistance to grace, distrust of providence, complaints in trials, love of creature comforts, seeking what is easiest, sensuality, weakness, fickleness, constant carelessness—in a word, no truly solid and lasting virtue? Do you have anything resembling the humility and gentleness so strongly recommended by this divine master?

Look deep into your conscience, and it will reproach you for your impatience, your outbursts of temper; the source of self-love and self-satisfaction which has penetrated to the marrow of your bones and spoils all you do; a secret envy for wanting to be considered great, for wanting power and to lord it over others; a jealousy that goes to the point of hatred for whatever hurts your feelings or goes against your natural inclinations and distances your heart very far from that of Jesus. Is not that sufficient to wound deeply this gentle Savior? Or to undo the plan of his mercy toward you? Or to paralyze the efficacy of his precious graces or even to stop this flow altogether?

Ah, now at least be aware of your wretchedness. With a deep sigh, sincerely deplore your sorry state and take yourself to the Sacred Heart of Jesus to obtain forgiveness and to seek remedies for your miseries. Straightforwardly and ardently ask this gentle Savior for a humble heart that is aware of its nothingness and accepts the contempt it deserves; a gentle heart which knows how to control itself, to govern its movements, and to overcome its natural sensitivity; a loving heart, compassionate to the misfortunes of others and eagerly seeking ways to relieve them; a pure heart which gives the benefit of the doubt until evil clearly shows itself; a heart detached from the apparent goods of this world and longing only for the invisible goods of heaven; a heart patient and faithful to its duties, generous in carrying them out, and obedient to the suggestions of faith and the inspirations of grace.

Stop here with these thoughts, and follow the one that attracts you the most, but do not end without a firm, practical resolution as your conclusion.

Colloquy

End in a colloquy with our Savior, beginning with these words of the prophet: "Give me, oh my God, a new heart" (Ez 36:26).

Third Meditation for the Feast
of the Sacred Heart

The object of this meditation:
the love of the heart of Jesus for everyone

First Prelude

"I have loved you, my child, with an everlasting love" (Jer 31:3).

Second Prelude

Contemplate the divine Word in the bosom of his father, surrounded by the angels in their adoration and giving his consent
to the divine decree sending him on earth to redeem human sins.

Third Prelude

Hear this gentle Savior, who says to his father by the mouth of the
prophet: "My heart has but one desire, one longing: the salvation
of men and women" (Ps 27:4).

You will be convinced of the truth of these words and by those
which began your meditation if you consider the astonishing love that
our Lord had and continues to have for you. Notice especially to what
lengths that love led him and what proofs of that love he has given you in
the course of his life. Not content at becoming flesh like you in his Incarnation, your brother by his birth, your Savior by his circumcision, your
light by his epiphany, he wanted to abase himself even to the lowest level
of poverty, embracing the humblest, the most hidden, and the most lowly
way of living, giving himself over to the most arduous tasks—in short,
putting up with all the privations associated with the poor and the outcast
of society. Such was his hidden life.

Can it ever again be possible for you to remember without emotion the marvels of his love during his public life? He was compassionate toward every sort of misfortune and consoling toward every kind of

affliction. See him deeply moved at the lot of the widow of Nain and consequently giving back to her the son she mourned (Lk 7:15). See him kindly conversing with the Samaritan woman, explaining to her the complete truth of the New Law (Jn 4). See him weeping with the sisters of Lazarus and restoring him to life (Jn 11:35). See him welcoming the little children with fatherly affection and blessing them as the beloved children of his father (Mt 19:13–15; Mk 10:13–16). See him revealing himself to us in all his parables with very touching images. See him welcoming sinners with very great compassion and gentleness, encouraging them either by his teachings or by extraordinary favors. See him treating his most inveterate and treacherous enemies with kindness. See him praying for his enemies even on the cross, up to his last breath.

Our gentle master could have made satisfaction for us with but one drop of his blood, one tear, one sigh. But what was enough for divine justice was not enough for the love in his heart, and it was this love that made him anticipate, prolong, and intensify his passion in order to begin his sufferings early and thus to suffer more. Marvel at this excess of his love for you. He expiated your sins of thought by the thorns that were shoved down onto his head, the sins of your tongue by the gall and the vinegar given him to drink, the sins of your flesh by the scourging with whips that wounded his shoulders, all your injustices and evil deeds by his wounds and his most pitiful death. He expiated one last time all sins by the terrible thrust of a lance that pierced his heart, making a wound large enough for the last drops of his blood to flow out. Why? Because all sins have their beginning and their origin in the heart, and he wants to reach them and undo them at their source.

Stop here and consider that it is you alone who are guilty and that you are the one who deserves this terrible punishment.

Jesus' love goes further still. Victorious and glorious, conqueror of death and hell, the divine Redeemer ascended into heaven (Acts 1:9). Does this mean that he is leaving us orphaned on earth without his presence (Jn 14:18)? Oh, stunning legacy of his love! He ascends to his father, he sits at his right hand (Eph 1:20; Col 3:1), but he does not cease living and abiding with us. "He even makes it the delight" of his heart to do so (Ps 13:5). His wisdom and his power unite to bring about the greatest of miracles. In the Incarnation he became flesh to abide with you; in the Holy Eucharist he united himself with matter, and by that ineffable deed of love, he left us his body and blood until the end of the ages (Mt 28:20).

He did still more, and this is where there burst forth the most incomprehensible wonders of his love for us. He gave us his adorable flesh to be spiritual nourishment for our soul. He gifted us with heavenly bread to sustain our soul, to converse with us, and to make divine life grow within us. He gave us his blood to be our drink for extinguishing in us the fire of concupiscence and to grant us spiritual strength for our temptations. In view of such a wondrous deed, is it not true to say that we almost share in the divine nature and that, by sharing in our own substance, Jesus renews and completes in us once again the mystery of his own Incarnation?

And that is not all. The great sacrifice of the cross, the burnt offering of infinite price offered to his father for the salvation of the world, is made present again, not like it once was on one specific day, once only, in only one place on the earth, but every day, or rather every moment of every day, in a thousand different places and among all peoples who are willing to receive him. Given all that, is it an exaggeration to say with the saints that the heart of our God on the altar is a blazing furnace? That it is a burning hearth from which there continually comes forth a sacred fire to set our souls on fire? It is he himself who says to you, "What else do I desire than that this fire of divine love set your hearts ablaze?" (Lk 12:49).

Need more be added to these testimonies of love to show how lavish is the heart of Jesus toward us?

Ah, let me say this, all covered with shame: He chose us priests to speak to people about his love. He called us to the remarkable and formidable honor of making him present every day on the altar, of receiving him every day in our heart by Holy Communion. And finally, he confided to us the care of all souls for whom he gave up his life. How could our heart remain cold and icy in the presence of so many signs of tenderness and love? How could we be lukewarm and lax in the service of such a master? How could we let ourselves be guided only by our own moods or purely natural tendencies? Ah, let us take our poor, wretched heart and plunge it into this divine fire whose hearth is the Sacred Heart of Jesus. It will come forth from the fire a strong, sturdy apostle's heart, overflowing with an immense love for God and for neighbor.

And now, privately make the practical resolution to enter the brotherhood that is consecrated to the Sacred Heart or else to persevere in it if you are already a member of it. Also resolve to pray frequently or at least once a day five Our Fathers, Hail Marys, and the Creed along with this loving aspiration: "O Sacred Heart of Jesus, make me love you ever more deeply."

Spiritual Bouquet

"The wine of your love inebriates my heart, and the bread of your charity strengthens it."

Fourth Week: The Unitive Way

. . . .

Retreat of eight days before the end of the academic year or before the feast of the Assumption[19]

The *Exercises* of St. Ignatius have as their goal in its first part to reform your life; in the second, to conform your life to that of Jesus Christ; in the third, to confirm you in your good dispositions by the strength of Jesus Christ's example in his suffering and death. They have as their goal in this fourth and final week to transform you into your divine model by being united ever more closely to him in meditating on the glorious mysteries of his resurrected life and on the perfections of God.

The fruit of these exercises, therefore, will be to lift your thoughts and desires toward heaven, to set you on fire with divine love, and to have you taste beforehand the joys of union with the one who glorifies his saints in eternity. These holy meditations to which you will now give yourself belong to the unitive way.

Because St. Ignatius wanted everything in this retreat to convey joy and love, there are to be no special mortifications for the body except to follow the ordinary rules of moderation. You are even to enjoy the innocent pleasures of nature, which can only make you praise the Lord and thank him for his goodness to you.

Week Four: Day One

Meditation on the resurrection of Jesus Christ, model of the new life to be lived by a Salvatorist after his novitiate or his profession

First Prelude

"He is risen!" (Mk 16:6).

Second Prelude

Imagine that you see the tomb of Jesus Christ hewn in the rock, sealed with a large stone, and surrounded by guards. When it was morning on the third day after his death, Jesus Christ suddenly came forth all resplendent in glory, neither smashing the stone nor breaking its seals. Consider what must have been the astonishment and the great fear of the guards and how the Temple priests persuaded the guards with money to say that the body of Jesus was stolen away while they were sleeping (Mt 28:11–15).

Third Prelude

Beg this divine Savior to let you penetrate the mystery of his resurrection and to let you find in it not only a means to reawaken your faith, hope, and love, but especially to find the model of the new life you ought to be living as the fruit of your novitiate as well as of this retreat.

The resurrection of Jesus Christ is true, observable by the senses, and enduring. Such ought also to be the characteristics of your new life.

First, the resurrection is true because it is based on his word and was foretold by him. Furthermore, it is confirmed by his appearances to the apostles and the holy women, and especially to St. Thomas, who put his fingers into the scars of his wounds. It is confirmed by the testimony of more than five hundred witnesses who saw him ascend into heaven, by the miracles performed as proof of this truth, and by the death of a great crowd of martyrs who attested to it. This is not, therefore, some fictional or imaginary resurrection but real and undeniable for everyone in good faith.

And you, have you risen in the same way, namely, without hypocrisy and without disguise but truly having passed from death because of sin to life in grace? Is your heart no longer attached to anything contrary to the laws of God and your rules? Have you held on to any reservations in the sacrifice of yourself by means of the vows that ought to have made you die to the world and to the flesh? A truly resurrected Salvatorist no longer has anything in common with the children of the world. You will not find such a Salvatorist among those who are dead from the point of view of faith, because he does live, speak, and act like the living, that is, like the saints or, rather, like Jesus Christ himself. He is fervent in his service and courageous in overcoming temptations and mastering the difficulties he encounters.

A second characteristic of the resurrection of the Savior is that it was visible to all who saw it. To convince his disciples of that, he took on a sensate body and let himself be touched by them. That is the way you must be, so that if anyone comes up to you or sees you from however close, no one will see anything in your conduct that contradicts itself. There ought to be in you a quality of recollection and reserve, a way of speaking and acting that reveals at first glance the dispositions of your heart and that makes others who may have had their faith shaken previously say what Jesus Christ says about the prodigal son: "He was dead but, behold, now he lives again. He was lost and, behold, he has now been found again" (Lk 15:32).

Is that how it is with you? Be on your guard, especially if you have had the misfortune of scandalizing the world or your confreres, for it is in such a case that you ought to live now so exemplary a life that you appear before God as a suitable atonement for the harm done to his sovereign majesty, and before your fellow human beings as a stunningly bright reparation for your previous scandalous behavior.

And finally, Jesus Christ risen from the dead dies no more (Rom 6:9), but he endures eternally in this glorious and victorious state, very different from that of Lazarus and the son of the widow of Nain, who, although they miraculously came forth from their tombs, later had to return to them. Such, then, is Jesus Christ, the model you must imitate in the order of grace if you do not want to fall back into your former sins or find yourself once again as you were before your conversion.

Fervently ask the Savior for the grace of this steadfastness in goodness. Ask also through the intercession of Mary, by rejoicing with her and with the Church, in the resurrection of her divine son. Meditate on each word of the prayer *Regina coeli, laetare* and resolve to avoid henceforth every occasion of slackening off.[20]

Colloquy

Let your colloquy be similar to the second prelude.

Spiritual Bouquet

"Let us move forward on the pathway of a new life."

Week Four: Day Two

Meditation on the appearances of Jesus Christ, symbol of the secret visits of his grace in the soul of a Salvatorist united to him by love

First Prelude

"He appeared to his eleven disciples" (Mk 16:14).

Second Prelude

Imagine yourself in the upper room when the Savior appeared to St. Thomas (Jn 20:26–29), or in the garden when he appeared to Mary Magdalene (Jn 20:11–18), or in the company of the disciples on the way to Emmaus when he was recognized by them in the breaking of the bread (Lk 24:13–33).

Third Prelude

Beg this divine Savior to make you truly profit from the fruit of this meditation, and commend yourself also to the most ordinary witnesses of his resurrection as you try to profit from the presence of his grace by which he communicates himself so intimately to you.

Now, consider to whom Jesus Christ appeared, how he appeared, and why he appeared. In doing so you will find many rules for setting yourself on the unitive way, which you are about to begin.

First of all, to whom did Jesus appear? To some ordinary women, then to his apostles and some wavering disciples, and finally to some unbelievers like the soldiers who were guarding his tomb.

To these last he showed himself only via the angels whose appearance filled them with dread. That is the Savior's usual way even now of visiting souls and the way he sometimes makes his presence known to the senses.

He more often makes his presence known to ordinary and uneducated people who are devout and fervent, simply because they are usually better disposed to believe and open to believe more deeply than the learned of this world, who rely too much on themselves and are more likely to consider supernatural and extraordinary occurrences as fantasies and dreams. That is also why we see today so few people caught up in contemplation.

The author of the *Imitation* explains it this way: Few souls are given the favors of heavenly communing, because so few have the courage to renounce absolutely and decisively the perishable and created things of the world. There certainly are plenty who desire contemplation, but they do not give themselves to the exercises that will dispose them for it. The greatest obstacle is a lack of mortification. If you only knew how to release your heart from these base and useless attachments, you could begin to experience some heavenly sweetness.[21] Remember this short phrase with deep meaning: Let go of all, and you will find all. This "all" allows of no exceptions, however. Oh my soul, pay close attention to these words, and close off all your senses the better to hear your God who speaks to you and wants to be heard.

Consider next how Jesus Christ appeared, Sometimes he showed himself with his own countenance, and people recognized his face, his voice, and his ways of acting. People could even see the scars of his sacred wounds. At other times he borrowed the traits of other people. The resemblance of a gardener is one example when he appeared to Mary Magdalene. That of a traveler is another example when he appeared to the disciples of Emmaus. It was not long before he was recognized, however. A gesture, some action, or a word was enough for the heart of people to be moved, transported in love.

Ah, it is you, beloved master, gentle spouse. These were the cries uttered by the soul. On the other hand, when his presence was not revealed to the senses, people discerned it sometimes in the calm and the peacefulness, which accompanied his visit to the soul, making it hear this sweet greeting: "Peace be with you" (Jn 20:19). At other times it was in the joy and the consolation filling the soul: "The disciples rejoiced when they saw the Lord" (Jn 20:20).

Such is not the way, however, of the spirit of darkness. He stirs up dark thoughts, arouses feelings of anxiety, dread, and dejection. And so, now, go into yourself and try to recognize in the light of these characteristics which spirit governs your actions, and take advantage of these rules lest you be fooled by the illusions from the devil.

Thirdly, consider why Jesus Christ appeared. It was to strengthen the fragile faith of his apostles, to prepare them for a long separation, and to encourage them to do everything henceforth for his glory. St. Thomas gave a vivid proof of this. Although he had the greatest doubts of them all, he was among those who exhibited the liveliest faith. Having become an apostle on fire with zeal, he preached the Gospel to the most foreign and distant peoples, going as far as India, where he was martyred.

Then there was the model of penitents, the holy Magdalene who had loved Jesus very much and who courageously lived with the separation from him and led an angelic life accompanied by rapturous contemplation. Learn from these examples that prayer and union with God were the hearth where servants of the Gospel such as St. Dominic, St. Francis Xavier, and St. Vincent Ferrer conceived their very heroic plans and found the strength to carry them out.

Place a great value, then, on the visits of God's grace. Judge yourself unworthy to receive them, but do nothing, however, that might deprive you of them. And then, see what sacrifice you could make corresponding to the grace received.

Colloquy

Let your colloquy be with the disciples of Emmaus, conversing with Jesus Christ and exclaiming at the end of this appearance of the Savior: "Did not our hearts burn within us while he talked to us on the road?" (Lk 24:32).

Spiritual Bouquet

"Stay with us, Lord, for evening is near" (Lk 24:29).

Week Four: Day Three

Meditation on the ascension of Jesus Christ

First Prelude

"He ascended into heaven" (Lk 24:51; Acts 1:9).

Second Prelude

Imagine that you see the Savior in his last apparition on the Mount of Olives, taking his apostles to task for their lack of faith, promising them his Holy Spirit, giving them his blessing, and then being taken up to heaven in their presence. See the bright cloud as it hides him from their sight. See the two angels who appeared to the witnesses of this glorious mystery and proclaimed that this same Jesus will come again, in the way he was seen taken up to heaven, to judge the world (Acts 1:9–11).

Third Prelude

Ask Jesus Christ, the two angels, and the apostles to help you understand better the purpose of the ascension and benefit from this meditation.

Reflect on the several purposes that Jesus Christ intends for his ascension. First of all, he ascended to heaven to prepare a place for us — and what a place! Like him, in heaven we will no longer have to suffer any evil, to desire any good, or to fear any change. God himself will wipe away your tears (Rv 7:17; 21:4), and their source will have dried up forever. All the faculties of your soul and your body will be satisfied. In such blessedness you will enjoy eternal happiness, no longer apprehensive that any chance happening might one day change it all.

How can we not long for such a destiny? Work hard, therefore, to be worthy of it, and put into practice the related advice given by the pious author of the *Imitation*:

Write, read, sing, sigh, be silent, pray, courageously suffer adversity. Eternal life deserves to be won by these battles and even greater ones. Peace will come on the day known to the Lord, and it will not be a day like ours here below, which is followed by night, but a continuous light, an infinite clarity, a strong peace, and a secure rest. You will no longer have to say: "Who will deliver me from this body of death?" You will no longer have to exclaim: "Alas, how long is this exile of mine," because, "death having been destroyed," you will enjoy eternal salvation and because, in place of all anxiety, you will taste a blessed joy in the midst of a warm and wonderful companionship.

Oh, if only you could really taste these truths and let them truly enter deeply into your heart, how could you ever dare to complain even once? Is anything so difficult that you cannot endure it for the sake of winning eternal life? It is no little matter to lose or to gain the kingdom of God. Therefore, says our savior, lift up your eyes to heaven where I am and where all the saints are along with me. After having lived through mighty battles on earth, they now live in joy and solace, in security and peace. And they will dwell with me forever in the kingdom of my father.[22]

And that is not the only purpose of the ascension. Jesus Christ ascended to heaven to be your mediator before God. In heaven, as the chant of the Church puts it, he continually presents to his father his sacred wounds as if so many mouths begging grace and mercy for you. The apostle St. John presents him as a lamb that was slain before the throne of the eternal God (Rv 5:6), to whom he recalls unceasingly by his presence the remembrance of his sacrifice on Calvary and the price of our redemption.

And so, he is there as your friend, your protector, your ambassador, and your deputy, charged with pleading your cause and that of the whole world. He has become the mediator of all on earth, and only through him are all graces given, all prayers from on earth heard, and all homage received. Not even the patriarchs, prophets, apostles, martyrs, angels, nor Mary, their queen, have access to the Most High except through Jesus Christ. All of them, no doubt, pray for us. But they, as well as we, pray in the name of Jesus and are heard only because of his merits. How great our confidence ought to be after such a meditation. Can there be any excuse for not having recourse to them in all your needs?

Lastly, Jesus Christ ascends to heaven to teach us the way that leads there. Was it not from the top of the Mount of Olives that he was lifted up to paradise? That is, was it not from a mountain at whose base he sweated blood; where he was overwhelmed with anxiousness, sadness, and dread at accomplishing the will of his father; and where his agony was so severe that he needed the help of an angel to strengthen him (Lk 22:43)? Could there be any better way to teach you that glory and eternal happiness are won only through suffering, a suffering endured—as he did—for the sake of justice and truth, suffering made holy by patience and a perfect surrender to the divine will? The saints, too, following the example of St. Paul (2 Cor 11–12), boasted of their tribulations, passionately longing for the cross, so much so that St. Teresa exclaimed: "To suffer or to die!"[23]

Keep yourself, then, from imitating the world, which runs after every sort of covetousness and studiously avoids all pain and mortification. Instead, fix your eyes on Jesus Christ who died for you and on the last steps of his life, which he left imprinted on the top of the mountain from which he was taken up into heaven. Imagine him saying to you there:

"Come and see the way I have taken to arrive at this joy. Follow me. Do not take your eyes off my footprints. Take up your cross and carry it to the end of your course.

"Remember all that I did and suffered to receive the glory that I now enjoy and which I merited for you. I left the bosom of my father for that of a woman, left her womb for the manger in Bethlehem, left Bethlehem for Egypt, Egypt for Nazareth, Nazareth for diverse parts of Judea, going from there to the cross, from the cross to the tomb, from the tomb to this mountain top, and finally from this mountain to the bosom of my peaceful repose, where I now await you."

Colloquy and Spiritual Bouquet

After your colloquy with Jesus Christ and with the souls of the saints of old who accompanied him in his glorious ascension, take as your spiritual bouquet these words of the apostle: "This slight momentary affliction is preparing for us an eternal weight of glory beyond all comparison" (2 Cor 4:17).

Chapter 3

CHRISTIAN MEDITATIONS

Moreau's *Meditations* is in the same style as his *Spiritual Exercises*, but its subject matter makes it unique. Moreau, who was in dialogue over liturgical matters with his contemporary Dom Prosper Guéranger of Solesmes, was concerned with prayer flowing from the liturgical year and feeding back into it. These meditations follow Moreau's adapted Ignatian outline but are not within the overall structure of the Ignatian *Spiritual Exercises*. Rather, the *Meditations* follow the principal Sundays of the liturgical year.

Moreau began work on these meditations in 1854 but revised and republished them in 1859. The following are from the 1859 edition. This edition was intended for the meditative practice of the religious of Holy Cross. Moreau worked on a third version in 1872, the year before his death. The time and care he invested in writing and revising these mediations reveals the centrality of the liturgy for Moreau in the spiritual lives of his religious. While he strives to connect the liturgy with Church teaching and the wider theological tradition, he also seeks to draw practical import for the lives and ministry of his religious.

The structure of each meditation follows that of the *Spiritual Exercises* very closely. The topic is introduced with up to three preludes that prepare the individual for the substance of the meditation. These preludes might be imagining a scene from scripture, contemplating a figure from scripture, or even praying with a verse of scripture. They are followed by the body of the reflection and then conclude with a colloquy or spiritual bouquet in order to draw it to a close.

The liturgical calendar used by Moreau in his time and the *Missale Romanum*, reformed and instituted by Pope Paul VI, differ. In the calendar that Moreau followed, the lectionary for the cycle of readings involved two readings, normally an epistle (though at times a reading from the Old Testament) and a passage from one of the gospels. The readings for each Sunday are provided in the first footnote of each meditation. Other particular times and feasts are also explained in the notes. Parenthetical notes to scriptural passages and allusions have been inserted by the editors, as have footnotes to identifiable citations from the Fathers of the Church or other French thinkers.

K.G. and A.G.

Epiphany

· · · · · · · · · · · · ·

Meditation on the mystery

First Prelude

"Magi came from the East" (Mt 2:1).

Second Prelude

Let us imagine these illustrious personages prostrate in front of the crèche, at the feet of the infant Jesus, offering him their gifts (Mt 2:11).

Third Prelude

Let us ask the grace of sharing in these sentiments of adoration, love, and thanksgiving that so filled the Magi toward the infant Jesus.[1]

The Epiphany has always been considered as one of the major feast days of the year owing as much to its antiquity, which goes back to the fourth century, as to the great mystery which the feast day forever commemorates. That is why the Church celebrates it with extraordinary solemnity.

What, then, is its purpose? It is to remember the call of the Gentiles to Christianity and to be the yearly remembrance of this marvelous event. Therefore, this day ought to be for all of us a day of joy and spiritual delight. The Church invites us to these sentiments and wants us to celebrate this feast day with great solemnity and singular devotion.

To do that worthily and fruitfully, let us meditate on the mysterious ways of providence toward the Magi, considering what we are taught by these wise men who are our models and ancestors in the faith.

Without wasting time to ponder either their number or their dignity, we will look more closely at the example of their virtues: (1) the promptness and persistence of their faith, (2) their detachment from themselves and from all their possessions, and (3) the symbolic meaning of their gifts.

1. How admirable the promptness and persistence of their faith! Their eyes no sooner beheld the miraculous star shine brilliantly before them than they set out, hastening their steps, eager to arrive at the place to which the star was calling them. There was no stopping for vain discussions on the nature of this extraordinary phenomenon. Rather, enlightened by faith and traditions common throughout the East, they recognized in this heavenly body the prophetic star foretold from long ago as the sign of the coming of the Lord promised to Abraham and to their ancestors. They held no doubts that the Virgin would bring forth a child (Mt 1:23–25; Is 7:14), that the shoot which is to sprout from the stump of Jesse would be born (Is 11:1), in short, that the promises of God would be fulfilled. They therefore set out in the direction that this star lays out for them.

They arrive in Jerusalem, and here, by the mysterious design of providence, the heavenly body that was guiding their course suddenly disappeared. Ought not this sudden and unexpected event have made them give up on their project and persuade them that it was all illusory? No doubt, that is what would have happened were they to have listened only to human wisdom and earthly prudence. But led on by heavenly counsel, they hope against all hope; and they will not be deceived in their expectations.

And so they continue their journey and enter the capital of Judea. Perhaps they were expecting to find it still resounding with word of the event that brought them there. Indeed, who would not have imagined the banks of the Jordan deeply moved at the birth of the Messiah, the people crowding together around his cradle, and the priests chanting hymns of joy?

There was none of that, however. Mary brought into the world the Redeemer of Israel; the shepherds came to adore him; the wise men of the Gentiles are coming to prostrate themselves at his feet. But the House of Jacob does not recognize its Savior. How great a temptation, a new trial for the Magi! And yet, nothing shakes their bountiful resolve. Always open to grace and full of honest courage, they are not afraid to ask Herod himself where the newborn king, the one who is to rule over Judah, is to be found. Then, with knowledge from the synagogue's response of the place of birth of Jesus Christ, the object of their desires, they continue on their way with the same diligence with which they began. And they do not wait long for the reward of their perseverance: a new appearance of the miraculous star going on before them to the entry of the stable, above which it halted.

And now let us return in earnest to ourselves and see whether we have a faith prompt and persistent like the faith we have just admired in the Magi. Therefore, let us look to see if we have the same openness to the inspirations of grace, which is really our guiding star, the lamp that enlightens us with a truly divine light.

Yet, how often we have willingly closed our eyes and resisted the inner voice that calls to us. Alas, how many delays. How often we are culpable and even rash in putting off the work of our conversion or our sanctification. Even now, do we not hear our conscience reproaching us for the thousand infidelities of today? God himself asks of us more promptness in our obedience, greater attention to our spiritual exercises, greater modesty in our outward appearance, deeper recollection in our times of silence, greater gentleness and charity for our confreres, more respect for our superiors, less self-seeking and seeking out esteem from others—in a word, greater religious spirit.

How do we answer these urgent questions? Are we not used to remaining just as we were when we entered religion? Heavens preserve us from losing our first fervor!

What to do, then? We know what the Lord wants of us. We see him just as the predestined of the Gentiles did, and even more clearly than they did—for, after all, as a sign of his will, they had only an unknown heavenly body, whereas we have so many touching exhortations, so many edifying examples, so many salutary warnings. And instead of saying just once as they did, "We have seen and we are on our way," we hesitate or come to a complete stop. Ah, let it be no longer like that. Let us walk as long as we have the light (Jn 12:35); and, finally, let us be obedient to the voice that cries out to us: Show yourselves worthy of the calling that you have embraced (Eph 4:1). In that way we are imitating the Magi who are our models not only in the promptness and persistence of their faith but also in the detachment from themselves and from all their possessions.

2. Indeed, what ought we to think when we see these men renowned for their wisdom—even if they were not princes as we commonly thought—what ought we to think, I was saying, when we see them leave and forsake their kingdom, their family, their relatives, and all that they held most dear in order to seek out some infant king as yet unknown to them, for whose existence they had no other proof except the appearance of a star? To how much unfavorable gossip must not such a project have exposed them? What sort of judgment must the other wise men of their country have held of them?

In spite of all that, in the conviction that God is calling them by the heavenly body that is brilliantly shining for their sakes and by the secret movement that touches their hearts, these generous men rise above all considerations of vainglory and forget about caring for their own reputation in order to carry out the orders from heaven.

And there is more. Trampling underfoot all human respect, they leave their homeland, as Abraham did in another age, to go into a strange, far-distant place. Accordingly, they forsake all they possess, at least for a certain time, without even knowing whether they would ever see again the places which have been so dear to them.

So it is that no honors, riches, comforts, relatives, and friends—nothing—can hold them back, not even fear of the dangers involved in making such a long trip. Carrying out the divine will is the unique purpose to which they apply themselves. So great is the generosity of their sacrifice that they could say to Jesus Christ when they meet him, being as truthful as the apostles: Here we are. We have left everything to follow you (Mt 19:27).

Now let us compare our own behavior and feelings to those of the Magi. It is true that we have left all that we possessed in the world to come and find in withdrawal from the world the God who calls us there. Closed off from all else in this house, just as the disciples of the Savior did at Jerusalem in another age, we are being prepared, far from our families and from the world, to put into practice the designs that providence can have on us.

But have we really set aside all those earthly interests in order to busy ourselves no longer with any but those of Jesus Christ and his Church? Do we not still cling to the bonds of flesh and blood? Would we obey with the same promptness and the same eagerness a superior who would send us to an institution or a mission far away, poor, difficult, and wearisome? On the contrary, do we not offer our services rather out of completely natural motivation, for temporal advantages, in whatever we undertake, seeking not the glory of God and the salvation of souls but our very own satisfaction—we ourselves, as the apostle puts it, but not Jesus our good master (Mk 10:17; Lk 18:18)?

Are we not slaves to human respect, even up in the sanctuary? Do we not have even a kind of disdain for these little things, however strongly recommended by our Lord? Do we not step back from even the lightest of sacrifices, especially when it comes to keeping silence? Therefore, let us seriously scrutinize ourselves on those points of our rules so easily neglected and be renewed in the resolution of being more faithful to the practices at which we fail the most often.

3. In the third place, let us consider the mysterious meaning of the gifts offered by the Magi. Let us admire once more the faith of these blessed predestined men from among the Gentiles. Let us enter the stable of Bethlehem with them. They probably expected to find a rich palace, a magnificent cradle, and numerous servants making up the court of the new king.

What must have been their surprise when, in place of this sumptuous display, they found only an infant wrapped in poor linen cloths, outstretched on a little straw that he wet with his tears, and lying in a crèche (Lk 2:7). But their faith, which had already overcome so many obstacles, was in no way shaken by that. Beyond the humbling veils of poverty and the frailties of infancy, they discover the Messiah promised to the world from the beginning of the ages. Falling at his feet, their faces prostrate on the ground, they adore him with sentiments of deepest respect and vibrant recognition. The sacred text continues: "Then, opening their coffers, they offered him gifts of gold, incense and myrrh," thus giving witness by the very nature of their gifts that they recognized in Jesus Christ the reality of a mortal body, the majesty of an eternal God, and the powerfulness of a legitimate king (Mt 2:11).

The holy Fathers of the Church have always considered the gold, incense, and myrrh offered by the Magi as mysterious symbols of charity, prayer, and mortification, which ought to be characteristic of us. We also find in them the homage we ought to give Jesus Christ on this solemnity: a heart burning bright with love, an ardent zeal for the growth of the kingdom of Jesus in souls, and the acts of penance, which, for us, consist especially in an exemplary fidelity to our vows and to our duties.

"Yes, reign over us, O divine child! Establish in each of us your empire of love that, adorned with the virtues of that time of blessings, we may be capable of offering you in the crèche of our poor hearts the gold of true charity, the incense of fervent prayer, and the myrrh of mortification made holy by obedience. And when you come down to be born in a real way in our hearts through Holy Communion, may you be able to find there nothing but the virtues symbolized by these gifts. May you be able to find in us the same faith, the same obedience, the same detachment, the same respect that you found in the Magi. O gentle child, from this time forward, prepare our hearts for these virtues."

Colloquy

Our colloquy is to be made with Mary and Joseph, witnesses of this marvel. Our prayer to them will be to obtain for us from their divine son sentiments and virtues in accordance with the spirit of this feast day, and let us be united with them in adoring the infant Jesus.

Spiritual Bouquet

"They offered him gifts of gold, incense, and myrrh" (Mt 2:11).

Third Sunday after Epiphany

. . . .

Meditation on the leprosy of sin

First Prelude

"Lord, if you will to do so, you can cure me" (Mt 8:2; Mk 1:40; Lk 5:12).

Second Prelude

Imagine a man stricken with one of the most shameful and most disgusting diseases, leprosy. Imagine him asking to be cured with loud cries and having his request granted by Jesus Christ on condition that he show himself afterward to the priests.

Third Prelude

Let us ask the grace of having as vivid awareness of the maladies of our soul as of our body and to enter into the dispositions needed to be cured of them. And then, the better to take in the teaching that the divine wisdom gives us symbolically in today's gospel, let us meditate on its allegorical meaning, considering first what this disease is and what it signifies.[2]

What is this leprosy with its double reference of physical and moral? Considered physically, this infirmity consists in a large-scale alteration of the skin that is covered up as if with a pasty material of a brown or grayish color and bristling with nodules, ridges, and hideous folds. Fear of contagion obliged the leper to be separated from everyone else, and the Law was very strict about this. It forbade the sick from having anything to do with anyone else. Everything they touched was profaned or soiled and had to be subjected to legal cleansing. They could have their dwellings only at a certain, determined distance from city enclosures. In this isolation from all other human society, they lived as if under civil interdiction and excommunication.

In its moral and allegorical sense, leprosy has always been considered as representing mortal sin. As a matter of fact, those who give themselves over to mortal sin become truly diseased in soul, all covered with ugly stains in the sight of God and faith, cut off, if not from the body of the Church, at least from its inner unity, which is formed by charity, deprived of the right to sit at the holy table with their fellow believers. They are sadly relegated to the desert of their consciences and the solitude of their remorse, condemned to wander in convoluted and difficult paths, far from the road frequented by those who are going to heaven, all other Christians being forbidden to seek out their company for fear of being soiled by approaching them or coming into contact with them. Understand by that just how much our soul becomes horrifying and hideous before God because of mortal sin.

There were also the ten lepers spoken of elsewhere in the Gospel who dared not come close to Jesus (Lk 17:12ff.). They stopped at a respectable distance from him, raised their voices, and cried out: "Jesus, our Master, have pity on us."

It is the same desire to be delivered from this terrible malady that brings the leper whose story we are meditating on to say to the Savior: "Lord, if you will to do so, you can cure me" (Mt 8:2; Mk 1:40; Lk 5:12). With what faith and what confidence he makes this prayer. Is he not in fact confessing by this moving prayer the divine mission of Jesus Christ, its great power, and the firm hope he has of his prayer being answered?

If, then, we have the misfortune of being slaves to mortal sin, let us have as great a desire as the leper of being delivered from that sin. Let us lift up our voice from the depths of the abyss where we are now, like the prophet David (Ps 130:1), or better, like this leper, and let us beg our Savior for the grace of being cured. Let us ask, crying out until we are answered. It is clear that with a will weak, unsure, hesitant, and fickle, we will never break the chains of sin. It is neither lukewarm prayers (Rv 3:16) that touch the heart of God nor weak sighs that accomplish the work of our conversion. It is not the idle chatter of our lips or the actual cry from the mouth that we have to have heard. Rather it is the cry of the

heart, and I mean of a heart broken by sorrow, a heart without consolation since it has not regained spiritual health and the goodness that it has
lost. Therefore, let us cry out to the Lord if we have the misfortune of
having become his enemies and of being tarnished by this hideous leprosy
of sin. Let us cry out to him, like this leper, with the same faith, the same
hope: "Lord, if you will to do so, you can cure me."

"O divine physician of our souls, have pity on us. We will not
cease calling on you until you have answered our prayer, until you have
stretched out your divine hand on our head and you have made us hear
these consoling words: 'I do will it. Be cured' (Mt 8:3; Mk 1:41; Lk 5:13)."

That is exactly what the minister of the sacrament of Penance does if
grace leads us to his feet, just as obedience led the leper before the priests
to whom Jesus sent him to verify his malady and his cure. The divine
master holds to this procedure precisely to teach us that, even though he
could cure the leprosy of sin without the intervention of his ministers, he
wanted sinners to present themselves to the priests of the New Law, no
longer only to make them recognize the evil or its termination, but really
to heal their entire selves.

Therefore, let us go in all our illnesses, let us go and find this loving
physician, this spiritual father; but let us go there like the leper with a
lively faith, a strong desire for our healing, a firm trust, a sincere humility
that brings us to make known the state of our conscience without hiding
anything, and especially a strong and generous resolution never again to
fall into the same sins.

Colloquy

O my divine Savior, let yourself be touched at the sight of my misery, and
sympathize with all my ills as you have sympathized with those of that
happy sick man whom you have deigned to heal by your word and one
sole act of your will. Say also to my soul, which is just as ill and covered
with sores: "I do will it. Be cured." That is the prayer I make to you now,
all confounded at the remembrance of my sins, keenly regretting not having died before having committed a single one of them, continuing to hope

for their pardon from your infinite mercy, promising you with the help of your grace to avoid them in the future.

Spiritual Bouquet

"Lord, if you will to do so, you can cure me."

Sixth Sunday after Epiphany

· ·

Meditation on the minor virtues

First Prelude

"A grain of mustard seed is the smallest of all grains, and it grows into a tree" (Mt 13:31–32; Mk 4:30–32; Lk 13:18–19).

Second Prelude

Let us imagine Jesus Christ before us, presenting to the people this parable with its figure of the smallest of grains becoming after some time the largest of green plants. It represents not only the Church, weak in the beginning but then developing rapidly and spreading out over all the earth, but the parable is also teaching us with this symbol the progress of virtuous souls who, by putting into practice the least of the virtues, arrive very soon at the greater ones.

Third Prelude

Let us pray for fidelity to the little things as the fruit of this meditation.[3]

Let us consider how fidelity to the least of our duties is good preparation for the exercise of the greatest virtues and how that fidelity itself is a great virtue which, from a certain point of view, is preferable to the more sublime.

First of all, it leads us to the greater virtues in accord with this sacred pronouncement: "Whoever is faithful in the smallest things will also be faithful in the greater" (Lk 16:10). And how is that? The answer is that God grants so much more help to the faithful soul that it has greater zeal for the least task. Not a day goes by and there are almost no moments in which he does not favor this soul in a special way. It follows that grace, now more abundant, increases courage, and courage, sustained by watch-fulness and fervor, leads to even more heroic virtues in about the same way, says St. Augustine, as miners who at first find only clay but with perseverance finish by discovering the richest of metals.

How valuable and consoling such a meditation is for a soul that is truly religious. If its entire life is an uninterrupted series of acts of fidelity, its whole life will be an increase of merit. And over the course of several years lived out in this fidelity, what scope, what abundance, what fill of merits and treasures will it not have attained for eternity? Let us develop this thought a little further.

No one outdoes God in generosity. The more precise we are in car-rying out his commands, the more attentive he is to pour out his favors on us. Every act carried out with this in view does not fail to have its recompense, and this reward is always an increase of graces. A first grace is gained, attracts another one even greater, and this second grace, when well received, merits still another. Thus, day-by-day fidelity brings an increase of grace and at the same time makes us grow in courage.

Now let us say a few words about earlier times of the Church, the times of Nero and Decius, and recall the triumph of the first martyrs. Now, there was generosity for you and heroic perseverance. They affronted the cruelty of these tyrants and scorned the fury of their executioners. Far from being terrified by their blades, flames, or racks, they did not even tremble because of death itself. Some would not even wait for death to come, for they looked for it with greater longing than the sensual person longs for the most exquisite meal.

Where did they get this unconquerable courage? Could this have been their first try at virtue? Most assuredly not. They had prepared for war before they ever went into battle. A thousand previous victories gained over themselves gave them assurance of this final glorious triumph. They knew that they would have been tempting God if they were to offer themselves for torture before they were prepared for it. They knew that it would have been blind presumption to claim the title of martyr before having carried out everything needed for the title of Christian. Finally, they knew that virtue has stages and that we do not strive for the highest before having passed through the lowest.

And that is not all. Alongside courage grows vigilance. From how many illusions is there not protection for the religious who makes it a rule to neglect nothing at all in the service of God and his work? He is always guarding against suggestions to vanity and selfishness. Nothing essential escapes his attention, because he has the habit of considering important the slightest actions of obedience. Attentive to the smallest of tasks, how could he fail to accomplish the more important tasks and the greater virtues?

With the opposite line of reasoning, contempt for the littlest things or neglect of them leaves us open for a great fall. "One abyss begets another" (Ps 42:8), says the Holy Spirit, and slight faults are often the source of greater disorders. St. Bernard says that no one becomes bad all of a sudden. It is only little by little that we fall into vice. First of all, we slacken in the less important things. Fervor slows down, tapers off, and finally we succumb to a violent temptation. Judas would never have sold his master if he had on principle fought against his love of money. Demas would never have renounced his religion if he had avoided the entertainments and the lures of the world.[4] How true it is, then, that we go from contempt for the smallest of things to even greater excesses, just as we rise from fidelity to the smallest observances to the greatest of virtues. Lastly, let us add that this fidelity is itself an outstanding virtue.

Judging from the above, we have here a sure rule. We now give consideration to our motive, intention, and dispositions. The motive we have in view is to please God, giving witness to our reverence and affection for him. Does there exist a nobler motive? And if there is anything great outside of God, is it not, says St. Basil, whatever is done for him? It is of little concern to us that the world treats that as a mere trifle—that world which makes so much out of cases of the least proprieties, that world which punishes with rigorous severity the omission of the smallest courtesies, that world which is so scrupulous in regard to etiquette. Yes, indeed, let the world make a fuss over these mere nothings, but let us make serious efforts to serve with the greatest of care the God who is so magnanimous in his rewards.

And let us not forget that intention is the life and soul of our actions. Consequently, before God, their worth and their merit are measured by the degree of purity of intention with which we act. What a consoling reality for so many souls who are hidden in secret before the face of God but unknown and perhaps scorned by the world!

Rejoice, you humble souls, for you are building up treasures to be counted out in your favor on the day consciences are revealed. Although those who belong to the world will appear before God with empty hands, you will have yours brimming with a rich harvest of merit. That is a truth often forgotten because we are always inclined to judge things by their appearances or their external brilliance without taking into account the intention behind it.

We name little, vile, or base actions that, in the eyes of faith, are great, noble, and sublime; whereas, following through on that same kind of error, we call brilliant, generous, heroic what is often only the fruit of pride and ambition. Let us hold fast to this tenet: Whatever is not for God is lost for heaven. The most-highly praised exploits of the first of the conquerors, deprived of this intention, are not worth even the smallest act done in the service of God.

In short, the dispositions with which we put this smaller virtue into practice make of this practice itself a great virtue. It is, as a matter of fact, the coming together of a thousand small traces of beauty that make up a perfect work in the natural order. Likewise, in the order of grace, the assembling of small virtues forms but one consummate holiness. Thus, the merit of the valiant woman whose portrait is sketched out for us by the sage consists solely in the carefulness and great attention she gives to doing her daily tasks (Prv 31:10–31). Glorious Mary, the masterpiece of the Almighty and the wonder of grace, came to the fullness of perfection only by an infinity of observances of rather common piety, if we were to consider them one by one, but when taken all together they raise her to the highest degree of sanctity. It is then that we understand this word of Jesus Christ: "Because you have been faithful in the few things I entrusted to you, I will put you in charge of greater affairs" (Mt 25:21).

For you see, the merit of the small virtues—and I would even say their superiority to more dazzling actions—lies in their requiring a more constant mortification and a more solid charity and humility.

First of all, the mortification is more continual. The greater the virtues, the more infrequent the occasions to put them into practice. To dispose of all your goods, to wear sackcloth and a hair shirt, to give your life for an enemy, and to confess Jesus Christ before tyrants are all virtues for rare occasions indeed. But to do all things for love of God as the most perfect motive and the one most pleasing to God; to put up with the faults of our neighbors and to adapt to their moods; never to speak badly of others or to speak of ourselves or in our own favor; to lead the way for people who have failed us and to seek to serve those for whom we feel aversion; never to sadden others but to give in and be silent; to suffer with resignation and in the spirit of penance the troubles that come with the conditions of our lives; to accept without ever complaining the annoyances and weariness of our work; to answer kindly those who allow themselves indiscrete or offensive questions; to welcome the refusal of service with graciousness and the bestowal of a favor with thanks; to have only the lowest of opinions of self and willingly to give way to those who are of lesser standing; to forgo our own views, ideas, projects, and judgments; to let go of our desires, feelings, tastes, and dislikes; to give up our comforts, conveniences, whatever feels good, delicacies, and satisfactions; to renounce our wills, exuberant show of emotions, sensitivities, and doing what comes naturally—in a word, to renounce everything—now those are virtues for all times and places. And what great opportunities for dying to self are contained in them!

Also in these virtues is a very sound humility. The desire to be noticed, the appetite to make ourselves famous, and the urge to win glory are almost always the driving force of our great deeds. We want to be in the public eye and rise in public standing regardless of the cost.

As a matter of fact, even among those who are not eaten up with this kind of ambition, there is another stumbling block that is both more dangerous to virtue and more cloaked in secrecy. It consists in this: that, being too predisposed to believe in our own worth, we have a secret self-satisfaction and congratulate ourselves on an alleged virtue by which we consider ourselves above what is ordinary.

But, alas, on what slippery slopes we find self-love! Is there a place so blessed as to be safe from its seduction? On the contrary, in little things we do not perceive anything like that. Rather, everything nourishes and sustains humility. Just as little things pass without much notice, so we are not tempted to make them into our trophies, and just as each of them taken singly has only a limited worth, so presumption and vanity scarcely find it worth their while.

In short, these small virtues are the indication of a more purified charity. That is the result of what we have just been saying. For the great virtues, it is the magnificence of the action that animates and strengthens. The external context works powerfully on us and by its great stimulus raises us up beyond ourselves so that our spirits are often ruled and carried away by this natural commotion. On the other hand, the ordinary virtues leave nothing to nature because nothing acts externally on us, nothing human sustains these virtues. Grace alone is their driving power. We can be faithful to them only out of love for God.

Since that is so, let us change our way of thinking, and, in place of denigrating the little virtues as perhaps we have done in the past, let us have a great esteem for them. But let us not stop at that. Let us do the least of our duties with this faithfulness, and let us never deliberately fail to do any of them. Let us recall that small faults offend God and that any offense of God is always a great evil. Let us never forget that a slight infidelity can be the start of our damnation. But if one of these infidelities manages to get away from us, let us humble ourselves before God and make amends by being more careful, and let us impose on ourselves some mortification so that we may not fall again. Thus we will acquire merits that more-outstanding deeds would never have obtained for us. Thus we will merit to enter into the joy of God (Mt 25:23) because we will have been this good and faithful servant who has carried out the least of his duties. May this also be our resolution.

Spiritual Bouquet

"Because you have been faithful in the little things, enter into the joy of your Lord" (Mt 25:23).

Sexagesima Sunday

· ·

Meditation on the Word of God

First Prelude

"The seed is the word of God" (Lk 8:11).

Second Prelude

Let us adore Jesus Christ as he himself explains the parable of the seed, thereby teaching us what dispositions we need to welcome this divine seed as well as what makes it sterile.

Third Prelude

Let us ask for the grace of really understanding the preeminence of the Word of God, that we may hear it with greater reverence and docility.[5]

What is the divine word?[6] It is the very Word of God communicating itself to the human race, whether interiorly through inspiration or exteriorly through the articulation of language, thus sowing eternal truths in our minds. What could be more splendid and more worthy of our attention and awe?

On this point St. Caesarius of Arles exclaimed:

> I ask you, which of these two things, the word of God or the body of Jesus Christ, seems to be of greater worth? If your answer is correct, you will say that the word of Jesus Christ does not seem to you less awesome than his body. Consequently, we ought take no less care in not allowing to fall from our heart the word of Jesus Christ which is proclaimed to us than we do to prevent the body of Christ which is presented to us from falling on the ground. For the one who listens with scant attention to the sacred word is

no less guilty than the one who through personal fault lets the very body of the savior fall to the ground.[7]

Therefore, try to deepen the hidden rapport between the mystery of the Eucharist and the minister of the divine word. This rapport consists in three things: (1) the truth of the body of our Lord in what is given to us at the altar and the truth of his word in what is preached to us from the pulpit; (2) that, just as we must open the mouth of our heart even more than that of our body to receive this celestial food worthily, so must we open wider the ears of the heart (that is, our attention) than the ears of our head (that is, our outer ones) to listen closely to the sacred word; and finally (3) that, just as we must receive so deeply the Eucharistic food that it is clear from our external behavior that we have been nourished at the table of the Son of God, so must we also profit from the sacred word in such a way that our life clearly indicates that we have been instructed in the school of this divine master.

We will understand better the first truth if we consider our churches as having two stately and venerable thrones: the altar and the pulpit—the altar where we present our requests to God and the pulpit where we discover God's will; the altar where priests speak to God on our behalf and the pulpit where they speak to us on behalf of God; the altar where Jesus Christ is adored in the truth of his body and the pulpit where he is recognized in the truth of his teachings. From the one as from the other of these two thrones, we are served a celestial food.

From the altar Jesus Christ preaches to us without words but no less eloquently in using a language of actions to make us recall the memory of his passion and to teach us to sacrifice ourselves with him. In the pulpit he gives us instruction with spoken words by means of his ministers.

At the altar, the word of the priest, through the power of the Holy Spirit, transforms the gifts that are presented there into the body of Jesus Christ, and in the pulpit, the same word ought to transform us in a hidden manner, making us become the mystical body and members of the Lord.

It is fitting that it be this way, for if Jesus Christ had not been revealed to mere mortals in these two ways, he could never have been revealed to the whole world, even though he wanted to be the Savior of all. For, in the truth of his fleshly body, he showed himself only to one corner of the earth, to the peoples of Judea. It is only by the truth of his word that he became known by the entire universe, just as it is only by his word that he makes himself known to us as we await the blessed day when we will see him in glory. Consequently, there is no less sin in desiring or in preaching the word of Jesus Christ in any way other than the divine preacher has taught in his Gospel and by his Church than in celebrating or asking to have celebrated the sacred mysteries in any way other than Jesus Christ has ordained it.

Such a conclusion is very fitting to make us understand the preeminence of the sacred word, making preachers and hearers alike tremble — the first at preaching it and the others at hearing it and making use of it to their profit.

"Grant us, then, O my God, the grace of finding the source of all our religious teaching in your holy scriptures, without ever altering, watering down, or twisting their sacred meaning or their holy expressions."

The second rapport between the word of God and the Eucharist is that both have to penetrate the heart, although by different paths — namely, the one by the mouth and the other by the ears. That is why the one who comes to the altar opening only the mouth of the body and closing to Jesus Christ the mouth of his heart drinks and eats his own judgment (1 Cor 11:29). A person likewise receives condemnation who, when listening to the preaching of Jesus Christ, pays attention only with the external ears and shuts off the interior sense of hearing.

To listen interiorly is to listen attentively because, besides the voiced sound that hits the ears, there is a hidden voice that speaks interiorly. It is this spiritual and inner discourse that forms the real preaching, and without it everything mortals say is but meaningless noise, for God alone can teach us the truth. Angels and human beings can only point it out to us, somewhat like pointing out objects in a room or important features on a painting but with our eyes not distinguishing much of anything unless the sun sheds its light clearly on these objects.

If it is true that, among the great number of things that strike our understanding and in spite of all the care we take to sort out what is true from what is false, he alone of whom it is written that he enlightens

everyone coming into the world (Jn 1:9) can make us discern correctly
how attentive we ought to be to his voice within us, although without dis-
regarding the sensate and external word that he has us hear.

On the contrary, just as we revere the water of Baptism that washes
us clean, the oil of Confirmation that makes us strong, and the visible
form of the Eucharistic bread that nourishes us for eternal life, so ought
we reverence the voice of those who preach to us, seeing that it becomes,
as it were, the vehicle of the voice of Jesus Christ. But this external and
reverent help is but one part of our duty. We must always take care that
fuzzy thinking or a dissipated imagination does not prevent us from listening with the heart to the divine master who speaks then from within us.

"It is at this point, O my Savior, that my soul understands this recommendation so often renewed to your hearers: 'Whoever has ears to
hear, let him hear' (Mt 11:15; 13:9, 43; Mk 4:9, 23). Indeed, you do not
speak to the deaf, but you know, O divine teacher, that there are some
who in seeing do not see and in hearing do not hear (Mt 13:13; Mk 4:12;
Lk 8:10). You know that there are inner ears where the human voice does
not penetrate and where you alone have the right to make yourself heard.
These are the ears we need to open for hearing you, and this is the grace
we ask of you."

But of what use is the grace to us if we listen to Jesus Christ but do
not faithfully obey his word by putting into practice what he teaches us?
Therefore, we must prove by our behavior that the Savior does nourish us
by his word, just as we much prove by our actions, after having received
Holy Communion, that he has nourished us with his body and his blood.
It is not enough just to gather from his heavenly teachings some vague
longings or weak feelings, even strong but fleeting ones, or phlegmatic
emotions.

Just staying put and enjoying these sentiments is no proof that the
Lord has spoken to us. After all, the human voice can go that far and
a skillfully handled instrument can indeed arouse these emotions. How
then can we know that we have really been taught by God? By our deeds.
Our great master's method of teaching does not consist only in clearly
pointing out the truth but in the infusion of charity in such a way that

those in the school of Jesus Christ soon begin to show it in their words and actions.

"You alone, O my Savior, can grant both the knowledge of what we must do and the grace to do it. Please teach us in this way and make of us so many faithful listeners. When you will ask us to account for your word, you will not be satisfied with sterile and fruitless feelings that never produce solid resolutions, with these flowers that always deceive our hopes because we never see them produce any fruit, with these fruits that never ripen but are the playthings of the wind and the prey of animals. No, you do not want any of these trees in the garden of your Church, which is why you cut them down and throw them onto the fire. O Jesus, make us worthy disciples of your Gospel.

"Do not let so much instruction, advice, and insight that you never cease to give us go to waste toward our growth in holiness, and let them not produce in us only that indifference or the kind of hardening of heart that makes us insensitive to all these graces, lest they become not only useless for us but also dangerous and deadly through our abuse of them."

Spiritual Bouquet

"Whoever has ears to hear, let him hear."

Friday after the Third Sunday of Lent

. . . .

Meditation on the mystery of the
five wounds of our Lord

First Prelude

"He was wounded for our iniquities" (Is 53:5).

Second Prelude

Imagine that cruel scene taking place at Calvary when they pierced the Savior's hands and feet and opened his side with the thrust of a lance.

Third Prelude

Ask Jesus Christ for the grace of sharing in the dispositions of his soul while they were wounding him in this way.[8]

Let us consider the purpose of Jesus Christ in letting himself be nailed to the cross as well as what sentiments remembrance of the five wounds ought to inspire in us.

His intention was to expiate the sin of the first man who misused his feet in going to the tree of the knowledge of good and evil, which he was never to approach. He misused his hands in picking the forbidden fruit and bringing it to his mouth. And he misused his heart in tasting a sensual pleasure by giving in, through a tender but culpable affection, to the insistence of his spouse. He thus identified with her in the consummation of the same act of disobedience (Gn 3:1–7).

Now, could Jesus Christ better satisfy divine justice for this sin of sensuality than in nailing to another tree a figure of the first one, his body weighed down with all our iniquities, and in watering this tree with the last drops of blood and water remaining in him? See how he lets his sacred limbs be pierced by these executioners without complaining but with the docility of a lamb led to the slaughter.

Stripped of his garments one last time, he is hurriedly placed on the cross to which they fasten his hands and feet with large nails that make large wounds. Who could ever comprehend the horrible suffering at that moment? The suffering that comes from having feet and hands pierced all the way through by iron nails; from being fastened and hung in that way on a gibbet that, when raised up, is let fall into a hole hollowed out to hold its base; from hanging there three whole hours, at the end of which he was given the thrust of a lance that created in his side a large, deep wound, as if it were not enough for him to die from such an appalling torture. No, our minds cannot comprehend, and no voice could express such cruel pain.

And if we ask our Savior why he had to receive these atrocious wounds, we will hear him tell us: "So that nothing is lacking to the satisfaction that I offer my father for your sins. By the pains of my pierced hands, I expiate all the sins you have committed through the sense of touch. By the cruel wounds of my feet, I expiate all the steps that you have taken along the path of wickedness. By the wound of my side, I expiate all the evil desires and all the disordered affections of your heart."

"O Jesus, bless us with your pierced hands. Nail, nail again to your feet and to your Sacred Heart our ungrateful feet and hearts so that they wander away from you no more. Above all, make us love you and show ourselves thankful for so many blessings by greater zeal for serving you."

These, then, are the sentiments that the sight of the five wounds ought to inspire in us: love and gratitude. How can we remain cold and indifferent before such a remarkable sight? Is it not here, as St. Paul wrote, that "the love of Jesus Christ impels us" (2 Cor 5:14)? Does not each of his wounds seem impelled to cry out to us: "See how much I love you; see what I have suffered for your sake. What are you doing for me? What more must I do to soften your hearts and draw you up to myself, if my wounds and the blood flowing from them cannot soften them and bring me your gratitude?"

Woe to us if we remain insensitive to this language of a God so loving, for one day it will be changed into curses against us. We will have to look upon these wounds which our eyes have averted, contemplating their scars in the glorified humanity of Jesus Christ who will have become our judge. To our shame and eternal damnation the blood that flowed on the cross will only serve to make the blood in our own veins seethe on the burning coals of eternity.

Let us be touched, therefore, at the sight of these sacred wounds, meditating on them often, making ourselves at home with them. Let us go there often, taking refuge in them lovingly in all our temptations. Let us try to imitate that great lover of Jesus when he wrote to a great saintly lady: "Whenever you are concerned about my health, whenever you want news of me and would like to converse with me, go to the wounds of our Lord, for that is where you will find me."[9]

Colloquy

As a colloquy, recite the prayer before the crucifix that is in our directory.[10]

Spiritual Bouquet

"I live by faith in him, who loved me and gave his life for me" (Gal 2:20).

Fourth Sunday of Lent

· ·

Meditation on the behavior of Jesus Christ
and of the people in the multiplication
of the loaves and the fishes

First Prelude

"Jesus took the loaves and distributed them to those who were
seated there" (Jn 6:11).

Second Prelude

Imagine this crowd of people that, regardless of where Jesus
went, ran after him, eagerly listening to him with such focused
attention that they forgot to eat. The Savior, touched by this
eagerness, worked a miracle there to give them something to eat.

Third Prelude

Ask for the grace to imitate the actions of Jesus Christ and of the
people in this situation.[11]

Three things are to be noted in the behavior of the people St. John
speaks about here in his gospel: their eagerness to follow our Savior, their
faith in him, and their gratefulness. Indeed, St. Mark, who records the
same story, says that Jesus, faced with the crowd coming and going to be
with him in such great numbers that he hardly found time to eat with his
apostles, had to withdraw into deserted places to find some moments of
rest (Mk 6:31–32).

Whereas the heads of synagogues, the Pharisees, and the doctors
of the Law spurned his teaching, or were present only inconspicuously,
or only to take him by surprise as he spoke and to make accusations
against him later, the people were eagerly trying to get close to him. They
were anxious to hear him, not afraid of being taken for his followers or

of compromising themselves in the eyes of official authority. Is that how we like to get close to our Savior, crowding around him in the sanctuary where he dwells, both during Divine Office when we invoke his name and during sermons when his words are taught? Do we go there only to be instructed in his law, to be filled with his sayings, and to be thoroughly filled in his presence with the fervor whose source he is? Or do we go only by habit, out of curiosity, or for fear of compromising ourselves with those who would perceive our absence?

Let us continue our admiration of the actions of these faithful hearers of the Word incarnate. Seeing the miraculous multiplication of the loaves and fishes, the crowd exclaimed, "This is undoubtedly the prophet who is to come into the world" (Jn 6:14). Could the crowd even think of doubting the reality of the miracle? They do believe in him, although this vivid impression is not going to last very long. They believe with simplicity, with the good sense natural to most people, but the hypocritical doctors and the Pharisees dismiss everything as dubious or attribute to magic and the devil whatever is supernatural in the marvels performed by our Savior. Do we have this kind of simple and lively faith without which all our religious beliefs crumble, a faith that is, as it were, the very life of the upright?

Carried away in their first fervor, the grateful people move beyond the conviction that Jesus is Messiah to the desire to proclaim him king, persuaded, no doubt, that in him they have found the powerful liberator who was to come to triumph over all the enemies of Judea and to deliver them from the yoke of the Romans (Jn 6:15). Although Jesus Christ resists the imprudent wishes of this multitude, the intention of these people is thereby no less a proof of their gratitude. Is it thus that we know how to give thanks for the blessings of our Savior and to serve his interests without human respect or cowardly fear? Does he truly reign as king over our minds and hearts? Are we working to spread his kingdom to all souls? We have more than enough material here for our reflections.

The Savior's behavior toward the crowd he miraculously fed is no less worthy of our attention and our imitation. He teaches the crowd, he feeds it by his prayer, and he slips away from the honors they want to bestow on him.

He teaches the crowd. That is what he was doing for three days. Since he wants to present an image of the Holy Eucharist in the multiplication of loaves, he begins by putting the faith of his apostles to the test by asking them: How can we feed so large a crowd with five loaves and two fishes (Jn 6:5, 9)? Thus, he distributed the bread of his word before giving them material bread, thereby teaching us to instruct the poor when we visit them and bring them relief in their temporal needs.

Moreover, when our Savior is about to work the miracle needed to feed his numerous hearers, he starts praying as was his custom at the beginning of all his actions and especially of his meals. It was not, however, for himself that he used to invoke his father, seeing that he possessed the same almighty power and that this external assistance was in no way needed in order to use it. It was, therefore, something he wanted to teach us. And how many of us probably do not know how to profit from it! At least let us learn today to call upon the help of God in our main work and to thank him afterward.

Finally, in order to evade the crowd's making him king, Jesus Christ withdraws to a mountain. Could there be a better way to teach us that his kingdom is not of this world as well as the means to curb in us the ambition that makes us seek out distinguished jobs and high-ranking positions? Let us try to restrain our self-centered desires, to be content with the position that obedience has assigned us, and to be persuaded that these thoughts come only from pride and the devil who constantly tries to wear us down in this matter.

Spiritual Bouquet

We will take as our spiritual bouquet these words: "Realizing that they would come and carry him off to make him king, Jesus slipped away" (Jn 6:15).

Friday after Passion Sunday

. . . .

Meditation on the mystery of the transfixion or compassion of the Blessed Virgin

First Prelude

"A sword of sorrow will pierce your soul" (Lk 2:35).

Second Prelude

Imagine the most holy Virgin showing you her heart pierced by seven swords.

Third Prelude

Ask Our Lady of Seven Sorrows for the grace to experience consciously the sorrows of her divine son.[12]

Let us call to mind the Seven Sorrows of Mary: (1) the prophecy of the elderly Simeon to this noble mother concerning the passion and the death of Jesus Christ and prefigured by a sword (Lk 2:34–35), (2) the flight into Egypt (Mt 2:13), (3) the loss of the child Jesus in the Temple (Lk 2:43–48), (4) the encounter with our Savior carrying his cross, (5) his being raised up on that infamous tree (Jn 19:26–27), (6) his being taken down from the cross and being laid in the arms of this desolate Virgin, and (7) his burial and Mary's subsequent being alone (Mt 27:59–60).

What did the Church intend by having us honor the memory of this long and sorrowful martyrdom? Was not its intention to make us share in the sufferings of the mother of God and to inspire in us a horror for sin, which is their cause? But to arouse in us this compassion, we need to understand the effect produced in the heart of Mary by this sevenfold sword. And who is there that could ever come close to expressing it? We would need to understand the exalted love that Mary had for her adorable son and her burning thirst and ardent zeal for our salvation. No one could plumb the depths of the tender love of the mother of God for her son or the no-less incomprehensible love she has for us.

1. However that may be, let us meditate on these sorrows one at a time, imagining first of all the blow Mary suffered when Simeon spoke to her in the prophecy of what awaited her and her divine son: This child will be the downfall and the rising of many, and a sword of sorrow will pierce your soul (Lk 2:34–35). At once, there passed before her eyes the sight of the persecutions our Savior had to undergo, the horrors of Calvary, and the misfortune of so many souls who would not profit from it all. We ourselves would prove to be a cause for affliction or consolation for Mary depending on the use we make of it for our redemption. Where, in fact, are we in relation to this event? How desolate the heart of this good mother if she has to experience seeing us among the damned.

2. Shortly afterward, she learns that Herod wants to kill Jesus, and so she takes the divine child in her arms. All troubled again at what the angel had announced to Joseph, she hastens to flee into a foreign land, being searched for everywhere by the accomplices of the barbaric king who pursues her. How anguished must have been this mother beyond compare! Could she not think she heard the soldiers' fierce cries in the dark shadows of the night? Is she not trembling at the fright painted all over her face that might betray her love and the treasure she carries away in her arms? Does she not dread the length and the difficulty of the desert roads, the hunger, the thirst, the ferocious beasts? No doubt she abandoned herself confidently to divine providence, but would her heart feel any less suffering? Therefore, let us learn to suffer with our mother with the same resignation and to flee the dangers to which our salvation is exposed.

3. Mary is next given over to a trial even more bitter. Jesus was in Jerusalem at the age of twelve, and after the feast his parents began their journey back to Nazareth. They soon perceived that their divine son, whom they thought was in the company of their relatives, was not on the return journey with them. What a shock that must have been for Mary. She retraces her steps, questions all passersby, and searches at the homes of relatives and friends. In spite of all that, she finds her divine

child only three days later. Do we seek out God with the same diligence when we have lost him?

4. In any case, an even greater sorrow was awaiting this desolate Virgin. In this situation, we have to borrow the tenderness of a mother in order to feel, however imperfectly, what the heart of Mary must have suffered. She learns that Jesus Christ has been handed over to these executioners. She hurries to his side to get one last goodbye. She already hears the shouts of a raging people. She moves forward, making her way through the crowd. The weapons shine their glare into her eyes. She sees the inscription of his condemnation. She comes still closer.

Oh, heavens above, what an encounter! What a blow pierces her soul as she beholds Jesus bowed down under the weight of the cross—his head crowned with thorns, his face ravaged, his tunic stained with blood, the way he walks marked by drops of blood! Then, Jesus raises his eyes and meets those of his mother. Their hearts also meet and speak more than their mouths, which probably remain silent in sorrow. Oh my soul, what feelings ought such a sight inspire in you, who have contributed perhaps to making Mary's heart experience these cruel sorrows!

5. That is not all. Our Savior climbs to Calvary, and his holy mother climbs there with him. He is raised up on the cross. Can you see her standing there at the foot of this instrument of torture, her hands folded, her eyes fixed on her dying son, unable to take them off his body covered with wounds, off the thorns crowning his head, off the nails piercing his feet and his hands, off his eyes drooping with death, off his mouth slightly opened to let sound the words of his last wishes, off the wound made in his side by the lance? All this for three hours already! Queen of martyrs, I throw myself at your feet to ask your pardon for having thus martyred you by my sins. I beg you to obtain pardon for me from your divine son by granting me your own pardon.

There remains for our meditation (6) the taking down of Jesus from the cross and (7) Mary's being alone during the time Jesus Christ's body is in the tomb. But silence seems more appropriate here when everything becomes silent and alone. They placed the body of Jesus at the feet of Mary, who took on her knees and between her arms the head of our Savior. After pressing her lips to his sacred wounds and mixing her tears with the last drops of blood still coming from the wounds, after assisting and taking part in the burial as much as she could, Mary withdrew with the holy women who were with her, and she remained plunged in sadness.

"O Mary, share with us some spark of the burning love that was ablaze in your heart. You are our mother. Make us love you as your grateful children."

Spiritual Bouquet

To become imbued with these sentiments, we will want to sing several of the more touching stanzas of the *Stabat*, and we will take the following one for our spiritual bouquet: "Therefore, O Mother, source of love, make me share in the intensity of your sorrow that I may weep with you."[13]

Quasimodo Sunday

· ·

Meditation on interior peace and exterior peace

First Prelude

"Peace be with you" (Jn 20:19, 21, 26).

Second Prelude

Imagine Jesus Christ coming into the Cenacle where his apostles were gathered and greeting them with peace.

Third Prelude

Pray for interior peace.[14]

What is interior peace? How much is it needed? What are the means of acquiring it and keeping it? Such are the reflections we are going to make.

Interior peace is a habitual disposition of the soul that makes us completely despise the enjoyments of the world and of the flesh, makes us rise above thoughts of sadness and discouragement which sometimes well up from our self-love, and preserves us from this eager, natural impulse as well as from those preoccupations which trouble and disturb the mind. In short, it establishes calmness in the soul along with that gentle quiet, which is the fruit of victory over our passions and the disordered longings of our heart. Having said that, I hasten to add that this interior peace is absolutely necessary if we are to be prepared to receive the graces belonging to our exercises of piety and to make them bear fruit after having received them.

Inner peace disposes us for grace, because the most efficacious means of strengthening us in virtue and of grounding us in the land of the saints where we have been planted, the easiest way to draw the Spirit of God to us and to be enriched by his gifts, is to implore help from on high very often and especially to listen to the interior voice that speaks to us during prayer.

Without the kind of peace I have just described, we can neither effectively ask for divine light and favors by the fervor of our prayers nor during the meditation listen to the Holy Spirit who speaks to our heart. To present ourselves before the Lord and to offer him prayers worthy of being heard, we need to follow the example of the prophet-king and to have previously found our heart, for our minds cannot at the same time be both filled with things of earth and attentive to things of heaven. But, how could anyone find his heart unless he takes care to calm the desires of his heart as soon as they begin?

If people search out their hearts only as they present themselves before the divine majesty, they will find only the stirrings that they allowed to enter their souls well before then. Sometimes it might be a project already planned and an eagerness to accomplish it without delay. At other times it might be some business they can hardly wait to get at with ready determination. At still other times it might be a humiliation they think they suffered and that they mull over, wanting to forget it as soon as possible. It might even be some moodiness, discontent, resentment, or even some innocent hobby they desired too intently or had become too engrossed in. How can an interior so stirred up and agitated make room for prayer, especially those prayers that pierce the heavens and bring down the dew of heavenly blessings? Even more so, how can this kind of inner life talk with God in meditation if it is all filled with itself?

It is only in recollected souls that the Lord makes his voice heard. That is why he leads into solitude the soul he wants to favor with his wordless conversations, according to these words: I will lead her into the wilderness and will speak to her heart (Hos 2:16). Why into the solitary wilderness? It fosters peace, inner calm, and recollection. Whoever has the good fortune to live with their passions in peaceful silence will hear the voice of the spouse even in the midst of the world and the bustle of this age.

On the other hand, the Levites in their cells before their crucifix or at the foot of the altar will know nothing of this happiness if they abandon themselves to the constant motion of their thoughts and the tumult of their souls' faculties. In such cases, let us not at all be surprised if we hear only rarely the one who speaks to us in prayer or if we find ourselves no longer attracted to our spiritual exercises. It is because we are doing little or nothing to maintain in ourselves a gentle and peaceful recollection. Rather, we let ourselves be preoccupied by a thousand desires and a thousand and one frivolous ideas. We do not give ourselves to the necessary discipline either to obtain or to maintain this inner peace.

To let grace bear fruit, we must prudently avoid occasions of sin, courageously overcome temptations when they present themselves, unceasingly do what is necessary to change our ways, and set about doing good deeds. Without inner peace, without constant vigil over all we do, can we continually work at all this and see success? No, says the prophet, because disorder and agitation, no matter what their origin, take away light for understanding and strength from the heart.

The heart not habitually at peace is like a battlefield where orders are poorly given and even more poorly carried out, where no one knows whether to take flight or attack. Such a heart is a path going in all directions at once if the seed of the divine word is trodden under the feet of those who pass by. Temptations come along; the devil is right behind; the soul is troubled. Without vigorous strength, the soul quickly loses the precious fruit of the graces it has received and sees taken away from it in the blink of an eye all the spiritual goods it had derived from meditation. From then on, it will give in to the dissipation that is its driving force, to the vain pleasures that evaporate its substance, to the melancholy that destroys its life, to the curiosity that keeps it focused on externals.

Ah, seeing that inner peace is so necessary that without it we can neither be disposed to receive any grace or bring it to fruition once received, let us not hesitate a moment longer to follow a pathway so useful to us and so pleasant. Let us courageously persevere on it, or, if we have not yet begun, let us find the means to enter upon it once and for all without ever leaving it.

The principal means are three: (1) humility, (2) love of God, and (3) obedience in conjunction with prayer.

1. Humility is first because Jesus Christ, truth itself, has indicated that it is first when he said: "Learn from me, for I am humble of heart, and

you will find rest for your souls" (Mt 11:28–29). How peaceful and happy we would be if, by putting this divine lesson into practice, we would come to snuff out at its origin the accursed passion of human respect that is ours by nature! Then, freed from human judgments, as calm and serene as a rock in the midst of the waves of opinions that come and go, we would let the world be stormy around us, let it exhaust its evil fury against us, but our happiness would not be disturbed by it all, because we would have learned to value only what God put in us and to judge ourselves for what we really are.

Let us, therefore, be humble, truly humble, and in our souls we will have peace, calm, and gladness. Without this fundamental virtue, we will always be prey to trouble and distress. Inner peace alone destroys at the very beginning, so to speak, the most ordinary of our anxieties and sorrows. Without it, we will always find, in contempt or contradiction, the source of a continual restlessness and a great bitterness, just like one of the favorites of Ahasuerus, who cried his heart out in despair at not having the respect of but one man in the entire empire (Est 5:9–14). There is also truth in the words of the holy author of the *Imitation of Christ*: Continual peace is reserved for the humble heart, but the proud is prey to confusion and restlessness.[15]

Let us enter the secret place of our conscience and seek the source of most of the little anxieties that trouble the calm of our soul. Do they not come from selfishness that exaggerates the good which is in us by making more of the evil that is in others, that makes us oversensitive to the slightest insult, the least humiliation, the smallest affront? Does this not come about, in a word, because our pride was wounded and because we have not yet understood the fullness of this truth from the mouth of our Savior, "Whoever exalts himself will be humbled" (Lk 14:11; 18:14; Mt 23:12)?

2. The second way to acquire or increase inner peace is love of God. We can say that by itself it encompasses all the other means because whoever loves fulfills the whole law (Mt 22:40; Rom 13:8). We have been made to love and to be loved. We need a beloved friend, and a heart properly raised can never do without one. This beloved friend can be none other than Jesus, who alone can make us happy, who alone is worthy to capture the affections of our soul and fulfill all its longings because he is

a thoroughly faithful friend, a beloved friend who is rich, powerful, and completely honest. He truly longed to give us this name. "You are my friends," he said to his apostles (Jn 15:14).

See how far his love for us took him. To calm our fears and to inspire confidence in us, he had to humble himself to becoming a slave and to clothe himself in the form of an infant (Phil 2:6–7). Yet, that is what Jesus did. He had to take on himself the weight of our sins to deliver us from death and had to find a nearly miraculous way of putting in our hearts the burning coals of charity. Yet, that is what Jesus did. He had to pour out all his blood to lighten our burden and to help us carry it. Yet, that is what Jesus did.

There was no action, no matter how painful, that his love for us would not make him do, no position so low or so wretched that his love would not make him undertake to attract our own love. And after so many proofs of his love, he asks in grateful response only that we go to him with confidence like children to their father. He invites us, calls us, and urges us to come to him to comfort us in our pain and to calm the bitterness of our hearts in his own heart.

Would we not have to be truly without any sensitivity at all to resist such touching invitations? Therefore, let us go to Jesus because it is he who courts us and because we can find peaceful happiness only in his embrace. It is there, lying against his adorable breast, that the beloved disciple dozed off in a gentle and peaceful sleep. It is there that true peace was found and continues to be found by an infinity of souls for whom the flesh, the world, and hell seem to have conspired in removing forever all hope of eternal rest. And it is from there that we ourselves will draw out a perfect conformity to the will of God whom we serve.

3. The third and last means for enjoying peace of soul is obedience in conjunction with prayer. That refers first of all to obedience to our rules. The apostle assures us that peace is with the one who follows the rule (Gal 6:16). This is also the sentiment of the holy author of the *Imitation of Christ* who says: "My son, set about doing the will of another rather than your own and you will acquire peace and rest."[16]

What a source of interior consolations it is to be able to give oneself this glorious testimony: I love my God, and I am loved by him; I never do anything except what he wants me to do. Insofar as we are faithful to our rules, we can use this language with confidence and without fear of deceiving ourselves, because to love God's will is to love God himself and because our rules are the expression of his holy will. As a certain Father of the Church said, whoever lives according to the rule lives according to God.

Furthermore, let us add prayer to this life lived according to a rule. In this we are only following the example of the Church as it continually asks for peace in the chants and supplications of the Divine Office. Sometimes it breaks the silence of its sacred mysteries to cry out through the mouth of the priest at the altar: "Lamb of God, grant us peace." At other times, the Church takes advantage of the times when its divine spouse is exposed outside the tabernacle in public adoration in order to tell him in song: "Lord, give peace to your servants, such peace as the world cannot have." At still other times, it offers peace to its children: "The peace of the Lord be with you always." Or also in the voice of the priests: "Peace be with you."

Let us recollect ourselves, therefore, and seek out this precious gift of peace, especially now when the Church asks for it so earnestly of its divine spouse for its children. And let us make the following resolutions: (1) to despise absolutely the pleasures of the world and of the flesh and to seek out consolation only in the love of God; (2) to mortify our intense eagerness, our overstimulation, and all the different anxious concerns that trouble or worry us; and (3) to make serious efforts to remain constantly faithful to our rules.

Spiritual Bouquet

"Peace be with you."

Fourth Sunday after Easter

···

Meditation on silence

First Prelude

"Let each one be slow to speak" (Jas 1:19).

Second Prelude

Let us recall that the Word made flesh remained silent for thirty years and that he did not break his silence except for legitimate reasons.

Third Prelude

Let us ask him for a spirit of silence and recollection.[17]

It is with good reason that St. James in today's epistle exhorts us to restrain our tongue by a slowness to speak that is full of wisdom and cautiousness. Nothing is more common than a readiness to make our thoughts known as soon as they come to us. Yet, nothing is more contrary to the spirit of the Gospel, for in the judgment of the same apostle, "If people think they are devout yet speak without thinking first, they have a piety that is vain and illusory" (Jas 1:26).

No doubt it was to remedy so great a disorder that the founders of religious orders prescribed certain times for silence when all unnecessary conversation was explicitly forbidden. And what could be more apt to prevent unnecessary words than those times of recollection when we are not allowed to talk except with God and with ourselves? It is also to make you decide on great fidelity to the rule of silence or to make you persevere in it that you are now going to meditate on the two principal reasons for practicing silence: the overall good of the community and your personal growth in holiness.

First of all, the overall good of the community requires it, as is easily shown by authority, the powers of reason of each of you, and experience.

1. The most respected and most compelling authorities say silence is necessary. Such is the evidence from the Desert Fathers, men of God so astute in the rule of their communities, and the evidence from all the founders of orders in both the East and the West, like St. Benedict, St. Bruno, St. Bernard, St. Francis of Assisi, St. Ignatius of Loyola, St. Francis de Sales, St. Vincent de Paul, and many others whose resplendent institutions were approved by the Church.

There is not one of these illustrious people who does not say that silence is essential and who does not regard it as the basis and foundation of religious life. In the language of early monasticism, it is the soul of peace and union of hearts, the pillar without which everything crumbles and is overturned. It is the only means to maintain order and discipline.

Furthermore, some sovereign pontiffs and celebrated councils have confirmed most solemnly this rule, so universally recommended to all religious. Is this not enough to confound those who dare treat the strict observance of silence as of little value, eccentric, ridiculous, and part of some misunderstood mystic rituals? Besides, does not our own reason witness to the necessity of silence?

2. Is it not clear that, in a community setting, everyone who lives there needs to cooperate to maintain the regular schedule, one of the greatest assets we enjoy in community? Is it not also clear that those who take liberties contrary to the good order of the community destroy, insofar as it is in them to do so, the wonderful harmony so pleasing to God's heart and the human heart as well? Such is the undesirable effect necessarily brought about by infractions of silence. Can we break the rule of silence without making some confrere do so at the same time? And if this example draws in several others, what then happens to the whole house except that it becomes a place of dissipation and a scandal to outsiders who come there? Besides that, what is the result of these furtive conversations held in secret? Here is what it is: these private talks and liaisons will open little by little the door to slander, to calumny, to complaining and grumbling, to intrigue and dissension—all of which are so distressing. Following upon all that come disharmony and confusion.

If, on the contrary, silence is faithfully observed, if we open our mouths only at the proper times, if we never enter one another's rooms without permission and only when necessary, if we go in recollection and modesty from one exercise to the next, is it not clear that we will see reign in such a house harmony, good common sense, cordial unity, and regularity? It was this that made St. Ephrem say that silence is the source of all things good; that made St. Bernard say that silence is the foundation of devotion and maintains it; that made St. Francis de Sales say that it is the safeguard of community life; that made all the masters of the spiritual life say that it is the binding power of regular discipline. Also, one of the fathers of the Company of Jesus charged with visiting the houses of the society terminated his inquiries once he was assured that silence was well observed, so persuaded was he that everything else depended on this fundamental point.[18] This reality is also based on experience.

3. As a matter of fact, why have the Carthusians been preserved up to this very day in their earliest fervor without ever having to be reformed?[19] It is because silence has always been strictly observed in their order. On the other hand, why did the famous Abbey of Clairvaux fall into laxity?[20] It is because they scorned silence. But without having to look backward into history, why, as the year rolls on and the time of vacation draws near, do we so often see devotion slacken off and a certain levity happen right in the middle of our most important exercises? It is because we have let go of our rule of silence.

At the beginning of the year or during a retreat, this practice seems sweet and easy. But, little by little, we tire of recollection, we give greater freedom to our senses, and we talk at the wrong times, resulting too often in some disheartening behavior.

St. Vincent de Paul, that apostle of France, that man so compassionate toward human weaknesses, would have preferred to remain with his confreres in a poorly outfitted house in Paris than to accept the house at Saint-Lazare under the conditions recommended to him. This was only because some of the proposals could lead one day to the breaking of silence. He said that he was afraid of impeding in that way the designs of God for his community.

If we do not want to turn away the designs of providence for our congregation, let us refrain from speaking when the rule prohibits it. Without that, we undermine regular discipline, we take away from the beauty of this institution, we destroy a practice essential to it, and we topple the walls that support it. In thus exposing the practice of silence to all the harmful things that could cause excessive use of the tongue, we deprive ourselves of one of the most fitting means of sanctification.

Not only does the general good order of the house require fidelity to silence, but our personal sanctification depends on it, too. What is needed to ensure our salvation and to attain ecclesiastical perfection? Three things: to avoid sin, to practice virtue, and to acquire the knowledge necessary for our work. Silence, such as our rules ordain, is absolutely indispensable for attaining this threefold end.[21]

1. To avoid sin. What is, in fact, the ordinary source of our faults? Is it not the failure of holding back the spitefulness of the tongue, this "world of iniquity" (Jas 3:6) as St. James says, from which come forth pride, flattery, lies, false statements, contempt, insults, careless words, slander, calumny—in a word, almost every sin we can commit? Is not "this world" like the interpreter of all human passions?

What remedy can we apply to all these evils if not silence? This is the powerful barrier against this devastating torrent. Those who let themselves be carried away by its turbulent force and speak at the wrong time will become, says scripture, like someone who gets on a high-spirited horse without bridle or bit (Jas 3:3; Ps 32:9), or again, like a traveler who sets sail at the mercy of wind and wave on a vessel without a rudder (Jas 3:4).

People who have no scruples about speaking at times when it is prohibited need to examine seriously their consciences in the evening. They will certainly find that their consciences will reproach them with many faults against their neighbor. Perhaps they will even see that they have said many unwarranted things in their unnecessary conversations with their confreres. If nothing else, they at least wasted their own time and made others lose theirs. If we have to make an exact account to our sovereign judge for every idle word, what accounting will he not require for so many conversations contrary to his good pleasure or even to his holy will?

2. In a very unique way, silence facilitates virtue and the practice of all the duties of our vocation. By remaining silent, we preserve an inner calm, a peacefulness of soul, and a recollection so necessary for prayer. By keeping silence, we progress along the ways of justice and knowledge, and we put into practice humility, mortification, patience, obedience, self-abnegation, and conformity to the will of God.

What a difference there is between religious who are exact keepers of silence and those who are not bothered by breaking silence from morning until night. The former become perfect human beings because, as St. James would have it, they can control all their passion and conquer all their enemies (Jas 3:6). The latter, however, who do not know how to control their tongue, are given to continual dissipation and, consequently, find only distaste and boredom in exercises of piety. They go backward instead of advancing along the path of perfection. Ultimately, they no longer go to the sacraments, or, if they do, it is to their misfortune. This is, no doubt, what made a writer cited by Bossuet say that the habitual breaking of silence can lead little by little to rejection, but that fidelity in keeping silence is enough to ensure salvation for a soul who observes it faithfully.

3. Finally, silence is necessary to be prepared for whatever work we might subsequently have as our assignment. And what striking examples come to mind as confirmation of this truth! First, we find an example not in the academic circles of Egypt but in the desert of Midian, where Moses, tending the flocks of his father-in-law, Jethro, is prepared for the great mission yet to be entrusted to him (Ex 3:1ff.). It is there—in the silence of the wilderness, oblivious of the halls of learning of Memphis, and giving himself to the contemplation of the future opprobrium of Jesus Christ—that Moses was being readied to deliver his people from the tyranny of Pharaoh.

Was it not also in the desert silence that the prophets were prepared for their exalted ministry? Did John the Baptist not leave behind at an early age ordinary family conversations, even the talks he could have had with our Savior, to bury himself in a solitary wilderness until the day he came out to show himself to the children of Israel? Was it not during a silence of thirty years that the Son of God was prepared for proclaiming his way of life to others? Was it not in silence that the apostles were prepared for the descent of the Holy Spirit? Was it not from the midst of that same silence in the Cenacle that thunderclaps went forth, shaking the desert, overturning the cedars of Lebanon, and setting the whole world on fire with the love of God? Was it not in the silence at Bethlehem, at the feet of the child Jesus, that St. Jerome learned Hebrew and acquired the depths of knowledge that made him the most capable of the holy interpreters of scripture? Was it not also in silence that St. Thomas, the "Dumb Ox" as he was called because of his love of silence, prepared himself to have the entire Catholic world listen to the booming voice of his learning? No doubt, all this ought to be enough to make us conclude that without silence we cannot prove ourselves worthy of our vocation.

Moreover, experience has shown that dissipated novices or professed acquire neither the depths of knowledge to which providence destined them nor the holiness to which they were called. They wasted their time and made others waste theirs, too. By often interrupting class lectures by their unnecessary interventions, they missed out on many explanations as well as many resolutions for which they will render account on the great day of the manifestation of consciences.

Therefore, let us keep silence for the general good of the community and for our own sanctification. Let us make the selfless resolution (1) never to speak unnecessarily and, if we are still novices, never to speak without permission during the times it is prohibited, and (2) to observe silence by watching carefully over our choice of words.

Spiritual Bouquet

"Let each one be slow to speak."

Fifth Sunday after Easter

· ·

Meditation on mental prayer

First Prelude

"Lord, teach us to pray" (Lk 11:1).

Second Prelude

Call to mind the solemn commitment Jesus Christ made in the Gospel to grant us whatever we ask of his father in his name as well as the reproaches Jesus made to his disciples for failing to use such a certain means of obtaining the graces of heaven (Jn 16:23–24).

Third Prelude

Ask for the grace of prayer.[22]

The frequent commands of our Savior, our personal needs and those of the entire Church, this very time of the Rogation Days we are about to begin—all of that joined to the example of our Lord and the saints shows us so well the importance and the necessity of prayer in general that we might stop and dwell on it awhile.[23]

Let us distinguish two different ways of praying: one, an external way, called vocal prayer, and the other called mental prayer because it is done in the mind and heart without vocalizing any word. It is true that vocal prayer requires the attention of the mind and the fervor of the heart. How sad for anyone who prays only with the end of the lips. In this first way of praying, we focus only for the moment on the things we say or ask for, without stopping at any one of them in particular. In meditation, on the other hand, we focus on only one primary truth in order to draw from it practical consequences and to arouse within us corresponding senti-ments. It is the necessity of this second kind of prayer that we need to grasp as one of the most essential acts of religious life. To do that, let us limit our references to precedent authority and to reason.

What great authority is that of Jesus Christ, of all the saints, of all the Doctors of the Church, the councils, and the apostles throughout the ages! This entire cloud of witnesses has but one voice for extolling the benefits, the importance, and the necessity of meditation. If you look at the Savior of the world in his retreat at Nazareth or in the Temple, if you go with him into the desert or into the lonely garden, or if you follow him through his time of preaching the Good News, everywhere you will see him praying and meditating. He would pass the nights in prayer, says St. Luke (Lk 6:12), and St. Mark adds that he would rise early in the morning to pray in a lonely place (Mk 1:35).

Even his suffering and sorrows of his most painful agony could not detour him from this holy occupation. In fact, it was then that he redoubled his recollection and fervor. It is true that we are dealing here with prayer that is vocal and external. But can we really believe that this ever interrupted his exalted contemplation? Furthermore, are we not aware that, in the judgment of the Fathers of the Church, after having taught us by his own behavior the practice of meditation, he then formally commanded us to pray this way? As St. Matthew puts it, "Whenever you pray, go to your room, close the door, and pray to your father in private" (Mt 6:6).

Moreover, from the time of the apostles until now, it is impossible to cite even one saint who was not also a person of prayer. You know that when the first preachers of the Gospel set out on this course scattered with brambles and thorns, they were to begin by sprinkling the ground with the sweat of their brow and to end by shedding their blood. But throughout their work they continually had recourse to prayer and to meditation. Not satisfied just to give this example to all who would come after them in apostolic ministry, they recommended explicitly the same thing to their own disciples, just as we see happening in the first Letter of St. Paul to Timothy, in which the teacher of the nations urges the faithful companion of his own work to reflect maturely on the rules of conduct that he had traced out for him (1 Tm 4:6–10).

Undoubtedly, it is according to the exalted lessons of these great masters that all people of God judged meditation so important, so beneficial, and so necessary. On this point, it is St. John Chrysostom who names prayer the channel of all grace, the destruction of all vice, the light of minds, the food of the soul, as well as its rich treasure. That is why St. Gregory forbids the ordination of any who have neither the inclination to prayer nor respect for this important practice, and he fears for those who confer on them Holy Orders.

St. Chrysostom considers as dead the soul that does not meditate, and his opinion is that without meditation it is impossible to be sustained in virtue. St. Bernard exhorts Pope Eugenius to lay hands for ordination only on those who are faithful to prayer, because he says that prayer purifies the mind, governs the movements of the heart, directs its actions, corrects its excesses, regulates its morals, and is the foundation for decency and good order in life.

Let us also take a look at St. Francis Xavier, who, at forty years of age, had already converted a million unbelievers and yet spent two hours every day in meditation. Fr. Avila used to turn away from the priesthood all who did not have the habit of meditation. In this, he was only in conformity with the spirit of the Church. At the Council of Milan, St. Charles Borromeo, the great reformer of ecclesiastical discipline, required an examination of young clerics about the substance and the different parts of meditative prayer.[24]

St. Francis de Sales prescribed meditation even for lay people. St. Vincent de Paul thought it so indispensable for anyone ministering at the altar that he held that the minister's salvation depended on such prayer. Gerson goes so far as to say that whoever does not pray cannot live as a good Christian without some sort of miracle. This does not seem farfetched to me, if we understand these words as referring to the essence of the practice of prayer that consists in reflecting on the truths of salvation and the means to it as well as in asking God for the grace to follow those means.

It is at least along these lines that Monseigneur de la Motte, Bishop of Amiens, required of those he ordained the promise of being faithful to prayer until death. It was along these same lines that Suárez, who would have willingly given away all his knowledge of theology for a half hour of prayer well done, judged prayer morally necessary for all Christians. Likewise, St. Aloysius Gonzaga spoke about perfection by saying that we could never attain it without recourse to prayer.

We will have no doubts whatsoever about this great truth if we recall the magnificent acclaim given to this religious practice by the Fathers of the Church. How can we not consider it necessary when they present it to us at times as a golden chain attached to heaven at one end and descending to the earth for the sake of raising our desires up to God and bringing his grace back down to us? At other times, they present it to us as that mysterious ladder of Jacob on which the angels ascend and descend, carrying our petitions to the Lord and bringing back to us his blessings (Gn 28:12). At still other times, they present it as the key to heaven, which opens its gate and its treasures.

Ah, if we are ever tempted to give up such a necessary exercise, let us remember that famous bull of Pope Benedict XIV, whose subject is to exhort the whole world to mental prayer, for it accords indulgences both to those who are accomplished in this practice and to those who teach it to others or who seek to be taught how to pray.[25] Let us recall especially that wonderful passage, which is like a summary of all that we have just been considering. Finally, reason itself will convince us of the truth of all this if we but reflect on the sanctity and the duties of our vocation.

As a matter of fact, just what is a priest or brother of Holy Cross? He is a person taken from the midst of others like him, removed from all temporal affairs and other business of this present life, in order to be pleasing to the Lord by the recitation of the Divine Office or the Little Office of the Blessed Virgin and to work for the fulfillment of the chosen—if not, like the priests, by the proclaiming of the Gospel, the administration of the sacraments, and the celebration of the holy mysteries, at least by the teaching and the formation of the young.

What great holiness is needed for such a vocation in anyone who is called to it! How great must be the liveliness of his faith, the strength of his hope, the ardor of his charity, the purity of his heart, the modesty and control over his senses, the rightness of his intentions, his detachment from creatures, and his love for the Church!

But how is he to acquire and preserve all these virtues and to live in a habitual union with God except by the exercise of prayer? It is precisely here that we find the source of the supernatural light by which we see the depths of our nothingness, the vanity of the world, and the infinite greatness of our divine master. It is here that faith is revived, that hope is nourished, and that charity is rekindled. It is here that we learn to detest sin, to give souls their true value. It is here that we discover the designs of heaven in order to fulfill them, whatever the cost.

On the other hand, how do we become lax, unfaithful, and often scandalous to others in the service of God? We do that by forgetting and despising the resolutions taken in the novitiate concerning the holy exercise of prayer. Each failure in this regard, each omission, leads to some other new and greater fault. We are a sick person refusing the medication, a soldier taken prisoner by the enemy who throws away his weapons, a traveler dried up with thirst who does not want to bend down to drink at the spring of living water which is at his feet.

If we slacken during vacation, if at that time we become lukewarm and careless about our spiritual progress, if we scandalize others just sometimes during the school year by our dissipation and withdrawal from the sacraments, then there is no doubt that we are far from being a person of prayer. Who are those among us who have the most virtues and possess the best spirit of their vocation? Is it not those who have the greatest longing for meditation, who dispense themselves from it the least, and who prepare for it most carefully by habitual recollection and union with God? Let us imitate them all the more, because without prayer we could never fulfill our obediences the way God wants.[26]

What public duties are there like ours? What obstacles there are to be overcome, what dangers to be averted, what distaste to be swallowed, what contradictions to be endured, what difficult personalities to be indulged, what prejudices to be undone! How many sinful people to be converted, how many blind to be brought to the light, how many weak to be strengthened, and how many upright to be led to perfection! Other than in prayer, where else can we find the strength, the apostolic courage, and the lifting of our spirits that are all indispensable for conducting ourselves with wisdom and letting ourselves be neither battered by fear nor seduced by selfishness nor discouraged by so much work that often bears no fruit?

Woe to anyone who would not persevere in the daily exercise of prayer! In prayer alone are we given to draw up the generosity of soul that will bring us gloriously triumphant out of such a terrible battle. In doing so, we follow the example of all the saints, especially of St. Dominic, St. Philip Neri, St. Francis Xavier, St. Jean-François Regis, and so many others who, after having worked all day long in their apostolic duties, would pass the night in prayer and would stop only when they would fall asleep. Oh, what sweetness they would find in an exercise we find perhaps only boring and distasteful, and yet, what brilliant success in their difficult and painstaking ventures!

Let us therefore make the resolution (1) to be faithful to this holy exercise until death and (2) to ask God for this grace.

Spiritual Bouquet

"Lord, teach us to pray."

Sixth Sunday after Easter

· ·

Meditation on preparing for the Holy Spirit

First Prelude

"The Spirit of truth will come to you" (Jn 16:13; 15:26).

Second Prelude

Imagine seeing Jesus Christ surrounded by his apostles on the evening before his death, there in the Cenacle, as he promises them the Holy Spirit to console them in his absence.

Third Prelude

Ask for the grace of preparing ourselves worthily for the descent of the Holy Spirit.[27]

We cannot succeed better in this preparation than by imitating the apostles. We are told in the story of their acts that they were preparing themselves for the coming of the promised comforter by retreat, prayer, and holy longings.

First, by retreat. Before leaving this earth, Jesus Christ had said to them: "Remain at rest in the city until you are clothed with power from on high" (Lk 24:49). Obedient to this command, they go down the mountain from which they saw the Savior ascend into heaven and withdraw with the seventy-two disciples to the Cenacle, which called to mind so many miracles of power and kindness.[28] It is there that they go on retreat, thoroughly convinced that the Spirit of God is not given to someone who is all flustered, but to one who is recollected and at peace.

If we want to receive the Holy Spirit on the day of Pentecost, let us also take care during these days of preparation before Pentecost to make the community where we live like a holy sanctuary and another Cenacle. Strictly banished from there are the fuss of the world, dissipation, and all those comings and goings that unnecessarily disturb silence. Then, let us enter more seriously into ourselves, recollect our senses even more, and practice better the rule of modesty. And if our work calls us outside the house, let us form within our soul a blessed solitude the way St. Teresa of Avila did who, even in the midst of her travels and her numberless works, had found the secret of becoming an interior oratory where she conversed unceasingly with God.

To the retreat, let us join prayer. The sacred writer says that together the apostles persevered in prayer (Acts 1:14). And what prayer theirs was, led by the holy Virgin and accomplished in the expectation of the gifts of the Holy Spirit! Let us judge by this togetherness and this perseverance how great was the ardor of their prayers. It was, therefore, not an ordinary prayer but a prayer whose fervor was proportionate to the excellence of the gift they awaited.

The same Spirit will descend next Sunday to the hearts he will find ready to receive him. Let us beg him to prepare our hearts himself for his coming, so that he may pour out in us that wisdom which makes us enjoy the things of God and makes us live a virtuous life. May he pour out in us the understanding that makes us thoroughly familiar with the mysteries of God, the gift of counsel that brings light to our doubts and guides us on our ways, the strength that makes us strong against temptations and trials, the knowledge that in the light of faith makes us see every truth, the piety that makes the Lord's yoke easy and his burden light (Mt 11:30), and the child's fear that is the beginning of wisdom (Prv 1:7; 9:10; Sir 1:16; Ps 111:10; Jb 28:28).[29]

For that to happen, that prayer must come from the heart. It consists less in the words than in the longings or in the aspirations, these pulses of the soul that need neither long formulas nor an abundance of words. Prayer is an ardent and continual longing. That is how the apostles practiced it in their retreat. The writer of their story, it is true, tells us nothing more except that they were praying, but even this silence gives us enough for understanding what the nature of their prayer was and the fervor of their longing. For what sort of human word could have expressed their prayers all afire and these holy yearnings, which carried their souls up before the divine comforter that Jesus Christ had announced to them?

See here, then, the example we must imitate if we want to draw to us the gifts of the Holy Spirit. For that purpose, we will do well to go over again each day of this week the story of Pentecost.

"Come, Holy Spirit, fill the hearts of your faithful, and light in them the fire of your love. Send forth your spirit and all will be created, and you will renew the face of the earth.

"Has the earth ever had a greater need of this renewal? In the first days of creation, when darkness still covered the face of the abyss, you were swept over the waters, and your almighty strength brought order into the chaos (Gn 1:2). When you came down upon the apostles, the thickest darkness once again enveloped the world lost in ignorance and sin, but your heavenly ray pierced through this terrible darkness and brightened on the earth a day more beautiful than when it first welcomed the sun. Today this world is still blind even in the midst of your light and still corrupt for all its knowledge.

"Come, then, O creator Spirit, and renew the face of this world, ignorant, self-centered, and materialist. Fill with your gifts those whom you call to know you and to be converted."

Spiritual Bouquet

"Come, Holy Spirit."

Pentecost

. . . .

Meditation on the mystery

First Prelude

"They were filled with the Holy Spirit" (Acts 2:4).

Second Prelude

Imagine now this rushing wind that rocked the Cenacle; see the tongues of fire that came down upon the apostles; recognize their transformation into new men.

Third Prelude

Let us penetrate the thoughts and sentiments of the *Veni, Sancte Spiritus*, and let us ask this creator Spirit, as the fruit of this period of prayer, to be enlightened, purified, and set ablaze just like the apostles.[30]

The Feast of Pentecost has this special quality: the mystery we celebrate now is renewed, in fact, every day. It is not only to the disciples gathered together in the Cenacle that our Savior promised the Holy Spirit, but to all who over the centuries will be found worthy of this glorious promise. This same Spirit still truly comes down to souls well disposed, no longer in a visible way as on the apostles, but in a way no less real for being invisible.

The Spirit brings with him, not the external gifts that were necessary for that era for building up of the religion, but the same graces of conversion and sanctification that will be necessary until the end of time. It remains only for us to achieve the same wonderful effects he brought about interiorly in each of the members of the gathering in the Cenacle who were (1) enlightened, (2) purified, and (3) strengthened.

1. The first effect of the descent of the Holy Spirit is that they were enlightened. And what indeed were the apostles before the coming of the divine Paraclete? They were but the most ignorant of people, assembled from the lowest class of society, lacking education and even understanding. After spending three years in the school of their divine master, they had not yet understood his mysteries or penetrated his sayings, and they were greatly mistaken about the nature of his promises. Yet, no sooner do they receive the Holy Spirit than they are accomplished in their knowledge of salvation. The truths they had not comprehended are being laid bare in front of them, and they grasp the whole of the religion: its dogmas, its morals, its sacraments, its ceremonies, and the meaning of everything Jesus Christ promised them or proclaimed to them.

All of that was suddenly made clear to them, without special study on their part and without any external kind of instruction. The behavior of the divine Spirit is still that way today in souls open to his inspiration. Sometimes he fills them with astonishing insights that make them superior to the highly learned and to the most renowned philosophers. Several saints have spoken about this, saying that they learned more at the foot of the crucifix than in discussions with others or in books.

Let us imitate them, then, having recourse to this same Spirit, and without neglecting the natural means of learning, let us call upon the Spirit's help in our own studies. Let us ask him to speak to us in our meditations, our spiritual reading, spiritual conferences, and the sermons we hear preached.

2. Moreover, let us take note that the knowledge received so miraculously by the apostles not only enlightened their minds. It also purified them, and this is the second effect produced by the Holy Spirit in them. He is not only the Spirit of Truth but also the Spirit who makes us holy. This is the meaning of the tongues of fire that came to rest on their heads, communicating to their hearts the sacred fire, namely, charity, whose symbol is fire.

Up to that time, the apostles were seen as ambitious, jealous, and quarreling—wanting the first places, envious of those who seemed to be preferred to them by their divine master, and giving in to frequent disputes among themselves. But the moment the life-giving Spirit came upon them, they were changed. All their weaknesses ceased, all their faults disappeared, and they become models for us and saints of most sublime virtue. Strangers to the world in which they are living, beyond all passion and all attraction for this world, they now dare to speak to the entire human race: "Be imitators of us as we are of Jesus Christ" (2 Thes 3:9).

The Holy Spirit would bring about in us the same effects, if we knew how to draw him to us and how to correspond to his grace. As his sacred fire comes down into our hearts, it would consume all our disordered yearnings and all our carnal desires. With his action in us destroying all that is impure in our souls, he transforms us into pure gold, without alloy. It is characteristic of divine charity to purify from all stains and to metamorphize, to coin a word, into a new nature. The old self dies, and from the ruins comes forth, shining and pure as a butterfly from its tomb, the new self alive with the life of Jesus Christ, or rather Jesus Christ himself living in the self reborn and purified by his grace. Is that the state of your soul?

3. The last effect of the descent of the Holy Spirit on the apostles is to strengthen them and to raise them above all human fear. These men so fainthearted only moments before, these cowards who shamefully abandoned their master, these disciples of whom the most zealous had denied him three times in a row, now they are preaching his resurrection and proclaiming his divinity along with his way of life in public squares, in synagogues, in the Temple, and before the court tribunals. They declare everywhere to the Jews that the one they just crucified is their Messiah and their God.

Not only are they no longer afraid to experience the lot of their master by exposing themselves to possible death for his sake, but they long for the happiness of sharing in it. They will not be satisfied until they pour out their own blood for the sake of his name, after having proclaimed that name to the ends of the world.

Who gave them this supernatural strength that makes them both lambs and lions, lambs to suffer much and lions to fight against the world and the devil? It is the Holy Spirit who came down upon them with the fullness of his gifts. This same Spirit is just as necessary for us, if not to hold up under violent persecutions, at least to subdue our passions and to overcome the flesh and its lustful desires, the world and its scandals, the devil and his accomplices.

Let us, who are as ignorant, as stained with sin, and as weak as the apostles were before Pentecost, beg the Spirit to pour out in us the light that enlightened them, the purity of conscience that increased their worth, and the strength that brought them new life. Let us call him to us with the same bright and burning desire that set afire the hearts of the apostles in the Cenacle. Let us then move on before him or at least let us prepare a dwelling place not unworthy of this divine Spirit, and let us say to him with a holy impatience: "Come, Holy Spirit, by your grace make possible for us what is impossible for us according to our nature."

Spiritual Bouquet

Let these words serve as our spiritual bouquet.

First Sunday after Pentecost

· ·

Meditation on the mystery of the Most Holy Trinity

First Prelude

In the name of the Father, and of the Son, and of the Holy Spirit (Mt 28:19).

Second Prelude

Imagine the vision of the prophet Isaiah as he sees the seraphim covering up their faces with their wings in the presence of the majesty of the Most High, exclaiming to one another: "Holy, Holy, Holy is the Lord God of Hosts" (Is 6:3).

Third Prelude

Ask for the grace of honoring worthily and fittingly the most adorable Trinity.[31]

Let us look at the homage we owe to the three divine persons united in one and the same nature. Our homage ought to be most especially that (1) of our faith, (2) of our love, and (3) of our imitation of the Trinity.

1. The homage of our faith comes first because, if the Trinity has been revealed to us, our duty ought to be to give bold evidence of our submission and our belief. The fact of this revelation is attested to by the most respected of authorities and, century after century, builds up testimony in its favor. What do I mean?

From the moment of creation, when God was pleased to spread out beyond himself that life which is in him as its source and its fullness, the august Trinity manifested itself with the words: "Let us make man in our image" (Gn 1:26). That is the thinking of Tertullian, Origen, St. Basil, St. Ephrem, St. Irenaeus, St. Justin, Clement of Alexandria, and most exegetes. Moreover, the Doctors of the Church saw a manifestation of this ineffable mystery in that mysterious vision of the patriarch of believers. When three men were approaching him and he saw them, he prostrated himself and adored but one, crying out: "Lord!" (*Domine!* [Gn 18:1ff.]).

Lactantius goes so far as to assure us that several philosophers recognized three principles in the Godhead.[32] St. Augustine says he read in the books of the Platonists what St. John wrote at the beginning of his gospel, that the Word was eternally in God and that the Word was God and that everything was made by this Word (Jn 1:1–3). He then adds that heaven inspired this knowledge even in pagan prophetesses and that proof of this is found in their oracles. However that may be, a great number of theologians maintain that wise men and women of the Gentiles had some notion of this truth, and that it was known, albeit imperfectly, by the prophets and the most learned of the Jews. That is how providence prepared some people for the clear and formal revelation that Jesus Christ was to make of this fundamental dogma in the fullness of time.

To Christianity alone was reserved the glorious privilege of making known the distinction of the divine persons. We, its children, believe what it teaches us because the eternal Word has revealed it and because that is the unanimous and universal understanding of all Catholic nations. Even if there were no other proof than the useless efforts to combat and destroy this belief, that alone would suffice to show beyond a doubt the truth of this dogma.

It is in vain that Arianism, upheld by those great masters of the world, the emperors Constantius [II] and Valentius, did all it could to remove it from people's hearts.[33] This truth has triumphed over all the subtleties of that heresy in spite of the cruelest of persecutions. For the past eighteen hundred years, peoples have been taught and baptized in the name of the Father, and of the Son, and of the Holy Spirit, according to the command given by our Lord to his apostles (Mt 28:19).

What more need do we have now except to ban all further scrutiny, all reflection, and all curiosity, believing simply what the Church teaches us about this mystery we are using for our meditation? That is how we render to God the homage of our faith, homage that will be for him all the more glorious insofar as we proclaim that it is a mystery beyond all our comprehension and all concepts of human understanding.

This we know as truth, that the Father has no source and that the Word is truly his Son, not by adoption but by nature, not by succession in time but from all eternity, not by creation but by generation both unique and personal. We know that the Holy Spirit proceeds from the Father and the Son as from but one and the same principle. We know that the Son, although begotten, remains completely in the Father, and the Holy Spirit remains completely in both the one and the other. But these are hidden truths that humans would never have suspected without revelation, hidden truths that were not clearly known and manifested until the coming of the Messiah. Faced with them, both the greatest of the learned and the simplest of the faithful will forever have to reduce the faculty of reason to nothing.

2. The second homage we owe to the most holy Trinity is love. What could be more fitting than to love what is supremely lovable and is for us an inexhaustible source of blessings? Where can we find more loving kindness than in each of the persons of the adorable Trinity? And who has ever loved us with so marvelous a love? Who could ever conceive of so many perfectly attractive qualities: a beauty ever ancient and ever new, beyond all change and incapable of the least variation; an immensity that nothing can encompass; a powerful force that nothing can stop; a splendor beside which any other light vanishes; a goodness that overflows without measure, the effects of which will be eternally impossible for human language to express?

Oh, how great are the mysteries of charity! The Trinity is totally taken up, so to speak, with raising us up to the Godhead. Our creation is the work of the Father, our redemption the work of the Son, and our sanctification the fruit of the working of the Holy Spirit. It is this divine Spirit that gives everyone grace, without ever losing anything of its own fullness, just like the sun whose light spreads out and divides out onto different objects without losing any of its own heat.

It is this divine Spirit who enlightens all minds and leads them to the knowledge of the true religion. It is he who inspires prophets, gives wisdom to lawgivers, consecrates pontiffs, calls back to life those spiritually dead, and makes an evangelist out of a publican converted to the faith. Out of a sinner, he makes a master of godly knowledge—out of a persecutor, the apostle of the nations, the hero of the faith, and a vessel of election. With the Spirit's life-giving breath, the weak become strong, the poor wealthy, and the simple and the ignorant wiser than all the sages in the world.

Glory be to this divine Spirit, as it was in the beginning, is now, and will be forever and ever. Glory, too, to this eternal Word, to this only Son who, without being separated from the Father, eternally goes out like the ray of the daystar and comes among us to exercise his office of lawgiver, Savior, pontiff, and mediator between heaven and earth. Glory also to this fertile and universal principle, to this Father without peer who has adopted us as his children, who has loved us so much that he delivered his Son to death for us (Jn 3:16), and who calls us to share his happiness in the company of the elect.

It is there, oh my soul, it is in this blessed eternity that, lovingly lost in the bosom of the three persons of the ineffable Trinity, we will meditate without ever becoming weary on these inexpressibly attractive qualities and these blessings beyond number. For it is only in eternity that we can truly know how loving the three persons are and how much they have loved us. In what transports of love and thanksgiving we will be at the sight of so many marvelous things!

Oh, how we will then intone with all our heart that canticle of praise that the Church puts so often in our mouths: Glory be to the Father, and to the Son, and to the Holy Spirit! O my God, why did I have to repeat these words full of mystery so often without attention, without faith, without awe? And especially, why did I have to trace on my body the sign of my redemption and call upon the indivisible Trinity so many times without comprehending the admirable mystery it was to call to mind and without being penetrated with the movements of love and thanksgiving that it ought to have inspired in me?

3. Let us now hasten to offer this adorable Trinity one last homage, that of imitating the Trinity. This is actually the best way of honoring the Trinity. How ought we imitate the most holy Trinity if not principally in that ineffable union which is like its indissoluble bond, which excludes every opposing sentiment, every contrary desire, and so marvelously makes the three divine persons unite for the same end? What a monstrous

inconsistency it would be if, all of us being children of the same Father, we were to live together as if we were strangers; if, all of us being sisters and brothers of the same Son of God, we were not united by such a strong and delightful bond; if, all of us wanting to be animated by the same Holy Spirit, we were to surface contrary desires and affections.

Let us, therefore, have but one heart and one soul. Let us banish everything that could trouble our peace and harmony, such as envy, jealousy, false stories, slander, and calumny. Let us reflect carefully on that. Such things will certainly be the object of a terrible accounting when we die. How frightened we, then, would be when the priest comes to bring strength for our soul in that terrible moment, and, with crucifix in his hand, he says, "Go now, O Christian soul, in the name of God the almighty Father who created you; in the name of Jesus Christ, who suffered for you; in the name of the Holy Spirit, who has placed his gifts in you."[34] Oh, what would we feel then if our conscience were to reproach us for having abandoned this tender Father to whom we owe complete devotion as our Creator? Or for having crucified once again this only Son to whom we owe complete attachment as our Savior? Or for having saddened this Holy Spirit to whom we owe complete attention as our sanctifier?

On the other hand, with what great confidence would we not be filled at the remembrance of our past deeds if they served the glory of the Father, by a humble submission to his will? Or served the glory of the Son, by a holy conformity to his example? Or served the glory of the Holy Spirit, by a constant fidelity in carrying through on his divine inspirations?

Therefore, let us make these selfless dispositions our own, and, further, let us make the resolution (1) to avoid whatever would be capable of spoiling fraternal charity; (2) to make the Sign of the Cross with greater respect and devotion; and finally (3) to renew our attention when praying the *Gloria Patri, et Filio, et Spiritui Sancto* (Glory be to the Father, and to the Son, and to the Holy Spirit).

Spiritual Bouquet

This prayer will serve as our spiritual bouquet.

Thursday after the Most Holy Trinity

· ·

Meditation on the procession of the Feast of the Blessed Sacrament or of the Most Holy Body of Christ

First Prelude

It is the feast day of the Body of Jesus Christ.

Second Prelude

Imagine the scene where Jesus Christ is saying to his disciples: "My flesh is real food, and my blood is real drink" (Jn 6:55).

Third Prelude

As the fruit of this prayer, ask for the grace of honoring in a fitting way the body of Jesus Christ.[35]

Three sentiments in particular ought to inspire us during the procession of the Blessed Sacrament: (1) a lively faith, (2) a grateful love, and (3) a desire to make just amends to the Holy Eucharist.[36]

1. First of all, let our faith be intense and full of life. Without such faith, how can we assist at this attractive ceremony in a way that is pleasing to our divine master, useful to our souls, and edifying for the faithful? Is it not by the holy impulses of our heart, the burning fire of our sentiments, and the recollection of our senses that we will be able to draw the attention of Jesus Christ toward us, merit his blessings, and edify the public who will be watching us in procession? Faith alone can form these joyful dispositions by inspiring in us a strong and lively belief in the dogma of the real presence.

In the presence of the adorable host, it is faith that will capture our imagination and our thoughts and will hold all the powers of soul and body respectfully submissive, fixed, and almost totally subdued. It is faith that will make Jesus Christ as present to our view as he was to the Israelites when he went down into their midst on Mount Sinai, cloaked in all the magnificent display of his power (Ex 19:16–19). Finally, it is faith that will remove the curtain hiding him from our sight and will make him as visible in the monstrance as when Jesus Christ in the flesh was traveling from village to village in Judea.

Of course all of us believe in this adorable mystery, but do all of us believe in it strongly enough? Alas, we need to admit that our faith in this mystery is, indeed, weak, seeing that it makes so little difference in our external behavior and that the least visible sign given by Jesus Christ of his sacramental existence would completely shock us, seizing us with fear. And if he were to appear suddenly there in the midst of the procession in glory and majesty, just as one day he will so appear on the clouds of heaven (Mt 24:30; 26:64), no one would dare follow after him, because our souls are soiled by sin. No one would dare turn his head away, laugh, or speak.

Indeed, if such a miracle were to happen, we would all fall prostrate at his feet, we would beat our breasts, our eyes would stream with tears, our faces would be pale and dejected, and our whole bodies would tremble. And so it is true that this hidden God (Is 45:15) could reproach us for our lack of faith and speak to us from the midst of the mysterious darkness that hides him only from unbelievers, saying with even greater reason than to his disciples, "Where is your faith?" (Lk 8:25).

Yes, all who are deeply conscious of the real presence make it visible in a thousand different ways in their external behavior, their movements, their posture, and especially by where they look, keeping their sight devoutly on the sacred host or modestly lowered. In a word, they appear convincing and convinced, edifying the faithful and bringing them to reverence this glorious sacrament.

Whereas if the opposite is true, the indifference of others, their almost disrespectful ways, their appearance of being distracted and scattered, thereby manifesting the weakness of their faith, weaken or destroy the faith of the laity, who always judge severely those who ought to set them an example. Because of their poor example, they often have an unfavorable impression of religion.

Therefore, let us visibly show great faith as we take part in this procession, and let us say over and over again to ourselves what the prince of the apostles said, "You are the Christ, Son of the living God" (Mt 16:16). Or, let us rouse ourselves to devotion by thoughts of faith and devout reflections such as these: Behold the one who was born of Mary. Behold the body that was in her womb and which she carried in her arms. Behold the flesh that was crucified for me and the blood that was poured out on Calvary. Let us go through the different events in the life of our Lord that we might have more reasons for reviving our faith and enkindling our love. This latter disposition is the second one we ought to have for accompanying the Blessed Sacrament.

2. Yes, we need an intensely burning love, because this mystery is all about charity. This is where the Savior of the world makes clear how great is his love for us. And what a love it is! Has there ever been a love more generous, more tender, with greater strength, or with greater selflessness?

Yes, it is a generous love. He is God, and he gives us his divinity. He has a body and gives it to us as food, blood and gives it to us as drink. In this food and drink, he hands over to us his virtues, and he applies his merits to us.

And it is a tender love. It is hard to distinguish tenderness from the object that is loved. Yet, Jesus, knowing that the hour for returning to his father had come (Jn 13:1), did not want to totally leave us. Rather, he instituted this adorable sacrament in order to remain with us to the end.

It is a strong love as well, for he needed his almighty power to work the wonder of the consecration. He also was not unaware of the insults and offenses he would have to drink century after century by so many wicked and immoral people, by so many unbelievers and heretics, by so many Christians unworthy of the name, and even by so many unworthy priests.

Finally, it is a selfless love. What need did he have of us and of our worship? Oh, how inexhaustible are the divine mercy and charity! Can love ever go further? Could we ever refuse our gratitude to a God who loves us with such generosity, tenderness, and selflessness?

May our hearts catch on fire as we walk along with him just as it happened to the disciples on the way to Emmaus. May we in turn be able to say with them: "Were not our hearts burning inside us as he was talking to us?" (Lk 24:32). Oh, if we truly love him, how fervent will be our prayer, how infrequent and minor will be our distractions, what a great many things we will have to tell him!

Love it is, therefore—love for love. How can we not let ourselves be aware of his love in the midst of this religious ceremony? Sometimes even the ungodly are touched by it, as Diderot, who would one day write:

> I have never seen that long line of priests in sacerdotal garments; those young acolytes dressed in their white albs, girded with their large, blue cinctures and sprinkling flower petals in front of the Blessed Sacrament; the crowd of people that went before and came behind them keeping a religious silence; so many people bended over with their foreheads to the ground; I have never heard this solemn and poetic chant intoned by the priests and repeated affectionately by an infinity of voices of men, women, young girls, and children without my very soul being moved, thrilled by it, and without tears coming to my eyes. [37]

3. Finally, let us make just amends, for such is the Church's purpose in this solemn procession, and everything says it is our duty to enter into the Church's view of things and its intentions: gratitude, zeal, and even justice.

The virtue of gratitude obliges us to make reparation, insofar as we can, for the shameful treatment received by the body of the Savior on our behalf during his passion. And could we flatter ourselves in loving him if the memory of so many offenses did not bring us to honor him the best we could? Could we ever believe that we have here the same flesh that was covered with disgrace and shame for our salvation, lacerated with whips, profaned by the hands of the executioners, and immolated on the cross, without hastening to worship and adore him? That is, without fulfilling the purpose of this solemnity? For, as St. Francis de Sales said, we do not celebrate this solemnity except to make true reparation to the body of

Jesus for all the humiliations he suffered in the streets of Jerusalem when he was dragged from one tribunal to another.

But it is zeal and even justice that more particularly oblige us to make these just amends. This is the role of zeal, because it ought to commit us to giving as much glory and honor to the divine Eucharist as heretics and bad Catholics insult it by their irreverent acts, sacrileges, and profanations. Who can really say how often in these past eighteen centuries this adorable Savior has been insulted, outraged, and desecrated?

Let us remember now his places of worship that have been torn down, the altars overturned, the tabernacles smashed, the sanctuaries sullied, the sacred vessels used for unholy purposes, and the sacred species scattered on the floor of the church or even trampled underfoot. Or, rather, let us forget all these horrors lest we spend our time only on the insults toward Jesus Christ on the altar of which we are guilty. For if it is the place of our zeal to make reparations, as much as we can, for the offenses which he received from others, how much more just it is for us to work at making just amends for those that stem from us and over which we ought never cease shedding tears. How deeply our consciences reproach us on this account, not to mention the times we might have received Communion unworthily when we approached the sacrament without a clear conscience or the irreverent acts we might have committed in the celebration of these marvelous mysteries. Let us remember, too, all the lukewarm Communions taken with negligence and without preparation, to which we brought only a dissipated spirit and a heart cold and indifferent; and useless Communions, too, that brought about no change in us but served only to let us become overly casual with holy things; and all those Communions that made us neither more faithful to our rules nor more humble or more charitable to our confreres.

What has been the result of all our Communions taken since we entered religious life? Do we not still have to reproach ourselves for having lived too long a time estranged from this divine sacrament? Is this not because, through lack of devotion or awareness, through stubborn attachment to ourselves and to things of this world, we have not wanted to make the least effort to overcome the obstacles that prevent us from receiving Communion? And how terrible if we have turned others away from receiving Communion by our speech and our example, mocking those who received Communion often and attributing bad intentions to them.

Therefore, we now need to make reparations by receiving Communion more piously, more fervently, and more frequently, but above all by just amends for all that irreverence, all those distractions, all that half-heartedness, all those sins and outrageous behavior. With this end in view, let us join in the procession of the Blessed Sacrament because if this is a ceremony right for making reparations or just amends to the body of Jesus Christ, then we are going to be witnesses of that by our actions.

The Lord is going to be present as a king in the midst of his subjects, as a father among his children, and as a shepherd reviewing his flock. What do I mean? He is going to come forward as a conqueror in the midst of an army drawn up for battle but for totally peaceful ends in view. So, then, look at his retinue: the leaders of the world plus his ministers go ahead of him and walk with him; some wealthy people humbly follow behind him and bow in his presence; people crowd around him just as in the days of his life on earth. All is subdued in humble submission. Everything is submissive before him, proclaiming his splendor and majesty: the streets strewn with flowers, houses all decorated, altars set up along his path, the canopy over him, the swinging of censers, the sound of church bells, the harmonious sound of voices and instruments.

What, then, is still missing in this triumph of his? Ah, the only thing that he desires the most and without which all this magnificent display is nothing in his eyes: the realm of our hearts. Let us be filled, therefore, with the dispositions we need for accompanying the most Blessed Sacrament, dispositions which I sum up in three principal ones: a living faith, a grateful love, and a spirit of sacrifice that brings us to make just amends to our Lord.

Spiritual Bouquet

"I am with you" (Mt 28:20).

Chapter 4

CHRISTIAN EDUCATION

I n 1856, Moreau wrote *Christian Education* to standardize the quality, character, and religious content of a Holy Cross education. He first gathered reports from the Holy Cross brothers who were teaching, assessed what he found, and then composed the treatise. These brothers were engaged most frequently in primary education.

This treatise represents Moreau's most extensive single writing on the subject of education. Although Moreau presents some of his overall philosophy or vision of education in this text, his purpose is primarily pedagogical—namely, the formation of Holy Cross religious to be teachers. At the same time, the practical concerns addressed and emphasized by Moreau also reveal the virtues of teachers and goals of a Christian education, which makes *Christian Education* best read alongside his other writings on education, including, in particular, Circular Letter 36.

The treatise is composed of three parts, with the first and third part included in this collection. The first part covers the virtues that relate to the vocation of teaching and also how to educate students who pose particular educational challenges. The second part, not included in this collection, gives detailed instruction on the operation and management of schools, including the layout of classrooms, admission procedures, and how to conduct a lesson. The third section contains Moreau's thinking on religious instruction and the catechism, along with his final thoughts on education as a work of the resurrection.

Scripture references have been added in parentheses. All notes to other sources have been added by the editors.

K.G. and A.G.

Preface

· · · · · · · · · · ·

M ay this short work on education, intended for the institutions of the congregation, attain the end that I proposed for myself in composing it: the formation of the heart of the young person and the development of religious sensibility. For I have never understood the education of youth otherwise, persuaded that the first duty of the teacher is to make Christians and that society has a much greater need of the virtuous than of the knowledgeable. Knowledge does not yield virtue, while virtue allies itself well with knowledge and ensures the good use of it. What is more, if there is, indeed, an era where the necessity of such an education is making itself known, it is certainly in ours where the pursuit of pleasure and immorality are ravaging us. Christian education alone can remedy this evil and hasten the return to the beliefs and practices of religion by bringing up the coming generations in these principles. It is for the sake of coming together with all our efforts to this blessed result, and of regularizing instruction given in our institutions, that I have conceived and executed the plan of this new pedagogy. I say a "plan" because this is not just an essay, as I had indicated in my circular letter of May 29, 1856, and I have the intention of completing it according to the observations that will be communicated to me and the personal assessments that I invite the teaching brothers to make to me on this work. We will perhaps find that the canticles occupy too great a place and that I attach to it too much importance.[1] But experience has shown that pious hymns are one of the most effective ways for the moral formation of the young. Also, they fill the mind and the heart with honest thoughts and sentiments. They contribute powerfully, if they are well executed, to maintaining order in a school, to dissolving the monotony of schoolwork, and in making it more enjoyable to the children. Even though these hymns are distributed in an order that seems more appropriate for institutions of secondary education than for primary schools, they can just as well be of service to the latter by omitting the canticles that would not be adapted to them. It seems to me, anyway, that the adept teacher will find in this variety even some resources of which he can use a great deal.

Introduction

· · · · · · · · · · · · · · · · · ·

Those who teach justice to many will shine like the stars for all eternity. (Dn 12:3)

P edagogy, thus derived from two Greek words, that for *child* and that for *leading*,[2] is the art of forming youth—that is to say, for a Christian, to make of youth people who are conformed to Jesus Christ, their model. For education—which, according to its etymology, can mean to pull out of ignorance or disorder—consists precisely in reforming human nature, tainted by original sin, by giving to reason the light that illuminated it before the fall of our first father, and by giving our hearts proper guidance to our feeling. This notion, founded on the Catholic faith, suffices to give the highest form of pedagogy and to make understood that it is the *art of arts*. To what extent is it important to you to form yourself in it before practicing it? From that point on, is it not a grave obligation for your superiors to lay out for you in advance the proper conduct to have, in order to correct the inexperience that you will have in leaving the novitiate? Is it not urgent also to end the diversity that reigns in the administration of our schools by teaching those who must direct them to do so in a uniform manner? It is this reflection especially that has inspired this little treatise, whose rules I make obligatory for all our institutions, as soon as they are published; and because it is the fruit of lengthy experience, you will be able to learn these useful principles for the education of children. In order to proceed with the most order and method possible, we will speak in this text first and foremost of teachers and students, then of the administration and direction of a school. Finally, we will speak of the formation of students in the Christian life and of the means to ensure their perseverance in it.

Part One

· · · · · · · · · · · · · ·

On Teachers and Students

One could consider teachers and students in themselves or in their relationship to each other; this is what I am going to do by speaking sequentially of them both respectively in two different chapters.

Chapter One: On Teachers in Themselves and in Their Relationship to Their Students

Every teacher, in order to succeed in this very difficult art of educating children, must have certain qualities and avoid certain faults of which I will speak in as many different articles. However, one can reduce to ten the qualities that are indispensable to teachers for worthily fulfilling their mission to students—and, consequently, the faults into which they can fall in not acquiring them. These qualities are: vocation, faithfulness, knowledge, zeal, vigilance, seriousness, gentleness, patience, prudence, and firmness.

Article 1: A vocation to be a teacher

Since God alone provides the means for the successful accomplishment of any task, it seems evident that a person needs to be called by God to be an effective teacher. Without this call to teaching, how will anyone be able to put up with everything that teachers face daily? From the time the school year begins, teachers do not have a moment's rest or a moment free. Every good teacher is preoccupied with the care and the progress of students, with their schoolwork, and with the small and bothersome difficulties that inevitably arise in dealing with young people. Teachers will find it difficult to care seriously for their own spiritual needs and their own interests.

Relationships with young people are always difficult. Sometimes those who deal with young people attach themselves too closely to the young and end up giving themselves over strictly to human affections. Finding among their students young people who are frank and open, who are moving toward accomplishing good things, who respond well to the care they are providing, some teachers forget the place of God in the relationship between teacher and student. Learning this often surprises teachers, since it is easily hidden by enthusiasm, kindness, and even duty.

Teachers who experience close relationships with their students become totally occupied with them. Every place they go the students come to mind; no matter what they do, they think of the students. Teachers like these often enter into unhealthy relationships of all kinds with their students, often without realizing what is happening.

Christian educators really need a call from God in order to deal with all that they face in working with young people. How else can teachers possibly work toward building Christian values in the young as well as toward giving them the knowledge they need? For the religious, this call to education comes in obedience.

Article 2: Faithfulness

Faithfulness is a virtue that draws us to fulfill faithfully our duties to God. St. Paul has said that piety is necessary for everyone because it is the opening to all that God has promised us.

What about teachers without this virtue? They are left with only their own resources, complete their tasks without real excitement and even with negligence, and are unable to teach all of the values and responsibilities contained in a Christian education. They have no concern or desire to teach or to practice the life of a Christian; prayer and the sacraments are not important to them. While these teachers may be able to help students develop intellectually, and though they may pass on some knowledge that is useful in life, the important knowledge that students need—the knowledge that leads them to the totality and completeness of the Christian life—is neglected. Such teachers may develop scholars, but they will not develop Christians. They have forgotten the essence of their mission—the development of the heart and the soul, on which good values depend. Consequently, their true goals are forgotten. The tender plants that these teachers have to cultivate will show real potential in their hands, but for lack of real care they will perish because they have not received the true nourishment they need.

How different, on the contrary, is the result with those students who have been given truly reverent teachers! Convinced that the Lord himself has given them the students they are instructing and are responsible for, reverent teachers will try above all to bring their students to the completeness of the Christian life. Such teachers see their students' souls more than they see their students' bodies. They know that young people have been won at the price of the shedding of the Lord's blood, and they consider them adopted children of God and temples of the Spirit. Their enthusiasm for their work increases because of this. Their major duty becomes instruction in the faith, and with untiring patience they help students learn to pray. They do not cease reminding students of Christian commitments, the works of God, and the effects of the sacraments. Finally, this kind of teacher helps students become able to deal with the values they will find opposed to Christianity and inspires in students a devotion to the sacred.

The Lord will bless such efforts and reward such enthusiasm with the greatest results. Anyone entering a Christian school will be able to note the reverence of the students. They grow from day to day both in knowledge and in Christian values. Those who have formed students in such a way "will shine like the stars of the heavens for all eternity" (Dn 12:3).

Article 3: Knowledge

If, as St. Paul says, "knowledge without faith makes one proud" (1 Cor 8:1) and thus becomes dangerous, it is likewise true that faith without knowledge makes a teacher useless and compromises the honor of the teacher's mission. That is why Daniel, speaking of the reward prepared for those who teach others, does not assume that teachers must be merely "just," and hence reverent, but also "learned and knowledgeable." Without knowledgeable teachers, what can be said to families who want their children to acquire all the learning needed to earn a good position in life? "You cannot give what you do not already have." This axiom applies to teaching as well—it would be useless for a person who did not possess the knowledge sufficient to achieve the goals of instruction to try to teach.

Teachers themselves should definitely have enough knowledge and instruction to be able to deal with questions that are only indirectly connected with the subjects they are presenting and be able to make lessons interesting and complete. In order to succeed in acquiring a superior degree of knowledge, teachers must have a constant desire for self-improvement and lose no opportunity to satisfy this ambition when it is not detrimental to their other duties.

To teach with success, teachers must know good methods, be skillful in applying these methods, have clear ideas, be able to define exactly, and possess language that is easily understood and correct. All of these skills are acquired and perfected only through study. I think we must assume that good teachers are not content simply with obtaining a degree or a credential to show their capabilities, but that they also try to increase their knowledge even further by studying as much as they can. In this way teachers are able to meet the qualifications required of them.

Article 4: Zeal

Zeal is the great desire to make God known, loved, and served, and thus to bring knowledge of salvation to others. Activity flows from this virtue. Teachers who possess it fulfill the duties of their profession with enthusiasm, love, courage, and perseverance. When they see young people who lack knowledge and Christian values, they experience what St. Paul felt when he wrote to those he had evangelized: "My children for whom I labor again and again until Christ is within you" (Gal 4:19). That statement, in fact, is the goal of all Christian education. To reach it, teachers must neglect nothing.

Teachers who have this virtue will be happy only when their students progress in the knowledge of virtue. All day and each day they will work at this great and difficult task of Christian education. When they pray, when they study, when they receive the sacraments, it will be especially for "their young people." This will be done without distinction or regard for any student as special, because such teachers know that all students are equally important to God and that their duty is to work with each with the same devotion, watchfulness, and perseverance.

If at times you show preference to any young person, it should be the poor, those who have no one else to show them preference, those who have the least knowledge, those who lack skills and talent, and those who are not Catholic or Christian. If you show them greater care and concern, it must be because their needs are greater and because it is only just to give more to those who have received less. You must be "all things to all people" (1 Cor 9:22), like St. Paul—little with the little, great with the great, seeing in all only the image of God imprinted within them like a sacred seal that you must preserve at all cost.

Teachers animated by such a spirit do not simply follow what is generally accepted in the profession but have a thousand little ways to encourage progress in even the weakest and least talented students and challenge all students to their highest performance.

Such teachers know how to maintain silence when required, to keep students at work when required, and to maintain proper order without using punishments—neither threats nor reprimands. Such teachers use any occasion to provide models for young people and to communicate about God, Jesus Christ, and the students' souls. Since the zeal of these teachers is guided by love, they do everything with strength and with gentleness: with strength because they are courageous and unshakable in the midst of any difficulties they face, and with gentleness because they are tender and compassionate like Jesus Christ, the model for all teachers, who loved to be bothered by young people.

Without this virtue of zeal among teachers in a school, everything changes. Everything falls apart. There is ignorance, disorder, bad conduct, and the true corruption of young people. These are what families experience through the faintheartedness and indifference of teachers without zeal. They are put in the midst of young people and cause the ruin of a great number of them. Thus, the virtue of zeal is necessary for a Christian teacher.

Article 5: Vigilance

The word "vigilance" is connected with watchfulness and hence signifies alertness. It is a virtue that makes us attentive to our duties. Vigilant teachers forget nothing of what they ought to do and do not become distracted from what they ought to be thinking about, seeing, hearing, or doing. There is nothing more necessary for teachers than this constant watchfulness over themselves and their students. Teachers need to watch themselves in order to conduct themselves as they should in front of young people, who closely study their teachers' faults and notice any weaknesses. Do not forget that young people are naturally observant and that they see all and hear all. Teachers are greatly mistaken if they believe that they do not have to be concerned with what students see or hear if the students are occupied with all of the distractions that go with being young.

Teachers need to watch, above all, over the young people placed in their care. Indeed, they are the spiritual parents of these young people. How else will teachers be able to carry out their responsibilities to the families that rely on them to help develop good values in their children? From the moment teachers accept charge of young people for their education, they become guardians. This vigilance does involve some annoying, tiring, and disquieting things, especially for those who are new to the profession. Until they have responsibility for their first classes, teachers do not realize the concerns that often bother those in positions of responsibility and authority. When they are put in charge of a class, they often experience a loss of calm and peace and create anxieties for themselves that are contrary to what should be motivating them. Looking out for students becomes a heavy responsibility and a real problem, since it leads teachers to dislike their work and even question their calling. I caution young teachers not to take this virtue to the extreme.

Teachers must keep their vigilance within reasonable limits and not imitate those who are always in a state of great alarm, often over some childish prank that they are unable to evaluate correctly. Those who are too vigilant are unaware that a great talent of good teachers is often to pretend not to notice what he or she does not want to be obliged to punish. An indulgence prudently managed is worth much more than outbursts and the punishments that follow them. Always avoid this embarrassing vigilance. It is revolting to students and unbearable for teachers. Let your watchfulness and attention be calm, without overconcern, without agitation or trouble, without great constraint or affectation. But also avoid the opposite, which involves carelessness, distraction, unwillingness to act, and tardiness, which are all contrary to this virtue of vigilance.

Article 6: Seriousness

Seriousness comes through faithfulness to self-control. It is impossible for teachers to be truly serious unless they are able to control their exterior selves. Seriousness, however, does not force a person into pedantry or affectation. Teachers should carefully avoid mean and threatening looks, gloomy and scowling faces, angry voices, and bitter, biting, and satirical words. The aim of seriousness is not to intimidate students, to keep them from showing themselves as they really are, to make them afraid of making mistakes, or to hinder the development of good qualities that might exist in them. Seriousness does not in any way exclude kindness, tenderness, or an affable way with students, which can win them over and lead them with docility.

Seriousness is a virtue that assumes a mental maturity and wisdom in the one who possesses it, along with a real faith in the presence of God. It is a virtue that requires noble sentiments and true humility. It will give you the dignity in attitude that inspires respect, commands attention, and enables you to exercise the authority and leadership that you need.

Although seriousness does not rule out affection for young people, neither does it permit too great a familiarity with them, and it does not allow unseemly clowning, childish pranks and jokes, and ridiculous punishments that will discredit the teacher and earn the dislike of students.

Teachers who wish to maintain this virtue in their lives guard against giving any particular student too great attention. This is the way one most often loses this virtue. It is the responsibility of a young teacher especially to develop this virtue in order not to lose the dignity of the mission of teaching and the respect that the teacher is owed by students.

Article 7: Gentleness

It was the Lord himself who said, "Blessed are the meek, for they shall inherit the earth" (Mt 5:5). There is no other conclusion to be reached than that, in the overseeing of the mind and heart of a young person and in the effective use of authority in a school, a teacher needs to possess gentleness. Gentleness is the filling of the soul with the Spirit so as to moderate the anger that arises when a person feels irritated toward those who have caused some injury. It is the result of a patience that never tires and of a self-control that keeps everything under the guardianship of reason and faith.

Given that, one can understand the need of such a virtue in teachers, for to fulfill their mission successfully, teachers must make themselves liked by their students. Gentleness is the only way in which they will succeed in the task of bringing out love in their students. You are aware of the statement, "Love causes love." As people, we are built so that we cannot resist a person who displays true affection for us. Young people are very impressionable and are especially prone to this. They relate easily and happily with those from whom they hope and expect to receive reciprocal love and confidence. Feelings of love and respect between teachers and students are the result of charity and gentleness, inseparable virtues that cannot exist independently of one another. St. Francis de Sales himself says that meekness is "the very flower of charity."[3]

Teachers who are meek and who follow the example of Jesus Christ lose none of their authority and do not stress what is hard and severe in authority. They put themselves in their students' places. They try to persuade their students that they will find in their teachers tender and devoted friends who understand them. Considering themselves as taking the place of those who have entrusted young people to them, gentle teachers borrow from the father and the mother positive feelings toward young people. Everything in such teachers bears the stamp of this virtue. They avoid judging with harshness and anger, and they do not rely on exaggerated confidence in themselves. They are always guided by a heart full of compassion and kindness and make their decisions without stubbornness or injustice. They do not say things that will hurt the feelings of young people and do not make fun of students, as people who often feel injured by the statements or actions of another do. Gentleness overcomes those tendencies to self-love and shuts out the desire for revenge. Gentleness permits teachers to endure all the adversities, unpleasant experiences, and occurrences that go hand in hand with schooling and to proceed with complete calmness of spirit.

Gentleness begets a number of other good qualities: sensibility, good will, and a pleasant manner of acting and speaking. Gentleness permits teachers to remove what is harsh from a command, permits teachers to participate in activities with young people, leads teachers to be able to talk and discuss matters with students, permits teachers to sympathize with students who are often upset over things that are not important, and permits teachers to assist students when they are not feeling well or when they are depressed. Teachers filled with meekness can show an interest and an affection for young people that will win hearts. In class such teachers treat students with politeness, answer their questions with patience, and help keep students from punishments as much as possible by keeping them out of situations that are likely to lead them to misbehavior and punishment.

Gentle teachers will never be seen to inflict punishment when they are overly angry and upset. They will never push to the limit a student who is ready to react with anger and an outburst. Since these teachers are more disposed to reward than to punishment, whenever someone guilty of an offense wishes to return to a positive relationship, they pardon the student and show even more respect and friendship to that student than before.

Gentle teachers also look upon school as their mission. Far from being a source of boredom and disappointment, classes become a real pleasure. This simply supports the statement of the wise person who said,

"Do everything with gentleness and you will attract not only the respect but the love of other people."

Teachers who have drawn such gentleness from Jesus Christ will be blessed and happy. They will truly be the important people in their school, and they will cause Jesus Christ to be the important person there. Loved by their students and respected by the parents, who will be so happy to have found such excellent teachers for their children, they will be rewarded with blessings from the entire school community and will go through life "doing good works." Their memory will remain engraved upon the hearts of those students whom they have brought to the fullness of Christianity, and they will be a model to imitate and an example to follow.

Sad results flow from teachers who lack these qualities. Teachers who make no effort to acquire the gentleness of mind and heart that was recommended by Jesus Christ are really to be pitied. In their classes, they are annoyed and angered over every little thing. They shout, talk harshly, and carry on in all kinds of ways. Their rude and harsh approach intimidates and frightens students without their realizing that these actions can compromise them in the eyes of their students and the students' families. They injure their students by making fun of their inadequacies, or their families, or their ethnic background. They call their students names. They impose exaggerated and unjust punishments on some; they require of others assignments and duties beyond the range of their abilities or experience. They cause students to lose a love of learning and to develop a distaste for school. Such conduct on the part of teachers earns them scorn and dislike; students try to find all kinds of ways of getting away from them and look for all kinds of ways to displease them. Not only will these teachers be unable to bring students to the fullness of Christianity, but they will also be unable to give students the knowledge and the instruction that are owed them. It would have been better if such teachers had never entered a classroom and attempted the difficult art of teaching.

Article 8: Patience

Anyone who knows young people easily recognizes the necessity of patience, which is the only thing that permits a teacher to rise above the difficulties inherent in educating youth. Patience is most necessary in directing a group of young people from very diverse backgrounds and training. Teachers often need to speak to one student and to answer another student and probably several others at the same time, to help others reason out situations when they seem often to have little use for reason, to repeat many times the same thing without seeing any results, to calm those who are too lively, to move forward those who move slowly, to correct those who need correcting, to prepare others to accept responsibility—and it seems that all of this goes on at the same time. Teachers seem not to have a moment for themselves amid the activity that is constantly going on in a school.

Without the virtue of patience, teachers would have difficulty enduring the qualities that are so natural to young people: making life difficult for a teacher, refusing to follow directions, upsetting the class, promoting a bad spirit among other students, and ridiculing and making fun of teachers. Some students mock teachers' voices and gestures; some will complain without cause to their parents, who will immediately assume that what they are being told is the truth. The many difficulties that teachers face would dishearten those who have entered teaching with real hopes of accomplishment, but teachers need to remember that they have received a call and to resist such trials with all the means given to them through patience. If you know how to build patience, a calmness will come to you and peace will exist around you. Patience is the shield against which all these difficulties are blunted.

Teachers who do not know patience cannot restrain themselves, and they often show their lack of patience in harsh or imprudent words. They often carry on in all sorts of ways, even becoming violent, and in a burst of anger—as ridiculous as scandalous—will lose all control. They will even go so far as to abuse their students physically. Losing self-control lowers them in the eyes of their students. The first cause of all of that is a lack of patience. With a little more energy and self-control, teachers can prevent these excesses. Little by little, time will calm first prejudices, soften reactions, and lead to reasonable conclusions. Right reason always ends by triumphing over all obstacles. It is through patience that "you will possess your soul in peace."

Article 9: Prudence

Prudence is the virtue that helps us decide the best way of reaching our goals and that helps us work against obstacles standing in the way of reaching them. To understand the necessity of prudence, we only have to reflect on our purpose as Christian educators. We cannot compromise our mission or hinder its progress by acting imprudently in directing our schools.

Society does not permit us the luxury of mistakes in this area. Often it takes just a minor imprudent act to ruin the reputation of a solidly established school. Teachers and administrators must take extra care to employ prudence so that they do not prejudice the people in the area around the school. It would be helpful to new teachers if they had a greater experience of people and events in the area before they come to teaching, but only a limited experience is possible. Teachers in a school are of necessity in contact with three different groups of people: the students, the parents, and the society in which the school exists. These groups place different demands upon the school and the teachers that must be satisfied in order for the school to exist in reasonable peace with each group. No matter what skilled teachers do, it is likely that some opposition will arise against them from time to time, especially among those who already look upon a particular school with an unfavorable bias. Teachers should expect to be criticized regularly in their careers. Some people will complain about their way of teaching; others will complain about their discipline. Some will say that their students do not make any progress; others will say that they are unjust in giving awards.

Teachers who always act with prudence will know how to make light of all this complaining insofar as it is false and unjust, and they will be able to take care of those areas in which they should make some improvement. The best way to avoid such accusations is to use the following principles: study and distinguish the makeup of students in order to treat each one according to his or her specific needs, and prepare classes well. By reviewing the materials that make up the subject matter of lessons, there will be no confusion of ideas, and there will be clarity of expression on the part of the teacher. These two principles will assist teachers who believe that their mission is important. It is impossible for a teacher to educate well without fully preparing for the task daily. Cleverness can never substitute adequately for preliminary work and preparation, and most of the time teachers who rely on their own cleverness fall into the use of old materials, repetitions, and digressions. Often some teachers have the illusion that the lesson or material is so simple, so easy, and so elementary that they require no preparation.

No teaching, however, requires more preparation than the teaching of young people. There is nothing more difficult than helping young minds begin building a fund of knowledge—minds often with small capacity and very few ideas. It is not easy to help students with inattentive and unskilled minds move toward study and reflection. Teachers must practice becoming like young people, borrowing their language, taking their ideas, and placing all they say into the young people's limited area of knowledge. This kind of teaching requires real skill and devotion. Teachers who do not prepare for it are acting outside of the counsels of prudence.

Consider teachers who are imprudent enough and presumptuous enough to dare running a class without looking ahead to what they are going to say or do. They enter the class without books or materials. They tend to talk at the top of their voice when they should be silent, saying whatever comes into their minds without considering the worth of what is being said or the importance of their opinions. They do not ask for anyone's advice and do not even listen to those with more experience. There exists great disorder in their explanations, making them incoherent and practically unintelligible to the students. They deny one day what they have rashly advocated on a previous day, and they often contradict what they have said before. The result of all this is boredom and dislike on the part of students. The students are condemned to listen, yawn, or sleep and do not know what to do during the class. They waste their time and begin to take on a dislike of learning and study. This dislike may stay with them for a long time, since that is one of the peculiarities of youth. The impressions and experiences of youth tend to leave an indelible trace during an entire life. It is important for young people, then, to learn early the habits of work and application. A skillful and prudent teacher is able to profit from this peculiarity of youth and give students a good and solid education from the beginning.

Prudence, then, is of the greatest importance. Experience is one sure path for acquiring it, but there is another upon which we must all rely: an openness to the Lord, especially in prayer. Ask the Lord for prudence; pray to the "author of all wisdom" that you will be given the light and necessary graces to direct and lead you in everything with the prudence and wisdom necessary to teach.

Article 10: Firmness

The Bible, in speaking of the way in which God governs the world, says that providence guides everything with "strength" and with "gentleness." That is the model that teachers must follow if they wish to succeed in educating young people.

Without gentleness, they will never truly get their students to have the love of work, application, and good behavior that are all essential conditions of success. On the other hand, if they lack firmness and steadfastness, they will not be able to maintain discipline in class. This virtue is needed to raise teachers above all the difficulties inherent in education and to help them remain unshakable in the course of their duties without becoming discouraged in a task that is troublesome and tiring.

Teachers always must keep an eye on their classes in order to stop any movement toward disorder, wherever it occurs. If students find too great a weakness in a teacher or a softness in demanding compliance, they will permit themselves disorders of all sorts. They will laugh at the threats of such teachers and not even perform the penances given, because they know that the teacher will not push them to the limit and will end by giving in. From the time you enter the school, then, hold to a firm and assured course, know how to make yourself obeyed, and communicate to students that you absolutely demand compliance with your regulations.

Conclusion

From what has been said above, one can conclude that the teacher's mission is difficult and requires hard work. It requires a great devotion in order to continue in the calling as a teacher. With the eyes of faith, consider the greatness of the mission and the wonderful amount of good that one can accomplish. And also, consider the great reward promised to those who have taught the truth to others and have helped form them into justice: "They will shine eternally in the skies like the stars of the heavens" (Jer 12:3). With the hope of this glory, we must generously complete the Lord's work.

Chapter Two: Students and Student-Teacher Relations

It would be a serious mistake to open a school imagining that all the students will be alike in character and conduct. Providence varies all of its works. If two plants of the same family, apart from similar characteristics, have obvious differences, it is no less true that in the group of students given to you there are no two who have the exact same mind and heart. It will do little good, then, to use the same procedures in working with every student. You would be like a doctor who always gives the same remedy for every illness.

This in itself should be enough to point out the importance of beginning the year or semester by studying your students. If you are taking the place of another teacher in a class, it is important to gain all of the information the other teacher can give you about the students. In order to facilitate this study, which requires a lot of attention, there are some things you can look for to help you understand the different types of students you will be educating. You can use the following information to determine the most suitable way to approach each student. Never forget that all teaching lies in the best approach to an individual student, that all the successes you find will be in direct proportion to the efforts you have made in this area. In the different natures of young people, one can actually distinguish several characteristics marking them as poorly brought up or spoiled by their parents, unintelligent, self-centered, opinionated, insolent, envious, without integrity, immature, lazy, or in poor health.

Article 1: Young people who are spoiled or have poor upbringing

There are young people for whom parents show little care. These young people never do what their parents want, never follow directions, and murmur at the least thing that goes against what they think they desire. They are often dirty, disgusting, and unpolished. They are sometimes impertinent, impolite, teasing, and extravagant, openly yawning, making faces, mimicking the faults of teachers and students. They are children spoiled by indulgence who will tire at the least hint of work and who will become disconcerted at the least punishment. They have become accustomed to seeing their least wishes satisfied and having all their little whims gratified.

Often students who have been poorly brought up are those from rich families, who think of themselves as being so superior as to give themselves an air of authority over their fellow students and independence from their teachers, and who believe that they have a right to special consideration and attentions. If it happens that someone makes fun of their ridiculous pretensions, they complain to their parents of poor treatment.

Such young people have great need of being formed by proper education. To achieve this requires much patience, kindness, and charity. A teacher will have to treat them with considerable indulgence, because if they have all these faults, it is not due to a shallow spirit, or bad judgment, or a poor internal disposition, but it is because they have been left to grow up without direction. You must show them a lot of kindness, display an interest in them, and correct them when necessary, but always in a fatherly manner; when you do correct them, give them only easy punishments that will really help them.

It is also good to have contact with parents in such situations in order to anticipate the accusations and recriminations of the young person and to support your own authority with theirs. This is a troublesome and delicate task. Expect to have a lot of duplicity and annoyance, but strengthen yourself by remembering the example given by our Lord. He also educated, not only children and young parents, but also persons already advanced in age and consequently possessing all the prejudices and the bad habits that people so often pick up in the course of their lives.

In fact, recall that the apostles, chosen and formed in the school of our Lord, were unsophisticated, unlettered, taken from the lowest class of society, and combined a lack of education with a lot of ambition, self-love, and egotism. Admire the unchanging gentleness and untiring zeal that the Lord always showed. In all his teaching and actions, he tried only to inform them, to instruct them, and to make new men of them. As teachers, then, meditate on this example and try to pattern your own teaching after it.

Article 2: Unintelligent young people

It is rare that a teacher will meet any young people so lacking in intelligence and memory that they can understand and retain practically nothing. These young people make no sound except when they think they are being punished. They are often sly, pouting, and surly; they do not mix well with companions their age, do not take part in games, and keep themselves apart. A young person like this presents teachers with great obstacles. It is difficult to win the confidence of these young people because they lack openness and are often insensitive to signs of interest and affection. If they inconvenience you in class and bother their fellow students, you will need to work with administrators to ask their parents to withdraw them from the school. But if they are not a source of trouble for the class, it is great benefit to them that you will leave them in peace, limiting yourself to what is possible and being content with the little that they are able to accomplish.

Article 3: Self-centered young people

You will sometimes meet students totally concerned with themselves, often looking at themselves in a mirror, combing and arranging their hair artfully, possessing an affected walk, having touchy or extremely timid characteristics, constantly excusing themselves, and never recognizing any faults they might have. These young people can often be described as two-faced, lying, presumptuous, and bold. In class they will often be the first to attempt to answer questions; when they make mistakes, they will get angry and pout for some time. At the least correction they will feel hurt and wounded. They will always be ready to quarrel with their companions and will always use a lofty and superior tone of voice. These actions and attitudes point out to a teacher a self-centered young person. The teacher's task is to correct this, and there are ways experienced teachers have found to bring about this result. If you find this in one of the students, then rarely speak to the student. When you do speak to the student, do so very seriously. If the student makes an error, do not fail to point it out; when doing this, however, help the student see that the resulting pouting and hurt feelings are ridiculous. Be careful always about not allowing the student to respond to your corrections as a teacher, and help the student understand the ridiculousness of his or her feelings and pouting in private as well as in public. Always, however, approach the student in a way that holds him or her in respect.

Article 4: Self-opinionated young people

Sometimes there are students who refuse to carry out responsibilities given them, who are stubborn to the point that all threats and punishments seem to have no effect on them, and who lay open resistance to a teacher's authority. There are others who eventually give in but do so with such bad grace that they murmur aloud and make noises which disturb their fellow students' attention. Sometimes, those who give in to the teacher assume a posture that is a kind of defiance of the teacher by putting their heads down on their desks, by making ridiculous faces, or by imitating the gestures of the teacher when the teacher is not watching.

Teachers should first avoid as much as possible giving occasion for such scenes, which can harm the good order of the class and undermine the authority of the teacher. If a teacher has not been able to foresee and prevent this situation, the teacher should refrain from responding too severely until convinced of the seriousness of a student's behavior and the punishment deserved. When a teacher finds it necessary to punish a student in this situation, the teacher should wait until the student's excited state is calmed down and he or she can be talked to without arousing a greater state of disrespect. The teacher has everything to gain by playing for time, since pushing the student to the limit will gain the teacher nothing. When the teacher notices that the young person is calmer, the teacher should use that moment to speak with him or her, bringing the student, in an offhand way, to admit to both the original problem and the resistance to the teacher's authority. A teacher will in this way help the student understand that a punishment is necessary only to repair the poor example he or she has given to other students.

Be sure to carry out the punishment while displaying great concern for the student, even if you ask the student to apologize publicly for the behavior. If the student persists in his or her disobedience, the student should be referred to other school authorities so that they can consider ways of helping the young person. A teacher should always take the opportunity to speak with the student's parents about the situation so that the teacher's authority is not compromised. Dismissal from school, however, should be used only as a last resort, after all other means of working with the student have been tried. Teachers and schools should proceed in the same way when dealing with students for whom penalties seem to be counterproductive.

Article 5: Insolent young people

Teachers may have to deal with certain young people who border on insolence, know no rule of politeness, and have no discretion or regard for anyone. They have a way of getting worked up over nothing, of being irritated at the slightest correction. When they become upset, their faces flare up, their eyes move around like two hot coals, their bodies bristle up, and their whole being is agitated. These students so easily lose control of themselves that even the language of reason and kindness cannot make them recover at those times. Teachers should consider themselves fortunate if that is all they experience from such young people. Many of these students, heated up with anger, burst out with all kinds of insults, threats, and bad language and seem ready to go to any lengths in dealing with a teacher.

The best thing for a teacher to do in such a situation is to keep a profound silence, showing by a sad and postured air that the teacher pities the insolent young person and is waiting until the first fire of anger is put out. That is the moment for the teacher to act and to make the student feel the weight of the teacher's authority. By words of severity and firmness, the teacher should make the student realize the fault, the unworthiness of the conduct, the shame that should be felt, and the results that he or she will then experience. If a teacher can have the student in this way admit to the wrongdoing, the teacher will have gained more respect and authority than was ever lost in the public display.

The teacher should then be content with a punishment of short duration, but one that is of the sort to impress the student by its severity. On such occasions, teachers should never fail to hold up for their students the virtue of politeness by praising it and pointing out that they attach great value to it. It is a fine opportunity to give students a lesson in being civil to another person, with confidence that at another time it will be remembered to the teacher's advantage.

Article 6: Envious young people

There are some young people, envious by nature, who are unable to see clearly that any fellow student may possess superior talent or merit. They build and hold a feeling of hatred for any fellow student who may appear superior. They speak to such students in a cold way, and the presence of these students annoys them. No matter what the other student does, they are offended; even the thought of another's success causes deep feelings of hate and distress. They often go further and join to their animosity a spirit of strife. Since they cannot endure those fellow students who cause the jealousy, they seek quarrels with them and find fault with all they say and do. They are unable to see in their fellow students anything but faults and go so far as to distort their best intentions. From disputes they pass to fits of passion and fighting.

Was it not jealousy that led Cain to kill his brother and the sons of Jacob to throw Joseph into a cistern in order to expose him to death and then to sell him to foreigners? The secret of success in dealing with the poor slaves of self-love lies in winning their confidence. This is a difficult task and requires great prudence. These young people are by nature filled with suspicion and are erratic in their judgments. Try to build a positive relationship with them as far as this is possible. Then in all ways act with the utmost patience because this fault penetrates deeply, like a vigorous plant that can be cut or destroyed on the outside but cannot be totally destroyed as long as its roots remain in the ground.

Profit by the control you exercise over such students to help them sense on every occasion how much this passion debases them in the eyes of others and how much it offends God, who loves everyone as they were created. Every time they happen to fall into this vice, impose on them as a penance some small prayer in which they ask God's pardon for their fault and the grace not to fall again. Do not forget also to require of them as punishment to show themselves more gentle and charitable toward those of whom they are jealous and even to give clear signs of repentance by congratulating the others and saying something nice to them.

Article 7: Young people without integrity

Although most of the young people you educate will have an admirable candor, a purity, and an innocence, be sure that there are others who, even if still quite young, have already tasted the fatal fruit of the tree of knowledge of good and evil. The demon has already had access to the souls of these young people, and in an age so young they know a thousand secrets and have aged in the path of depravity. We even find parents, often religious ones, who in blind security are asleep in this regard and indirectly foster the vices of their children by laziness. These poor parents abandon their children to take care of themselves and give them liberty to visit anyone or make no choice of the companions that show up. They are unaware that it is enough to have one dissolute character in their children's midst to spread the poison of malice and corrupt weak or impressionable natures.

Among the many young people in a school, it is hardly possible not to find some affected with this poison. It is your task as the shepherd of the young flock to redouble your care, attention, and vigilance in order to keep these sheep from spreading their evil to all those who are healthy and doing well. You will never be able to display too much zeal and activity in discerning the young people who are the plague of your school and whose influence you must at all price prevent and destroy. Look on them as devouring wolves that the devil has introduced into the sheepfold, which is confided to your care, in order to surprise and kill the tender lambs that rely on you for their security. Experience will also teach you that these hearts have a particular skill in recognizing one another, in guessing at and attracting one another. Surely the nature of evil favors these unions and friendships, for they quite soon have an understanding. A few words uttered by chance are enough to be understood; they already know one another and their friendship is formed. Since crime is the principle and bond of this union, your duty is to break it and prevent the results.

By what characteristics, then, will you recognize these young truants, and by what means will you be able to keep them apart, foil their tricks, or, if possible, work to remedy the situation? At first you will be aware of them from a certain desire they have to be together, to be a separate group, with an air of defiance and a certain separation from their teachers or prefects. You will also know them by their gestures and their attitude, by a type of isolation and staying apart, by an air too calm and quiet to be ordinarily associated with healthy young people of their age. Undoubtedly that will not be enough to let you make a sure judgment or allow your suspicions to become evident facts, but it will be enough to awaken your attention and further open your eyes.

Even if you have suspicion, do not give in to spying. That is tantamount to remedying one evil with another. By acting in that way, you would spread among them the seeds of defiance, disunion, and hypocrisy. But try to see and hear everything yourself; try to surprise them at times when they see themselves not in view of a teacher and are not keeping up any sort of guard. Times of recreation, extracurricular events, field trips—those are the times that you must especially exercise vigilance. If you are vigilant, you will succeed in clarifying your suspicions and reaching a good judgment or a reasonable opinion about the condition of these young people.

If their inclinations are well enough known to you, you should at once bring this to the attention of the school administration. Administrators then will need to work with the father and mother of the student, in order to help them improve their son or daughter's state by purifying the heart and enlightening the intelligence. For that, there will be a need for continued surveillance. To give this heart the goodness it has lost and to inspire in it hatred of whatever eats at the goodness, you must have recourse to all means of prudence, to all the resources of charity, and, above all, to the efficacy of prayer. If, in spite of all that, the student is unable to correct his or her condition or if you are seriously concerned that the student will have a bad effect upon the others, it will be necessary for the student to be dismissed from the school.

Article 8: Immature young people

The greatest number of your students will be immature and giddy. That is a mark of youth and a characteristic proper to it. Do not be alarmed, then, and keep from wanting always to bring students to a seriousness that is against nature. In connection with this, most of them resemble those butterflies in our garden that are always flying but whose flight is not regulated at all. They leave one flower, return to it, and then quit it to go to another, finding their nourishment and enjoyment in all sorts of places. You should take into consideration their immaturity and act toward them as a wise parent toward a child, with great kindness, patience, and tenderness. Rarely does a wise parent chastise, but a look and tone of voice take the place of reprimands and punishments, making known what the parent really thinks. These are the delicate devices that truly form the hearts of young people and give them nobility of character and loftiness of feelings.

Learn to put yourself within reach of immature young people, treating them with the indulgence that their age deserves, while distinguishing slight faults from those that reflect malice and dangerous tendencies. An immature young person should not be led by way of penalties, because, being susceptible only to transitory impressions, they soon lose the memory of the correction. The young person shortly after falls into the same fault, while not showing real obstinacy. As for these natures, the art of education consists in removing from them the occasions in which they most often fail. Thus, in class, be careful to place them between the best-behaved and most serious students in order to remove from them all the small objects that distract and amuse them.

Generally these students have a good heart. Make use of this excellent quality to win their affection and confidence so that they will consider you less as a teacher than as a father or a friend. Above all, know how to arouse their striving by promising and giving them, at opportune times, rewards that flatter them. A skillful teacher knows how to draw a lot of gain from this procedure, for young people are easily led in this way. Wisely used, small rewards and praise can produce the most astonishing results in students. Also, consider how consoling it is for a teacher to be appreciated by the students, to see that they obey less out of fear of penalties than out of fear of displeasing or of not earning the small rewards and praises that are handed out to those students who behave well. It is indeed easy for the teacher who really knows how to educate children to get immature young people to this goal. Most of the time the majority of them need only reflection and more developed reasoning to become excellent students.

Article 9: Lazy young people

Laziness is not only avoiding work and desiring to waste time away on all those enjoyments that are so natural for the young, but above all laziness is a softness and an indolence that makes students sometimes apathetic and incapable of anything that is serious, noble, and generous. This quality in some students is one of the most irritating, since it amounts to removing the hope of one day seeing the acquisition of good habits. Every good habit is brought about by doing violence to oneself in a series of acts. That is the way one can break in a fiery horse and make it gentle, docile under the master's hand, untiring in work. What good use can one expect from a horse without this vigor?

Lazy students lack the active push that each of us needs from ourselves. They do not have the energetic zest that carries ardent students a long distance. They must then be pressured, sharpened as much by the promise of rewards as by threat of the punishments that they deserve. This twofold way of dealing with lazy students ought, however, to be used with discretion and prudence, for there are young people who, if pushed too abruptly or too far, will resist such efforts and will become obstinate, believing that the impossible is being asked of them. They will then do nothing of what is requested of them. Every hope of then getting them to progress will be lost. The teacher, perhaps thinking them totally inept, will then abandon them to decay for lack of care and nurture.

Thus, a teacher should avoid excessive zeal with lazy students and practice combining firmness with wise leniency. Teachers must be aware of the natural trouble that lazy students have with work and let no opportunity to overcome this problem pass by. Teachers must let words and counsel call lazy students to their obligation toward work; they must also join to that their own example and the example of others, using every possible way to encourage what is most noble in the young people entrusted to their care.

Article 10: Young people in weak health

In dealing with young people who are in poor health, one must give them compassion, interest, and attention. It is important to lessen some of the requirements for them, to plan for them, and to see to it that they always find cleanliness in the school. It is especially important that the air be clean and often renewed. In anything related to instruction—although teachers should keep them in regular classes—they should be less demanding of these students when assigning duties and lessons. Even when the student is at fault, teachers should be somewhat indulgent as long as other students do not read this as injustice.

In general, teachers should treat such students like those who are extremely gentle and somewhat timid in character. These young people are not generally inclined to waste time as much as others, and their misfortune prevents them generally from getting into some of the difficulties that their fellow students face. The example of those who do well and the natural fear of penalties and punishments they see given out are usually enough to deter them from laziness and encourage them to complete their assigned work. It is often easy to keep such students in good order without severe punishment. Their physical condition, usually well known to others, will serve as an excuse for the teacher's special way of dealing with them. A teacher can always use this reason in dealing with questions raised about equality of treatment.

Conclusion

The considerations discussed above can assist teachers in distinguishing the qualities of their students, in knowing students' faults, and in guiding teachers in developing good order in the classroom and school. But these alone are not enough to give teachers a complete knowledge of teaching and the education of young people, a knowledge that each teacher must grasp in order to fulfill worthily the role of a teacher. In conducting a class, there are a thousand details, a thousand circumstances, that teachers run into in practice that cannot even be conceived of before the circumstances arise. These will naturally disconcert a young teacher completely new to teaching and inexperienced in the ways students act.

It is necessary then to join to what has already been said about some other counsels related to the running of a school. They can help a young teacher make up for the lack of experience that is naturally lacking in those who are beginning to teach and that often weakens the authority they need for success. Young teachers must not come to believe that it is age, body size, tone of voice, or threats that give teachers authority and inspire respect among students. It is none of these external advantages but rather a character that is fair, firm, and modest, one that is consistent at all times and that never acts without reason or through outbursts. It is these qualities that keep everything in order, establish good discipline, see that regulations are observed, make reprimands few, and forestall punishments.

Actually, the authority a teacher exercises over students depends, above all, on the way in which the teacher begins. Nobody knows a teacher then; they wait to see how the teacher presents himself or herself and then judge the teacher. Teachers who do not grasp this favorable moment, who do not put themselves in charge of the class from the first day, will then have all the trouble in the world in getting back the authority that they did not seize in the first place. The ideas contained here are meant to help teachers not fall into this trap because of a lack of good principles.

Part Three

· · · · · · · · · · · · · · ·

On the Formation of School Children in the Christian Life and the Means to Ensure Their Perseverance

Until now, it has yet been only a matter of instruction, and you have not at all addressed the mind of your students in order to initiate them into the first stages of human knowledge. You have, therefore, not at all yet learned to turn them into Christians conformed to Jesus Christ; and nevertheless, such is the principal goal of your mission to young people. Indeed, what would it matter to children to know how to read, write, calculate, or draw, or to learn a couple of ideas on history, geography, geometry, physics, and chemistry, if they are unaware of their duties to God, to others, and to society? Or that in knowing them, they would not align their behavior to said duties? And yet, it is to you, after the pastor of the parish, to teach all of this to your charges, and to coax them, as much as it is in your power, to practice it—which is what you will do in teaching them the catechism and in bringing them to prayer, to the singing of canticles, to attendance at church, to the discipline of the sacraments, and to the gatherings of youth of which your rule speaks.

The art of the catechist, which consists in knowing well how to dialogue with children on religion, and this method, also being the best for instructing them in other subjects, you will do well to know intimately, as well as the example that I cite on this matter at the end of this treatise.[4]

Chapter One: On the Catechism

If you want to understand the case that you must make for the catechism, listen to a disciple of modern philosophy, Geoffrey, who—after having taken lessons from his master, lost like his master in the wash of human opinion for having abandoned Christian teaching—wrote very soon before his death:

> There is a small book that we teach to children, and on which we question them as to the Church; read this small book that is the catechism, you will find in it a solution to all questions that I have asked, all of them without exception. Ask a Christian whence comes the human race, he knows; where it is going, he knows; how it goes, he knows. Ask a poor child, who in his life has never even thought about such things, why he is here on earth, and what he will become after his death, he will give you a sublime response that he will not understand, but that is no less admirable. Ask him how the world was created and for what purpose, why God put animals or plants here; how the earth was populated; if it was by one family or by several; why people speak multiple languages; why they suffer, why they fight one another, and how all of this will end. He knows. Origins of the world, origins of the human race, the matter of the soul, the destiny of humans in this life and in the next, the relationship between us and God, our duties toward our brothers and sisters, the rights of humans over creation—nothing will elude him. And, when he has grown, he will hesitate little more on the subject of natural law, political law, or on the law of peoples; for all this emerges, all this flows from Christianity with clarity and as from itself. That is what I call a great religion; I believe it to be so based on this evidence that it leaves none of these questions that interest humanity without an answer.

Article 1: On the excellence of the catechism, on its nature, and on the necessity of explaining it

But this catechism whose praises you have just heard me sing is less an informal instruction than a summary of scholastic theology. It contains, in effect, but definitions, divisions, and enumerations of parts. In writing it in this way, it was believed that one had to sacrifice clarity to theological solidity and precision; but pastors of souls were obliged to explain in their everyday lessons and to put in the grasp of children what would be unintelligible to them in the formulas that they learn by heart. For this reason, it is important, not only to conduct and to watch over your students of catechism in the parish, but also to make sure that they know the lessons that they must recite to the Church, and to try to get them to understand every last word with clear, short, and solid explanations, avoiding any figurative, technical, specialized, or haphazard expression and relying frequently on comparisons, examples, and edifying stories. For this task, you may avail yourself of the *Explanation of the Catechism* by Monsieur Guillois, the former pastor of Pré in Le Mans, taking care, however, to avoid the details that are not directly connected to the lessons that you will teach or that would be above the age and intelligence of your students.[5]

Article 2: The importance and necessity of the catechism

When one considers how many children have today the joy to receive the benefit of an education in a religious school, and, in particular, in the schools of the brothers, one is surprised as much as one is upset to see so few children, once they have become young people and adults, persevere in the faith and in piety. For this perseverance is something so rare that it is difficult to recognize in society the vestiges of the good that such an education would seem as if it should produce. Must we not conclude that there is in the way in which we form the young, even on the part of the brothers, deep imperfections and considerable gaps? Without a doubt, we could, with plenty of reason, find other causes of evil in the development of the passions at the time when Christian young people leave our schools in order to enter into the world once and for all; they enter into the corruption of morals, a corruption hastened by the evil discourse that sullies their ears, the lascivious songs that they hear in every range, the scandalous examples that seduce their hearts, and the association with the opposite sex. Without a doubt, one could find another cause of such a great evil in the short amount of time that children spend under the guidance of the brothers, whose schools they leave too early, even at the age when they need most the brothers' tutelage; for it is ordinarily around the age of twelve, thirteen, or fourteen years that these poor children are pulled out of school and are exposed all alone and without defense to the violence of their passions, to the seductions and the corruption of the world. But without insisting on the heavy responsibility that weighs also upon the clergy, as well as on the necessity and the means of allowing the brothers to prolong their religious influence on the young, which I will explain in the last chapter of this third part, we will see how you must perform this beautiful and great work of the catechist.

Begin by convincing yourself that the Christian life depends on an enlightened faith, a living and firm faith that you have found through education, and that this first of the three theological virtues is, according to the Council of Trent, the root and the foundation of our justification.[6]

If, therefore, this faith is missing in teachers, it will cause harm to their students, and there will be among them but little to no piety at all, or a piety based on routine that has nothing profound or generous in it. From that moment, there will only be disorder in the generations educated in this way, only vocations for God's Church that are lost or scandalously unfaithful. Yet, you have only the means of the catechism to enlighten their faith, to animate it, and to reinforce it in the souls of your students. It is there, as I said before, where the whole of Catholic education compressed down resides, and consequently, you have a most serious obligation to provide to your students an instructive and interesting catechism, whether it be of your own creation, or by the priests in the parish, or better yet in taking them to church at appropriate days and times.

Article 3: On the manner of teaching the catechism

If you are responsible for teaching the catechism to your students — and if you are a director, this sublime task belongs to you by right, rather than to your assistants — treat them as baptized children, whose intelligence is enlightened by the Holy Spirit and whose good will is helped along by grace. And from that moment, instruct them with zeal and dignity, ensuring by your attitude and expression, by your language, and by a recollected exterior and the singing of canticles to make them understand the importance of the education you impart to them and the respect that they must bring while listening to the Word of God.

Proceed soon after in questioning them and soliciting from them explanations, as it follows, remembering to preach, but examining them almost continually by your requests. Target the level of the most ignorant. Never determine anything as a mortal or venial sin, but limit yourself to responding that it is more or less a serious sin. Remember, in a word, that you will answer to God for the ignorance in which you leave them by your own fault and for the sins to which this ignorance will lead them.

Have the children of the same grade make the Sign of the Cross by your own example. After reminding them by the intervention of one among them of the previous lesson, address the first question of the catechism, which must always be that of the diocese, and which you will always have to have in hand so that it remains clear while you are examining them.

As for the posture of the one who answers, demand that the student be standing, with arms crossed and eyes fixed on you. Take care to pose your question before choosing the one who will respond to it, in order that all pay attention, waiting in suspense. If the one whom you have questioned is not able to respond, choose another, without repeating the question to which everyone should have listened and retained; and, if you have not yet succeeded, pose the same question to two or three others; then, in case of failure, you yourself give the answer and have all who were not able to respond repeat it. It is especially necessary to use this method with regard to children who do not yet know how to read fluently.

When a question requires more explanation, develop it with follow-up questions that are short and precise, and have them respond to these other questions in the same manner that I have just explained. Have them recite and explain to them the lessons of the catechism in the order that we follow in the Church if it is a matter of children who have not yet made their First Communion, in order to put them in a position to know and understand the lessons that we will then ask of them. Do not neglect, however, to come back from time to time to the most important points, according to the needs or deficiencies of the children, especially as First Communion approaches.

Make sure that all your students are tested in this way every day—and, if possible, several times in the same catechism—but especially the most unlearned and those who have the most difficulty in retaining their lessons. It is then especially that we must keep from laughing about those who cannot respond, or who respond poorly. Avoid punishing in the moment, but only make a note of those who would need it to punish them later, encouraging, on the other hand, with rewards all of the other students.

Article 4: On how long the catechism should last

A quite sad experiment has proved that the brothers, in general, no longer apply themselves as much to the religious instruction and education of the children who are entrusted to them as before the creation of primary schools run by secular teachers. The focus that religious have had to give to the profane side of studies, and the fear of succumbing without it in their committed struggle, appears to have cooled their zeal for religious education. Too often we have seen the catechism sacrificed, or at the very least the time that one should devote to it has been shortened in order to busy oneself almost exclusively with certain specialties that should come second. Nevertheless, the goal, which we have put forth in founding institutes of this nature, which we have wanted in particular in the ministry of Holy Cross, and which the Church who has approved it has the right to expect of you, is principally that the children that you educate be solidly instructed in religion, formed by the practices of the Christian life, and placed on the path to perseverance in virtue after they have gone out from your schools.

May you never lose sight of this important goal and understand that the struggle with secular schools obliges you to focus more than before on the profane part of your lessons. The otherwise redoubtable struggle with unbelief, systematic immorality, socialism, communism, and anarchism obliges all the more to extend, rather than narrow, the sphere of religious education of your charges. Be sure to cut nothing from the half hour of catechism with which you begin each class in the mornings and evenings, including the opening song and the prayer; watch that your children never fail to miss Christ, who gives himself to the Church. Dedicate on Saturday evenings a half hour to examine your students by way of review on the whole of the lessons learned during the week. Question them also on Mondays about the catechism and the sermon presented at Church the evening before.

Chapter Two: On Prayer, Sacred Music, and Attendance at the Liturgy

If it is important to form your students in social appearances by teaching them and having them observe the rules of politeness and Christian civility toward others, how much more important is it to teach them and to have them put into practice their duties toward God? Would it not be the greatest of indecencies to refuse him the respect, the love, and the obedience that are due to him, as well as to his Church? And would it not be the guiltiest negligence on your part not to be preoccupied by the manner in which the children entrusted to your care should acquit themselves? This is why the truly religious educator places first and foremost among his obligations teaching students not only to observe God's laws and the laws of his Church, without ever being embarrassed to do so, but also to pray as is fitting, to sing in church or to recite pious canticles in one's school, and to attend devotedly the Divine Office; to reverence the cross, images of the holy Virgin, and the ministers of religion that they encounter; to take off one's hat in front of a passing procession, to prostrate oneself before the holy viaticum that one takes to the sick, to make worthily the Sign of the Cross, to take and to give holy water, according to need, with respect and devotion.

Do not be surprised, then, to see me insist here on prayer, on pious or sacred hymns, and on attendance at prayer.

Article 1: On prayer

St. Augustine said that those who know how to pray well also know how to conduct themselves. From this, we must conclude that if there are so few children living as good Christians upon leaving school, it is that certainly they have not been formed in prayer, or they have abandoned this holy exercise upon their entrance into the world, or at the least they have greatly neglected it. What are, in effect, the schools where prayer is regarded as the most essential duty of Christian education and where by consequence prayer is done? Where are the students who have become young people left unto themselves, who pray as it would be necessary to do so in order to persevere in virtue? Alas, they have just barely received their First Communion and their initial instruction, and, no longer finding as they did earlier among family the practice of common prayer, at least in the evening, they neglect these pious practices, forget them little by little, and end up leaving them behind. Thus, you see people today: the majority no longer pray, because they do not know any prayers. Follow them into our churches, into our liturgies—what an air of discomfort and unease! They do not know how to bend a knee or to strike the breast, or even how to make upon themselves the sign of a Christian. One would say that they are completely foreign to Catholic worship. Their look is distracted and indifferent and their lips are mute, because they have forgotten all manner of prayer.

Bring therefore special care to the teaching of prayers in use in the diocese to the children in your school, for the morning and the evening, before and after meals. Have them recite them in common, at the sound of the bell, at the beginning of class in the morning and at the end of class in the evening, keeping watch so that they all follow the prayer leader, with a tone so moderate that the voice of the leader can still be heard, and that they stop at all the pauses he or she makes in order to avoid confusion. Then, stand with head uncovered, in front of your seat, with a solemn exterior, with arms crossed; and make sure to speak, be it in general or specifically, in order to correct or to punish, being content to show by a sign or to mark in your record those who misbehaved. You will then warn them or punish them when the exercise is done.

You would do well, if you have a class in scripture, to require that the students kneel on the benches, and those at the farthest tables to do so on the tables themselves, in order that you can better observe the attitude of each student, all before you in good order, arms crossed and eyes modestly lowered. If, on the contrary, you are conducting a class of little ones, you should make sure that your children are kneeling on the floor, properly aligned along the benches, without leaning on them, or sitting on their heels, or turning their head, or touching each other.

As for the manner of proceeding to have your students learn prayers of common usage, begin by the Sign of the Cross, the Our Father, the Hail Mary, the Apostles' Creed, and the Acts of Faith, Hope and Love, and of Contrition, prayers that you might have them recite only at the first grade. In the second grade, add the Confiteor, the Ten Commandments, and the prayers before and after meals. In the third grade, have them learn and recite the Our Father, the Hail Mary, the Creed, and the Confiteor in Latin; the supplementary prayers used in the diocese for the morning and evening; and the responses at Mass and during the Rosary. For the Rosary, you might have them recite it only on Saturdays, and you might split it up by decades, reciting the first after morning prayer; the second, before the canticle recited at dismissal; the third, after the opening canticle at the evening class; the fourth, after the canticle sung toward the middle of class; and the fifth, before the canticle of dismissal—taking care to remind them at each stage of the mysteries of the Rosary.

Article 2: On sacred hymns

It is so natural for us to translate our most lively feelings by song that canticles are found everywhere and in every time, be it as a supreme homage to the divinity or as a means of encouragement toward duty and virtue. Thus, one sees in the books of the saints that song figures into the praises that those most eminent in dignity and piety addressed to God. In this way the patriarchs consecrated their tongues to him by religious canticles, and Moses relays those canticles that were sung to the sound of instruments after the miraculous passage across the Red Sea (Ex 15) and soon before his death (Dt 32:1–44). One also finds in the Old Testament the canticles of Deborah (Jgs 5); of Hannah, the mother of Samuel (1 Sm 2:1–20); of Judith (Jdt 16:1–17); of Isaiah (Is 12); of Ezekiel (Ez 36:24–28); of Habakkuk (Hb 3:1–19); and of the three young men in the furnace (Dn 3:26–56), as well as the Song of Songs of Solomon, who had composed five thousand of them, and the hundred and fifty psalms of David that resonate still today in Jewish synagogues and in all the Christian churches as the most magnificent praise of God's works and the most shining avowal of the misery of humanity.

The New Testament also includes three beautiful canticles, labeled "gospel canticles" because they are taken from the gospels: that of Zachary (Lk 1:68–79), of the holy Virgin (Lk 1:46–55), and of Simeon (Lk 2:29–32). Did not our Lord even deign to sing, when he along with the apostles sang a hymn after the institution of the Blessed Eucharist and before going to the garden (Mt 26:30; Mk 14:26)? Yes, without a doubt, for this song resided not only in the recitation of a prayer but in a prayer recited in song and in a canticle of thanksgiving. Moreover, St. Augustine said regarding this moment that the divine master was not content to have given us an example, but that he wanted to continue teaching his apostles, to commission them in the practice thereof, and to give them individually and to the entire Church a formal commandment. It is probably because of this that St. Paul so strongly recommends to Christians to engage themselves in their fervor by the psalms and by spiritual canticles (Eph 5:19), and that since then this holy discipline has been observed in all Catholic places of worship.

It is true that sacred canticles from the Bible, incorporated from the very origins of Christianity into the liturgy of the Church, were until the ninth century the only ones that we sang in holy places, because they were proclaimed in Latin, the language that everyone spoke at the time or at least understood. But because this language has been corrupted, except in monasteries and in schools for secular clergy, and even though the Church had preserved this language intact in its liturgy, the faithful who no longer understood it were no longer able to associate the movements of their heart with the sentiments expressed by the prayers and the hymns of public worship. That is what has allowed little by little the entrance of popular idiom into our churches, not only for the preaching of the Word of God, but also for certain non-liturgical hymns, like the canticles that one sings today between liturgies, before or after sermons, or in the course of catechism.

It is enough to tell you how important it is that you form your students in the hymnody of the Divine Office and in the songs of the canticles used in Christian schools and in well-organized catechism lessons. For, by them, you enter into the intentions of Jesus Christ, you serve the Church in multiplying its cantors, and you support the zeal of its pastors. Besides, it is an excellent way to bring back the practice of having the entire assembly of the faithful participate in the hymns of the Church instead of just a few singing them, a practice that has unfortunately fallen into disfavor. In turn, you will infuse the souls of your students with healthy thoughts and generous feelings; for if after having sung the great mysteries of our faith, the young also celebrate the deeds of the saints, the virtues and sacrifices of the heroes of the faith, these same young will automatically find within themselves the desire to imitate them, stirred as they are by the attraction of reward or the horror of eternal chastisement.

Apply yourself, therefore, to the proper execution of ecclesiastical hymnody and of appropriate canticles in your school, especially in times of retreats to prepare for First Communion. Have care to teach the tunes to your students, either on Sundays or feasts, or in bringing them together for this an hour before the liturgy, or for a half hour each day, morning and evening, in the middle of class. At the start of class, do not forget the canticle to the Holy Spirit, "Descend upon us," or any other recommended song instead of *Veni, Sancte Spiritus*; and for the end, sing "Mary, O Tender Mother," or better yet, the one that should replace it. You must require that everyone have in hand their book of canticles, and you should make sure that they sing in a low voice, without screaming, with much order and harmony. And if there are several classes near one another in your institution, have them sing in alternating fashion the canticles that have multiple couplets or refrains. If all this is done well, if especially your children respond in concert with one another, you yourself will be touched by these earthly choirs that emulate concerts of angels in heaven and whose pious notes will resound to God, filling your school with the fragrance of edification and virtue.

Blessed are the Christian youth to whom this developed practice of singing the hymns of Zion inspires a profound aversion to the dissolute hymns of Babylon. St. Augustine explained in these terms the effect that liturgical song produced within his soul: "Only tears did I shed while hearing hymns sung! How much was my heart moved by the solemn hymns of the Church! While song resonates in my ears, the truth penetrates my heart and so vibrantly animates it. I began to reflect and to burst into tears, nevertheless finding myself amidst an ineffable joy."[7] Form your students, therefore, in religious hymnody, especially on Sundays and on vacation days. By this, you will put an end to bad songs that are so often in use by youth, particularly in the countryside; you will incline your students to the good; you will inspire in them good feelings; you will preserve them from many bad thoughts and words; and you will make them familiar with the knowledge of the truths of the faith. But in order to succeed in this exercise, choose first of all three or four intelligent students with a good voice and a good ear, and make of them leaders who then help you to form others. Encourage them with rewards, and attempt to have them frequently practice these canticles during periods of recreation.

Article 3: On attendance at the liturgy

If it is not possible for you to take your students to church on the usual days to attend the holy Mass, whether because of distance, or because of a lack of time, or because the hour at which one says it does not go with the class schedule, or, even yet, because we are having a sung Mass instead of a low Mass, you should not at least fail to get them to Mass on Sundays or on holy days of obligation. On those days, you should bring them all together at school at the time of the parish Mass and for Vespers, placing them in two rows, in silence and with a composed and modest exterior, and not forgetting to hand out a rosary to those who do not yet know how to read. The student charged with said distribution should also be the one who collects the rosaries after the liturgy and will keep them during school.

In the absence of one or several brothers, you should have a monitor enter the church first, while another walks last on the sides, in order that both can watch the students who have entered or who are outside and to keep them from wandering off. You should also have one student walk at the front who is always asked to offer holy water to the students of the class who follow behind him or her. Make sure that as they come to their places they remain standing, arms crossed, and that they kneel when the signal is given, after which you should give them the sign to bow modestly to adore Jesus Christ in the Eucharist. According to need, certain chosen students among the most wise should be designated to prepare in advance the places they will occupy and to arrange the benches or the chairs that need to be made available, such that all the ones in the same row, as much as from the front and the side, are all in a perfect line with respect to one another.

During the liturgy, make sure that all recite their Rosary while meditating upon the mysteries or that they follow along in their book, without turning their head from one side to another. Make sure that they sing, if it is possible, especially the psalms; that they do not make any noise as they rise, kneel, or sit; that they sign themselves properly at the beginning of the Mass and at the two gospels; and that they follow the movements of the choir. When the bells ring to signal the moment of the consecration, those who have books should put them under their arms, and those who have a rosary should bring their arms in. Then they should join their hands and bow respectfully in adoration of the Blessed Sacrament.

If it is a matter of a low Mass, you should keep your students kneeling from the Introit to the gospel, standing from the gospel to the Sanctus, and kneeling for the rest of the Mass. In any case, you should have them leave the church as they entered, and they should return home two by two, as at the end of school, without ever shaking in this holy place the dust from their knees.

Chapter Three: On the Regular Reception of the Sacraments

The regular reception of the sacraments is the best way to salvation that our Lord instituted, whether to correct bad habits, or to acquire virtue, or to persevere in it. This means must be used, therefore, with zeal and wisdom, not only by confessors, but also by religious educators, who must bring their students to this practice no less by their example than by their exhortation. Remember this, and may you never forget it. Only then will you give all your efforts to procuring good confessors to your students, so that they will go to confession frequently and so that they will do so at ease, with the care and tenderness that growth of the soul in Jesus Christ requires. In order that this important action takes place more properly, it is desirable that it happen for an entire grade on a free day, in the morning, after a low Mass.

For the confession of the children who have not yet made their First Communion, it is important that you prepare them for it by inspiring in them the fear of God, by forming their conscience, and by engendering in them a horror of evil. Make them understand as much as possible how much sin, that seems to them such a small thing, is a great evil, and to what great misfortune they expose themselves in ceding to those first inclinations to bad tendencies, especially that of anger, gluttony, sloth, pride, disobedience, and shameful vice. It is at this time that one must get along with the confessors, in order to bring to them every month the children who talk to them. During the three months before their First Communion, the most important period in the life of a young student, it should be every fifteen days. Thus, when the time comes for the retreat preparing them for this important act, you must increase the zeal, the prayer, and the exhortation, relying on those truths that most effectively inspire in them penitence, the most profound contrition for the past, and the firm will toward a complete conversion. The grace of God, so abundant at this time, is a powerful aid to the schoolmaster who knows how to pray for this intention and to choose, with the lessons of the catechism that correspond to the activities of the retreat, the appropriate canticles for the occasion.

As for Communion for those who have moved on from the first grade, it is in the purview of the confessor alone to take care of it. But in order to make themselves worthy, your students should continue to go to confession at least once a month, or even more often if they would like; for they are getting to the age where they will undergo many more struggles and temptations, and where, consequently, they need all the more to be sustained and strengthened by the sacraments. Do, therefore, everything that depends on you in order to ensure that this grace is granted them. For fear that they create an obstacle for themselves by losing their attention near the confessional, if they perchance were waiting their turn in a large number and without supervision, only allow them to go in groups of four or five at a time, progressively. Thus, the confessor gives you back the sheets on which you should have listed their names and which they should bring you with a signature so that you can keep track in the register of confessions.

Chapter Four: On Gatherings of Youth

A means of perseverance no less important than the preceding ones, since it has as a goal to complete these other means, would be to extend Christian education to your students after they have left your school. Toward this, there already exist several very worthy, and unfortunately too rare, initiatives of encouragement, but perhaps they are too imperfect still for attaining the ends for which they have been proposed. Here follows what one can do better and more effectively, in my judgment.

It would be to establish, in the cities and the towns where you direct your schools, places where children could be welcomed on Sundays and feasts (at least after Vespers), as well as on vacation days, and even, if it were possible, every evening in the winter when they no longer have to go to class. You might have in these spaces innocent amusements that would serve as an attraction to draw in the youth. After the games would come a shorter religious exercise, like evening prayer, preceded by a canticle and a small reading with a commentary or a familiar lesson, always mixed with an edifying story. What would be better yet would be to have in these locales, if not a chapel, at least an oratory where this exercise could be done and where an intelligent, zealous priest could preside after having sought out the students to see them, to get to know them, to speak to them, and to win over their hearts. He could have a small apartment on site to listen to them one-on-one or to hear their confessions when they need it.

These gatherings could be supervised by you or one of your assistants, without, however, your having to break your rule of conduct, until you might be able to find several monitors from among the oldest and wisest in your school. Or better yet, you could entrust this task to a few members of the Conference of St. Vincent de Paul, who could exercise a real apostolate among the youth. These children, becoming accustomed to frequenting these places while you are their teachers, would then take this on as a habit, finding there good friends and interesting amusements, and they would continue still to come in great number, especially on Sundays and feast days, after having left the benches of your classrooms. From that point, you would likewise continue to benefit them with Christian instruction to sustain them against the temptations of adolescence and against the seductions of this world, by helping them to persevere in virtue and in the regular reception of the sacraments until such time when, grown into adults, the exercises of the piety of their parish church would be for them sufficient.

This is what you can and must do for your students, if you truly have zeal for their salvation. Make haste, therefore; take up this work of the resurrection, never forgetting that the particular goal of your institution is, above all, to sanctify youth. By this, you will contribute to preparing the world for better times than our own, for these children who today attend your school are the parents of the future and the parents of future generations. Each one of them carries within him or her a family. Influence them, therefore, by all the means of instruction and sanctification that I have just explained. Then, and only then, will you be able to hope to achieve the end of your vocation by the renewal of the Christian faith and of piety. Fiat! Fiat!

Chapter 5

CIRCULAR LETTERS

In order to communicate with the members of Holy Cross around the world, Basil Moreau wrote circular letters. "Circular" describes the geographical reach of the letter. The practice of writing these letters is common in apostolic religious communities even today, as well as in the Church itself—papal "encyclicals" come from a similar tradition and origin. Though Moreau might write a letter on the occasion of any feast or important event during the year, it was often his practice to write a letter around the New Year, reflecting particularly on Christmas, Epiphany, and a new year of imitating Christ. In these letters, he took care to respond—in general terms—to letters he had received from the members of Holy Cross, who not only extended to Moreau their greetings but also disclosed frankly their life and ministry situations.

Moreau's circular letters vary widely in content. They provided a means of updating members of Holy Cross around the world on news such as new ministries and the status of existing ones. In this way, those in Algeria might learn the happenings of Bengal and Indiana, and vice versa. The letters also demonstrate the governance of Holy Cross as it grew, particularly Moreau's efforts to lead an international congregation from Sainte-Croix, Le Mans, France. They gave Moreau a forum for providing ongoing instruction for his priests, brothers, and sisters in living the religious life. For this reason, there are passages about the vows of poverty, chastity, and obedience. Moreau's theological reflections also emerge in his recounting of events. He frequently gives recourse to trust in divine providence, that the crosses he describes in the letters will themselves become hope, and that his religious should be working to become models of Christ to the world. In this way, Moreau's letters not only recounted the growth of his religious congregation but also provided a theological lens through which he hoped his membership would understand that growth.

The letters are numbered chronologically from the time they were written. Subheadings within the text have been added. Where Moreau quotes a scriptural or patristic source, references have been added in parentheses or in a footnote.

K.G. and A.G.

Circular Letter 14

. . . .

Notre-Dame de Sainte-Croix, Le Mans
September 1, 1841

My dear brothers in Jesus Christ:[1]

On the eve of attaining the end I had in view in transferring your novitiate from Ruillé to Sainte-Croix and in organizing the magnificent establishment that this transfer has given us, I feel the need of laying before you in writing the plan of government that I have definitely adopted. I also wish to sketch for you a summary of your duties and, at the same time, to tell you what I have done in return for the confidence with which you have honored me.

Far from me be the thought of attributing to myself the merit of the truly providential works that have just arisen under my direction. After God, who alone is the author of all good, it is to the devotedness of my fellow priests and to your own spirit of cooperation that we owe the astounding work of Holy Cross as it exists today. I have been but a simple instrument, which the Lord will soon break that he may substitute for it others more worthy. In his plan, they are to develop or, at least, to solidify what I have begun. In the midst of the most painful trials, I have never lost hope in providence or in your fidelity to the sublime vocation that God has given you. I have counted on the apostolic spirit of the virtuous priests who have willingly shared my labors, on the cooperation of all the members of your institute, and on the charity of the faithful. The five years of experience which have just passed are sufficient evidence that my trust was not in vain.

Nevertheless, this important work which has been entrusted to us is not yet completed. It still calls for many sacrifices and much labor. I am well aware of all that still remains to be done to form our subjects to the religious life, to afford them an intellectual formation in keeping with the needs of the times, and to establish uniformity in their conduct and their teaching methods.

Qualities of a Perfect Life in Christ

I firmly trust, however, that the same God who has begun this work under such favorable auspices will carry it through to its completion. This he will do, provided that you strive constantly after the perfect life. This perfect life is characterized by obedience, discipline, punctuality, community spirit, zeal for the interior life, edification, and devotion to work. The perfection of this life stands out, particularly in that purity of intention that seeks not self but God alone; aims only at heaven and not at anything earthly; strives for nothing but the happiness of possessing Jesus and belonging to him and to his Blessed Mother; and directs all interests, goods, and rights to the sole honor of the divine master and the salvation of souls. Obedience will so completely animate the whole tenor of such a life that no one will engage in any activity except at the will of the superior. This kind of life will be marked by devotion to regularity and punctuality, by a constant and universal fidelity to the rules and constitutions of the society in a spirit of love rather than of fear, and in a spirit of faith rather than for human motives.

This life will promote community spirit by humility, meekness, and charitable forbearance with others. It will follow scrupulously the maxim of the pious author of the *Imitation*: "We must mutually support, console, aid, instruct, and admonish one another."[2] Such a life will give edification by its modesty, its sacrifices of personal viewpoints, its self-forgetfulness, its religious gravity, and its careful avoidance of all criticism, unkind jesting, and even the slightest trace of frivolity. It will be a life of devotion to the work of teaching or of any other employment, to punctuality to the common exercises, and to the shunning of idleness. Lastly, it will be an interior life, elevated to God by the habitual practice of acts of faith, hope, and charity, after the example of Jesus Christ, who is to be the particular model of our conduct. Unless we wish to ruin the work of Holy Cross, it is absolutely essential for us to lead with our Lord a life hidden in God.

Now this perfect life, on which I cannot insist too much, will reenact before our eyes the life of our Savior, which was divine in every detail. Our life of obedience will reflect his life of subjection to the miseries of our humanity, even to disgrace, sufferings, and death. Our spirit of discipline will imitate his habitual conformity to the will of his father, while our community spirit will reflect his life in the company of our Blessed Lady, St. Joseph, and his apostles. Our life of edification will reproduce his life of good example in the midst of the world, and our spirit of work will mirror his labors and his cross. Lastly, our interior life will emulate his hidden life at Nazareth, which is so fraught with lessons for us and so calculated to inspire us with a holy fear of all outside ministry. Oh, to what marvels of grace your young society would give rise if you could succeed in thus reproducing the life of Jesus Christ!

You are associated with the apostolate of the priests of Holy Cross by the services which you render through your various acts of obedience, either to them personally or to their students, as well as by the instruction you give to the numerous children in your own schools. As an institute of primary teachers, your expansion is no longer confined to France alone, but has spread over into Africa and America. With the sisters who devote themselves to housework and the care of the sick in our principal establishments, you are united in a spirit of zeal and prayer, and these are bonds of union between you and the community of the Good Shepherd, where the spirit of the Gospel lives in the religious, is preserved in the orphans, and is rekindled in the penitents.[3] The development of your institute has been greatly aided by the Association of St. Joseph, which the sovereign pontiff, at the express wish of the good bishop of the diocese, has deigned to encourage by the grant of numerous indulgences. From all this you can see, my dear sons in Jesus Christ, what a source of blessings, success, and merits is yours. You can appreciate the beauty and glory of your calling if you but know how to make yourselves worthy of it by faithfully imitating the hidden and public life of our Lord.

Union

Assuredly, all these different works, with which your society is connected in varying degrees, contain many elements of disintegration. Considering them only from the standpoint of human reason, it is difficult to explain how they could begin, organize, develop, and harmonize up to the present. This is particularly true in view of our slender pecuniary resources, the unfavorable political situation, and differences of personal temperament, not to mention the ill will of several who tried in vain to ruin what was being undertaken in a manner that seemed to them so patently imprudent.

But the same spirit that gave movement to the wheels of the mysterious chariot in the vision of Ezekiel—the same spirit that propelled, one before the other, the symbolic animals of varied forms in such a way that, without ever pausing in their onward course and without ever retracing their steps, they tended always to the same end, though by ways apparently most opposed to one another (2 Kgs 2:11–12)—this self-same spirit, I say, seems to have breathed on the different instruments of the work of Holy Cross. Here, notwithstanding differences of temperament and talent, the inequality of means, and the differences of vocation and obedience, the one aim of the glory of God and the salvation of souls inspires almost all the members and gives rise to a oneness of effort that tends toward that more perfect union of hearts which is the foundation of the unity and strength of Holy Cross.

What is true of a palace whose foundations have been laid and which is rising gradually until completion is verified, likewise, in a great work of charity. It is not one alone who builds; nor is it one stone, or one single beam of wood, that forms it. Each worker contributes something from his own trade; each stone is cut to fit into its one appointed place; and each piece of wood is arranged and placed so as to enhance the general effect of the entire building. Union, then, is a powerful lever with which we could move, direct, and sanctify the whole world, if the spirit of evil, who has been allowed to exercise his power over this earth, does not set himself up against the wondrous effects of this moral force.

In fact, why are the political parties that are disturbing society today powerful enough to bring about revolutions and upheavals? Is it not because they know the secret of uniting and working for one same end? Would it not, then, be disgraceful for you and for me not to do for the cause of good, for God, and for eternity what the children of the world do every day for the cause of evil, for the world, and for the short day of this life? Ah, we who are disciples of a God who died for the salvation of souls who are perishing, we do not realize all the good we could do for others through union with Jesus Christ in the spirit of our rules and constitutions. It is this touching mystery of religious union that our Savior unveiled for us in the Gospel when he explained the incorporation of all the faithful with his divine person in the mystical body of which he is the head and we the members. Since we form with him but one body and draw life from the same Spirit, he urges us to remain united in him, like the vine and branches, borne by the same root and nourished by the same sap, and forming together but one plant.

Read this beautiful simile in the fifteenth chapter of St. John. There you will find all the motives which could induce you to tighten the cords that keep the works of Holy Cross closely united to one another. First of all, there is the motive of family pride, for it is our duty to avoid the disgrace of sterility and to win for ourselves the glory of sturdy growth. Just as the branch cannot bear fruit of itself unless it be united to the vine, so neither can we unless we are united in Jesus Christ, the vine of which we are the branches.

We have, too, the motive of holy fear. If we cut ourselves off from this mystic vine, or if we deserve this penalty and thus become divided among ourselves, we, thereby, expose ourselves to the risk of ruining God's work and of bringing down on ourselves the chastisements of his eternal justice. There is, moreover, the consideration of our own personal interests and those of the community. From this union there will flow down upon us, as from a rich spring, every grace and blessing.

Finally, there is the motive of gratitude toward the author and finisher of our vocation. The fruits of our justice and sanctity will glorify God, just as the fruits on a tree are, at the same time, the glory of the tree itself and of the gardener. Beholding the fruits of our mutual union, the world will glorify God; and in his jealousy at such great spiritual and temporal prosperity, the devil will endeavor to destroy it at its very root and to disrupt these works by sowing dissension in the minds and hearts of the members. For he knows full well that all his efforts will come to naught so long as we remain steadfast in holy union.

Woe, then, and anathema to the priest, brother, or sister who, by word or action, would attempt to separate establishments that God has willed to unite under the same general authority. Here we have a striking representation of the hierarchy of the heavenly spirits, wherein all the different choirs of angels are arranged in three orders, which are mutually subordinated one to another. Our association is also a visible imitation of the Holy Family, wherein Jesus, Mary, and Joseph, notwithstanding their difference in dignity, were one at heart by their unity of thought and uniformity of conduct. A fearful judgment is in store for whoever would thus paralyze the prosperous development of the three works, for they have been founded on such close mutual relationships as to constitute but one work by their common interests and unity of ideal.

From all this, it follows that, just as in the adorable Trinity — of which the house of Notre-Dame de Sainte-Croix is still another image — there is no difference of interests and no opposition of aims or wills, so among the priests, brothers, and sisters there should be such conformity of sentiments, interests, and wills as to make all of us one in somewhat the same manner as the Father, Son, and Holy Spirit are one. This was the touching prayer of our Lord for his disciples and their successors: "That they all may be one, as you, Father, in me and I in you" (Jn 17:21). This it is which prompts me to say to you, my dear sons in Christ, as the apostle said to the Philippians: "If, therefore, there is any comfort in Christ, any encouragement from charity, any fellowship in the spirit, any feelings of mercy, fill up my joy by thinking alike, having the same charity, with one soul and one mind. Do nothing out of contentiousness or vainglory; but in humility, let each one regard the others as his superiors, each one looking not to his own interests but to those of others" (Phil 2:1–4).

Hence, unless you wish to see everything crumble and fall into ruin, the rules and constitutions must establish between you and the priests of Holy Cross, between the particular superiors and the superior general, the same interdependence as that which exists between the branches of a tree and its trunk, between the rays of the sun and its fire, between brooks and their source. Now, since this trunk, this sun, this source, which signify the common origin of these three works, is of itself, as a mere instrument, without light, vitality, or water, it must be closely united to God through Jesus Christ, and to Jesus Christ through Mary and Joseph, in order to receive light, the sap of the spiritual life, and the saving waters of divine grace.

Consecration of the Three Societies

Furthermore, in order the better to cement this union and this imitation of the Holy Family, I have consecrated and do hereby consecrate anew, as far as lies in my power, the Auxiliary Priests to the Sacred Heart of Jesus, the shepherd of souls; the brothers to the Heart of St. Joseph, their patron; and the sisters to the Heart of Mary pierced with the sword of sorrow.

Relations between Priests and Brothers

I have not the slightest intention to subject the brothers to the priests in such a way that any priest would have the right to give orders to any brother, or that the brothers would be obliged to obey all the priests indiscriminately. Even though the brothers owe respect and deference to all the priests without exception, because of their sacerdotal character, still the priests cannot give orders to the brothers unless they have been elected to an office or employment to which this right is attached. In addition, both priests and brothers shall always show themselves grateful for the least favors that they receive from one another.

This, then, my dear sons in Jesus Christ, is the plan of government that God wishes to be followed in the administration of Notre-Dame de-Sainte-Croix. You see in this outline a brief sketch of what he has inspired me to undertake in answer to your patient waiting. Thank him with me for bringing me into contact with your beautiful spirit of devotion to the Christian education of youth by allowing your venerable founder to ask and obtain my consent, notwithstanding my unwillingness, to shoulder a burden which his ill health had made him powerless to carry.[4]

Manual of the Brothers of St. Joseph

The better to second the designs of heaven in this important undertaking and to enable you to meditate continually on the obligations of your vocation, I have drawn up a small manual, which will be as a spiritual mirror, showing each one what he must be in order to cooperate to the best of his ability in the development of the work of Holy Cross. What I offer you today is not an extensive collection of practices and reflections; still less is it a course of instruction on all the duties of your state. In the works of the venerable de La Salle or his followers, and in those of Rodriguez, you have admirable treatises that will amply suffice for all the needs of your congregation.[5] Still, I felt that a manual containing all your prayers and ceremonies, your rules and constitutions, and certain customs special to your society would be as acceptable to you as it would be useful. Consequently, I composed it hurriedly and, so to speak, without stopping, leaving to others the work of perfecting it. Receive it as a pledge of my fatherly interest, my absolute devotedness, and my ardent desire to increase your happiness by contributing to your sanctification and the glory of your institute. May you draw from it the spirit of your vocation; and each time that you take it in hand, ask God that, after having worked for others, I myself may not become a castaway.

Yours devotedly,

B. Moreau

Rector, Missionary Apostolic[6]

Circular Letter 23

· ·

Mayet, France
January 4, 1845

My dear sons and daughters in Jesus Christ:

The swift cycle of rapidly moving years does not weaken my affection and devotion for you. On the contrary, it provides new impetus to my sentiments of love for all the members of our association. While warning me of the shortness of my days, the passing years awaken my zeal for our common aims, as I behold the little time that remains to attain them. I cannot consider this rapid succession of weeks and months without deep and lively emotion. Yes, I will admit here in all simplicity that the return of the New Year and the Feast of St. Basil surprises me like a man who awakens with a start. The recurrence of these years makes me realize very vividly the distance I have already traveled and the little time that separates me from the end of my career. What? — I say to myself — the year just begun is already gone, and I am obliged to date this circular on the fourth day of 1845. What is this shadow of the world which passes by and disappears under my very eyes?

New Year's Wishes

It seems but yesterday that on the New Year and the feast of my illustrious patron I received the good wishes of the dear family of Notre-Dame de Sainte-Croix, and now, once again, mine is the pleasant duty of renewing my gratitude to these priests, brothers, and sisters for all the kind things they tell me. I assure them, in turn, of my sincere gratitude for their filial affection and of my fervent good wishes for their eternal happiness. This same affection will remain throughout the few days, which, perhaps, still remain to me to live in their midst; it will be equally true of the long and happy life that you have just wished me. How true it is, O God, that our life passes like a shadow, and that its moments are like drops of water that fall to the earth and disappear in its depths. Consequently, we must hasten to make better use of our days than ever before, in order to make amends for anything in the past which could have impeded the action of divine providence on our newborn association. Our duty for the present is to seize upon everything that can contribute to realizing God's designs in our regard, and to see now what reasons we have for hope or fear in the future.

These, my dear sons and daughters in Jesus Christ, are the thoughts that well up within my mind as I behold the end of one year and the beginning of another. They are, indeed, very serious thoughts, and well do they deserve each one's careful meditation, particularly since we are in greater need than ever before of renewing ourselves in the spirit of our vocation. Let us not forget that the development of the work entrusted to us depends upon our acceptance of the inspirations of grace and our fidelity in seconding the designs of divine providence. In the future, then, far from dwelling with vain complacency on any success achieved thus far, let us humble ourselves for the hindrances that we may have placed, even inadvertently, in the way of still greater success, and let us strive with complete self-distrust to consolidate and perfect what has been begun.

It is, moreover, God's plan in regard to our community that, while we always remain in breathless suspense as to the future destiny of Notre-Dame de Sainte-Croix, we should not count on individual talents to ensure the successful cultivation of the portion of his vineyard to which he has visibly called us, but rather on the religious spirit. Our confidence should rest not on pecuniary resources but on the protection promised to those, who, above all else, seek holiness and the kingdom of God. This is undoubtedly why the road we travel is often steep and difficult, why periods of consolation are ordinarily shorter than those of trial, and why the year just past has bristled with cruel thorns, which have wounded us to the heart.

Trials

I cannot, in fact, qualify by any other name those scandals that have grieved my soul and made me fear that the Spirit of God will end by abandoning a society wherein certain members have become worldly minded. I refer to useless or unauthorized expenses and the violation of the most essential points of the rule without regard for the vows of obedience and of poverty; to the voluntary or forced departure of those novices on whom I had lavished so much affection and interest; to the unexpected death of Br. André, who was so worthy to be a model of all the other children of St. Joseph; and to the equally regretted deaths of Br. Joachim and Br. Paul in America.[7] I speak also of the separation from those who recently left us to bring, as primary teachers, the knowledge of Jesus Christ to the children of Oran, Bône, and Phillippeville in Algeria.

Then, too, there were the anxieties occasioned by the sickness of two of our beloved sons, whom God in his all-compassionate goodness has finally restored to health. We experienced no small alarm over the storm and the shipwreck that almost claimed our latest colony for Notre-Dame du Lac among its victims. Besides, an ill-willed newspaper printed a letter dictated by inexperience and a self-love that was too sensitive to the insults and contempt which we shall count ourselves happy to receive in return for our religious devotedness. I cannot forget the numerous complaints that caused me to close a store which, without any burden for the motherhouse, I had opened in the interests of Notre-Dame de Sainte-Croix, and forced me against my will to abandon certain building projects, which were already started, only to resume them almost immediately. I suffered from the almost incredible delays, which, notwithstanding my repeated insistence, marked the sending of various articles of clothing to the brothers in our various schools. Finally, there was the unavoidable anxiety occasioned by the large number and the youth of the students entrusted to the zeal of those in charge of our splendid institute, and by the poor health of the reverend mother prioress of the Good Shepherd.

Crosses

These are, doubtless, a goodly number of crosses for one year, not to mention those which from time to time are provided by ill will, lying, and slander. Far from complaining of these trials, we must learn to love them, for if we bear them as we should, they are worth their weight in gold. These nails and thorns will be changed later into the many precious stones that will make up the crown of glory reserved for those who have been faithful to the duties of their vocation and have worn lovingly, even to the end, their Savior's crown of thorns. I know not what new crosses await us during the coming year. Whatever they may be, let us not forget that the heaviest crosses contribute most to the general good of our work and to the welfare of each one of us. We must bear in mind that since our divine model remained nailed to the cross even to his last sigh, we too must desire to stay with our cross even unto death. We should not bother about what the world may say of us, for if in one sense we do not deserve its blame, in another sense we have merited it only too well by our infidelities to the inspirations of grace. At such moments, let us remember that the life of all the saints was a mixture of sweetness and bitterness and that, according to the expression of one of the most lovable of them all, the heart of the servant of God is like an anvil, made to be struck and to live on blows and outrages.

Consolations

Heaven, however, knowing our weakness, has not been sparing of its consolations in the midst of all these trials. Since what concerns me personally also interests our entire association, I shall tell you very frankly, my dear sons and daughters in Jesus Christ, that I am more than joyful when I recall all the edifying things I saw and heard during the general retreats of recent years. I rejoice, too, when I recall the courageous departure of our humble confrere almost on the morrow of his profession, and of those beloved brothers and pious daughters of Our Lady of Sorrows who have cheerfully abandoned everything they held most dear in order to carry on abroad the work for which we were founded.

I am consoled when I recall the readiness with which, at my request, it was agreed to put under a common name the property that I had at first destined for the priests of Holy Cross, and thus to do away with any distinction between priests, brothers, and sisters. In this regard, however, the accounting method shall not be changed, lest injustice be done to anyone in case of possible division. It is also heartening to see increased uniformity in the matter of rising, food, and quality of the clothing, and to watch the spiritual advancement of several subjects whose perseverance I had previously regarded as doubtful. I was happy over the kind and unexpected manner in which the two councils of the Propagation of the Faith have just settled claims which were only too well founded on my part.[8] I rejoice at the blessings showered on our apostolic ministry, even in the very parish whence this circular letter is dated, although I am far from being able to meet the needs of the large numbers of the faithful who, by reason of natural character, habits, and religious prejudice, form, as it were, a people distinct from all others.

Another source of consolation is the excellent spiritual and temporal status of the community of the Good Shepherd. Under the government of its superioress, and thanks to the wisdom of its directors and the generosity of a kind soul, it no longer occasions me any of the worries that are inseparable from a work in its infancy.[9] Finally, I joyously bless the merciful providence of God when I behold our conventual church. It will soon be completed and will embody in its general plan all the ideas that have guided the foundation of Notre-Dame de Sainte-Croix.

The rearing of this temple of stone, however, would only sadden me if, as it rises, it were not the image of the invisible and spiritual edifice that all of us are bound to build and of which we are to be the living stones. Faith, first of all, has laid the foundations. It is for hope to lift them up to heaven, for chastity to clothe its walls with dazzling whiteness, for obedience to unify all the parts, and for charity to crown the complete edifice. May the virtues of fortitude, temperance, prudence, and justice be its four unshakable columns.

In this temple, there must also be an altar, whereon we may offer spiritual sacrifices through the immolation of our carnal desires. Let us be the tabernacle wherein God dwells since "his kingdom is within us" (Lk 17:21). In our hearts, may the mysterious lamp be fed unceasingly by the oil of good works, and may it be kept constantly burning. Through the prayers prescribed by our rule, may our hearts exhale the aroma of pure incense, and may our guardian angels bear them up to the very throne of the Lamb without stain. Finally, let us heed within us the preaching of the Holy Spirit by the anointing of his grace, and let us always bear in mind that, like the visible temple that is rising on the grounds of Notre-Dame de Sainte-Croix and which will soon be consecrated, we, too, have received our consecration in the waters of Baptism and were stamped with the zeal of the children of God. Let us take care, then, that nothing defiled come in contact with this temple, lest we behold on the temporal and spiritual affairs of our community the execution of the terrible threat: "Whoever profanes this holy temple, God will destroy" (1 Cor 3:17). Then, of all these buildings which have been undertaken at such great expense, there will not remain a stone upon a stone.

Let us, then, continue with noble courage, my dear sons and daughters in Jesus Christ, on the difficult path that we have chosen. We should rely confidently on him who has called us to so glorious a task, find encouragement in the hope of a better life, and keep our eyes fixed on that changeless eternity where no longer there will be succession of days, weeks, months, and years.

Articles

With these thoughts in mind, after conferring with my local council while on a visit to Sainte-Croix, and after the solemn Mass, which was celebrated in honor of my holy patron, I have ordered and do hereby order the following:

Article 1

The visitation of all our houses in France will begin this year and continue in the following years, conformably to the constitutions and rules.

Article 2

The brothers who have not as yet held conferences will organize these meetings in the place, at the time, and in the manner most convenient. They will submit their programs for my approval at the time of the next general retreat. The minutes of these conferences will then be read in public.

Article 3

Those who have been guilty of useless or unauthorized expenses will reimburse the community for the harm thus done to it by practicing more rigid economy.

Article 4

It is forbidden to take meals or refreshments in the city of Le Mans at the time of the general retreat, either when arriving, or when leaving, or on the occasion of any other trip whatsoever.

Article 5

During the week following the reception of this circular letter, each one will read over the notes and resolutions of the last retreat, as also the letter of St. Ignatius on obedience.

Article 6

The prohibitions concerning the use of tobacco, dessert wines, liqueurs, and coffee are reaffirmed for all who have not obtained a dispensation from me personally.

Article 7

The brother directors of schools are explicitly urged to organize a solemn distribution of prizes for their pupils, either at the end of the school year or after the First Communion ceremonies.

Article 8

All correspondence carried on without the knowledge of the local superior, unless it be with the rector or the respective particular superiors, is and remains formally forbidden to all without exception, unless they have special permission from me.

Article 9

In encouraging vocations for their institute, the brothers should not forget the qualities required by their constitutions for the admission of candidates. Before sending them to the motherhouse, they will try to obtain (1) a written promise, signed by the father, mother, or guardian of the postulant, to reimburse the community for the expenses of their training in the novitiate if they should be sent away from the society or leave of their own accord; (2) their birth certificate, certifying that they are fifteen years of age, completed; (3) a certificate of good life and conduct from their pastor; (4) their baptismal record; and (5) their vaccination certificate.

Article 10

The brothers in parishes, who come to Notre-Dame de Sainte-Croix in the course of the year, should apply for their room to the local superior of the brothers at the motherhouse. This is now Fr. Vérité or, in his absence, Fr. Pattou, in case I should not be on hand to receive them at the boarding school. Their particular superior, Fr. Chappé, usually resides at the Novitiate of St. Joseph.

Article 11

The brother directors of schools who may need religious habits for themselves or for their brothers at the time of the general retreat should apply for them in July; otherwise, they may be kept waiting.

Article 12

Motives of prudence have prompted me to substitute the word "association" for that of "congregation" in order to express the union of our three societies.

Article 13

I forbid you, under holy obedience, to communicate this circular to anyone outside of our association.

Article 14

I have learned that certain brothers are overburdened with schoolwork to the detriment of their exercises of piety, or even of their health, and that these same brothers, besides their work of perfecting, are being forced to act as sacristans and choirmasters. I hereby authorize and order these brothers to inform the pastors who treat them in this fashion that, according to articles 404, 405, and 407 of their constitutions, no such duties can be exacted of any of our brothers without a dispensation from me. This I will never grant unless the brothers themselves are willing to accept it.

In conclusion, I call your attention to Articles 1, 3, 4, 5, 6, 7, 8, 9, 10, and 12 of my circular letter of January 5, 1844.

Letters

I should like to bring to your attention the following letters which will give you news of our foundations abroad:

LETTER OF FR. GRANGER

New York
October 3, 1844

Reverend Father Founder:

At last we have reached this land that is the object of all our desires. O how beautiful and clear is the American sky! Now, better than ever, we understand all that God has done for us. Yes, like a tender mother, his providence has directed all our steps. . . . But I must stop; no pen can express the varied sentiments which well up within my heart. . . .

Our crossing, dear Father, was quite short, since it took hardly more than thirty-one days, but it was full of hard trials. The first fifteen days could not have been finer; we almost complained of having such beautiful weather. Br. Vincent remarked occasionally that God did not find us equal to big hardships. He was right, but providence, which arranges everything gently, did not fail to carry out its merciful designs on us. At last, it found us worthy to suffer something for the Lord Jesus.

Up to the Newfoundland banks, nothing extraordinary happened. With the exception of some rough weather, everything went very pleasantly. It was on St. Michael's night that we had our first taste of bad weather. About ten o'clock a storm arose. I got out of bed and went up on deck with Br. Vincent. The whistling of the wind and the roar of the waves struck terror into my soul. I imagined that the waves were going to wash over the ship, but nothing happened. With the wind in the right direction, we were making about five leagues an hour. That very night I had quite a narrow escape when I fell headlong near the opening of a trapdoor some ten feet deep, but the angel of the Lord put his hand on me and broke my fall. Nevertheless, we learned much that night, for we were taught greater confidence in the holy angels and, particularly, in St. Michael. Those who travel by sea should take him as secondary patron.

October the fourth, the Feast of St. Francis of Assisi, was also marked by a new trial. A violent wind, which made the ship rock, blew for several hours. At noon, the main mast was broken into three pieces, along with the main yard. This caused great alarm among everyone, passengers and crew alike. Our colony went to confession; I myself hurried to ask the favor of absolution from an Italian priest who shared my room. Then I distributed a goodly number of miraculous medals to arouse confidence. They were received eagerly and gratefully. At two o'clock, we were getting ready for dinner when a strong wind pitched the vessel on her side for a full minute. The rebound hurled a heap of copper against one of the partitions, and the copper rolled up against it with a great crash and shattered it. For a moment, we thought we were lost. We feared the ship had been ripped open, and we offered up the sacrifice of our lives. I hastened to offer my services, but my fears were soon dispelled. St. Francis was praying for us.

Finally, the last trial, the biggest one of all, came during the night of the first Sunday and lasted all the first Monday of October. The sky had been overcast all day; perfect calm reigned on the sea. About six in the evening a storm broke. We got up at nine when the rocking of the ship threatened to throw us out of bed. Oh, how confidence in Our Lady gives courage! I got up, convinced that we would not be lost; Mary had been invoked fervently all day long throughout the entire world, for it was the Feast of the Holy Rosary. We were dreadfully frightened. At times we rolled about the ship with the objects we grasped to steady ourselves. The ship, riding now on one side, now on the other, seemed at every moment on the point of being swallowed up by the waves. An entire row of beds was thrown out into the middle of the ship, and all those in the upper berths were pitched out. Only one was hurt, but he suffered no broken bones. Br. Vincent and I went into the midst of the debris; we prayed aloud; a Protestant family gathered about us, happy to be near us. Soon the ship was transformed into a church. Some forty Germans were reciting their beads in common. On all sides the most heartfelt prayers went up to God and to his mother. Faith was reawakened, and danger made everyone pious. Oh, but the night was long. It was a battle between life and death; one sail was ripped. The storm abated about six in the morning, after lasting twelve hours. If it meant traveling under similar circumstances, I must say that we would very willingly make the sacrifice of a return to France.

Since that time, we have had no damage to the ship, but the winds, which were against us almost continually after we passed the banks of Newfoundland, kept us eight extra days at sea. For the rest, if we have had crosses, consolations have not been wanting. With the exception of Sr. Mary of the Circumcision, who was almost constantly in bed, and of Br. Justin, who scarcely left his either, all of us were in good health, at least for the first fortnight. I was a little unwell. Only twice the seasickness affected me, but on those two occasions it was bad. Br. Augustus, however, was worse than I. As to Br. Vincent, providence took care of him. He was our guardian angel. May God reward him for what he did for us and for many others.

During the first ten days, we made all our exercises regularly. Providence had so arranged our cabins that, without leaving theirs, the sisters could go to confession, hear holy Mass, and receive Holy Communion. We had holy Mass nine times.

Sunday, the Feast of the Holy Name of Mary, I had the happiness of baptizing a newborn child of German Catholic parents. To the name of Philip I added that of Mary in memory of the feast of the day. After the severe trials we had undergone, a great change came over the boat. On all sides we were asked for medals. Those who received them kissed our hands, while tears of emotion filled many eyes. The people hung the medals around their necks and vied with one another in showing us deference and doing us favors. May God and Our Lady reward them.

All our little colony edified me greatly and, I think, edified the whole boat as well. Our sisters showed great courage. They often said that, even knowing what sufferings would be theirs, they would gladly leave France again to come to America. Beginning with the first Sunday in October, the beads were said in common by the Germans. During the great storm, Br. Vincent made a promise to have one thousand Hail Marys recited at Notre-Dame de Sainte-Croix and at Notre-Dame du Lac. You will use your own judgment in regard to the promise.

From what I have said, dear Father, you can easily see what gratitude we owe to God, Mary, and the holy angels. A Protestant asked me for a medal, even though just a few days previously he had been bitter in his remarks on holy images. Our sisters went on deck, but no remarks were made. In the storm, I lost the letters you gave me for Fr. Sorin and Fr. Cointet, as also the obediences of the priests and the other letters in my case.[10] The letter for the Bishop of Vincennes has been saved, as also the faculties for Fr. Sorin. Happily, Br. Vincent had taken charge of them. During the frightful night described above, I lost my beautiful crucifix. I beg you to send me another at the next opportunity. I believe that the stole I brought to Sainte-Croix has remained with the sisters.

Now we are experiencing that truth of the Gospel which says that for the father and the mother we have left for Jesus Christ, we find a hundred others out here. The Parmentier home is like our father's house. They are so kind that we really have to be on our guard against all the attention they shower on us. Today I sang the high Mass at St. Paul's Church. Oh, how sweet it was to sing the praises of God in his holy temple! The music was grand. I believed I was at St. Julian's. . . .[11] There are Catholics everywhere; they have their schools beneath the churches. In very truth, all light flows from the church. Fr. Nicholas, the pastor, has given us most generous hospitality. He sees a glorious future for our brothers in America, but he says that we must form good subjects from the viewpoint of piety and learning. The vice-consul of France was kindness itself; he accompanied us personally to the Customs House. At the suggestion of

Mme. Parmentier, our sisters intend to change their religious garb for lay clothes.

All join with me in sending you affectionate regards. Please remember us to all at Sainte-Croix, to the priests, brothers, sisters, and boarders. My kindest regards to the bishop, to Fathers Heurte-bize and Bouvier. The sisters want to be remembered to their dear Sisters of Holy Cross and those of the Good Shepherd. M. Saint-Michel sends greetings to his friend, M. Gauthier. M. Launay, my companion in profession, is close to my heart, and also Fr. Drouelle, my monitor. To be brief, greet all those whose names I could write. We expect to be at Notre-Dame du Lac in a week.

Finally, very reverend Father, accept the good wishes and the respectful homage of your beloved sons and daughters, especially that of your beloved son,

P. Granger

LETTER OF BR. MARCELLUS

Bône, Algeria
December 14, 1844

Reverend Father:

Doubtless the long time during which you did not know whether I was dead or alive must have worried you greatly, for the danger of a child is always a source of great anxiety for the most tender of fathers. I am more than happy to calm your fears in my regard and to inform you that I am now completely well again. It is true that my condition was very serious, but by a miracle of providence, doubtless wrought by your prayers and those of my friends in France, divine goodness was pleased to spare me this time and to postpone to some future date the death of a child who, at the approach of the New Year, feels increasing within him the fervent good wishes that he always addresses to heaven for you.

Br. Marcellus

FROM THE PROPAGATION OF THE FAITH

La Flèche, France
December 31, 1844

Dear Reverend Father:

If you have not received a more prompt reply to the protest that you lodged with the Paris Council of the Propagation of the Faith, complaining of the disposition made of our last allowance and asking for an advance grant that may serve to repair the harm which has resulted from this error, it is only because the matter has been the object of a long correspondence between the two Councils of Paris and Lyons. The recent termination of this correspondence has resulted in a decision in accordance with your wishes.

The two councils grant you, reverend Father, an advance of four thousand francs on your next allocation. I have the honor to enclose for you a letter from the treasurer of Paris for Abbé Dubois, who is requested to give you the above-mentioned sum if he actually has it on hand. In case he has not, our treasurer will complete this sum by sending you the balance whenever you wish.

I am happy, reverend and dear Father, to have been able to contribute to a result which you are so justified in desiring. I am also happy to advise you that you will very probably no longer have to be afraid of your allocations not being granted in accordance with your wishes. The Council of Lyons, after a very thorough discussion of the matter, will not, I hope, repeat the error that caused you serious trouble this year.

Permit me to offer you and all the members of your holy congregation our best wishes for the year beginning tomorrow. In return, I ask a memento for myself in your good prayers.

If, on my return to Paris, I can stop at Le Mans, I will not fail to come in person to offer you the expression of the sentiments of respect and affection with which I have the honor to be, very dear and reverend Father,

Your humble and obedient servant,
De Labouillerie
[Secretary of the Paris office of the Propagation of the Faith]

Conclusion

The present circular letter will be sent out by the proper authority to all the members of our association. It shall first be read in chapter or at the spiritual reading and will thereafter be preserved in the archives of each particular house.

Given while on retreat, the day, month, and year as above.

B. Moreau
Rector

Circular Letter 25

· ·

Notre-Dame de Sainte-Croix, Le Mans
January 5, 1846

My dear sons and daughters in Jesus Christ:

It is always with lively joy and gratitude that I receive your good wishes for New Year's and my feast day. This is so, because this twofold occasion brings me the happiness of knowing the state of your soul in regard to God, your vocation, and myself. It likewise affords me a valuable opportunity to renew the assurance of my fatherly affection for you and to speak about the general interests of our association. Notwithstanding my numerous occupations, the duties of my office and my sentiments of affection for you demand that I suggest new ways and means of improving the work of Holy Cross. That is why I ordinarily make use of this annual circular to offer such observations as cannot be postponed until the general retreat.

Besides, I am, after the example of St. Paul, happy to show you from time to time my care and anxiety for all of you, whether you have known me personally or, as is the case for several of our dear family at Notre-Dame du Lac in America, have never come in direct contact with me. I do this in order that your consolation may rest firmly in God, that we may be perfectly united by charity and cling to Jesus Christ, as trees to their roots or buildings to the foundations, in constant fidelity to our sacred obligations. For although I am separated in body from most of you, I have you ever present in mind and heart. Thus, it is from this intimate union with you that I draw the courage I need in the midst of all my labors and trials. Yes, my dear sons and daughters in Jesus Christ, your devotedness to our common undertaking and your friendship for me give me strength. I am without anxiety for the future so long as my affection for you and my zeal for the work of God are faithfully echoed in your hearts.

For these reasons, I am always pleased to have a thorough account of your dispositions and to be able, at least once a year, to read your souls in the letters of direction that reveal them to me. I prefer this to all the usual compliments and assurances of affection. May God bless all those who thus confide to me the secrets of their conscience and console me by their progress in the virtues of the holy state they have embraced. They should not be surprised and, much less, discouraged at the attacks unleashed against them by the world, the flesh, and the devil. Rather, let them generously resist the onslaughts of the enemies of their sublime vocation, bearing in mind the words of the archangel to the venerable father of young Tobias, who had fallen blind in the midst of his charitable labors: "Because you were acceptable to God, it was necessary that temptations should prove you" (Tb 12:13).

Unfortunately, more than one departure saddens my heart each year and forces me to repeat the warning of the apostle: "Wherefore he who thinks himself to stand, let him take heed lest he fall" (1 Cor 10:12). Until now you have experienced only ordinary temptations. Greater combats are yet in store for you. But God is faithful; he will not suffer you to be tempted beyond your strength. He will always give you the means to resist your temptations in such a way that you will be able to overcome them. Hence, laying aside the burden of sin that can retard our advance, let us run with constancy in the way which is opened up before us. Let us keep our eyes ever fixed on Jesus, the author and reward of our faith, who, at the sight of the glory that his father proposed to him, endured the sorrows of the cross. Consider well what great contradictions he suffers for sinners, lest you succumb in discouragement under the weight of your afflictions. In your combats to remain faithful to your vocation, you have not yet resisted unto blood as did our Savior and the martyrs (Heb 12:4).

Have you forgotten the consoling words which Wisdom addresses to you as her children: "My child, despise not the correction of the Lord and reject it not when he chastises you" (Prv 3:11)? It is true that when chastisement is resented, it causes sadness rather than joy. Afterward it brings forth salutary fruits of justice. Hence, lift up your faltering hands, you who are tempted to discouragement. Strengthen your trembling knees, and direct your steps into the path of virtue. Seek after holiness, without which no one will see God. Take care that not one of you be unfaithful to divine grace, and that no bitter root work its shoots into your midst to harm and infect many with its poison.

Now, my dear sons and daughters in Jesus Christ, this is what would happen if any we were to disregard our rules and constitutions, put off at will our rising and retiring, neglect our meditation, give up frequent Communion, make useless visits, or become too familiar with our students. For this last point, all should follow the *Conduite des écoles*, the principles of the manual, and the recommendations of the superiors.[12] I beg of you never to allow such scandalous conduct to go on in your midst without at once notifying me, and I ask you to profit by the New Year to renew yourselves in the spirit of your vocation.

Spirit of Zeal

This spirit consists in great zeal for your own sanctification and that of your students. Such zeal is generous and never sacrifices duty to laziness, worldliness, or sensuality. It will be active and enlightened and will spare no labors for the honor of the institute, the progress of the students, and the success of its foundations. It should be full of moderation and firmness and undismayed by trials or the fear of displeasing those who are unfamiliar with the works of God. Let it be ardent in spreading the Association of St. Joseph and devotion to this powerful protector. This zeal must be pure and disinterested, always seeking the welfare of the community rather than personal advantage. It must be faithful in attendance at the conferences that have been organized by the authority of superiors and in acquiring the knowledge necessary to fulfill your duty.

Besides, this zeal must be prompt in maintaining the rules and constitutions in all their vigor, by example even more than by words. It must encourage vocations and assist in training good subjects for the association. In the material order, this spirit of zeal will see that the deeds of foundations are carefully preserved, that bills and salaries are paid when they fall due, and that an honest effort is made to balance the annual budget and to find new sources of income when expenditures exceed receipts. Lastly, your zeal must be shown in upholding the authority of superiors and, when the situation demands it, in cooperating with and defending the administration of the motherhouse. Unfortunately, in these bad times, our administration is beset with many difficulties. So many contradictions try our patience and so much grief fills our days that our only consolation is in the readiness with which our religious undertake to defend the interests of Notre-Dame de Sainte-Croix.

As for myself personally, am I not entitled to this readiness on your part, my dear sons and daughters in Christ? You call me "Father," and does not this title give me the right to count on your cooperation and devotedness? When a superior is the victim of calumny, broken down by injustice and discouraged by ingratitude, from whom can he ask aid and support if not from those very ones whose own interests are at stake and who are the natural defenders of his government? These thoughts then show how grossly certain brothers misunderstand their vocation when, instead of justifying and upholding the administration of Notre-Dame de Sainte-Croix, they themselves take sides with her enemies and detractors.

Trials

Thanks be to God, my dear sons and daughters in Jesus Christ, that most of you have understood more clearly your obligations toward me, as well as toward the community and toward yourself. Very few of you will have to apply these present observations to yourselves. I should not have had much to suffer during this past year if it had not been God's will to try me in other ways. For I must count among the trials of the year 1845 the departure of several subjects who could have done great good for the association; the deaths of Br. Anselm, of the worthy superioress of the Good Shepherd, and of two promoters, Mme. Leguicheux of Fresnay and Mlle. Maurice of Le Mans, who were outstanding for their devotedness to our two associations. It was a cross to be obliged to engage in deplorable but necessary controversies with certain authorities who disregarded our rights, and to accept the loss of an annual grant of two thousand francs formerly made by an institution, which is so financially embarrassed that it can no longer pay. We have been tried by the attempts of persistent and jealous opponents to thwart the development of, and even to destroy, our excellent boarding school, as well as by the loss of vocations, which at first appeared solid but were later shaken by the attraction of the world or by the ambitious pretext of entering the ecclesiastical state. All these are indeed heavy crosses, even without mentioning the lies that were broadcast far and wide about our administration and our priestly ministry.

Consolations

But in the midst of so many trials, the blessings of God have not been wanting. I am pleased to regard as a special blessing the intimate and ever-growing union that exists among the three branches of the great family of Holy Cross. I find consolation in the recollection and the spirit of obedience that you showed at the last general retreat, in the eagerness with which many of you answered an appeal to their spirit of sacrifice to replace at Oran a brother who deceived our expectations, and in your hurrying to the assistance of our beloved colony of America or to found a novitiate in Canada. Other blessings are found in the kindness of the two central councils of the Propagation of the Faith in agreeing once more to honor our request for a subsidy in favor of our houses abroad. God's goodness is manifest in the success of our retreats and missions in the diocese and in the admirable devotedness of the promoters of our two associations. I feel special satisfaction over the prosperity of the Good Shepherd community, due to the generosity of a noble soul, who has become for it almost a second providence, and to the wise direction of three worthy priests, who, although not of our society, are aiding this good work with a zeal deserving all our gratitude. We have reasons for encouragement in the number and docility of the students of our institution and, lastly, in the completion of the conventual church and the reception of many postulants at the Solitude of St. Joseph. Nor must we forget the return to Notre-Dame du Lac of Fr. Badin, Vicar General of Bardstown, Kentucky, who has recently pleaded the interests of Notre-Dame before the Central Council of the Propagation of the Faith at Lyons. The memorandum that he presented on this occasion gives further proof that the Lord is with Fr. Sorin, the superior of this important foundation.

But the more divine providence is pleased to bless the works that it has confided to us and for which we are jointly responsible, the more keenly do I feel the weight of my responsibility and the more deeply I am convinced of the need of personal holiness if I am not to be an obstacle to God's designs for each one of you. Pray, then, for me, my dear sons and daughters, and pray also for one another, in order that we may accomplish all the good we can, and that the many souls in whose salvation we are privileged to cooperate may at last attain eternal life.

Regular Visitation

I would find great happiness in going personally to exhort you to show yourselves worthy of your vocation if I could make the regular visitation of our houses, especially abroad. Hindered as I am, however, by occupations, which keep me almost continually at the motherhouse, it is in vain that I look forward to this happy moment with all the ardor of my heart. I rejoice, nevertheless, at that article of our constitutions that obliges the reverend Father rector to visit each and every house of the association at least once, because I hope this visitation will realize a dream, which is always before me. This dream is to go personally to all our houses, even to the remote and the least important, in order to get firsthand assurance of the condition of each and, as far as I can, to find ways and means to procure for you surroundings that will compensate for the life of retirement and denial to which you have so generously devoted yourselves.

I have already visited, although much too rapidly, almost all our schools in France, but I have been unable to go farther. These are the omissions that I hope to remedy and the void in my life which I hope to fill. I know full well the difficulties of so long an absence from the motherhouse, but I feel that sooner or later my presence will be necessary in Algeria and in America. In carrying out this general visitation I shall spare neither time nor trouble. Work does not frighten me, for love makes it light, and grace helps me to bear up under it. This love I hope to find in my heart, and the grace I trust to obtain from your prayers. Pray, then, I beg you again, and ask the Lord to send worthy laborers into his vineyard.

Articles

With this in mind, in order to maintain the rules in their full vigor among us, and after consultation with my particular council, I have felt it my duty to order and do hereby order the following:

Article 1

The three invocations in use in the association will be said this year for the intention of obtaining (1) the subjects and money necessary for each of the three societies, (2) fidelity to the rules and constitutions, and (3) perseverance for those among us who are exposed to greater dangers to their vocation.

Article 2

The regulations of my circular letter of January 4, 1845, shall be read attentively in order to ensure even more faithful conformity to them.

Article 3

We are not to explain or have the children in our schools recite any catechism other than the one in use in the diocese wherein we are employed. It is never permitted to a brother, who may have students of different religions in his class, as in Algeria, to read, or have read, or even to allow in his class, other works than those approved by the ordinary or by the reverend Father rector of the association.

Article 4

Those who feel capable of passing the examination for their teacher's license will do well to present themselves at the next opportunity before the commission of their department. They should bring their birth certificate, duly legalized, and register the day before the opening of the examinations.

Article 5

The brothers are allowed to show their rules to their confessors.

Article 6

I permit the brothers to receive Holy Communion more often than the rules stipulate when their confessors counsel them to do so. They may also apply to their respective pastors for a dispensation from fasting.

Article 7

Permission will never be granted to the brothers to act as secretaries in mayor's offices or to exercise any other function not mentioned in their manual. They are not allowed to act as subdeacon at the altar.

Article 8

It will henceforth be useless to ask for permission to play any other instrument than those authorized by the rules. We wish to restrict the brothers to learning vocal music and plainchant.

Article 9

In France, used clothing and personal linen that are no longer serviceable must in the future be brought back to the motherhouse and presented to the one in charge of the clothes room before they can be replaced.

Article 10

Brothers in parishes are strictly forbidden to wear or to possess lay clothing. Nor are they to take away with them the cloaks, which, at the request of the directors, have been heretofore permitted in certain houses.

Article 11

According to the terms of the instruction already received and later reaffirmed, the brothers of Bône and Philippeville will, before January and August, send in to the brother director of the school of Oran the statistics of their school so that a general table can be drawn up and sent to the motherhouse for the first of January and the fifteenth of August. The same ruling holds good for the chronicles.

Article 12

In America, the instructions brought by Br. Augustine on the question of the accounts as well as the chronicles and statistics shall be most carefully observed. This article and the preceding are absolutely essential and must be carried out immediately.

Article 13

The inventory books should be kept accurately, checked annually, and brought to the general retreat. I was greatly grieved to learn that not all the chronicles were left at Notre-Dame de Sainte-Croix.

Article 14

All requests for clothing should be made exclusively by the directors to Fr. Pattou before July first.

Article 15

The new colony for America will be made up of at least three sisters, three brothers, and two ecclesiastics. They will leave at a date to be determined later.

It is important to add on page 235 of the manual the surname and Christian names of the son or the ward who makes the ten-year contract.[13] Those who have any observations to make regarding that part of the manual which does not contain the rules are invited to send them in before February 15.

The present circular shall be forwarded through the proper channel to all the members of our association. It will be read, first of all, in chapter or at spiritual reading, and afterward preserved in the archives of each particular house.

Given at Notre-Dame de Sainte-Croix on the day, month, and year as above.

B. Moreau
Rector

Circular Letter 34

· ·

Notre-Dame de Sainte-Croix, Le Mans
June 19, 1848

My dear sons and daughters in Jesus Christ:

Hardly has the news of the death of Br. Theodosius reached the distant members of our association, when I am again obliged to ask your suffrages for the repose of two souls whom the Lord has just called to himself after fortifying them with the sacraments of the Church. I myself had been in a position to appreciate their genuinely religious and devoted spirit. I refer to Br. Mary Basil, a novice who died at the motherhouse on the seventeenth of this month at the age of only eighteen, and the superioress of the sisters at Bertrand in the United States. She had been sent to Fort Wayne, about twenty-five leagues from Notre-Dame, for special medical treatment under an excellent physician, but she died there last April 29 at the age of forty and is sincerely mourned by all for her lively faith, inexhaustible charity, tireless activity, ardent zeal, and prudence. So well was she fitted for her important post that she leaves a void that will be difficult to fill.

Crosses

Thus is Jesus Christ pleased to try his work; only a religious spirit that understands the power of his cross can sustain our courage in the midst of all these trials. Happy, indeed, are we if we know how to profit by them and to understand the unspeakable advantage of becoming more and more conformed to the image of the divine Christ crucified. For those who live by faith, the cross is a treasure more valuable than gold and precious stones. If we were truly worthy of our vocation, far from dreading these crosses, we would be more eager to accept them than to receive a relic of the very wood that our Savior sanctified by his blood. Let us not allow ourselves, then, to be discouraged by trials, no matter how numerous or bitter they may be. Afflictions, reverses, loss of friends, privations of every kind, sickness, even death itself, "the evil of each day," and the sufferings of each hour—all these are but so many relics of the sacred wood of the true cross that we must love and venerate. We must enclose these precious souvenirs in a reliquary made of charity that is patient, resigned, and generous, and which, in union with the divine master, suffers all things and supports all things. Thus will we appease his justice.

May we never lose sight of this language of the Gospel. May we meditate on it, especially at those times when heaven may impose hard sacrifices on our poor human nature. Let us, then, renew our confidence and our courage by recalling the examples left by those whom we mourn. Let us also pray for them, in order that if perchance God's justice still retains them in the flames of purgatory, he may be pleased to give them the possession of the happiness reserved for their fidelity to him. And let us give special remembrance to the souls whom this circular letter recommends to your prayers.

Hence, tomorrow, Tuesday, a Mass will be sung for Br. Mary Basil, at which the boarders will assist, since this young novice had for some time acted as prefect in the study hall and dormitory for the younger children. For the other details, you will conform to Article 356 of the rule. For the superioress, whose death is so deeply mourned, in addition to the suffrages prescribed by rule, the same service will be celebrated at Notre-Dame du Lac and at St. Laurent of Montreal as at the motherhouse.

The colony, which left Le Havre on the sixth of this month for Canada, is composed of Fr. Drouelle, as visitor; Br. Pascal, master of novices; Brothers Bruno, Maur, John, and Honorius; and Sisters Mary of the Redemption, Mary of the Coronation, and Mary of the Resurrection. Fr. Dugoujon, who is on his way to Guadeloupe as prefect apostolic, will be accompanied by Abbé Bisson, who is a novice, and by Br. Prosper.

Given at Notre-Dame de Sainte-Croix, Le Mans, on the day, month, and year as above.

B. Moreau
Rector

Circular Letter 36

· ·

Notre-Dame de Sainte-Croix, Le Mans
April 15, 1849

My dear sons and daughters in Jesus Christ:

May the grace of our Lord, the blessing of his mother conceived without sin, and the protection of St. Joseph be ever with you.

Full Teaching Rights for Sainte-Croix

In my last circular letter I held out to you certain hopes and asked the help of your most fervent prayers that they might be realized. The details that I then made known to you on this subject must have evidenced my great confidence in the minister of public instruction and worship. I am now happy to inform you that my hopes have not been deceived. With the fatherly and merciful goodness, which he has so often shown toward Notre-Dame de Sainte-Croix, God has heard your prayers and mine. You have already guessed my meaning. Full teaching rights have been decreed for our institution.[14]

For a long time, as you know, I had been taking steps to obtain this concession that I deemed absolutely necessary for an establishment which was to serve as the motherhouse of our association. All of us had much to suffer from the state of affairs that obliged us to give up our dear students at the most critical period of their Christian training and to turn over their minds to a philosophical teaching so opposed to the principles we were striving to inculcate while they were under our care. Too many tragic examples had taught us the dangers of the false philosophy that is so widespread today; too many young souls had been tarnished by the lessons of that human wisdom which often ends in skepticism or pantheism. At the sight of all this, we could hardly help being sad and anxious at the realization that we must soon expose to this baneful influence students whom we loved so dearly and whom we dreaded to send back into the world without being fortified against all its seductions. Moreover, this anguish of ours was shared by the families who honored us with their confidence. How many good mothers had expressed their fears on this point. Our Lord has heeded the sorrow of their watchful care and of ours and has deigned to bring it to an end. May he be blessed for his goodness.

M. de Falloux, a man whom the religious world has learned to respect and admire, and who ranks among the most generous defenders of true liberty and sane doctrine, has been made head of public instruction in France. One of his first official acts was to grant us our most ardent desire. In fact, encouraged by a letter of M. Langlais, a lawyer of Paris; emboldened by a reply of the illustrious founder of the Committee for the Defense of Religious Liberty; and relying on the friendship with which Messieurs Henri and Charles de Riancey honored me, I went to Paris, full of confidence in the good will of the new minister of the republic. On January 12, at nine in the morning, he granted me an interview. One hour later, upon the recommendation of the deputy of La Sarthe and in the presence of all the directors gathered around the council table, he granted me, with a kindness I shall never forget, that complete teaching liberty which we had coveted so long and so fervently.

Ideals of Education

Consequently, we may, henceforth, take our beloved students from the elementary courses through the profound studies of philosophy that completes their education and which, if well directed, can exercise such a great influence in the afterlife. We can state in a word the kind of teaching we hope to impart. We recognize no genuine philosophical system save that which is based on Catholic faith. While we accept whatever is good and true in university teaching, we declare that its principles are not dogmas, because the university is immersed in a psychology whose theories are more or less opposed to the doctrines of the Church, and because the university believes in no other revelation than that of individual or collective reason.[15] Even though we base our philosophy course on the data of faith, no one need fear that we shall confine our teaching within narrow and unscientific boundaries. No, we wish to accept science without prejudice and in a manner adapted to the needs of our times. We do not want our students to be ignorant of anything they should know. To this end, we shall shrink from no sacrifice. But we shall never forget that virtue, as Bacon puts it, is the spice which preserves science.[16] We shall always place education side by side with instruction; the mind will not be cultivated at the expense of the heart. While we prepare useful citizens for society, we shall likewise do our utmost to prepare citizens for heaven.

Such are our plans, my dear sons and daughters in Jesus Christ. If we put no obstacles in the way of his designs, God will bless them, for he himself has inspired whatever has been undertaken up to the present for the completion of this important work. Yes, I have the firm confidence that God will bless our educational program since he is giving us the means to realize it. We cannot fail to recognize the special protection of his providence in the fact that we now have all the teachers necessary for our project and that he has crowned with success all the candidates whom we presented for the various examinations since receiving full teaching rights. Out of eight candidates who took the examination for teachers, six passed with very high grades. Four professors of our college who went to Paris for the baccalaureate returned home with their diplomas.[17] Surely these successes should not make us proud, but they do console us, because we see therein a new proof of God's protection on the work to which all of us have consecrated our lives.

Gratitude

This divine protection will strike you as still more tangible and will make you redouble your gratitude when I tell you that the District Committee of Laval, which, since 1830, has obstinately refused to accept our brothers as public school teachers, unanimously decided, in extraordinary session on May 17, to admit them for the future, provided they comply with the ordinary legal requirements. Our sincere thanks go out to all the committee members, particularly to the prefect, to the pastor of Saint-Vénérand, and to M. Quatre-barbes, M. de Vaujuas, and M. de Chalais, who so kindly interested themselves in our cause. But it is God's own hand that has guided everything, and he it is whom we must thank above all. Hence, my dear sons and daughters in Jesus Christ, I beg you to unite your thanks with ours in order that we may draw down more abundant blessings from heaven upon our work, and above all not stop their flow by a want of gratitude. St. Bernard says: "Ingratitude is like a scorching wind which dries up the rivers of grace."[18]

The best way to show God our gratitude and love, St. Gregory tells us, is to express them by deeds, by the practice of good works. For all of us, "good works" are summed up in the observance of our rules. Permit me, then, in conclusion, to remind you of certain points that some members seem to have forgotten. I refer, first of all, to the reading of newspapers.[19] It is not at all advisable to introduce this practice into our houses; it is a source of much distraction and of very little profit. Those whose work obliges them to be abreast of current events should keep themselves informed on world happenings. No one can find fault with them for so doing, since they are not acting out of empty curiosity but rather out of necessity. As for the others, that is, for all who are not in charge of houses but who are employed as assistant teachers or as coadjutor brothers, the reading of newspapers would mean giving in to a natural desire for news and exposing themselves to manifold dangers against the spirit of their vocation.

On this point, as on all others, Jesus Christ should be our model, since our likeness to this divine master is the foundation of our predestination to eternal glory. Do we read anywhere in his life that in his associations with others he was curious for worldly news? No, indeed. On the contrary, no one ever practiced more merciless mortification in this regard. Yet, what stirring events attracted the attention of the world and filled the minds of Jews, Romans, and Greeks. But our Savior announced only the great and glad tidings that he had brought into the world and spoke unceasingly of the kingdom of God. The apostles, who imitated him so closely, also devoted themselves solely to prayer and preaching the Gospel, and they showed no more interest in the world and its great ones than they would have if such were nonexistent.

Now, just because St. Luke found fault with those who, like the Athenians and those who visited them, "spend all their leisure telling or listening to something new" (Acts 17:21), do not imagine that I would have you be strangers to what is happening before our eyes and is so reassuring for the future. No, not at all. All of us, however, must restrain our eagerness to get news. We must leave to superiors and directors the task of keeping us informed of what it is important for us to know and thus observe faithfully Article 410 of our rule, which forbids us to adopt political opinions or to read partisan newspapers. This article of the rule recently drew the praise of the Committee for Primary Instruction, which was organized by M. de Falloux. From this you will understand, my dear sons and daughters, that far from authorizing subscriptions to certain newspapers, as I have been frequently asked to do, I renew the prohibition just mentioned. I make a single exception for *L'Ami de la Religion*. This paper may be read, but not subscribed to, by directors of schools, wherever they can find someone to lend it to them. It may also be read by all the ecclesiastics in our various houses, professed or not, who have duties outside the novitiate. The superiors of these houses have permission to take out a subscription.

I also deem it my duty to forbid all our religious to publish anything whatsoever without my approval. I make an exception for the catalogues of our educational houses abroad. In these cases, it will be sufficient to have the written permission of the local superior in each individual instance.

Refutation of a False Charge

As some of you have been uneasy regarding the recent calumnies against the motherhouse in the *Courrier de la Sarthe*, I publish herewith the reply, which the newspaper was obliged to insert in its columns. It will enable you to give the lie to whoever might attempt to deceive your good faith in this matter.

Extract from the Newspaper
L'Union

April 9, 1849

To the Editor:

In your edition of April 5, you reprinted the lie of the *Courrier* regarding the house of which I am superior. You also carried my own reply, which, though somewhat forceful and to the point, contained no more than I felt obliged to say in the circumstances. This reply was addressed directly to the *Courrier*, which refused to publish it on the grounds that it was too insolent. Frankly, I did not think the *Courrier* was so scrupulous in matters of this kind. But, pray tell me, which expression is so shocking? A careful rereading of the letter, which I felt obliged to write and which you have faithfully reprinted, reveals only one word that strikes me as being somewhat hard for the *Courrier* to stomach. I called the statements of this newspaper "lies." Surely, for an editor who is privileged to wield a pen and to use it in the service of others, the charge of falsehood is a serious one. If I did not prove my charge, I, in turn, would fear being classed as a calumniator. The question, then, is to see if my charge is founded in fact.

I hereby declare unhesitatingly that my charge is well founded, and I defy anyone to prove the contrary. Here then is one fact, since the *Courrier* asks us for facts:

I, the undersigned, public watchman of the Commune of Holy Cross, hereby declare that the institution of M. l'Abbé Moreau had nothing to do with the unfortunate incident that took place last Sunday, April 2, in Rue Notre-Dame. I have also heard it said very positively that the editor of the Courrier knew the facts of the case before he published in his paper the article, which attacked the said institution. Given at Sainte-Croix, April 5, 1849.

Leveau, Public Watchman

Now if it be true, as I could prove if need be, that the *Courrier* knew the truth, and the whole truth, in this deplorable affair, and if, as I heard it said to the public watchman, the editor of the *Courrier* was requested not to drag the establishment of Sainte-Croix into this affair, since it was in no way implicated — how else can we describe the language of a man who dares to publish as true what he knows to be false?

For the rest, Mr. Editor, the *Courrier* is wasting its time in trying to embitter the working classes against us. Anyone who has seen or who sees the house of Notre-Dame at close range knows well that the men who live there are not in the habit of carrying clubs and mauling the republicans who go singing past its walls.

Perhaps this letter, simple as it is, will provoke further attacks from the *Courrier.* The prospect does not frighten me; I even pardon them in advance. Once the editor, by the requested insertion, retracts the lie, which gave rise to a police investigation and aroused the hatred of the workmen against me, he can count on my unbroken silence, no matter what he may invent in the future.

Accept, Mr. Editor, the homage of my esteem.

B. Moreau

Under orders from the bailiff, the *Courrier* reproduced the above letter. It did so, however, only while recounting an old story taken from a pamphlet printed in Paris, under the title *Acts of the Apostles*, and which it kindly inserted in its issue of July 24, 1844. It pretends to clear itself on the score of the watchman's affidavit by saying that the accusation against Notre-Dame de Sainte-Croix was formal and the explanation weak. We are in a position, if he so desires, to prove that he was fully aware of publishing a falsehood and that if he has not been actually sued for libel, he owes it only to our Christian patience.

Criticism of the General Administration

I have also heard rumors accusing me of not keeping my resolution to postpone all new foundations until 1850 and of not trying to surround myself at the motherhouse with brothers who are best able to defend their interests in the general administration of the association. If you had received all the requests for teaching brothers that have come to me and which I have always answered with categorical refusals even though, strictly speaking, I did have some licensed teachers at my disposal; if you were acquainted with my confidential information to certain school directors regarding their possible imminent recall to the motherhouse; if you stopped to reflect on the way in which, for the last three years, I have turned over to three brothers the complete control of all particular and general accounts as well as the treasury, you would not be long in discrediting these rumors, which are, at least, inconsiderate. You would also recognize the sincerity of my intentions and the wisdom of my conduct.

I rejoice and am consoled in advance at the thought that I shall soon be able to prove by deeds that I could not have acted otherwise without compromising the interests of our congregation. Then, you will see that I was not speaking empty words when I repeated in our annual retreats that the day would come when the brothers' society would be represented in our councils by its ablest members and by those most worthy of unlimited confidence. In any case, I could have answered this particular complaint by reminding you that the actual members of the administration of Sainte-Croix are elected by the chapters and not by me alone.

Spirit of Faith

Lay aside then my dear sons and daughters in Jesus Christ, all these worries so characteristic of a soul not yet sufficiently guided by faith and all these anxieties of a heart still lacking confidence in the work of God. Let us, at long last, be "children of the light" (1 Thes 5:5; Eph 5:8); let us turn our attention only to the conquest of the kingdom of heaven by devoting ourselves unreservedly to the works of our vocation. If each member strives to do his best by punctually following the rules, wherever obedience has placed him, we shall soon have new triumphs to relate. You will contribute more and more to ensuring these triumphs by redoubling your devotion to St. Joseph and by spreading his association, which I recommend more than ever to your zeal. Pray, too, for the vocations that are coming either for Sainte-Croix or the Good Shepherd; in this latter house, subjects are sorely needed.

For these reasons, I have ordered and do hereby order as follows:

1. On the Saturday following the reception of this present circular, each priest will say a Mass of thanksgiving for all the favors granted the association since the twelfth of January and, especially, for the concession of full teaching rights.

2. The other members of the association, whatever may be their status, will offer a Communion for the same intentions.

The brothers in the houses that have not as yet forwarded to the motherhouse the data required by our circular of January 5, Nos. 1, 2, 3, 4, and 5 (although they should have sent them without delay), or those who have sent No. 1 and not No. 3 (which is the case with the greatest number), will forward them within a week, at the latest, after the reception of the present circular. Hardly anyone has as yet furnished for the month of January the statement asked for in No. 6.

This circular letter shall be sent by the proper authorities to all the members of our association. It will be first read in chapter or at spiritual reading, and then preserved in the archives of each house.

Given at Notre-Dame de Sainte-Croix, on the day, month, and year as above.

B. Moreau
Rector

Circular Letter 79

· ·

Solitude of St. Joseph, Le Mans
January 1, 1857

My dear sons and daughters in Jesus Christ:

May the grace of our Lord, the blessing of his mother conceived without sin, and the protection of St. Joseph be ever with you.

The six days of vacation accorded our students in honor of the visits of Msgr. de Mérode, private chamberlain of His Holiness; of Msgr. de la Bouillerie, Bishop of Carcassonne; of Msgr. Wicard, Bishop of Laval; and of our own beloved bishop afford me an opportunity to withdraw into solitude in search of the retirement that is impossible in my ordinary occupations. It is from the depths of this retreat that I reply to your New Year's greetings.

Thus cut off from the noise of the world and the distractions of the usual New Year's visits, I can the more easily hearken to the sentiments that my affection for you inspires within me at this moment. What is more, I consider it my duty to express to you the hidden thoughts of my mind, because there is no time in our lives richer than this in the abundance of the sentiments which it evokes and the gravity of the reflections which it arouses.

New Year's Reflections

As I kneel before my crucifix and reflect on the year just ended and the one which is beginning, I am filled with indescribable sadness at the thought of the past twelve months. I am moved particularly by the thought that, for me, this new year will be followed by so few others that they appear as but a few days, or rather a few hours, in the passage of the centuries. With this thought before me, I feel myself spurred on not to lose a single one of these fleeting moments, in order that I may finish my course more faithfully than I began it. What — I exclaim — the fifty-seventh year, which seemed only beginning, is now closed forever, and its stream of days has rushed headlong into eternity! Yes, so it is. And yet, a whole lifetime is made up of only a small number of these fleeting years. A few more New Year's days for him who writes these lines, and twenty or thirty more for the youngest among you to whom I write these lines, and then there will come the last day of the year and of life. This short span of years would hardly be worth bothering about if our task in it were not to perfect our lives by endeavoring to cooperate with the designs of God.

Let us, then, take care to profit by this year and, in this way, to show our gratitude to God, who has deigned to prolong our life in this world. This is the debt we owe him for all the blessings that his providence has showered upon us during the year of 1856. In this manner, we can make up for time spent uselessly or wasted in frivolous occupations; we can atone for our abuse of grace and, perhaps, even for our grave faults, which are all the more serious for being committed in the very dwelling of the saints. The best way to profit by this precious time and to reap a great abundance of merits and consolations is the sincere resolution to observe the rule faithfully. When this is done, each one then can say like the master speaking of his father: "I do always the things which please him" (Jn 8:29). What sweeter satisfaction can there be for a religious soul? How easy and pleasant this life of obedience. How safe and meritorious.

Value of Obedience

Thus, my dear sons and daughters in Jesus Christ, in recalling the peace and contentment I experienced as a simple seminarian when I had nothing else to do but to follow the common rule and obey my superiors, I find myself longing for the past and envying that time when, at the beginning of my ecclesiastical career, I was allowed to make the sacrifice of my own will. When I compare my present dispositions with the sentiments that the goodness of God then inspired in me, I am grieved to see that for so many years my position has been so different. Not only do I find myself without a guide on the path along which providence has led me—I who was so happy to be led blindly by him whom God had given me for director at the Solitude of Issy—but, even more, I find myself placed, by a series of circumstances beyond my control, at the head of a large family, which is worthy of a better father.[20] Rather, I should say, I am in command of an army, which, if it is to battle and vanquish more surely the invisible enemy of all good, needs a more able and more courageous chief. Oh, how I pity those who look with envy on my position. If it is more in view, it is likewise more exposed to all the arrows of the enemy; against it, all the fury of battle is hurled. How fervently I would thank God if, at last, I could consign this burden into the hands of him whom providence would point out as my successor. How willingly I would bow under the yoke of obedience in anticipation of the day of eternity; I would shut myself up in the obscurity of a life of retreat and silence.

I tremble, moreover, when I reflect on the strict account I shall have to give of my administration. When my mind attempts to measure the great responsibility that weighs on me, I can find no peace save in blind trust in the God of mercies, from whom I expect the help that will compensate for my weakness. Certainly, this should be enough to convince you, my dear sons and daughters in Jesus Christ, how groundless is the fear of those who link the continued existence of our congregation with my person, or who contend that the association would cease at my death—as if God needed any particular instrument to carry out his designs. Is it not written: "The foolish things of the world has God chosen, that he may confound the wise; and the weak things of the world has God chosen, that he may confound the strong" (1 Cor 1:27)?

Thus, I have the firm hope that God will, in his own quiet and strong way, finish what he deigned to begin twenty-two years ago, and I hope that my resignation or my death, far from stopping his work, will only bring his action into clearer relief and will, perhaps, even remove certain obstacles occasioned by the struggles I have had to face.

But there is one condition which is essential for the future of our congregation, a condition without which not even providence will act. This condition is your own generous cooperation and your faithful correspondence with the grace of vocation. Now, among the religious virtues demanded by this spirit, there is one which I cannot recommend too highly: obedience to your rules and your superiors. This obedience must be constant and daily; it must be a practical obedience resulting in true abnegation. If it is such, it will be a source of personal merit and the best means of drawing down the blessings of heaven on the entire association. What untold good we would do for souls if we were penetrated with the spirit and the letter of our rules, if we allowed ourselves to be guided by them with the simplicity and docility of a child obeying its nurse. This is the spirit we should have in the work of God, for we are only too fortunate to have been chosen to be his instruments.

The Religious Rule

Moreover, let us remember that our regularity will not only determine the general welfare of our association, but it will also influence our spiritual interests and the success of our apostolate. Take away the rules, and order disappears. What laws are for the physical and moral world, rules are for the religious life. They are even more than simple laws, because they enter into the smallest details of our actions, direct our conduct in even the most trifling circumstances, and aim to make all of us one in heart and spirit. The rules are the guarantee of order, economy, stability, and union. If all the rules were perfectly kept, what a beautiful spectacle we would present for both heaven and earth! In our own way we would exemplify that marvelous order that Balaam admired in the company of the Israelites: "How lovely are your tents, O Israel!" (Nm 24:5). What a source of edification the sight of our virtues would be for all our brethren, and how fragrant the good odor of Jesus Christ that we would diffuse in the world! How many souls we would win to Jesus Christ by the eloquence of our actions, many times more persuasive and powerful than mere eloquence of words! How many vocations we would attract and win for our association! These would be only some of the fruits of our fidelity to our rules, my dear sons and daughters in Jesus Christ, but they are sufficient

motives to set us off on this path, the path of the saints and of Jesus
Christ, the path which leads to heaven.

At the beginning of the new year, then, let us take a holy and firm
resolution to steep ourselves anew in the religious spirit by generously
offering to God all the little sacrifices demanded by our rules. This is my
most ardent wish for the family entrusted to me. I shall go further and say
that it is the only object of my good wishes and prayers. How grateful I
would be to God if he permitted me to see these desires realized among
the children of Holy Cross. What overflowing joy would fill my heart!
How sweet a reward for my concern! I would thank divine providence a
thousand times for having granted me such a consolation in my old age.
And so, in the name of the divine master, who did not give his disciples
peace as the world gives, I do not wish you a happy New Year with the
joy of the world. My prayers for you ask neither the happiness of this
earth nor the honors and riches which worldly persons so avidly seek, for
as the pious author of the *Imitation* says:

> It is vanity, therefore, to seek after riches, which must perish, and
> to trust in them. It is vanity also to lay one's self out for honors,
> and to raise one's self to a high station. It is vanity to follow the
> desires of the flesh, and to covet that for which we must afterward
> be grievously punished. It is vanity to wish for a long life and to
> take little care of leading a good life. It is vanity to mind only this
> present life and not to look forward to those things that are to
> come. It is vanity to love that which passes with all speed, and not
> to hasten thither where everlasting joy abides.[21]

No, my dear sons and daughters in Jesus Christ, I shall not wish you the
empty success, which only the world would acclaim; before God, such
achievements are dead and useless. My tenderness for you inspires me
with another language.

The Cross

A happy New Year in the eyes of faith is one which will count for eternity by the abundance of its merits, its holy use of time, and the practice of good works. Allow me, then, to remind you of those serious warnings of the Gospel that the sensuality of our age tends to push more and more into the background. Allow me to hope that yours will be the heritage of Jesus Christ, the heritage which his saints, our forebears in God, have bequeathed to us. It is a heritage of humiliation, poverty, and suffering, of trials, temptations, labors, and persecutions of all kinds. In vain shall we seek any way leading to heaven other than the road of Calvary. The whole teaching of the Gospel is summed up in the science of the folly of the cross, which St. Paul announced to the Gentiles when he preached to them only Jesus and him crucified, a scandal to the Jews and folly to the Gentiles (1 Cor 1:23). Would it be proper, then, for us who aspire to walk in the footsteps of so many illustrious models, to refuse the burden of the cross that they have so gloriously borne?

The saints, to quote again the author of the *Imitation*, served God in hunger and thirst, in cold and nakedness, in labor and weariness, in countless trials and tribulations.[22] And we, disciples of the same master, what have we to suffer, what mortifications have we to practice, what weariness have we to bear? Is not the life of these generous athletes of the faith an open condemnation of our own? Let us, at least, learn to atone for our weakness by accepting generously and wholeheartedly the little sacrifices entailed by the life we have embraced. By exemplary exactitude to our rules and exercises, let us show that we know how to appease the justice of God and to compensate in our humble way for the privations of a life of penance. Be assured, my dear sons and daughters in Jesus Christ, that we must make expiation for our sins either here or hereafter. Even now we can satisfy the claims of penance against us if, during this new year, we practice charity according to the rule, forgive our mutual offenses, and, if need be, make noble amends for our own faults. For we must ever bear in mind that the happiness of our community life and the necessary condition of all our success depend on fraternal charity and union. This union must not only embrace the members of each house but, with still greater reason, must extend to all the houses of the congregation, since they are all but different branches of one same tree.

The duty of expiation will be satisfied if superiors gain the good will of their subjects and know how to win their confidence by the sweet bonds of affection, never forgetting that they are responsible before God for the souls of their subjects and are bound to provide for their spiritual need with paternal solicitude, especially in what regards fidelity to their exercises of piety. All of us can do penance if we scrupulously fulfill the grave obligations of our vows of obedience, poverty, and chastity; if we frequent the sacraments, those veritable wellsprings of life, as prescribed in the calendar; and if, in all our institutions, we emulate the motherhouse in its strict observance of the rule of silence.

We can placate the anger of God by punctuality in rising and fidelity to meditation, particular examen, community meals, spiritual reading, prompt retiring, and the monthly retreat. Let us recite the Little Office, or the prayers substituted for it, with true devotion, and let us, under proper direction, conscientiously employ the time set aside for study. Fidelity to the rule demands that we should not leave the house or write letters without the knowledge of our superior or director and that we never miss holy Mass, the visit to the Blessed Sacrament, or the hour of adoration.

The spirit of penance requires, furthermore, that those of us who are permitted to do so know how to mortify their senses by observing the fasts prescribed by the Church and the rule, and that those who are dispensed content themselves on those days with the ordinary breakfast and give up something at dinner or supper. Modesty must shine forth in our whole exterior and prevent any affectation in our demeanor, particularly in the care taken of the hair.

The Rule and Education

If we are faithful to our rule, we must take care that the ten thousand children confided to our care are educated according to its norms and that familiarity with them should be guarded against at all times. Our rules certainly ensure the necessary training for the mind, but their first and foremost concern is with the formation of the heart through the development of those religious dispositions that alone can make a good person and a Christian. Hence, our sublime but difficult mission should be fulfilled with that happy blending of gentleness and firmness, prudence and vigilance, which is the secret of all successful education. We can count on God's help if we devise means of making virtue attractive for youth, by establishing and multiplying among them those pious and charitable associations that afford an outlet for praiseworthy activity and, at the same time, make the practice of virtue easy by rendering it pleasant. Among these associations, I recommend particularly those of St. Joseph and of the holy infancy. Hence, we must secure solid vocations for our work and attract to our boarding schools students or pupils who are willing to be taught. We are faithful to our duties to God, finally, if we form our novices and postulants to the religious life according to the rule and directory, and if in all our houses the affairs of temporal administration are treated in council or chapter, according as the rule prescribes, without incurring any extraordinary expense not authorized by legitimate authority.

Regular Discipline

To these points of rule, my dear sons and daughters in Jesus Christ, I attach a very special importance. I ask you to pay special attention to them during the new year, for I know full well from the replies to the questionnaire sent to each establishment that some of our houses leave much to be desired on many of these points. Nevertheless, all of them are essential for regularity and good order. May the new year be marked by greater fidelity to the practices and duties I have just mentioned. May it mean for each one of you new progress along the road of perfection in which we are all striving to advance.

In exchange for your good wishes, I offer you these prayers from the very bottom of my heart. If they are heard, all the days of this year will be, in the language of the holy scripture, full days: *Invenientur in eis dies pleni* ("There will be found in them full days" [Ps 73:10]). Each day and each hour will merit for you in eternity that treasure of merits and that immense weight of glory of which the great apostle speaks. I shall go further and add that a year lived in this way will be a year of happiness, because you will taste therein the peace of our Lord promised to those who love and observe his law. You will likewise experience that ineffable joy which expands the heart of the just man and makes it celebrate an endless feast.

Consecration of the Conventual Church

But our greatest incentive to make good use of the new year is the thought that it will be signaled by an event that will redound to the glory of our entire congregation. At last I can announce that the consecration of our conventual church has been fixed for Wednesday, June 10. I doubt if we shall ever have a more memorable day, or witness a more touching spectacle. Already, in spirit, I can see the dawn of that day whose vigil we shall consecrate by prayer and fasting; I behold in vision the majestic procession of bishops and abbots as it circles around this new temple, accompanied by the chant of solemn hymns. I see the holy relics carried in triumph while the assembly invokes the entire heavenly court. I hear the terrible exorcisms being pronounced against the powers of darkness; I see the crosses painted on twelve columns, the mystical sprinklings, the holy anointings, the lighting of candles, and the scattering of ashes on the holy pavement, on which the officiating prelate will then proceed to trace the mysterious letters of a twofold alphabet. Everything in this new edifice will be sanctified: the foundations on which it rests, the walls which give it shape, the vaulted ceiling which crowns it, the sanctuary where the venerable bishop will offer up the Holy Sacrifice for the first time, and, lastly, the altars on which the adorable victim will thereafter be immolated.

But to what purpose would be the blessing of these stones, cut and arranged at such expense, if we, the living and spiritual temples which these stones represent, were not found pure and holy in the eyes of the sovereign majesty? Is it not especially in our hearts that he wishes to set up his throne and to reside as in his true sanctuary? Will it be possible that, even then, there will be souls in the congregation who are inhabited and possessed by the demon? Let us bear in mind that, as it is written, we are the temples of God, that his Spirit dwells in us, and that this temple is sacred (1 Cor 3:16).

These temples of ours are much more sacred than the material edifice where we gather to pray. On the day of our Baptism were we not exorcised, anointed, washed, and purified by the sacramental waters of Baptism so as to become spiritual temples? And has not Holy Communion made us many times more-sacred receptacles of Jesus Christ than the consecrated vessels that contain his body and blood in our churches? Unlike the sacred vessels, we do not merely contain this flesh and blood; we really make it part of ourselves. That is why, as St. Paul says, God will destroy whosoever violates his holy temple (1 Cor 3:17). What a terrible misfortune it would be if the Savior of the world, when he comes for the solemn dedication of his church in union with all the elect of heaven, purgatory, and earth, should find even one single member of the family of Holy Cross cast off as a worthless stone, unfit for the edifice for which it had been fashioned.

To escape this terrible fate, we must constantly strive, by purifying ourselves in the sacrament of Penance and by frequently approaching the Eucharistic table where a God gives himself to be the food of our souls, to become true temples of the Holy Spirit. God grant that, on the day of the dedication that I now announce to you, there may not be a single one among you, my dear sons and daughters in Jesus Christ, who will not have answered this appeal. If it be so, then not only the conventual church of the motherhouse will be consecrated, but the entire congregation will itself be dedicated to the Lord.

In conclusion, my dear brothers and sisters in Jesus Christ, I should like to reply to those who have asked why I spent so much money in the construction of this church. The reason is that I wished to leave to the family of Holy Cross a temple where at times all its members might meet in common prayer, and a sanctuary to arouse the respect and build up the piety of the pupils in the college attached to the motherhouse, and which, at the same time, would be of service to the people of the neighborhood. My idea was to erect a lasting memorial of our love and gratitude to Jesus Christ, the sole founder of our congregation, whose Sacred Heart has been made the object of our titular feast; to Mary, whose protection over our work has always been so evident; and, finally, to St. Joseph, who has so often showed himself its guardian. Besides, from the very beginning, I have often thought that, if I could build a dwelling place for God, which would be as worthy of him as our limited resources would allow, his providence would never leave us without a home in the different places to which he would call us, and, above all, he would deign to admit us into the abode of his glory. Finally, I felt that we could find no better use for the proceeds of our lottery, which, after all, was authorized exclusively for this purpose, or for the funds that I had accumulated from the generous gift of one of my fellow priests and the legacy left to me by Fr. Dubignon.[23]

Financial Administration

I need not add that the temporary financial difficulties of Notre-Dame de Sainte-Croix cannot be blamed on the expenses incidental to the construction of this church. On the contrary, my dear sons and daughters in Jesus Christ, the interest of truth obliges me to declare to all who endeavored to calumniate my administration when work on our chapel was suspended that prudence alone advised me to stop building. Besides, our difficulties of last year were not caused by lack of foresight but by the unusually high cost of living and the unpaid loans made to several of our houses some years past. In this connection, it is good for the congregation at large to know that I loaned 13,500 francs to Notre-Dame du Lac, which today is demanding the return of the amount I have received in partial payment; 11,713 francs to St. Laurent, Canada; 5,072 francs to the houses of New

Orleans; 9,000 francs to the Novitiate of Montjean, which is now located in the magnificent chateau of Maulévrier; 10,000 francs for the purchase and remodeling of our house of studies in Rome; and 45,000 francs to our college in Paris. Add to these loans the expenses incurred by the mother-house in the training of subjects for these different foundations.

On this occasion, I must remind the superiors of all our houses, especially in America, that our constitutions forbid them to build, purchase, or alienate property, or to contract loans or mortgages, without the formal authorization of the superior general. The superior general strongly condemns all that has been done to this point contrary to these rules, which are so full of wisdom and of foresight, and he hereby forbids every superior, in virtue of holy obedience, to incur any extraordinary expense in the future without proper permission. Neither can I overlook any longer the negligence of some of our chapters or councils abroad, which fail to make daily entries of their receipts and expenses, to balance their accounts weekly, and to fill out carefully and in proper form the quarterly statistics to be sent to our general steward. Whoever continues in this line of conduct seriously compromises his administration; furthermore, he not only endangers his salvation, but he also exposes himself to inflicting grave injury upon the interests of others.

I also wish to observe that useless correspondence and traveling are as contrary to economy and religious poverty as they are to the spirit of seclusion and recollection. But while, on the one hand, superiors and directors must put an end to these abuses immediately, on the other hand, they should permit their subjects to correspond freely with their relatives, provided such correspondence is necessary and prepaid. Needless to say, relatives are expected to prepay the postage of their own correspondence. In this connection, I recommend that unusually heavy paper not be used, particularly such as often comes from our houses in America. As for France, I recommend that everyone watch the weight of his letters so that they will not be surcharged for lack of sufficient postage. If they are, these charges will be refused by the motherhouse.

Perpetual Adoration

Lastly, among the practices of piety in use in our congregation, there is one which I cannot recommend strongly enough, my dear sons and daughters in Jesus Christ, because its faithful practice is the richest source of divine blessings for us and for our houses. I refer to the perpetual adoration of the Blessed Sacrament. Hence, I call the attention of each and all of our members to this pious exercise and place upon superiors the responsibility of seeing that it is carried out every day as follows: in the United States, from 6:00 a.m. to 8:00 a.m.; in Canada, from 4:00 p.m. to 6:00 p.m.; in Italy, from 1:00 p.m. to 2:00 p.m.; in Bengal, from 2:00 p.m. to 3:00 p.m.; in New Orleans, from 3:00 p.m. to 4:00 p.m.; and elsewhere, according to the local meridian.

I close this letter by convoking the following capitulants at Notre-Dame de Sainte-Croix on June 9 next:[24] *[Editor's note: the priest, brother, and sister capitulant lists for the upcoming general chapter are not included here for reasons of space.]*

Preparation for Consecration

In order to prepare ourselves in a holy manner for the dedication of our conventual church, to give thanks to God, and to profit by this great solemnity, there will be at Notre-Dame de Sainte-Croix, first of all, a three-day retreat for the community, though it will be particularly for the students, especially those who are preparing for First Communion. (The ceremony of First Communion is postponed this year to Tuesday, June 9). Secondly, there shall be an octave of high Masses and of benedictions preceded by a sermon. During this octave, there will be special exercises for the associates of St. Joseph, in the morning for the women and in the evening for the men.

On Tuesday, the vigil of our great solemnity, all the members of the congregation who are not legitimately prevented will fast. The next day, all, without exception, will receive Holy Communion if possible and renew their vows in private during their thanksgiving. That same day will be a holiday, with a walk for the students. In the evening, before or after night prayer, the *Te Deum* shall be sung or recited, and if possible, the facade of the house shall be illuminated.[25]

Altar Wine

Since it is very important to provide our houses abroad with pure wine for the Holy Sacrifice as well as for the use of the sick, I am happy to assure all the superiors that, if they address their requests directly to the steward of Notre-Dame de Sainte-Croix, their orders will be filled promptly and conscientiously and at lower prices than they have hitherto had to pay. On this matter, I have had an understanding with a trustworthy individual. This proposition may be of special interest to our mission in Bengal, to Notre-Dame du Lac, and to New Orleans. This same offer can be made to other religious communities in these localities; the motherhouse will accept responsibility for meeting all orders.

Various Prescriptions

Before closing this letter, I believe it my duty (1) to postpone all new foundations for at least two years in order the better to train our subjects and to bring back to the novitiate those who need further formation; (2) to remind directors of schools that they may not allow their unlicensed teaching brothers to devote to the study of music the time necessary to prepare for their examination; (3) to forbid all subjects to keep money or to dispose of it contrary to the rule on the vow of poverty; (4) to demand the repayment of money already advanced before authorizing any extraordinary expense in our houses abroad; (5) to command, in virtue of the vow of obedience, all who are in charge of accounts to enter their receipts and expenses daily, without any omission, and to send their quarterly reports to the general steward, after having made them out conscientiously and after having had them signed by the proper authority.

This circular letter shall be read in its entirety at the chapter or the spiritual reading following its reception and shall afterward be preserved in the archives of each house.

Given at Notre-Dame de Sainte-Croix under our signature, the seal of the congregation, and the countersignature of our secretary, on the day, month, and year as above.

Moreau

Superior General

Lamy

Secretary General

Circular Letter 96

· ·

Solitude of the Savior, Le Mans
June 16, 1858

Dear fathers and brothers:

May the grace of our Lord, the blessing of his mother conceived without sin, and the protection of St. Joseph be ever with you.

It is with a heart full of shame and regret that I reply to all the expressions of kindness and affection that your charity inspired you to send me on my feast day. The simple remembrance of what my holy patron was and what I have been up to the present in the Congregation of Holy Cross fills me with confusion. My conscience cries out, in fact, that for these last twenty-two years I have not ceased to be more or less of an obstacle to the grace that should have flowed into your souls through my ministry. If I heeded only this inner voice, I would write to His Holiness this very day and, with an earnestness inspired by the conviction of my wretchedness, would lay the burden of my generalship at his feet.

On the other hand, another voice tells me that by such an action I would occasion you anxiety and demoralize your spirit of generous service. It is this which keeps me at the perilous post where divine providence has placed me and prevents me from yielding to the sadness which threatens to overwhelm me in the solitude in which I write these lines. Have pity on my shortcomings, dear fathers and well-beloved brothers, and ask our Lord to give me the qualities I lack so that I may govern the congregation according to the fullness of my desires.

Ask him, particularly, that before his justice summons me to give an account of my administration, his mercy may grant me the grace to provide a more perfect religious formation to those whom he sends to us. For when I look out from the heart of this retreat over the distant lands where zeal has led you and keeps you so courageously, I regret that I have been unable to keep you a little while longer at the motherhouse before exposing you to all the dangers of a world where so much bad example entices to evil, where so many false principles echo in your ears, and where the wicked spirit already finds so much unconscious acquiescence in your poor hearts. Oh, what a misfortune to risk one's self-vigilance, reflection, and modesty, which is the fruit of solitude! Going out into the world without this habit is like marching unarmed against the enemy and foolhardily risking a one-sided battle where defeat is inevitable. This explains why between our annual retreats there are so many failures and defeats.

Spirit of Prayer

Be eager, then, dear fathers and well-beloved brothers, to come and renew your zeal in the annual retreat, which you will make whenever obedience calls. Try to make this retreat as soon as vacation begins. In its shadows, let us love to hide ourselves for a few days from the eyes of the world. Let us cherish the silence that marks those on retreat and love the sacred walls of this solitude where we spent such quiet days and which now shelter us from the main attacks of the enemy.

To the love of retreat let us join a love of prayer, for without prayer even the most charming solitude is as a land without water, producing only briars and thorns. But a desert watered by prayer grows and flourishes, takes on an air of joy, and is adorned with delicious fruits, because it draws down the blessings of heaven on those who dwell there. In fact, it is in order to pray better that we, like the apostles in the Cenacle, gather together at this time under the protection of Mary. It was, moreover, to teach us how to pray, to form thus within us a new heart, that providence gave us the period of the novitiate. Since that happy time, if you have been faithful to your rules, prayer should be the beginning and the end of your studies. It should awake with you and take its place at your bedside. It should accompany you even in your recreations and perfume all your occupations as with a divine balm. This is why you were given the admirable book of the Little Office of the Blessed Virgin, or the Breviary, at the reception of the habit.[26] From it, we are to pray several times a day, and it is to rest at our side in the tomb, as if still to pray in our stead when our mouths are closed in death and no longer opened to sing the praises of God. Directors and superiors should see to it, then, that each religious makes his meditation daily at least during the allotted time, because meditation is the prayer par excellence in which God speaks to our heart and our heart speaks to him without words. Without meditation no one will ever be a good religious.

Spirit of Study

Yet, we shall accomplish very imperfectly the designs of providence on each of us if to the love of retirement and prayer we do not apply ourselves at the same time, as did St. Basil, to cultivating our intellects and enriching our minds with the knowledge proper to our state and acquired for the honor of our congregation. How many things we have to learn! We have only to recall the duties of the priest or the teacher to understand how frightful would be our responsibility to religion, parents, and ourselves were we to neglect to acquire or preserve the knowledge proper to our vocation. Let us make good use of all our leisure time, so as to increase the fund of information that will make us more useful to the congregation and build up the reputation of its members. Above all, let us not only study, but let us also observe the liturgy and ceremonies of the Church, the rubrics, and sacred chant, and let us be faithful to our rules and constitutions. Such, moreover, is the example given us by the great doctor whose name I have the honor to bear. May we all imitate him as well as we can, each one within the limits of his obedience.

Perseverance

God grant that in the world we may not belie the good opinion formed of us during our novitiate or during the annual retreat. May we be ever faithful to our promises and always mindful of the holiness of our vocation. May no one fall into that serious error, all too common among us, of believing that there are two rules of conduct for the religious of Holy Cross, the one more rigid for the novitiate and the motherhouse, the other more elastic for the time we spend outside these houses when engaged in the active life. On the contrary, let us show ourselves such as we were, or, at least, should have been, in the quiet of solitude: humble, devoted to the rule, mortified, innocent, and occupied with study and prayer when we have no other duties to perform.

Since, however, our sad experience with the inconstancy of our hearts prevents us from trusting in even our better resolutions, let us go to him who holds in his hands the will of humans. Let us ask him to establish and confirm us in well doing and to proportion his grace to our needs and weaknesses. In a word, let us beg him to bring us out of the combat against the enemy of our salvation with an increase of virtue and merits, rather than as cowards who have yielded to temptation and thus dishonored the habit we wear.

In conclusion, I beg all superiors and directors to take my *Christian Education* and the rules for spiritual reading from now until the next retreat, to reestablish or maintain silence in the times and the places exacted by the rules, never to allow novices or postulants to go out alone, and, especially, never to tolerate under any pretext the least familiarity with the students. Furthermore, they should see to it that no teacher receives or sends away a student without their permission, and that no one who has struck a pupil escape the penances mentioned in the rule.

Lastly, I recommend to your prayers the soul of Br. Cyprian, professed, who was already dying when I visited Notre-Dame du Lac. He passed away at 4:00 a.m. on May 15, after receiving the sacraments of Penance, Holy Eucharist, and Extreme Unction. He was, his superior writes, an excellent religious, a true model of simple obedience and generosity, who suffered cruelly for eight months, but always with admirable patience. May his example encourage those who survive him in the congregation to obey without argument and without discouragement.

The present circular letter shall be read in its entirety at the chapter or the spiritual reading which follows its reception and then preserved in the archives of each house after being translated into English and German for our houses in America.

Given at Le Mans under our signature, the countersignature of our secretary general, and the seal of our congregation, the day, month, and year as above.

The Superior General

B. Moreau

By order:

The Secretary General

Lamy

P.S. I wish to remind all who correspond with the motherhouse that they must always stamp their letters, otherwise they will not be accepted.

I have not continued my visits since my return from America because unforeseen events have kept me at the motherhouse.

Those who have no opportunity to procure copies of the rules and constitutions at Notre-Dame de Sainte-Croix will receive them either during the annual retreat or by mail.

Circular Letter 137

· ·

Notre-Dame de Sainte-Croix, Le Mans *January 3, 1861*

May the grace of our Lord, the blessing of his mother conceived without sin, and the protection of St. Joseph be always with you.[27]

New Year's Wishes

It is a great consolation to me, dear fathers and well-beloved brothers, to begin each year with the good wishes you express for me and those which God inspires in me for you. Let me say for my part that if the warmth of these good wishes is to be in proportion to the motives of him who utters them, and to his interest in those to whom he offers them, no one in the world could wish you a happy New Year more sincerely or more fervently than myself. My good wishes are those of a father for apostles of Jesus Christ and for children whom I cherish with all my heart. I offer them to our Lord to the end that you may be happy on earth with the happiness of the just and happy in heaven with the blessedness of the elect. I offer these wishes for the prosperity of your houses, for your sanctification, and for the perfection of all the work entrusted to us. I do not, of course, forget the supreme head of the Church, who is so sorely tried and to whom as religious we owe all that we are today.

Yet, even though it is a pleasure to wish you happiness in this new year, I cannot repress a certain feeling of sadness, and my heart is heavy as I see the years succeed one another so rapidly and disappear so completely as to leave nothing behind but the recollection of the good or bad use we have made of them. In very truth, what food for deep and salutary reflection we find in this thought of the shortness of our days here below.

We seem almost able to touch the year that has just ended, and yet there is an eternity between it and the year which now opens before us. Ah, the years, which flit by so quickly, should lead us on to those that will never end, just as rivers carry us back to the depths of the ocean where they disappear. Since the years of time are given to us in order that we may merit happiness in the years of eternity, let us look seriously into the use we have made of the twelve months just passed, so that by making a holier use of the time still remaining to us, we may redeem whatever time we may have lost. How will God judge us for this year? Has the year of 1860 really been for us a religious and a holy year? Only if it has been such will it weigh in our favor in the scales of the sovereign judge, for years passed in lukewarmness and sin are not worth enough to be recorded in the book of life and merit a reward.

I thank God, dear fathers and well-beloved brothers, for the regularity, fervor, and generosity of the greater number among you. I beg him to grant you the grace of perseverance and to make you ever more perfect models, whom the other members of the community may always imitate. But my soul is troubled and saddened when I think of some who have hitherto shown so little religious spirit, so much slothfulness in rising, so little preparation for meditation, so little recollection in prayer, so little devotion during the sacrifice of the Mass, so little fidelity to the Little Office of the Blessed Virgin. They have evidenced much levity in their looks, much haste in their step, lack of reflection in their words, dissipation in times of work and silence, indiscretion in their conversation, and lack of mortification at their meals. It pains me to add that these same religious have shown little obedience of the mind, docility of will, or readiness to work. Even though they have pronounced the vows of obedience, chastity, and poverty, they have proved themselves slaves to the threefold concupiscence and, in a word, have manifested pride, ambition, jealousy, suspicion, irritability, stubbornness, and sensuality.[28]

Can it be true that there are some among you to whom we could apply these words of the apostle, which the world, especially in recent years, verifies in so terrifying a manner: "There are many among you who are enemies of the cross of Christ and who have no taste except for what is carnal and earthly" (Phil 3:18–19)? If such were the case, I would tremble for their salvation, and I would see in their conduct one of the greatest obstacles to the blessings of divine providence that the devil can place in the way of the family of Holy Cross. This opposition to good, this aversion to the cross, this idolatry of self, this love of one's own judgment, will, comforts, and conveniences—all this constitutes the inexhaustible source of all the relaxation, resistance to grace, temptations, falls, and sins, as well as all the calamities of our own time. Why? Because in the very words of the Gospel, self-abnegation and mortification of the flesh constitute the essential basis of all virtue and, consequently, of all moral good.[29] In fact, without it one cannot be—I shall not say a religious—even a good Christian.

As a matter of fact, dear fathers and well-beloved brothers, Christianity—and with still greater reason the religious life—is nothing else than the life of Jesus Christ reproduced in our conduct. What is the life of Jesus Christ? It is a poor crib and a cross of sorrow, and between this crib and this cross thirty years of abnegation and sacrifice. Living the life of Jesus Christ means struggling unto death against the flesh and sin and warring relentlessly against the world and all its vanities.

The first Christians understood this lesson well—they who sold their possessions and gave the price to the poor and then, with the cross on their shoulders, followed their divine master even up to Calvary. They reproduced the generous examples of the ancient prophets of whom St. Paul said that some were tortured, refusing to accept release, that they might find a better resurrection (Heb 11:35). Others experienced mockery and stripes—yes, even chains and prison. They were stoned, sawed asunder, tempted, and put to death by the sword. For long years, these heroes of the faith were seen like travelers and wanderers, clothed in sheepskins and goatskins, destitute, distressed, exiled from a world that was unworthy of them, wandering in deserts, mountains, caves, and holes in the earth. Now, would you know the secret of these austere virtues and of this heroic generosity? It is found entirely in the doctrine of self-renunciation, detachment from all things, and crucifixion of the flesh.

Exhortation to the Vows

Because this moral teaching of the Gospel is hardly known today, people's sole concern is for an easy and sensual life; they seek whatever gratifies the flesh and shun anything that mortifies it. This explains why we must witness the gradual and noticeable disappearance of greatness of soul, generosity of heart, ardency of zeal, and courage of sacrifice. What is still more deplorable is that this spirit of the world, buried in sensuality, works its way even into religious communities. As a result, some religious, after offering themselves through the vows of poverty, chastity, and obedience, hesitate to sacrifice the Isaac whom they should immolate completely unless they wish to frustrate the designs of providence on themselves, their house, or even the entire congregation. In their blindness, they fail to see that deliberate relaxation, sought out with all the subtleties of a mind clever at disguising sensuality under the outward pretense of imaginary need of prolonged rest or special food, weighs no less heavily in the scales of God than the mortal sins to which such laxness usually leads. I beg of God—and this is the most ardent wish of my heart—to open for such religious the eyes of faith and to make them see the pit which they are digging beneath their very feet: *Utinam saperent et intelligerent, ac novissima providerent* ("If they were wise, they would understand this; they would discern what the end would be" [Dt 32:29]).

As for you, my dear fathers and well-beloved brothers, who have guarded yourselves against this state of languor and softness by rising to the heights of your sublime vocation through fidelity to your rule, walk to the very end in the path of perfection upon which you have entered and love God with all your mind, and heart, and strength. If to all of this you add love of neighbor, which is inseparable from the love of our father who is in heaven, you will resist these encroachments of the examples and maxims of a world that is at enmity with the cross of Jesus Christ.

May all of us understand that ordinary virtue is no longer sufficient to save either us or the youth entrusted to us. If education was ever a difficult work from the Christian viewpoint, it is assuredly so today, when parents almost seem leagued together to ruin our young people by raising them in the school of a world wrapped up in materialism. Oh, who will grant us the grace to inspire these young souls with the spirit of renunciation and sacrifice and thus to save them from the corruption, which threatens those of every age and condition of life? To this end let us pray and work; let us be on our guard and sacrifice ourselves, fixing our eyes on our divine model, without ever allowing the grace of our vocation to grow weak within us.

The hour to rise from sleep is at hand (Rom 13:11). The Church is at grips with hell. Her supreme head is a captive in the midst of his own people, and everything indicates that the wrath of God and the fury of the populace are about to break loose.[30] I urge you, therefore, to pray more fervently than ever before, to make the novena to St. Michael, which you will find on the accompanying leaflet, and to recite the Little Office with special devotion and exactitude. I ask you also to be very orderly and economical in your administration and to receive graciously the drafts that are sent to you on the enclosed sheet.

I authorize and even command those whom their superiors or directors will have found sufficiently prepared to present themselves for the next examinations, either for the *brevet* or the baccalaureate.[31]

From the obligation of having a safe with two different locks, I dispense those directors whose only assistant is a novice. They must, nevertheless, still sign and forward their quarterly statement.

I beg of you not to neglect the teaching of singing, especially of religious chant.

Finally, I recommend that you send your proposed budgets sufficiently early for their consideration by the provincial chapters at their annual meeting, so that they may be subsequently returned to the different houses.

I conclude by revoking all prohibitions and commands that I may have hitherto issued in virtue of holy obedience.

This present circular shall be read in chapter and then preserved in the archives of each house.

Given at Notre-Dame de Sainte-Croix, the day, month, and year as above.

B. Moreau
Superior General

Circular Letter 179

. . . .

Notre-Dame de Sainte-Croix, Le Mans
January 10, 1865

Reverend fathers and dear brothers:

I am availing myself of my very first spare moments since the close of the provincial chapter of France to thank you for your New Year's greetings and to revive your confidence for the future of the work entrusted to us, notwithstanding its manifold trials during the year of 1864. I know full well that these troubles have caused you no little worry. Besides, it is my binding duty to encourage you to remain firm in fidelity to your vocation, in order that by withstanding the illusions of the devil and the allurements of the world or the flesh, you may obtain the reward that has been promised to virtue.

Be not surprised, then, at the violent storm that has been stirred up against the Congregation of Holy Cross by the enemy of all good. Neither should you be frightened over our financial crisis, which is lessening steadily, nor over the scandal given by some of our members and the defection of certain subjects who, like cowards, have abandoned the master after having been showered with his blessings.[32] You should not be disheartened by the incredible facility with which several religious have blackened and calumniated in the eyes of Rome the very congregation that received them into her bosom, instead of upholding her honor and her reputation by word and deed. These are ungrateful children who have torn the heart of their own mother and have deserved to have applied to them the words of Isaiah: "I have brought up children and have exalted them, but they have despised me" (Is 1:2).

For my own part, reverend fathers and dear brothers, I am not the least surprised by all these trials. Thanks be to God, they have only increased my confidence in him who alone has founded and maintained this congregation. He it is who will expand it more and more, provided we do not lend a helping hand to the devil who would destroy it because he sees us snatching souls from him. How, in fact, could he remain indifferent when he beholds the ten thousand students confided to our care and the many others who are saved from hell by our apostolic ministry? Hence, I am not surprised at the snares he lays for your faith, but Jesus Christ is faithful, and he will not permit you to be tempted beyond your strength. If we but know how to awaken him from his seeming sleep by our prayers, he will command the winds and the storm and we shall have once more the calm of bygone days (Mk 4:35–41). This peace of mind and heart has already made itself felt in the chapter over which I have just presided, and the members of the chapter found therein new light and encouragement.

Necessity of Crosses

Bear in mind and do not forget, reverend fathers and well-beloved brothers, that just as divine providence has willed its greatest works to begin in humility and abjection, it has also decreed that they should expand only at the price of difficulties and contradictions, trials, crosses, contempt, calumny, and detraction. Its purpose in so decreeing is that the first materials of these spiritual edifices may be tried as gold in the fire. Is not this the eloquent lesson of the touching mystery of Bethlehem, which we are now celebrating? What is the message of this stable, this crib, these swaddling clothes, and these poor shepherds? Did not persecution greet this infant God when he came into the world that he was to save by dying on the cross covered with opprobrium? Did not his apostles, too, drink of the bitter chalice of his passion? And was not the fruit of all this suffering the founding of the Church and the conversion of the Gentiles?

Consequently, although the trials undergone by the Congregation of Holy Cross have been numerous and cruel, yet, far from breaking or uprooting this growing plant, they should, on the contrary, strengthen and fortify it, make it fruitful, and at the same time purify the virtue of those who do not allow themselves to lose heart, and increase their knowledge of God. Hence, we must have the hope that we shall happily complete our course under the auspices of the Church, which has deigned to approve our undertaking and has just accorded us, in the decrees with which you are already familiar, a new proof of its solicitude for us.

Rejoice then instead of being worried or discouraged, when you find temptation striking at the congregation or at yourselves. Rejoice particularly if the devil attacks you through the senses by making them rebel against your soul. Far from believing thereby that you have missed your vocation, take advantage of the occasion to strengthen yourselves in it, for the greatest saints have undergone similar trials, especially St. Anthony, St. Benedict, St. Bernard, and St. Francis of Assisi.

Confidence in God

It follows that the many different trials to which we have been subjected are indubitable marks of the divine will in regard to our congregation and of the presence of our Lord in our midst. No one but God could have carried this institute through its many financial and moral crises. Were it not for his grace, how many of us, like many others, would have yielded to the temptation to turn back? What snares were laid in the path of inexperienced young brothers whose good dispositions gave such happy promise. Alas! Why did they have to become victims of the world and the devil? At least learn from their sad example, my dear brothers. I refer especially to those of you who write me occasionally: "I am too severely tempted against the most beautiful of all virtues to believe that God calls me to the vow of chastity." If the saints whom I have just mentioned had reasoned thus, where would they be today? Is not such a complaint a misunderstanding of the words of the archangel who said to the venerable father of young Tobias: "Because you were pleasing to God, it was necessary that temptation should try you" (Tb 12:13)?

Be glad, then, reverend fathers and dear brothers, that you have been found worthy to suffer in body and soul and to share in the sufferings of this institute. Be glad and increase your confidence in proportion to your suffering, just as I personally suffer more tribulations, since these trials are a sure guarantee of the divine will toward us and the work whose instruments we are. The devil roared in vain when he brought into our midst false brethren who raised against the motherhouse the arms of calumny, envy, ignorance, jealousy, love of money, corruption of heart, and even the indiscreet zeal of some good men who believed they were doing God's work when they tried to destroy us. Yet, in all this I have not, thank God, even for so much as one moment lost confidence in the future. Less than ever am I fearful when I reflect on what the Holy See has just done for us, without mentioning that out of the 210,000 francs owed by the former Br. Marie-Julien, there remain but 60,000 francs to be paid, as the provincial chapter, which I have just closed, attested for itself.[33] If I mention this fact, it is only to reassure those of you who are frightened at our financial condition. It is also to offset an accusation made against me in America, where someone is supposed to have said that no one knew what I have done with the funds of the congregation. God is my witness that since the beginning of Notre-Dame de Sainte-Croix I have always kept my council informed of our receipts and expenses. On this score my death will disclose nothing of which my councilors and the general chapter were not informed at the proper time and place, according as the events were taking place.

Therefore, even should persecution redouble rather than diminish, as is the case now, there would be no reason to fear for God's work. All the malice of the world and hell cannot change the will of the Lord, nullify his sovereign rights, render useless the work of his power, or make foolish the designs of his wisdom. No, my reverend fathers and well-loved brothers, a hundred times, no. For myself, my only fears are for our sins, the violation of our rules and constitutions, attachment to self-will, lack of self-denial, idleness, ambition, and pride, with which perhaps our consciences reproach us in moments of self-examination and for which Cardinal Barnabo reprimanded us in a recent letter.[34] Hence, it is that I am far from frightened when I see the slaves of these passions leave our ranks. I tremble for their salvation and grieve over their sad lot. I see in them the answer to the prayer that morning after morning we say to St.

Joseph: "Look down upon this house with a propitious eye; bring to it subjects who will glorify God, and do not suffer any unworthy therein."

I know, reverend fathers and well-beloved brothers, that almost all of those who left us regretted it later; some have even applied to me for readmission. I know, too, that some novices, who were shaken in their vocation by inordinate passions, may still continue to abuse grace and follow along the road that leads to perdition, instead of that into which divine mercy has led them. Yet, I shall have no fears for the congregation, and even if all of you had abandoned me on hearing of our catastrophes, I should have begun all over again as soon as I could, so convinced am I that what I have undertaken is the will of God. If, indeed, you had then looked back, Jesus Christ would have chosen other workers to take your place.

Nevertheless, thanks to his infinite goodness, you have persevered, and if I except two or three houses, I have received from all superiors and directors, not to speak of the provincial capitulants of France and some of the teaching brothers, the most touching assurances of affection and devotedness in their own name and in the name of their little families.

May those who have thus consoled me accept here and now my thanks and, I shall add, my felicitations. May they grow more and more devoted to the rule, frequent the sacraments or celebrate holy Mass worthily, perform their duties according to the rule, and be as economical as prudence may allow. If need be, they should make a loan for May 1, payable in three or four months, or even a year, with a guarantee of my signature in the latter case, in order to avoid all loans from notaries. In this way, our debt will be noticeably diminished.

As to vocations, pray much, encourage any you may find, and be assured that if we are the religious we should be, nothing necessary will ever be wanting to us. As our assurance of this, we have the very words of the Gospel.

Fr. Drouelle will inform you of the date of his arrival at our college at Paris. I have appointed the following as members of his council: Fr. Champeau, assistant, and Fr. Sauvayre, steward; Br. Arpajon and Br. Milly will complete the council. In case Br. Marcellus is called elsewhere, I appoint the Director of Tréport. Fr. Chappé will be at the Novitiate of the Savior before the end of this month, and later a suitable brother will be appointed to the Novitiate of St. Joseph. I have named Fr. Gillespie general steward and Fr. Dubourg general treasurer.

I shall not close without telling you how pleased I am with the school at Flers since its reorganization. I might add that if the superior can borrow a few thousand francs, we shall have no further worries about this house, and there shall be no need for recourse to notaries and bankers.

I commend to your prayers good Br. Sebastian, professed, who died after a most edifying sickness, fortified by the sacraments of the dying. His condition prevented the administration of viaticum, though he had received Communion the day before. I wish also to remind you that Br. Leopold, who preceded him to the grave, was entitled to the suffrages for general officers as mentioned in Article 366, page 425, of our rules.

I ask again that all who are engaged in the education of youth should read the first part of my *Christian Education* and follow it in their manner of conducting classes. I have in mind especially the part on punishments, which occasion so many abuses.

Jubilee and Fidelity to the Holy Father

Finally, I close by exhorting you, reverend fathers and dear brothers, to profit by the jubilee granted us, to renew yourselves in the spirit of your vocation, and to enable all those confided to your care to gain the indulgence.[35] Be on your guard against anyone who would dare to assert that the encyclical announcing this great grace is not opportune, and do not entertain the slightest doubt as to the doctrines it contains. By so doing you would certainly sin against the respectful obedience due to the Vicar of Christ, and even against faith. On the contrary, accept all its teachings and prepare yourselves to receive the abundant graces that it offers. As regards the dispensation from vows that it mentions, reread my observations on that point in my circular of November 4, 1864. Then, thank God for this new favor, being firmly convinced that no one better than Pius IX could be the judge of its necessity, because no one is better placed than he to sound the alarm from the heights of Zion, from which his watchful eye scans all the battlefields where Catholic truth is at grips with error, and from which, too, always alert, he hears all the thunders of the tempest that threatens to sink the ship of the Church, but which will abate before the suppliant voice of two hundred million Catholics.

In conclusion, I call the attention of the priests to Number III of our *Ordo.*

Given at Notre-Dame de Sainte-Croix, the day, month, and year as above.

Moreau
By order:
A. Séguin

P.S. I wish to make known to you the two following decisions of the provincial chapter of France in its session of last August:

Article 14

The very reverend superior general will be asked to form a permanent committee to establish uniformity of teaching method and the choice of class books for all our houses, while waiting for the members of the congregation to produce elementary works that deserve to be used in preference to others.

Article 18

The program of the annual examination, which our religious must undergo at retreat time, will be the same this year as last, but a deeper study of the subject matter shall be made.

The committee requested by the above-mentioned Article 14 is composed of the following:

Reverend Fathers: Charles, Chairman; LeCointe, Vice-Chairman; Saugon

Brothers: Gregory; Leonard; Andrew.

Moreau

Circular Letter 8 to the Sisters

· ·

Notre-Dame de Sainte-Croix, Le Mans
January 22, 1858

My dear daughters in Jesus Christ:[36]

May the grace of our Lord, the blessing of his mother conceived without sin, and the protection of St. Joseph be always with you.

Not the least of the consolations that God sent me during this past year was the general spirit of docility with which you accepted my proposal for the settlement of your financial interests and your new relations with the Congregation of Holy Cross. To this was added the providential consolation and noticeable expansion of the congregation in Louisiana, especially after all its trials, changes, and sufferings. We are still not far removed from those sad days that seemed to sound the death knell of this beloved colony, which had been decimated by pestilence or exhausted by sickness in that deadly climate. Nor have I yet forgotten the painful and cruel shock that the death of those two splendid priests inflicted upon me. They were taken away so unexpectedly from your affection and from the hopes that their talents and virtue inspired—and this at the very time that the devil was seeking to unsettle vocations, discourage those who remained, and sow discord in our ranks.

But thanks be to God. For he strikes only to heal and chastises only to spare, and at the very moment that everything seems lost, he reveals his mercy and lifts up those who have fallen. It was in this way that he has acted toward you, my dear daughters in Jesus Christ. After his arm had fallen heavily upon you, he opened his hand to shower abundant consolations upon your congregation. It was necessary that, as at Notre-Dame du Lac and at St. Laurent, you should undergo trials in order to be pleasing to him, for trials are like a divine seal that stamps all the works of God.

Far from seeing in them reasons for discouragement, recognize that these trials are so many marks of God's loving attention and that they are, as it were, the foundation on which he wishes to build this work. Now that the foundation has been laid, we must carry on this work of providence, help it reach its goal, and cooperate with whatever designs God may have for the development of your congregation.

Plan of Government

You are aware that I have already decided upon the principal bases on which your congregation will be organized, and, consequently, this government has assumed a form in keeping with your rule. It is important then that your institute should henceforth be governed according to the plan that I have outlined. Councils and chapters are to carry on their administration within the limits of their jurisdiction and the measure of their competence. The provincial chapter particularly must function conformably to my decisions and prescriptions. The father provincial, in agreement with the mother provincial, is to see to the execution of regulations or decisions and to take steps for all necessary convocations and all measures to be adopted. In a word, the government of your congregation should be inspired and activated by all the sisters who are to have part in it, without adopting any arbitrary measures or doing anything contrary to the rules and constitutions, which you will soon receive.

This is a duty incumbent most especially on the officers and capitulants. Such procedure is all the more necessary because it is the only means of learning the improvements to be made, the modifications to be adopted, or the needs to be met. For in these meetings, each sister must share her ideas with the others and make whatever suggestions her own experience or convictions may have shown to be necessary or useful. A summary of the suggestions made in chapter will be subsequently submitted to me, and later I shall communicate my decision on them. It seems to me that even if these first experiments in administration had no other effect than this, they would already have rendered great service to your congregation.

Necessity of Religious Spirit

But here, my dear daughters in Jesus Christ, I feel the need of opening my whole heart to you. I shall do so with that sincerity and openness that are inspired by your affection for me and by my own lively desire for your spiritual welfare. This administrative organization is doubtless of the utmost importance to ensure the continued existence of your community. Yet, I do not hesitate to declare that it would be powerless to sustain your congregation if it were not accompanied by, or rather based on, what is really the very life and soul of all communities. I mean the religious spirit.

In fact, what is the use of rules and regulations if they are not observed? To what use could we put a machine, no matter how wonderful its mechanism, if there were no mainspring? Above all, then, my dear daughters in Jesus Christ, strive to acquire the spirit of your vocation, and ground yourselves in genuinely religious dispositions. Your sanctification and your perfection depend entirely on the observance of your vows and rules. To imbue yourselves with their spirit and to put them into practice is the best—or rather, the only—way to please God and do his will. You can never be grateful enough to him for drawing you out of this corrupted and corrupting world in preference to so many others who are lost in it—for having led and admitted you into his house, received you into his family, adopted you into the number of his chosen children, and thus smoothed and cleared for you the road to heaven. You can find no better means to prove your gratitude than the faithful observance of your rules and constitutions, which are the expression of his will for you.

Union

There is one point to which I would call your attention very particularly. You are, to use the comparison of St. Paul, members of one same body (1 Cor 12:12–26). Consequently, your relations with your religious companions must be like those of the members of the body toward one another. Now see what happens in the body. If one member suffers, do not all the others hasten to the assistance of the injured member? All the members have the same end, which is to preserve the life of the body, although they have different functions and different means of cooperating in the attainment of this end. What would happen if a member rebelled against the head, refused to help another member, or to do its part for sustaining the body? Great harm would result for the whole body and, consequently, for the rebellious member as well.

This is a perfect picture of what a community should be. Between all its members and between them and their head, there should exist so intimate a union and so strong a love that one cannot suffer without all the others hastening to offer their assistance, sympathize in its suffering, and provide whatever remedies may be available. By that very fact, there exists among the religious of the same society such a spirit of solidarity that one member cannot undergo harm without all the others suffering likewise. In like manner, if each sister does her work to the best of her ability and within the sphere of her obedience, the community as a whole benefits thereby.

My dear daughters in Jesus Christ, take these principles as your rule of conduct. Love and practice charity as "the bond of perfection" (Col 3:14). "Help each other," says the apostle whom I have quoted, "in order to assist each other in good works" (Heb 10:24). At every moment, community life offers opportunities to practice this virtue. Such, for example, are the opportunities to do little favors for one another, to bear one another's burdens, to pardon the faults of one's neighbor, to bear patiently with her failings and her unevenness of temperament and character. Other opportunities are afforded by not taking offense at sharp or domineering remarks and by making the sacrifice of one's inclinations, likes, and dislikes. These and a thousand other situations that arise every day provide us with an opportunity to practice this admirable virtue, which was so highly recommended by our Lord, since he made it the distinctive mark of his disciples. What love he showed for us! He regards as done for himself whatever is done for even the least of his followers (Mt 25:40). Besides, what other means is there to enjoy peace, taste the happiness of community life, and give sweetness and pleasure to the yoke of religious life? Since you are children of one family, have but one heart and one soul, in order that you may be the consolation of your common father.

Fidelity to Silence

To this spirit of union join the practice of silence, which is the guardian and mainstay of religious discipline. Where this rule is well observed, we may conclude with certainty that there reign also fervor and regularity, in a word, the religious spirit. God dwells not in the midst of noise and dissipation. Without silence, there is no spiritual advancement, and it is noteworthy that those religious who are least regular in their conduct are the very ones who violate silence the most frequently. How many evils are caused by the tongue! How difficult it is to violate this rule without wounding either truth or charity! For it is in violations of silence that we find all the indiscreet confidences, criticism, detraction, complaints, and faultfinding, which have undermined and ruined so many vocations. In any case, silence cannot be broken without at least losing time and giving bad example. Strive to observe this essential rule, and correct those whom you may find violating it. Such correction is an act of zeal and charity that may help to forestall many sins.

Obedience

To these recommendations I add the counsel of obedience and respect for your superiors, who represent the authority of God in your regard.

By your prompt and generous obedience, try to lighten the account they shall have to render for your souls. Never put them under the necessity of issuing a real command or of using all their authority in dealing with you, for these procedures always give rise to irritation, to dissatisfaction, and, too frequently, to secret enmities. Above all, avoid cabals and factions, which are as dangerous for the community as they are for the individual religious who fall victims to these illusions of the devil. If you are under obligation to obey, your superiors have the duty to direct you and, when necessary, to command you, but always with that sweetness and moderation that add new weight to the command, while not endangering the firmness of authority.

Duties of Superiors

Superiors, consequently, should avoid whatever can wound their subjects. They should be on their guard especially against harshness, unnecessary severity, domineering manners, and fickleness. All of these faults result in loss of prestige, effect no corrections, and give rise to resentment and jealousy. Let superiors bear in mind that it is their duty to give good example and that they should never demand of others what they do not do themselves. They should be the first to keep the rules. In a word, their whole conduct should be inspired by a tender and affectionate charity.

I address these counsels in a special manner to those of you who share in the government of the congregation as capitulants or councilors. If you wish to draw down the Spirit of God upon your meetings, learn how to remain calm and practice little courtesies and mutual acts of politeness in your deliberations or discussions. Never defend your own viewpoint with too much vigor or obstinacy. Try, rather, to enlighten one another and to bring about the adoption of whatever decision impresses you as being most in keeping with equity, truth, or the well-understood interests of your houses, without yielding to self-seeking, jealousy, or prejudice. Whatever may be your motives to the contrary, always accept the opinion adopted by the majority. In such circumstances, recriminations are out of place and serve no purpose; too often, indeed, they indicate nothing but poorly concealed spite.

I wish to state here that I approve the changes of obedience made at New Orleans regarding the directress of the school at Opelousas and the stewardess of the asylum. By the simple fact of her appointment, the directress of this school becomes a member of the provincial chapter, along with the new stewardess, Sr. Mary of the Holy Angels.

I also hereby officially appoint a secretary for this chapter, but only for its next session. This secretary will be Sr. Mary of St. Michael, about whom I have heard most favorable reports. I trust that she will justify the confidence that I place in her and thus make us forget whatever may have been blameworthy in her conduct in the past. These are the only changes that I make in the members of this chapter; in fact, they only make the chapter complete. In addition, in order to help Fr. Sheil, who has already done so much for you, I have decided that while awaiting the arrival of two priests whom I intend to send him, he shall, in company with M. Raymond and under the presidency of the Archbishop of New Orleans, if his lordship deigns to accept, organize a provincial chapter that shall meet at the time of the general retreats of the brothers and the sisters, in order to establish temporarily the Vicariate of New Orleans.

Recollections of Visit

I feel the need of telling all the sisters of the Vicariate of Notre-Dame du Lac what pleasant remembrances I have of the visit I was able to pay them and how ardently I desire them to continue to profit from it by the careful observance of all my prescriptions. The only exceptions to these prescriptions are for those cases in which the superiors, with the majority vote of their council and of the vicar who takes the place of a provincial, shall see fit to modify them. Even in such cases, however, these modifications shall be submitted to me beforehand or, at least, presented for approval as soon as possible, unless the urgency of the matter demands otherwise. I shall also add that, outside the time of the regular visit, the provincial superior, as well as all other superiors in general, should avoid making any changes in houses outside their place of residence without previous consultation with the superiors or directresses of these houses and their councils. In case of disagreements, they should also ask the advice of the vicar or even of the provincial councilors.

For the rest, the new edition of your rules and constitutions, which has been submitted for the approbation of our bishop while awaiting that of the Holy See, will trace out for you on this point, as well as on the majority of other administrative details, the line of conduct you are to follow. In the meantime, it is important not to take any serious steps except in agreement with the councils or chapters and with the provincial. May I be permitted to add that, in case of divergence of opinion, it would be wise to ask the mother superior of St. Laurent in Canada for her viewpoint in similar circumstances, with a view to establishing the greatest possible uniformity in the government of the congregation.

I cannot close this circular letter without repeating anew my thanks to the sisters in Canada for the enjoyment they afforded me during my stay at St. Laurent by their spirit of union, their docility, and their regularity. I trust that, far from allowing these happy dispositions of grace to fade away, they will make them ever stronger under the direction of the superior general, who until the next general chapter will be Mother Mary of the Seven Dolors. Consequently, all the sisters of the congregation may henceforth correspond with her, although I reserve to myself the right to settle all important questions until such time as the motherhouse of the Marianites is organized.

Spirit of Vocation

In conclusion, I recommend to you once more the principles of conduct which I have indicated above, convinced as I am that never has it been more necessary or timelier for you to be imbued with their spirit. Just as your congregation is entering upon a new path, so you also must renew within yourselves the spirit of your vocation and fidelity to your duties. It is my inmost conviction that on you alone depends the future of your congregation; you hold its destiny in your hands. It is you who will shackle its upward flight or who will assist and hasten it according to the fervor or the laxity of your lives.

It is all the easier for you to enter upon this new path because, not being concerned with worries over temporal needs, you have more time and means for fidelity to your exercises. In addition, providence, whose unspeakable goodness toward you has been so admirable, has just provided the sisters at New Orleans with a new source of help in their spiritual needs. I shall not recall here all the claims by which Fr. Raymond has merited my esteem and confidence. The sisters at New Orleans know how generously and devotedly he offered and gave his priestly ministrations in the most difficult circumstances they have ever had to face. He promises for the future to give a still wider scope to the unselfish cooperation that he has continued up to the present, and he wishes to draw still closer the bonds which already unite him to the family of Holy Cross. Consequently, at his request, I have admitted him to the community of spiritual interests with us. May the sisters regard him henceforth as a father who is completely devoted to them, and they should have recourse to his experience and prudence whenever they feel the need of assistance. In order to facilitate their relations with this good priest and afford them greater freedom of action in receiving spiritual direction from him, I authorize them to correspond with him without being obliged to show their letters to their superiors or directresses; these latter may not unseal these letters if they are delivered to them.

Your good will is too well-known to me, my dear daughters in Jesus Christ, for me to entertain any doubts about the efforts you will make and the readiness you will show in carrying out the counsels that have been inspired in me by my desire to see you correspond ever more generously with the special graces which God has given you. In this way, you will acquire new claims to my esteem and affectionate interest.

Yours devotedly in J.M.J.,
The Superior General
B. Moreau
By order:

The Secretary General
Lamy

P.S. I have just learned of the death of Br. Louis-Marie, professed, who died at Vigna Pia on January 23, after receiving the last sacraments and, in addition, the apostolic benediction. The death of this good brother is a genuine loss for his house, where he rendered great services by his activity and generosity. Each one should acquit promptly for this dear soul the usual suffrages.

I take this occasion to correct an omission in my last circular, where I neglected to mention Br. Athanasius among those who answered my appeal of November 14.

This present circular shall be read in its entirety at the chapter or the spiritual reading following its reception, and then preserved in the archives of each house, after being translated into English and German for our houses in America.

Given under our signature, the countersignature of our general secretary, and the seal of our congregation, at Le Mans, the day, month, and year as above.

Circular Letter 16 to the Sisters

· ·

Thymadeuc, France
January 2, 1859

My dear sisters:

May the grace of our Lord, the blessing of his mother conceived without sin, and the protection of St. Joseph be always with you.

It is with a heart still full of the sweet memories of my trip to Canada, Notre-Dame du Lac, St. Mary's, Chicago, and Philadelphia that I take advantage of my retreat at Thymadeuc to thank you for your New Year's greetings and to announce the resumption of the general visit.[37] Perhaps you have been surprised at its being interrupted so long, but I have not been able to continue it since my return to France. To ensure its greater success, it was necessary, first of all, to organize more effectively the administration of each establishment and to regularize the accounting system of the motherhouse in conformity with the constitutions that the Holy See has deigned to give us and according to the prescriptions of my circular letter of February 1, 1857. It was necessary also to train stewards according to the new system, to draw up models for keeping the entries in a uniform manner, and to accompany them with the instructions necessary to make them intelligible. Besides, it was imperative to revise your rules, so as to harmonize them with our constitutions. Then, too, because the first edition of your meditations was exhausted, a second became all the more indispensable, since I insist that it be used exclusively, as the only one approved for your congregation. Finally, there was the work of getting the bookkeepers to change their old method for the new before January 1, 1858, which was the date I had set for this transfer. Now all this took no less than thirteen months, and I fear that I shall still find some of our houses backward in this regard.

I need not add that, on my return from America, I found a lawsuit pending in the Court of Laval. You will pray then that justice be done, and, particularly, that God's holy will be accomplished. It is this which preoccupies me above all in my prayers; though, of course, I do not forget the cherished family of which I have become the spiritual father. There is nothing in the world dearer to me than Holy Cross. Day and night, it is the object of all my desires and solicitude. This is my reason for sending you from the depths of my retreat some recommendations intended to establish on a firmer basis that harmony and cordial understanding without which you would be unable either to measure up to my confidence or to be of help in the salvation of souls.

Kinds of Authority in the Congregation

In the first place, to avoid disorder and confusion among inferior authorities, it is important to have clear ideas on hierarchical order in the government of the congregation. Now, there are three kinds of power in our congregation: that of jurisdiction, that of vocation, and that which results from the vows.[38]

The first is a spiritual power derived from the keys of the Church. It acts immediately on souls, binding and loosing consciences. Such is the power of the pope over all the faithful, of the bishops over their dioceses, and, under the direction of the bishops, of pastors over their parishioners. Now, this power, which the superior general has received from the Holy Father and which constitutes in him ordinary jurisdiction, is transmitted by the same superior general to all the Salvatorists for the religious of his congregation. They may not, however, exercise this power over outsiders or over you, unless the bishops of the dioceses where providence has placed you grant them this jurisdiction, because to hear the confessions of religious it is necessary, under pain of censure and nullity of the absolution, to obtain special faculties from the ordinary.

The power of vocation consists in the right every superior has to command his or her inferiors and to employ them as he or she deems just within the limits of the constitution and rules. Now, this right is enjoyed by all Salvatorists, Josephites, or Marianites who have any power whatever as superiors or directors. Without it, they would lack the authority of superiors and the right to the obedience of their subjects and so would be unable to govern the establishments entrusted to them. Thus, we readily recognize this power in all those who have been made superiors, from the general of the congregation down to the sister superior who has coadjutor religious under her direction.

It is imperative that you, who up until the present have been accustomed to address yourselves to me for almost everything, now follow the regular channels of authority. In other words, in each vicariate or province, you will have recourse to the vicaress or the mother provincial. She, in turn, will correspond with the mother general, and the latter with me. Hence it is that stewardesses, or superiors, of particular establishments who have no special stewards have the obligation of sending to the mother provincial at the end of each semester a general summary of receipts and expenses since January 1, 1858. This report must then be approved by the mother provincial and sent by her to the general stewardess, conformably to articles 1 and 2 of your constitution 10. All should remember that the particular and detailed accounts of each house, as well as its budgets, must be received and approved by the provincial chapter.

I have made it plain, my very dear sisters, that you must no longer correspond with me, neither for New Year's, nor for my feast day, nor for any spiritual or temporal matter, unless you are provincials. You should, on the contrary, address yourselves to your respective sister superior. I except the case where you would not thus find the help you need, for then you have the right of recourse not only to your mother general but also to me personally, and I shall consider it a duty as well as a pleasure to reply. Still, your letters must come to me through your superiors. These superiors, however, may never read, much less detain, such correspondence. By so doing they would abuse your confidence and their power of domination.

There is still a third power that results from profession and which I gladly call the power of religion, because it is exercised principally toward religious. It is the right we give a person to command, promising God to obey him in the person of the one on whom this right is bestowed. From this results the power of commanding in virtue of holy obedience. Now, this promise so binds us to obey a superior who commands, within the limits of the constitutions and rules, that we cannot fail to obey without sacrilege. For if we cannot refuse obedience to one who has the power of vocation without violating justice that obliges us to give to each one his or her due, we certainly go counter to the virtue of religion by refusing submission to one to whom we have vowed obedience. Religion obliges us to accomplish every vow that has not become illicit or which it is not morally impossible to keep. That is why in our congregation we cannot obtain a dispensation from our vows except from the superior general or the sovereign pontiff, who alone has over the universal Church the three powers just explained and who alone can dispense from the vow of perpetual chastity.

Obligations of Vows

Take great care then, my dear sisters, not to ask the bishops of the dioceses where obedience has placed you to dispense you from any of your vows, for they have no power to do so. On the other hand, do not imagine that it depends only on my will to grant dispensations. There must be serious reasons for the licit use of this power; otherwise, I myself would commit a grave sacrilege. For these reasons, novices must reflect carefully before contracting these sacred engagements of which, as Jesus Christ has said, not all are capable, but only those to whom grace has been given from on high. But if you have the happiness of belonging to the number of those privileged disciples, take courage and have confidence, for the divine master will not permit you to be tempted beyond your strength and will enable you always to emerge from the combat glorious and triumphant (Mt 19:12).

To merit this grace, we must constantly become more and more devoted to prayer and mortification. For along with vigilance, these are the two conditions on which our Savior has promised victory. This reminds me to recommend fidelity to Rules 14, 16, 19, and 23, because I am convinced that with prayer and the spirit of penance, each one of you

will save your soul. Without these dispositions, on the contrary, you yourselves will be lost in your efforts to save others, or at least you will deaden
the spirit of God among you. You will never attain your end, which is
religious perfection, and you will also retard the progress of the congregation, instead of cooperating in its expansion.

Example of Christ and the Saints

Consider the lives of Jesus Christ and the saints, our models. What assidu-
ity in prayer and what continual mortification were theirs! "They served
God," says the pious author of the *Imitation*, "in hunger and thirst, in cold
and nakedness, in work and fatigue, in vigils and fasting."[39] They work by
day and pass the night in long prayers. Is not all this still practiced by the
fervent religious in whose midst it is my privilege to taste the sweetness
of retreat? These worthy sons of St. Bernard, these austere Trappists,
eat only once a day, although they devote themselves to the most severe
manual labor and consecrate the greater part of the night to chanting the
Divine Office. Oh, what fervor they manifest in their exercises of piety!
What holy emulation they practice in their efforts to acquire virtue! What
fervor they put into the observance of the rules! What respect they profess for superiors, and what submission to their least prescriptions. What
is our life in comparison with theirs? At least, my dear sisters, let us learn
to carry courageously the yoke of the obedience that we have vowed and
to practice poverty in our furniture, clothing, and food. Let us not neglect
any of our spiritual exercises, least of all the reception of the sacraments
and our weekly hour of adoration.

Interior Life

Thus, sustained by grace, we shall be able to labor for our neighbor's salvation without endangering our own and to devote ourselves to works of
apostolic zeal without forgetting that work which should be our constant

care and without which the others cannot succeed or at least will be of no avail—that is, the work of our personal sanctification. "What will it profit a man to gain the whole world if he suffer the loss of his own soul?" asks Jesus Christ (Mt 16:26; Mk 8:36; Lk 9:25). Oh, give heed to this sacred oracle, you who so easily sacrifice piety to learning, meditation and the Little Office to study, rising in the morning to uselessly prolonged rest, silence to the itch for talking! To such, should we not say with the author already quoted that "we must first of all have zeal for our own advancement before we begin to show so much for that of others?"[40]

Works of Zeal

Speaking of zeal, I believe I ought to recommend for our houses of education only those works of piety and charity that exist in the institution attached to the motherhouse in order that we may establish a certain uniformity and avoid too great a multiplicity. I am greatly consoled to see how the months of the holy infancy, St. Joseph, and the Blessed Virgin are observed at Notre-Dame de Sainte-Croix. I am also pleased with the organization of the three associations, of the holy infancy among the students under twelve years of age, the propagation of the faith among the others, and St. Joseph among all without distinction of age. Try then to do the same, without adding anything further, and you will have done much for the sanctification of youth by spreading the spirit of prayer and the habit of Christian almsgiving.

Direct special attention to promoting devotion to St. Joseph, not only because of his high sanctity, but also because of the great privileges that God grants him in favor of those who piously invoke him. Of these, the first is the virtue of chastity obtained through his intercession or the victory over the temptations of the flesh and the senses, to which one may have had the misfortune to succumb in one's past life. The second is a special assistance against the demon at the last hour and the grace of a happy death. This is why I beseech all the members of the family of Holy Cross to pray often to this matchless patron of our congregation and to inspire this devotion in young people and Christian families. Recite with more fervor than ever the morning prayer, "I address myself to you, O St. Joseph," laying particular stress on the words: "Bring to the congregation subjects who will glorify God, and suffer not any unworthy herein." Besides, let us not forget that he is the model of the instructors of youth, since he was commissioned by heaven to watch over the infancy of our Lord and to provide for his wants.

I would be pleased to learn also that wherever there is a copy of the holy face, like those distributed at Rome, a special homage is paid to it, as is so happily the custom in the crypt of our conventual church. There, this image remains exposed to the veneration of visitors with a lamp burning in its honor, and before it, fervent servants of God come to recite the litany enclosed with this circular. It seems to me that this practice must be very pleasing to the Savior whose sufferings for our redemption we too easily forget. For this same reason, I recommend that all make the Stations of the Cross devoutly at least once a week, passing from one station to another without moral interruption. Were you to omit this last detail you would not gain the indulgences, even though you pray before all the stations on the same day. This point has been settled by Pius IX. This prescription refers likewise to the beads. His Holiness has further decided that to gain the indulgences attached to the prayer before a crucifix, "Behold me, O good Jesus," one must in addition pray piously for the intention of the pope.

Some have expressed surprise that the new edition of the rules did not speak of suffrages for deceased novices to be performed outside of the house where death takes place. I answer that, since the novices do not form part of the congregation and since deaths are multiplying in proportion to the growing number of subjects, I feared to overburden you with suffrages by asking more. The directory, however, exhorts you to do more, and charity will inspire you to make up for what I did not feel free to prescribe in favor of these dear dead.

Trials at New Orleans

This is also the place to recommend to your prayers three novices—two Josephites of New Orleans, Br. John and Br. Aloysius, and a Salvatorist of the motherhouse, M. Launay—who have fallen asleep in the Lord since my last letter. You will remember that in this letter I told you of the trials of Fr. Sheil, who lost seven subjects during the latest ravages of yellow fever. Thanks be to God, health has been restored to this devoted confrere, and his tribulations have served to renew the members of his community in the spirit of fervor and devotedness without discouraging the new vocations, which have presented themselves since the cessation of the destructive scourge.

Annual Retreats

To avoid the accumulation of accounts that has occurred at Notre-Dame de Sainte-Croix on the occasion of the general retreat, as well as to obviate the expenses incurred by transferring so many religious and the extreme difficulty of hearing so many directions in a few days, I decree that for the future you will gather at the provincial houses for the annual retreat, and that the accounts will be verified by the visitors and sent to the proper authorities at the time indicated by the rule. The retreats, then, will be held, as far as possible, at Notre-Dame de Sainte-Croix, Maulévrier, Paris, Saint-Laurent, Sainte-Marie-du-Lac, Philadelphia, Chicago, and New Orleans, even at Opelousas, although it is not a vicariate. This plan shall be followed unless the vicars think it better not to move to those of the above-mentioned localities where they have no residence. It is for them, after all, in agreement with the mother general and the mother provincial, to arrange for the retreat in the most economical manner possible and to the best interests of the province, just as it is their duty to indicate the time of the annual retreat and to grant extraordinary holidays or vacations in the houses subject to their authority. You will take advantage of the next retreat to elect delegates to the General Chapter of 1860.

Various Prescriptions

With a view to order and economy, I ask you not to use letterhead paper except for the administrative purposes or envelopes except when writing to ecclesiastical superiors or to the civil authorities. It is necessary, moreover, to avoid increasing the postage on letters by using excessively heavy paper, as happens in America. It is also against economy to use envelopes without necessity, as was done by several in returning my questionnaire on regular discipline. Instead of simply folding the sheet and writing the address on the blank side, they used envelopes and thus caused extra postage to be charged at the post office.

I must remind you here that no religious may, without violating the vows of obedience and poverty, correspond uselessly with anyone, whether members of the community or not, especially without knowledge of the superiors. Unnecessary traveling is also forbidden, as are also all reunions arranged purely for pleasure purposes. It is not permitted to serve an elaborate breakfast on Sundays or holidays or to introduce the slightest modification in the religious habit. The weekly holiday shall henceforth be on Thursday instead of Wednesday for the entire congregation, and extra free days shall not be granted without the permission of the superior.

I would like to be able to give you news of Fathers Dufal, Maniel, and Fourmond, who set out in the month of October for our mission in Dacca. To date, I have received none, except from Alexandria, where they arrived in good health. I can but recommend them and their companions to your prayers.

This present circular letter shall be read in its entirety in chapter or at the spiritual reading following its reception and then preserved in the archives of each house, after being translated into English or German for our houses in America.

Given under our signature, the countersignature of our general secretary, and the seal of our congregation, at Thymadeuc, on the day, month, and year as above.

The Superior General
B. Moreau
By order:
The Secretary General
Lamy

MOREAU CHRONOLOGY

	Events in Moreau's Life	Writings of Moreau	Wider Church and Political Events
1799	February 11: Born in Laigné-en-Belin	•	•
1800	•	•	March 21: Pope Pius VII installed
1801	•	•	July 15: Concordat between Rome and Napoleon
1814	October: Begins studies at the College of Château-Gontier (–1816)	•	•
1816	Begins studies at St. Vincent's Seminary in Le Mans (–1821)	•	•
1817	•	•	Lamennais publishes first volume of *Essai sur l'indifférence en matière de religion*
1820	May 27: Ordained subdeacon by Bishop de la Myre	•	March 19: Bishop de la Myre ordained Bishop of Le Mans September: Fr. Dujarié founds the Brothers of St. Joseph

	Events in Moreau's Life	Writings of Moreau	Wider Church and Political Events
1821	April 7: Ordained deacon by Bishop de la Myre August 12: Ordained priest by Bishop de la Myre October 11: Begin studies at St. Sulpice in Paris (–1822)	•	•
1822	July 21: Arrives at the Solitude of Issy (–1823)	•	•
1823	Appointed professor of philosophy at Tessé Gives retreat to the Brothers of St. Joseph	•	October 5: Pope Leo XII installed
1825	March: Receives first invitation to preach parish mission May 26: Appointed professor of dogma at St. Vincent's (–1830)	•	•
1829	•	•	April 5: Pope Pius VIII installed November 8: Bishop Carron ordained Bishop of Le Mans
1830	March: Transferred from dogma to scripture at St. Vincent's (–1836)	•	The July Revolution
1831	•	•	February 6: Pope Gregory XVI installed

	Events in Moreau's Life	Writings of Moreau	Wider Church and Political Events
1833	Establishes and serves as ecclesiastical superior of Our Lady of Charity of the Good Shepherd Monastery in Le Mans (–1858)	•	•
1834	•	•	March 21: Bishop Bouvier ordained Bishop of Le Mans
1835	January: Appointed assistant superior at St. Vincent's (–1836) June 19: Asked by Bishop Bouvier to oversee the Brothers of St. Joseph August: Founds the Auxiliary Priests August 31: Becomes superior of the Brothers of St. Joseph November 1: Moves the brothers' novitiate to Sainte-Croix	November 8: Circular Letter 1 on the vision of religious life •	•
1836	February: Auxiliary Priests preach their first retreat November: Establishes the Boarding School of Notre-Dame de Sainte-Croix in Le Mans August: First Brothers of St. Joseph make perpetual profession of religious vows	•	•

	Events in Moreau's Life	Writings of Moreau	Wider Church and Political Events
1837	March 1: Unites Brothers of St. Joseph and Auxiliary Priests in the Fundamental Act of Union, thus forming the Association of Holy Cross	•	•
1838	•	•	February 17: Death of Fr. Dujarié
1850	November 9: Mission to Rome	•	•
1852	November 27: Mission to East Bengal	•	•
1854	•	•	February 4: Death of Fr. Gabriel Mollevaut December 8: Pius IX declares dogma of Immaculate Conception in *Ineffabilis deus* December 28: Bishop Bouvier dies
1855	October: Experiences "dark night"	*The Exercises of Saint Ignatius and Meditations for Sunday and the Principal Feasts of the Year* (distinct volumes for sisters, priests, and brothers)	November 11: Bishop Nanquette ordained Bishop of Le Mans
1856	Mission to Poland	May 25: Circular Letter 77 on papal approbation *Christian Education*	•

	Events in Moreau's Life	Writings of Moreau	Wider Church and Political Events
1857	May 13: Pius IX approves the constitutions of the Congregation of Holy Cross May 13: Vatican separates sisters into a separate congregation June 17: Consecration of the conventual church in Sainte-Croix July–September: Visit to North America	September 25: Circular Letter 90 on his visit to North America	•
1858	Resigns as ecclesiastical superior of Good Shepherd Monastery	April 13: Circular Letter 94 promulgating new constitutions *Rules* (written to coordinate with the newly approved constitutions)	•
1859	•	*Catechism of the Christian Life and Religious Life for the use of the Congregation of Holy Cross* *Christian Meditations for Sunday and the Principal Feasts of the Year* (second edition)	•
1860	August: General Chapter does not accept 1858 *Rules* Attempts to resign as superior general	•	•

	Events in Moreau's Life	Writings of Moreau	Wider Church and Political Events
1861	Financial crisis precipitated by Br. Marie-Julien surfaces in Paris August: Vatican calls for official visitation of Holy Cross by French Bishops (–1862)	•	•
1862	September: Completion of official visitation of Holy Cross by French Bishops	•	June 3: Bishop Fillion installed as Bishop of Le Mans
1866	June 14: Cardinal Barnabo of the Propaganda Fide accepts Moreau's resignation as superior general	June 21: Circular Letter 188 announcing his resignation	•
1867	•	Last Spiritual Testament	February 19: Constitutions of the Marianites of Holy Cross approved
1868	September 1: Meeting with Pius IX in Rome	•	•
1869	April 28: Moves to a house owned by his sisters	•	July 26: Separation of the Sisters of the Holy Cross (US) from the Marianites in France
1872	August 12: Celebrates fiftieth anniversary of ordination	*Christian Meditations for the Use of the Faithful and the Secular Clergy*	•
1873	January 20: Dies		
1883	•	•	January 10: Vatican suspends the dependence of the Sisters of Holy Cross (Canada) on the Marianites in France

	Events in Moreau's Life	Writings of Moreau	Wider Church and Political Events
1955	Cause opened in Rome	•	•
2003	April 28: Declared Venerable by Pope John Paul II	•	•
2006	April 12: Approved for beatification by Pope Benedict XVI	•	•
2007	September 15: Beatified in Le Mans	•	•

Map of Moreau's France

NOTES

FOREWORD

1. Quotations from the foreword to or from documents included in the present volume are cited internally by page number.

INTRODUCTION

1. Basil Moreau, *Spiritual Exercises of Saint Ignatius for the Use of the Salvatorists* [hereafter SE], trans. Congregation of Holy Cross (unpublished manuscript), Week 2, Day 1. This translation is from the 1859 edition.

2. SE, Week 2, Day 1.

3. On the relationship between the French Revolution and the Catholic Church, see William Doyle, *The Oxford History of the French Revolution*, 2nd ed. (New York: Oxford University Press, 2002); Jeremy Jennings, *Revolution and the Republic: A History of Political Thought in France since the Eighteenth Century* (Oxford: Oxford University Press, 2011); Sylvia Neely, *A Concise History of the French Revolution* (Lanham, MD: Rowman & Littlefield Publishers, 2008); Simon Schama, *Citizens: A Chronicle of the French Revolution* (New York: Alfred A. Knopf, 1989); and Alec R. Vidler, *The Church in an Age of Revolution: 1789 to the Present Day* (Baltimore: Penguin Books, 1965), 11–21.

4. On the same day the monarchy was overthrown, Moreau wrote to his religious community, urging them "to remain calm," a refrain often repeated in subsequent circular letters. Moreau, Circular Letter (hereafter CL) 31, February 24, 1848, in *Circular Letters of the Very Reverend Basil Anthony Mary Moreau, Founder of the Religious of Holy Cross*, trans. Edward L. Heston (Notre Dame: Ave Maria Press, 1943), 1:136.

5. The Estates-General was composed of three estates: the clergy (the First Estate), the nobility (the Second Estate), and the common people (the Third Estate).

6. Doyle, *French Revolution*, 9–32, 36–42, 66–87; Neely, *French Revolution*, 7–12, 29–32; and Schama, *Citizens*, 60–64, 67–68.

7. Doyle, *French Revolution*, 96, 136–37; Neely, *French Revolution*, 62–63; Schama, *Citizens*, 62, 293; and Vidler, *Church in Revolution*, 14–15.

8. From 1789 to 1799, the French Revolution witnessed a chaotic cast of different governments, from the National Assembly (June 17, 1789–September 30, 1791) to the Legislative Assembly (October 1, 1791–September 19, 1792) to the National Convention (September 20, 1792–October 26, 1975) to the Directory (October 27, 1795–November 9, 1799). For the purpose of this brief sketch, "Revolution" and "French Revolution" will refer to these various revolutionary governments when more specific distinctions are not necessary. For a chronology of the various governments, see Neely, *French Revolution*, 249–57.

9. For example, at the time of the Estates-General, the clergy supported such reforms as higher stipends, unrestricted access for all clerics to positions of leadership in the Church, and elected synods for Church governance. They were supported by the Third Estate. Owen Chadwick, *The Popes and European Revolution* (Oxford: Clarendon Press, 1981), 445ff.

10. Three-quarters of the 303 clerical deputies elected to the First Estate were parish priests, while only forty-six were bishops. When many of these clerical deputies sided with the Third Estate, the momentum swung for the creation of the National Assembly. Doyle, *French Revolution*, 34–36, 99, 136–37; Vidler, *Church in Revolution*, 13; and E. E. Y. Hales, *Revolution and the Papacy: 1769–1846* (Notre Dame: University of Notre Dame Press, 1966), 70–71.

11. Doyle explains: "The clergy expected that the new order would confirm and reinforce the authority of the Catholic Church within the nation. The clerical consensus on these matters far outweighed the order's internal disagreements about the positions of parish priests." *French Revolution*, 99, 136–37. See Schama, *Citizens*, 485–86.

12. Doyle, *French Revolution*, 118–19, 136–37; and Neely, *French Revolution*, 80–88.

13. Among other provisions, the law, which spoke of respect for "the unity of the faith, and the communion to be maintained with the visible Head of the universal church," set clerical pay scales, reorganized the ecclesiastical map, provided for the election of parish priests and bishops without papal approval, and forbade any interaction between French citizens and a foreign bishop. Doyle, *French Revolution*, 136–44.

14. An overriding objection of many in the Church was that such major changes required ecclesiastical approval by either a council in France or the Pope. The leaders in the National Assembly did not want to submit a governmental act to external approval. The oath required that clergy swear "to be faithful to the nation, the king and the law, and to uphold with all their power the constitution declared by the National Assembly and accepted by the king." Doyle, *French Revolution*, 140–44; Hales, *Revolution and Papacy*, 81–82; and Chadwick, *Popes and Revolution*, 447.

15. Although exact figures are unknown, Vidler estimates that no more than half of the clergy ever took the oath. Nearly all the bishops, however, did not take the oath, and most fled into exile. *Church in Revolution*, 17. See also Chadwick, *Popes and Revolution*, 447; and Hales, *Revolution and the Papacy*, 76–77.

16. Doyle, *French Revolution*, 145–46.

17. Hales, *Revolution and Papacy*, 80–88; and Doyle, *French Revolution*, 146.

18. Estimates vary, but more than twelve hundred priests were killed during the Revolution, most during the Reign of Terror (September 5, 1793–July 28, 1794), and around thirty thousand, almost one-fifth of all the clergy, emigrated or were deported. Vidler, *Church in Revolution*, 17; Chadwick, *Popes and Revolution*, 448; Hales, *Revolution and Papacy*, 78; and Doyle, *French Revolution*, 146, 397.

19. Some scholars even argue that the clerical oath was a turning point in the course of the entire Revolution. Doyle, *French Revolution*, 144–46; Schama, *Citizens*, 491; and Chadwick, *Popes and Revolution*, 446–48.

20. Tony Catta, *Father Dujarié: Pastor of Ruillé-sur-Loir, Canon of Le Mans, Founder of the Communities of the Sisters of Providence, and the Brothers of St. Joseph, now the Brothers of Holy Cross*, trans. Edward L. Heston (Milwaukee: Catholic Life Publications, Bruce Press, 1960), 13–14; and James Connelly, *Basile Moreau and the Congregation of Holy Cross* (Portland, OR: Garaventa Center for Catholic Intellectual Life and American Culture, 2007), 17–18.

21. Although the laws against the Catholic Church were not enforced with the same rigor in Rennes as elsewhere, priests from the region, such as the pastor of Sainte-Marie-du-Bois, were still sent into exile; others were imprisoned; still others, such as the "Martyrs of Laval," were executed.

Those who refused to take the oath, then, had to minister in secret, usually hidden and protected by their congregants. Catta, *Father Dujarié*, 17–22; and Ephrem O'Dwyer, *The Curé of Ruillé: A Sketch of the Very Reverend James Francis Dujarié, Founder of the Sisters of Providence and the Brothers of Saint Joseph of Ruillé* (Notre Dame: Ave Maria Press, 1941), 42.

22. The details of this period of Dujarié's life are unclear. Much of what we know about his life during the Revolution comes from Moreau. Catta, *Father Dujarié*, 20–22; Connelly, *Basile Moreau*, 18; and O'Dwyer, *Curé of Ruillé*, 42–45, 47.

23. Doyle, *French Revolution*, 288; and Catta, *Father Dujarié*, 24–25.

24. Catta, *Father Dujarié*, 26–27; Connelly, *Basile Moreau*, 18; and O'Dwyer, *Curé of Ruillé*, 48–49.

25. Bishop de Maillé de la Tour-Landry ordained Dujarié. We have the record of Dujarié's ordination because the ordination records kept by the bishop were confiscated at his arrest and subsequently turned over to the National Archives. Catta, *Father Dujarié*, 28–30; and O'Dwyer, *Curé of Ruillé*, 52–53.

26. Catta, *Father Dujarié*, 31–32; Chadwick, *Popes and Revolution*, 449; Neely, *French Revolution*, 231–32; and Doyle, *French Revolution*, 385.

27. Catta notes these examples from summer and fall 1796. Catta, *Father Dujarié*, 31; and Neely, *French Revolution*, 225.

28. According to diocesan annals, both de la Haye and Dujarié assisted with the process of reconciling constitutional clergy with the Catholic Church. The form of retraction and its accompanying ritual varied case to case, with some in public and others in private. Some of the reconciled constitutional clergy were given new ministry assignments, whereas others lived as laymen afterward. Catta, *Father Dujarié*, 31–33.

29. The priest's name was Jacques Bigot. Catta, *Father Dujarié*, 33–34.

30. The concordat was not without controversy. For various groups of revolutionaries, the concordat seemed a betrayal of the Revolution's ideals. Napoleon, in fact, had to purge the legislature to ensure passage. For the Church, it had to make several concessions, including the forfeiting of land confiscated by the Revolution. Moreover, Napoleon added onto the concordat the seventy-seven "Organic Articles" in which, according to Doyle, "the power of the Pope to communicate with the French clergy was circumscribed even more closely than under the Gallican days before 1789." At the same time, the doctrinal and spiritual authority of the papacy was recognized. Doyle argues, "All [the concessions in the concordat], in any case, paled into insignificance beside the fact that free exercise of the faith in France had been restored, the hierarchy was back in place, and the authority of the papacy had received far more fulsome recognition from the heirs of a Godless revolution than ever it had won from the Most Christian Kings of the old regime." Doyle, *French Revolution*, 386–90, 396–98. See also Chadwick, *Popes and Revolution*, 487–90; and Hales, *Revolution and Papacy*, 139–54.

31. Doyle, *French Revolution*, 385.

32. Some children were still taught by local clergy and other teachers. This was the case, as will be shown, for the young Moreau. Catta, *Father Dujarié*, 53.

33. Catta, *Father Dujarié*, 54; and Connelly, *Basile Moreau*, 17.

34. The number of students in college dropped from fifty thousand in 1789 to only twelve to fourteen thousand in 1799. Doyle, *French Revolution*, 399.

35. Baptismal records indicate that the Moreau family preferred to delay their children's Baptisms for a priest who had not taken the oath. Victoire was the one exception. Etienne Catta and Tony Catta, *Basil Anthony Mary Moreau*, trans. Edward L. Heston (Milwaukee: Bruce Publishing Company, 1955), 1:8.

36. A parallel school for females was opened by the niece of a former pastor. As godmother to one of the Moreau children who did not survive infancy, she likely also provided funding for the education of the young Moreau. Catta and Catta, *Moreau*, 1:7–9.

37. Reestablished after its priest-rector was released from revolutionary incarceration in 1794, the school functioned as a preparatory seminary. Catta and Catta, *Moreau*, 1:17.

38. We know very little about Moreau's time at Château-Gontier. The surviving correspondences from those two years are with his sisters Cécile and Victoire. Basil Moreau, *Recueil Documentaire: Le très révérend Père Moreau d'après ses écrits, ses correspondants et les documents de l'époque 1799–1835* (New York: L'Administration Générale de Sainte-Croix, 1945), 29–32.

39. Catta and Catta, *Moreau*, 1:24n63.

40. The text was Bailly's *Institutiones Theologicae*. The rector of the seminary had to supply his own notes to complete some of the deficiencies in the text. Catta and Catta, *Moreau*, 1:24–25.

41. The "Declaration of Clergy of France of 1682" was led by the Archbishop of Paris and registered in the Parliament in Paris in March of that year. Although the ideas expressed were not new, the Declaration became the official rendering of the core Gallican ideas of the limitation of the pope's temporal authority concerning governmental power, general councils of the Church, and the canons and customs of local churches. "Declaration of the Gallican Clergy" in S. Ehler and J. Morrall, trans. and eds., *Church and State through the Centuries: A Collection of Historic Documents with Commentaries* (Westminster: Newman Press, 1954), 205–8. See also Catta and Catta, *Moreau*, 1:24.

42. Since Moreau was not yet the canonical age of twenty-four, the bishop gave him a dispensation for early ordination. Catta and Catta, *Moreau*, 1:27.

43. The Sulpicians, as members of the Society of Saint-Sulpice are commonly known, are a community of diocesan priests dedicated to the education of seminarians and parish work. They were founded by Olier in 1641 and take their name from the church of Saint-Sulpice in Paris, which serves as the community's headquarters and was the location of its first seminary. That seminary is where Moreau studied. For more details concerning the French School, see the section "Sulpician Spirituality and the French School" under "Intellectual and Spiritual Influences on Moreau."

44. The letter is dated March 5, 1822. Catta and Catta, *Moreau*, 1:40n42.

45. Moreau to Monsieur et très honoré Supérieur [Fillion], January 28, 1822, quoted in Catta and Catta, *Moreau*, 1:38. For the original letter in French, see Moreau, *Recueil Documentaire*, 49–50.

46. James Denn describes this text as exhibiting a stifled desire to evangelize. Bernard Mullahy suggests that it evidences the ardor of Moreau's zeal that would continue even after his work on the interior life the following year at Issy. Both of these analyses identify the character of zeal in the young Moreau but neglect the fact that Moreau is primarily concerned with education or teaching, even should that take the form of a sermon. Denn, *The Theology of Preaching in the Writings of Basil Anthony Moreau* (Rome: Catholic Book Agency, 1969), 18–19; and Mullahy, *The Spirituality of the Very Reverend Basil Anthony Moreau* (Notre Dame: Ave Maria Press, 1948), 18.

47. When Holy Cross accepted responsibility for the Church's mission in East Bengal, Moreau wrote: "One of the most urgent needs of this holy enterprise and one of the most efficacious means of assuring its success is to open schools where children can learn to practice religion at the same time that they learn reading, writing and arithmetic." Moreover, after the growth in holiness of the congregation's own members, the other two purposes Moreau gave for the congregation's existence in its rules were the sanctification of their brothers and sisters by preaching the divine Word, especially in country places and foreign missions, and the instruction of youth. CL 175, May 31, 1864, 2:322.

48. Moreau, *Recueil Documentaire*, 49–50.

49. Basil Moreau, "Counsels on the Study of Theology," in *The Very Reverend Basil Anthony Moreau, C.S.C.: Articles on his Life and Teaching*, ed. and trans. Thomas McDonagh and Leo Sullivan (Washington, DC: Holy Cross College, 1943), 51–56.

50. SE, Week 2, Day 1.

51. Moreau had taken private, personal vows before the subdiaconate, including vows of perpetual chastity, obedience, poverty, and a vow to fast on Fridays and to drink only water at lunch while in the seminary. These vows were "private" in the sense that Moreau made them on his own initiative and directly to God. Unlike religious priests, brothers, and sisters, diocesan priests do not profess public vows that the Church receives in the name of God. Diocesan priests, instead, promise to live celibately and to be obedient to their bishop, yet these promises, while public and binding for life, are not considered "vows" according the Church's technical definition. Catta and Catta, *Moreau*, 1:26.

52. Moreau, like many priests and religious of his time, practiced corporal mortification. He did this, however, under the guidance of his spiritual director. It remained a personal devotion and not one that he mandated for Holy Cross religious. In his writings, Moreau often uses the word "mortification," yet in a broader sense more akin to the virtue of temperance. For example, he uses "mortification" to characterize control of the senses, the virtues, the religious rule itself, and the vows of poverty, chastity, and obedience. In SE, Week 2, Day 3, he writes: "The practice of mortification" for his religious was "found entirely in living out the Rules of [the] Congregation." For further examples of this use of the term, see CL 45, 104, 131, 137, 138, and 169.

53. Catta and Catta, *Moreau*, 1:60–62.

54. Catta and Catta, *Moreau*, 1:63.

55. Much of this relationship happened by correspondence after the year at Issy. Moreau's letters to Mollevaut are presumed destroyed, but the letters from Mollevaut to Moreau are still extant. See Moreau, *Recueil Documentaire*, 95–186.

56. Catta and Catta, *Moreau*, 1:40.

57. See Jennings, *Revolution and the Republic*, 121.

58. Jennings, *Revolution and the Republic*, 121. Lamennais wrote in the first volume (1817) of his *Essai*: "Such is the necessary result of the absurd social contract thought up by philosophy, and which is in reality only a blasphemy declaring war against society and against God." See Jennings, *Revolution and the Republic*, 120ff.

59. Jennings, *Revolution and the Republic*, 121–22.

60. Moreau to Monsieur et très cher Supérieur [Fillion], June 27, 1822; Moreau to Monsieur et très cher Supérieur [Fillion], April 1, 1823, in Moreau, *Recueil Documentaire*, 52–55, 64–69.

61. The early influences of this position might be attributed to Moreau's family, who had rejected the constitutional clergy in favor of nonjurors. Moreau's first biographer, his nephew Charles Moreau, makes too quickly the point that Moreau accepted Lamennais's thinking enthusiastically and quickly took a stand for the prerogatives of the pope against Gallicanism. Moreau did indeed take up the Ultramontane position, but his engagement with Lamennais was more measured. The strongest evidence for his Ultramontanism comes later in his conflicts with Bishop Bouvier, treated below. Catta and Catta, *Moreau*, 1:76; and Charles Moreau, *The Very Reverend Father Basil Anthony Mary Moreau: Priest of Le Mans and His Works*, trans. Congregation of Holy Cross (Paris: Firmin-Didot, 1900), vol. 1, bk. 1, 17–19.

62. See Introduction, n41. The term "Gallicanism" had various meanings in the course of French history in the relations among the papacy, the French State, the French Bishops, the Jesuits, and the Sorbonne, to name a few. For background on the seventeenth-century development of

Gallican ideas, see Jotham Parsons, *The Church in the Republic: Gallicanism and Political Ideology in Renaissance France* (Washington, DC: Catholic University of America Press, 2004). For an introduction to eighteenth-century Gallicanism, see Jeffrey Burson, "The Catholic Enlightenment in France from the Fin de Siècle Crisis of Consciousness to the Revolution, 1650–1789," in *A Companion to the Catholic Enlightenment in Europe*, ed. U. Lehner and M. Printy (Leiden: Brill, 2010), 63–126.

63. This is how the move has been consistently interpreted by Moreau's biographers. Catta and Catta, *Moreau*, 1:96–99; and Thomas Barrosse, *Moreau: Portrait of a Founder* (Notre Dame: Fides Publishers, 1969), 34–42.

64. This change was the result of a meeting between Pius IX and Moreau on December 22, 1850, in Rome. See Catta and Catta, *Moreau*, 1:818–19.

65. At one point Bouvier was called to Rome concerning his theology and agreed to revise it, though Moreau did not wait for the revised version. Catta and Catta, *Moreau*, 1:871.

66. Moreau to Fillion, April 1, 1823, quoted in Catta and Catta, *Moreau*, 1:75.

67. Catta and Catta, *Moreau*, 1:96–97.

68. Bouvier wrote, "I had him [Moreau] removed as professor of dogma." M. Bouvier to M. Carrière (Superior of Saint-Sulpice), March 22, 1832, quoted in Catta and Catta, *Moreau*, 1:97n56. See also Catta and Catta, *Moreau*, 1:96–99.

69. Moreau wrote these words later for the *Annales de Sainte-Croix*. Catta and Catta, *Moreau*, 1:97.

70. Cécile Perreault, *To Become Another Christ: Identification with Christ according to Basil Moreau*, trans. Louis-Bertrand Raymond (Montreal: Fides Publishers, 1990).

71. Bernardin de Picquigny, *Explication des épîtres de saint Paul* (Paris: Chez Mequignon, 1813).

72. Perreault, *Another Christ*, 21–56.

73. Extant are Moreau's course notes concerning marriage (De matrimonio). His notes also exist on grace and sin (Tractatus de gratia). Archives of the Congregation of Holy Cross, University of Notre Dame.

74. An archival document listing the contents of Moreau's library runs for ten pages, with titles ranging from Augustine of Hippo's letters and the Hebrew Bible to a life of Voltaire and the philosophical work of Lamennais. Archives of the Congregation of Holy Cross, University of Notre Dame. For a greatly abridged version of this list, see Catta and Catta, *Moreau*, 1:102–3.

75. The extant manuscripts of *De religione et ecclesia* are incomplete. Archives of the Congregation of Holy Cross, University of Notre Dame.

76. Catta and Catta, *Moreau*, 1:103.

77. "Counsels on the Study of Theology," in McDonagh and Sullivan, *Moreau*, 51–56.

78. Moreau, CL 36, April 15, 1849, 1:161–62.

79. For an introduction see W. Thompson, ed., *Bérulle and the French School: Selected Writings*, trans. L. Glendon (New York: Paulist Press, 1989).

80. The relevant Tridentine text is Canon XVIII of the 23rd session of the Council of Trent, July 15, 1563. For a description of France, see Thompson, *Bérulle and the French School*, 11.

81. Though these primary figures serve as markers for this presentation of the French School of Spirituality, it is important to note that the French School from the outset involved women as well. These included Madeleine de Saint-Joseph (1578–1637), Marie de l'Incarnation Guyart (1599–1672), Louise de Marillac (1591–1660), and Marguerite Bourgeoys (1620–1700). Their influence is harder to trace on account of their thoughts surviving mostly in letters. See Raymond Deville, *The French School of Spirituality*, trans. Agnes Cunningham (Pittsburgh: Duquesne University Press, 1994), 214–35.

82. Thompson, *Bérulle and the French School*, 57.

83. The Gospel of John, the Pauline epistles, and the writings of St. Augustine and patristic theologians are considered common sources for the French School. Thompson, *Bérulle and the French School*, 36.

84. Thompson, *Bérulle and the French School*, 14, 16.

85. The technical term was *anéantissement*, literally an annihilation or abnegation in which one dies to an old self corrupted by sin and then is filled with grace at the center of one's being. Thompson, *Bérulle and the French School*, 35–47.

86. Moreau, CL 14, September 1, 1841, 1:43; and Wulstan Mork, *Moreau Spirituality* (Notre Dame: Sisters of the Holy Cross, 1973), 26–82.

87. Perreault, *Another Christ*, 23ff.

88. Jean-Jacques Olier, *Introduction à la vie et aux vertus Chrétiennes* (Paris: Langlois, 1657). For a translated excerpt of the larger work, see Thompson, *Bérulle and the French School*, 217–69.

89. Eudes's book was published in English as *The Admirable Heart of Mary* (Fitzwilliam, NH: Loreto Publications, 2008). For the French, see *Le cœur admirable de la très sacrée Mère de Dieu* (Paris: Lethielleux, 1935). In the case of Bérulle, he also spoke of the Trinity in terms of hearts; see Deville, *The French School*, 105–17.

90. St. Margaret Mary Alacoque (1647–1690) helped popularize devotion to the Sacred Heart, but Eudes first advanced the Feasts of the Heart of Mary and the Sacred Heart of Jesus. For this reason, Pius XI called him the "Father, the Doctor, and the Apostle of the liturgical devotion to the Sacred Hearts of Jesus and Mary." In addition to being a subject of devotion, the Sacred Heart in this period is also considered a Counter-Reformation affirmation of Catholicism. See Deville, *The French School*, 114–17.

91. Francis de Sales, "Treatise on the Love of God," quoted in Wendy Wright, "'That Is What It Is Made For': The Image of the Heart in the Spirituality of Francis de Sales and Jane de Chantal," in *Spiritualities of the Heart*, ed. Annice Callahan (New York: Paulist Press, 1990), 153.

92. The French School derived this understanding of *totus Christus* or the whole Christ, from patristic thinkers, especially Augustine's *Enarrationes in Psalmos*. See, for instance, a conference of Charles de Condren's (1588–1641) inspiration: *Théologie Chrétienne*, in Deville, *The French School*, 161–62. The classic work on the *totus Christus* is Émile Mersch, *The Whole Christ: The Historical Development of the Doctrine of the Mystical Body in Scripture and Tradition* (London: Dennis Dobson, 1949).

93. See the section "Circular Letter 14 and the Association of Holy Cross" under "Moreau's Leadership and Development of Holy Cross."

94. Deville, *The French School*, 144.

95. For a brief account of Moreau's work on parish missions, see Catta and Catta, *Moreau*, 1:397–405.

96. For the history of the founding of Holy Cross, see the section "The Early Developments of Holy Cross."

97. George Ganss, ed., *Ignatius of Loyola: The Spiritual Exercises and Selected Works* (New York: Paulist Press, 1991).

98. Edward Howells, "Relationality and Difference in the Mysticism of Pierre de Bérulle," *Harvard Theological Review* 102, no. 2 (April 2009): 228.

99. Robert P. Maloney, C.M., "Vincent de Paul and Jean-Jacques Olier: Unlikely Friends," *Vincentian Heritage Journal* 28, no. 1 (2008): 1, 13.

100. Moreau quotes à Kempis frequently in his writings. See, for instance, CL 14, 29, 79, 104, 132, and 169; SE, Week 1, Days 1, 7, 8; Week 2, Days 4, 7; Week 4, Day 2; *Christian Meditations*: Most Precious Blood of Our Lord, Octave of Easter.

101. Perreault, *Another Christ*, 16.

102. Perreault, *Another Christ*, 16.

103. Catta and Catta, *Moreau*, 2:234n104.

104. Catta and Catta, *Moreau*, 2:235.

105. Moreau worked on and off on his *Christian Meditations* starting in the 1850s. Guéranger provided a new idea for the arrangement of some of the content. Moreau's last edition (1872) of the *Christian Meditations* is conceived in concert with the structure of the liturgical year. Mullahy, *Spirituality of Basil Moreau*, 40–42; and Catta and Catta, *Moreau*, 2:235–36, 990.

106. Trappists are the Order of Cistercians of the Strict Observance. They observe the Rule of St. Benedict.

107. Catta and Catta, *Moreau*, 1:363.

108. Moreau, Sermon, "Meditation."

109. These young women first took religious vows in 1820. Their rule was approved in 1843, and they became officially known as the Sisters of Providence. Catta, *Father Dujarié*, 53–68; Connelly, *Basile Moreau*, 19; and O'Dwyer, *Curé of Ruillé*, 73–87.

110. Although the educational needs in France had given rise to a number of communities of teaching brothers, in addition to the Christian Brothers, many of these communities did not permit their members to go out individually. That left smaller, rural parishes unserved since they could not sustain more than one teacher. For this reason, Dujarié also had his brothers trained as sacristans, because a sacristan was entitled to a stipend from the state that would help the parish in supporting the brother. Catta, *Father Dujarié*, 107–8; O'Dwyer, *Curé of Ruillé*, 90–91; and Catta and Catta, *Moreau*, 1:289–91.

111. Catta, *Father Dujarié*, 108–13; and O'Dwyer, *Curé of Ruillé*, 92–94, 103–4, 135.

112. Their educational training included the basics of the catechism, reading, writing, grammar, and mathematics, while their spiritual formation consisted of a simple prayer and devotional life. Many, however, did not receive even this most basic training and formation. Perhaps as a result, from 1825 to 1828, for example, 155 candidates came to the community and sixty persevered and were sent out to teach. These numbers, however, were similar to those of other foundations of the day. Connelly, *Basile Moreau*, 21–22; O'Dwyer, *Curé of Ruillé*, 95–100, 135; and Catta, *Father Dujarié*, 109, 113–17, 142.

113. At their first annual retreat in 1822, the Brothers of St. Joseph began taking an annual vow (technically a promise) of obedience to their superior, but most did not take it. They only began taking formal religious vows after Moreau became their superior. O'Dwyer, *Curé of Ruillé*, 108–9; and Catta, *Father Dujarié*, 232.

114. O'Dwyer, *Curé of Ruillé*, 135.

115. A discrepancy exists in the secondary sources concerning the year of the retreat. Some sources, such as Charles Moreau and O'Dwyer, place the year at 1822. Catta and Catta place the year at 1823, pointing out that Moreau was still in Issy in 1822. The most plausible explanation seems that while the brothers held their first retreat in 1822, Moreau first assisted in 1823. Charles Moreau, *Moreau*, vol. 1, bk. 1, 44; O'Dwyer, *Curé of Ruillé*, 108; Catta and Catta, *Moreau*, 1:295–96; Catta, *Father Dujarié*, 138, 238n5; and R. P. Philéas Vanier, *Le chanoine Dujarié 1767–1838: Fondateur des Sœurs de la Providence de Ruillé-sur-Loir et des Frères de Saint-Joseph* (Montreal: Éditions Fides, 1948), 98n34.

116. When Charles X was driven from the throne in the summer of 1830, fears spread that France was on the brink of returning to the days of the Revolution. As a result, a number of the brothers left, and although the overall loss was not large, there was concern that more could leave

if immediate action were not taken. Catta, *Father Dujarié*, 193–97, 224; and Catta and Catta, *Moreau*, 1:297–300.

117. "Traité entre les frères de Saint-Joseph et leur Supérieur Général," September 1,1831, in Vanier, *Le chanoine Dujarié*, 388. For an English translation and commentary, see Catta, *Father Dujarié*, 225–26; and Catta and Catta, *Moreau*, 1:298–99.

118. Moreau and Fr. Vincent Brenot, a Jesuit missionary from Laval, led the annual retreat together that year. Catta, *Father Dujarié*, 232–35; O'Dwyer, *Curé of Ruillé*, 176–77; and Catta and Catta, *Moreau*, 1:303–6.

119. Catta and Catta, *Moreau*, 1: 304–11; and Catta, *Father Dujarié*, 235–36.

120. Br. André Mottais wrote Bishop Bouvier in November 1834 outlining plans for the community's future and identifying Moreau as the one to lead the brothers. See Frère André to Monseigneur [Bouvier], November 14, 1834, in Vanier, *Le chanoine Dujarié*, 458–59. For the text and critical study of his plan, see Vanier, *Le chanoine Dujarié*, 136–52. Then in June 1835, Br. Leonard directly approached Moreau about this possibility. Catta and Catta, *Moreau*, 1:309–12, 328–31; and Catta, *Father Dujarié*, 254–56, 258–61.

121. Moreau to Mon cher frère [Léonard], June 17, 1835, in Vanier, *Le chanoine Dujarié*, 469–70. See also Catta and Catta, *Moreau*, 1:311–12; and Catta, *Father Dujarié*, 258–59.

122. Showing respect to Dujarié both during and after the transition was of paramount concern for Moreau. For example, he insisted on receiving the superiorship of the brothers directly from Dujarié, thus upholding the latter's dignity as their founder. Catta, *Father Dujarié*, 262–64; and Catta and Catta, *Moreau*, 1:312–18.

123. Moreau quoted in Catta and Catta, *Moreau*, 1:317. See also Catta, *Father Dujarié*, 264–67.

124. For example, the day following his appointment, Moreau had the brothers elect a general council to advise him. Then, in his first circular letter to the community, Moreau addressed a number of the needed temporal and spiritual reforms. Moreau, CL 1, November 8, 1835, 1:1–6; Catta, *Father Dujarié*, 268–75; and Catta and Catta, *Moreau*, 1:317–18, 338–42.

125. CL 1, November 8, 1835, 1:2.

126. CL 1, November 8, 1835, 1:2. See also Catta and Catta, *Moreau*, 1:312, 342–44.

127. Catta and Catta, *Moreau*, 1:342–44, 353–54.

128. It was at that retreat that they chose the name "Auxiliary Priests" and envisioned their work preaching retreats and missions, as well as lending parochial assistance to ill pastors or to understaffed parishes on major feast days. They would fulfill their first preaching assignment in February 1836 at Teloché. Moreau to Mon cher frère [Léonard], June 17, 1835, in Vanier, *Le chanoine Dujarié*, 469–70; and Catta and Catta, *Moreau*, 1:312, 334–36.

129. Such citywide missions were held in other major French cities. Catta and Catta, *Moreau*, 1:33–40.

130. The fact that both Dujarié and Moreau envisioned a group of priests for parish missions and retreats is not surprising, given that it was a key aspect of the life of the Church at the time. Dujarié approached Moreau in 1823 to join his envisioned association of missionary priests. Dujarié imagined a small society of priests, four to six in number, under the patronage of the Sacred Heart, that would preach missions but would primarily serve as ecclesiastical superiors and provide spiritual assistance for the brothers and sisters. Although his full reasons are unknown, Moreau did not join. Catta, *Father Dujarié*, 170–78, 180–81; and Catta and Catta, *Moreau*, 1:319–23.

131. Catta and Catta, *Moreau*, 1:323–32.

132. Relatively short, the Fundamental Act deals mostly with temporal realities, including money and property. The document reflects the fears held by a number of the brothers that the

newer, significantly smaller society of priests was going to raid the brothers' scant resources. "Acte Fondamental Réglant les Intérêts Temporels des Prêtres et des Frères membres de l'association de Sainte-Croix," March 1, 1837, in Vanier, *Le chanoine Dujarié*, 519–22. For an English translation, see Charles Moreau, *Basil Moreau*, vol. 1, bk. 1, 76–78. See also Catta and Catta, *Moreau*, 1:328–30, 368–70; and Catta, *Father Dujarié*, 251–54.

133. Moreau turned first to the Sisters of Providence, which had been formally separated from the Brothers of St. Joseph in 1831 by Bishop Philippe-Marie Carron (then bishop of Le Mans) over concerns surrounding authority and the comingling of finances. Then Moreau turned to the Sisters at Evron. Both declined. Etienne Catta and Tony Catta, *Mother Mary of the Seven Dolors and the Early Origins of the Marianites of Holy Cross (1818–1900)*, trans. Edward L. Heston (Milwaukee: Catholic Life Publications, Bruce Press, 1959), 19–21; Catta and Catta, *Moreau*, 1:431–32; and Catta, *Father Dujarié*, 199–205, 207–20.

134. Bishop Bouvier rejected the educational role that Moreau envisioned for the sisters. As a result, the sisters' first constitutions explicitly spoke of them doing educational work and care of the sick "only in houses directed by Holy Cross priests in foreign lands." Having joined the priests and brothers in the United States in 1843, the sisters founded their first school in Bertrand, Michigan, in 1844. The first school administered by the sisters in France (Préval) did not begin until 1854, the year Bishop Bouvier died. Catta and Catta, *Mary of the Seven Dolors*, 50–60, 71–72, 260.

135. Bishop Bouvier explicitly rejected Moreau's plan to include the sisters in the first constitutions for Holy Cross and permitted only that a rule be drawn up for a society of women. Catta and Catta, *Mary of the Seven Dolors*, 20, 50–60; and Catta and Catta, *Moreau*, 1:432–34.

136. CL 94, April 13, 1858, 2:65–66.

137. Catta and Catta, *Moreau*, 1:323–24; and Catta, *Father Dujarié*, 179.

138. As Catta writes, "It is above all in this sense [of the religious life] that M. Moreau is definitely a founder." Catta and Catta, *Moreau*, 1:367–68. See also Barrosse, *Moreau*, 85–87.

139. Although obedience is one of the three religious vows, apostolic (nonmonastic) religious life consists in the profession of poverty, chastity, and obedience.

140. Catta, *Father Dujarié*, 168–82, 232–35, 247–48; Catta and Catta, *Moreau*, 1:303–6, 367–68; O'Dwyer, *Curé of Ruillé*, 176–77; and Connelly, *Basile Moreau*, 36.

141. Twelve brothers total, including Br. André Mottais, professed perpetual (lifelong) vows of poverty, chastity, and obedience that August. Catta, *Father Dujarié*, 142, 274–75; and Catta and Catta, *Moreau*, 1:354–56.

142. Moreau announced his intention to profess perpetual vows in his circular letter to open 1840. He had to overcome the opposition of both Bishop Bouvier, who was hesitant to have diocesan priests profess religious vows, as well as of some of his own Auxiliary Priests, who, while zealous for the work of Holy Cross, were hesitant about the structures and demands of religious life. The other priests to profess that evening were Pierre Chappé, Paul Celier, and Augustin Saunier. CL 9, January 1, 1840, 1:21; Catta and Catta, *Moreau*, 1:406–15; Connelly, *Basile Moreau*, 37; and Catta, *Father Dujarié*, 274–75.

143. Moreau's plans for the sisters were held up by Bishop Bouvier, whose reluctance stemmed in part from the wider proliferation of women's communities in the diocese. After assigning them to Holy Cross's new foundation in the United States, Moreau allowed two sisters, Mary of Calvary and Mary of the Heart of Jesus, to pronounce vows, albeit addressed to a "future superioress" since their constitutions had yet to be approved by a legitimate ecclesiastical authority. Connelly, *Basile Moreau*, 41–42; Catta and Catta, *Mary of the Seven Dolors*, 60–61; and Catta and Catta, *Moreau*, 1:432–41.

144. In 1839, three bishops of foreign-mission dioceses—the bishop-elect of the diocese of Vincennes, Indiana, the bishop of Montreal, Canada, and the bishop of Algiers—all approached Moreau to send members of Holy Cross to their lands. The first offer Moreau accepted was from Bishop Dupuch of Algiers. On April 28, 1840, four brothers and two priests left from Sainte-Croix for Algeria. They were to work in schools, orphanages, and an envisioned preparatory seminary. Catta and Catta, *Moreau*, 1:458, 464–72.

145. Catta and Catta, *Mary of the Seven Dolors*, 51–65.

146. The Congregation of the Sacred Hearts of Jesus and Mary, which had societies of priests, brothers, and sisters, is one example. Catta and Catta, *Moreau*, 448–51; and Catta, *Father Dujarié*, 176.

147. See the section "Circular Letter 14 and the Association of Holy Cross" under "Moreau's Leadership and Development of Holy Cross."

148. Catta and Catta, *Moreau*, 1:457–18.

149. Although Circular Letter 14 is formally addressed to the "brothers," since the few Auxiliary Priests were mostly in Le Mans and the sisters were just beginning their novitiate, it addresses Moreau's vision for all his religious—brothers, sisters, and priests. CL 14, September 1, 1841, 1:38–45. For the French versions of the circular letters, see Basil Moreau, *Lettres Circulaires du Très Révérend Père Basile Moreau Fondateur des Religieux et des Religieuses de Sainte-Croix*, 2 vols. (Montreal: Éditions Fides, 1941–42).

150. Barrosse, *Moreau*, 92–98. See also Catta and Catta, *Moreau*, 1:441–48.

151. See Phil 1:6.

152. This remains one of the most enduring themes of his circular letters. Even where the term "providence" is not used, he nevertheless refers to God's action, direction, and involvement in the nature and activity of the community. See the section "Divine Providence," under "Moreau's Spiritual Emphases."

153. CL 14, September 1, 1841, 1:38–39.

154. Perfection in the New Testament comes from the Greek *teleios* (e.g., Mt 5:48; 19:21), which means "to reach one's end" or "to be finished." Perfection is attained then in one's end in Christ. See the section "*Imitatio Christi:* The Centrality of the Cross," under "Moreau's Spiritual Emphases."

155. CL 14, September 1, 1841, 1:39.

156. Mork, *Moreau Spirituality*, 31–35.

157. Moreau uses the language of family when referring both to his own religious congregation, such as referring to the religious at Notre-Dame du Lac as "our family," as well as to the apostolates where the community served, such as the "family of Notre Dame" and the "family" at Notre Dame College in Sainte-Croix. CL 14, September 1, 1841, 1:43.

158. See Jn 15 and 1 Cor 12. Drawing upon the scriptural image of the vine and the branches, Moreau at times used the image of a tree and its branches to speak of the union of Holy Cross sisters, brothers, and priests with each other and with Christ.

159. CL 14, September 1, 1841, 1:41–42.

160. Catta and Catta, *Moreau*, 1:457–98, 798–809, 817–25, 886–51; and Barrosse, *Moreau*, 100–102.

161. CL 86, July 3, 1857, 2:1–10; and Catta and Catta, *Moreau*, 1:648–55; 2:225–28, 230–40.

162. For an example of the complexity and frequency of communication from Sainte-Croix to the missions, see Marvin R. O'Connell, *Edward Sorin* (Notre Dame: University of Notre Dame Press, 2001), 124–41.

163. Catta and Catta, *Moreau*, 2:990.

164. The Sacred Congregation for the Propagation of the Faith (Sacra Congregatio de Propaganda Fide) is now known as the Congregation for the Evangelization of Peoples (Congregatio por Gentium Evangelizatione).

165. Jean-Baptiste Bouvier, *Institutiones theologicae ad usum seminariorum* (Paris: Méquignon, 1853).

166. See the section "Formation in a Time of Debate," under "Moreau as Scholar and Teacher."

167. Moreau saw Sorin as one of his most talented missionaries. In 1852, Moreau appointed Sorin the new superior of the Bengal mission (parts of present-day India and present-day Bangladesh), which would likely have led to Sorin's consecration as a bishop. Sorin refused, and the other religious at Notre Dame protested with their own letters to Moreau. Moreau expressed that the very virtues they extolled in their superior made him perfect for the new mission. Sorin and the Indiana house then voted to separate themselves from Sainte-Croix; the bishop of Vincennes, Indiana, agreed to release them from their vows. Indications from Rome, however, suggested that the Vatican would side with Sainte-Croix over Indiana. Ultimately, Sorin retracted the secession, and Moreau subsequently revoked his new assignment to Bengal. Sorin would spend two months in Le Mans, and the two reconciled at that point. For the most thorough study of the relationship between Moreau and Sorin, see O'Connell, *Edward Sorin*.

168. The announcement of deaths from these epidemics colors the tone of Moreau's circular letters at the time. A good example is CL 69, which chronicles the eighteen deaths at Notre Dame and expresses the grief of both Sorin and Moreau. CL 69, November 4, 1854, 1:324–25.

169. "Dark night" is a technical term coming from St. John of the Cross (1542–1591). It references a mystical experience of a deep perception of God's absence. The most complete account of Moreau's dark night, including the reactions of other sisters and priests to Moreau's state, is given in Catta and Catta, *Moreau*, 2:96–114. Moreau's dark night came after the death of Bishop Bouvier but before the installation of Bishop Jean-Jacques Nanquette in November 1855.

170. Charles Moreau, *Moreau*, vol. 2, bk. 5, 32.

171. Barrosse's text reproduces in part Charles Moreau's. All of the following quotations, unless otherwise indicated, come from the account recorded by Fr. Séguin. Barrosse, *Moreau*, 224–28.

172. Moreau, CL 65, June 15, 1854, 1:306.

173. Moreau to Sorin, September 27, 1855, quoted in Barrosse, *Moreau*, 226.

174. De Jurien to Moreau, quoted in Barrosse, *Moreau*, 228.

175. CL 76, October 25, 1855, 1:340.

176. The sermon text is located in Charles Moreau, *Basil Moreau*, vol. 2, bk. 5, 32.

177. Moreau, CL 77, May 25, 1856, 1:357.

178. Moreau, CL 77, May 25, 1856, 1:356–57.

179. Moreau, *Christian Education* [hereafter CE], Introduction.

180. CE, part 1, chapter 1, article 4.

181. CE, part 3, chapter 4.

182. CL 77, May 25, 1856, 1:355.

183. The Vatican requested the alteration of the structure of Holy Cross before the constitutions were approved. The priests and brothers remained in one congregation, but the sisters had to be given a separate governance structure apart from the male religious. The Marianites of Holy Cross eventually were divided geographically with independent congregations related by a common heritage in Sainte-Croix. The Sisters of the Holy Cross were headquartered at Notre Dame, Indiana. The Sisters of Holy Cross were centered in Montreal, Canada. The Marianites of Holy Cross continued in France as well as Louisiana. On Vatican approval of Holy Cross, see Barrosse,

Moreau, 229–46. For a copy of the decree, see CL 86, July 3, 1857, 2:10. Although accepting the Vatican's decree for the separation of sisters from the priests and brothers, Moreau first and Sorin after him, as late as 1888, were still hoping the sisters, brothers, and priests could all be united in one congregation. O'Connell, *Edward Sorin*, 709.

184. CL 86, July 3, 1857, 2:10–11.

185. The rules and the *Catechism* still exist but are not included in the present volume because of the detailed nature of the *Rules* and because the *Catechism* is a compendium of teachings on religious life from the Catholic tradition and represents less of Moreau's original work. Archives of the Congregation of Holy Cross, University of Notre Dame.

186. CL 90, September 25, 1857, 2:38.

187. For a more detailed accounting of the 1860 General Chapter, see Catta and Catta, *Moreau*, 2:376–94.

188. Barrosse, *Moreau*, 273.

189. Barrosse explains that this was personally hurtful to Moreau as Moreau considered the rules one of his great contributions to the congregation. Barrosse, *Moreau*, 274.

190. Basil Moreau, quoted in Barrosse, *Moreau*, 275.

191. For two examples of protracted legal battles over benefactions, see Catta and Catta, *Moreau*, 1:660–65; 2:319–40.

192. Catta and Catta, *Moreau*, 2:418–420.

193. Sorin to Drouelle, February 8, 1861, quoted in Catta and Catta, *Moreau*, 2:415.

194. In CL 77, Moreau valued Holy Cross's assets at 1.2 million francs. In 1860, it was 1.5 million francs. The introduction of a 210,000 franc debt in addition to that already owed creditors was a great burden. CL 77, May 25, 1856, 1:354–55; and Connelly, *Basile Moreau*, 62.

195. Catta and Catta, *Moreau*, 2:257.

196. O'Connell, *Edward Sorin*, 642–45, 685–89, 694–98; Barrosse, *Moreau*, 292; and Catta and Catta, *Moreau*, 2:494ff.

197. O'Connell, *Edward Sorin*, 642–45.

198. Connelly, *Basile Moreau*, 62–63.

199. Bishop Nanquette had just began the visitation when he suddenly died in November 1861. Bishop Fillion, who succeeded him, completed the visitation. Connelly names Louis-Dom-inique Champeau, Victor Drouelle, and Edward Sorin, all of whom joined Holy Cross in their twenties and had since been assigned to Paris, Rome, and Notre Dame, respectively, as those who expressed their frustrations during the visitation. Connelly, *Basile Moreau*, 62–64.

200. Catta and Catta, *Moreau*, 2:505–26.

201. Catta and Catta, *Moreau*, 2:505–26; Barrosse, *Basil Moreau*, 326; and CL 188, June 21, 1866, 2:377.

202. CL 188, June 21, 1866, 2:377–8; and Barrosse, *Basil Moreau*, 327–29.

203. This visit and audience took place in 1868. Catta and Catta, *Moreau*, 2:835–63.

204. This living arrangement placed Moreau near Sainte-Croix as Holy Cross's assets in the town were auctioned and sold.

205. Sorin had written to Moreau in 1871, wishing him feast day (St. Basil) greetings and extending an invitation to leave the "mournful theater" of France. Sorin, still addressing Moreau as "Very Reverend Father" and signing his letter "your old devoted child," offered to provide for his arrangements. Sister of the Holy Cross, Mother Mary of St. Angela, also wrote to the founder and encouraged him to accept Sorin's invitation "to pass some quiet years among your spiritual children in America." Quoted in Catta and Catta, *Moreau*, 2:976–81; and Barrosse, *Moreau*, 380.

206. Catta and Catta, *Moreau*, 2:1009.

207. SE, Week 2, Day 1.

208. Moreau, Sermon, "Reception of the Habit for Carmelite Sisters," 1856. The young women would have changed garments in the course of the liturgy, exchanging their secular dress for religious dress. Moreau incorporates that liturgical action into his sermon.

209. Moreau will say a similar thing to his clerics, in his 1859 *Meditations*: "When you became a cleric, the clothes you wore in the world were taken from you and you put on a black garment unlike any the world uses," and for the profession of vows "you lay stretched out on the sacred floor like a corpse in a sepulcher. You have died to the earthly world. Never forget that." SE, Week 3, Day 7.

210. Mork, *Moreau Spirituality*, 83–181.

211. Perreault, *Another Christ*, 28n15, n16.

212. The most important personal example was Moreau's dark night of 1855.

213. CL 34, June 19, 1848, 1:141–42.

214. In a related manner, Moreau often uses the image of a tree with different branches to describe Holy Cross and its union with Christ. CL 11, January 8, 1841, 1:33.

215. CE, part 3, chapter 4.

216. CE, Conclusion.

217. From the sixth-century hymn written for the translation of a relic of the Holy Cross, *Vexilla regis prodeunt*: "*O, Crux Ave, Spes Unica!*" The word order is often modified in Holy Cross from the hymn text to *Ave Crux, Spes Unica*.

218. Examples of divine providence in the French School include Jean-Pierre de Caussade (1675–1751) and Louis-Marie Grignion de Montfort (1673–1716). Jean-Pierre de Caussade, *Abandonment to Divine Providence* (Notre Dame: Ave Maria Press, 2010); and Louis-Marie Grignion de Montfort, *True Devotion to Mary with Preparation for Total Consecration*, trans. Frederick William Faber (Charlotte, NC: Saint Benedict Press, 2010).

219. CL 36, April 15, 1849, 1:162.

220. CL 179, January 10, 1865, 2:348.

221. Robert J. Kruse, *Basil Moreau: The Cross (A Study in Spiritual Theology)* (Rome: Pontificia Universitas Gregoriana, 1964), 38.

222. CL 5, December 27, 1837, 1:11.

223. CL 20, January 5, 1844, 1:79.

224. CL 23, January 4, 1845, 1:89.

225. CL 143, July 7, 1861, 2:199.

226. CL 26, January 3, 1847, 1:113.

227. CL 14, September 1, 1841, 1:38, 42.

228. CL 170, August 22, 1863, 2:293.

229. CL 170, August 22, 1863, 2:293.

230. Moreau uses this idea in his *Spiritual Exercises*. For example, when reflecting on humility in the Incarnation, he writes of Christ leading the disciple through the steps of humility to union with neighbor and also with the triune God. SE, Week 2, Day 2.

231. This theme also runs through the *Spiritual Exercises*. See in particular SE, Week 2, Day 8.

232. Moreau asked for an hour of devotion from each of his religious before the Blessed Sacrament each day. See, for example, CL 37, June 14, 1839, 1:171.

233. Moreau also wrote often about the disposition for receiving the Blessed Sacrament, because he desired for his religious to receive Communion frequently. He exhorts them: "Rouse in yourself, therefore, the desire for frequent Communion but always in accord with your Rules."

Pope Pius X later urged frequent communion for the entire Church in *Sacra Tridentina*, promulgated on December 20, 1905. See SE, Week 1, Day 8; and Moreau, Sermon, "Holy Communion."

234. Moreau, "Holy Communion." For Moreau on the sacrament of Reconciliation, see Moreau, "Confession"; SE, Week I, Day 7; and SE, Week 1, Day 8.

235. Moreau, "Holy Communion."

236. Moreau, "Holy Communion."

237. This is a frequent theme in the fourth week of Moreau's *Spiritual Exercises*. SE, Week 4. See also Mork, *Moreau Spirituality*, 26–82.

238. CL 14, September 1, 1841, 1:41.

239. The virtues of teachers that Moreau treats are faithfulness, knowledge, zeal, vigilance, seriousness, gentleness, patience, prudence, and firmness. CE, part 1, chapter 1, article 4.

Chapter 1: Sermons

1. Moreau takes these ways from the four weeks from the *Spiritual Exercises* of St. Ignatius. What follows draws upon Moreau's own version of the *Spiritual Exercises* that he wrote for his congregation.

2. "Manifestations" refers to Jesus' resurrection appearances to the disciples.

3. "V." and "R." are abbreviations in liturgical prayer denoting "versicle" and "response." The leader of prayer says the versicle, while the congregation together says the response.

4. The invitatory is the psalm prayed at the beginning of the first hour of the Divine Office or the Liturgy of the Hours.

5. The proper of the Mass consists of the prayers "proper" to a given celebration of the Mass, whether those are of a particular liturgical season or saint.

6. Formerly known in Latin as *jejunia quattuor temporum* or "fasts of the four seasons," Ember Days were four separate series of Wednesdays, Fridays, and Saturdays within the same week that were set aside as days of fasting and prayer (until the reforms of the Second Vatican Council). The weeks in which the Ember Days fall are (1) between the third and fourth Sundays of Advent, (2) between the first and second Sundays of Lent, (3) between Pentecost and Trinity Sunday, and (4) the week beginning the Sunday after September 14 (the Feast of the Exaltation of the Cross). The *Te Deum*, as part of the Liturgy of the Hours, and the *Gloria in excelsis*, as part of the Mass, are usually prayed on Sundays and other major solemnities in the Church.

7. For more examples of colloquies, see chapter 2, Spiritual Exercises.

8. Derived from the "little prayer" of Fr. Charles de Condren (1588–1641), this prayer was written by Jean-Jacques Olier (1608–1657), one of the leading thinkers of the French School and a major influence on Moreau.

9. *Dies irae* or "Day of Wrath" is a thirteenth-century Latin hymn that was used as the sequence for the Requiem Mass and in the Liturgy for All Souls' Day until the liturgical reforms of the Second Vatican Council.

10. See p. 61.

11. Vincent de Paul, *St. Vincent de Paul: Correspondance, entretiens, documents*, ed. Pierre Coste (Paris: Librairie Lecoffre, 1920–1925), 3:56.

12. Tertullian, *Apologeticum*, 39.7.

13. Thomas à Kempis, *The Imitation of Christ*, 1.16.

14. Moreau's preaching here is very similar to his CL 14.

15. Jacques-Bénigne Bossuet (1627–1704) was a renowned French bishop, preacher, and orator.

16. From the Latin root *laesa maiestas*, literally meaning "injuried majesty," the term refers to an offense of crime violating the dignity of a ruler.

17. Clement I, *Epistle to the Corinthians*, 57; Ignatius of Antioch, *Letter to the Philadelphians*, 8:1.

18. *Didache*, chapter 4.

19. Louis Bourdaloue (1632–1704) was a famous Jesuit preacher known as "the king of preachers and the preacher of kings," since he was repeatedly invited to preach Advent and Lenten sermons in Versailles.

20. Council of Trent, Session 22, Doctrine concerning the Sacrifice of the Mass (September 17, 1562), 6. In Moreau's time, many people did not receive Communion weekly, let alone daily. Moreau regularly exhorted both his religious as well as lay men and women, at the retreats he preached, to go to Communion frequently, even daily.

21. Moreau is playing on the word "pasch," which means a "passing over," in terms of religious life.

22. à Kempis, *Imitation*, 1.18.

23. à Kempis, *Imitation*, 1.18.

24. à Kempis, *Imitation*, 2.12.

25. à Kempis, *Imitation*, 1.18.

26. Moreau's reference to Ps 77:10 is a literal translation of *nunc coepi* in the Vulgate (76:11).

27. This seems to be an indication of Moreau's either paraphrasing or quoting scripture from memory. He substitutes *dilexit* for *amabat*.

28. St. Margaret Mary Alacoque (1647–1690) promoted devotion to the Sacred Heart of Jesus after a series of visions. Moreau is preaching before her beatification (1864) and canonization (1920) as well as before the Feast of the Sacred Heart was celebrated universally in the Church (1856). Hence, he shows a certain prudence in referring to Margaret and her visions and teaching.

29. St. Claude de la Colombière (1641–1682) was the Jesuit spiritual director of Margaret Mary Alacoque.

30. Pius VI, *Auctorem fidei*, August 28, 1794.

31. Only in 1856, at the direction of Pope Pius IX, was the devotion to the Sacred Heart of Jesus extended to the universal Church. Until then, celebration of the devotion was left to local discretion.

32. This sermon can be dated to 1841. The dogma of the Immaculate Conception was not formally declared until thirteen years later on December 8, 1854, by Pope Pius IX in *Ineffabilis deus*.

33. This pronouncement was made at the First Council of Ephesus, which was held in 431. Nestorius, the patriarch of Constantinople, conceived of the loose union between Christ's human and divine natures. Though he denied it, he is accused of a two-person, two-nature Christology. He suggested that Mary could be called the Christ-bearer, but only as the bearer of the flesh the Word assumed. As part of its repudiation of Nestorius, the council declared Mary as *Theotokos* (God-bearer), maintaining that Christ's human and divine natures were united in one person.

34. The Seraphic Order is another name given to the Franciscans, since their founder, St. Francis of Assisi, had a vision in which a seraph appeared to him.

35. Jean Charlier de Gerson (1363–1429), who served as the chancellor of the University of Paris, was one of the more prominent theologians at the Council of Constance (1414–1418).

36. Francisco Suárez (1548–1617), a Spanish Jesuit who was a leading figure of the Salamanca movement and was regarded as one of the great scholastics after St. Thomas Aquinas, wrote on St. Joseph in his work.

37. Lapide (1567–1637) was a Flemish Jesuit who wrote commentaries on all the books of the Bible, minus Job and the Psalms.

38. In the time of Moreau, the Sacred Congregation of Rites was the Vatican congregation responsible for overseeing the liturgy and the other sacraments, as well as the process for the canonization of the saints. In 1969, Pope Paul VI divided it into two separate congregations: the Congregation for the Causes of Saints and the Congregation for Divine Worship. The *A cunctis* (literally, "everybody") prayer is for the Tridentine Mass.

39. Moreau is referencing the Basilica of the Holy House in Loreto, Italy, where it is believed the house of the Holy Family was moved in the thirteenth century.

40. Moreau seemingly references as one what are actually two separate scriptural stories involving the miraculous movement of the sun: the first when the sun stopped at Joshua's prayer (Jos 10:12–13) and the second when the sun moved back ten degrees for King Hezekiah at the command of Isaiah (2 Kgs 20:10–11).

41. The Church has never officially declared that St. Joseph was assumed, body and soul, into heaven. Yet, in a homily on the Feast of the Ascension on May 26, 1960, Blessed John XXIII said that it could be "piously believed" that St. Joseph, along with St. John the Baptist, were assumed into heaven at the time of the Lord's ascension. John XXIII, "Homily for the Canonization of Saint Gregory Barbarigo," May 26, 1960.

42. Moreau preached to a Carmelite community on the occasion of new sisters entering the novitiate and receiving their habits. The sermon dates from 1856.

CHAPTER 2: SPIRITUAL EXERCISES

1. Ignatius, *Spiritual Exercises*, annotation 10.

2. Ignatius, *Spiritual Exercises*, annotation 91.

3. The sacrament of Extreme Unction is known today as the Anointing of the Sick.

4. One instance of Augustine on this topic is *City of God*, 5.18.

5. Irenaeus, *Against Heresies*, 3.18.7.

6. Ignatius, *Spiritual Exercises*, annotation 234.

7. The book of Esther in the Vulgate is six chapters longer than the recognized length of the book today. Moreau was paraphrasing one of these later chapters.

8. This comes from Gregory of Nyssa's *On Perfection*, a treatise in letter form that worked through Pauline theology. See St. Gregory of Nyssa, *Ascetical Works*, trans. Virginia Woods Callahan, The Fathers of the Church, vol. 58 (Washington, DC: Catholic University of America Press, 1999), 93–124.

9. This and the following sayings of Martin of Tours all come from the writings of Sulpicius Severus, the chronicler known for his biography of Martin of Tours. These citations come from Sulpicius's Letter 3 to Bassula, in which he describes the death of Martin of Tours.

10. The Solitude was the name of the building used for the Holy Cross novitiate.

11. Gregory of Nyssa, *On Perfection*.

12. Bernardin de Picquigny, *Explication des épîtres de saint Paul* (Paris: Chez Méquignon, 1813).

13. François de Ligny, *Histoire de la vie de Notre Seigneur Jésus-Christ* (Avignon: Joseph-Thomas Domergue, 1774); the English translation: *The History of the Life of Our Lord and Savior Jesus Christ: From His Incarnation until His Ascension: Denoting and Incorporating the Words of the Sacred Text from the Vulgate* (New York: D. & J. Sadlier, 1869); Jean-Baptiste de Saint-Jure, *Le livre des élus ou Jesus*

crucifié (Paris: Chez la veuve de Gabriel-Charles Berton, 1759), and *De la connaissance et de l'amour du fils de Dieu Notre-Seigneur Jésus-Christ* (Paris: Chez Sebastien Crmoisy, 1641).

14. A paraphrase of Augustine, *Confessions*, 11.2.2-3.

15. Moreau is drawing on Ignatius, *Spiritual Exercises*, annotation 234.

16. "State of life" refers to the permanent way or form of life into which a vocation places a person. Traditionally, the three states of life are lay, religious, and clerical. The novices in the course of their novitiate would be discerning whether or not God was calling them to become a religious brother or religious priest.

17. St. Margaret Mary Alacoque (1647–1690).

18. This is attributed to St. Peter Damian (1007–1072).

19. Though the Assumption of Mary was not made a dogma of the Catholic Church until 1950, the celebration of the feast can be traced to as early as the fourth century. It was widely popular in France in the nineteenth century.

20. The *Regina Coeli* is the Marian antiphon sung at the end of Compline, the last office of the day in the Liturgy of the Hours, from Easter through Pentecost.

21. à Kempis, *Imitation*, 3.31.

22. à Kempis, *Imitation*, 3.47.

23. Teresa of Avila, *Autobiography*, chapter 40.

CHAPTER 3: CHRISTIAN MEDITATIONS

1. The epistle and gospel readings for the Feast of the Epiphany were Is 60:1–6 and Mt 2:1–12.

2. Depending on the date of Easter, there were up to six Sundays following the Feast of the Epiphany and before Septuagesima, which marked the third Sunday before Ash Wednesday and thus began the countdown to the season of Lent. The epistle and gospel readings for the Third Sunday after the Epiphany were Rm 12:16–21 and Mt 8:1–13.

3. The epistle and gospel readings for the Sixth Sunday after the Epiphany were 1 Thes 1:2–10 and Mt 13:31–35.

4. Demas was involved in ministry as a coworker of St. Paul (Col 4:14). While with Paul in his first imprisonment in Rome (Phlm 1:24), he would later desert Paul after having become "enamored of the present world" (2 Tm 4:10).

5. Sexagesima was the second Sunday before Ash Wednesday. It was part of a three-week period, beginning with Septuagesima the week prior, leading into Lent. The name, which means "the sixtieth," derived from an approximation of the days (fifty-seven) leading to the celebration of Easter. The epistle and gospel readings for Sexagesima were 2 Cor 11:19–12:9 and Lk 8:4–15.

6. Moreau uses *parole* in referring to the scriptures, and it is translated here as "word." When referring to the incarnate Son of God, Moreau uses *Verbe*, and it is translated here as "Word."

7. Caesarius of Arles, Sermon 78.2.

8. The epistle and gospel readings for the Friday after the Third Sunday of Lent were Nm 20:1–3; 6–13; and Jn 4:5–42.

9. These words are attributed to a letter from St. Francis de Sales (1567–1622) to St. Jane Frances de Chantal (1572–1641). The two together founded the Institute of the Visitation of the Blessed Virgin.

10. This prayer, also known by its first two Latin words, *En ego*, was frequently said kneeling before a crucifix or after Communion or Mass.

11. The epistle and gospel readings for the Fourth Sunday of Lent were Gal 4:22–31; 6–13; and Jn 6:1–15.

12. The epistle and gospel readings for the Friday after Passion Sunday, which was the Sunday before Palm Sunday (or Passion Sunday II), were Jer 17:13–18 and Jn 11:47–54.

13. The *Stabat* or *Stabat mater dolororsa* is a thirteenth-century hymn about the sorrows of Mary, traditionally sung as a part of the Stations of the Cross.

14. Quasimodo Sunday was the Sunday immediately following the celebration of Easter, thus concluding the Easter Octave. The epistle and gospel readings for Quasimodo Sunday were 1 Jn 5:4–10 and Jn 20:19–31.

15. à Kempis, *Imitation*, 1.6.

16. à Kempis, *Imitation*, 3.13.

17. The epistle and gospel readings for the Fourth Sunday after Easter were Jas 1:17–21 and Jn 16:5–14.

18. The Company of Jesus is one of the formal names of the Jesuits.

19. Formally the Order of St. Bruno, the Carthusians were founded by St. Bruno of Cologne (1030–1101) in 1084. They follow their own rule, rather than the rule of St. Benedict as many other monastic communities. Unlike many monastic and religious communities, as Moreau notes, the Carthusians have never undergone a reform.

20. The Abbey of Clairvaux is a Cistercian monastery in Ville-sous-la-Ferté in northeastern France. It was founded by St. Bernard (1090–1153) in 1115. After several centuries, the monastery was reformed by Denis Largentier beginning in 1615.

21. Rule 20 of the 1858 rules addressed silence, which included "Grand Silence" from Evening Prayer until after meditation the following morning, as well as directions on places of the house in which one was always to keep strict silence, such as the chapel, or only to speak in a low voice, such as in the sacristy or living quarters.

22. The epistle and gospel readings for the Fifth Sunday after Easter were Jas 1:22–27 and Jn 16:23–30.

23. The Rogation Days were four days set apart in the liturgical year for invoking God's mercy, often in solemn procession. Following the Second Vatican Council, their celebration was left to the decision of individual episcopal conferences. The Major Rogation was celebrated April 25, while the three Minor Rogations were celebrated the Monday, Tuesday, and Wednesday leading up to the Feast of the Ascension. The Fifth Sunday of Easter fell right before the Minor Rogations and thus was often called "Rogation Sunday." The name for the days comes from the Latin verb *rogare*, meaning "to ask," which was a part of that Sunday's gospel: "Ask, and you will receive" (Jn 16:24).

24. Moreau writes Milan here, though seemingly referencing reforms that Borromeo made in Milan after the Council of Trent. Called to Rome and made a cardinal by his uncle, Pope Pius IV, Borromeo (1538–1584) was responsible for organizing the final sessions of the Council of Trent (1562–1563). As Archbishop of Milan he implemented those reforms in his diocese, with particular attention to the establishment of seminaries for the better education and training of clergy.

25. Benedict XIV, *Quemadmodum nihil*, December 16, 1746.

26. The word "obediences" refers to the tasks or responsibilities assigned to a religious by his or her superiors. The word flows from the vow of obedience taken by religious. Obediences can be as simple as one's house chores or as significant as one's ministerial assignments.

27. The Sixth Sunday after Easter was also the Sunday that fell in between the celebrations of the Ascension and Pentecost. The epistle and gospel readings for this Sunday were 1 Pt 4:7–11 and Jn 15:26–16:4.

28. The Cenacle is also where, by tradition, Jesus celebrated the Last Supper with his disciples.

29. In this paragraph, Moreau has written of the seven gifts of the Holy Spirit, which are derived from Is 11:2–3.

30. The epistle and gospel readings for the Feast of Pentecost were Acts 2:1–11 and Jn 14:23–31.

31. The First Sunday after Pentecost was also Trinity Sunday. The epistle and gospel readings for this Sunday were Rom 11:33–36 and Mt 28:18–20.

32. Lucius Caecilius Firmianus Lactantius was a late third-, early fourth-century Christian author who became a religious advisor to Constantine I, the first Christian emperor of Rome.

33. Arianism, named for Arius, the priest who promoted this teaching, was a late third-, early fourth-century heresy that held that the Son of God was subordinate to God the Father, thereby undoing any sense of God being triune. It was first declared heretical by the First Council of Nicaea in 325, a declaration that was later reaffirmed by the First Council of Constantinople in 381.

34. These words are part of the Prayer of Commendation said by the priest when a person is near death.

35. The epistle and gospel readings for this feast were 1 Cor 11:23–29 and Jn 6:56–59.

36. Processions with the Blessed Sacrament, often elaborate and led through the neighborhoods surrounding the church, marked the celebration of this feast.

37. Denis Diderot, "Lépicié," in *Essais sur la peinture* (Paris: Chez Fr. Buisson, 1796), 304. Diderot (1713–1784) was a prominent philosopher in the French Enlightenment; his writings often expressed a negative or critical view of organized religion.

CHAPTER 4: CHRISTIAN EDUCATION

1. With *Christian Education*, Moreau included a book of hymns or songs (*Cantiques a l'usage de l'institution de Sainte-Croix et des écoles de la congrégation*). The hymns occupy 179 pages, whereas, by way of comparison, the three parts of *Christian Education* together are 154 pages.

2. Moreau here, using a substantive, *conduite*, plays on the Greek *agōgē*. The usage implies also learning to conduct oneself.

3. Francis de Sales, *Introduction to the Devout Life*, part 3, chapter 8.

4. At the end of the text, Moreau provides one sample lesson, which he compiles from two other sources. Moreau cites a historical passage retelling the story of the finding of Jesus in the Temple (Lk 2:41–52) from de Ligny's *Histoire de la vie de notre seigneur Jésus-Christ* (Avignon: Joseph-Thomas Domergue, 1774). Then Moreau provides a sample dialogue between teacher and student concerning the text. The example comes from Bernard Overberg's *Manuel de pédagogie et de méthodique générale: ou, guide de l'instituteur primaire* (Lege: L. Grandmont-Donders, 1845).

5. In 1859, three years after writing *Christian Education*, Moreau would write his own catechism for use by the congregation. *Catéchisme de la vie chrétienne et de la vie religieuse à l'usage de la Congrégation de Sainte-Croix* (Le Mans: Imprimerie Étiembre et Beauvais, 1859).

6. Council of Trent, Session 6, Decree on Justification, 8 (January 13, 1547).

7. Augustine, *Confessions*, 9.6.14.

CHAPTER 5: CIRCULAR LETTERS

1. This letter, though outlining the plan for the whole Congregation of Holy Cross, was addressed to the Brothers of St. Joseph, whose leadership Moreau assumed from Fr.

Jacques-François Dujarié. At this point, the Auxiliary Priests were few in number and the sisters were just beginning their novitiate. Many future circular letters were addressed either to all three branches of Holy Cross or to the brothers and the priests.

2. à Kempis, *Imitation*, 1.16.

3. The Congregation of the Good Shepherd was founded in Angers by St. Euphrasia Pelletier (1796–1868), and Moreau became the superior of their house in Le Mans from 1833 until 1854. These sisters are distinct from those who would later become the sisters, or Marianites, of Holy Cross.

4. Dujarié was the founder of the Brothers of St. Joseph.

5. St. Jean-Baptiste de La Salle (1651–1719) was the founder of the Institute of the Brothers of the Christian Schools (known as the "Christian Brothers"). He was canonized in 1900. It was to his community, which managed to survive the French Revolution, that Dujarié sent some of his earliest brothers for training and instruction as well as for a model of a rule they could follow.

6. Moreau's title changed in his circular letters according to the status of Holy Cross. When Holy Cross operated under diocesan jurisdiction, Moreau was known as "missionary apostolic." Moreau became the superior general when Holy Cross came to be under Vatican control. The congregation was fully recognized when its constitutions were approved on May 13, 1857.

7. Br. André Mottais (1800–1844) was one of the first brothers in Dujarié's community. He played an instrumental role in assisting with leadership of the community and then with the subsequent change to Moreau's leadership. Moreau continued to rely on Mottais's leadership.

8. The Sacred Congregation for the Propagation of the Faith (Sacra Congregatio de Propaganda Fide) oversaw missionary endeavors for the Catholic Church.

9. St. Euphrasia Pelletier. See chapter 5, Circular Letters, n3 above.

10. For the use of the word "obediences" in this context, see 3. Christian Meditations, n26. Obediences here refer to the formal communication of ministerial and living assignments from their superiors to members of the Congregation.

11. The cathedral of Le Mans.

12. Moreau is referencing the text of Jean-Baptiste de La Salle, *Conduite des écoles chrétiennes*. De La Salle worked on the text through his later years, and it was published posthumously in 1720. Beginning with André Mottais, the Brothers of St. Joseph had sought out the Christian Brothers as a model for education. Moreau's own *Christian Education* would not be written for another ten years.

13. The reference is to the civil law that granted exemption from military service to those young men who obligated themselves to devote at least ten years to teaching in primary schools. The Brothers of St. Joseph enjoyed this exemption.

14. Teaching rights certified that Notre-Dame de Sainte-Croix could prepare students for the study of rhetoric and philosophy as any *lycée* or royal college did. Moreau had worked for nearly a decade against both civil and ecclesiastical opposition to obtain these full teaching rights. At the civil level, anticlericals on area educational boards had attempted to block Moreau's efforts. At the ecclesiastical level, Bishop Bouvier saw Moreau's starting a school as competing with his seminaries, which at the time educated a significant population of students who were not pursuing Holy Orders. During this time, Moreau continued to develop the school and the qualifications of its faculty. By the 1850s, Notre-Dame de Sainte-Croix had become academically the best school in its region.

15. When Moreau speaks of "university" here, he is not speaking of the concept of a university in general but of the French universities at the time. These universities—not including seminaries—had undergone their own revolutionary reforms and played a role in the granting

and regulation of full teaching rights. Moreau would be misunderstood to be against university education here. The issue, rather, was university education that was opposed to faith, which he thought to be the case in France at the time.

16. Moreau paraphrases Francis Bacon (1561–1626), *Of the Proficience and Advancement of Learning, Divine and Human*, I.3.

17. In order to aid the effort for full teaching rights, a friend in the Ministry of Public Instruction helped Moreau to get their students seated for exams; otherwise, admission was based on a university-approved educational institution. Moreau also sent faculty for degrees in order to meet faculty qualifications.

18. Bernard of Clairvaux, *Sermon 51 on the Song of Songs*.

19. In addition to the spiritual realities about which Moreau speaks, the reading of various partisan newspapers could create the perception of a religious congregation's political alliance in post-Revolutionary France. As Moreau will explain, those who played a role in granting Holy Cross full teaching rights were pleased, in part, by this nonpartisan stance reflected in the prohibition against (largely) partisan newspapers.

20. Fr. Gabriel Mollevaut, who was rector at the Solitude in Issy the year that Moreau spent there (1822–1823) and had been Moreau's spiritual director since then, died in 1854.

21. à Kempis, *Imitation*, 1.1.

22. à Kempis, *Imitation*, 1.18.

23. In 1837, Fr. Dubignon designated Moreau as the sole heir in his will. Upon Dubignon's death in 1847, when it became known that his legacy was to go solely to Moreau and Holy Cross, a controversy arose because Holy Cross was seen as supporting foreign missions, draining money from the local church. Moreau had to agree to pay parts of the inheritance to the local seminary as restitution for Dubignon's prior food and board. A second bequest of the Dubignon family, this one from Dubignon's sister, was also the cause of a lawsuit between 1857 and 1861.

24. A general chapter is a regular legislative meeting, attended by representatives or capitulants from the wider community, that serves as the highest governing body of Holy Cross. For example, it is the body that elects the superior general of the congregation.

25. The *Te Deum* is an early Christian hymn of praise, typically sung as part of the Divine Office on Sundays and other major solemnities. It is also a tradition to sing it in celebration of a special blessing.

26. The priests were required, by the Church, to pray the Divine Office. For the brothers, the Little Office of the Blessed Virgin was considered acceptable, in part because it was in French, whereas at that time the Divine Office was only prayed in Latin.

27. The letter was printed without a formal salutation. The second sentence of the letter indicates the addressees were the priests and brothers of Holy Cross.

28. The threefold concupiscence (1 Jn 2:16) references the three desires the fruit produced in Adam and Eve (Gn 3:6) at the fall. Christ overcame these three desires in his temptations in the desert in the Synoptic gospels. The religious vows of poverty, chastity, and obedience—as well as the Gospel practices of almsgiving, fasting, and prayer, respectively—are understood as actions undertaken for the reformation of those desires in Christ.

29. See explanatory note concerning Moreau and corporal mortification in the introduction: Introduction, n52.

30. Moreau is alluding to the conflict between Pius IX and Victor Emmanuel and the loss of land of the papal states in the 1860s.

31. These exams provided credentials not only to the faculty members but also to the schools. See chapter 5, Circular Letters, n17.

32. Moreau is referencing Christ.

33. Br. Marie-Julien, working in Paris, had invested a fifth of the congregation's net worth in a scam. See the introduction, "Moreau from 1860 to 1866, 1. Financial Woes."

34. Moreau included the letter from Cardinal Barnabo, the prefect of the Propaganda Fide, in CL 177, November 22, 1864, 2:333–336.

35. In his encyclical *Quanta cura* and the *Syllabus errorum* ("Syllabus of Errors") released in conjunction with it, Pope Pius IX addressed, among a number of diverse issues, the intersection between Church and state, condemning some political positions related to freedom of speech and religion, democracy, and socialism. He closed the encyclical by declaring 1865 a jubilee year and offering a plenary indulgence. Pius IX, *Quanta cura*, December 8, 1864: 10.

36. One manuscript copy has a salutation including the male religious. Perhaps because of the content of the letter or the announcements of the postscript, this letter might have been sent out to all of Holy Cross.

37. Moreau had gone to the Cistercian monastery at Thymadeuc, approximately 150 miles to the west of Le Mans, for retreat.

38. Moreau is teaching the sisters the sorts of authority that exist in the Church and those which they exercised. It was particularly important for Moreau to inform the sisters of their authority as a congregation because it was coming into conflict at different points with local bishops who preferred to have the sisters under diocesan control rather than the level of an international congregation. These three types of authority—*potestas jurisdictionis, dominativa, and domestica*—still exist in modern canon law concerning religious institutes. See Canon 596§1.

39. à Kempis, *Imitation*, 1.18.

40. à Kempis, *Imitation*, 2.3.

SELECTED BIBLIOGRAPHY

Published Primary Sources

French

Moreau, Basil. *Catéchisme de la vie chrétienne et de la vie religieuse à l'usage de la Congrégation de Sainte-Croix.* Le Mans: Imprimerie Étiembre et Beauvais, 1859.

——. *De tout un peu: Moreau et Mollevaut, extraits divers.* Edited by R. P. Philéas Vanier, C.S.C. Québec: Scolasticat Sainte-Croix, 1923.

——. *Exercices de Saint-Ignace et méditations à l'usage des Joséphites, de Marianites et des Salvatoristes.* 3 vols. Le Mans: Gallienne, 1855.

——. *Lettres Circulaires du Très Révérend Père Basile Moreau: Fondateur des Religieux et des Religieuses de Sainte-Croix.* 2 vols. Montreal: Éditions Fides, 1941–42.

——. *Méditations à l'usage des Frères de Saint-Joseph du Mans, d'après la méthode de Saint-Ignace.* Le Mans: Gallienne, 1848.

——. *Méditations chrétiennes a l'usage des fidèles et du clergé séculier avec approbation de l'Ordinaire.* Montreal: Oratoire Saint-Joseph, 1932. First published 1872 by Ed. Monnoyer.

——. *Pédagogie chrétienne à l'usage des Joséphites de la Congrégation de Sainte-Croix.* Le Mans: Imprimerie Julien, Lanier et Cie, 1856.

——. *Recueil de cantiques à l'usage des Joséphites de la Congrégation de Sainte-Croix.* Le Mans: Imprimerie Julien, Lanier et Cie, 1856.

——. *Recueil Documentaire: Le très révérend Père Moreau d'après ses écrits, ses correspondants et les documents de l'époque (1799–1835).* Edited by R. P. Philéas Vanier, C.S.C. New York: L'Administration Générale de Sainte-Croix, 1945.

——. *Sermons publiés par ordre du chapitre général (1920) de la Congrégation de Sainte-Croix.* Montreal: Congrégation de Sainte-Croix, 1923.

English

Moreau, Basil. *Circular Letters of the Very Reverend Basil Antony Mary Moreau: Founder of the Religious of Holy Cross.* Translated by Edward L. Heston. 2 vols. Notre Dame: Ave Maria Press, 1943–44.

——. *Our Light and Our Way: Conferences for Religious.* Translated by M. Eleanore. Milwaukee: Bruce Publishing Company, 1936.

Secondary Sources

Barrosse, Thomas. *Moreau: Portrait of a Founder*. Notre Dame: Fides Publishers, 1969.

Bednarczyk, Paul. "Basil Anthony Moreau and the Eucharist: A Recovery for Contemporary Apostolic Religious Life within the Congregation of Holy Cross." MA diss., Fordham University, 1990.

Bergeron, Henri-Paul. *Basile Moreau, fondateur des religieux et des religieuses du congrégations Sainte-Croix*. Rome: Congrégation de Sainte-Croix, 1979.

———. *Basil Moreau: Founder of the Congregations of Holy Cross*. Translated by Eveline Swaile. Rome: Congregation of Holy Cross, 1985.

Bernoville, Gaëtan. *Basile Moreau et la Congrégation de Sainte-Croix*. Paris: Grasset, 1952.

Beston, William. *Moreau: The "Suffering Servant" of Holy Cross, and the Inspirer of Union and Community Spirit*. Wilkes-Barre, PA: King's College, 1973.

Catta, Etienne, and Tony Catta. *Basil Anthony Mary Moreau*. Translated by Edward L. Heston. 2 vols. Milwaukee: Bruce Publishing Company, 1955.

———. *Le T.R.P. Basile-Antoine Moreau (1799–1873) et les origines de la Congrégation de Sainte-Croix*. 3 vols. Montreal: Éditions Fides, 1950.

———. *Mother Mary of the Seven Dolors and the Early Origins of the Marianites of Holy Cross (1818–1900)*. Translated by Edward L. Heston. Milwaukee: Catholic Life Publications, Bruce Press, 1959.

Catta, Tony. *Father Dujarié: Pastor of Ruillé-sur-Loir, Canon of Le Mans, Founder of the Communities of the Sisters of Providence, and the Brothers of St. Joseph, Now the Brothers of Holy Cross (1767–1838)*. Translated by Edward L. Heston. Milwaukee: Catholic Life Publications, Bruce Press, 1960.

———. *Le Père Dujarié (1767–1838): Curé de Ruillé-sur-Loir, Chanoine honoraire du Mans, Fondateur des Communautés des Sœurs de la Providence et des Frères de Saint-Joseph, Maintenant Frères de Sainte-Croix*. Paris: Éditions Fides, 1958.

Connelly, James. *Basile Moreau and the Congregation of Holy Cross*. Portland, OR: Garaventa Center for Catholic Intellectual Life and American Culture, 2007.

Cousineau, Albert. *Principes de vie sacerdotale et religieuse: À l'école du vénéré Père Basile Moreau, fondateur de la Congrégation de Sainte-Croix*. Montreal: Éditions Fides, 1952.

Denn, James. *The Theology of Preaching in the Writings of Basil Anthony Moreau*. Rome: Catholic Book Agency, 1969.

Donahue, James. *Basil Anthony Moreau, C.S.C.: Founder of the Congregation of Holy Cross, Missionary and Educator*. Notre Dame: Ave Maria Press, 1937.

Fitzgerald, Gerald. *Juxta Crucem: The Life of Basil Anthony Moreau, 1799–1873*. New York: P. J. Kennedy & Sons, 1937.

Fontenelle, Renatus. *Articles produits par Mgr. R. Fontenelle, postulateur en la cause du serviteur de Dieu Basile-Antoine Moreau, fondateur et premier supérieur général de la Congrégation de Sainte-Croix*. Montreal: Éditions Fides, 1948.

Frechet, Léandre. *Jesus the Christ in the Writings of Basil Moreau, C.S.C.* Translated by Alan Harrod. Rome: Congregation of Holy Cross, 1985.

———. "Saint Joseph d'après le P. Basile-Antoine Moreau, C.S.C." *Cahiers de Joséphologie* 22, no. 1 (1974): 1–89.

Giallanza, Joel, ed. *A Simple Tool: The Mission and Message of Father Basil Moreau*. Rome: Instituto Salesiano Pio XI, 1998.

Grisé, Jacques. *Basile Moreau: homme d'action, homme de Dieu*. Québec: Éditions Fides, 2004.

Kruse, Robert J. *Basil Moreau: The Cross (A Study in Spiritual Theology)*. Rome: Pontificia Universitas Gregoriana, 1964.

Lalande, Graziella. *Like a Mighty Tree*. Translated by Eveline Swaile. Montreal: Éditions Fides, 1989.

————. *Qui êtes-vous, Basile Moreau?* Montreal: Éditions Fides, 2010.

Legault, André. *Le Pére Moreau 1799–1872, fondateur des religieux et des religieuses de Sainte-Croix*. Montreal: Éditions Fides, 1945.

MacEoin, Gary. *Father Moreau: Founder of Holy Cross*. Milwaukee: Bruce Publishing Company, 1962. Republished as *Basil Moreau: Founder of Holy Cross*. Notre Dame: Ave Maria Press, 2007.

Moreau, Charles. *Le Très Révérend Père Basile-Antoine Moreau, prêtre du Mans, et ses œuvres*. 2 vols. Paris: Firmin-Didot, 1898–1900.

————. *Lettre contradictoires sur la vie et les œuvres du T.R. père Basile Moreau, prête du Mans*. Mayenne: Imprimerie Ch. Colin, 1901.

————. *The Very Reverend Father Basil Anthony Mary Moreau: Priest of Le Mans and His Works*. Translated by the Congregation of Holy Cross. Paris: Firmin-Didot, 1900.

Morin, Robert, et al. *Basile Moreau*. Le Mans: *s.n.*, 1962.

Mork, Wulstan. *Moreau Spirituality*. Notre Dame: Sisters of the Holy Cross, 1973.

————. *Spiritualité Moreau*. Translated by Germain de Serres. Rome: Congrégation de Sainte-Croix, 1986.

Mullahy, Bernard. *The Spirituality of the Very Reverend Basil Anthony Moreau*. Notre Dame: Ave Maria Press, 1948.

O'Connell, Marvin R. *Edward Sorin*. Notre Dame: University of Notre Dame Press, 2001.

O'Dwyer, Ephrem. *The Curé of Ruillé: A Sketch of the Very Reverend James Francis Dujarié, Founder of the Sisters of Providence and the Brothers of Saint Joseph of Ruillé*. Notre Dame: Ave Maria Press, 1941.

Perreault, Cécile. *Devenir un autre Christ: L'identification à Jésus-Christ selon Basile Moreau*. Montreal: Éditions Fides, 1988.

————. *To Become Another Christ: Identification with Christ according to Basil Moreau*. Translated by Louis-Bertrand Raymond. Montreal: Fides Publishers, 1990.

Proust, Jean. *Le Bienheureux Basile Moreau: Fondateur des congrégations de Sainte-Croix*. Montreal: Éditions Fides, 2007.

Vanier, R. P. Philéas. *Le chanoine Dujarié 1767–1838: Fondateur des Sœurs de la Providence de Ruillé-sur-Loir et des Frères de Saint-Joseph*. Montréal: Éditions Fides, 1948.

INDEX

Adam, 192–93
Aloysius Gonzaga, St., 307
Altar wine, 437
Ambrose, St., 138, 148
Amends
making, 325–27
Articles
in circular letters, 392–95, 409–12, 455
Ascension of Jesus Christ meditation, 254–57
Augustine, St., 101, 148, 161, 170, 186, 189, 227, 272, 318
Authority
kinds of, in Congregation, 467–69
Auxiliary Priests, 26–27
Avila, Fr., 306

Barnabo, Cardinal, 43
Barrosse, Thomas, 30
Basil, St., 184, 273, 317
Benedict, St., 137, 299
Benedict XIV, Pope, 307
Bernard, St., 141, 161, 273, 299, 300, 306
Bernardine of Siena, St., 183–84, 188
Bérulle, Pierre de, 8, 17–18, 21
Blessed Sacrament, Feast of
meditation for procession of, 322–27
Bonaparte, Napoleon, 2, 6
Bonaventure, St., 161
Bourdaloue, Pére, 111–12
Bouvier, Jean-Baptiste, 8, 12–13, 13–14, 21, 22, 25
refusal to recommend association for Vatican approval, 33–34
Brothers of St. Joseph
founding of, 24
Fundamental Act of Union, 26–27
joining Holy Cross, 26–27
manual of, 386
Moreau assumes leadership of, 25
relations with priests, 385–86
vows and, 28
Bruno, St., 299

Caesarius of Arles, St., 277–78
Canons of Hippolytus, 108
Canticles
Christian education and, 369–72
Carmelite Sisters, sermons on reception of habit
Christ, the new self sermon, 195–200
introduction, 191
old self sermon, 192–95
Carthusians, 105, 300
Catechism
excellence and nature of, 362–63
importance and necessity of, 363–64
length of, 366–67
manner of teaching, 364–66
Catholic Church
authority in, 467
changes for, following French Revolution, 3–5
power of, before French Revolution, 3
Ultramontanism vs. Gallicanism, 12–13
Catta, Etienne, 8
Catta, Tony, 8
Champeau, Louis-Dominique, 42
Charity
characteristics of, 102–3
Charles Borromeo, St., 306
Chastity
chastity vow sermon, 144–49
malice of impurity, 147–48
vow of, and Carmelite Sisters, 198
Christ, the new self sermon, 195–200
Christian education. See Education, Christian
Christian meditations. See Meditations
Circular letters, 377–475
altar wine, 437
annual retreats, 473
Articles, 392–95, 409–12, 455
confidence in God, 451–54
consecration of conventual church, 432–34
consolations, 390–92, 407–8
criticism of general administration, 422
crosses, 390, 413–14, 429–30
duties of superiors, 461–62
example of Christ and saints, 470

exhortation to the vows, 447–48
fidelity to silence, 460
financial administration, 434–35
full teaching rights for Sainte-Croix, 415–16
gratitude, 417–19
ideals of education, 416–17
interior life, 470–71
jubilee and fidelity to Holy Father, 454–55
kinds of authority in Congregation, 467–69
Letter 8 (to the Sisters), 456–65
Letter 14 (to the Sisters), 29–32, 379–86
Letter 16, 466–75
Letter 23, 387–402
Letter 25, 403–12
Letter 34, 47, 413–14
Letter 36, 415–23
Letter 77, 38–39
Letter 79, 424–38
Letter 96, 439–43
Letter 137, 444–48
Letter 179, 449–55
letter from Propagation of the Faith, 401–2
letter of Fr. Granger, 396–400
necessity of crosses, 450–51
necessity of religious spirit, 458
New Year's reflections, 424–25
New Year's wishes, 387–88, 444–46
obedience, 460–61
obligations of vows, 469–70
perpetual adoration, 436
perseverance, 441–43
plan of government, 457–48
preparation for consecration, 436–37
qualities of perfect life in Christ, 380–81
recollections of visit, 462–63
refutation of false charge, 419–21
regular discipline, 431–32
regular visitation, 408–9
religious rule, 427–28
rule and education, 430–31
spirit of faith, 422–23
spirit of prayer, 440–41
spirit of study, 441
spirit of vocation, 463–64
spirit of zeal, 405–6
trials, 389, 406–7
trials at New Orleans, 473
union, 382–85, 459–60
value of obedience, 425–27
various prescriptions, 437–38, 474–75
works of zeal, 471–72
Civil Constitution of the Clergy
  oath of, 4, 5
Clairvaux, Abbey of, 300
Clement I, Pope, 108
Clement of Alexandria, 317
Communion. See also Eucharist

Christian education and, 374–75
generous king sermon, 121–26
Institution of the Eucharist sermon, 128–30
introduction, 120–21
Most Holy Body of Christ meditation,
  322–27
sacramental presence sermon, 126–27
Community spirit sermons
charity and, 102–3
example of Jesus on passion for esteem,
  95–101
introduction, 78–82
perfect life, 79
power of union, 80–81
pride sermon, 82–95
recreation and, 103
virtues sermon, 101–5
Confession
act of going to confession, 109–110
Christian education and, 374–75
frequent, 111–14
general, 110–11
historical perspective on, 106–8
necessity of, 108–9
prayers and steps for good confession,
  115–19
as proof of Jesus' love for us, 106
sermons on, 106–19
Confession sermons
fruits of frequent confession sermon, 110–14
introduction, 106–10
making a good confession sermon, 115–19
Congregation of Holy Cross. See Holy Cross,
  Congregation of
Consolations, 390–92
in circular letters, 390–92, 407–8
Constitutional clergy, 4, 5
Contemplation, 60, 64–67
Conventual church
consecration of, 432–34, 436–37
Crosses
centrality of cross for Moreau, 45–49
in circular letters, 390, 413–14, 429–30,
  450–51
conforming interior and exterior life to
  Christ, 45–46
imitation of Christ and, 46–48
resurrection that follows, 48–49

Dark night, Moreau's, 34–37
de Jurien, Countess, 36–37
de la Hayem, Jacquet, 5–6
de la Myre, Bishop, 8
de Ligny, Fr., 226
Desert Fathers, 299
Diderot, 325

Discipline
  regular discipline, in circular letter, 431–32
Divine providence, 49–50
Doyle, William, 7
Drouelle, Fr., 42
Dufal, Pierre, 40
Dujarié, Jacques-François
  founding Brothers of St. Joseph, 24
  life of, 5–7
  vision for Brothers, 27–28

Education, Christian, 37–38, 329–76
  on attendance at liturgy, 372–73
  as daily labor of Holy Cross, 30–31
  education as evangelizing, 9–10
  French Revolution and, 7
  full teaching rights for Sainte-Croix, 415–16
  on gatherings of youth, 375–76
  ideals of education, 416–17
  importance and benefits of catechism,
    361–67
  introduction and preface, 329–33
  on prayer, 367–69
  regular reception of sacraments, 373–75
  rule and education, 430–31
  on sacred hymns, 369–72
  students with educational challenges,
    348–60
  as synthesis of faith and reason, 15–16
  virtues of successful teachers, 334–48
Enlightenment
  from Holy Spirit, 314
Entering the Heart of Jesus sermon, 162–66
Ephrem, St., 300, 317
Epiphany
  mystery of, meditation, 261–66
Esteem
  passion for, 89–91, 92, 95–101
Eucharist. See also Communion
  Most Holy Body of Christ meditation,
    322–27
Eudes, John, 17, 18–19
Eugenius, Pope, 306
Example of Jesus sermon, 95–101
Exterior peace meditation, 292–97

Faith
  lively faith and Blessed Sacrament, 322–24
  spirit of, in circular letter, 422–23
Faithfulness
  as virtue for teachers, 335–36
Feast of Sacred Heart
  meditations on, 239–47
Fidelity
  to smallest of things, 271–76

Fillion, Charles-Jean, 43
Fillion, Louis-Jean, 9
Financial administration, 434–35
Firmness
  as virtue for teachers, 347–48
Francis de Sales, St., 18, 19, 100, 299, 300,
    325–26
Francis of Assisi, St., 161, 299
Francis Xavier, St., 91, 94, 306, 309
French Revolution
  Catholic Church and, 2–5
French School of Spirituality, 8
  influence on Moreau, 17–20
Frequent confession, 111–14
Fruits of Frequent Confession sermon, 110–14
Fundamental Act of Union, 26–27

Gallicanism, 12–13
General confession, 110–11
Generous king sermon, 121–26
Gentleness
  as virtue for teachers, 341–43
Glories of St. Joseph sermon, 182–89
God
  confidence in, 451–54
  love of, and inner peace, 295–96
  trust in divine providence, 49–50
  Word of God meditation, 277–81
Granger, Fr.
  letter of, 396–400
Gratitude
  in circular letters, 417–19
  Gratitude sermon, 132–36
  making amends, 325–26
  Sacred Heart of Jesus and, 154–55
Gregory, St., 306
Gregory of Nyssa, St., 224–25
Guéranger, Prosper, 21

Heart of Jesus sermon, 158–62. See also Sacred
    Heart of Jesus
  Entering the Heart of Jesus sermon, 162–66
  Heart of Jesus sermon, 158–62
Hidden life of Jesus
  meditation on, 233–38
Holy Communion sermons
  Generous king sermon, 121–26
  Institution of the Eucharist sermon, 128–30
  introduction, 120–21
  Sacramental presence sermon, 126–27
Holy Cross, Congregation of
  from 1860 to 1866, 40–42
  Articles, 392–395, 409–12
  Auxiliary Priests and the Fundamental Act
    of Union, 26–27

Brothers of St. Joseph founding and early
   years, 24–26
confidence in God, 451–54
consecration of conventual church, 39,
   432–34, 436–37
consecration of three societies, 385
consolations, 390–92, 407–8
crosses, 390, 413–14, 429–30, 450–51
early developments of, 23–29
financial administration, 434–35
financial crisis, 40–41, 449, 452
founding of, 26–27
full teaching rights for Sainte-Croix, 415–16
growth years of, in 1850s, 33–34
joining Brothers of St. Joseph and, 26–27
Magna Carta of (Circular Letter 14), 30–32
manual of brothers of St. Joseph, 386
missionary expansion years, 33
Moreau's resignation and last years, 42–44
refutation of false charge, 419–21
regular discipline, 431–32
regular visitation, 408–9
relations between priests and brothers,
   385–86
religious rule, 427–28
religious union, 382–85
rule and education, 430–31
Sisters joining with, 27–29
trials, 389, 406–7
union of, and Holy Family, 52
value of obedience, 425–27
Vatican approval of, 33–34, 38–39
vision of union of members, 31–32
vows of poverty, chastity and obedience, 28
Holy Family
   union with Holy Trinity, 51–52
Holy Spirit
   enlightenment, 314
   mystery of, meditation, 313–16
   Pentecost meditation, 313–16
   preparation for meditation, 310–12
   purification, 314–15
   strength from, 315–16
Holy Trinity
   imitating, 320–21
   love and, 319–20
   mystery of meditation, 317–21
   union with Holy Family, 51–52
   as vision for union for Holy Cross, 31
Humility
   inner peace and, 294–95
   virtue of, 104
Hymns
   Christian education and, 369–72

Ignatius of Antioch, St., 108
Ignatius of Loyola, St., 227, 299

influence on Moreau, 20–21
St. Ignatius on mental prayer sermon, 60–71
spiritual exercises of, 58, 201
Illuminative way spiritual exercises, 203–38
   call of Jesus and his kingdom, 209–14
   hidden life of Jesus Christ in general, 233–38
   imitation of Christ, 214–22
   introduction to, 58–59, 203
   means for imitating Christ and establishing
      his kingdom in oneself, 222–27
   during novitiate preceding Feast of St.
      Joseph, 203–9
   what imitation of Christ means for you,
      228–32
Imitation of Christ, 45–49, 214–32
Immaculate Conception sermon, 168–71
Immaculate Heart of Mary sermons, 167–74
   Immaculate Conception sermon, 168–71
   introduction, 167–68
   Love of Mary's Heart sermon, 171–74
Impurity, malice of, 147–48
Incarnation, 46
Institution of the Eucharist sermon, 128–30
Interior life, 470–71
Interior peace meditation, 292–97
Irenaeus, St., 317

Jane Frances de Chantal, St., 100
Jean-François Regis, St., 309
Jerome, St., 303
Jesus Christ
   appearances of Jesus Christ meditation,
      251–54
   ascension of meditation, 254–57
   call of Jesus Christ meditation, 209–14
   Christ, the new self sermon, 195–200
   conforming interior and exterior life to
      Christ, 45–46
   Entering the Heart of Jesus sermon, 162–66
   Example of Jesus sermon on passion for
      esteem, 95–101
   Heart of Jesus sermon, 158–62
   hidden life of meditation, 233–38
   imitation of Christ, 1, 45–49, 214–32
   institution of Eucharist, 128–30
   love of heart of, for everyone, 244–47
   as model for life, 31–32, 470
   Most Holy Body of Christ meditation,
      322–27
   multiplication of loaves and fishes
      meditation, 285–87
   mystery of five wounds of the Lord
      meditation, 282–84
   prayers of, as example, 305

qualities of perfect life in Christ, 380–81
resurrection of Jesus Christ meditation,
    249–51
sacramental presence of, in Communion,
    126–27
Sacred Heart of, 151–66
union with, through chastity, 145–46
John Chrysostom, St., 306
Joseph, St., 175–90
    death of, 188
    devotion to, 471–72
    as father of Jesus, 183–86
    glories of St. Joseph sermon, 182–89
    new Joseph sermon, 189–90
    obedience of, 179–80
    poverty of, 180–82
    purity of, 177–78
    virtues of St. Joseph sermon, 176–82
Justice
    making amends, 326
    Sacred Heart of Jesus and, 152–54
Justice, gratitude, and obedience sermon,
    152–58
Justin, St., 317

Knowledge
    of teachers, 336–37
Kruse, Robert, 50

Lactantius, 318
La Grande Trappe of Mortagne, 22
Lamennais, Hugues-Félicité Robert de, 11–14
Le Mans, Diocese of, 6, 7
Leprosy
    meditation on leprosy of sin, 267–70
Le Provost, Julien, 7–8
Letters. See Circular letters
Liturgical year meditations
    Epiphany, 261–66
    Fifth Sunday after Easter, 304–9
    First Sunday after Pentecost, 317–21
    five wounds of our Lord meditation, 282–84
    Fourth Sunday after Easter, 298–303
    Fourth Sunday of Lent, 285–87
    Friday after Passion Sunday, 288–91
    Friday after Third Sunday of Lent, 282–84
    interior and exterior peace meditation,
        292–97
    introduction, 259–60
    leprosy of sin, 267–70
    loaves and fishes meditation, 285–87
    mental prayer meditation, 304–9
    minor virtues, 271–76
    mystery of Most Holy Trinity meditation,
        317–21
    mystery of transfixion, 288–91

Pentecost, 313–16
preparation for Holy Spirit meditation,
    310–12
Quasimodo Sunday, 292–97
Sexagesima Sunday, 277–81
silence meditation, 298–303
Sixth Sunday after Easter, 310–12
Sixth Sunday after Epiphany, 271–76
Third Sunday after Epiphany, 267–70
Thursday after the Most Holy Trinity,
    322–27
Word of God meditation, 277–81
Liturgy
    attendance of, and Christian education,
        372–73
Loaves and fishes, meditation on, 285–87
Louis XVI, King, 2, 3
Love
    of God, and inner peace, 295–96
    grateful love and Blessed Sacrament, 324–25
    Holy Trinity and, 319–20
    Love of Mary's Heart sermon, 171–74
Luers, John Henry, 42

Making a Good Confession sermon, 115–19
Marcellus, Brother
    letter of, 400
Marie-Julien, Brother, 41
Martin, St., 220
Mary
    Immaculate Conception sermon, 168–71
    Immaculate Heart of Mary sermons, 167–74
    Love of Mary's Heart sermon, 171–74
    mystery of transfixion or compassion of
        Blessed Virgin meditation, 288–91
    Seven Sorrows of, 288
Meditations, 259–327
    on appearances of Jesus Christ, 251–54
    on ascension of Jesus Christ, 254–57
    benefits of, 22, 76–77
    call of Jesus Christ and his kingdom, 209–14
    contemplation, 60, 64–67
    for Feast of the Sacred Heart, 239–47
    on hidden life of Jesus, 233–38
    imitation of Christ, 214–32
    importance of, to saints, 306
    on interior and exterior peace, 292–97
    introduction, 57–60
    on leprosy of sin, 267–70
    on love of heart of Jesus for everyone,
        244–47
    memory, understanding and will, 60–64
    on mental prayer, 304–9
    on minor virtues, 271–76
    on Most Holy Body of Christ, 322–27

on multiplication of loaves and fishes, 285–87
on mystery of Epiphany, 261–66
on mystery of five wounds of the Lord, 282–84
on mystery of Most Holy Trinity, 317–21
on mystery of Pentecost, 313–16
on mystery of transfixion or compassion of Blessed Virgin, 288–91
other approaches to meditation sermon, 73–77
on preparing for Holy Spirit, 310–12
on procession of Feast of Blessed Sacrament, 322–27
on resurrection of Jesus Christ, 249–51
St. Ignatius on mental prayer, 60–71
on silence, 298–303
Sulpician approach to, 71–73
on Word of God, 277–81
Memory
meditation and, 60, 62–63
Mental prayer
St. Ignatius on, 60–71
Missionary endeavors, 33
Mollevaut, Gabriel, 11
Moreau, Basil
aims and organization of Holy Cross, 29–32
assumes leadership of Brothers of St. Joseph, 25
Auxiliary Priests and the Fundamental Act of Union, 26–27
Brothers of St. Joseph's early years and, 24–26
centrality of cross, 47–49
dark night of, 34–37
disagreement over governance of sisters, 41–42
divine providence, 49–50
early developments of Holy Cross, 23–29
early evidence of importance of teaching, 9
education as evangelizing, 9–10
education as synthesis of faith and reason, 15–16
financial crisis, 41
French Revolution background and, 2–7
imitation of Christ, 45–49
intellectual and spiritual influences on, 16–23
intellectual formation of, 7–11
life as imitation of Christ, 1, 31–32
life from 1860 to 1866, 40–42
map of France, 483
ordination of, 8
as professor, 13–14
resignation and last years, 42–44
scholarly development, 11–13, 14–15
Solesmes and La Trappe influence, 21–22

spiritual emphases of, 45–53
St. Ignatius of Loyola's influence, 20–21
Sulpician spirituality and French School influence, 17–20
synthesis of various theological influences, 22–23
time line of life, writings and church events, 476–82
Ultramontane position, 12–13
virtue of zeal, 52–53
Moreau, Charles, 40
Moreau, Louis, 8
Mortal sin
leprosy representing, 268
Mortification, 104, 105
Most Holy Trinity
meditation on mystery of, 317–21

Nanquette, Bishop, 39
New Joseph sermon, 189–90
New Orleans
trials at, 473
New self sermon, 195–200
Newspapers
extract from L'Union, 420–21
reading, 418–19
New Year's wishes, 387–88, 444–46
Nonjuring clergy, 4, 5

Obedience
Carmelite Sisters vow of, 198
Holy Cross vow of, 28
inner peace and, 296–97
obedience vow sermon, 136–44
promptness in, 138–39
Sacred Heart of Jesus, 156–57
of St. Joseph, 179–80
universal, 140
value of, in circular letters, 425–27, 460–61
Old self sermon, 192–95
Olier, Jean-Jacques, 8, 17, 18
Origen, 317
Other approaches to meditation sermon, 73–77

Passion Sunday, 288–91
Patience
as virtue for teachers, 344–45
Paul, St., 100, 146, 148
Peace
interior and exterior peace meditation, 292–97
Penance. See Confession
Pentecost
mystery of meditation, 313–16
Perfect life, 79

Perpetual adoration, 436
Perreault, Cécile, 14, 21
Perseverance
  in circular letter, 441–43
Philip Neri, St., 309
Picquigny, Bernardin de, 14, 226
Pius IX, Pope, 13, 43, 454–55, 472
Pius VI, Pope, 4, 157
Poverty
  Carmelite Sisters vow of, 198
  Holy Cross vow of, 28
  poverty vow sermon, 149–50
  of St. Joseph, 180–82
Prayers
  application of five senses, 60, 67–69
  contemplation, 60, 64–67
  by Jesus, 305
  for making a good confession, 115–19
  mental prayer meditation, 304–9
  by saints, 305
  St. Ignatius on mental prayer sermon, 60–71
  spirit of, in circular letter, 440–41
  teaching students in Christian education, 367–69
  vocal prayer, 304
Pride
  as enemy of community spirit, 88
  example of Jesus sermon, 95–101
  passion for esteem, 89–91, 92, 95–101
  Satan and, 82, 84
  sermon on, 82–95
  vainglory, 84, 87, 91, 94
  vanity, 91–92
Priests
  relations with brothers, 385–86
Propagation of the Faith
  letter from, 401–2
Prosper Guéranger, Dom, 259
Prudence
  as virtue for teachers, 345–47
Purgative way, 58–59, 203
Purification
  from Holy Spirit, 314–15
Purity
  of St. Joseph, 177–78

Quasimodo Sunday, 292–97

Recreation
  community spirit and, 103
Reign of Terror, 5
Religious rule, 427–28
Religious spirit
  necessity of, 458
Renewal of the vows sermons

chastity sermon, 144–49
gratitude sermon, 132–36
introduction, 131–32
obedience sermon, 136–44
poverty sermon, 149–50
Resurrection
  meditation on, of Jesus Christ, 249–51
  that follows the cross, 48–49

Sacramental Presence sermon, 126–27
Sacraments
  Christian education and, 373–75
  as proof of Jesus' love for us, 106
Sacred Heart of Jesus, 151–66
  devotion to, 156–57, 158, 239–44
  Entering the Heart of Jesus sermon, 162–66
  Eudes on, 18–19
  Heart of Jesus sermon, 158–62
  introduction, 151–52
  Justice, gratitude, and obedience sermon, 152–58
  love of, for everyone, 244–47
  meditations for the Feast of, 239–47
Saint-Jure, Fr., 227
Saints. *See also specific saints*
  importance of prayer to, 305–7
  as model for life, 470
St. Joseph sermons, 175–90
  glories of St. Joseph sermon, 182–89
  introduction, 175–76
  new Joseph sermon, 189–90
  virtues of St. Joseph sermon, 176–82
Salvatorists, 201
Satan
  pride and, 82, 84
Senses
  application of, in prayer, 60, 67–69
Seriousness
  as virtue for teachers, 340–41
Sermons, 55–200
  chastity sermon, 144–49
  Christ, the New Self sermon, 195–200
  on community spirit, 78–105
  on confession, 106–19
  entering the Heart of Jesus sermon, 162–66
  example of Jesus sermon, 95–101
  fruits of frequent confession sermon, 110–14
  generous king sermon, 121–26
  glories of St. Joseph sermon, 182–89
  gratitude sermon, 132–36
  Heart of Jesus sermon, 158–62
  on Holy Communion, 120–30
  Immaculate Conception sermon, 168–71
  on Immaculate Heart of Mary, 167–74
  Institution of the Eucharist sermon, 128–30

justice, gratitude, and obedience sermon, 152–58
love of Mary's Heart sermon, 171–74
making a good confession sermon, 115–19
on meditation, 57–77
new Joseph sermon, 189–90
obedience sermon, 136–44
old self sermon, 192–95
other approaches to meditation sermon, 73–77
poverty sermon, 149–50
pride sermon, 82–95
on reception of the habit for Carmelite Sisters, 191–200
on renewal of the vows sermons, 131–50
sacramental presence sermon, 126–27
on Sacred Heart of Jesus, 151–66
St. Ignatius on mental prayer sermon, 60–71
St. Joseph sermons, 175–90
Sulpician approach to meditation sermon, 71–73
virtues of St. Joseph sermon, 176–82
virtues sermon, 101–5
Seven Sorrows of Mary, 288–91
Sexagesima Sunday, 277–81
Silence
to avoid sin, 301–2
benefit of, for community, 298–301
to facilitate virtue, 302
fidelity to, 460
meditation on, 298–303
to prepare for assignment, 302–3
Sin
leprosy of sin meditation, 267–70
silence to avoid, 301–2
Sisters of Holy Cross
annual retreats, 473
disagreement over governance of, 41–42
duties of superiors, 461–62
example of Christ and saints, 470
fidelity to silence, 460
interior life, 470–71
joining Holy Cross, 27–29
kinds of authority in Congregation, 467–69
necessity of religious spirit, 458
obedience, 460–61
obligations of vows, 469–70
plan for government of, 457–58
recollections of visit, 462–63
spirit of vocation, 463–64
trials at New Orleans, 473
union, 459–60
various prescriptions, 474–75
vows, 28
works of zeal, 471–72
Solesmes, 21–22
Sorin, Edward, 28, 34, 41, 42, 43

Sorrow
Seven Sorrows of Mary, 288–91
Spiritual way exercises, 201–57
illuminative way, 203–38
introduction, 58–59, 201–2
meditations for the Feast of the Sacred Heart, 239–47
St. Ignatius of Loyola's influence, 20–21
Unitive way, 248–57
Strength
from Holy Spirit, 315–16
Students
educational challenges of, 348–60
teaching to pray, 367–69
Study
spirit of, 441
Sulpician approach to meditation sermon, 71–73
Superiors, duties of, 461–62

Teachers
virtues for successful, 334–48
vocation of, 334–35
Teresa of Avila, St., 91, 189, 194, 256
Tertullian, 317
Thomas, St., 303
Thomas à Kempis, 21
Trials
in circular letters, 389, 406–7
Trinity. See Holy Trinity

Ultramontanism, 12–13
Understanding
meditation and, 60, 63
Unitive way spiritual exercises, 248–57
appearances of Jesus Christ meditation, 251–54
ascension of Jesus Christ meditation, 254–57
introduction to, 58–59, 248
meditationon resurrection of Jesus Christ meditation, 249–51
model of new life after novitiate, 249–51
symbol of secret visits of his grace, 251–54
Urban VIII, Pope, 17–18

Vainglory, 84, 87, 91, 94, 101
Vanity, 91–92
effects of, 91–92
Vatican
approval of Holy Cross, 33–34
Vigilance
as virtue for teachers, 339–40
Vincent de Paul, St., 14, 18, 21, 100, 232, 299, 300, 306

Virtues
    charity, 102–3, 104
    humility, 104
    minor virtues meditation, 271–76
    mortification, 104, 105
    silence facilitating, 302
    for successful teachers, 334–48
    virtues of St. Joseph sermon, 176–82
    virtues sermon, 101–5
Visitations
    regular, in circular letter, 408–9
Vocal prayer, 304
Vocation
    authority and power of, 467–68
    silence to prepare for, 302–3
    spirit of, 463–64
    teaching as, 334–35
Vows. *See also* Renewal of the vows sermons
    authority and power of, 468–69
    Brothers of St Joseph and, 28
    exhortation to, 447–48
    Holy Cross and, 28
    obligations of, 469–70

Will
    meditation and, 60, 63–64
Word of God
    meditation on, 277–81
Worldly goods
    vanity of, 428

Zeal
    spirit of, 405–6
    as virtue for teachers, 337–39
    virtue of, 52–53
    works of, 471–72

Biblical Index

The Old Testament
Genesis
  1:2, 312
  1:26, 317
  3:1–7, 282
  3:5, 82, 230
  3:6, 48
  3:22, 86
  4:1–16, 72
  6:5–9:17, 72
  12:1, 133
  14:18–20, 72
  18:1ff, 318
  22:1–19, 72
  27:15–16, 198
  28:12, 307
  32:4–33:20, 72
  37:1–28, 72
  37:9, 186
  41:15–37, 175
  41:43, 175
  41:55, 175, 189
  42:1–45:25, 189
  49:8–10, 72
Exodus
  1:8–2:10, 72
  3:1ff, 302
  12:3–11, 131
  12:14, 131
  13:21–22, 131
  14:15–20, 131
  15, 369
  16:3–15, 131
  19:16–19, 323
  19:16–20:17, 131
  25:18–22, 178
  25:40, 158, 205
Leviticus
  23:29, 137
Numbers
  20:1–11, 131
  24:5, 427
  27:12–23, 72
Deuteronomy
  26:19, 96
  30:4–19, 119

  32:1–44, 369
  32:29, 447
Judges
  5, 369
  6:15, 236
1 Samuel
  2:1–20, 369
2 Samuel
  6:22, 99
2 Kings
  2:11–12, 79, 382
  10:15, 239
Tobit
  12:13, 404, 451
Judith
  16:1–17, 369
Esther
  5:9–14, 295
  14:14, 212
2 Maccabees
  1:3, 214
Job
  10:14, 186
Psalms
  2:7, 72
  13:5, 245
  16, 22, 72
  16:6–7, 145
  20:8–9, 174
  22, 155
  22:1, 237
  22:6, 236
  24:10, 95
  25:7, 134
  27:4, 244
  27:10, 199
  32:9, 301
  36:8–9, 144
  38; 40, 237
  42:8, 273
  45:14, 168
  49:13, 85, 194
  62:9, 166
  68:4, 129
  68:11, 129

68:29, 142
69:21, 98
72:10–11, 72
73:10, 432
73:27, 123
77:10, 142
82:6, 87
84:11, 99
85:10, 153
95:6–7, 125
95:8, 152
96:4–5, 84
100:3, 61
103:2, 105
104:30, 153
111:10, 62, 311
116:12, 125, 134
118:22, 75
119:106, 142
119:120, 65
130:1, 268
145:9, 119
Proverbs
1:7; 9:10, 311
3:11, 404
8:31, 127
9:10, 62
16:4, 96
23:26, 239
28:14, 148
31:10–31, 274
Songs
5:1, 121
Sirach
1:16, 311
Isaiah
1:2, 449
6:3, 317
7:14, 262
11:1, 262
12, 369
28:16, 75
29:13, 160
35:4–6, 72
35:5, 71
40:3, 72
45:15, 323
48:11, 95
52:13–53:12, 72
53:2, 236
53:5, 127, 282
61:1, 71
61:1–3, 72
63:3, 211
63:4, 164
63:15, 120
Jeremiah

12:3, 348
12:11, 57
23:5, 72
31:3, 244
31:15, 72
46:27–28, 72
Lamentations
1, 155
3:30, 98
Ezekiel
1:15–21, 139
10:14–19, 186
18:23, 115
36:24–28, 369
36:26, 243
44:1–3, 72
Daniel
1–3, 85
2:44, 72
2:48, 121
3:26–56, 369
12:3, 333, 336
Hosea
2:14, 241
2:16, 293
11:1, 72
Joel
2:17, 166
3:18, 106
Micah
5:1, 72
Habakkuk
3:1–19, 369
Zechariah
12:10, 151, 164
13:6, 164
Malachi
3:1–4, 72
4:2, 236

The New Testament
Matthew
1:21, 185
1:23–25, 262
2:1, 261
2:11, 261, 266
2:13, 179, 288
2:14, 180
3:3, 62
5:5, 341
5:6, 181
5:11, 96, 99
5:28, 148
5:38–44, 78
6:1, 96
6:3–4, 16–18, 96

6:6, 305
6:10, 210
7:14, 140
8:2, 267–68
8:3, 269
8:4, 98
8:8, 122, 125
8:19, 206, 212, 215
8:20, 212, 221, 230
8:22, 216
9:9, 210
9:36, 120
10:37–38, 198
11:4, 71
11:4–6, 75
11:6, 74
11:12, 140
11:15; 13:9, 43, 280
11:19, 236
11:28, 127
11:28–29, 295
11:30, 311
12:24, 236
13:13, 280
13:31–32, 271
13:55, 97, 235
15:8, 160
16:16, 324
16:19, 107
16:24, 198, 216
16:26, 471
17:5, 242
19:12, 469
19:13–15, 245
19:21, 197
19:27, 264
19:29, 211
22:1–14, 124
22:11–14, 109
22:13, 124
22:14, 124
22:40, 295
23:12, 87, 295
23:37–38, 165
24:30; 26:64, 323
24:31, 65
25:21, 105, 274
25:23, 140, 276
25:32, 66
25:34, 219
25:34–35, 66
25:35–36, 184
25:40, 460
25:41, 219
25:41–44, 66
26:30, 370
27:59–60, 288
28:11–15, 249

28:19, 317–18
28:20, 127, 246, 327
Mark
1:35, 305
1:40, 267–68
1:41, 269
4:9, 23, 280
4:12, 280
4:30–32, 271
4:35–41, 450
5:28, 125
6:3, 97, 235
6:31–32, 285
6:34, 120
8:36, 471
9:23, 125
10:13–16, 245
10:17, 265
10:18, 98
12:17, 126
14:26, 370
15:34, 237
16:6, 249
16:14, 251
Luke
1:34, 178
1:41, 234
1:43, 125
1:46, 168
1:46–55, 370
1:48, 169
1:68–79, 370
2:7, 265
2:19, 167–68, 171
2:19, 51, 19
2:29–32, 370
2:33, 183
2:34, 75
2:34–35, 179, 288–89
2:35, 173, 288
2:43–48, 288
2:46, 221
2:46–49, 134
2:47, 235
2:48, 183
2:51, 186, 235
3:23, 235
5:8, 123
5:12, 267–68
5:13, 269
6:12, 305
6:15, 236
6:20–22, 197
6:26, 96
6:40, 212
7:15, 245
7:39, 236
8:10, 280

8:11, 277
8:25, 323
9:23, 137
9:25, 471
10:3, 213
10:42, 213
11:1, 304
12:49, 246
12:50, 98
13:14, 236
13:18–19, 271
14:11; 18:14, 295
14:17, 120
15:2; 7:34, 236
15:18–19, 125
15:32, 250
16:10, 271
16:13, 231
17:12ff, 268
17:21, 392
18:8, 57, 237
18:18, 265
19:25, 173
21:25, 67
21:27, 65
22:19–20, 129
22:30, 213
22:43, 256
23:2, 236
23:11, 237
24:13–33, 252
24:29, 254
24:32, 254, 325
24:49, 310
24:51, 254
John
  1:1–3, 318
  1:9, 280
  1:10, 235
  1:11–12, 125
  1:14, 196
  1:46, 236
  3:16, 172, 320
  3:19, 236
  4, 245
  4:24, 61
  6:5, 9, 287
  6:11, 285
  6:14, 286
  6:15, 286–87
  6:42, 97
  6:55, 120, 322
  6:56, 128, 207
  6:69, 123
  7:15, 97, 235
  7:41, 236
  7:52, 236
  8:29, 425

8:46, 108
8:48, 236
9:16, 236
9:17, 236
9:29, 236
10:19, 236
10:24, 236
10:33, 236
11:28–29, 139
11:35, 245
11:36, 154
11:48, 236
12:35, 263
12:43, 97
13:1, 324
13:4–10, 128
13:12–15, 128
13:15, 215–16, 228, 232, 242
13:16, 212
14:6, 46, 146, 191, 199, 215
14:18, 245
15:5, 206
15:14, 296
16:13; 15:26, 310
16:23–24, 304
17:20–23, 78
17:21, 46, 199, 384
17:21–23, 146
19:15, 98
19:26, 174
19:26–27, 288
19:27, 174
19:34, 151
20:11–18, 251
20:13, 237
20:19, 253
20:19, 21, 26, 292
20:20, 253
20:23, 106
20:26–29, 251
20:28, 212, 231
20:29, 127
21:7, 137
21:16, 124
30:23, 107
Acts
  1:9, 237, 245, 254
  1:9–11, 255
  1:14, 311
  1:15–26, 212
  2:4, 313
  5:41, 99, 219
  11:26, 216
  14:22, 140
  17:21, 419
Romans
  5:1–5, 208
  6:3–5, 217

6:9, 250
6:16, 143
7:14–25, 177
7:24, 86
8:1, 208
8:3, 97
8:4–6, 208
8:9, 225
8:10–11, 208
8:14, 99
8:14–15, 216
8:16–17, 208
8:22–23, 195
8:24, 196
8:28, 217
8:29–30, 58, 159, 205, 217
8:35, 39, 125
8:39, 216
9:19, 209
11:17, 208
13:8, 295
13:11, 448
13:14, 145, 198
15:19, 213
1 Corinthians
1:18–24, 75
1:20–25, 99
1:23, 429
1:27, 426
2:2, 222
3:16, 433
3:17, 392, 433
4:3, 100
4:15, 97
6:18, 148
7, 145
8:1, 336
9:19, 143
9:22, 338
9:24–25, 140
9:27, 92
10:12, 404
11:26, 129
11:29, 279
12:12–13, 217
12:12–26, 459
12:27, 206
13:4ff, 102
14:15, 19, 70
15:52, 66
16:22, 225
2 Corinthians
1:3, 119
2:17, 96
3:18, 216
4:4, 84, 216
4:10–11, 217
4:17, 257

5:14, 283
5:21, 237
11–12, 256
11:2, 143
11:16–30, 219
12:7, 60
12:9, 196, 217
12:10, 100
Galatians
1:10, 100
2:20, 14, 146, 199, 206, 208, 217, 284
3:26–27, 4:5, 216
3:27, 217
4:19, 217, 337
5:20–21, 194
5:24, 118
5:26, 88, 95
6:16, 296
Ephesians
1:5, 216
1:16–17, 224
1:20, 245
2:4, 172
3:18, xi
4:1, 264
4:15, 217
4:21, 196
4:21–24, 191
4:24, 197
5:8, 422
5:19, 370
5:20, x
6:12, 214
Philippians
1:6, 142
2:1–4, 384
2:5, 146, 159, 198
2:6–7, 296
2:6–8, 118, 197
2:7–8, 230
2:8, 136, 141
2:10, 240
3:10, 213
3:18–19, 445
4:13, 76
Colossians
1:24, 173
2:3, 97, 123, 234, 240
2:9, 240
3:1, 245
3:3, x, 176, 234–35, 238
3:9–10, 222, 230
3:14, 459
3:22, 138
1 Thessalonians
4:3–5, 147
5:5, 422

2 Thessalonians
  3:9, 315
1 Timothy
  1:17, 95
  4:6–10, 305
  2 Timothy
  2:22, 148
  4:8, 142
Titus
  3:5, 119
  Hebrews
  10:24, 459
  10:37, 238
  11:35, 446
  12:4, 140, 404
James
  1:19, 298
  1:26, 298
  3:3, 301
  3:4, 301
  3:6, 301–02
  1 Peter
  1:22, 138
  1:24, 95
  2:24, 127
  5:8, 220
  1 John
  2:16, 229
  2:16–17, 194
  3:2, 87
  Jude
  20–21, 119
Revelation
  1:7, 219
  2:4–5, 136
  2:7, 238
  2:17, 238
  3:16, 141, 268
  3:20, 238
  5:6, 256
  7:14, 213
  7:17; 21:4, 255
  14:3–4, 145
  22:20, 125, 238

Blessed Basil Moreau (February 11, 1799–January 20, 1873) was the French priest who founded the Congregation of Holy Cross in 1837. Born at the end of the French Revolution, Moreau lived and worked in a time of many cultural, political, and religious shifts. As a professor of philosophy and theology, Moreau saw a fundamental need for educators who were also adept at communicating faith. His own writings, sermons, circular letters, and spiritual exercises reveal the work of a skilled thinker and teacher, who was instructing his fellow priests, brothers, and sisters in Holy Cross about both education and ongoing formation in the spiritual life. Moreau's writings reflect his French milieu but also his concern for the world; he quickly sent members of his congregation around the globe to make God known, loved, and served. Today, members of Holy Cross live and work in sixteen countries on five continents. Moreau was beatified on September 15, 2007, in Le Mans, France.

Rev. Kevin Grove, C.S.C., received a Master of Divinity degree from the University of Notre Dame in 2009 and was ordained a priest in the Congregation of Holy Cross in 2010. Fr. Grove is a doctoral candidate at the University of Cambridge. He is the coeditor of *The Cross, Our Only Hope* and *You Have Redeemed the World*.

Rev. Andrew Gawrych, C.S.C., received a Master of Divinity degree from the University of Notre Dame in 2007 and was ordained a priest in the Congregation of Holy Cross in 2008. As a priest, he has worked both in parish and vocations ministry. He is the editor or coeditor of several Holy Cross books, including *The Cross, Our Only Hope; The Gift of Hope; The Gift of the Cross;* and *You Have Redeemed the World*.

Founded in 1865, Ave Maria Press,
a ministry of the Congregation of
Holy Cross, is a Catholic publishing
company that serves the spiritual and
formative needs of the Church and its
schools, institutions, and ministers;
Christian individuals and families; and
others seeking spiritual nourishment.

For a complete listing of titles from

Ave Maria Press

Sorin Books

Forest of Peace

Christian Classics

visit www.avemariapress.com

 ave maria press® / Notre Dame, IN 46556
A Ministry of the United States Province of Holy Cross